SHORTER LEXICON OF THE
GREEK NEW TESTAMENT

SHORTER
LEXICON
OF THE
GREEK NEW TESTAMENT

F. WILBUR GINGRICH

Walter Bauer

THE UNIVERSITY OF CHICAGO PRESS

CHICAGO AND LONDON

This book is an abridgement of *A Greek-English Lexicon of the New Testament and Other Early Christian Literature* by William F. Arndt and F. Wilbur Gingrich, published 1957 by The University of Chicago Press, a translation and adaptation of Walter Bauer's *Griechisch-deutsches Wörterbuch zu den Schriften des Neuen Testaments und der übrigen urchristlichen Literatur.*

Library of Congress Catalog Card Number: 65-24434

The University of Chicago Press, Chicago & London
The University of Toronto Press, Toronto 5, Canada

Printed in the United States of America

To my wife

FOREWORD

This book is a condensed version of the translation and adaptation of the late Walter Bauer's *Griechisch-deutsches Wörterbuch zu den Schriften des Neuen Testaments und der übrigen urchristlichen Literatur* by the late William F. Arndt and me, published in 1957 under the title, *A Greek-English Lexicon of the New Testament and other Early Christian Literature*.

The scope of this smaller book is limited to the words of the New Testament itself, to the exclusion of the Apostolic Fathers and other pieces of early Christian literature included in the larger lexicon. The variant readings of the Nestle (now Nestle-Aland) text of the New Testament are included in this work, together with a few others.

The emphasis is here placed upon the bare meanings of the words; for more information the user must consult the unabridged lexicon or other works. A large number of more or less difficult inflectional forms have been included.

An asterisk (*) at the end of an entry means that all the occurrences of the word in the New Testament have been noted. Where this is not the case, it will be found that a more or less representative list of occurrences is given.

The writer wishes to acknowledge gratefully the assistance of the following students in his advanced Greek classes at Albright College in checking references and various other matters: James W. Adam, Guy W. Camp III, Michael L. Ervin, James F. Getz, Fred A. Grater, Paul F. Jacobs, Faith King, John King, Robert W. Martin, Gene M. Miller, Joanne E. O'Dell, Eugene H. Stecher, Richard E. Stetler, David N. Treaster, and Dennis L. Trout.

F. WILBUR GINGRICH

READING, PENNSYLVANIA

ABBREVIATIONS

BOOKS OF THE NEW TESTAMENT

Ac = Acts of the Apostles	Mk = Mark
Col = Colossians	Mt = Matthew
1 Cor = 1 Corinthians	Phil = Philippians
2 Cor = 2 Corinthians	Phlm = Philemon
Eph = Ephesians	1 Pt = 1 Peter
Gal = Galatians	2 Pt = 2 Peter
Hb = Hebrews	Ro = Romans
J = John	Rv = Revelation
1 J = 1 John	1 Th = 1 Thessalonians
2 J = 2 John	2 Th = 2 Thessalonians
3 J = 3 John	1 Ti = 1 Timothy
Jd = Jude	2 Ti = 2 Timothy
Js = James	Tit = Titus
Lk = Luke	

The few abbreviations used for books of the Old Testament are easily understood without explanation.

GENERAL

acc. = accusative	opt. = optative
act. = active	pass. = passive
aor. = aorist	passim = here and there
dat. = dative	perf. = perfect.
e.g. = exempli gratia, for example	perh. = perhaps
f = following	pl. = plural
ff = following, of more than one	pluperf. = pluperfect
fig. = figurative(ly)	prep. = preposition
fut. = future	pres. = present
gen. = genitive	prob. = probably
gener. = generally	ptc. = participle
Gk. = Greek	q.v. = quod vide, which see
H. = Hellenistic	sing. = singular
imperf. = imperfect	subj. = subjunctive
ind. = indicative	subscr. = subscription, short
inf. = infinitive	statement at end of a book
intrans. = intransitive	subst. = substantive(ly)
inscr. = inscription, title	s.v. = sub verbo, under the word
lit. = literal(ly)	trans. = transitive
mid. = middle	v.l. = varia lectio, variant
mng. = meaning	reading
nom. = nominative	voc. = vocative
oft. = often	w. = with

SHORTER LEXICON OF THE GREEK NEW TESTAMENT

A

A, α *alpha*, first letter of the Greek alphabet. α' as numeral = *one* or *first*, in titles of 1 Cor, etc. See also ἄλφα.

Ἀαρών, ὁ indecl. *Aaron*, brother of Moses (Ex 4: 14) Lk 1: 5; Ac 7: 40; Hb 5: 4; 7: 11; 9: 4.*

Ἀβαδδών, ὁ indecl. (Heb. = 'destruction') *Abaddon*, Gk. Ἀπολλύων *Destroyer*, the ruling angel in hell Rv 9: 11.*

ἀβαρής, ές, gen. **οῦς** *not burdensome* ἀβαρῆ ἐμαυτὸν ὑμῖν ἐτήρησα *I kept myself from being a burden to you* 2 Cor 11: 9.*

ἀββά (Aram.) vocative case *abba* = (*O*) *father*, a specially intimate term Mk 14: 36; Ro 8: 15; Gal 4: 6.*

Ἅβελ, ὁ indecl. (Heb.) *Abel* (Gen 4) Mt 23: 35.

Ἀβιά, ὁ indecl. (Heb.) *Abijah.*—**1.** Son of Rehoboam (1 Ch 3: 10) Mt 1: 7a, b.—**2.** Founder of the class of priests to which Zechariah belonged (1 Ch 24: 10) Lk 1: 5.*

Ἀβιαθάρ, ὁ indecl. (Heb.) *Abiathar* priest at Nob (1 Sam 22: 20ff) Mk 2: 26.*

Ἀβιληνή, ῆς, ἡ *Abilene* the territory around the city of Abila, northwest of Damascus Lk 3: 1.*

Ἀβιούδ, ὁ indecl. (Heb.) *Abiud* Mt 1: 13a, b.

Ἀβραάμ, ὁ indecl. (Heb.) *Abraham* father of the Hebrew people (Gen 12: 1–3) and fig. of the Christians Ro 4: 1ff.

ἄβυσσος, ου, ἡ *unfathomable depth, abyss, underworld* abode of the dead Ro 10: 7; of demons Lk 8: 31; Rv 11: 7.

Ἅγαβος, ου, ὁ *Agabus* a Christian prophet Ac 11: 28; 21: 10.*

ἀγαγεῖν, ἀγάγετε, ἀγαγών 2 aor. act. inf., imperative, and participle of ἄγω.

ἀγαθοεργέω (contracted form ἀγαθουργέω) *do good* 1 Ti 6: 18; *confer benefits* Ac 14: 17.*

ἀγαθοεργός, όν *doing good;* used as a noun Ro 13: 3 v.l.*

ἀγαθοποιέω—1. *do good* Lk 6: 9; τινά *to someone* 6: 33.—**2.** *do what is right* 1 Pt 2: 15, 20.

ἀγαθοποιΐα, ας, ἡ *doing good* 1 Pt 4: 19.*

ἀγαθοποιός, όν *doing good;* used as a noun *one who does good* 1 Pt 2: 14.*

ἀγαθός, ή, όν *good*—**1.** of persons: of God *perfect, complete* Mk 10: 18. *Morally good, upright* of Christ J 7: 12; of men Mt 12: 35; Ac 11: 24. *Kind, benevolent* 1 Pt 2: 18.—**2.** of things: *fertile* Lk 8: 8; *sound* Mt 7: 17f; *beneficial, wholesome* 7: 11; *useful* Eph 4: 29; *fortunate* 1 Pt 3: 10; *clear*

1 Ti 1: 5; *firm* Tit 2: 10; *dependable* 2 Th 2: 16. *Better* Lk 10: 42.—**3.** neut., used as a noun *what is good* in a moral sense Ro 2: 10. *Advantage* 8: 28. *Goods, property* Lk 12: 18. *Good deeds* J 5: 29.

ἀγαθουργέω see ἀγαθοεργέω.

ἀγαθωσύνη, ης, ἡ *goodness, uprightness* Ro 15: 14; Eph 5: 9; 2 Th 1: 11. *Generosity* Gal 5: 22.*

ἀγαλλίασις, εως, ἡ *rejoicing, exultation.* ἔλαιον -εως = oil used for anointing on festive occasions Hb 1: 9.

ἀγαλλιάω *rejoice, be overjoyed, exult* w. dat. *rejoice in* or *because of* Lk 10: 21, *with* 1 Pt 1: 8.

ἄγαμος, ου, ὁ and ἡ *an unmarried man* or *woman* 1 Cor 7: 8, 11, 32, 34.*

ἀγανακτέω *be aroused, be indignant* or *angry;* perh. = *express displeasure* Mk 14: 4; Lk 13: 14.

ἀγανάκτησις, εως, ἡ *indignation* 2 Cor 7: 11.*

ἀγαπάω *to love*—**1.** of persons: God J 3: 16, Jesus Mk 10: 21, and man 2 Cor 12: 15 *love, cherish, show the greatest solicitude for,* of the finest and most typical Christian virtue (more frequent and typically Christian than φιλέω, but prob. equivalent to it in J 21: 15–17).—**2.** of the love for things *love, long for, value* Lk 11: 43; J 12: 43; 2 Ti 4: 8.— **3.** *prove* or *show love (for)* J 13: 1; 1 J 3: 18; 4: 7.

ἀγάπη, ης, ἡ—**I.** *love,* the highest Christian virtue 1 Cor 13: 13; Gal 5: 22.—**1.** of God and Christ to each other J 15: 10; 17: 26, and to men Ro 5: 8. The essence of God 1 J 4: 8, 16. —**2.** of men, to God or Christ J 5: 42, or to other men 2 Cor 8: 7.—**3.** as an abstract quality Ro 13: 10; 1 Cor 8: 1; 13: 1–3.— **II.** *a love-feast,* a common meal of the Christian church with

religious significance Jd 12; 2 Pt 2: 13 v.l.

ἀγαπητός, ή, όν *beloved, dear :* of children, friends, fellow-Christians 1 Cor 4: 17; Col 4: 14; 3 J 2, 5, 11. Of the Messiah, with strong inclination toward the mng. *only-beloved* Mt 3: 17.

Ἀγάρ, ἡ indecl. *Hagar* (Gen 16), symbol of the Mosaic law Gal 4: 24, 25.*

ἀγγαρεύω *requisition, press into service* (originally for the Persian royal post; in Rom. times for any military or civil service), then *force, compel* Mt 5: 41; 27: 32; Mk 15: 21.*

ἀγγεῖον, ου, τό *vessel, flask, container* Mt 25: 4; 13: 48 v.l.*

ἀγγελία, ας, ἡ *message* 1 J 1: 5; *command* 3: 11.*

ἀγγέλλω *announce, report* J 20: 18; 4: 51 v.l.*

ἄγγελος, ου, ὁ—**1.** *messenger, envoy* Lk 7: 24.—**2.** *angel,* a supernatural being who acts as messenger Mt 1: 20, guardian Ac 12: 15, mediator Gal 3: 19, and generally as the servant of God. Also of servants of Satan Mt 25: 41.

ἄγγος, ους, τό *vessel, basket* Mt 13: 48.*

ἄγε (pres. imperative of ἄγω, used as interjection) *come* Js 4: 13; 5: 1.*

ἀγέλη, ης, ἡ *herd* of swine Mt 8: 30–32.

ἀγενεαλόγητος, ον *without genealogy* Hb 7: 3.*

ἀγενής, ές, gen. οῦς *base, low, insignificant,* lit. *not of noble birth* 1 Cor 1: 28.*

ἁγιάζω *make holy, sanctify, consecrate, dedicate, purify :* of things Mt 23: 17, 19; of persons J 10: 36; 1 Cor 7: 14; Hb 9: 13. οἱ ἡγιασμένοι = the Christians as *sanctified, purified* Ac 20: 32. *Treat as holy,* · *hold in reverence* Mt 6: 9; 1 Pt 3: 15.

ἁγιασμός, οῦ, ὁ *holiness, consecration, sanctification* as a process Ro 6: 19, 22, or a result 1 Ti 2: 15. Christ its originator 1 Cor 1: 30.

ἅγιος, ία, ον *set apart for* or *by God,* morally or ceremonially *holy.*—1. of things *sacred, consecrated* 1 Cor 3: 17. Neut. as noun τὸ ἅγιον perh. *holy food* Mt 7: 6. τὰ ἅγια *sanctuary, temple* Hb 9: 12.—2. of persons: of God *unapproachable, morally perfect* J 17: 11. Of Christ Mk 1: 24. οἱ ἅγιοι *God's people, saints* the Christians Ro 1: 7. Of pers. gener. *pure, upright, worthy of God* Eph 1: 4.

ἁγιότης, ητος, ἡ *holiness, moral purity* 2 Cor 1: 12; Hb 12: 10.*

ἁγιωσύνη, ης, ἡ *holiness, uprightness* Ro 1: 4; 2 Cor 7: 1; 1 Th 3: 13.*

ἀγκάλη, ης, ἡ *arm,* bent as to receive something Lk 2: 28.*

ἄγκιστρον, ου, τό *fishhook* Mt 17: 27.*

ἄγκυρα, ας, ἡ *anchor* lit. Ac 27: 29, 30, 40; fig. Hb 6: 19.*

ἄγναφος, ον *unbleached, unshrunken* of cloth not yet treated by the fuller (γναφεύς, q.v.) Mt 9: 16; Mk 2: 21.*

ἁγνεία, ας, ἡ *purity,* esp. *chastity* 1 Ti 4: 12; 5: 2.*

ἁγνίζω *cleanse, purify* ceremonially Ac 21: 24, 26; morally Js 4: 8.

ἁγνίσθητι 1 aor. pass. imperative of ἁγνίζω.

ἁγνισμός, οῦ, ὁ *purification,* ceremonial Ac 21: 26.*

ἀγνοέω *not to know, be ignorant* Ro 2: 4. W. neg. *know* (*quite well*), *be sure* Ro 1: 13; 2 Cor 2: 11. *Not to understand* Mk 9: 32. *Sin in ignorance* Hb 5: 2. *Disregard* 1 Cor 14: 38.

ἀγνόημα, ατος, τό *sin committed in ignorance* Hb 9: 7.*

ἄγνοια, ας, ἡ *ignorance,* excusable Ac 3: 17; 17: 30; *wilful* Eph 4: 18; 1 Pt 1: 14.*

ἁγνός, ή, όν *holy, pure* (first ceremonially, then ethically) Phil 4: 8; Js 3: 17. *Chaste* Tit 2: 5. *Innocent* 2 Cor 7: 11.

ἁγνότης, ητος, ἡ *purity, sincerity* 2 Cor 6: 6; 11: 3 v.l.*

ἁγνῶς *purely, sincerely* Phil 1: 17.*

ἀγνωσία, ας, ἡ *ignorance, lack of spiritual discernment* 1 Cor 15: 34; 1 Pt 2: 15.*

ἄγνωστος, ον *unknown* Ac 17: 23.*

ἀγορά, ᾶς, ἡ *market place,* the center of civic life. 'When they come' is to be understood w. ἀπ' ἀγορᾶς Mk 7: 4. The Agora at Athens Ac 17: 17.

ἀγοράζω *buy, purchase,* lit. Mt 13: 44; fig. 1 Cor 6: 20.

ἀγοραῖος, ον *pertaining to a market,* used only as a noun. οἱ ἀ. *idlers, rabble* Ac 17: 5. ἀ. (supply 'days' or 'sessions') ἄγονται *the courts are in session* 19: 38.*

ἄγρα, ας, ἡ *catching, a catch* Lk 5: 4, 9.*

ἀγράμματος, ον *illiterate* in the sense *uneducated* Ac 4: 13.*

ἀγραυλέω *live out of doors* Lk 2: 8.*

ἀγρεύω *to catch* fig. Mk 12: 13.*

ἀγριέλαιος, ἡ *wild olive tree* Ro 11: 24; perh. as adj., with 'branch' to be supplied 11: 17.*

ἄγριος, ία, ιον *wild* Mt 3: 4; Mk 1: 6; Jd 13.*

Ἀγρίππας, α, ὁ *Agrippa,* i.e. Herod Agrippa II Ac 25 and 26 passim. His father, Herod Agrippa I, is called simply Herod in Ac 12: 1ff.

ἀγρός, οῦ, ὁ *field* Mt 6: 28; Lk 17: 7; *country* as apposed to city or village Mk 15: 21. Pl. *farms, hamlets* Lk 9: 12.

ἀγρυπνέω *keep oneself awake,* fig. *be on the alert* Mk 13: 33. *Keep watch* (*over*), *guard, care for* Eph 6: 18; Hb 13: 17.

ἀγρυπνία, ας, ἡ sleeplessness 2 Cor 6: 5; 11: 27.*

ἄγω—1. lead, bring, take or bring along Mt 21: 7; Ac 17: 15; 20: 12; to trial or punishment Ac 6: 12; 9: 2. Fig. lead, guide Ro 2: 4; Gal 5: 18. Of time spend Lk 24: 21 (supply 'Jesus' as subj.); of court sessions hold Ac 19: 38.—2. go, always hortatory subjunctive let us go Mk 1: 38; J 11: 7, 15f.

ἀγωγή, ῆς, ἡ way of life, conduct 2 Ti 3: 10.*

ἀγών, ἀγῶνος, ὁ athletic contest, race fig. Hb 12: 1; struggle, fight Phil 1: 30. ἐν πολλῷ ἀγῶνι under a great strain 1 Th 2: 2. Care, concern Col 2: 1.

ἀγωνία, ας, ἡ agony, anxiety Lk 22: 44.*

ἀγωνίζομαι engage in an (athletic) contest 1 Cor 9: 25; fight, struggle, strive J 18: 36; Col 4: 12; 1 Ti 4: 10; strain every nerve Lk 13: 24.

Ἀδάμ, ὁ indecl. (Heb.) Adam (Gen 1: 27ff) Ro 5: 14. ὁ ἔσχατος Ἀδάμ the last Adam = Christ 1 Cor 15: 45.

ἀδάπανος, ον free of charge 1 Cor 9: 18.*

Ἀδδί, ὁ indecl. (Heb.) Addi Lk 3: 28.*

ἀδελφή, ῆς, ἡ sister: lit. Lk 10: 39f; fig. Ro 16: 1; 2 J 13.

ἀδελφός, οῦ, ὁ brother: lit. J 1: 41; fig. Mk 3: 35; Phil 1: 14. Fellow countryman Ro 9: 3; neighbor Mt 5: 22ff.

ἀδελφότης, ητος, ἡ brotherhood (group of believers) 1 Pt 2: 17; 5: 9.*

ἄδηλος, ον unseen Lk 11: 44; indistinct 1 Cor 14: 8.*

ἀδηλότης, ητος, ἡ uncertainty 1 Ti 6: 17.*

ἀδήλως adv. uncertainly, without a definite goal 1 Cor 9: 26.*

ἀδημονέω be anxious, be distressed Mt 26: 37; Mk 14: 33; Phil 2: 26.*

ᾅδης, ου, ὁ Hades (Heb. Sheol), the underworld as the place of the dead Lk 16: 23; personified Rv 20: 13f.

ἀδιάκριτος, ον unwavering, impartial Js 3: 17.*

ἀδιάλειπτος, ον unceasing, constant Ro 9: 2; 2 Ti 1: 3.*

ἀδιαλείπτως adv. unceasingly, constantly Ro 1: 9; 1 Th 1: 2; 2: 13; 5: 17.*

ἀδιαφθορία, ας, ἡ sincerity, integrity Tit 2: 7 v.l.*

ἀδικέω do wrong Col 3: 25; ὁ ἀδικῶν the evildoer Rv 22: 11. Be in the wrong Ac 25: 11. Do wrong to someone, treat someone unjustly Mt 20: 13; Ac 7: 26; Gal 4: 12. Injure, harm, damage, spoil Rv 9: 4, 10, 19; if he has caused you any loss Phlm 18.

ἀδίκημα, ατος, τό misdeed, crime, wrong Ac 18: 14; 24: 20; Rv 18: 5.*

ἀδικία, ας, ἡ injustice Ro 9: 14; wrong (ironic) 2 Cor 12: 13; wickedness, wrongdoing, unrighteousness Ro 6: 13; 1 Cor 13: 6; 1 J 5: 17. The gen. ἀδικίας = unjust Lk 16: 8, 9 (cf. 11); 18: 6.

ἀδικοκρίτης, ου, ὁ unjust judge Tit 1: 9 v.l.*

ἄδικος, ον unjust, unrighteous Mt 5: 45; 1 Cor 6: 1; 1 Pt 3: 18; dishonest, untrustworthy Lk 16: 10.

ἀδίκως adv. unjustly. undeservedly 1 Pt 2: 19; 2: 23 v.l.*

Ἀδμίν, ὁ indecl. (Heb.) Admin Lk 3: 33.*

ἀδόκιμος, ον failing to stand the test, unqualified, worthless 2 Cor 13: 5–7; disqualified 1 Cor 9: 27; unworthy Ro 1: 28; useless Hb 6: 8.

ἄδολος, ον unadulterated, pure 1 Pt 2: 2.*

Ἀδραμυττηνός, ή, όν belonging to Adramyttium, a seaport in northwest Asia Minor, on the Aegean Sea Ac 27: 2.*

'Αδρίας, ου, ὁ the Adriatic Sea (the sea between Crete and Sicily is included in it) Ac 27: 27.*

ἁδρότης, ητος, ἡ abundance, lavishness 2 Cor 8: 20.*

ἀδυνατέω be powerless, only impersonal it is impossible Mt 17: 20; Lk 1: 37.*

ἀδύνατος, ον powerless, weak of persons Ac 14: 8; Ro 15: 1. Impossible of things Ro 8: 3; Hb 6: 4, 18.

ᾄδω sing Eph 5: 19; Rv 5: 9.

ἀεί adv. always 2 Cor 6: 10; 1 Pt 3: 15; continually, constantly Ac 7: 51; 2 Cor 4: 11.

ἀετός, οῦ, ὁ eagle Rv 12: 14; vulture Lk 17: 37.

ἄζυμος, ον free from yeast or leaven fig. 1 Cor 5: 7. As a noun, pl. unleavened bread Lk 22: 1; fig. 1 Cor 5: 8. The festival of unleavened bread Mk 14: 1, immediately following the Passover and often identified with it Lk 22: 1, 7.

'Αζώρ, ὁ indecl. Azor Mt 1: 13f.

"Αζωτος, ου, ἡ Azotus, the O.T. Ashdod (Is 20: 1), a Philistine city on the coast of S. Palestine Ac 8: 40.*

ἀηδία, ας, ἡ enmity, lit. 'unpleasantness' Lk 23: 12 v.l.*

ἀήρ, ἀέρος, ὁ air Ac 22: 23; 1 Cor 9: 26; Eph 2: 2.

ἀθᾶ see μαρὰν ἀθᾶ.

ἀθανασία, ας, ἡ immortality 1 Cor 15: 53f; 1 Ti 6: 16.*

ἀθάνατος, ον immortal 1 Ti 1: 17 v.l.*

ἀθέμιτος, ον unlawful Ac 10: 28; illicit, wanton 1 Pt 4: 3.*

ἄθεος, ον without God Eph 2: 12.*

ἄθεσμος, ον lawless, unprincipled 2 Pt 2: 7; 3: 17.*

ἀθετέω—1. declare invalid, nullify, set aside Mk 7: 9; Gal 2: 21; thwart, confound 1 Cor 1: 19.— 2. reject, ignore of persons Lk 10: 16; break faith with Mk 6: 26.

ἀθέτησις, εως, ἡ annulment technical legal term Hb 7: 18; removal 9: 26.*

'Αθῆναι, ῶν, αἱ Athens the intellectual capital of the Greek world Ac 17: 15f.

'Αθηναῖος, α, ον Athenian Ac 17: 21f.*

ἀθλέω compete in a contest 2 Ti 2: 5.*

ἄθλησις, εως, ἡ contest, struggle fig. Hb 10: 32.*

ἀθροίζω collect, gather Lk 24: 33.*

ἀθυμέω be discouraged, lose heart Col 3: 21.*

ἀθῷος, ον innocent Mt 27: 4, 24.*

αἴγειος, εία, ειον of a goat Hb 11: 37.*

αἰγιαλός, οῦ, ὁ shore, beach Mt 13: 2; Ac 27: 39.

Αἰγύπτιος, ία, ιον Egyptian Ac 7: 24.

Αἴγυπτος, ου, ἡ Egypt Mt 2: 13– 15; = Jerusalem Rv 11: 8.

ἀΐδιος, ον eternal, everlasting Ro 1: 20; Jd 6.*

αἰδώς, οῦς, ἡ modesty 1 Ti 2: 9; reverence, respect Hb 12: 28 v.l.*

Αἰθίοψ, οπος, ὁ Ethiopian Ac 8: 27.*

αἷμα, ατος, τό blood. σάρξ καὶ αἷμα a (mere) human being Gal 1: 16; human nature Hb 2: 14. Pl., of physical descent J 1: 13. Murder Rv 6: 10; bloody deed Mt 27: 6. As a means of purification, of animals Hb 10: 4, or of Christ Col 1: 20; 1 Pt 1: 19.

αἱματεκχυσία, ας, ἡ the shedding of blood Hb 9: 22.*

αἱμορροέω suffer from a flow of blood or hemorrhage Mt 9: 20.*

Αἰνέας, ου, ὁ Aeneas Ac 9: 33f.*

αἴνεσις, εως, ἡ praise Hb 13: 15.*

αἰνέω to praise Rv 19: 5.

αἴνιγμα, ατος, τό lit. riddle, then indistinct image; ἐν αἰ. dimly 1 Cor 13: 12.*

αἶνος, ου, ὁ *praise* Mt 21: 16; Lk 18: 43.*

Αἰνών, ἡ indecl. *Aenon, a place probably in the upper Jordan valley* J 3: 23.*

αἴξ, αἰγός, ὁ, ἡ *goat* Lk 15: 29 v.l.*

αἵρεσις, εως, ἡ *religious sect* Ac 5: 17; 26: 5; perh. *heretical sect* Ac 24: 5, 14; 28: 22. *Dissension, division* 1 Cor 11: 19; Gal 5: 20. *Opinion, dogma* 2 Pt 2: 1.

αἱρετίζω *choose, select* Mt 12: 18.*

αἱρετικός, ή, όν *factious, causing divisions*, perh. *heretical* Tit 3: 10.*

αἱρέω only mid. *choose* 2 Th 2: 13; *prefer* Phil 1: 22; Hb 11: 25.*

αἴρω—1. *raise, lift, take up, pick up* Mt 16: 24; Lk 17: 13; J 8: 59; *keep in suspense* J 10: 24; *weigh* (anchors) Ac 27: 13; *take or carry along* Mt 16: 24; 27: 32. The transition to mng. 2 may be seen in J 1: 29, where αἴ. means both *take up* and *remove.*—2. *take or carry away, remove* Lk 6: 29; J 2: 16; 19: 38. *Do away with* J 19: 15; *sweep away* Mt 24: 39; *conquer, take over* J 11: 48; *expel* 1 Cor 5: 2; *cut off* J 15: 2. Supply τι *something* Mt 9: 16.

αἰσθάνομαι *understand* Lk 9: 45.*

αἴσθησις, εως, ἡ *insight, experience* Phil 1: 9.*

αἰσθητήριον, ου, τό *sense, faculty* Hb 5: 14.*

αἴσθωμαι 2 aor. subjunctive of αἰσθάνομαι.

αἰσχροκερδής, ές *fond of dishonest gain* 1 Ti 3: 8, 3 v.l.; Tit 1: 7.*

αἰσχροκερδῶς adv. *in fondness for dishonest gain* 1 Pt 5: 2.*

αἰσχρολογία, ας, ἡ *evil speech*, in the sense of *obscene* or *abusive speech* Col 3: 8.*

αἰσχρός, ά, όν *shameful, disgraceful* 1 Cor 11: 6; 14: 35; Eph 5: 12. *Dishonest* Tit 1: 11.*

αἰσχρότης, ητος, ἡ *indecency* Eph 5: 4.*

αἰσχύνη, ης, ἡ *modesty, shame* 2 Cor 4: 2; *shame, disgrace, ignominy* Phil 3: 19; Hb 12: 2; Rv 3: 18; *disgrace* Lk 14: 9. *Shameful deed* Jd 13.*

αἰσχύνομαι *be ashamed* Lk 16: 3; 1 Pt 4: 16. *Be put to shame, be disgraced* 1 J 2: 28;=be disappointed 2 Cor 10: 8; Phil 1: 20.*

αἰτέω *ask, ask for, request* Mt 27: 20; Ac 16: 29; *make a request of* someone 13: 28. W. double acc. *ask someone for something* Mt 7: 9. The classical meaning *demand* may fit some passages, e.g. 1 Cor 1: 22.

αἴτημα, τος, τό *request* Lk 23: 24; Phil 4: 6; 1 J 5: 15.*

αἰτία, ας, ἡ—1. *cause, reason* Mt 19: 3; Ac 10: 21; *relationship* Mt 19: 10.—2. legal term *charge, ground for complaint, accusation* J 18: 38; Ac 25: 18, 27.

αἰτίαμα, τος, τό (see αἰτίωμα) Ac 25: 7 v.l.*

αἰτιάομαι *to charge* Ro 3: 9 v.l.*

αἴτιος, ία, ον *responsible, guilty* only as noun: masc. *cause, source* Hb 5: 9. Neut. *cause* Ac 19: 40; *guilt, complaint* Lk 23: 4, 14; αἰ. θανάτου *reason for capital punishment* vs. 22.*

αἰτίωμα, τος, τό *charge, complaint* Ac 25: 7.*

αἰφνίδιος, ον *sudden* Lk 21: 34; 1 Th 5: 3.*

αἰχμαλωσία, ας, ἡ *captivity* Rv 13: 10. Abstract for concrete, (many) *captives, prisoners of war* Eph 4: 8; Hb 7: 1 v.l.*

αἰχμαλωτεύω *take captive* Eph 4: 8; 2 Ti 3: 6 v.l.*

αἰχμαλωτίζω *capture* in war: lit. *scatter as captives* Lk 21: 24. Fig. *take captive, subdue* Ro 7: 23; 2 Cor 10: 5; *mislead* 2 Ti 3: 6.*

αἰχμάλωτος, ώτου, ὁ *captive* Lk 4: 18.*

αἰών, αἰῶνος, ὁ—1. *very long time,*

eternity: in the past, *earliest times, ages long past* Lk 1: 70; ἐκ τοῦ αἰῶνος *since the world began* J 9: 32. In the future εἰς τὸν αἰῶνα *to eternity, eternally* J 6: 51, 58. εἰς τοὺς αἰ. τῶν αἰώνων *for evermore* Ro 16: 27; Hb 13: 21.—**2.** *age, era*: ὁ αἰὼν οὗτος, etc. *this present* (evil) *age*, before the παρουσία Mt 12: 32; 13: 22; Lk 16: 8; 2 Cor 4: 4; Gal 1: 4. ὁ αἰὼν ὁ ἐρχόμενος, etc. *the* (happy) *age to come*, after the παρουσία Mk 10: 30; Eph 1: 21. —**3.** *world, material universe* 1 Ti 1: 17; Hb 1: 2.—**4.** the *Aeon*, a powerful evil spirit Eph 2: 2; perh. Col 1: 26.

αἰώνιος, ία, ον *eternal, everlasting: without beginning* Ro 16: 25; *without beginning or end* 16: 26; *without end* Mt 25: 46; Lk 10: 25; Hb 13: 20.

ἀκαθαρσία, ας, ἡ *impurity, refuse:* lit. Mt 23: 27. *Immorality, viciousness* Ro 1: 24; Gal 5: 19.

ἀκαθάρτης, ητος, ἡ *uncleanness* Rv 17: 4 v.l.*

ἀκάθαρτος, ον *impure, unclean:* ceremonially Ac 10: 14, vs. 28; 1 Cor 7: 14. Morally Eph 5: 5; of demons Mk 1: 23.

ἀκαιρέομαι *have no time, no opportunity* Phil 4: 10.*

ἀκαίρως adv. *out of season, inopportunely* 2 Ti 4: 2.*

ἄκακος, ον *innocent, blameless* Hb 7: 26; *unsuspecting* Ro 16: 18.*

ἄκανθα, ης, ἡ *thorn-plant* Mt 13: 7; 27: 29.

ἀκάνθινος, η, ον *made of thorns* Mk 15: 17; J 19: 5.*

ἄκαρπος, ον *unfruitful, useless, unproductive* lit. Jd 12; fig. Mk 4: 19; 1 Cor 14: 14; Eph 5: 11.

ἀκατάγνωστος, ον *above reproach* Tit 2: 8.*

ἀκατακάλυπτος, ον *uncovered, unveiled* 1 Cor 11: 5, 13.*

ἀκατάκριτος, ον *without a proper trial* Ac 16: 37; 22: 25.*

ἀκατάλυτος, ον *indestructible, indissoluble*, hence *endless* Hb 7: 16.*

ἀκατάπαστος, ον of uncertain mng., perh. *insatiable* 2 Pt 2: 14 v.l.*

ἀκατάπαυστος, ον *unceasing, restless*, w. gen. *unable to cease from* 2 Pt 2: 14.*

ἀκαταστασία, ας, ἡ *disturbance* 2 Cor 6: 5; *disorder, unruliness, unrest* 1 Cor 14: 33; 2 Cor 12: 20; Js 3: 16; *insurrection* Lk 21: 9.*

ἀκατάστατος, ον *restless* Js 3: 8; *unstable* 1: 8.*

ἀκατάσχετος, ον *uncontrollable* Js 3: 8 v.l.*

Ἀκελδαμάχ (Aram.=*field of blood*) *Akeldama* Ac 1: 19.*

ἀκέραιος, ον *pure, innocent* lit. 'unmixed' Mt 10: 16; Ro 16: 19; Phil 2: 15.*

ἀκηδεμονέω found nowhere else than Mk 14: 33 v.l., for ἀδημονέω, q.v.*

ἀκλινής, ές *unwavering* τ. ὁμολογίαν ἀ. κατέχειν *hold fast the confession without wavering* Hb 10: 23.*

ἀκμάζω *become ripe* Rv 14: 18.*

ἀκμήν adverbial acc. (of ἀκμή 'present moment') *even yet, still* Mt 15: 16; Hb 5: 13 v.l.*

ἀκοή, ῆς, ἡ—1. (*the faculty of*) *hearing* 1 Cor 12: 17. *The act of hearing, listening* 2 Pt 2: 8; ἀκοῇ ἀκούσετε *you will indeed hear* Mt 13: 14. The organ of hearing, the *ear* Mk 7: 35; Ac 17: 20.—**2.** *that which is heard: fame, report, rumor* Mt 4: 24; 14: 1; 24: 6. *Account, report, preaching* J 12: 38; Gal 3: 2, 5; Hb 4: 2; 1 Th 2: 13.

ἀκολουθέω *follow* Mt 21: 9; *accompany* J 6: 2; *follow* as disciple Mk 1: 18; 2: 14.

ἀκουσθεῖσι dat. pl., 1 aor. pass. ptc. of ἀκούω.

ἀκουστός, ή, όν *audible*, hence *known* Ac 11: 1 v.l.*

ἀκούω hear, lit. Mt 11: 5. Heed, listen to 18: 15, understand 1 Cor 14: 2; Gal 4: 21. Learn of Ro 10: 18; pass. be reported 1 Cor 5: 1; learn (a body of teaching) 1 J 1: 5; 2: 7, 24. Give (someone) a (legal) hearing J 7: 51; Ac 25: 22.

ἀκρασία, ας, ἡ lack of self-control 1 Cor 7: 5; self-indulgence Mt 23: 25.*

ἀκρατής, ές without self-control, dissolute 1 Ti 3: 3.*

ἄκρατος, ον unmixed, in full strength Rv 14: 10.*

ἀκρίβεια, ας, ἡ exactness κατὰ ἀ. strictly Ac 22: 3.*

ἀκριβέστερον see ἀκριβῶς.

ἀκριβής, ές strict Ac 26: 5.*

ἀκριβόω ascertain (exactly) Mt 2: 7, 16.*

ἀκριβῶς adv. accurately, carefully, well Lk 1: 3; Eph 5: 15. Comparative ἀκριβέστερον more exactly, more accurately Ac 18: 26; 24: 22.

ἀκρίς, ίδος, ἡ locust, grasshopper Mk 1: 6; Rv 9: 3, 7.

ἀκροατήριον, ου, τό audience room, auditorium Ac 25: 23.*

ἀκροατής, οῦ, ὁ a hearer, one who hears or listens to Ro 2: 13; Js 1: 22, 23, 25.*

ἀκροβυστία, ας, ἡ foreskin, uncircumcision Ac 11: 3; Ro 2: 25ff; pagan, heathen in conduct Col 2: 13. Heathendom, the Gentiles Ro 4: 9; Col 3: 11.

ἀκρογωνιαῖος, α, ον lying at the extreme corner. ἀ. λίθος cornerstone or capstone Eph 2: 20; 1 Pt 2: 6.*

ἀκροθίνιον, ου, τό spoils, booty Hb 7: 4.*

ἄκρον, ου, τό top Hb 11: 21; tip Lk 16: 24; extreme limit, end Mt 24: 31; Mk 13: 27.*

'Ακύλας, acc. αν, ὁ Aquila (accent on first syllable), a friend of Paul, husband of Priscilla Ac 18: 2, 18, 21 v.l.,

26; Ro 16: 3; 1 Cor 16: 19; 2 Ti 4: 19.*

ἀκυρόω make invalid, cancel Mt 15: 6; Mk 7: 13; legal term Gal 3: 17.*

ἀκωλύτως adv. without let or hindrance Ac 28: 31.*

ἄκων, ἄκουσα, ἄκον unwilling; to be translated as an adv. unwillingly 1 Cor 9: 17.*

ἅλα see ἅλας.

ἀλάβαστρος, ου, ὁ and ἡ, also ἀλάβαστρον, ου, τό alabaster flask Mt 26: 7; Mk 14: 3; Lk 7: 37.*

ἀλαζονεία, ας, ἡ pretension, arrogance Js 4: 16; pride 1 J 2: 16.*

ἀλαζών, όνος, ὁ boaster Ro 1: 30; 2 Ti 3: 2.*

ἀλαλάζω wail loudly Mk 5: 38; clash, clang 1 Cor 13: 1.*

ἀλάλητος, ον unexpressed, inexpressible στεναγμοὶ ἀ. sighs too deep for words Ro 8: 26.*

ἄλαλος, ον mute, dumb Mk 7: 37; 9: 17, 25.*

ἅλας, ατος, τό (v.l. ἅλα Mt 5: 13 and elsewhere. The classical ἅλς is represented only by the v.l. ἁλί Mk 9: 49) salt lit. Lk 14: 34; fig. Mt 5: 13a; Col 4: 6.

ἁλεεῖς, οἱ see ἁλιεύς.

ἀλείφω anoint Mk 16: 1; Lk 7: 38, 46; Js 5: 14.

ἄλειψαι 1 aor. mid. imperative 2nd sing. of ἀλείφω.

ἀλεκτοροφωνία, ας, ἡ cock-crow in genitive of time = the period from midnight to 3 a.m. Mk 13: 35.*

ἀλέκτωρ, ορος, ὁ cock, rooster Mk 14: 30; J 18: 27.

'Αλεξανδρεύς, έως, ὁ an Alexandrian Ac 6: 9; 18: 24.*

'Αλεξανδρῖνος, η, ον Alexandrian Ac 6: 9 v.l.; 27: 6; 28: 11.*

'Αλέξανδρος, ου, ὁ Alexander: (1) Mk 15: 21. (2) Ac 4: 6. (3) 19: 33. (4) 1 Ti 1: 20; 2 Ti 4: 14.*

ἄλευρον, ου, τό wheat flour Mt 13: 33; Lk 13: 21.*

ἀλήθεια, ας, ἡ truth: truthfulness, dependability, uprightness Ro 15:

8; 2 Cor 7: 14; *truth* as opposed to untruth Mk 5: 33; Eph 4: 25. Moral and, religious *truth* as revealed in Christianity J 1: 17; 3: 21; 14: 6; 1 Cor 13: 6; Eph 4: 24. *Reality* Phil 1: 18; 2 J 1. With ἐν, ἐπί, κατά *in reality, truly, certainly* Mt 22: 16; Mk 12: 14; Lk 22: 59; Ro 2: 2.

ἀληθεύω *be truthful, tell the truth* Gal 4: 16; Eph 4: 15.*

ἀληθής, ές *true* J 19: 35; Phil 4: 8; 2 Pt 2: 22; *dependable* J 5: 31f; Tit 1: 13. *Truthful, righteous, honest* Mt 22: 16; J 3: 33; 2 Cor 6: 8. *Real, genuine* Ac 12: 9; 1 Pt 5: 12.

ἀληθινός, ή, όν *true, dependable* Hb 10: 22; Rv 6: 10; *true, in accordance with truth* J 4: 37; 19: 35; Rv 19: 9; *genuine, real* Lk 16: 11; J 4: 23; 17: 3; 1 Th 1: 9; Hb 8: 2.

ἀλήθω *grind* Mt 24: 41; Lk 17: 35.*

ἀληθῶς adv. *truly, really, actually* Mt 14: 33; Lk 9: 27; 1 J 2: 5. As adj.=*real* J 1: 47; 8: 31.

ἁλιεύς, έως, ὁ *fisherman* lit. Mk 1: 16. Fig. ποιήσω ὑμᾶς ἁ. ἀνθρώπων *I will make you fish for men* Mt 4: 19.

ἁλιεύω *to fish* J 21: 3.*

ἁλίζω *to salt, make salty, season* Mt 5: 13; Mk 9: 49.*

ἁλίσγημα, ατος, τό *pollution* (ceremonial) Ac 15: 20.*

ἀλλά adversative particle *but* (stronger than δέ): most frequently after a negative, as Mt 5: 17; Mk 9: 37; Eph 1: 21. Followed by οὐ, in strong contrast to a preceding positive statement 1 Cor 10: 23. *Yet, and yet* J 1: 31; 8: 26; 12: 27; *rather* Lk 1: 60; *instead of that* 1 Cor 6: 6; *nevertheless* Ro 5: 14; *except* Mk 4: 22; 2 Cor 1: 13; *certainly, at least* Mk 14: 29; Ro 6: 5. Strengthening an imperative *now* Mt 9: 18; Mk 9: 22.

Alone, or with καί, γε καὶ, or οὐδέ, emphatically introducing what follows *indeed, why!, and not only this, but also* 2 Cor 7: 11 (6 times); J 16: 2; 1 Cor 3: 2. Elliptical ἀλλά (τοῦτο γέγονεν, e.g.) ἵνα *but* (*this has happened,* e.g.) *in order that* Mk 14: 49 J 1: 8.

ἀλλάσσω *change, alter* Ac 6: 14 Gal 4: 20; *exchange* Ro 1: 23.

ἀλλαχόθεν adv. *at* (lit. 'from') *another place* J 10: 1.*

ἀλλαχοῦ adv. *elsewhere, in another direction* Mk 1: 38.*

ἀλληγορέω *speak symbolically* or *allegorically* Gal 4: 24.*

ἁλληλουϊά (Heb.) *praise the Lord* (Yahweh), transliterated 'hallelujah' Rv 19: 1, 3, 4, 6.*

ἀλλήλων reciprocal pron., genitive pl. *each other, one another* J 13: 34; Js 4: 11.

ἀλλογενής, ές *foreign*; used as noun *foreigner* Lk 17: 18.*

ἀλλοιόω *change* Lk 9: 29 v.l.*

ἅλλομαι *leap up* Ac 3: 8; 14: 10; of water *well up* J 4: 14.*

ἄλλος, η, ο *other, another, different* Mt 13: 5, 24; 1 Cor 9: 27; 15: 41; *more, additional* Mt 4: 21; 25: 20. οἱ ἄλλοι *the rest* 1 Cor 14. 29. ἄλλοι – ἄλλο *some*—*one thing, some*—*another* Ac 19: 32; 21: 34. Contrary to the best classical usage, ἄ. invades the domain of ἕτερος (q.v.) and means *other* of two Mt 5: 39; 12: 13; it is used interchangeably with ἕτερος 2 Cor 11: 4, and prob. also Gal 1: 7, for which see ἕτερος.

ἀλλοτριεπίσκοπος, ου, ὁ a rare word of uncertain meaning; among those suggested are *busybody, informer, revolutionist* 1 Pt 4: 15.*

ἀλλότριος, ία, ιον *belonging to another, strange, foreign* Lk 16: 12; Ac 7: 6; 2 Cor 10: 15; Hb 11: 9. *Hostile, enemy* Hb 11: 34.

ἀλλόφυλος, ον *foreign, Gentile, heathen* as noun Ac 10: 28; 13: 19 v.l.*

ἄλλως adv. *otherwise*; τὰ ἄ. ἔχοντα *the opposite* 1 Ti 5: 25.*

ἀλοάω *thresh* 1 Cor 9: 9, 10; 1 Ti 5: 18.*

ἄλογος, ον *without reason* of animals 2 Pt 2: 12; Jd 10. *Contrary to reason, absurd* Ac 25: 27.*

ἀλόη, ης, ἡ *aloes* J 19: 39.*

ἅλς, ἁλός, ὁ see ἅλας.

ἁλυκός, ή, όν *salty*; *a salt spring* Js 3: 12.*

ἄλυπος, ον *free from grief* or *anxiety* Phil 2: 28.*

ἅλυσις, εως, ἡ *chain*, also *handcuffs* Mk 5: 3; Ac 28: 20; generally *captivity, imprisonment* Eph 6: 20; 2 Ti 1: 16.

ἀλυσιτελής, ές *unprofitable*, perhaps *harmful* Hb 13: 17.*

ἄλφα, τό indecl. *alpha*, first letter of the Greek alphabet;=*beginning* or *first* Rv 1: 8, 11 v.l.; 21: 6; 22: 13.*

Ἀλφαῖος, ου, ὁ *Alphaeus*—1. The father of Levi the tax-collector Mk 2: 14; Lk 5: 27 v.l.—2. The father of James, one of the twelve Mt 10: 3; Mk 3: 18; Lk 6: 15; Ac 1: 13.*

ἅλων, ωνος, ἡ *threshing floor* and the threshed grain upon it Mt 3: 12; Lk 3: 17.*

ἀλώπηξ, εκος, ἡ *fox* lit. Mt 8: 20; Lk 9: 58; fig. 13: 32.*

ἅλωσις, εως, ἡ *capture, catching* 2 Pt 2: 12.*

ἅμα adv. *at the same time, together* Ac 24: 26; Ro 3: 12; Phlm 22. Prep. w. dat. *together with* Mt 13: 29; 1 Th 5: 10, ἅ. πρωΐ *early in the morning* Mt 20: 1.

ἀμαθής, ές *ignorant* 2 Pt 3: 16.*

ἀμαράντινος, η, ον *unfading*, perhaps *made of amaranth* 1 Pt 5: 4.*

ἀμάραντος, ον *fadeless* 1 Pt 1: 4.*

ἀμαρτάνω *do wrong, sin* 1 Cor 7: 28: against God Lk 15: 18; Christ and the brethren 1 Cor 8: 12; oneself 6: 18; the law Ac 25: 8. ἁ. ἁμαρτίαν *commit a sin* 1 J 5: 16.

ἁμάρτημα, τος, τό *sin* (lit. 'the result of sinning') Mk 3: 28f.

ἁμαρτία, ας, ἡ *sin:* a sinful *deed* Mt 26: 28; Ac 3: 19; 1 Cor 15: 17; 1 Th 2: 16; Js 2: 9; *sinfulness* J 1: 29; 9: 41; 1 J 1: 7; almost personified in Paul, Ro 5: 12; 6: 12–14, 23. σῶμα τῆς ἁ. *a body ruled by sin* 6: 6.

ἁμάρτυρος, ον *without witness* Ac 14: 17.*

ἁμάρτω 2 aor. subj. act. of ἁμαρτάνω.

ἁμαρτωλός, όν *sinful* Mk 8: 38; Ro 7: 13. ὁ ἁ. *sinner*: of one not free from sin Hb 7: 26; of one not careful in the observance of ceremonial duties *unobservant* or *irreligious person* Mt 9: 10f; Lk 15: 1f; of one especially sinful 7: 37, 39;=*heathen* Lk 6: 32–34 (cf. Mt 5: 47); Gal 2: 15.

Ἀμασίας, ου, ὁ (Heb.) *Amaziah* Mt 1: 8 v.l.; Lk 3: 23ff v.l.*

ἄμαχος, ον *peaceable, not quarrelsome* 1 Ti 3: 3; Tit 3: 2.*

ἀμάω *reap, mow* Js 5: 4.*

ἀμέθυστος, ου, ἡ or ὁ *amethyst*, a precious stone of violet color Rv 21: 20.*

ἀμελέω *neglect* w. gen. 1 Ti 4: 14; Hb 2: 3; w. inf. 2 Pt 1: 12 v.l. *Disregard* w. gen Hb 8: 9. *Pay no attention* Mt 22: 5.*

ἄμεμπτος, ον *blameless, faultless* Lk 1: 6; Phil 3: 6; Hb 8: 7.

ἀμέμπτως adv. *blamelessly* 1 Th 2: 10; 5: 23.*

ἀμέριμνος, ον *free from care* 1 Cor 7: 32; ἁ. ποιεῖν τινα *keep someone out of trouble* Mt 28: 14.*

ἀμετάθετος, ον *unchangeable* Hb 6: 18; τὸ ἁ. *unchangeableness* 6: 17.*

ἀμετακίνητος, ον *immovable* 1 Cor 15: 58.*

ἀμεταμέλητος, ον *not to be regretted* 2 Cor 7: 10; *not to be taken back, irrevocable* Ro 11: 29.*

ἀμετανόητος, ον *unrepentant* Ro 2: 5.*

ἄμετρος, ον *immeasurable*; εἰς τὰ ἄ. *beyond limits* 2 Cor 10: 13, 15.*

ἀμήν (Heb.) asseverative particle *truly*, only with words of Jesus Mt 5: 18; Mk 3: 28; Lk 4: 24; J 1: 51. Liturgical formula *amen = so let it be* 1 Cor 14: 16; 2 Cor 1: 20; Gal 6: 18; 1 Pt 4: 11. ὁ ἄ. of Jesus, explained by the following clause Rv 3: 14.

ἀμήτωρ, ορος *without a mother* Hb 7: 3.*

ἀμίαντος, ον *undefiled, pure, unsullied* Hb 7: 26; 13: 4; Js 1: 27; 1 Pt 1: 4.*

'Αμιναδάβ, ὁ (Heb.) indecl. *Amminadab* Mt 1: 4; Lk 3: 33.*

ἄμμον, ου, τό *sand* Ro 4: 18 v.l.*

ἄμμος, ου, ἡ *sand* Mt 7: 26; Ro 9: 27; Rv 20: 8.

ἀμνός, οῦ, ὁ *lamb* used only in reference to Jesus J 1: 29, 36; Ac 8: 32; 1 Pt 1: 19.*

ἀμοιβή, ῆς, ἡ *(adequate) return, recompense* 1 Ti 5: 4.*

ἄμορφος, ον *misshappen, ugly* 1 Cor 12: 2 v.l.*

ἄμπελος, ου ἡ *vine, grapevine* Mk 14: 25; fig. J 15: 1, 4, 5.

ἀμπελουργός, οῦ, ὁ *vine-dresser, gardener* Lk 13: 7.*

ἀμπελών, ῶνος, ὁ *vineyard* Mk 12: 1f; 1 Cor 9: 7; perh. *orchard* Lk 13: 6.

'Αμπλιᾶτος, ου, ὁ (v.l. 'Αμπλιᾶς) *Ampliatus* common as a slave name Ro 16: 8.*

ἀμύνομαι *retaliate*; another possibility is *help, come to the aid of* Ac 7: 24.*

ἀμφιάζω *dress, clothe* Lk 12: 28.*

ἀμφιβάλλω *cast* a net Mk 1: 16.*

ἀμφίβληστρον, ου, τό a circular *casting-net* Mt 4: 18; Mk 1: 16 v.l.*

ἀμφιέζω variant form of ἀμφιάζω.

ἀμφιέννυμι *dress, clothe* Mt 6: 30; 11: 8; Lk 7: 25.*

'Αμφίπολις, εως, ἡ *Amphipolis* capital city of southeast Macedonia Ac 17: 1.*

ἄμφοδον, ου, τό *street* (lit. 'quarter of a city') Mk 11: 4; Ac 19: 28 v.l.*

ἀμφότεροι, αι, α *both* Lk 6: 39; Eph 2: 16. *All* (even when more than two are involved) Ac 19: 16; 23: 8.

ἀμώμητος, ον *blameless, unblemished* 2 Pt 3: 14; Phil 2: 15 v.l.*

ἄμωμον, ου, τό *amomum* an Indian spice plant Rv 18: 13.*

ἄμωμος, ον *unblemished* Hb 9: 14; 1 Pt 1: 19; *blameless* Eph 1: 4; Phil 2: 15; Rv 14: 5.

'Αμών, ὁ indecl. (Heb.) *Amon* Mt 1: 10 v.l.*

'Αμώς, ὁ indecl. (Heb.) *Amos*— 1. Lk 3: 25.—2. Mt 1: 10; Lk 3: 23ff v.l.*

ἄν an adverb incapable of translation by a single English word, denoting that the action of the verb is dependent on some circumstance or condition; its effect upon the meaning of its clause varies with the construction.—1. With the indicative— a. imperfect or aor. to indicate repeated action in past time, in relative and temporal clauses: ὅσοι ἄν ἥψαντο αὐτοῦ, ἐσῴζοντο *whoever touched him was cured* Mk 6: 56; cf. Ac 2: 45; 4: 35.— b. In the apodosis of contrary to fact (unreal) conditions, with imperfect tense for present time, aor. or plup. for past time: εἰ ἤν προφήτης, ἐγίνωσκεν ἄν *if he were a prophet, he would (now) know* Lk 7: 39. εἰ ἔγνωσαν, οὐκ ἄν ἐσταύρωσαν *if they had known him, they would not have crucified him* 1 Cor 2: 8. Plup. 1 J 2: 19. ἐλθών Lk 19: 23 and ἐπεί Hb 10: 2 are equivalents of a protasis.—**2.** With the subjunctive—**a.** in the protasis of conditional relative clauses of the future more vivid type ὃς ἂν ἐσθίῃ . . . ἔνοχος ἔσται *whoever eats will be guilty* 1 Cor 11: 27, or the present general type ἃ ἂν ἐκεῖνος ποιῇ, ταῦτα καὶ ὁ υἱὸς ὁμοίως ποιεῖ *whatever he does, the Son does also* J 5: 19. Similarly with temporal clauses ὅταν = ὅτε + ἄν *whenever* Mt 15: 2. ἡνίκα ἄν *as often as* 2 Cor 3: 15. ὡς ἄν *as soon as* 1 Cor 11: 34. ἕως ἄν *until* Mt 10: 11.—**b.** in purpose clauses with ὅπως, with no appreciable change in meaning Lk 2: 35.—**3.** With the optative: rare and literary in the N.T. In a main clause εὐξαίμην ἄν *I might wish* Ac 26: 29 (potential optative); in a rhetorical question πῶς γὰρ ἂν δυναίμην *how could I?* Ac 8: 31; in an indirect question τί ἂν ποιήσαιεν τῷ 'Ιησοῦ *what they might do with Jesus* Lk 6: 11.—**4.** ἄν for ἐάν = *if* J 5: 19a; 13: 20; 20: 23.

ἀνά prep. with acc., originally 'up, along' etc.—**1.** Alone, in distributive sense ἀνὰ δύο *two by two* Lk 10: 1; ἀνὰ πεντήκοντα *by fifties* 9: 14; ἀνὰ δηνάριον *a denarius each* Mt 20: 9f. Fixed as an adverb ἀνὰ εἷς ἕκαστος *each one singly* Rv 21: 21.—**2.** In combinations ἀνὰ μέσον w. gen. *among* Mt 13: 25; ἀ. μ. τῶν ὁρίων *into the (midst of the) district* Mk 7: 31; *between* 1 Cor 6: 5, w. omission of the second member; *in the center of* Rv 7: 17. ἀνὰ μέρος *in turn* 1 Cor 14: 27.

ἀνάβα 2 aor. act. imperative, 2nd sing. of ἀναβαίνω.

ἀναβαθμός, οῦ, ὁ *step*; pl. *flight of stairs* (from the temple to the tower Antonia) Ac 21: 35, 40.*

ἀναβαίνω *go up* Ac 1: 13, esp. to Jerusalem or the temple Mt

20: 17f; J 7: 14. *Climb up* Lk 19: 4. *Come up* Mt 3: 16; Mk 4: 7; Ac 21: 31. *Ascend* Ac 2: 34; 10: 4. ἀ. ἐπὶ τὴν καρδίαν *enter the mind* 1 Cor 2: 9. ἀ. ἐν τῇ καρδίᾳ *arise in the heart* Lk 24: 38.

ἀναβάλλω *defer, postpone*. ἀ. αὐτούς *he put them off, he adjourned their trial* legal term Ac 24: 22.*

ἀναβέβηκα perf. act. of ἀναβαίνω.

ἀναβήσομαι fut. mid. (dep.) of ἀναβαίνω.

ἀναβιβάζω *bring up, pull up* Mt 13: 48.*

ἀναβλέπω—**1.** *look up* Mt 14: 19; Mk 8: 24; Ac 22: 13.—**2.** *regain one's sight* Mt 11: 5; Mk 10: 51; Ac 9: 12, 17f. *Receive sight, become able to see* J 9: 11, 15, 18.

ἀνάβλεψις, εως, ἡ *recovery of sight* Lk 4: 18.*

ἀναβοάω *cry out* Mt 27: 46; Mk 15: 8 v.l.

ἀναβολή, ῆς, ἡ *delay, postponement* Ac 25: 17.*

ἀνάγαιον, ου, τό *a room upstairs* Mk 14: 15; Lk 22: 12.*

ἀναγγέλλω *report* Ac 14: 27; 2 Cor 7: 7. *Make known* Ac 19: 18; *proclaim* J 16: 13; 1 Pt 1: 12; *preach* Ac 20: 20.

ἀναγεννάω *cause to be born again* 1 Pt 1: 3, 23.*

ἀναγινώσκω *read* Mk 12: 26; J 19: 20; Ac 8: 28, 30 (the eunuch was reading aloud to himself); *read (aloud) in public* Lk 4: 16; Col 4: 16.

ἀναγκάζω *force, compel* Ac 26: 11; Gal 2: 3, 14; *invite, urge strongly* Mt 14: 22.

ἀναγκαῖος, α, ον—**1.** *necessary, urgent* 1 Cor 12: 22; Tit 3: 14.—**2.** *intimate, close* Ac 10: 24.

ἀναγκαστῶς adv. *by compulsion* 1 Pt 5: 2.*

ἀνάγκη, ης, ἡ—**1.** *necessity* Hb 7: 12; *compulsion* 2 Cor 9: 7. ἀ. ἔχω *I must* Lk 14: 18. ἀ. with ἐστίν understood = *it is necessary, one must* Hb 9: 16, 23.—

2. *distress, calamity* Lk 21: 23; 1 Cor 7: 26.

ἀναγνούς, ἀναγνῶναι, ἀναγωσθῆναι 2 aor. ptc. and inf. act., 1 aor. pass. inf. of ἀναγινώσκω.

ἀναγνωρίζω *learn to know again* Ac 7: 13 v.l.*

ἀνάγνωσις, εως, ἡ public *reading* in synagogue Ac 13: 15; 2 Cor 3: 14 or church 1 Ti 4: 13.*

ἀνάγω—**1.** *lead* or *bring up* Mt 4:1; Ac 9: 39; Ro 10: 7. *Bring before* Ac 12: 4. ἀ. θυσίαν *bring an offering* 7: 41.—**2.** mid. or pass. *put out to sea, set sail* Ac 13: 13; 18: 21.

ἀναδείκνυμι *show clearly* Ac 1: 24; *appoint* Lk 10: 1.*

ἀνάδειξις, εως, ἡ *commissioning, installation* Lk 1: 80.*

ἀναδέχομαι *accept, receive* Hb 11: 17; *welcome* Ac 28: 7.*

ἀναδίδωμι *hand over, deliver* Ac 23: 33.*

ἀναζάω *come to life again* Ro 14: 9 v.l.; Rv 20: 5 v.l.; fig. Lk 15: 24, 32 v.l. *Spring into life* Ro 7: 9.*

ἀναζητέω *look for, search for* Lk 2: 44f; Ac 11: 25.*

ἀναζώννυμι *bind up, gird up* the long robes to facilitate work or walking, fig. 1 Pt 1: 13.*

ἀναζωπυρέω *rekindle* 2 Ti 1: 6.*

ἀναθάλλω *grow again* or *cause to grow again, revive* Phil 4: 10.*

ἀνάθεμα, ατος, τό—**1.** *something dedicated to the deity, a votive gift* Lk 21: 5 v.l.—**2.** What is dedicated to a divinity may be either blessed or cursed (cf. Joshua 6: 17; 7: 12 LXX as an example of the latter sense, which came to predominate). So in the N.T. *cursed, a curse, anathema* Ac 23: 14; Ro 9: 3; 1 Cor 12: 3; 16: 22; Gal 1: 8f.*

ἀναθεματίζω *bind with an oath* or *under a curse* Ac 23: 12, 14, 21; intransitive *curse* Mk 14: 71.*

ἀναθεωρέω *look at* or *examine*

carefully Ac 17: 23; *consider* Hb 13: 7.*

ἀνάθημα, ατος, τό a *votive gift* Lk 21: 5.*

ἀναίδεια, ας, ἡ *persistence*, lit. 'shamelessness' Lk 11: 8.*

ἀναίρεσις, εως, ἡ *murder, killing* Ac 8: 1; 13: 28 v.l.; 22: 20 v.l.*

ἀναιρέω—**1.** *take away, abolish* Hb 10: 9. *Do away with, kill, murder* Mt 2: 16; Ac 16: 27; 2 Th 2: 8.—**2.** mid. *take up (for oneself), adopt* Ac 7: 21.

ἀναίτιος, ον *innocent* Mt 12: 5, 7; Ac 16: 37 v.l.*

ἀνακαθίζω *sit up* Lk 7: 15; Ac 9: 40.*

ἀνακαινίζω *renew, restore* Hb 6: 6.*

ἀνακαινόω *renew* 2 Cor 4: 16; Col 3: 10.*

ἀνακαίνωσις, εως, ἡ *renewal* Ro 12: 2; Tit 3: 5.*

ἀνακαλύπτω *uncover, unveil* 2 Cor 3: 14, 18 (see Exodus 34: 34).*

ἀνακάμπτω *return* Mt 2: 12; Lk 10: 6; Ac 18: 21; Hb 11: 15. *Turn back again* 2 Pt 2: 21 v.l.*

ἀνάκειμαι *lie down, recline* Mk 5: 40 v.l.; at table Mt 9: 10; J 12: 2. ὁ ἀνακείμενος *guest* Lk 22: 27.

ἀνακεφαλαιόω *sum up, recapitulate* Ro 13: 9; *gather up, unite* Eph 1: 10.*

ἀνακλίνω act. *cause to lie down* or *recline* Lk 12: 37; *put to bed* 2: 7. Mid. and pass. *lie down, recline* at a meal Mt 8: 11; Mk 6: 39.

ἀνακόπτω *hinder, restrain* Gal 5: 7 v.l.*

ἀνακράζω *cry out* Mk 1: 23; 6: 49; Lk 23: 18.

ἀνακραυγάζω *cry out* Lk 4: 35 v.l.*

ἀνακρίνω—**1.** *question, examine* Ac 17: 11; 1 Cor 10: 25, 27.—**2.** *judge, call to account* 1 Cor 2: 14f; 14: 24.—**3.** legal term *examine, investigate* Ac 12: 19; 28: 18; *conduct an examination* Lk 23: 14.

ἀνάκρισις, εως, ἡ preliminary investigation, hearing Ac 25: 26.*

ἀνακυλίω roll away Mk 16: 4.*

ἀνακύπτω stand erect, straighten oneself lit. Lk 13: 11; J 8: 7, 10; fig. Lk 21: 28.*

ἀναλαμβάνω take up Ac 1: 11; take Eph 6: 13, 16; take along Ac 7: 43; 2 Ti 4: 11; take on board Ac 20: 13f.

ἀναλημφθείς 1 aor. pass. ptc. of ἀναλαμβάνω.

ἀνάλημψις, εως, ἡ ascension; perhaps death, departure; lit. taking up Lk 9: 51.*

ἀναλίσκω or ἀναλόω consume Lk 9: 54; Gal 5: 15; 2 Th 2: 8 v.l.*

ἀνάλλομαι jump up Ac 14: 10 v.l.*

ἀναλογία, ας, ἡ right relationship, proportion κατὰ τὴν ἀ. in agreement with or in proportion to Ro 12: 6.*

ἀναλογίζομαι consider, think of Hb 12: 3.*

ἄναλος, ον without salt, tasteless Mk 9: 50.*

ἀναλόω see ἀναλίσκω.

ἀνάλυσις, εως, ἡ departure i.e. death, lit. 'dissolution' 2 Ti 4: 6.*

ἀναλύω loose, untie Ac 16: 26 v.l. Return, depart Lk 12: 36; depart=die Phil 1: 23.*

ἀναλῶσαι 1 aor. act. inf. of ἀναλίσκω (ἀναλόω.).

ἀναμάρτητος, ον without sin J 8: 7.*

ἀναμένω wait for 1 Th 1: 10.*

ἀναμιμνήσκω remind τινά τι someone of something 1 Cor 4: 17; cf. 2 Ti 1: 6. Mid. and pass. remember Mk 11: 21; 14: 72; Hb 10: 32.

ἀνάμνησις, εως, ἡ reminder Hb 10: 3; remembrance, memory Lk 22: 19; 1 Cor 11: 24f.*

ἀνανεόομαι be renewed Eph 4: 23.*

ἀνανήφω come to one's senses, lit. 'become sober again' 2 Ti 2: 26.*

Ἀνανίας, ου, ὁ (Heb. Hananiah) —1. A member of the Jerusalem church, husband of Sapphira Ac 5: 1.—2. A Christian of Damascus who helped Paul 9: 10; 22: 12.—3. A Jewish high priest (47–59 AD) 23: 2; 24: 1.

ἀναντίρρητος, ον not to be contradicted, undeniable Ac 19: 36.*

ἀναντιρρήτως adv. without raising any objection Ac 10: 29.*

ἀνάξιος, ον incompetent, unfit, lit. 'unworthy' 1 Cor 6: 2.*

ἀναξίως adv. in a careless or unworthy manner 1 Cor 11: 27, 29 v.l.*

ἀναπαήσομαι 2 fut. pass. ind. of ἀναπαύω.

ἀνάπαυσις, εως, ἡ—1. stopping, ceasing ἀνάπαυσιν οὐκ ἔχουσιν λέγοντες they say without ceasing Rv 4: 8; cf. 14: 11. Rest Mt 11: 29.—2. a resting-place Mt 12: 43; Lk 11: 24.*

ἀναπαύω act. cause to rest, give someone rest, refresh w. acc. Mt 11: 28; 1 Cor 16: 18; Phlm 20. Pass. be set at rest, be refreshed 2 Cor 7: 13; Phlm 7. Mid. rest, take one's rest or one's ease Mt 26: 45; Mk 6: 31; Lk 12: 19; remain quiet Rv 6: 11; rest upon 1 Pt 4: 14.

ἀναπείθω induce, incite, lit. 'persuade wrongly' Ac 18: 13.*

ἀνάπειρος, ον Hellenistic Gk. for ἀνάπηρος, q.v.

ἀναπέμπω send (up) to one in a higher position Lk 23: 7; Ac 25: 21; 27: 1 v.l. Send back Lk 23: 11, 15; Phlm 12.*

ἀνάπεσε,-εῖν 2 aor. act. imperative and inf. of ἀναπίπτω.

ἀναπηδάω jump up, stand up Mk 10: 50.*

ἀνάπηρος, ον crippled, as noun a cripple Lk 14: 13, 21.*

ἀναπίπτω lie down, recline esp. at a meal, take one's place to eat Mk 6: 40; Lk 11: 37; J 13: 12. Lean (back) J 13: 25.

ἀναπληρόω make complete, fill up the measure of 1 Th 2: 16.

Make up for 1 Cor 16: 17; Phil 2: 30. *Take* or *fill* a place 1 Cor 14: 16. *Fulfill, carry out* Mt 13: 14; Gal 6: 2.*

ἀναπολόγητος, ον *without excuse* Ro 1: 20; 2: 1.*

ἀναπράσσω *demand, exact* a payment Lk 19: 23 v.l.*

ἀναπτύσσω *unroll* of a book in scroll form Lk 4: 17 v.l.*

ἀνάπτω *kindle* Lk 12: 49; Js 3: 5; Ac 28: 2 v.l.

ἀναρίθμητος, ον *innumerable* Hb 11: 12.*

ἀνασείω *stir up, incite* Mk 15: 11; Lk 23: 5.*

ἀνασκευάζω *upset, unsettle* Ac 15: 24.*

ἀνασπάω *pull up* Ac 11: 10; *pull out* Lk 14: 5.*

ἀνάστα 2 aor. act. imperative of ἀνίστημι.

ἀνάστασις, εως, ἡ *rise, rising* Lk 2: 34. *Resurrection* of the dead Mt 22: 31; Lk 20: 35; J 11: 24f; Ac 1: 22; Ro 6: 5; 1 Cor 15: 12f; Rv 20: 5f.

ἀναστατόω *disturb, upset, trouble* Ac 17: 6; 21: 38; Gal 5: 12.*

ἀνασταυρόω *crucify again* Hb 6: 6.*

ἀναστενάζω *sigh deeply* Mk 8: 12.*

ἀνάστηθι 2 aor. act. imperative of ἀνίστημι.

ἀναστρέφω—1. *overturn, upset* J 2: 15 v.l.—2. *return* Ac 5: 22; 15: 16.—3. mid. and pass. *turn here and there, stay, live* in a place Mt 17: 22 v.l. Thus *conduct* or *behave oneself, live, act,* always with moral or religious coloring 2 Cor 1: 12; 1 Ti 3: 15; Hb 13: 18; 2 Pt 2: 18.

ἀναστροφή, ῆς, ἡ *way of life, conduct, behavior* Gal 1: 13; Js 3: 13; 1 Pt 2: 12.

ἀνασῴζω *save* Hb 10: 14 v.l.*

ἀνατάσσομαι *draw up, compile,* lit. 'arrange in proper order' Lk 1: 1.*

ἀνατεθραμμένος perf. pass. ptc. of ἀνατρέφω.

ἀνατείλας 1 aor. act. ptc. of ἀνατέλλω.

ἀνατέλλω—1. *cause to rise* Mt 5: 45.—2. intransitive *spring up, rise* Mt 13: 6; Mk 16: 2; 2 Pt 1: 19; *dawn* Mt 4: 16. *Come up* Lk 12: 54. *Be descended* Hb 7: 14.

ἀνατέταλκα perf. act. ind. of ἀνατέλλω.

ἀνατίθημι mid. *lay* a matter *before* someone for consideration Ac 25: 14; Gal 2: 2.*

ἀνατολή, ῆς, ἡ—1. *rising* of a star: ἐν τῇ ἀνατολῇ *in its rising,* when it rose Mt 2: 2.—2. *rising* of the sun, *east, orient* Mt 2: 1; 8: 11; Rv 7: 2; 21: 13. Fig. ἀ. ἐξ ὕψους *the dawn from heaven,* i.e. the Messiah Lk 1: 78.

ἀνατολικός, ή, όν *eastern* Ac 19: 1 v.l.*

ἀνατρέπω *overturn* lit. J 2: 15; fig. *upset, ruin* 2 Ti 2: 18; Tit 1: 11.*

ἀνατρέφω *bring up, care for, rear* Lk 4: 16 v.l.; Ac 7: 20, 21; 22: 3.*

ἀναφαίνω *cause to appear;* ἀναφάναντες τὴν Κύπρον *we came within sight of Cyprus,* i.e. we *sighted* it Ac 21: 3. Pass. *appear* Lk 19: 11.*

ἀναφάναντες 1 aor. act. ptc. of ἀναφαίνω.

ἀναφέρω—1. *take* or *lead up* Mk 9: 2.—2. *offer up* (as) a sacrifice Hb 7: 27; 1 Pt 2: 5.—3. *bear, take away* sins Hb 9: 28 (cf. Is 53: 12).

ἀναφωνέω *cry out* Lk 1: 42.*

ἀναχθείς 1 aor. pass. ptc. of ἀνάγω.

ἀνάχυσις, εως, ἡ *stream, flood,* lit. 'pouring out' 1 Pt 4: 4.*

ἀναχωρέω *go away* Mt 2: 13. *Withdraw, retire, take refuge* 2: 14; J 6: 15; Ac 23: 19. *Return* Mt 2: 12.

ἀνάψας 1 aor. act. ptc. of ἀνάπτω.

ἀνάψυξις, εως, ἡ refreshing, relief, rest Ac 3: 20.*

ἀναψύχω revive, refresh 2 Ti 1: 16; intr. be refreshed Ro 15: 32 v.l.*

ἀνδραποδιστής, οῦ, ὁ kidnapper, slave-dealer 1 Ti 1: 10.*

'Ανδρέας, ου, ὁ Andrew one of the twelve Mk 3: 18; 13: 3; J 1: 40, 44.

ἀνδρίζομαι act in a manly or courageous way 1 Cor 16: 13.*

'Ανδρόνικος, ου, ὁ Andronicus Ro 16: 7.*

ἀνδροφόνος, ου, ὁ murderer 1 Ti 1: 9.*

ἀνέβην 2 aor. act. ind. of ἀναβαίνω.

ἀνεγκλησία, ας, ἡ blamelessness ἀ. τοῦ θεοῦ blamelessness before God Phil 3: 14 v.l.*

ἀνέγκλητος, ον blameless, irreproachable 1 Cor 1: 8; Col 1: 22; 1 Ti 3: 10; Tit 1: 6f.*

ἀνέγνων 2 aor. act. ind. of ἀναγινώσκω.

ἀνέδειξα 1 aor. act. ind. of ἀναδείκνυμι.

ἀνεζωσάμην 1 aor. mid. ind. of ἀναζώννυμι.

ἀνέθαλον 2 aor. act. ind. of ἀναθάλλω.

ἀνεθέμην 2 aor. mid. ind. of ἀνατίθημι.

ἀνέθην 1 aor. pass. ind. of ἀνίημι.

ἀνεθρεψάμην 1 aor. mid. ind. of ἀνατρέφω.

ἀνεῖλα, ἀνεῖλον 2 aor. act. ind. of ἀναιρέω.

ἀνείς 2 aor. act. ptc. of ἀνίημι.

ἀνειχόμην imperf. mid. of ἀνέχω.

ἀνεκδιήγητος, ον indescribable 2 Cor 9: 15.*

ἀνεκλάλητος, ον inexpressible 1 Pt 1: 8.*

ἀνέκλειπτος, ον unfailing, inexhaustible Lk 12: 33.*

ἀνεκτός, όν bearable, tolerable; comp. ἀνεκτότερος more tolerable Mt 11: 22, 24; Lk 10: 12, 14.

ἀνελεήμων, ον unmerciful Ro 1: 31; Tit 1: 9 v.l.*

ἀνελεῖν, ἀνέλω 2 aor. act. inf. and subj. of ἀναιρέω.

ἀνέλεος, ον merciless Js 2: 13.*

ἀνεμίζω pass. be moved by the wind Js 1: 6.*

ἄνεμος, ου, ὁ wind Mt 11: 7; 14: 30; Ac 27: 14; the four directions or cardinal points Mk 13: 27; fig. Eph 4: 14.

ἀνένδεκτος, ον impossible Lk 17: 1.*

ἀνενέγκαι aor. act. inf. of ἀναφέρω.

ἀνέντες 2 aor. act. ptc. of ἀνίημι.

ἀνεξεραύνητος, ον unfathomable, inscrutable Ro 11: 33.*

ἀνεξίκακος, ον bearing evil without resentment, patient 2 Ti 2: 24.*

ἀνεξιχνίαστος, ον inscrutable, mysterious Ro 11: 33. Fathomless, inexhaustible Eph 3: 8; lit. 'not to be tracked out.'*

ἀνέξομαι fut. mid. ind. of ἀνέχομαι.

ἀνεπαίσχυντος, ον who does not need to be ashamed 2 Ti 2: 15.*

ἀνέπεσα aor. act. ind. of ἀναπίπτω.

ἀνεπίλημπτος, ον beyond reproach 1 Ti 3: 2; 5: 7; 6: 14.*

ἀνέπτυξα 1 aor. act. ind. of ἀναπτύσσω.

ἀνέρχομαι go up J 6: 3; Gal 1: 17, 18.*

ἀνέσεισα 1 aor. act. ind. of ἀνασείω.

ἄνεσις, εως, ἡ rest, relaxation 2 Cor 2: 13; 7: 5; 8: 13; 2 Th 1: 7. Freedom, relief Ac 24: 23.*

ἀνέστην 2 aor. act. ind. of ἀνίστημι.

ἀνετάζω examine someone, give someone a hearing Ac 22: 24, 29.*

ἄνευ prep. w. gen. without Mk 13: 2 v.l.; 1 Pt 3: 1; 4: 9. Without the knowledge and consent of Mt 10: 29.*

ἀνεύθετος, ον unfavorably situated, poor Ac 27: 12.*

ἀνευρίσκω find after searching Lk 2: 16; Ac 21: 4.*

ἀνέχομαι put up with, bear with, endure Mt 17: 17; 1 Cor 4: 12;

2 Cor 11: 1. *Hear* or *listen to willingly* Hb 13: 22. *Accept* a complaint Ac 18: 14.

ἀνεψιός, οῦ, ὁ *cousin* Col 4: 10.*

ἀνέῳγα, ἀνέῳξα 2 perf. act. ind. and 1 aor. act. ind. of ἀνοίγω.

ἀνήγαγον 2 aor. act. ind. of ἀνάγω.

ἀνήγγειλα, ἀνηγγέλην 1 aor. act. ind. and 2 aor. pass. ind. of ἀναγγέλλω.

ἄνηθον, ου, τό *dill* Mt 23: 23.*

ἀνῆκα 1 aor. act. ind. of ἀνίημι.

ἀνήκω *be proper* or *fitting* impersonal Eph 5: 4; Col 3: 18. τὸ ἀνῆκον *what is proper, one's duty* Phlm 8.*

ἀνήμερος, ον *savage, brutal,* lit. 'untamed' 2 Ti 3: 3.*

ἀνήνεγκον 2 aor. act. ind. of ἀναφέρω.

ἀνήρ, ἀνδρός, ὁ *man,* normally an adult (1 Cor 13: 11) male (Ac 8: 3, 12). Specialized senses: *husband* Mk 10: 2, 12; *bridegroom* Rv 21: 2; in address, pl. *gentlemen* Ac 27: 10, 21, 25; ἄνδρες ἀδελφοί *brethren* 15: 7, 13. Pleonastic ἀνὴρ ἁμαρτωλός = simply *a sinner* Lk 5: 8. Rarely *person* = ἄνθρωπος, see Lk 11: 31; Js 1: 12.

ἀνῃρέθην 1 aor. pass. ind. of ἀναιρέω.

ἀνήφθην 1 aor. pass. ind. of ἀνάπτω.

ἀνήχθην 1 aor. pass. ind. of ἀνάγω.

ἀνθέξομαι fut. mid. ind. of ἀντέχομαι.

ἀνθίστημι *set oneself against, oppose, resist, withstand* Lk 21: 15; Ro 13: 2; Gal 2: 11; Js 4: 7; *stand one's ground* Eph 6: 13.

ἀνθομολογέομαι *praise, thank* Lk 2: 38.*

ἄνθος, ους, τό *flower;* ἀ. χόρτου *wild flower* Js 1: 10, cf. 11; 1 Pt 1: 24.*

ἀνθρακιά, ᾶς, ἡ *a charcoal fire* J 18: 18; 21: 9.*

ἄνθραξ, ακος, ὁ *charcoal;* ἄνθρακες πυρός *burning embers* Ro 12: 20 (cf. Pr 25: 22).*

ἀνθρωπάρεσκος, ον as subst., *one who tries to please men* at the sacrifice of principle Eph 6: 6; Col 3: 22.*

ἀνθρώπινος, η, ον *human* Ac 17: 25; 1 Cor 2: 13; Js 3: 7. A temptation *common to man,* i.e. bearable 1 Cor 10: 13. Speak *in human terms* Ro 6: 19. *Commonly accepted* 1 Ti 3: 1 v.l.; 1: 15 v.l.

ἀνθρωποκτόνος, ου, ὁ *murderer* J 8: 44; 1 J 3: 15.*

ἄνθρωπος, ου, ὁ *human being, man, person;* pl. *people* Mt 5: 13, 16; Mk 10: 27; 1 Cor 1: 25; 2 Cor 3: 2; Phil 2: 7; *mankind* in general Mk 2: 27. In address, w. a connotation of familiarity *friend* Lk 5: 20; of impatience 22: 58, 60; of contempt, almost = *fellow* Mk 14: 71; J 5: 12. Indefinite, almost = τὶς *someone* J 4: 29; 1 Cor 4: 1; w. negative *nobody* J 5: 7; 7: 46. *Everyone* Ro 14: 20. Restricted to adult males *man, husband* Mt 19: 5, 10; 1 Cor 7: 1. *Son* Mt 10: 35. May be omitted in translating such combinations as ἀ. φάγος = simply *a glutton* Lk 7: 34; cf. Mt 13: 52; 18: 23; Ac 21: 39. κατὰ ἄ. *in a human way* 1 Cor 9: 8; *in accordance with (mere) human thought* Gal 1: 11.

ἀνθυπατεύω *be proconsul* Ac 18: 12 v.l.*

ἀνθύπατος, ου, ὁ *proconsul* governor of a senatorial province in the Roman Empire Ac 13: 7; 18: 12.

ἀνιέντες pres. act. ptc. of ἀνίημι.

ἀνίημι—1. *unfasten, untie* Ac 16: 26; 27: 40.—**2.** *abandon, desert* Hb 13: 5.—**3.** *give up, stop* Eph 6: 9.*

ἀνίλεως, neut. **ων,** gen. **ω** *merciless* Js 2: 13 v.l. for ἀνέλεος.*

ἄνιπτος, ον *unwashed,* i.e. ceremonially unclean Mt 15: 20; Mk 7: 2, 5 v.l.*

ἀνίστημι—1. trans. *raise, erect, raise up* Ac 9: 41. Of the dead *raise (up), bring to life* J 6: 39f; Ac 2: 24; 13: 34. In the sense *cause to appear* or *to be born* Mt 22: 24; Ac 3: 22.—2. intr. (2 aor. and all mid. forms) *rise, stand up, get up* Mt 26: 62; Lk 11: 7f; *rise* from the dead Mk 9: 10, 31; 1 Th 4: ·16. Short for *stand up and go* Mk 14: 60; Lk 4: 38. In the sense *appear, come* Mt 12: 41; Hb 7: 11, 15. Weakened to *set out, get ready* Mk 2: 14; Lk 1: 39; Ac 8: 26; 10: 20.

Ἄννα, ας, ἡ *Anna* Lk 2: 36.*

Ἄννας, α, ὁ *Annas* high priest 6–15 A.D., father-in-law of Caiaphas Lk 3: 2; J 18: 13, 24; Ac 4: 6.*

ἀνόητος, ον *foolish, senseless* Lk 24: 25; Gal 3: 1; 1 Ti 6: 9.

ἄνοια, ας, ἡ *foolishness* 2 Ti 3: 9; *fury* Lk 6: 11.*

ἀνοίγω—1. trans. *open* Mt 3: 16; J 9: 10; Ac 5: 19; 14: 27; Rv 5: 9.—2. intr. (only 2 pf. ἀνέῳγα) *open (itself), be open* J 1: 51; 1 Cor 16: 9. στόμα ἡμῶν ἀνέῳγεν *our mouth is open,* i.e. we have spoken freely 2 Cor 6: 11.

ἀνοικοδομέω *build up again* Ac 15: 16.*

ἄνοιξις, εως, ἡ the act of *opening* ἐν ἀ. τοῦ στόματός μου *when I open my mouth* Eph 6: 19.*

ἀνοίσω fut. of ἀναφέρω.

ἀνοιχθήσομαι fut. pass. of ἀνοίγω.

ἀνομία, ας, ἡ *lawlessness, sin* as a frame of mind Ro 6: 19a; 1 J 3: 4. *A lawless deed* Mt 13: 41; Ro 6: 19b; Hb 10: 17.

ἄνομος, ον simply *without law* 1 Cor 9: 21a, b; *lawless, godless, criminal* Lk 22: 37; Ac 2: 23; 1 Ti 1: 9. ἄ. θεοῦ *rejecting God's law* 1 Cor 9: 21c. ὁ ἄ. = the Antichrist 2 Th 2: 8.

ἀνόμως *without the law* Ro 2: 12.*

ἀνόνητος, ον *useless* 1 Ti 6: 9 v.l.*

ἀνορθόω *rebuild, restore* lit. *make erect again* Ac 15: 16. Of a crippled woman Lk 13: 13; *strengthen* Hb 12: 12.*

ἀνόσιος, ον *unholy, wicked* 1 Ti 1: 9; 2 Ti 3: 2.*

ἀνοχή, ῆς, ἡ *forbearance, clemency* Ro 2: 4; 3: 26.*

ἀνταγωνίζομαι *struggle* Hb 12: 4.*

ἀντάλλαγμα, ατος, τό that which *is given* in *exchange, an equivalent* Mt 16: 26; Mk 8: 37.*

ἀνταναπληρόω *fill up, complete* Col 1: 24.*

ἀνταποδίδωμι *give back, repay, return* Lk 14: 14; Ro 12: 19; 1 Th 3: 9.

ἀνταπόδομα, ατος, τό *repayment* Lk 14: 12; *retribution* Ro 11: 9.*

ἀνταπόδοσις, εως, ἡ *repaying, reward* Col 3: 24.*

ἀνταποκρίνομαι *answer in turn, make reply* Lk 14: 6; *answer back* Ro 9: 20.*

ἀντεῖπον 2 aor. only *speak against, contradict* Lk 21: 15; *say in reply* Ac 4: 14.*

ἀντέχω *cling to, be devoted to* Mt 6: 24; Lk 16: 13. *Take an interest in, pay attention to* Tit 1: 9; *help* 1 Th 5: 14.*

ἀντί prep. w. gen., orig. mng. local, *opposite*—1. *instead of, in place of* Mt 2: 22; Lk 11: 11; Js 4: 15.—2. *for, as, in place of* Mt 5: 38; Ro 12: 17; 1 Cor 11: 15; *after or upon* J 1: 16.—3. *for, in behalf of* Mt 17: 27; 20: 28. ἀνθ᾿ ὧν *because* Lk 1: 20; 2 Th 2: 10; *therefore* Lk 12: 3; cf. Eph 5: 31. (*In exchange*) *for* Hb 12: 16.

ἀντιβάλλω *put* or *place against, exchange* ἀ. λόγους *discuss* Lk 24: 17.*

ἀντιδιατίθημι mid. *oppose oneself, be opposed* 2 Ti 2: 25.*

ἀντίδικος, ου, ὁ *enemy, opponent* in a lawsuit or generally Mt 5: 25; Lk 12: 58; 18: 3; 1 Pt 5: 8.*

ἀντίθεσις, εως, ἡ *opposition, objection, contradiction* 1 Ti 6: 20.*

ἀντικαθίστημι intr. *oppose, resist* Hb 12: 4.*

ἀντικαλέω *invite in return* Lk 14: 12.*

ἀντίκειμαι *be opposed* Gal 5: 17; 1 Ti 1: 10. ὁ ἀντικείμενος *the opponent* Phil 1: 28; cf. Lk 13: 17; 21: 15; 1 Cor 16: 9; 2 Th 2: 4; 1 Ti 5: 14.*

ἄντικρυς adv., used as improper prep. w. gen. *opposite, off* Ac 20: 15.*

ἀντιλαμβάνω mid. *come to the aid of, help* Lk 1: 54; Ac 20: 35. *Take part in, devote oneself to* or perh. *enjoy, benefit by* 1 Ti 6: 2.*

ἀντιλέγω *speak against, contradict* Ac 13: 45; 28: 19, 22; Tit 1: 9; 2: 9; *deny* Lk 20: 27. *Oppose, be obstinate* Lk 2: 34; J 19: 12; Ro 10: 21.*

ἀντίλημψις, εως, ἡ *help* pl. *helpful deeds* 1 Cor 12: 28.*

ἀντιλογία, ας, ἡ *contradiction, dispute* Hb 6: 16; 7: 7. *Hostility, rebellion* 12: 3; Jd 11.*

ἀντιλοιδορέω *revile in return* 1 Pt 2: 23.*

ἀντίλυτρον, ου, τό *ransom* 1 Ti 2: 6.*

ἀντιμετρέω *measure in return* Lk 6: 38.*

ἀντιμισθία, ας, ἡ *exchange* τὴν αὐτὴν ἀ. πλατύνθητε *widen your hearts in the same way in exchange* 2 Cor 6: 13. *Penalty* Ro 1: 27.*

'Αντιόχεια, ας, ἡ—1. *Antioch in Syria, on the Orontes River* Ac 11: 19–26; 13: 1; Gal 2: 11.— 2. *Antioch in Pisidia in Asia Minor* Ac 13: 14; 2 Ti 3: 11.

'Αντιοχεύς, έως, ὁ *a man from Antioch in Syria* Ac 6: 5.*

ἀντιπαρέρχομαι *pass by on the opposite side* Lk 10: 31f.*

'Αντιπᾶς, ᾶ, ὁ *Antipas* Rv 2: 13.*

'Αντιπατρίς, ίδος, ἡ *Antipatris* a city in Judaea Ac 23: 31.*

ἀντιπέρα adv., used as improper prep. w. gen. *opposite* Lk 8: 26.*

ἀντιπίπτω *resist, oppose* Ac 7: 51.*

ἀντιστῆναι 2 aor. act. inf. of ἀνθίστημι.

ἀντιστρατεύομαι *be at war with* Ro 7: 23.*

ἀντιτάσσω mid. *oppose, offer resistance* Ac 18: 6; Ro 13: 2; Js 4: 6; 5: 6; 1 Pt 5: 5.*

ἀντίτυπος, ον *serving as a counterpart to, corresponding to* 1 Pt 3: 21. As a noun *copy, antitype, representation* Hb 9: 24.*

ἀντίχριστος, ου, ὁ *the Antichrist* 1 J 2: 18, 22; 4: 3; 2 J 7; pl. 1 J 2: 18.*

ἀντλέω *draw water* J 2: 8, 9; 4: 7, 15.*

ἄντλημα, ατος, τό *bucket* for drawing water J 4: 11.*

ἀντοφθαλμέω *look directly at, face* Ac 27: 15; 6: 10 (11) v.l.*

ἄνυδρος, ον *waterless* Mt 12: 43; Lk 11: 24; 2 Pt 2: 17; νεφέλαι ἄ. *clouds that yield no rain* Jd 12.*

ἀνυπόκριτος, ον *genuine, sincere*, lit. *without hypocrisy* or *insincerity* Ro 12: 9; 1 Ti 1: 5; Js 3: 17.

ἀνυπότακτος, ον *not made subject, independent* Hb 2: 8. *Undisciplined, disobedient, rebellious* 1 Ti 1: 9; Tit 1: 6, 10.*

ἄνω adv. *above* J 8: 23; Ac 2: 19; Gal 4: 26; Col 3: 1f; ἕως ἄνω *to the brim* J 2: 7. *Upward* J 11: 41; Phil 3: 14; Hb 12: 15.

ἀνῶ 2 aor. subj. act. of ἀνίημι.

ἄνωθεν adv.—1. *from above*, esp. *heaven* Mk 15: 38; J 19: 23; Js 3: 15.—2. *from the beginning* Lk 1: 3; *for a long time* Ac 26: 5.—3. *again, anew* Gal 4: 9. In J 3: 3, 7 ἀ. is purposely given a double meaning *again* and *from above*.

ἀνωτερικός, ή, όν *upper, inland, interior* Ac 19: 1.*

ἀνώτερος, έρα, ον neut, as adv.

higher, i.e. to a better place Lk 14: 10; *above, earlier* Hb 10: 8.*

ἀνωφελής, ἐς *useless* τὸ ἀ. *uselessness* Hb 7: 18; *harmful* Tit 3: 9.*

ἀξίνη, ης, ἡ *ax* Mt 3: 10; Lk 3: 9; 13: 7 v.l.*

ἄξιος, ία, ον *worthy* Mt 10: 37f; 1 Ti 1: 15; 4: 9; Hb 11: 38; *to be compared* Ro 8: 18; *in keeping with* Lk 3: 8; *deserving* Lk 12: 48; 23: 15; Ac 25: 11, 25; Ro 1: 32; *fit* Lk 15: 19; *good enough* J 1: 27. Impers. ἄξιόν ἐστι *it is worth while, proper* 1 Cor 16: 4.

ἀξιόω *consider worthy* Lk 7: 7; Hb 10: 29; *make worthy* 2 Th 1: 11. *Consider fitting*, hence *ask, desire, request* Ac 15: 38; 28: 22.

ἀξίως adv. *worthily, in a manner worthy of* Ro 16: 2; Phil 1: 27; Col 1: 10.

ἀόρατος, ον *unseen, invisible* Ro 1: 20; Col 1: 15f; Hb 11: 27.

ἀπαγγέλλω *report, announce, tell* Mt 11: 4; Mk 6: 30; Lk 7: 18; Ac 12: 14; *proclaim* Mt 12: 18; *confess* 1 Cor 14: 25.

ἀπάγχω mid. *hang oneself* Mt 27: 5.*

ἀπάγω—1. trans. *lead away* Lk 13: 15. As legal term *bring before, arraign* Mt 26: 57; Mk 14: 53; Ac 23: 17. *Lead away* to trial, prison or execution Mk 14: 44; Lk 23: 26; Ac 12: 19.—Pass. *be misled* 1 Cor 12: 2.—2. intr. of a road *lead* Mt 7: 13f.

ἀπαίδευτος, ον *stupid* lit. 'uneducated' 2 Ti 2: 23.*

ἀπαίρω pass. *be taken away* Mk 2: 20.

ἀπαιτέω *ask for* or *demand* something *back* Lk 6: 30. Of life regarded as a loan 12: 20.*

ἀπαλγέω *become callous* Eph 4: 19.*

ἀπαλλάσσω act. *free, release* Hb 2: 15. Pass. *be released, be cured* Ac 5: 15 v.l.; *come to a settlement* with someone Lk 12: 58; intr. *leave, depart* Ac 19: 12.*

ἀπαλλοτριόω pass. *be estranged, alienated* Eph 2: 12; 4: 18; Col 1: 21.*

ἀπαλός, ή, όν *tender* Mt 24: 32; Mk 13: 28.*

ἀπαντάω *meet* Mk 14: 13; Lk 17: 12.*

ἀπάντησις, εως, ἡ the act of *meeting* someone; εἰς ἀπάντησιν *to meet* Mt 25: 6; 27: 32 v.l.; Ac 28: 15; 1 Th 4: 17.*

ἅπαξ adv. *once* 2 Cor 11: 25; Hb 9: 27. ἔτι ἅ. *once more* = for the last time 12: 26f. ἅ. καὶ δίς *once and again, repeatedly* Phil 4: 16; 1 Th 2: 18. *Once for all* Hb 10: 2; 1 Pt 3: 18; Jd 3, 5.

ἀπαράβατος, ον *permanent, unchangeable* Hb 7: 24.*

ἀπαρασκεύαστος, ον *unprepared* 2 Cor 9: 4.*

ἀπαρθῇ 1 aor. pass. subj. of ἀπαίρω.

ἀπαρνέομαι *deny, disown, repudiate* Mk 14: 30f, 72; Lk 12: 9.

ἀπαρτί adv. *exactly, certainly* conjectural emendation for ἀπ' ἄρτι Rv 14: 13.*

ἀπάρτι see ἀπ' ἄρτι s.v. ἄρτι.

ἀπαρτισμός, οῦ, ὁ *completion* Lk 14: 28.*

ἀπαρχή, ῆς, ἡ *first-fruits*, the first of any crop or offspring of livestock, consecrated before the rest could be used Ro 11: 16 (cf. Num 15: 18–21). Fig. Ro 16: 5; 1 Cor 15: 20; Rv 14: 4; *foretaste* Ro 8: 23.

ἅπας, ασα, αν used in Attic Gk. for πᾶς after consonants; this distinction is not always maintained in the N.T. *all, whole, every* Mt 24: 39; Mk 8: 25; Lk 8: 37; 23: 1; Ac 4: 31; 16: 3, 28; Js 3: 2.

ἀπασπάζομαι *take leave of, say farewell to* Ac 21: 6; 20: 1 v.l.*

ἀπατάω *deceive, cheat, mislead* Eph 5: 6; 1 Ti 2: 14; Js 1: 26.*

ἀπάτη, ης, ἡ—1. *deception, deceitfulness* Col 2: 8; 2 Th 2: 10; Hb 3: 13; ἐπιθυμία τ. ἀπάτης

deceptive desire Eph 4: 22. In
Mt 13: 22; Mk 4: 19 ἡ ἀ. τοῦ
πλούτου may mean *the seduction
which comes from wealth* or
(see 2 below) *pleasure.*—**2.** *pleasure, pleasantness* 2 Pt 2: 13;
perhaps Mt 13: 22; Mk 4: 19
(see 1 above) and possibly Hb
3: 13.*

ἀπάτωρ, gen. ορος *without father*
Hb 7: 3.*

ἀπαύγασμα, ατος, τό act. *radiance,
effulgence* pass. *reflection;* the
act. is prob. preferable in Hb 1:
3.*

ἀπαφρίζω *cast off like foam* Jd 13
v.l.*

ἀπέβην 2 aor. act. ind. of ἀποβαίνω

ἀπέδετο Hellenistic form for ἀπέ-
δοτο, 2 aor. mid. ind., 3 sing.,
of ἀποδίδωμι.

ἀπεδίδουν imperf. act. ind. of
ἀποδίδωμι.

ἀπεδόμην 2 aor. mid. ind. of
ἀποδίδωμι.

ἀπέθανον 2 aor. act. ind. of
ἀποθνῄσκω.

ἀπεῖδον 2 aor. act. ind. of ἀφοράω.

ἀπείθεια, ας, ἡ *disobedience, dis-
belief* Ro 11: 30, 32; Hb 4: 6, 11.
υἱοὶ τῆς ἀ. *disobedient sons,* i.e.
men Eph 2: 2; 5: 6; Col 3: 6
v.l.*

ἀπειθέω *disobey, be disobedient*
or *disloyal* Ro 10: 21; 11: 30f;
Hb 3: 18; 11: 31. The mng.
disbelieve (in the Christian gospel), *be an unbeliever* is probable
for such passages as J 3: 36; Ac
14: 2; Ro 15: 31.

ἀπειθής, ές *disobedient* Ac 26: 19;
Ro 1: 30; Tit 1: 16.

ἀπειλέω *threaten, warn* Ac 4: 17;
1 Pt 2: 23.*

ἀπειλή, ῆς, ἡ *threat* Ac 4: 17 v.l.,
29; 9: 1; Eph 6: 9.*

I. ἄπειμι (εἰμί) *be absent* or *away*
1 Cor 5: 3; 2 Cor 13: 2, 10;
Phil 1: 27.

II. ἄπειμι (εἶμι) *go, come* lit. 'go
away' Ac 17: 10.*

ἀπειπάμην mid. of ἀπεῖπον.

ἀπεῖπον *disown, renounce* 2 Cor 4:
2.*

ἀπείραστος, ον *incapable of being
tempted* κακῶν *by evil* Js 1: 13.*

ἄπειρος, ον *unacquainted with*
Hb 5: 13.*

ἀπεκατέστην 1 aor. act. ind. of
ἀποκαθίστημι.

ἀπεκδέχομαι *await eagerly* Ro
8: 19, 23, 25; Phil 3: 20; Hb 9:
28.

ἀπεκδύομαι *take off, strip off*
fig. Col 3: 9. *Disarm* 2: 15.*

ἀπέκδυσις, εως, ἡ *removal, strip-
ping off* fig. Col 2: 11.*

ἀπεκρίθην 1 aor. pass. ind. of
ἀποκρίνομαι.

ἀπεκτάνθην 1 aor. pass. ind. of
ἀποκτείνω.

ἀπελαύνω *drive away* Ac 18: 16.*

ἀπελεγμός, οῦ, ὁ *refutation, dis-
credit, disrepute* Ac 19: 27.*

ἀπελεύθερος, ου, ὁ *freedman* fig.
1 Cor 7: 22.*

ἀπεληλύθειν, ἀπελθών pluperf.
act. ind. and 2 aor. act. ptc. of
ἀπέρχομαι.

᾽Απελλῆς, οῦ, ὁ *Apelles* Ro 16: 10.*

ἀπελπίζω *give up hope, despair* Eph
4: 19 v.l. In Lk 6: 35 μηδὲν
ἀπελπίζοντες = *expecting nothing
in return;* cf. vs. 34.*

ἀπέναντι improper prep. w. gen.
opposite Mt 27: 61; *before* Ro
3: 18; *against, contrary to* Ac
17: 7.

ἀπενεγκεῖν 2 aor. act. inf. of
ἀποφέρω.

ἀπεπνίγην 2 aor. pass. ind. of
ἀποπνίγω.

ἀπέραντος, ον *endless* 1 Ti 1: 4.*

ἀπερισπάστως adv. *without dis-
traction* 1 Cor 7: 35.*

ἀπερίτμητος, ον *uncircumcised,*
fig. = obdurate Ac 7: 51.*

ἀπέρχομαι *go away, go* Mt 8: 21,
33; 19: 22; Mk 1: 35; 5: 17; Ro
15: 28; *leave* Mk 1: 42; *pass
away* Rv 21: 1, 4; *go out and
spread* Mt 4: 24. ἀ. ὀπίσω *follow*

Mk 1: 20; *go in search of* Jd 7; ἀ. εἰς τὰ ὀπίσω *draw back* J 6: 66; 18: 6.

ἀπεστάλην, ἀπέσταλκα, ἀπέστειλα 2 aor. pass. ind., 1 perf. act. ind., 1 aor. act. ind. of ἀποστέλλω.

ἀπέστην 2 aor. act. ind. of ἀφίστημι.

ἀπεστράφην 2 aor. pass. ind. of ἀποστρέφω.

ἀπέχω—1. act., trans. *receive* a sum *in full* and give a receipt for it (commercial term) Mt 6: 2, 5, 16; Lk 6: 24; Phil 4: 18.— *Keep* Phlm 15. Among the possibilities for ἀπέχει in the difficult passage Mk 14: 41 are *it is enough* and, taking 'Judas' as the subj. and 'his money' as the obj., *he has received.*—**2.** act., intrans. *be distant* lit. Mt 14: 24; Lk 7: 6; 15: 20; 24: 13; fig. Mt 15: 8.—**3.** mid. *keep away, abstain* Ac 15: 20, 29; 1 Th 4: 3; 1 Ti 4: 3; 1 Pt 2: 11.

ἀπήγξατο 1 aor. ind. mid. of ἀπάγχομαι.

ἀπῇεσαν imperf. act. ind. of ἄπειμι (εἶμι).

ἀπήλασα 1 aor. act. ind. of ἀπελαύνω.

ἀπήλγηκα perf. act. ind. of ἀπαλγέω.

ἀπῆλθα, ἀπῆλθον 2 aor. act. ind. of ἀπέρχομαι.

ἀπηλλάχθαι perf. pass. inf. of ἀπαλλάσσω.

ἀπίδω 2 aor. subj. act. of ἀφοράω.

ἀπιστέω—1. *disbelieve, refuse to believe* Lk 24: 11, 41; Ac 28: 24; 1 Pt 2: 7.—**2.** *be unfaithful* Ro 3: 3; 2 Ti 2: 13.

ἀπιστία, ας, ἡ—1. *unfaithfulness* Ro 3: 3.—**2.** *lack of faith, unbelief* Mk 6: 6; 9: 24; Ro 11: 20; 1 Ti 1: 13. καρδία ἀπιστίας *an unbelieving heart* Hb 3: 12.

ἄπιστος, ον—1. *unbelievable, incredible* Ac 26: 8.—**2.** *faithless, unbelieving* Mk 9: 19; J 20: 27; 1 Cor 6: 6; 7: 12–15; 14: 23f; Rv 21: 8.

ἁπλότης, ητος, ἡ *simplicity, sincerity, frankness* Eph 6: 5; Col 3: 22; 2 Cor 1: 12 v.l. ἀ. εἰς Χριστόν *sincere devotion to Christ* 2 Cor 11: 3. *Generosity, liberality* Ro 12: 8; 2 Cor 8: 2; 9: 11, 13.*

ἁπλοῦς, ῆ, οῦν lit. 'single, sincere', then *clear, sound, healthy,* with the connotation *generous* (opp. πονηρός; see Mt 20: 15) Mt 6: 22; Lk 11: 34.—Superl. ἁπλούστατος *quite innocent, guileless* Mt 10: 16 v.l.*

ἁπλῶς adv. *without reserve, generously* Js 1: 5.*

ἀπό prep. w. gen. *from, away from, out of* (separation, departure, origin) Mt 17: 25f; Mk 5: 17; 8: 11; Lk 1: 52; 16: 18; 22: 71; Ac 2: 5; 1 Th 1: 8. *Because of, from, with* (cause, manner) Lk 21: 26; 22: 45; J 21: 6; Ac 11: 19. *With* (means) Lk 15: 16 v.l.; *by* (agent), direct Ac 2: 22, indirect Js 1: 13. As substitute for the partitive genitive *of, some of* Mt 27: 21; Mk 7: 28; J 21: 10; for the genitive of material Mt 3: 4.—ἀ. τῶν καρπῶν *by the fruit* Mt 7: 16, 20. ἀφ' ἧς or οὗ *since, when* Lk 7: 45; 13: 25; 24: 21. ἀ. ἐτῶν δώδεκα *for twelve years* Lk 8: 43. ἀ. μιᾶς *alike, unanimously* Lk 14: 18. ἀ. σταδίων δεκαπέντε (*by*) *fifteen stades* J 11: 18. ἀνάθεμα ἀ. Χριστοῦ *separated from Christ by a curse* Ro 9: 3. ἀ. μέρους *in part* Ro 11: 25. The extraordinary expression ἀπὸ ὁ ὤν κ.τ.λ. Rv 1: 4 may be due to the writer's reverence for the divine name, which he leaves undeclined; it is one of the many grammatical peculiarities of this book.

ἀποβαίνω *get out,* lit. 'go away' Lk 5: 2; J 21: 9. *Turn out, lead* (to) Lk 21: 13; Phil 1: 19.*

ἀποβάλλω *throw off* Mk 10: 50; *lose, throw away* Hb 10: 35.*

ἀποβλέπω look, pay attention Hb 11: 26.*

ἀπόβλητος, ον rejected (as unclean) 1 Ti 4: 4.*

ἀποβολή, ῆς, ἡ rejection Ro 11: 15; loss Ac 27: 22.*

ἀπογίνομαι die fig. 1 Pt 2: 24.*

ἀπογραφή, ῆς, ἡ census, registration Lk 2: 2; Ac 5: 37.*

ἀπογράφω register, record Lk 2: 1, 3, 5; Hb 12: 23.*

ἀποδείκνυμι exhibit, display 1 Cor 4: 9; prove Ac 25: 7; proclaim 2 Th 2: 4; recommend, attest Ac 2: 22.*

ἀπόδειξις, εως, ἡ proof. ἀ. πνεύματος proof consisting in possession of the Spirit 1 Cor 2: 4.*

ἀποδεκατεύω tithe, give one tenth of Lk 18: 12.*

ἀποδεκατόω—1. tithe, give one tenth of Mt 23: 23; Lk 11: 42.— 2. Collect a tithe (one tenth) from Hb 7: 5.*

ἀπόδεκτος, ον pleasing, pleasant 1 Ti 2: 3; 5: 4.*

ἀποδέχομαι—1. welcome, receive favorably Lk 8: 40; 9: 11; Ac 18: 27; 21: 17; 28: 30. Accept Ac 2: 41.—2. acknowledge, praise 24: 3.*

ἀποδημέω go on a journey Mt 25: 14f; Lk 20: 9; be away, absent 2 Cor 5: 6 v.l.

ἀπόδημος, ον away on a journey Mk 13: 34.*

ἀποδίδωμι—1. give away, give (up) or (out) Mt 27: 58; Lk 16: 2; Ac 4: 33; pay (out) Mt 20: 8; Mk 12: 17; fulfil 1 Cor 7: 3; keep Mt 5: 33; yield Rv 22: 2.— 2. give or pay back, return Lk 9: 42; 12: 59; 19: 8. Render, recompense Mt 6: 4, 6, 18; Ro 2: 6; 12: 17; Rv 18: 6.—3. mid. sell Ac 5: 8; 7: 9; Hb 12: 16.

ἀποδιορίζω divide, separate οἱ ἀποδιορίζοντες those who cause a division Jd 19.*

ἀποδοκιμάζω reject (after scrutiny), declare useless Mt 21: 42; Lk 9: 22; Hb 12: 17.

ἀποδοχή, ῆς, ἡ acceptance, approval 1 Ti 1: 15; 4: 9.*

ἀποδώῃ, ἀποδῷς 3 sing. 2 aor. opt. act. of ἀποδίδωμι; 2 sing. 2 aor. subj. act. of the same.

ἀποθανεῖσθε, ἀποθάνῃ, ἀποθανεῖν from ἀποθνῄσκω: 2 pl. fut. mid. ind.; 3 sing. 2 aor. subj. act. and 2 aor. act. inf.

ἀπόθεσις, εως, ἡ removal, getting rid of fig. 1 Pt 3: 21; 2 Pt 1: 14 (euphemistic for death).*

ἀποθήκη, ης, ἡ storehouse, barn Mt 3: 12; Lk 12: 18.

ἀποθησαυρίζω store up, lay (up) 1 Ti 6: 19.*

ἀποθλίβω press upon, crowd Lk 8: 45.*

ἀποθνῄσκω die—1. lit., of physical death Mt 8: 32; 9: 24; Ro 14: 8; Hb 10: 28; Rv 14: 13. Decay 1 Cor 15: 36.—2. fig. be freed from Ro 6: 2; Gal 2: 19; Col 2: 20. Of mystical death with Christ Ro 6: 8. Of losing the true, eternal life Ro 7: 10; Rv 3: 2; oft. in J: 6: 50, 58; 8: 21, 24; 11: 26.—3. be about to die, face death, be mortal 1 Cor 15: 31; 2 Cor 6: 9; Hb 7: 8.

ἀποκαθιστάνω and ἀποκαθίστημι restore, reestablish Mk 9: 12; Ac 1: 6. Cure Mk 3: 5; intr. 2 aor. act. be cured 8: 25; bring back, restore Hb 13: 19.

ἀποκαλύπτω reveal, disclose Mt 10: 26; Lk 17: 30; Ro 1: 17; 1 Cor 3: 13; Gal 1: 16; 1 Pt 5: 1.

ἀποκάλυψις, εως, ἡ revelation, disclosure Lk 2: 32; Ro 8: 19; Gal 1: 12; 2: 2; Eph 3: 3; 1 Pt 1: 7, 13.

ἀποκαραδοκία, ας, ἡ eager expectation Ro 8: 19; Phil 1: 20.*

ἀποκαταλλάσσω reconcile Eph 2: 16; Col 1: 20, 22.*

ἀποκατάστασις, εως, ἡ restoration Ac 3: 21.*

ἀπόκειμαι be stored up, put away lit. Lk 19: 20. Fig. Col 1: 5; be reserved 2 Ti 4: 8. Impers.

ἀπόκειταί τινι *it is reserved* or *certain for someone, one is destined* Hb 9: 27.*

ἀποκεφαλίζω *behead* Mk 6: 16, 27.

ἀποκλείω *close, shut* Lk 13: 25.*

ἀποκόπτω *cut off, cut loose* Mk 9: 43, 45; J 18: 10, 26; Ac 27: 32. *Make a eunuch of, castrate* Gal 5: 12.*

ἀπόκριμα, ατος, τό *official report, decision, sentence* 2 Cor 1: 9.*

ἀποκρίνομαι *answer, reply* Mt 3: 15; 8: 8; Mk 7: 28; 9: 6; Lk 4: 4; 23: 9; J 1: 21; 3: 5. Hebraistically with εἰπεῖν and λέγειν = *continue* Mt 22: 1; 26: 25 or *begin, speak up* Mk 9: 5; J 5: 19; Ac 5: 8 or left untranslated Mt 16: 16; Mk 7: 28; Lk 23: 3.

ἀπόκρισις, εως, ἡ *answer* Lk 2: 47; J 1: 22.

ἀποκρύπτω *hide, conceal* Lk 10: 21; 1 Cor 2: 7.

ἀπόκρυφος, ον *hidden, secret* Mk 4: 22; Lk 8: 17; Col 2: 3.*

ἀποκτείνω or ἀποκτέννω *kill* Mt 14: 5; Lk 11: 47; J 8: 22; 16: 2; *deprive of spiritual life* Mt 10: 28; 2 Cor 3: 6. Fig. Eph 2: 16.

ἀποκυέω *give birth to, bring into being* fig. Js 1: 15, 18.*

ἀποκυλίω *roll away* Mt 28: 2; Mk 16: 3; Lk 24: 2.*

ἀπολαλέω *speak out freely* Ac 18: 25 v.l.*

ἀπολαμβάνω *receive* Gal 4: 5. As 'commercial' term Lk 16: 25; 23: 41; Ro 1: 27. *Receive in return, get back* Lk 6: 34; 15: 27. *Take aside* Mk 7: 33. *Welcome* 3 J 8 v.l.

ἀπόλαυσις, εως, ἡ *enjoyment* 1 Ti 6: 17; Hb 11: 25.*

ἀπολείπω *leave behind* 2 Ti 4: 13, 20; Tit 1: 5; *desert* Jd 6. *Remain* Hb 4: 9; 10: 26; impers. *it is certain* 4: 6.*

ἀπολεῖται, —ολέσαι, —ολέσῃ fut. mid. ind., 1 aor. act. inf. and subj. of ἀπόλλυμι.

ἀπολείχω *lick, lick off* Lk 16: 21 v.l.*

ἀπόλλυμι—1. act. *destroy, ruin, kill* Mt 2: 13; Ro 14: 15; 1 Cor 1: 19. *Lose* Mt 10: 39, 42; 2 J 8.—2. mid. and pass. *be lost, perish, die, be ruined* Mt 8: 25; 9: 17; 26: 52; Lk 15: 24; J 11: 50; Js 1: 11; *pass away* Hb 1: 11.

Ἀπολλύων, ονος, ὁ *Apollyon, the Destroyer* (see Ἀβαδδών) Rv 9: 11.*

Ἀπολλωνία, ας, ἡ *Apollonia* a city in Macedonia Ac 17: 1.*

Ἀπολλῶς, ῶ, ὁ (short for Ἀπολλώνιος, which is a v.l. in Ac 18: 24) *Apollos* Ac 18: 24; 19: 1; 1 Cor 1: 12; 3: 4–6, 22; 4: 6; 16: 12; Tit 3: 13.*

ἀπολογέομαι *speak in one's own defense, defend oneself* Lk 21: 14; Ac 19: 33; 24: 10; Ro 2: 15; 2 Cor 12: 19. περί τινος *against something* Ac 26: 2.

ἀπολογία, ας, ἡ *defense* Ac 25: 16; Phil 1: 7, 16; 2 Ti 4: 16; 1 Pt 3: 15; *answer, reply* 1 Cor 9: 3.

ἀπολούω mid. *wash oneself* 1 Cor 6: 11; *wash away* Ac 22: 16.*

ἀπολύτρωσις, εως, ἡ *release* Hb 11: 35. Fig. *redemption* (lit. 'buying back'), *deliverance, ransoming* Lk 21: 28; Ro 3: 24; 8: 23; Eph 1: 7; Hb 9: 15. *Redeemer* 1 Cor 1: 30.

ἀπολύω—1. *release, set free, pardon* Mt 18: 27; 27: 15–26; Lk 6: 37; 13: 12.—2. *let go, send away, dismiss* Mt 15: 23, 32, 39; Mk 8: 9; Ac 4: 23. Euphemistic for *let die* Lk 2: 29. *Divorce* Mk 10: 2, 4, 11f.—3. mid. *go away* Ac 28: 25. In Hb 13: 23 Timothy *has been set free* or *sent away* or *has gone away*.

ἀπολῶ, ἀπολωλός fut. ind. act., 2 perf. act. participle of ἀπόλλυμι.

ἀπομάσσω mid. *wipe off* in protest Lk 10: 11.*

ἀπομένω *remain behind* Lk 2: 43 v.l.*

ἀπονέμω *assign, show, pay* 1 Pt 3: 7.*

ἀπονίπτω *wash off* mid. (*for*) *oneself* Mt 27: 24.*

ἀποπίπτω *fall, drop* (*from*) Ac 9: 18.*

ἀποπλανάω *mislead* Mk 13: 22; pass. *wander away* 1 Ti 6: 10.*

ἀποπλέω *sail away* Ac 13: 4; 20: 15.

ἀποπλύνω *wash off* or *out* Lk 5: 2 v.l.*

ἀποπνίγω *choke* trans. Mt 13: 7; Lk 8: 7. Pass. *drown* 8: 33.*

ἀπορέω *be at a loss, in doubt, uncertain* Lk 24: 4; J 13: 22; Ac 25: 20; 2 Cor 4: 8. πολλὰ ἠπόρει *he was very much disturbed* Mk 6: 20. ἐν ὑμῖν *because of you* Gal 4: 20.*

ἀπορία, ας, ἡ *perplexity, anxiety* Lk 21: 25.*

ἀπο(ρ)ρίπτω intr. *throw oneself down* Ac 27: 43.*

ἀπορφανίζω *make an orphan of* fig. 1 Th 2: 17.*

ἀποσκευάζω *pack up* Ac 21: 15 v.l.*

ἀποσκίασμα, ατος, τό *shadow* Js 1: 17.*

ἀποσπάω—1. lit. *draw* Mt 26: 51. —2. fig. *draw away, attract* Ac 20: 30. Pass. *be parted* 21: 1; *withdraw* Lk 22: 41.*

ἀποσταλῶ, ἀποσταλείς 2 aor. pass. subj. and ptc. of ἀποστέλλω.

ἀποστασία, ας, ἡ *rebellion, abandonment, apostasy* Ac 21: 21; 2 Th 2: 3.*

ἀποστάσιον, ου, τό *divorce* Mt 5: 31; 19: 7; Mk 10: 4.*

ἀποστάτης, ου, ὁ *deserter, apostate* Js 2: 11 v.l.*

ἀποστεγάζω *unroof* ἀ. τ. στέγην *remove the roof* Mk 2: 4.*

ἀποστεῖλαι, ἀποστείλω, ἀπόστειλον 1 aor. act. inf., subj., imperative of ἀποστέλλω.

ἀποστέλλω *send, send away* or *out* Mt 13: 41; 14: 35; Mk 8: 26; 12: 2, 13; Lk 1: 19, 26; J 3: 28;

Ac 5: 21; 1 Cor 1: 17; esp. on a divine mission Mt 10: 5; Mk 9: 37; J 3: 17, 34; Ac 3: 20. *Put in* Mk 4: 29. ἀποστείλας ἀνεῖλεν *he had* the boys *killed* Mt 2: 16; similarly Mk 6: 17; J 11: 3; Ac 7: 14; Rv 1: 1.

ἀποστερέω *steal, rob, defraud* Mk 10: 19; 1 Cor 6: 7f; Js 5: 4 v.l. *Deprive* 1 Cor 7: 5; 1 Ti 6: 5.*

ἀποστῇ, ἀποστῆναι 2 aor. act. and inf. of ἀφίστημι.

ἀποστήσομαι fut. mid. ind. of ἀφίστημι.

ἀποστολή, ῆς, ἡ *apostleship, office of an apostle* Ac 1: 25; Ro 1: 5; 1 Cor 9: 2; Gal 2: 8.*

ἀπόστολος, ου, ὁ—1. *delegate, envoy, messenger* Lk 11: 49; J 13: 16; 2 Cor 8: 23; Eph 3: 5; Phil 2: 25; Hb 3: 1; Rv 2: 2; 18: 20.—2. *apostle*, one holding the highest office in the Christian communities (1 Cor 12: 28f), esp. of Jesus' original 12 disciples (Mt 10: 2; Ac 1: 26; Rv 21: 14), but also of other prominent leaders outside their number Ac 14: 14; Ro 1: 1; 16: 7; Gal 1: 19.

ἀποστοματίζω *question closely, interrogate* or *watch closely* Lk 11: 53.*

ἀποστρέφω—1. trans. *turn away* 2 Ti 4: 4; *remove* Ro 11: 26; *mislead* Lk 23: 14; *return, put back* Mt 26: 52. In Ac 3: 26 the usage may be trans. or intrans. —2. mid. and pass. *turn away from, reject, repudiate* Mt 5: 42; Tit 1: 14; Hb 12: 25; *desert* 2 Ti 1: 15.*

ἀποστυγέω *hate, abhor* Ro 12: 9.*

ἀποσυνάγωγος, ον *expelled from the synagogue* ἀ. ποιεῖν *excommunicate* J 16: 2. ἀ. γενέσθαι *be excommunicated* 9: 22; 12: 42.*

ἀποτάσσω mid. *say farewell* (*to*), *take leave* (*of*) Mk 6: 46; Lk 9: 61; 2 Cor 2: 13. Fig. *renounce, give up* Lk 14: 33.

ἀποτελέω *bring to completion, perform* Lk 13: 32. Fig. pass. *come to completion, be fully formed* or *matured* Js 1: 15.*

ἀποτίθημι mid. *take off* lit. *take off and lay down* Ac 7: 58; fig. *lay aside, rid oneself of* Ro 13: 12; Hb 12: 1. *Put* in prison Mt 14: 3..

ἀποτινάσσω *shake off* Lk 9: 5; Ac 28: 5.*

ἀποτίνω *pay the damages, make compensation* Phlm 19.*

ἀποτολμάω *be bold, come out boldly* Ro 10: 20.*

ἀποτομία, ας, ἡ *severity* Ro 11: 22.*

ἀποτόμως adv. *severely, rigorously* 2 Cor 13: 10; Tit 1: 13.*

ἀποτρέπω mid. *turn away from, avoid* 2 Ti 3: 5.*

ἀπουσία, ας, ἡ *absence* Phil 2: 12.*

ἀποφέρω *take, bring* or *carry (away)* Lk 16: 22; Ac 19: 12; 1 Cor 16: 3; Rv 17: 3; *lead away* Mk 15: 1.

ἀποφεύγω *escape, escape from* 2 Pt 1: 4; 2: 18, 20.*

ἀποφθέγγομαι *speak out, declare* Ac 26: 25; *under inspiration* 2: 4, 14.*

ἀποφορτίζομαι *unload* Ac 21: 3.*

ἀπόχρησις, εως, ἡ *consuming, using up* Col 2: 22.*

ἀποχωρέω *go away* with ἀπό *leave, desert* Ac 13: 13; *depart* Mt 7: 23; Lk 20: 20 v.l.; *withdraw* 9: 39.*

ἀποχωρίζω *separate* Mt 19: 6 v.l. Pass. *be separated* Ac 15: 39; *be split* Rv 6: 14.*

ἀποψύχω *breathe out, stop breathing,* hence either *faint* or *die* Lk 21: 26.*

'Αππίου φόρον *Appii Forum,* the *Forum of Appius,* a market town on the Appian Way, 43 Roman miles from Rome Ac 28: 15.*

ἀπρόσιτος, ον *unapproachable* 1 Ti 6: 16.*

ἀπρόσκοπος, ον *blameless* Phil 1: 10; *clear* Ac 24: 16; *giving no offense* 1 Cor 10: 32.*

ἀπροσωπολήμπτως adv. *impartially* 1 Pt 1: 17.*

ἄπταιστος, ον *without stumbling* Jd 24.*

ἅπτω—1. *light, kindle* Lk 8: 16; Ac 28: 2.—2. mid. *touch, take hold of, hold* w. gen. as obj. 2 Cor 6: 17; Col 2: 21 (perh. = *eat*); *cling to* J 20: 17; of sex relations 1 Cor 7: 1. *Touch* for blessing or healing Mt 9: 21, 29; 17: 7; Mk 10: 13 (here perh. *hold*); Lk 7: 14; 22: 51. *Harm, injure* is poss. for 1 J 5: 18.

'Απφία, ας, ἡ *Apphia* a Christian woman, prob. the wife of Philemon, at Colossae Phlm 2.*

ἀπωθέω mid. *push aside* lit. Ac 7: 27. Fig. *reject, repudiate* 7: 39; 13: 46; Ro 11: 1f; 1 Ti 1: 19.*

ἀπώλεια, ας, ἡ *destruction, ruin, annihilation* Ac 8: 20; esp. of the eternal destruction of the wicked Mt 7: 13; Phil 1: 28; Hb 10: 39; 2 Pt 3: 7; Rv 17: 8, 11. *Waste* Mk 14: 4.

ἀπώλεσε, ἀπώλετο 1 aor. act. and 2 aor. mid. ind. of ἀπόλλυμι.

ἀπωσάμην 1 aor. mid. ind. of ἀπωθέω.

"Αρ see 'Αρμαγεδδών.

ἀρά, ᾶς, ἡ *curse* Ro 3: 14.*

ἄρα *inferential particle,* sometimes with γε and οὖν: *so, then, consequently, you see, as a result* Mt 7: 20; 18: 1; Lk 1: 66; Ro 5: 18; 7: 21; 8: 1; 1 Cor 15: 14; Gal 6: 10; Hb 12: 8. After ἐπεί *for otherwise* 1 Cor 5: 10; after εἰ *if, on the other hand* 15: 15. In indirect questions εἰ ἄ. *whether (perhaps)* Mk 11: 13; Ac 8: 22.

ἆρα *interrogative particle* indicating anxiety or impatience, introducing direct questions only, usually incapable of direct translation, as Lk 18: 8; Ac 8: 30; cf. ἆ. Χριστὸς ἁμαρτίας διάκονος; *is Christ, then, a servant of sin?* Gal 2: 17.*

’**Αραβία, ας, ἡ** *Arabia:* in Gal 1: 17 prob. the Nabataean kingdom south of Damascus; in 4: 25 the Sinai peninsula.*

’’**Αραβοι** in Ac 2: 11 v.l. could have been wrongly formed from the gen. pl. ’Αράβων.*

ἄραι, ἄρας, ἄρατε 1 aor. inf., ptc., imperative act. of αἴρω.

’**Αράμ, ὁ** indecl. *Aram* Mt 1: 3f; Lk 3: 33 v.l.*

ἄραφος, ον *seamless* J 19: 23.*

’’**Αραψ, βος, ὁ** an *Arab* Ac 2: 11.*

ἀργέω *be idle, grow weary, delay* 2 Pt 2: 3.*

ἀργός, ή, όν *idle, unemployed* Mt 20: 3, 6; *idle, lazy* 1 Ti 5: 13; Tit 1: 12; *useless* Js 2: 20; 2 Pt 1: 8; *careless* Mt 12: 36.*

ἀργύριον, ου, τό *silver,* always of money except 1 Cor 3: 12. Of silver money generally Ac 3: 6; 7: 16. Of particular silver coins *silver shekel* (worth about 4 drachmas; see below) Mt 26: 15; *silver drachmas* (worth normally 18 to 20 cents, nine or ten pence) Ac 19: 19. Of *money* in general Mt 25: 18, 27; Lk 9: 3.

ἀργυροκόπος, ου, ὁ *silversmith* Ac 19: 24.*

ἄργυρος, ου, ὁ *silver* as a material in general Ac 17: 29; 1 Cor 3: 12 v.l.; Js 5: 3; Rv 18: 12. As money Mt 10: 9.*

ἀργυροῦς, ᾶ, οῦν (*made of*) *silver* Ac 19: 24; 2 Ti 2: 20; Rv 9: 20.*

’’**Αρειος πάγος, ὁ** *the Aeropagus* or *Hill of Ares* (Ares, the Greek god of war = the Roman Mars, hence the older 'Mars' Hill'), northwest of the Acropolis in Athens Ac 17: 19, 22. The council which met there from early times was also known as the Aeropagus; in Roman times it supervised education and visiting lecturers, and it is not improbable that Paul was brought before it for this reason.*

’**Αρεοπαγίτης, ου, ὁ** *Aeropagite,* member of the council of the Areopagus Ac 17: 34.*

ἀρέσαι, ἀρέσει 1 aor. act. inf. and fut. ind. of ἀρέσκω.

ἀρεσκεία, ας, ἡ *desire to please* Col 1: 10.*

ἀρέσκω—1. *strive to please, accommodate,* almost = *serve* w. dat. Ro 15: 2; 1 Cor 10: 33; Gal 1: 10.—2. *please, be pleasing* Mk 6: 22; Ac 6: 5; Ro 8: 8; 1 Cor 7: 32f.

ἀρεστός, ή, όν *pleasing, desirable* J 8: 29; Ac 6: 2.

’**Αρέτας, α, ὁ** *Aretas*; the one mentioned in 2 Cor 11: 32 is Aretas IV, king of Nabataean Arabia c. 9 BC to 40 AD.*

ἀρετή, ῆς, ἡ *moral excellence, virtue* Phil 4: 8; 2 Pt 1: 5; for 1 Pt 2: 9 *praise* or *manifestation of divine power* are both poss.; the latter is preferable for 2 Pt 1: 3.*

ἄρῃ 1 aor. subj. act. of αἴρω.

ἀρήν, ἀρνός, ὁ *lamb* Lk 10: 3.*

ἀρθῆναι, ἀρθῇ, ἄρθητι 1 aor. pass. inf., subj. and imperative of αἴρω.

ἀριθμέω *count* Mt 10: 30; Lk 12: 7; Rv 7: 9.*

ἀριθμός, οῦ, ὁ *number, total* Lk 22: 3; Ac 4: 4; 16: 5; Rv 13: 17f.

’**Αριμαθαία, ας, ἡ** *Arimathaea* a city in Judea Mt 27: 57; Mk 15: 43; Lk 23: 51; J 19: 38.*

’**Αρίσταρχος, ου, ὁ** *Aristarchus* of Thessalonica Ac 19: 29; 20: 4; 27: 2; Col 4: 10; Phlm 24.*

ἀριστάω *eat breakfast* J 21: 12, 15; *eat a meal, dine* Lk 11: 37; 15: 29 v.l.*

ἀριστερός, ά, όν *left* (opposite to right) Mt 6: 3. ἐξ ἀ. *on the left* Mk 10: 37; Lk 23: 33. ὅπλα ἀ. *weapons used by the left hand,* i.e. *for defense* 2 Cor 6: 7.*

’**Αριστόβουλος, ου, ὁ** *Aristobulus*

οἱ ἐκ τῶν 'Αριστοβούλου *those who belong to* (*the household of*) *A.* Ro 16: 10.*

ἄριστον, ου, τό *breakfast* Lk 14: 12; *noon meal* Mt 22: 4; *meal generally* Lk 11: 38; 14: 15 v.l.*

ἀρκετός, ή, όν *enough, sufficient* Mt 6: 34; 10: 25; 1 Pt 4: 3.*

ἀρκέω act. *be enough, sufficient* Mt 25: 9; J 6: 7; 14: 8; 2 Cor 12: 9. Pass. w. dat. *be satisfied* or *content with* Lk 3: 14; 1 Ti 6: 8; Hb 13: 5; 3 J 10.*

ἄρκος, ου, ὁ, ἡ *a bear* Rv 13: 2.*

ἅρμα, ατος, τό *chariot* Ac 8: 28f, 38; Rv 9: 9.*

'Αρμαγεδ(δ)ών indecl. *Armageddon* a mystic place name, sometimes identified with Megiddo and Jerusalem Rv 16: 16.*

ἁρμόζω *join* or *give in marriage, betroth* mid. for act. 2 Cor 11: 2.*

ἁρμός, οῦ, ὁ *joint* Hb 4: 12.*

ἄρνας acc. pl. of ἀρήν.

ἀρνέομαι—1. *deny* Lk 8: 45; J 1: 20; 2 Ti 3: 5; 1 J 2: 22. ἀ. ἑαυτόν *disregard oneself* Lk 9: 23, but *be untrue to oneself* 2 Ti 2: 13.—2. *repudiate, disown* Mt 10: 33; 1 Ti 5: 8; 2 Ti 2: 12; Tit 1: 16.—3. *refuse* Hb 11: 24.

'Αρνί, ὁ indecl. *Arni* Lk 3: 33.*

ἀρνίον, ου, τό *lamb, sheep* fig. J 21: 15; Rv 5: 6, 8, 12f.

ἀρνῶν gen. pl. of ἀρήν.

ἆρον 1 aor. act. imperative of αἴρω.

ἀροτριάω *to plow* Lk 17: 7; 1 Cor 9: 10.*

ἄροτρον, ου, τό *a plow* Lk 9: 62.*

ἁρπαγή, ῆς, ἡ *robbery, plunder* Hb 10: 34; *greediness* Lk 11: 39. In Mt 23: 25 either *greediness* or *plunder* (what has been stolen) is possible.*

ἁρπαγμός, οῦ, ὁ prob. = ἅρπαγμα *a thing to be seized* or *greatly desired, a prize, a piece of good fortune* Phil 2: 6; *robbery* is next to impossible.*

ἁρπάζω *steal, carry off, drag away, take* or *snatch away* Mt 12: 29; J 10: 12, 28f; Jd 23; *tear out* Mt 13: 19. Of the Holy Spirit or other divine agency *catch up, carry away* Ac 8: 39; 2 Cor 12: 2, 4; Rv 12: 5. Perh. *seize* or *claim for oneself* Mt 11: 12.

ἅρπαξ, αγος adj. *rapacious, ravenous* Mt 7: 15. As noun *robber, swindler* Lk 18: 11; 1 Cor 5: 10f; 6: 10; Tit 1: 9 v.l.*

ἀρραβών, ῶνος, ὁ (Semitic loanword) *first instalment, deposit, down payment, pledge* fig. 2 Cor 1: 22; 5: 5; Eph 1: 14.*

ἄρραφος see ἄραφος.

ἄρρην see ἄρσην.

ἄρρητος, ον *too sacred to tell* 2 Cor 12: 4.*

ἀρρωστέω *be ill, sick* Mt 14: 14 v.l.*

ἄρρωστος, ον *sick, ill* Mt 14: 14; 1 Cor 11: 30.

ἀρσενοκοίτης, ου, ὁ *a male homosexual, sodomite, pederast* 1 Cor 6: 9; 1 Ti 1: 10.*

ἄρσην, εν gen. **ενος** *male* Mt 19: 4; Mk 10: 6; Lk 2: 23; Ro 1: 27; Gal 3: 28; Rv 12: 5, 13.*

'Αρτεμᾶς, ᾶ, ὁ *Artemas* Tit 3: 12.*

"Αρτεμις, ιδος, ἡ *Artemis* a Greek goddess (Diana is her Roman name) Ac 19: 24, 27f, 34f.*

ἀρτέμων, ωνος, ὁ *sail*, prob. *foresail* Ac 27: 40.*

ἄρτι adv. *now, just.* Of the immediate past *just* Mt 9: 18; Rv 12: 10, or the immediate present *at once, immediately, now* Mt 26: 53; J 13: 37. In H. Gk. it is extended to refer to the present in general *now, at the present time* J 9: 19, 25; 1 Cor 13: 12; 1 Pt 1: 6, 8; as adj. 1 Cor 4: 11. ἀπ' ἄρτι *from now on* J 13: 19; Rv 14: 13 (see ἀπαρτί). ἕως ἄρτι *up to the present time, until now* Mt 11: 12; J 2: 10; 1 Cor 4: 13.

ἀρτιγέννητος, ον *new born* 1 Pt 2: 2.*

ἄρτιος, ία, ον complete, capable, proficient 2 Ti 3: 17.*

ἄρτος, ου, ὁ bread, loaf (of bread) Mt 26: 26; Mk 6: 38, 44, 52; Lk 9: 3; Hb 9: 2. Food in general Mk 3: 20; Lk 15: 17; 2 Th 3: 8, 12. In a mystical sense J 6: 31ff, 35, 51.

ἀρτύω season, salt lit. Mk 9: 50; Lk 14: 34; fig. Col 4: 6.*

Ἀρφαξάδ, ὁ indecl. Arphaxad Lk 3: 36.*

ἀρχάγγελος, ου, ὁ archangel 1 Th 4: 16; Jd 9.*

ἀρχαῖος, αία, αῖον ancient, old, former Lk 9: 8, 19; Ac 15: 7, 21; 2 Pt 2: 5; Rv 12: 9; 20: 2; of long standing Ac 21: 16. οἱ ἀ. the men of ancient times Mt 5: 21, 27 v.l., 33. τὰ ἀ. what is old 2 Cor 5: 17.*

Ἀρχέλαος, ου, ὁ Archelaus son of Herod I, ethnarch of Judaea, Samaria and Idumaea from his father's death in 4 BC to 6 AD, when he was deposed by the emperor Augustus Mt 2: 22.*

ἀρχή, ῆς, ἡ—1. beginning, origin Mt 19: 4; 24: 8; Mk 1: 1; 13: 8; Lk 1: 2; J 1: 1; 15: 27; Ac 11: 15. ἀρχὴν λαμβάνειν begin Hb 2: 3. στοιχεῖα τῆς ἀ. elementary principles 5: 12. ὁ τῆς ἀ. τοῦ Χ. λόγος elementary Christian teaching 6: 1. ἀ. τῆς ὑποστάσεως original conviction 3: 14. ἀ. τῶν σημείων first of the signs J 2: 11. τὴν ἀρχήν = ὅλως at all 8: 25. Fig. Col 1: 18. First cause Rv 3: 14. Concrete = corner Ac 10: 11.—2. ruler, authority Lk 12: 11; 20: 20; Tit 3: 1. Of angels and demons Ro 8: 38; 1 Cor 15: 24; Col 2: 10, 15.—3. Rule, domain, sphere of influence Jd 6.

ἀρχηγός, οῦ, ὁ either leader, ruler, prince or originator, founder; the former is more likely for Ac 5: 31; for 3: 15 either is poss. The latter is more likely for Hb 2: 10; 12: 2.*

ἀρχιερατικός, όν highpriestly Ac 4: 6.*

ἀρχιερεύς, έως, ὁ high priest head of the Jewish religion and president of the Sanhedrin Mk 14: 60f, 63; J 18: 19, 22, 24. The pl. denotes members of the Sanhedrin who belonged to highpriestly families Mt 2: 4; Lk 23: 13; Ac 4: 23. Fig. of Christ Hb 2: 17; 4: 14.

ἀρχιλῃστής, οῦ, ὁ robber chieftain J 18: 40 v.l.*

ἀρχιποίμην, ενος, ὁ chief shepherd 1 Pt 5: 4.*

Ἄρχιππος, ου, ὁ Archippus Col 4: 17; Phlm 2.*

ἀρχισυνάγωγος, ου, ὁ leader or president of a synagogue a layman whose duty it was to take care of the physical arrangements for the worship services Mk 5: 22; Lk 13: 14; Ac 13: 15.

ἀρχιτέκτων, ονος, ὁ master builder 1 Cor 3: 10.*

ἀρχιτελώνης, ου, ὁ chief tax collector Lk 19: 2.*

ἀρχιτρίκλινος, ου, ὁ head waiter, butler; in the context of J 2: 8f prob. toastmaster, master of the feast.*

ἄρχω—1. act. rule w. gen. Mk 10: 42; Ro 15: 12.—2. mid. begin Mt 4: 17; Lk 15: 14; 24: 27; Ac 8: 35; 10: 37. At times ἄ. is pleonastic and adds little to the meaning of the sentence, e.g. ὦν ἤρξατο ὁ Ἰησ. ποιεῖν = simply what Jesus did rather than what Jesus began to do Ac 1: 1. Cf. Mt 26: 37; Lk 7: 15, 24, 38.

ἄρχων, οντος, ὁ ruler, lord, prince Mt 20: 25; Ac 4: 26; Rv 1: 5. Of authorities, officials gener., both Jewish Mt 9: 18; Lk 8: 41; 14: 1; 18: 18; J 3: 1; Ac 3: 17 and Gentile Ac 16: 19. Of evil spirits Mt 9: 34; 12: 24; Lk 11: 15; J 12: 31; 14: 30; Eph 2: 2. The ἄρχοντες of 1 Cor 2: 6, 8 may be demonic powers or earthly rulers. Of a judge Lk 12: 58.

ἄρωμα, ατος, τό pl. *spices, aromatic oils* or *salves* Mk 16: 1; Lk 23: 56; 24: 1; J 19: 40.*

ἀσάλευτος, ον *immovable* Ac 27: 41; *unshaken* Hb 12: 28.*

Ἀσάφ, ὁ indecl. *Asaph* or *Asa* Mt 1: 7f; Lk 3: 23ff v.l.*

ἄσβεστος, ον *inextinguishable* Mt 3: 12; Mk 9: 43, 45 v.l.; Lk 3: 17.*

ἀσέβεια, ας, ἡ *impiety, godlessness* Ro 1: 18; 11: 26; 2 Ti 2: 16; Tit 2: 12; Jd 15, 18.*

ἀσεβέω *act impiously* 2 Pt 2: 6; Jd 15.*

ἀσεβής, ές *impious, godless* 2 Pt 3: 7; Jd 15. Mostly as a noun ὁ ἀ. *the godless* (*man*) Ro 5: 6; 1 Ti 1: 9; 1 Pt 4: 18.

ἀσέλγεια, ας, ἡ *licentiousness, debauchery, sensuality* Mk 7: 22; Ro 13: 13; 2 Pt 2: 2, 7, 18.

ἄσημος, ον *obscure, insignificant* Ac 21: 39.*

Ἀσήρ, ὁ indecl. *Asher* Lk 2: 36; Rv 7: 6 (see Gen 30: 13).*

ἀσθένεια, ας, ἡ *weakness* 1 Cor 15: 43; 2 Cor 11: 30; Hb 5: 2; 11: 34. *Sickness, disease* Mt 8: 17; Lk 5: 15; J 5: 5; Ac 28: 9; Gal 4: 13. Fig. *timidity* Ro 6: 19; 1 Cor 2: 3.

ἀσθενέω *be weak.* Bodily *be sick* Mt 10: 8; 25: 39; J 11: 1ff; Ac 9: 37; Phil 2: 26f. Gener. Ro 8: 3; 2 Cor 12: 10; 13: 3. Fig. Ro 4: 19; 14: 1f; 2 Cor 11: 29. Economically *be in need* Ac 20: 35.

ἀσθένημα, ατος, τό *weakness* Ro 15: 1.*

ἀσθενής, ές *weak.* Bodily *sick, ill* Lk 10: 9; Ac 4: 9; 1 Cor 11: 30. Gener. *weak* Mk 14: 38; 1 Pt 3: 7; = unimpressive 2 Cor 10: 10. Fig. Ro 5: 6; 1 Cor 1: 25, 27; 4: 10; 9: 22; Hb 7: 18.

Ἀσία, ας, ἡ *Asia* a Roman province in western Asia Minor

Ac 2: 9; 19: 10, 22, 26f; Ro 16: 5; 2 Cor 1: 8.

Ἀσιανός, οῦ, ὁ *a man from* the Roman province of *Asia* Ac 20: 4.*

Ἀσιάρχης, ου, ὁ *Asiarch* a wealthy and influential man, prob. connected with the imperial cult Ac 19: 31.*

ἀσιτία, ας, ἡ *lack of appetite*; πολλῆς ἀ. ὑπαρχούσης *since almost nobody wanted to eat* Ac 27: 21.*

ἄσιτος, ον *without eating* Ac 27: 33.*

ἀσκέω *do one's best,* lit. *practise* Ac 24: 16.*

ἀσκός, οῦ, ὁ *wine-skin* Mk 2: 22.

ἀσμένως adv. *gladly* Ac 2: 41 v.l.; 21: 17.*

ἄσοφος, ον *unwise, foolish* Eph 5: 15.*

ἀσπάζομαι *greet, welcome* Mk 9: 15; Lk 1: 40; *take leave of* Ac 20: 1; *hail, acclaim* Mk 15: 18; *pay one's respects to* Ac 25: 13; *be fond of, cherish* Mt 5: 47. Imperative, w. acc. *greetings to* someone, *remember me to* someone Ro 16: 3, 5ff; Phlm 23; Hb 13: 24; 3 J 15.

ἀσπασμός, οῦ, ὁ *greeting* Mt 23: 7; Lk 1: 29; 11: 43; 1 Cor 16: 21.

ἄσπιλος, ον *spotless, without blemish* lit. 1 Pt 1: 19; fig. 1 Ti 6: 14; Js 1: 27; 2 Pt 3: 14.*

ἀσπίς, ίδος, ἡ *asp, Egyptian cobra* Ro 3: 13.*

ἄσπονδος, ον *irreconcilable* 2 Ti 3: 3; Ro 1: 31 v.l.*

ἀσσάριον, ου, τό *assarion* a Roman copper coin, worth about one-sixteenth of a denarius, roughly one cent Mt 10: 29; Lk 12: 6.*

Ἀσσάρων, ωνος a variant form of Σαρων Ac 9: 35 v.l.*

ἆσσον adv. (comparative of ἄγχι) *nearer* Ac 27: 13.*

Ἄσσος, ου, ἡ *Assos* a seaport in northwest Asia Minor Ac 20: 13f.*

ἀστατέω be unsettled, homeless, a vagabond 1 Cor 4: 11.*

ἀστεῖος, α, ον beautiful, well-formed Hb 11: 23. In Ac 7: 20 ἀ. may mean acceptable, well-pleasing. However, if τῷ θεῷ is to be taken as a superlative, the meaning would be a wonderfully beautiful child.*

ἀστήρ, έρος, ὁ star Mt 2: 2; Rv 1: 16; 9: 1.

ἀστήρικτος, ον unstable, weak 2 Pt 2: 14; 3: 16.*

ἄστοργος, ον unloving, without affection Ro 1: 31; 2 Ti 3: 3.*

ἀστοχέω miss the mark περὶ τὴν πίστιν with regard to the faith 1 Ti 6: 21; cf. 2 Ti 2: 18. Deviate, depart w. gen. from something 1 Ti 1: 6.*

ἀστραπή, ῆς, ἡ lightning Mt 24: 27; Rv 4: 5; light, ray Lk 11: 36.

ἀστράπτω flash, gleam Lk 17: 24; 24: 4.*

ἄστρον, ου, τό star, constellation Ac 7: 43; 27: 20; Hb 11: 12.

Ἀσύγκριτος, ου, ὁ Asyncritus Ro 16: 14.*

ἀσύμφωνος, ον not harmonious fig. at variance Ac 28: 25.*

ἀσύνετος, ον senseless, foolish Mk 7: 18; Ro 1: 21, 31.

ἀσύνθετος, ον faithless, untrustworthy, perh. undutiful Ro 1: 31.*

Ἀσύνκριτος see Ἀσύγκριτος.

ἀσφάλεια, ας, ἡ security, safety Ac 5: 23; 1 Th 5: 3. Fig. certainty, truth Lk 1: 4.*

ἀσφαλής, ές certain, safe, secure, firm Phil 3: 1; Hb 6: 19; definite Ac 25: 26. τὸ ἀ. the certainty, the truth 21: 34; 22: 30.*

ἀσφαλίζω mid. fasten Ac 16: 24. Make secure Mt 27: 64–66. Guard Ac 16: 30 v.l.*

ἀσφαλῶς adv. securely Ac 16: 23; under guard Mk 14:44; beyond a doubt Ac 2: 36.*

ἀσχημονέω behave disgracefully,

dishonorably, indecently 1 Cor 7: 36; 1 Cor 13: 5. For the latter passage feel that one ought to be ashamed is also possible.*

ἀσχημοσύνη, ης, ἡ shameless deed, indecent act Ro 1: 27; shame = private parts Rv 16: 15.*

ἀσχήμων, ον shameful, unpresentable. τὰ ἀ. the private parts 1 Cor 12: 23.*

ἀσωτία, ας, ἡ debauchery, dissipation Eph 5: 18; Tit 1: 6; 1 Pt 4: 4.*

ἀσώτως adv. dissolutely, loosely Lk 15: 13.*

ἀτακτέω be idle, lazy lit. 'be out of order' 2 Th 3: 7.*

ἄτακτος, ον idle, lazy lit. 'disorderly' 1 Th 5: 14.*

ἀτάκτως adv. idly, in idleness 2 Th 3: 6, 11.*

ἄτεκνος, ον childless Lk 20: 28f.*

ἀτενίζω look intently, fix one's eyes Lk 4: 20; Ac 7: 55; 13: 9; 2 Cor 3: 7, 13.

ἄτερ prep. w. gen. without, apart from Lk 22: 6, 35.*

ἀτιμάζω dishonor, treat shamefully, insult Mk 12: 4; Lk 20: 11; J 8: 49; Ac 5: 41; Ro 2: 23; Js 2: 6; degrade Ro 1: 24.*

ἀτιμάω means the same as ἀτιμάζω Mk 12: 4 v.l.*

ἀτιμία, ας, ἡ dishonor, disgrace, shame 1 Cor 11: 14; 15: 43; 2 Cor 6: 8. πάθη ἀτιμίας shameful passions Ro 1: 26. εἰς ἀ. for (a) dishonor(able use) Ro 9: 21; 2 Ti 2: 20. κατὰ ἀ. λέγω to my shame I must confess 2 Cor 11: 21.*

ἄτιμος, ον unhonored, dishonored, despised 1 Cor 4: 10; 12: 23. οὐκ ἄ. εἰ μή honored everywhere, except Mt 13: 57; Mk 6: 4.*

ἀτιμόω means the same as ἀτιμάζω. Pass. be disgraced Mk 12: 4 v.l.*

ἀτμίς, ίδος, ἡ mist, vapor Ac 2: 19; Js 4: 14.*

ἄτομος, ον lit. indivisible. ἐν ἀ. in a moment 1 Cor 15: 52.*

ἄτοπος, ον *out of place. Improper, wrong, evil* Lk 23: 41; Ac 25: 5; 2 Th 3: 2. *Unusual, surprising* Ac 28: 6.*

'Αττάλεια, ας, ἡ *Attalia* the seaport of Perga in Pamphylia Ac 14: 25.*

αὐγάζω *see* 2 Cor 4: 4; less likely *shine forth.**

αὐγή, ῆς, ἡ *dawn* lit. 'light' Ac 20: 11.*

Αὔγουστος, ου, ὁ *Augustus* (Lat. = revered) a title given Octavian, the first Roman emperor (31 BC–14 AD) in 27 BC; Lk 2: 1.*

αὐθάδης, ες *self-willed, stubborn, arrogant* Tit 1: 7; 2 Pt 2: 10.*

αὐθαίρετος, ον *of one's own accord* 2 Cor 8: 3, 17.*

αὐθεντέω *have authority, domineer over* w. gen. 1 Ti 2: 12.*

αὐλέω *play the flute* Mt 11: 17; Lk 7: 32; 1 Cor 14: 7.*

αὐλή, ῆς, ἡ *courtyard* Mk 14: 54; J 18: 15; *fold* for sheep J 10: 1, 16; *house* or *farm* Lk 11: 21; (*outer*) *court* Rv 11: 2; *palace* Mt 26: 3.

αὐλητής, οῦ, ὁ *flute-player* Mt 9: 23; Rv 18: 22.*

αὐλίζομαι *spend the night, find lodging* Mt 21: 17; Lk 21: 37; *spend some time* is also possible for the Lk passage.*

αὐλός, οῦ, ὁ *flute* 1 Cor 14: 7.*

αὐξάνω and αὔξω—1. trans. *grow, cause to grow* or *increase* 1 Cor 3: 6 f; 2 Cor 9: 10.—2. intrans., act. and pass. *grow, increase* Mk 4: 8; Lk 13: 19; J 3: 30; Ac 6: 7; 2 Cor 10: 15; Col 1: 6, 10.

αὔξησις, εως, ἡ *growth, increase* Eph 4: 16; Col 2: 19.*

αὔξω *see* αὐξάνω.

αὔριον adv. *tomorrow* Ac 23: 20; Js 4: 13. With the article and ἡμέρα to be supplied ἡ αὔ. *the next day* Mt 6: 34 b; Lk 10: 35. In the sense *in a short time, soon* Lk 12: 28; 1 Cor 15: 32.

αὐστηρός, ά, όν *severe, strict,* *exacting, austere* both in favorable and unfavorable senses Lk 19: 21f.*

αὐτάρκεια, ας, ἡ *sufficiency* 2 Cor 9: 8; *contentment, self-sufficiency* 1 Ti 6: 6.*

αὐτάρκης, ες *content, self-sufficient,* either meaning is possible for Phil 4: 11.*

αὐτοκατάκριτος, ον *self-condemned* Tit 3: 11.*

αὐτόματος, η, ον *by itself* of something that happens without visible cause Mk 4: 28; Ac 12: 10.*

αὐτόπτης, ου, ὁ *eyewitness* Lk 1: 2.*

αὐτός, αὐτή, αὐτό—1. *self* intensive, setting the word it modifies off from everything else, emphasizing and contrasting. αὐτὸς 'Ιησοῦς *Jesus himself* Lk 24: 15. Cf. Mk 12: 36f; Lk 24: 36; Ac 24: 15; 1 Cor 11: 13; Hb 13: 5. αὐ. ἐγώ *I alone* 2 Cor 12: 13. *Of oneself, of one's own accord* J 2: 25; 16: 27; *thrown on one's own resources* Ro 7: 25. καὶ αὐτός *even* Ro 8: 21; Hb 11: 11. αὐ. τὰ ἔργα *the very deeds* J 5: 36; cf. Mt 3: 4; Lk 13: 1. αὐτὸ τοῦτο *just this* 2 Cor 7: 11. Adverbial accusative τοῦτο αὐ. *for this very reason* 2 Cor 2: 3; cf. 2 Pt 1: 5. As an emphatic personal pronoun Mt 5: 4ff.—2. In the oblique cases, as a third pers. personal pronoun, esp. in the gen., used as a possessive pronoun *him, her, it* Mt 4: 23; 8: 1; Mk 1: 10; Lk 2: 22; J 15: 2; 1 Cor 8: 12; Rv 2: 7, 17. Used, as it seems to speakers of English, superfluously (pleonastically) with relative pronouns ἣν οὐδεὶς δύναται κλεῖσαι αὐτήν *which no one can close* (*it*) Rv 3: 8; cf. Mk 1: 7; J 6: 39; Ac 15: 17.—3. preceded by the article ὁ αὐτός, ἡ αὐτή, τὸ αὐτό *the same* Mt 5: 46; 26: 44;

Lk 6: 33; Ro 2: 1; Eph 6: 9.
τὸ αὐ. λέγειν *agree* 1 Cor 1: 10.
τὸ αὐτό as adv. *in the same way*
Mt 27: 44. ἐπὶ τὸ αὐτό *at the
same place, together* Mt 22: 34; 1
Cor 11: 20; *to the total* Ac 2: 47.
κατὰ τὸ αὐτό *together* of place
and time 14: 1.
αὐτοῦ adv. *here* Mt 26: 36. *There*
Ac 18: 19.
αὐτόφωρος, ον *(caught) in the act*
in the expression ἐπ' αὐτοφώρῳ
J 8: 4.*
αὐτόχειρ, ρος *with one's own hand*
Ac 27: 19.*
αὐχέω *boast* Js 3: 5.*
αὐχμηρός, ά, όν *dark* 2 Pt 1: 19.*
ἀφαιρέω *take away, remove, rob*
Lk 1: 25; 10: 42; Ro 11: 27;
Hb 10: 4; Rv 22: 19; *cut off* Mk
14: 47.
ἀφανής, ές *invisible, hidden* Hb 4:
13.*
ἀφανίζω *cause to disappear, destroy* Mt 6: 19f; *render invisible*
or *unrecognizable* or *disfigure* 6:
16. Pass. *disappear* Js 4: 14;
perish Ac 13: 41.*
ἀφανισμός, οῦ, ὁ *disappearance,
destruction* Hb 8: 13.*
ἄφαντος, ον *invisible* Lk 24: 31.*
ἀφεδρών, ῶνος, ὁ *latrine* Mt 15:
17; Mk 7: 19.*
ἀφεθήσομαι fut. pass. ind. of
ἀφίημι.
ἀφειδία, ας, ἡ *severe* (lit. *unspar-
ing*) *treatment* Col 2: 23.*
ἀφεῖλον, ἀφελεῖν 2 aor. act. ind.
and inf. of ἀφαιρέω.
ἀφεῖναι 2 aor. act. inf. of ἀφίημι.
ἀφελότης, ητος, ἡ *simplicity* Ac
2: 46.*
ἀφελπίζω see ἀπελπίζω.
ἀφελῶ 2 fut. act. ind. of ἀφαιρέω.
ἄφεσις, έσεως, ἡ *release* Lk 4: 18.
Pardon, cancellation of an obligation, a punishment, or guilt,
hence *forgiveness* of sins Mk
1: 4; 3: 29; Lk 3: 3; Ac 10: 43;
Eph 1: 7.
ἀφέωνται perf. pass. ind. of ἀφίημι.

ἀφή, ῆς, ἡ *ligament* Eph 4: 16;
Col 2: 19.*
ἀφῆκα 1 aor. ind. act. of ἀφίημι.
ἀφθαρσία, ας, ἡ *incorruptibility,
immortality* Ro 2: 7; 1 Cor 15:
42, 50, 53f; 2 Ti 1: 10. ἐν ἀ. *in
immortality* or *forever* Eph 6: 24.
ἄφθαρτος, ον *imperishable, incor-
ruptible, immortal* Ro 1: 23; 1
Cor 9: 25; 15: 52; 1 Pt 1: 4;
imperishable quality 1 Pt 3: 4.
ἀφθονία, ας, ἡ *freedom from envy,*
hence *willingness* Tit 2: 7 v.l.*
ἀφθορία, ας, ἡ *soundness, purity*
Tit 2: 7.*
ἀφίδω 2 aor. subj. act of ἀφοράω.
ἀφίημι—1. *let go, send away* Mk
4: 36; *give up* Mt 27: 50; *utter*
Mk 15: 37; *divorce* 1 Cor 7: 11ff.
Cancel, pardon Mt 18: 27, 32;
remit, forgive sins, etc. Mt 6: 12,
14f; Mk 3: 28; Lk 12: 10; Ro 4:
7; 1 J 1: 9; 2: 12.—2. *leave* lit.
Mt 4: 11; 19: 27; Mk 13: 34;
Lk 10: 30; *abandon* Mk 14: 50.
Let someone *have* something Mt
5: 40. Fig. *give up, abandon* Ro
1: 27; Hb 6: 1; Rv 2: 4; *neglect*
Mt 23: 23.—3. *let, let go, permit,
tolerate* Mk 5: 19; Ac 5: 38; Rv
2: 20; 11: 9. *Let* someone *go on*
J 11: 48. The imperatives ἄφες,
ἄφετε are used with the subjunctive, esp. in the first person
ἄφες ἐκβάλω τὸ κάρφος *let me
take out the speck* Mt 7: 4; ἄφες
ἴδωμεν *let us see* 27: 49; also
with ἵνα and the third person
ἄφες αὐτήν, ἵνα τηρήσῃ αὐτό *let
her keep it* J 12: 7.
ἀφικνέομαι *reach* = become known
to Ro 16: 19.*
ἀφιλάγαθος, ον *not loving the
good* 2 Ti 3: 3.*
ἀφιλάργυρος, ον *not loving money,
not greedy* 1 Ti 3: 3; Hb 13: 5.*
ἄφιξις, εως, ἡ *departure* Ac 20:
29.*
ἀφίστημι—1. trans. (1 aor. act.)
cause to revolt, mislead Ac 5: 37.
—2. intrans. (middle, and 2 aor.,

perf. and pluperf. act.) *go away,
withdraw* Lk 2: 37; 13: 27; Ac
12: 10; ἀπό τινος *desert someone* Ac 15: 38. *Fall away, become apostate* Lk 8: 13; Hb 3:
12. *Keep away* Lk 4: 13; 2 Cor
12: 8; *abstain* 2 Ti 2: 19.

ἄφνω adv. *suddenly* Ac 2: 2; 16:
26; 28: 6.*

ἀφόβως adv. *fearlessly* Lk 1: 74;
Phil 1: 14; *without cause to be
afraid* 1 Cor 16: 10; *boldly* or
shamelessly Jd 12.*

ἀφομοιόω *make like* or *similar*
Hb 7: 3.*

ἀφοράω *look away, fix one's eyes*
trustingly Hb 12: 2; *see* Phil
2: 23.*

ἀφορίζω *set apart, take away,
separate, exclude* Mt 13: 49; 25:
32; Lk 6: 22; Ac 19: 9; 2 Cor 6:
17; Gal 2: 12. *Set apart, appoint*
Ac 13: 2; Ro 1: 1; Gal 1: 15.*

ἀφοριῶ Attic fut. of ἀφορίζω.

ἀφορμή, ῆς, ἡ *occasion, pretext,
opportunity* Ro 7: 8, 11; 2 Cor
11: 12; 1 Ti 5: 14.

ἀφρίζω *foam at the mouth* Mk 9:
18, 20.*

ἀφρός, οῦ, ὁ *foam* Lk 9: 39.*

ἀφροσύνη, ης, ἡ *foolishness, lack
of sense* Mk 7: 22; 2 Cor 11: 1,
17, 21.*

ἄφρων, ον, gen. ονος *foolish, ignorant* Lk 11: 40; 2 Cor 11: 16, 19;
1 Pt 2: 15.

ἀφυπνόω *fall asleep* Lk 8: 23.*

ἀφυστερέω *withhold, keep back*
Js 5: 4.*

ἀφῶμεν 2 aor. subj. act. of
ἀφίημι.

ἄφωνος, ον *silent, dumb* Ac 8: 32;
1 Cor 12: 2. *Incapable of speech*
2 Pt 2: 16; *incapable of conveying
meaning* 1 Cor 14: 10.*

Ἀχάζ, ὁ indecl. *Ahaz* Mt 1: 9; see
2 Kings 16: 1ff.*

Ἀχαΐα, ας, ἡ *Achaia* a Roman
province created 146 BC, including the most important
parts of Greece, i.e. Boeotia,
Attica and the Peloponnesus
Ac 18: 12, 27; Ro 15: 26; 2 Cor
1: 1.

Ἀχαϊκός, οῦ, ὁ *Achaicus* 1 Cor 16:
17, 15 v.l.*

ἀχάριστος, ον *ungrateful* Lk 6:
35; 2 Ti 3: 2.*

Ἀχάς v.l. for Ἀχάζ.

ἀχειροποίητος, ον *not made by*
(human) *hand, spiritual* Mk 14:
58; 2 Cor 5: 1; Col 2: 11.*

Ἀχελδαμάχ see Ἀκελδαμάχ.

ἀχθῆναι, ἀχθήσεσθαι 1 aor. pass.
inf. and 1 fut. pass. inf. of ἄγω.

Ἀχίμ, ὁ indecl. *Achim* Mt 1: 14.*

ἀχλύς, ύος, ἡ *mistiness, dimness of
sight* Ac 13: 11.*

ἀχρεῖος, ον *useless, worthless* Mt
25: 30; *unworthy, miserable* Lk
17: 10.*

ἀχρειόω pass., fig. *become depraved, worthless* Ro 3: 12.*

ἄχρηστος, ον *useless, worthless*
Phlm 11.*

ἄχρι, ἄχρις—1. improper prep. w.
gen. *until* Mt 24: 38; Lk 4: 13;
Ro 1: 13; Gal 4: 2; *to* Hb 6: 11;
within Ac 20: 6; *before* Ro 5: 13;
as far as Ac 22: 22; Hb 4: 12;
to, unto Ac 22: 4; Rv 2: 10.—
2. conj. *until* (*the time when*)
with or without οὗ Ac 7: 18;
Ro 11: 25; Gal 3: 19; *as long as*
Hb 3: 13.

ἄχυρον, ου, τό *chaff* Mt 3: 12;
Lk 3: 17.*

ἀψευδής, ές *free from all deceit,
trustworthy* Tit 1: 2.*

ἀψίνθιον, ου, τό and ἄψινθος, ου,
ἡ *wormwood* Rv 8: 11b; as name
of a star and masc. Rv 8: 11a.*

ἄψυχος, ον *inanimate, lifeless* 1
Cor 14: 7.*

B

β' as numeral = *two, second* superscriptions of 2 Cor, etc.

Βάαλ, ὁ indecl. *Baal,* Hebrew for 'lord' Ro 11: 4.*

Βαβυλών, ῶνος, ἡ *Babylon* lit. Mt 1: 11f; fig., probably with reference to Rome 1 Pt 5: 13; Rv 14: 8; 18: 10, 21.

βαθέως genitive of βαθύς.

βαθμός, οῦ, ὁ *step*; fig. *rank, standing* 1 Ti 3: 13.*

βάθος, ους, τό *depth* lit. Mt 13: 5; Lk 5: 4; fig. Ro 8: 39; 11: 33; κατὰ βάθους *reaching down into the depths* = *extreme* 2 Cor 8: 2.

βαθύνω *make deep* and intrans. *go down deep*; the latter is preferable in Lk 6: 48.*

βαθύς, εῖα, ύ *deep* lit. J 4: 11; fig. Ac 20: 9; Rv 2: 24. ὄρθρου βαθέως *early in the morning* Lk 24: 1.*

βάϊον, ου, τό *palm branch* (Coptic loanword) J 12: 13.*

Βαλαάμ, ὁ indecl. *Balaam* 2 Pt 2: 15; Jd 11; Rv 2: 14; see Num 22–24.*

Βαλάκ, ὁ indecl. *Balak* Rv 2: 14; see Num 22: 2ff.*

βαλλάντιον, ου, τό *money-bag, purse* Lk 10: 4; 12: 33; 22: 35f.*

βάλλω—1. *throw* Mt 3: 10; 5: 29f; 13: 48; Rv 2: 10; 6: 13; *sow, scatter* Mk 4: 26; *cast* 15: 24. Fig. *drive* 1 J 4: 18. Pass. *lie* Mt 9: 2; Lk 16: 20.—**2.** *put, place, lay, bring* Mt 10: 34; Mk 7: 33; Lk 13: 8; J 13: 2; Rv 2: 14; *pour* Mt 9: 17; J 13: 5; Rv 12: 15f; *swing* Rv 14: 19; *deposit* Mt 25: 27.—**3.** intrans. *rush down, break loose* Ac 27: 14.

βαπτίζω *dip, immerse*—**1.** of Jewish ritual washings, mid. and pass. *wash one's hands* Mk 7: 4 v.l.; Lk 11: 38.—**2.** *baptize,* of ritual immersion by John the Baptist and Christians Mt 3: 11, 13f, 16; 28: 19; Mk 6: 14, 24; J 4: 1f; Ac 2: 38, 41; 8: 12f, 36, 38; 1 Cor 1: 14–17; 15: 29.—**3.** fig. Mt 3: 11; 1 Cor 10: 2; 12: 13. Of martyrdom Mk 10: 38f.

βάπτισμα, ατος, τό *baptism* Mt 3: 7; Mk 1: 4; Ac 18: 25; Ro 6: 4; Eph 4: 5; 1 Pt 3: 21. βαπτίζεσθαι βάπτισμα *undergo a baptism* Lk 7: 29. Fig., of martyrdom Mk 10: 38f.

βαπτισμός, οῦ, ὁ *dipping, ceremonial washing* Mk 7: 4, 8 v.l.; Hb 9: 10; *baptism* 6: 2.

βαπτιστής, οῦ, ὁ *Baptist,* always as a surname of John Mt 3:1; 11:11f; Mk 6: 25; Lk 9: 19.

βάπτω *dip, dip in* Lk 16: 24; J 13: 26; Rv 19: 13; for the latter passage *dye* is also possible.*

βαρ Aramaic = *son* Mt 16: 17 v.l.*

Βαραββᾶς, ᾶ, ὁ *Barabbas* Mt 27: 16f; Lk 23: 18; J 18: 40.

Βαράκ, ὁ indecl. *Barak* Hb 11: 32; see Judg 4f.*

Βαραχίας, ου, ὁ *Barachiah* Mt 23: 35.

βάρβαρος, ον *speaking a foreign, unintelligible language* adj. or noun 1 Cor 14: 11. As noun *a person who is not Greek, foreigner, barbarian* Ac 28: 2, 4; Ro 1: 14; Col 3: 11.*

βαρέω *weigh down, burden,* pass., fig. *be burdened, be overcome, become heavy* Lk 9: 32; 21: 34; 2 Cor 1: 8; 1 Ti 5: 16.

βαρέως adv. of βαρύς; *with difficulty* ἀκούειν *be hard of hearing* Mt 13: 15; Ac 28: 27.*

Βαρθολομαῖος, ου, ὁ *Bartholomew* one of the 12 apostles Mt 10: 3; Mk 3: 18; Lk 6: 14; Ac 1: 13. Often identified w. Nathanael.*

Βαριησοῦς, οῦ, ὁ *Bar-Jesus* a false prophet Ac 13: 6.*

Βαριωνᾶ or **Βαριωνᾶς, ᾶ, ὁ** *Bar-Jona* Mt 16: 17.*

Βαρναβᾶς, ᾶ, ὁ *Barnabas* discoverer and companion of Paul Ac 4: 36; 9: 27; 11: 22, 30; 12: 25; chapters 13–15 passim; 1 Cor 9: 6; Gal 2: 1, 9, 13; Col 4: 10.*

βάρος, ους, τό *weight, burden* fig. Mt 20: 12; Ac 15: 28; Gal 6: 2; Rv 2: 24; *fulness* 2 Cor 4: 17; *importance* ἐν β. εἶναι *insist on one's importance* 1 Th 2: 7.*

Βαρσαββᾶς, ᾶ, ὁ *Barsabbas* a patronymic of two different men Ac 1: 23; 15: 22.*

Βαρτιμαῖος, ου, ὁ *Bartimaeus* Mk 10: 46.*

βαρύνω *burden, grieve* Ac 3: 14 v.l.; 28: 27 v.l.; 2 Cor 5: 4 v.l.*

βαρύς, εῖα, ύ *heavy, weighty* fig. Mt 23: 4; *burdensome, difficult* 1 J 5: 3; *severe* 2 Cor 10: 10; *weighty, important* Mt 23: 23; Ac 25: 7; *fierce, savage* Ac 20: 29.*

βαρύτιμος, ον *very expensive, very precious* Mt 26: 7.*

βασανίζω *torture, torment* Mt 8: 6, 29; 2 Pt 2: 8; Rv 12: 2; 14: 10; *press hard* Mt 14: 24.

βασανισμός, οῦ, ὁ *torture, torment* Rv 9: 5; 14: 11; 18: 7, 10, 15.*

βασανιστής, οῦ, ὁ *torturer, jailer* Mt 18: 34.*

βάσανος, ου, ἡ *torture, torment* Lk 16: 23, 28; *great pain* Mt 4: 24.*

βασιλεία, ας, ἡ—**1.** *kingship, royal power* or *rule, kingdom* Lk 19: 12, 15; 1 Cor 15: 24; Hb 1: 8; Rv 1: 6; 17: 12.—**2.** *kingdom,* territory ruled over by a king Mt 4: 8; Mk 6: 23; Lk 21: 10.— **3.** *the royal reign* or *kingdom* of God or the heavens (the expressions are equivalent) Mt 3: 2; 5: 3, 10, 19f; Mk 4: 11; Lk 8: 1; J 3: 3, 5; Ac 28: 23, 31; Ro 14: 17; 1 Cor 4: 20; Gal 5: 21. It is thought of as present Mt

12: 28; Lk 11: 20 or future Mt 3: 2; Lk 21: 31.

βασίλειος, ον *royal* 1 Pt 2: 9. τὰ β. *the (royal) palace(s)* Lk 7: 25.*

βασιλεύς, έως, ὁ *king* lit. Mt 2: 1; 17: 25; Mk 6: 14; J 6: 15; Ac 12: 1; 2 Cor 11: 32; Hb 7: 1f; Rv 1: 5. Of the Roman emperor 1 Ti 2:2; 1 Pt 2: 13, 17. Fig. of God and Christ Mt 2: 2; J 1: 49; 1 Ti 1: 17; Rv 17: 14.

βασιλεύω *be king, rule* w. gen. *over* or *of something* Mt 2: 22; also w. ἐπί and gen. or acc. Lk 19: 14, 27; Rv 5: 10. Fig. Ro 5: 14. Of God and Christ Rv 11: 15. In aor. (ingressive) *become king* Rv 11: 17; 19: 6.

βασιλικός, ή, όν *royal* Ac 12: 20f; Js 2: 8; *royal official* J 4: 46, 49.*

βασιλίσκος, ου, ὁ *petty king* v.l. in J 4: 46 and 49.*

βασίλισσα, ης, ἡ *queen* Mt 12: 42; Lk 11: 31; Ac 8: 27; Rv 18: 7.*

βάσις, εως, ἡ *the* (human) *foot* Ac 3: 7.*

βασκαίνω *bewitch* with the evil eye Gal 3: 1.*

βαστάζω—**1.** *pick up* J 10: 31.— **2.** *carry, bear* lit. Lk 11: 27; 22: 10; J 19: 17; fig. Mt 20: 12; J 16: 12; Gal 6: 2; *bear patiently, put up with* Ro 15: 1; Rv 2: 3. β. κρίμα *bear one's judgment, pay the penalty* Gal 5: 10.—**3.** *carry away, remove* Mt 3: 11; 8: 17; J 20: 15; *steal* J 12: 6.

βάτος, ου, ὁ and ἡ *thorn-bush* Lk 6: 44; Ac 7: 30, 35. ἐπὶ τ. β. *in the passage about the thorn-bush* Mk 12: 26; Lk 20: 37.*

βάτος, ου, ὁ *bath* a Hebrew liquid measure = between 8 and 9 gallons Lk 16: 6.*

βάτραχος, ου, ὁ *frog* Rv 16: 13.*

βατταλογέω *babble* Mt 6: 7; Lk 11: 2 v.l.*

βδέλυγμα, ατος, τό *abomination, detestable thing* esp. of idolatry Lk 16: 15; Rv 17: 4f; 21: 27.

β. τῆς ἐρημώσεως *the detestable thing causing desolation* Mt 24: 15; Mk 13: 14.*

βδελυκτός, ή, όν *abominable, detestable* Tit 1: 16.*

βδελύσσομαι *abhor, detest* Ro 2: 22; perf. pass. ptc. ἐβδελυγμένος *abominable* Rv 21: 8.*

βέβαιος, α, ον *firm, strong, secure* lit. Hb 6: 19. Fig. *reliable, dependable, certain* Ro 4: 16; 2 Cor 1: 7; Hb 2: 2; 2 Pt 1: 10; *valid* Hb 9: 17.

βεβαιόω *confirm, establish* 1 Cor 1: 6, 8; Col 2: 7; *fulfill* Ro 15: 8; *strengthen* 2 Cor 1: 21; *guarantee* Hb 2: 3.

βεβαίωσις, εως, ή *confirmation* Phil 1: 7; *confirmation, guarantee* Hb 6: 16.*

βεβαμμένος pf. pass. ptc. of βάπτω.

βέβηλος, ον *profane, worldly, godless* 1 Ti 1: 9; 4: 7; 6: 20; 2 Ti 2: 16; *irreligious* Hb 12: 16.*

βεβηλόω *desecrate, profane* Mt 12: 5; Ac 24: 6.*

βέβληκα pf. act. ind of βάλλω.

βέβρωκα pf. act. ind. of βιβρώσκω.

Βεεζεβούλ, ὁ indecl., with variant readings Βεελζεβούβ and Βεελζεβούλ *Beelzebub*, i.e. Satan Mt 10: 25; 12: 24, 27; Mk 3: 22; Lk 11: 15, 18f.*

Βελιάρ, ὁ indecl., with v.l. Βελιάλ *Belial*, i.e. Satan or the Antichrist 2 Cor 6: 15.*

βελόνη, ης, ή *needle* Lk 18: 25.*

βέλος, ους, τό *arrow* Eph 6: 16.*

βελτίων, ον *better*; neut. as adv. *very well* 2 Ti 1: 18; Ac 10: 28 v.l.*

Βενιαμ(ε)ίν, ὁ indecl. *Benjamin* Ac 13: 21; Ro 11: 1; Phil 3: 5; Rv 7: 8.*

Βερνίκη, ης, ή *Bernice* sister and companion of Herod Agrippa II Ac 25: 13, 23; 26: 30.*

Βέροια, ας, ή *Beroea* a city in Macedonia Ac 17: 10, 13.*

Βεροιαῖος, α, ον *from Beroea*, as noun *the Beroean* Ac 20: 4.*

Βεώρ, ὁ indecl. *Beor* 2 Pt 2: 15.*

Βηθαβαρά, ή *Bethabara* v.l. for Βηθανία in J 1: 28.*

Βηθανία, ας, ή *Bethany*—**1.** a village on the Mount of Olives, nearly 2 mi. from Jerusalem Mt 21: 17; 26: 6; Mk 11: 11f; Lk 24: 50; J 12: 1.—**2.** place on the east side of the Jordan where John baptized J 1: 28.

Βηθαραβά error for Βηθαβαρά.

Βηθεσδά, ή indecl. *Bethesda* a pool in Jerusalem J 5: 2 v.l.*

Βηθζαθά, ή indecl. *Bethzatha* J 5: 2.*

Βηθλέεμ, ή indecl. *Bethlehem* a town in Judaea, about 4½ miles south of Jerusalem Mt 2: 1, 5f, 8, 16; Lk 2: 4, 15; J 7: 42.*

Βηθσαϊδά(ν), ή indecl. *Bethsaida* the name of a city (perh. two cities) near the Sea of Galilee Mt 11: 21; Mk 6: 45; 8: 22; Lk 9: 10; 10: 13; J 1: 44; 12: 21. Also as v.l. for Βηθζαθά J 5: 2.*

Βηθφαγή, ή indecl. *Bethphage* a place on the Mount of Olives Mt 21: 1; Mk 11: 1; Lk 19: 29.*

βῆμα, ατος, τό—**1.** *step, stride* οὐδὲ β. ποδός *not even a foot of ground* Ac 7: 5.—**2.** *tribunal, judicial bench* Mt 27: 19; J 19: 13; Ac 18: 12, 16f; 25: 6, 10, 17; Ro 14: 10; 2 Cor 5: 10; *speaker's platform* Ac 12: 21, 23 v.l.*

βήρυλλος, ου, ὁ, ή *beryl* a precious stone of sea-green color Rv 21: 20.*

βία, ας, ή *force, violence* Ac 21: 35; 27: 41; *use of force* 5: 26; cf. 24: 7 v.l.*

βιάζω mid. *force one's way, enter forcibly* Lk 16: 16; pass., prob. *be forcibly entered, suffer violence* (w. other possibilities) Mt 11: 12.*

βίαιος, α, ον *violent, strong* Ac 2: 2.*

βιαστής, οῦ, ὁ *a violent, impetuous man* Mt 11: 12.*

βιβλαρίδιον, ου, τό *little book* Rv 10: 2, 9f, vs. 8 v.l.*

βιβλιδάριον, ου, τό v.l. for βιβλαρίδιον in the Rv passages above.

βιβλίον, ου, τό *book, scroll* Lk 4: 17; J 20: 30; Gal 3: 10; 2 Ti 4: 13; Rv 5: 1ff; 6: 14; 13: 8. β. ἀποστασίου *a certificate of divorce* Mk 10: 4.

βίβλος, ου, ἡ *book, scroll* esp. *sacred book* Mt 1: 1; Mk 12: 26; Lk 3: 4; Ac 7: 42; 19: 19; Phil 4: 3; Rv 3: 5.

βιβρώσκω *eat* J 6: 13.*

Βιθυνία, ας, ἡ *Bithynia* a Roman province in northern Asia Minor Ac 16: 7; 1 Pt 1: 1.*

βίος, ου, ὁ—**1.** *life, everyday life* Lk 8: 14; 1 Ti 2: 2; 2 Ti 2: 4; 1 Pt 4: 3 v.l.—**2.** *livelihood, property* Mk 12: 44; Lk 8: 43 v.l.; 15: 12, 30; 21: 4. β. τοῦ κόσμου *worldly goods* 1 J 3: 17. ἀλαζονεία τοῦ β. *pride in one's possessions* 2: 16.*

βιόω *live* 1 Pt 4: 2.*

βίωσις, εως, ἡ *manner of life* Ac 26: 4.*

βιωτικός, ή, όν *belonging to (daily) life, ordinary* Lk 21: 34; 1 Cor 6: 3, 4.*

βλαβερός, ά, όν *harmful* 1 Ti 6: 9.*

βλάπτω *harm, injure* Mk 16: 18; Lk 4: 35.*

βλαστάνω, βλαστάω *sprout, put forth* trans. *produce* Js 5: 18. Intrans. *bud, sprout* Mt 13: 26; Mk 4: 27; Hb 9: 4.*

Βλάστος, ου, ὁ *Blastus* Ac 12: 20.*

βλασφημέω in relation to men *revile, defame, slander* Ro 3: 8; 1 Cor 10: 30; Tit 3: 2. In relation to a divine being *speak irreverently of, blaspheme* Mt 9: 3; 27: 39; Mk 3: 29; Ac 19: 37; Ro 2: 24; 14: 16; 2 Pt 2: 10.

βλασφημία, ας, ἡ *slander, abusive speech, blasphemy* Mt 12: 31; 26: 65; J 10: 33; Eph 4: 31; Rv 13: 5f; *a reviling judgment* Jd 9.

βλάσφημος, ον *slanderous, scurrilous, blasphemous* Ac 6: 11; β. κρίσιν φέρειν *pronounce a defaming judgment* 2 Pt 2: 11. As noun *blasphemer* 1 Ti 1: 13.

βλέμμα, ατος, τό *glance, look* βλέμματι *by what he saw* 2 Pt 2: 8.*

βλέπω *see, look (at)*—**1.** *be able to see* J 9: 7, 15, 25; Ac 9: 9; Ro 11: 8; Rv 3: 18.—**2.** *see, look at* Mt 5: 28; 7: 3; Mk 5: 31; Lk 9: 62; 10: 23f; Ac 9: 8f; Ro 8: 24f; Rv 1: 11f; *look on* Ac 1: 9. βλέπων βλέπω *see with open eyes* Mt 13: 14. βλέπων οὐ βλέπει *though he looks he does not see* Lk 8: 10.—**3.** *watch, beware of* Mk 13: 9; Phil 3: 2; *see to it, take care* Mt 24: 4; Gal 5: 15; *perceive* Mt 14: 30; *discover, find* Ro 7: 23; Hb 3: 19.

βληθήσομαι fut. pass. ind. of βάλλω.

βλητέος, α, ον verbal adj. from βάλλω *must be put* Lk 5: 38; Mk 2: 22 v.l.*

Βοανηργές *Boanerges* Mk 3: 17.*

βοάω *call, shout, cry out* Mt 3: 3; Mk 15: 34; Lk 18: 7; J 1: 23; Ac 8: 7.

Βόες, ὁ indecl. *Boaz* Mt 1: 5; cf. Ruth 4: 21.*

βοή, ῆς, ἡ *cry, shout* Js 5: 4.*

βοήθεια, ας, ἡ *help* Hb 4: 16; nautical term *support,* perh. in the form of cables Ac 27: 17.*

βοηθέω *come to the aid of, help* w. dat. Mt 15: 25; Mk 9: 22, 24; Ac 16: 9; 21: 28; 2 Cor 6: 2; Hb 2: 18; Rv 12: 16.*

βοηθός, όν *helpful,* as noun *helper* Hb 13: 6.*

βόησον 1 aor. act. imperative of βοάω.

βόθρος, ου, ὁ *pit, cistern* Mt 15: 14 v.l.*

βόθυνος, ου, ὁ *pit* Mt 12: 11; 15: 14; Lk 6: 39.*

βολή, ῆς, ἡ *a throw* λίθου β. *a stone's throw* Lk 22: 41.*

βολίζω *take soundings* Ac 27: 28.*
βολίς, ίδος, ἡ *missile, arrow, javelin* Hb 12: 20 v.l.*
Βόος, ὁ indecl. *Boaz* Lk 3: 32.*
βόρβορος, ου, ὁ *mud, filth* 2 Pt 2: 22.*
βορρᾶς, ᾶ, ὁ *the north* ἀπὸ β. *on the north* Rv 21: 13 but *from (the) north* Lk 13: 29.*
βόσκω act. *feed, tend* Mk 5: 14; J 21: 15, 17. Pass. *graze, feed* Mk 5: 11.
Βοσόρ, ὁ indecl. *Bosor* 2 Pt 2: 15 v.l.*
βοτάνη, ης, ἡ *vegetation* Hb 6: 7.*
βότρυς, υος, ὁ *bunch of grapes* Rv 14: 18.*
βουλευτής, οῦ, ὁ *member of a council* in this case the Sanhedrin Mk 15: 43; Lk 23: 50.*
βουλεύω mid. *deliberate, consider* Lk 14: 31. *Decide, plan* Ac 27: 39; 15: 37 v.l.; 2 Cor 1: 17; *plot* J 11: 53; 12: 10; Ac 5: 33 v.l.*
βουλή, ῆς, ἡ *plan, purpose* Lk 7: 30; Eph 1: 11; *resolution, decision* Ac 2: 23; 5: 38; 20: 27; 27: 12, 42; Hb 6: 17; *motive* 1 Cor 4: 5.
βούλημα, ατος, τό *intention, will* Ac 27: 43; Ro 9: 19; 1 Pt 4: 3.*
βούλομαι *wish, be willing, want, desire* Mt 1: 19; 11: 27; Lk 22: 42; Ac 5: 28; 25: 20, 22; 1 Cor 12: 11; 1 Ti 6: 9; Phlm 13. βουληθείς *according to his will* Js 1: 18. βούλεσθε ἀπολύσω; *shall I release?* J 18: 39.
βουνός, οῦ, ὁ *hill* Lk 3: 5; 23: 30.*
βοῦς, βοός, ὁ *ox* Lk 14: 5, 19; J 2: 14f; 1 Cor 9: 9.
βραβεῖον, ου, τό *prize* lit. 1 Cor 9: 24; fig. Phil 3: 14.*
βραβεύω *rule* Col 3: 15, lit. 'award prizes, judge, control.' *
βραδύνω intr. *hesitate, delay* 1 Ti 3: 15; *hold back in hesitation* 2 Pt 3: 9.*
βραδυπλοέω *sail slowly* Ac 27: 7.*
βραδύς, εῖα, ύ *slow* Lk 24: 25; Js 1: 19.*

βραδύτης, ητος, ἡ *slowness* 2 Pt 3: 9.*
βραχίων, ονος, ὁ *arm* fig. Lk 1: 51; J 12: 38; Ac 13: 17.*
βραχύς, εῖα, ύ *short, little:* of distance Ac 27: 28; of time Lk 22: 58; Ac 5: 34; Hb 2: 7, 9; of quantity J 6: 7. διὰ β. *in a few words* Hb 13: 22.*
βρέφος, ους, τό *baby, infant* Lk 1: 41, 44; 2: 12, 16; 18: 15; Ac 7: 19; 2 Ti 3: 15; fig. 1 Pt 2: 2.*
βρέχω *wet* Lk 7: 38, 44. Of rain *fall* Rv 11: 6. *Send rain, cause to rain* Mt 5: 45; Lk 17: 29. Impersonal βρέχει *it rains* Js 5: 17.*
βροντή, ῆς, ἡ *thunder* Mk 3: 17; J 12: 29; Rv 6: 1; 10: 3f.
βροχή, ῆς, ἡ *rain* Mt 7: 25, 27.*
βρόχος, ου, ὁ *noose* fig. *restraint* 1 Cor 7: 35.*
βρυγμός, οῦ, ὁ *grinding, gnashing* Mt 8: 12; 25: 30; Lk 13: 28.
βρύχω *grind, gnash* Ac 7: 54.*
βρύω *pour forth* Js 3: 11.*
βρῶμα, ατος, τό *food, solid food* lit. Lk 3: 11; Ro 14: 15; 1 Cor 6: 13; Hb 9: 10; 13: 9; fig. J 4: 34; 1 Cor 3: 2.
βρώσιμος, ον *eatable* Lk 24: 41.*
βρῶσις, εως, ἡ—1. *eating* Ro 14: 17; 1 Cor 8: 4. As a general term for *consuming,* β. may mean corrosion, or a destructive insect or worm Mt 6: 19f.—2. *food* lit. Hb 12: 16; fig. J 6: 27, 55.
βυθίζω *sink* Lk 5: 7; *plunge* 1 Ti 6: 9.*
βυθός, οῦ, ὁ *the deep, open sea* 2 Cor 11: 25.
βυρσεύς, έως, ὁ *tanner* Ac 9: 43; 10: 6, 32.*
βύσσινος, η, ον *made of fine linen* as noun *fine linen garment* Rv 18: 12, 16; 19: 8, 14.*
βύσσος, ου, ἡ *fine linen* Lk 16: 19; Rv 18: 12 v.l.*
βωμός, οῦ, ὁ *altar* Ac 17: 23.*

Γ

γ' as numeral = *three, third* in the superscription of 3 J.

Γαββαθᾶ indecl. *Gabbatha* J 19: 13.*

Γαβριήλ, ὁ indecl. *Gabriel* Lk 1: 19, 26.*

γάγγραινα, ης, ἡ *gangrene, cancer* fig. 2 Ti 2: 17.*

Γάδ, ὁ indecl. *Gad* Rv 7: 5 (Gen 30: 11).*

Γαδαρηνός, ή, όν *from Gadara* a city in Transjordania; ὁ Γ. *the Gadarene* Mt 8: 28; Mk 5: 1 v.l.; Lk 8: 26 v.l., 37 v.l.*

Γάζα, ης, ἡ *Gaza* a city in southwest Palestine Ac 8: 26,*

γάζα, ης, ἡ (Persian loanword) *the* (royal) *treasury* Ac 8: 27.*

γαζοφυλακεῖον or **γαζοφυλάκιον, ου, τό** *treasury* J 8: 20; *contribution box* or *receptacle* Mk 12: 41, 43; Lk 21: 1.*

Γάϊος, ου, ὁ *Gaius*—**1.** Ro 16: 23; 1 Cor 1: 14.—**2.** Ac 19: 29.—**3.** Ac 20: 4.—**4.** 3 J 1.*

γάλα, γάλακτος, τό *milk* lit. 1 Cor 9: 7. Fig. 3: 2; Hb 5: 12f; 1 Pt 2: 2.*

Γαλάτης, ου, ὁ *a Galatian* Gal 3: 1.*

Γαλατία, ας, ἡ *Galatia* a district in Asia Minor settled by the Celtic Galatians 1 Cor 16: 1; Gal 1: 2; 2 Ti 4: 10 (where *Gaul* may be meant); 1 Pt 1: 1.*

Γαλατικός, ή, όν *Galatian* Ac 16: 6; 18: 23.*

γαλήνη, ης, ἡ *a calm* on the sea Mt 8: 26; Mk 4: 39; Lk 8: 24.*

Γαλιλαία, ας, ἡ *Galilee* the northern third of Palestine Mt 4: 18; Mk 1: 9, 14, 28; Lk 5: 17; J 2: 1, 11; Ac 9: 31.

Γαλιλαῖος, α, ον *Galilean* Mt 26: 69; Mk 14: 70; Lk 13: 1f; J 4: 45; Ac 5: 37.

Γαλλία, ας, ἡ *Gaul* v.l. in 2 Ti 4: 10 for Γαλατία.*

Γαλλίων, ωνος, ὁ *Gallio* proconsu of Achaia 51–52 AD Ac 18: 12, 14, 17.*

Γαμαλιήλ, ὁ indecl. *Gamaliel*, i.e. Rabban Gamaliel the Elder, a renowned teacher of the law Ac 5: 34; 22: 3.*

γαμέω *marry, enter matrimony* of both men and women Mt 5: 32; 19: 10; Mk 10: 12; 12: 25; Lk 16: 18; 1 Cor 7: 9f, 28, 34. Pass. *get married, be married* 7: 39.

γαμίζω *give in marriage* Mt 24: 38; Mk 12: 25 v.l. This may be the sense in 1 Cor 7: 38, but it is even more likely that γ. here = γαμέω and means simply *marry*. Pass. *be given in marriage, be married* Mt 22: 30; Mk 12: 25; Lk 17: 27; 20: 35.*

γαμίσκω *give in marriage* Mt 24: 38 v.l. Pass. *be given in marriage* Mk 12: 25 v.l., Lk 20: 34 in text, 35 v.l.*

γάμος, ου, ὁ *wedding celebration* γ. ποιεῖν *give a wedding celebration* Mt 22: 2; cf. verses 3, 4, 9; J 2: 1f. ἔνδυμα γ. *wedding garment* Mt 22: 11f. *Wedding banquet* Rv 19: 7, 9; *banquet* Lk 12: 36. *Wedding hall* Mt 22: 10 v.l. *Marriage* Hb 13: 4.

γάρ conjunction used to express cause, inference or continuation, or to explain; never comes first in its clause.—**1.** cause or reason: *for* Mt 2: 2; 3: 2f; Mk 1: 22; J 2: 25; Ac 2: 25; 1 Cor 11: 5. καί γάρ simply *for* Mk 10: 45; J 4: 23; 1 Cor 5: 7 but *for also, for even* Mt 8: 9; Lk 6: 32f; 2 Cor 2: 10. γάρ καί *for also, for precisely* 2 Cor 2: 9. In questions γάρ can be left untranslated as in 1 Pt 2: 20 or prefixed by *what!* as in 1 Cor 11: 22 or *why!* in Mt 27: 23.—**2.** explanatory

for, you see Mt 12: 40, 50; Mk
7: 3; Ro 7: 2; Hb 3: 4.—**3.** inferential certainly, by all means,
so, then Hb 12: 3; Js 1: 7; 1 Pt
4: 15. οὐ γάρ no, indeed! Ac 16:
37.—**4.** continuation or connection indeed, to be sure, but
Ro 2: 25; 5: 7; 1 Cor 10: 1; Gal
1: 11.

γαστήρ, τρός, ἡ belly—**1.** fig.
glutton Tit 1: 12.—**2.** womb Lk
1: 31. ἐν γαστρὶ ἔχειν be pregnant Mt 1: 18, 23; 1 Th 5: 3;
Rv 12: 2.

γέ emphatic particle, enclitic yet,
at least Lk 11: 8; 18: 5. Even,
as a matter of fact Ro 8: 32. εἴ γε
if indeed, inasmuch as 2 Cor 5: 3;
Gal 3: 4; Eph 3: 2. εἰ δὲ μή γε
otherwise Mt 6: 1; 9: 17; 2 Cor
11: 16. μενοῦν γε rather Ro 9: 20.
μήτι γε not to mention, let alone
1 Cor 6: 3. Often γε cannot be
translated into English.

γεγένημαι perf. mid. ind. of
γίνομαι.

γέγονα perf. act. ind. of γίνομαι.

Γεδεών, ὁ indecl. Gideon Hb 11: 32
(Judg 6–8).*

γέεννα, ης, ἡ Gehenna, Valley of
Hinnom a ravine south of Jerusalem, a place of fire for the
punishment of the wicked, hell
Mt 5: 22, 29f; 23: 15; Mk 9: 45,
47; Js 3: 6.

Γεθσημανί indecl. Gethsemane an
olive orchard on the Mount of
Olives Mt 26: 36; Mk 14: 32.*

γείτων, ονος, ὁ and ἡ neighbor Lk
14: 12; 15: 6, 9; J 9: 8.*

γελάω laugh Lk 6: 21, 25.*

γέλως, ωτος, ὁ laughter Js 4: 9.*

γεμίζω fill Mk 4: 37; 15: 36; J 2:
7; Rv 8: 5.

γέμω be full w. gen. or acc. Mt
23: 25, 27; Lk 11: 39; Ro 3: 14;
Rv 17: 3, 4; 15: 7.

γενεά, ᾶς, ἡ clan, race, kind Lk
16: 8; perh. nation Mk 13: 30.
Generation, contemporaries Mt
12: 41f; 17: 17; Mk 9: 19; Lk

21: 32; Hb 3: 10. Age, period of
time Mt 1: 17; Lk 1: 48, 50;
Col 1: 26. Perh. family or origin
Ac 8: 33.

γενεαλογέω derive descent Hb 7:
6.*

γενεαλογία, ας, ἡ genealogy, pedi-
gree 1 Ti 1: 4; Tit 3: 9.*

γενέθλια, ίων, τά birthday or
birthday celebration Mk 6: 21 v.l.*

γενέσθαι 2 aor. mid. inf. of
γίνομαι.

γενέσια, ίων, τά birthday celebration Mt 14: 6; Mk 6: 21.*

γένεσις, εως, ἡ birth Mt 1: 18;
Lk 1: 14. In Mt 1: 1 γ. may
mean origin or descent, and the
expression βίβλος γενέσεως may
mean genealogy as Gen 5: 1.
πρόσωπον γ. natural face Js
1: 23. τροχὸς τῆς γ. course of life
3: 6.*

γενετή, ῆς, ἡ birth J 9: 1.*

γένημα, ατος, τό product, fruit,
yield of plants lit. Mt 26: 29; Mk
14: 25; Lk 12: 18 v.l.; 22: 18;
fig. 2 Cor 9: 10.*

γεννάω—1. be or become the father
of, beget lit. Mt 1: 2ff, 20; J 8:
41; 9: 34; Ac 7: 8, 29. Fig. J 1:
13; 1 Cor 4: 15; Phlm 10; 1 J 2:
29.—**2.** of women: bear Lk 1: 13,
35, 57; Ac 2: 8; 22: 28.—**3.** fig.
cause, produce 2 Ti 2: 23.

γέννημα, ατος, τό that which is
produced or born of living
creatures, offspring, brood Mt 3:
7; 12: 34; 23: 33; Lk 3: 7.*

Γεννησαρέτ, ἡ indecl. Gennesaret
the plain south of Capernaum
Mt 14: 34; Mk 6: 53; also the
lake adjacent to this plain Lk
5: 1 (called Sea of Galilee in Mk
1: 16).*

γέννησις, εως, ἡ birth v.l. in Mt
1: 18, Lk 1: 14 and 1 J 5: 18.*

γεννητός, ή, όν born γ. γυναικῶν
all mankind Mt 11: 11; Lk 7:
28.*

γένος, ους, τό race, stock—**1.** descendants Ac 4: 6. τοῦ γὰρ καὶ

γένος ἐσμέν *we, too are descended from him* 17: 28. *Family* 7: 13.—**2.** *nation, people* Mk 7: 26; Ac 7: 19; Gal 1: 14; 1 Pt 2: 9.—**3.** *class, kind* Mt 13: 47; 1 Cor 12: 10.

Γερασηνός, ή, όν *from Gerasa* a city in Peraea, east of the Jordan. ὁ Γ. the *Gerasene* Mt 8: 28 v.l.; Mk 5: 1; Lk 8: 26, 37.*

Γεργεσηνός, ή, όν *from Gergesa* a town on the eastern shore of the Sea of Galilee. ὁ Γ. *the Gergesene* v.l. in Mt 8: 28, Mk 5: 1 and Lk 8: 26, 37.*

γερουσία, ας, ἡ *council of elders* in Ac 5: 21 the Sanhedrin in Jerusalem.*

γέρων, οντος, ὁ *old man* J 3: 4.*

γεύομαι w. gen. or acc. *taste, partake of, enjoy* Lk 14: 24; J 2: 9; Ac 20: 11; Col 2: 21; *eat* Ac 10: 10. Fig. *come to know, experience* Mk 9: 1; J 8: 52; Hb 2: 9; 1 Pt 2: 3; *obtain* Hb 6: 4.

γεωργέω *cultivate* Hb 6: 7.*

γεώργιον, ου, τό *cultivated land, field* fig. 1 Cor 3: 9.*

γεωργός, οῦ, ὁ *farmer* 2 Ti 2: 6; Js 5: 7. *Tenant farmer, vinedresser* Mt 21: 33ff, 38, 40f; J 15: 1.

γῆ, γῆς, ἡ *soil, earth, ground* Mt 5: 18; 10: 29; 13: 5, 8, 23; Mk 8: 6; Lk 6: 49; 13: 7; J 12: 24; Col 1: 16; Hb 6: 7; 2 Pt 3: 13. (*Dry*) *land* Mk 4: 1; 6: 47; J 6: 21; Ac 27: 39, 43f; *land, region, country* Mt 2: 6; Mk 15: 33; Ac 7: 3f, 6, 36. The inhabited *earth* Lk 21: 35; Ac 1: 8; *men, humankind* Mt 5: 13; Lk 18: 8; Ro 9: 28; Rv 14: 3.

γῆρας, ως or **ους**, dat. **γήρει** or **γήρᾳ, τό** *old age* Lk 1: 36.*

γηράσκω *grow old* J 21: 18; Hb 8: 13.*

γίνομαι capable of many translations in various contexts, of which these are typical:—**1.** *be born* or *produced* Mt 21: 19; J

8: 58; Ro 1: 3; 1 Cor 15: 37; Gal 4: 4. *Arise, come about, occur, come* Mt 8: 26; Mk 4: 37; Lk 4: 42; 23: 19, 44; J 6: 17; Ac 6: 1; 11: 19; 27: 27; 1 Ti 6: 4; Rv 8: 5, 7.—**2.** *be made* or *created, be done* Mt 6: 10; 11: 20f; Lk 14: 22; J 1: 3; Ac 19: 26; 1 Cor 9: 15; Hb 11: 3; *be established* Mk 2: 27.—**3.** *happen, take place* Mt 1: 22; 18: 31; Lk 1: 38; 8: 34; J 10: 22; Ac 7: 40; 28: 9. Expressions like γέγονε ἐμοί τι *something has come to me* = *I have* or *have received something* Mt 18: 12; Mk 4: 11; Lk 14: 12; 1 Cor 4: 5. μὴ γένοιτο *by no means, far from it, God forbid* lit. 'may it not be' Lk 20: 16; Ro 3: 4, 6, 31; Gal 2: 17. καὶ ἐγένετο and ἐγένετο δέ, with or without καί following, is usually felt to be superfluous and is left untranslated; older versions rendered it *it came to pass* Mt 7: 28; 9: 10; Lk 2: 1, 6, 46; 8: 1, 22.—**4.** *become* Mt 5: 45; 24: 32; Mk 1: 17; 6: 14; Lk 6: 16; J 1: 12, 14; 1 Cor 13: 11; Gal 3: 13; Col 1: 23; Hb 5: 5. *Come, go* Mk 1: 11; Lk 1: 44; Ac 13: 32; 20: 16; 21: 35; Gal 3: 14.—**5.** *be* largely = εἰμί: Mt 10: 16; Mk 4: 19; Lk 6: 36; 17: 26, 28; J 15: 8; Ac 22: 17; Gal 4: 4; 1 Th 2: 8; Hb 11: 6. With dat. of a person *belong* Ro 7: 3f. *Appear* Mk 1: 4; J 1: 6.

γινώσκω—1. *know, come to know* Mt 13: 11; Lk 12: 47f; J 8: 32; 14: 7; Ac 1: 7; 19: 35; 1 Cor 3: 20; 13: 9, 12; 2 Cor 5: 16; 1 J 4: 2, 6. Imperative γινώσκετε *you may be quite sure* Mt 24: 33, 43; J 15: 18.—**2.** *learn* (*of*), *ascertain, find out* Mt 9: 30; Mk 6: 38; 15: 45; Lk 24: 18; J 4: 1; Ac 21: 34.—**3.** *understand, comprehend* Mk 4: 13; J 8: 43; 10: 6; Ac 8: 30; 21: 37; 1 Cor 2: 8, 11, 14.—**4.** *perceive, notice, realize* Mk

5: 29; 7: 24; Lk 8: 46; J 6: 15; Ac 23: 6.—**5**. *acknowledge, recognize* Mt 7: 23; J 1: 10; *choose* 1 Cor 8: 3; Gal 4: 9.—**6**. euphemistically, of sex relations *know* Mt 1: 25; Lk 1: 34.

γλεῦκος, ους, τό *sweet new wine* Ac 2: 13.*

γλυκύς, εῖα, ύ *sweet* Js 3: 11f; Rv 10: 9f.*

γλῶσσα, ης, ἡ *tongue*—**1**. lit. as an organ of speech Mk 7: 33, 35; Lk 16: 24; 1 Cor 14: 9; Js 1: 26; Rv 16: 10.—**2**. *language* Ac 2: 11; Phil 2: 11; Rv 5: 9. The expressions γλῶσσαι, γένη γλωσσῶν, ἐν γ. λαλεῖν etc. refer to the broken, ecstatic speech of those overcome by strong religious emotion. The latter expression is usually rendered *speak in tongues*. Ac 19: 6; 1 Cor 12: 10; 13: 1, 8; 14: 1–27, 39.

γλωσσόκομον, ου, τό *money-box* J 12: 6; 13: 29.*

γναφεύς, έως, ὁ *bleacher, fuller* one who cleans woolen cloth Mk 9: 3.*

γνήσιος, ία, ον *true* lit. 'legitimate' Phil 4: 3; 1 Ti 1: 2; Tit 1: 4. τὸ γ. *genuineness, sincerity* 2 Cor 8: 8.*

γνησίως adv. *sincerely, genuinely* Phil 2: 20.*

γνοῖ 2 aor. subj. act. of γινώσκω, Hellenistic form.

γνούς, γνόντος 2 aor. act. ptc. of γινώσκω.

γνόφος, ου, ὁ *darkness* Hb 12: 18.*

γνῶ 2 aor. act. subj. of γινώσκω.

γνώμη, ης, ἡ—**1**. *purpose, intention, mind* 1 Cor 1: 10; Rv 17: 13; *decision, resolve* Ac 20: 3; Rv 17: 17.—**2**. *opinion, judgment* 1 Cor 7: 25, 40; 2 Cor 8: 10; Ac 4: 18 v.l.—**3**. *previous knowledge, consent* Phlm 14.*

γνωρίζω *make known, reveal* Lk 2: 15; J 15: 15; Ac 7: 13; Ro

9: 22f; Eph 6: 19, 21; Phil 4: 6; *know* Phil 1: 22.

γνώριμος, ον *acquainted (with), known (to)* J 18: 16 v.l.*

γνῶσις, εως, ἡ *knowledge* Lk 1: 77; 11: 52; Ro 11: 33; 1 Cor 8: 1, 7, 11; 12: 8; 2 Cor 6: 6; 10: 5; 2 Pt 1: 5f; 3: 18; *personal acquaintance with* w. gen. Phil 3: 8. Heretical *knowledge* of the Gnostics 1 Ti 6: 20.

γνώσομαι fut. mid. (deponent) of γινώσκω.

γνώστης, ου, ὁ *one acquainted (with), expert (in)* w. gen. Ac 26: 3.*

γνωστός, ή, όν *known* Ac 2: 14; 4: 10; 9: 42; 19: 17. As noun *acquaintance, friend, intimate* J 18: 15f; Lk 2: 44. τὸ γ. *what can be known* Ro 1: 19.

γογγύζω *grumble, mutter, complain* Mt 20: 11; Lk 5: 30; J 6: 41, 43, 61; 1 Cor 10: 10; *speak secretly, whisper* J 7: 32.*

γογγυσμός, οῦ, ὁ *grumbling, complaint, displeasure* Ac 6: 1; Phil 2: 14; 1 Pt 4: 9; *secret talk, whispering* J 7: 12.*

γογγυστής, οῦ, ὁ *grumbler* Jd 16.*

γόης, ητος, ὁ *swindler, impostor* lit. 'sorcerer' 2 Ti 3: 13.*

Γολγοθᾶ, ἡ acc. Γολγοθᾶν *Golgotha* Aram., translated 'place of a skull' Mt 27: 33; Mk 15: 22; J 19: 17.*

Γόμορρα, ων, τά and **ας, ἡ** *Gomorrah* (Gen 19: 24ff) Mt 10: 15; Mk 6: 11 v.l.; Ro 9: 29; 2 Pt 2: 6; Jd 7.*

γόμος, ου, ὁ *cargo* Ac 21: 3; Rv 18: 11f.*

γονεύς, έως, ὁ only pl. in NT οἱ γονεῖς, έων *parents* Mk 13: 12; J 9: 2f; 2 Cor 12: 14.

γόνυ, γόνατος, τό *knee* Lk 5: 8; Eph 3: 14; Hb 12: 12. τιθέναι τὰ γ. *bow the knees* Mk 15: 19; Lk 22: 41; Ac 9: 40.

γονυπετέω *kneel down (before)* Mt 17: 14; 27: 29; Mk 1: 40; 10: 17.*

γράμμα, ατος, τό—1. *letter* of the alphabet 2 Cor 3: 7; Gal 6: 11. γράμματα οἶδεν *he knows how to read and write* J 7: 15. τὰ γ. *(higher) learning* Ac 26: 24.—2. *document, piece of writing* in the form of a *letter, epistle* Ac 28: 21; a *promissory note* Lk 16: 6f. *Book* J 5: 47. ἱερὰ γ. *sacred Scriptures* of the O.T. 2 Ti 3: 15. *Letter* of the literally correct form of the Mosaic law Ro 2: 27, 29; 7: 6; 2 Cor 3: 6.*

γραμματεύς, έως, ὁ—1. *secretary, clerk* a high official in Ephesus Ac 19: 35.—2. *an expert in the law, a scholar versed in the law, scribe* Jewish Mt 2: 4; 23: 2, 13ff; Mk 2: 16; Lk 9: 22; Ac 6: 12; 1 Cor 1: 20. Of their Christian counterparts Mt 13: 52; 23: 34.

γραπτός, ή, όν *written* Ro 2: 15.*

γραφή, ῆς, ἡ *writing* in the N.T. always *Holy Scripture*, the O.T. Mt 21: 42; Mk 14: 49; Lk 24: 27; J 20: 9; Ac 8: 32; 1 Cor 15: 3f; Gal 3: 8, but including Paul's letters 2 Pt 3: 16. Individual *passage of Scripture* Lk 4: 21; Ac 8: 35; Js 2: 8.

γράφω *write* Mt 4: 4, 6f, 10; J 19: 22; Ac 1: 20; Ro 15: 15; 1 Cor 7: 1; 3 J 13. *Write down, record* J 20: 30; Rv 1: 11, 19. *Compose, write* Mk 10: 4; J 21: 25b; 2 Pt 3: 1. *Cover with writing* Rv 5: 1. *Write about* J 1: 45.

γραώδης, ες *characteristic of old women* γ. μῦθοι *tales such as old women tell* 1 Ti 4: 7.*

γρηγορέω *be* or *keep awake* lit. Mt 24: 43; Mk 13: 34; 14: 37; Lk 12: 37. Fig. *be on the alert,*

be watchful Mt 26: 41; Mk 14: 38; Ac 20: 31; 1 Cor 16: 13; Rv 16: 15; *be alive* 1 Th 5: 10.

γυμνάζω *exercise, train* fig. 1 Ti 4: 7; Hb 5: 14; 12: 11; 2 Pt 2: 14.*

γυμνασία, ας, ἡ *training* 1 Ti 4: 8.*

γυμνητεύω v.l. for γυμνιτεύω.

γυμνιτεύω *be poorly dressed* 1 Cor 4: 11.*

γυμνός, ή, όν—1. *naked, stripped, bare* Mk 14: 52; Ac 19: 16; Rv 16: 15. τὸ γ. *the naked body* Mk 14: 51.—2. *without an outer garment* J 21: 7.—3. *poorly dressed* Mt 25: 36; Js 2: 15.—4. *bare, uncovered* 1 Cor 15: 37; 2 Cor 5: 3; Hb 4: 13.

γυμνότης, ητος, ἡ *nakedness* Rv 3: 18. *Destitution, lack of sufficient clothing* Ro 8: 35; 2 Cor 11: 27.*

γυναικάριον, ου, τό *idle, silly woman* lit. 'little woman' 2 Ti 3: 6.*

γυναικεῖος, α, ον *feminine* σκεῦος γ. *wife* 1 Pt 3: 7.*

γυνή, αικός, ἡ *woman*—1. of any adult female Mt 9: 20; Lk 1: 42; Ac 5: 14; 1 Cor 11: 3, 5ff; 14: 34f. The voc. γύναι Mt 15: 28; Lk 22: 57; J 2: 4 is by no means disrespectful, but there is no satisfactory English equivalent for it, and it is best to omit the word in translation.—2. *wife* Mt 5: 28, 31f; Lk 1: 5, 13, 18, 24; 1 Cor 7: 2ff; Col 3: 18f.

Γώγ, ὁ indecl. *Gog* Rv 20: 8 (Ezk 38 and 39).*

γωνία, ας, ἡ *corner* Mt 6: 5; Rv 7: 1. κεφαλὴ γωνίας *corner-stone* or *keystone* Mk 12: 10; Ac 4: 11; 1 Pt 2: 7.

Δ

Δαβίδ see Δαυίδ.

δαιμονίζομαι be possessed by a demon κακῶς δαιμονίζεται is cruelly tormented by a demon Mt 15: 22. The ptc. ὁ δαιμονιζόμενος the demoniac 9: 32; Mk 1: 32; J 10: 21.

δαιμόνιον, ου, τό—1. a deity, divinity Ac 17: 18.—2. demon, evil spirit Mt 11: 18; Mk 1: 34, 39; Lk 9: 49; J 7: 20; 1 Cor 10: 20f; 1 Ti 4: 1; Js 2: 19; Rv 16: 14; 18: 2.

δαιμονιώδης, ες demonic Js 3: 15.*

δαίμων, ονος, ὁ demon, evil spirit Mt 8: 31; Mk 5: 12 v.l.; Rv 18: 2 v.l.

δάκνω bite fig. Gal 5: 15.*

δάκρυον, ου, τό tear Lk 7: 38, 44; Ac 20: 19; 2 Cor 2: 4; 2 Ti 1: 4; Hb 5: 7; Rv 21: 4.

δακρύω weep J 11: 35.*

δακτύλιος, ου, ὁ a ring Lk 15: 22.*

δάκτυλος, ου, ὁ finger Mt 23: 4; Mk 7: 33; Lk 11: 20; 16: 24; J 20: 25.

Δαλμανουθά, ἡ indecl. Dalmanutha a place of uncertain location near the Sea of Galilee Mk 8: 10.*

Δαλματία, ας, ἡ Dalmatia a Roman province across the Adriatic from S. Italy 2 Ti 4: 10.*

δαμάζω subdue lit. Mk 5: 4; tame Js 3: 7. Fig. tame, control 3: 8.*

δάμαλις, εως, ἡ heifer, young cow Hb 9: 13.*

Δάμαρις, ιδος, ἡ Damaris Ac 17: 34.*

Δαμασκηνός, ή, όν from Damascus οἱ Δ. the Damascenes 2 Cor 11: 32.*

Δαμασκός, οῦ, ἡ Damascus capital city of Coelesyria Ac 9: 2f; 22: 5f; 2 Cor 11: 32; Gal 1: 17.

Δάν, ὁ indecl. Dan Rv 7: 5 v.l. (Gen 30: 6).*

δαν(ε)ίζω act. lend (money) Lk 6: 34f. Mid. borrow (money) Mt 5: 42.*

δάν(ε)ιον, ου, τό loan Mt 18: 27.*

δαν(ε)ιστής, οῦ, ὁ money-lender, creditor Lk 7: 41.*

Δανιήλ, ὁ indecl. Daniel Mt 24: 15; Mk 13: 14 v.l. (Dan 1: 6f).*

δαπανάω spend freely Mk 5: 26; Ac 21: 24; 2 Cor 12: 15; spend wastefully Lk 15: 14; Js 4: 3.*

δαπάνη, ης, ἡ cost, expense Lk 14: 28.*

δαρήσομαι 2 fut. pass. of δέρω.

Δαυίδ, ὁ indecl. David Mt 1: 6; 9: 27; Mk 2: 25; Lk 20: 42, 44; Ac 2: 29; Ro 1: 3; Rv 3: 7.

δέ adversative particle, never first in its clause and Mt 1: 2ff; but Mt 6: 1; 1 Cor 2: 15. Simply indicating a transition now, then Mk 5: 11; Lk 3: 21; 1 Cor 16: 12; that is Ro 3: 22; 1 Cor 10: 11; Phil 2: 8. After a neg. rather Lk 10: 20; Ac 12: 9, 14; Eph 4: 15; Hb 4: 13, 15. δὲ καί but also, but even Mt 18: 17; Mk 14: 31; J 2: 2; Ac 22: 28; 1 Cor 15: 15. καὶ . . . δέ and also, but also Mt 16: 18; J 6: 51; Ac 22: 29; 2 Ti 3: 12. For μέν . . . δέ see μέν. δέ may often be omitted in translation.

δέδεκται perf. mid. ind. of δέχομαι.

δεδώκει pluperf. act. ind. of δίδωμι, without augment.

δεηθείς 1 aor. pass. ptc. of δέομαι.

δέησις, εως, ἡ entreaty, supplication, prayer Lk 1: 13; Ro 10: 1; Eph 6: 18; 1 Ti 2: 1; 1 Pt 3: 12.

δεῖ impersonal verb it is necessary, one must or has to Mt 17: 10; Mk 14: 31; Lk 2: 49; Ac 9: 6; 1 Cor 11: 19; one ought or should Mt 18: 33; Lk 18: 1; Ac 5: 29; 2 Ti 2: 6, 24. δέον neut. ptc. what one should δέον ἐστίν=

δεῖ Ac 19: 36; εἰ δέον *if it must be* 1 Pt 1: 6. The impf. ἔδει *had to* Lk 15: 32; J 4: 4; *should have, ought to have* Mt 18: 33; Ac 27: 21; 2 Cor 2: 3.

δεῖγμα, ατος, τό *example* Jd 7.*

δειγματίζω *expose, disgrace* Mt 1: 19; *mock, expose* Col 2: 15.*

δείκνυμι, δεικνύω *show, point out, make known* Mt 8: 4; Lk 22: 12; J 14: 8f; 1 Cor 12: 31; Hb 8: 5; Rv 1: 1. *Explain, prove* Mt 16: 21; Ac 10: 28; Js 2: 18.

δειλία, ας, ἡ *cowardice* 2 Ti 1: 7.*

δειλιάω *be cowardly, timid* J 14: 27.*

δειλινός, ή, όν *in the afternoon* τὸ δειλινόν *toward evening* Ac 3: 1 v.l.*

δειλός, ή, όν *cowardly, timid* Mt 8: 26; Mk 4: 40; Rv 21: 8.*

δεῖνα, ὁ, ἡ, τό *so-and-so* of a person or thing one cannot or does not wish to name *a certain man, somebody* Mt 26: 18.*

δεινός, ή, όν *fearful, terrible* as noun *affliction* ending of Mk in the Freer ms. 8.*

δεινῶς adv. *fearfully, terribly* Mt 8: 6. δ. ἐνέχειν *act in a very hostile manner* Lk 11: 53.*

δειπνέω *eat, dine* Mt 20: 28 v.l.; Lk 17: 8; 22: 20; 1 Cor 11: 25; Rv 3: 20.*

δειπνοκλήτωρ, ορος, ὁ *host* at a banquet Mt 20: 28 v.l.*

δεῖπνον, ου, τό *dinner, supper* the main *meal* of the day, eaten toward evening Lk 14: 12; J 21: 20; 1 Cor 11: 20f; (*formal*) *dinner, banquet* Mt 23: 6; Lk 14: 17, 24; J 12: 2; 13: 2; Rv 19: 9, 17.

δεῖπνος, ου, ὁ as v.l. for δεῖπνον Lk 14: 16; Rv 19: 9, 17.*

δεισιδαιμονία, ας, ἡ *religion* Ac 25: 19.*

δεισιδαίμων, ον, gen. ονος *religious* comparative degree δεισιδαιμονεστέρους ὑμᾶς θεωρῶ *I perceive that you are very religious people* Ac 17: 22.*

δέκα indecl. *ten* Mt 20: 24; Mk 10: 41; Lk 17: 12; Rv 12: 3.

δεκαδύο indecl. *twelve* Ac 19: 7 v.l.; 24: 11 v.l.

δεκαέξ indecl. *sixteen* Rv 13: 18 v.l.*

δεκαοκτώ indecl. *eighteen* Lk 13: 4, 11.

δεκαπέντε indecl. *fifteen* J 11: 18; Ac 27: 5 v.l., 28; Gal 1: 18 (ἡμ. δεκ. means *two weeks*).*

Δεκάπολις, εως, ἡ *Decapolis* a league originally consisting of ten Greek cities, nearly all of which were southeast of the Sea of Galilee Mt 4: 25; Mk 5: 20; 7: 31.*

δεκατέσσαρες indecl. *fourteen* Mt 1: 17; 2 Cor 12: 2; Gal 2: 1.*

δέκατος, η, ον *tenth* J 1: 39; Rv 11: 13; *tithe* Hb 7: 8f.

δεκατόω *collect* or *receive tithes from* w. acc. Hb 7: 6; pass. *pay tithes* 7: 9.*

δεκτός, ή, όν *acceptable* Phil 4: 18; *welcome* Lk 4: 24; Ac 10: 35; *favorable* Lk 4: 19; 2 Cor 6: 2.*

δελεάζω *lure, entice* Js 1: 14; 2 Pt 2: 14, 18.*

δένδρον, ου, τό *tree* Mt 7: 17ff; Mk 8: 24; Lk 13: 19; Rv 7: 1, 3.

δεξιοβόλος a word of uncertain meaning, found only as a v.l. for δεξιολάβος in Ac 23: 23 and nowhere else.*

δεξιολάβος, ου, ὁ an extremely rare word of uncertain meaning; *bowman, slinger, bodyguard* are among the meanings suggested Ac 23: 23.*

δεξιός, ά, όν *right* as opposed to left Mt 5: 30; Ac 3: 7; Rv 10: 2. τὰ δ. *the right side* Mk 16: 5. ἡ δ. *the right hand* Mt 6: 3; Rv 1: 17, 20; δ. διδόναι *give the right hand* as a pledge of mutual trust Gal 2: 9. ἐκ δ. *on the right side* Mt 20: 21, 23. ὅπλα δ. *weapons for offense* (e.g. swords) 2 Cor 6: 7.

δέομαι *ask, pray, beg* Mt 9: 38; Lk 8: 38; Ac 8: 24; 10: 2; 2 Cor

8: 4; 10: 2. δέομαί σου *I beg of you* Gal 4: 12 can sometimes = *please* Lk 8: 28; Ac 21: 39.

δέον see δεῖ.

δέος, ους, τό *fear, awe* Hb 12: 28.*

Δερβαῖος, α, ον *from Derbe* Ac 20: 4.*

Δέρβη, ης, ἡ *Derbe* a city in Lycaonia, in the Roman province of Galatia Ac 14: 6, 20; 16: 1.*

δέρμα, ατος, τό *skin* Hb 11: 37.*

δερμάτινος, η, ον *(made of) leather* Mt 3: 4; Mk 1: 6.*

δέρρις, εως, ἡ *skin* Mk 1: 6 v.l.*

δέρω *beat, strike* Mk 12: 3, 5; Lk 22: 63; J 18: 23; Ac 22: 19; 1 Cor 9: 26; 2 Cor 11: 20. δαρήσεται πολλάς *he will receive many blows* Lk 12: 47, cf. verse 48.

δεσμεύω *bind* Lk 8: 29; Ac 22: 4; *tie up* Mt 23: 4.*

δεσμέω v.l. for δέσμευω, with the same meaning Lk 8: 29.*

δέσμη, ης, ἡ *bundle* Mt 13: 30.*

δέσμιος, ου, ὁ *prisoner* Mk 15: 6; Ac 16: 25, 27; Phlm 1, 9; Eph 4: 1.

δεσμός, οῦ, ὁ *bond, fetter* of a physical defect Mk 7: 35; Lk 13: 16. Lit., pl. Lk 8: 29; Ac 26: 29, 31; Hb 11: 36. *Imprisonment, prison* Phil 1: 7, 13f; 2 Ti 2: 9; Phlm 10, 13.

δεσμοφύλαξ, ακος, ὁ *warden, keeper of the prison* Ac 16: 23, 27, 36.*

δεσμωτήριον, ου, τό *prison, jail* Mt 11: 2; Ac 5: 21, 23; 16: 26.*

δεσμώτης, ου, ὁ *prisoner* Ac 27: 1, 42.*

δεσπότης, ου vocative δέσποτα *lord, master, owner* 1 Ti 6: 1f; 2 Ti 2: 21; 1 Pt 2: 18. Of God Lk 2: 29; Rv 6: 10; of Christ Jd 4.

δεῦρο adv. of place *come, come here* Mk 10: 21; J 11: 43; Ac 7: 3, 34; Rv 17: 1. Of time *until now* ἄχρι τοῦ δ. *thus far* Ro 1: 13.

δεῦτε adv. (serves as pl. of δεῦρο) *come! come on!* Mt 11: 28; 25:

34; 28: 6; Mk 1: 17; 6: 31; J 21: 12.

δευτεραῖος, αία, ον *on the second day* Ac 28: 13.*

δευτερόπρωτος, ον a word of doubtful meaning (lit. 'second-first') and genuineness, found only as v.l. in Lk 6: 1.*

δεύτερος, α, ον *second* Mt 22: 26; Lk 12: 38; 19: 18; J 4: 54; Ac 12: 10; 1 Cor 15: 47; 2 Cor 1: 15; Hb 8: 7; Rv 2: 11. Neut. as adv. *(for) the second time* Mt 26: 42; J 3: 4; 21: 16; 2 Cor 13: 2; Jd 5; *secondly* 1 Cor 12: 28.

δέχομαι *take, receive* Mt 18: 5; Lk 16: 4, 6f; 22: 17; Ac 7: 59; 22: 5; 2 Cor 7: 15; 11: 4; Phil 4: 18. *Welcome* Mk 6: 11; J 4: 45; Col 4: 10. *Accept, approve* Mt 11: 14; Mk 10: 15; Lk 8: 13; 2 Cor 6: 1; 8: 17. *Put up with, tolerate* 2 Cor 11: 16.

δέω *bind, tie* lit. Mt 13: 30; J 19: 40; of arrest and imprisonment Mk 6: 17; Ac 9: 2, 14, 21; 21: 11; Col 4: 3. Fig. Lk 13: 16; Ac 20: 22; Ro 7: 2; 1 Cor 7: 27. *Forbid* Mt 16: 19; 18: 18.

δή emphatic particle; never comes first in its clause *indeed* Mt 13: 23; *now, then, therefore* Lk 2: 15; Ac 6: 3 v.l.; 13: 2; 15: 36; 1 Cor 6: 20.*

δηλαυγῶς *very clearly* Mk 8: 25 v.l.*

δῆλος, η, ον *clear, plain, evident* Mt 26: 73. With ἐστίν understood 1 Cor 15: 27; Gal 3: 11; 1 Ti 6: 7 v.l.*

δηλόω *make clear, reveal, show* 1 Cor 3: 13; Hb 9: 8; 2 Pt 1: 14; *give information* 1 Cor 1: 11; *indicate* Hb 12: 27.

Δημᾶς, ᾶ, ὁ *Demas* Col 4: 14; 2 Ti 4: 10; Phlm 24.*

δημηγορέω *deliver a public address* Ac 12: 21.*

Δημήτριος, ου, ὁ *Demetrius*—1. a Christian 3 J 12.—2. a silversmith at Ephesus Ac 19: 24, 38.*

δημιουργός, οῦ, ὁ craftsman, maker, Creator Hb 11: 10.*

δῆμος, ου, ὁ people, populace, crowd Ac 12: 22; 17: 5; perh. popular assembly 19: 30, 33.*

δημόσιος, ία, ιον public Ac 5: 18. δημοσίᾳ publicly Ac 16: 37; 18: 28; 20: 20.*

δηνάριον, ου, τό (Latin) denarius a Roman silver coin normally worth about 18 cents; it was a working man's average daily wage Mt 20: 2, 9f, 13; Mk 6: 37; Lk 10: 35; J 12: 5; Rv 6: 6.

δήποτε adv. with relative whatever J 5: 4 v.l.*

δήπου adv. of course, surely Hb 2: 16.*

Δία, Διός accusative and genitive of Ζεύς.

διά prep. w. gen. and acc. through—
A. w. gen.—I. of place through Mt 12: 43; Lk 5: 19; 6: 1; J 10: 1f; Ac 9: 25; 20: 3; Ro 15: 28; 1 Cor 3: 15; throughout 2 Cor 8: 18; out of Mt 4: 4.—II. of time—
1. to denote extent through, during, throughout Lk 5: 5; Ac 23: 31; Hb 2: 15. διὰ παντός always, continually, constantly Mk 5: 5; Ac 10: 2; 2 Th 3: 16; Hb 9: 6. During Ac 5: 19.—
2. to denote an interval after Mk 2: 1; Ac 24: 17; Gal 2: 1.—
III. of means, instrument, agency by means of, through, with—1. of means, instrument, manner Ac 1: 16; 15: 27; 20: 28; 1 Cor 16: 3; 1 Pt 1: 7; 2 J 12; in Lk 8: 4.—2. of attendant circumstance with Ro 2: 27; 8: 25; 14: 20; 2 Cor 2: 4; in a state of Ro 4: 11.—3. of cause through, because of, by means of Ro 3: 20; 7: 5; 1 Cor 1: 21; 4: 15; Gal 2: 16; 5: 6—4. of persons through (the agency of), by Mt 2: 15; Ac 11: 28; Ro 1: 5; 1 Cor 1: 9; Gal 1: 1; 3: 19; Hb 2: 2; in the presence of 2 Ti 2: 2; represented by Ro 2: 16.—

B. w. acc.—I. of place through Lk 17: 11.—II. to indicate the reason because of, for the sake of Mt 10: 22; Mk 2: 27; Lk 23: 25; Ac 21: 34. Out of Mt 27: 18; J 7: 13; Phil 1: 15. διὰ τί; why? Mk 2: 18; Lk 5: 30; J 7: 45; 1 Cor 6: 7.

διαβαίνω go through, cross, come over Lk 16: 26; Ac 16: 9; Hb 11: 29.*

διαβάλλω bring charges Lk 16: 1.*

διαβεβαιόομαι speak confidently, insist 1 Ti 1: 7; Tit 3: 8.*

διαβλέπω look intently or open one's eyes (wide) Mk 8: 25; see clearly Mt 7: 5; Lk 6: 42.*

διάβολος, ον slanderous 1 Ti 3: 11; 2 Ti 3: 3; Tit 2: 3. As noun ὁ δ. the slanderer, specifically the devil Mt 4: 1, 5, 8, 11; J 13: 2; Ac 13: 10; Eph 4: 27; 1 Ti 3: 7; 1 Pt 5: 8.

διαγγέλλω proclaim far and wide Lk 9: 60; Ro 9: 17; Mk 5: 19 v.l. Give notice of Ac 21: 26.*

διαγίνομαι pass, elapse Mk 16: 1; Ac 25: 13; 27: 9.*

διαγινώσκω decide, determine Ac 24: 22. ἀκριβέστερον δ. determine by thorough investigation 23: 15.*

διαγνωρίζω give an exact report Lk 2: 17 v.l.*

διάγνωσις, εως, ἡ decision Ac 25: 21.*

διαγογγύζω complain, grumble (aloud) Lk 15: 2; 19: 7.*

διαγρηγορέω awake fully, perh. keep awake Lk 9: 32.*

διάγω live, spend (one's life) 1 Ti 2: 2; Tit 3: 3; Lk 7: 25 v.l.*

διαδέχομαι receive in turn Ac 7: 45.*

διάδημα, ατος, τό diadem, crown Rv 12: 3; 13: 1; 19: 12.*

διαδίδωμι distribute, give Lk 11: 22; 18: 22; J 6: 11; Ac 4: 35; Rv 17: 13 v.l.*

διάδος 2 aor. imper. act of διαδίδωμι.

διάδοχος, ου, ὁ *successor* Ac 24: 27.*

διαζώννυμι *tie around* δ. ἑαυτόν *tie* (a towel) *around oneself* J 13: 4, cf. 5; *put on* 21: 7.*

διαθήκη, ης, ἡ—1. *last will and testament* Gal 3: 15; Hb 9: 16f. Gal 3: 17 shades into sense 2.— 2. *covenant* only in the sense of a *declaration of (God's) will* or *decree* in which God alone sets the conditions, not an agreement between equals. *Covenant* Lk 22: 20; 1 Cor 11: 25; 2 Cor 3: 6, 14; Gal 4: 24; Hb 8: 8; 9: 4, 15; *declaration of will* Lk 1: 72; Ac 3: 25; Ro 11: 27; *ordinance* Ac 7: 8; *decree, assurance* Ro 9: 4; Eph 2: 12.

διαίρεσις, εως, ἡ *apportionment, allotment* or *variety, difference* 1 Cor 12: 4, 5, 6.*

διαιρέω *divide, distribute, apportion* Lk 15: 12; 1 Cor 12: 11.*

διακαθαίρω *clean out* Lk 3: 17.*

διακαθαρίζω *clean out* Mt 3: 12; Lk 3: 17 v.l.*

διακατελέγχομαι *refute* (*completely*) w. dat. Ac 18: 28.*

διακελεύω *order* w. dat. J 8: 5 v.l.*

διακονέω w. dat. of pers.—1. *wait on* someone *at table* Lk 12: 37; 22: 26f; J 12: 2.—2. *serve* generally, lit. and fig. Mt 4: 11; Mk 10: 45; Ac 19: 22; 2 Ti 1: 18; 1 Pt 1: 12; *wait on* Mt 27: 55. *Take care of* Ac 6: 2; 2 Cor 3: 3. *Help, support* Mt 25: 44; Lk 8: 3; Hb 6: 10.—3. *serve as deacon* 1 Ti 3: 10, 13.

διακονία, ας, ἡ—1. *service* Ac 6: 4; 2 Cor 11: 8; Eph 4: 12; Hb 1: 14; Rv 2: 19; specif. domestic Lk 10: 40. *Service, office, ministry* Ac 1: 17; 20: 24; 1 Cor 12: 5; 2 Cor 5: 18. *Aid, support, distribution* Ac 6: 1; 11: 29; δ. τῆς λειτουργίας *kind contribution* 2 Cor 9: 12.—2. *office of a deacon* as an official of the church Ro 12: 7.

διάκονος, ου, ὁ, ἡ—1. *servant* Mt 20: 26; 22: 13; Mk 9: 35; specifically *waiter* J 2: 5, 9. Fig. 2 Cor 6: 4; 11: 23; Col 1: 23, 25. *Helper* Gal 2: 17; Eph 6: 21; 1 Ti 4: 6; *agent* Ro 13: 4.— 2. *deacon* as a church official Phil 1: 1; 1 Ti 3: 8, 12; *deaconess* Ro 16: 1.

διακόσιοι, αι, α *two hundred* Mk 6: 37; J 6: 7; 21: 8.

διακούω w. gen. *give* someone *a hearing* Ac 23: 35.*

διακρίνω—1. act.—a. *make a distinction, differentiate* Ac 11:12; 15: 9; *single* out 1 Cor 4: 7.— b. *pass judgment* 14: 29; *judge correctly* Mt 16: 3; *recognize* 1 Cor 11: 29; *render a decision* 6: 5. —2. mid. and aor. pass.—a. *take issue, dispute* Ac 11: 2; Jd 9.—b. *doubt, waver* Mt 21: 21; Ro 4: 20; Js 1: 6; Jd 22; *hesitate* Ac 10: 20.

διάκρισις, εως, ἡ—1. *distinguishing, differentiation* 1 Cor 12: 10; Hb 5: 14.—2. *quarrel* Ro 14: 1; Ac 4: 32 v.l.*

διακωλύω *prevent* imperfect *he tried to prevent* Mt 3: 14.*

διαλαλέω *discuss* Lk 1: 65; 6: 11.*

διαλέγομαι—1. *discuss, conduct a discussion* Mk 9: 34; Ac 19: 8f; 20: 7; 24: 12.—2. *speak, preach* 18: 4; Hb 12: 5.

διαλείπω *stop, cease* Lk 7: 45.*

διάλεκτος, ου, ἡ *language* Ac 2: 6, 8; 21: 40; 26: 14.

διαλιμπάνω by-form of διαλείπω *stop, cease* Ac 8: 24 v.l. and 17: 13 v.l.*

διαλλάγηθι 2 aor. pass. imperative of διαλλάσσομαι.

διαλλάσσομαι *become reconciled* Mt 5: 24.*

διαλογίζομαι *consider, ponder, reason, discuss, argue* Mt 16: 7f; Mk 2: 6, 8; 8: 16f; 11: 31; Lk 1: 29; 20: 14.

διαλογισμός, οῦ, ὁ—1. *thought, opinion, reasoning, design* Mk

50   διαλύω–διαστρέφω

7: 21; Lk 2: 35; 6: 8; Ro 1: 21;
14: 1. κριταὶ δ. πονηρῶν perh.
*judges who hand down corrupt
decisions* Js 2: 4.—**2.** *doubt, dispute, argument* Lk 9: 46; 24:
38; Phil 2: 14.
διαλύω *break up, disperse* Ac 5:
36; 27: 41 v.l.*
διαμαρτύρομαι—1. *charge, warn,
adjure* w. dat. of the person Lk
16: 28; 1 Ti 5: 21; 2 Ti 2: 14; 4:
1.—**2.** *testify (of), bear witness
(to)* solemnly Ac 8: 25; 20: 21,
24; 28: 23; 1 Th 4: 6; Hb 2: 6.
διαμάχομαι *contend sharply* Ac 23:
9.*
διαμένω *remain (continually)* Lk
1: 22; Gal 2: 5; 2 Pt 3: 4;
continue Hb 1: 11. δ. μετά *stand
by* Lk 22: 28.
διαμερίζω *divide, distribute* Mk
15: 24; Lk 11: 17f; 22: 17; Ac
2: 3, 45.
διαμερισμός, οῦ, ὁ *dissension, dis-
unity* Lk 12: 51.*
διανέμω *spread (a report)* lit.
'distribute' Ac 4: 17.*
διανεύω *nod, beckon* Lk 1: 22.*
διανόημα ατος, τό *thought* Lk 11:
17; 3: 16 v.l.*
διάνοια, ας, ἡ *mind, understanding,
intelligence* Mk 12: 30; Eph 4:
18; Hb 8: 10; *insight* 1 J 5: 20;
disposition, thought Lk 1: 51;
2 Pt 3: 1; *attitude* Col 1: 21;
sense, impulse Eph 2: 3.
διανοίγω *open* Mk 7: 34; Lk 2: 23;
24: 31, 45; Ac 7: 56; 16: 14.
Explain, interpret Lk 24: 32;
Ac 17: 3.*
διανυκτερεύω *spend the whole
night* Lk 6: 12.*
διανύω *complete,* perh. *continue*
Ac 21: 7.*
διαπαντός = διὰ παντός; see διά.
διαπαρατριβή, ῆς, ἡ *mutual* or
constant irritation 1 Ti 6: 5.*
διαπεράω *cross (over)* Mt 9: 1; 14:
34; Mk 5: 21; 6: 53; Lk 16: 26;
Ac 21: 2.*
διαπλέω *sail through* Ac 27: 5.*

διαπονέομαι *be (greatly) disturbed,
annoyed* Ac 4: 2; 16: 18; Mk
14: 4 v.l.*
διαπορεύομαι *go, walk* or *pass
through* Mk 2: 23 v.l.; Lk 6: 1;
13: 22; Ac 16: 4; Ro 15: 24;
go by Lk 18: 36.*
διαπορέω *be greatly perplexed, be at
a loss* Lk 9: 7; Ac 2: 12; 5: 24;
10: 17; Lk 24: 4 v.l.*
διαπραγματεύομαι *gain by trading,
earn* Lk 19: 15.*
διαπρίω lit. 'saw through'; fig.
cut to the quick, infuriate Ac 5:
33; 7: 54.*
διαρθρόω *render capable of arti-
culate speech* Lk 1: 64 v.l.*
διαρπάζω *plunder thoroughly* Mt
12: 29; Mk 3: 27.*
δια(ρ)ρήγνυμι and **διαρήσσω** *tear*
Mt 26: 65; Mk 14: 63; Lk 5: 6;
Ac 14: 14; *break* Lk 8: 29.*
διασαφέω *explain* Mt 13: 36; *tell in
detail, report* 18: 31; Ac 10: 25
v.l.*
διασείω *extort money by violence
(from)* lit. 'shake violently' Lk
3: 14.*
διασκορπίζω *scatter, disperse* Mk
14: 27; J 11: 52; Ac 5: 37;
waste, squander Lk 15: 13.
διασπαρείς 2 aor. pass. ptc. of
διασπείρω.
διασπάω *tear apart* Mk 5: 4; Ac
23: 10.*
διασπείρω *scatter* Ac 8: 1, 4; 11:
19.*
διασπορά, ᾶς, ἡ *dispersion, dia-
spora* of Jews J 7: 35; of
Christians Js 1: 1; 1 Pt 1: 1.*
διαστέλλω mid. *order, give orders*
Mk 5: 43; 7: 36; Ac 15: 24; pass.
τὸ διαστελλόμενον *the command*
Hb 12: 20.
διάστημα, ατος, τό *interval* Ac 5:
7.*
διαστολή, ῆς, ἡ *difference, distinction* Ro 3: 22; 10: 12; 1 Cor
14: 7.*
διαστρέφω *make crooked* fig. Ac
13: 10. διεστραμμένος *perverted,*

depraved Mt 17: 17; Lk 9: 41; Ac 20: 30; Phil 2: 15. *Mislead* Lk 23: 2; *turn away* Ac 13: 8.*

διασῴζω *bring safely (through)* Ac 23: 24; 27: 44; 1 Pt 3: 20; *rescue, save* Ac 27: 43; 28: 1, 4; *cure* Mt 14: 36; Lk 7: 3.*

διαταγείς 2 aor. pass. ptc. of διατάσσω.

διαταγή, ῆς, ἡ *ordinance, direction* Ro 13: 2. εἰς διαταγὰς ἀγγέλων *by directions of angels,* i.e. *by God's directing angels* Ac 7: 53.*

διάταγμα, ατος, τό *edict, command* Hb 11: 23.*

διαταράσσω *confuse, perplex (greatly)* Lk 1: 29.*

διατάσσω *order, direct, command* in act. and mid. Mt 11: 1; Lk 3: 13; Ac 18: 2; 24: 23; 1 Cor 7: 17; 9: 14; 11: 34; *arrange* Ac 20: 13. διαταγεὶς δι' ἀγγέλων *ordered through angels* Gal 3: 19.

διαταχθείς 1 aor. pass. ptc. of διατάσσω.

διατελέω *continue, remain* Ac 27: 33.*

διατεταχέναι perf. act. inf. of διατάσσω.

διατηρέω *keep, preserve* Ac 15: 29; *treasure* Lk 2: 51.*

διατί = διὰ τί; see διά.

διατίθημι only mid. **διατίθεμαι** *decree, ordain* Ac 3: 25; Hb 10: 16; διαθήκην δ. *issue a decree* 8: 10. *Assign, confer* Lk 22: 29. *Make a will* ὁ διαθέμενος *the testator* Hb 9: 16f.*

διατρίβω *spend* (lit. 'rub away') time, etc. Ac 14: 3, 28; 16: 12; 20: 6. *Stay, remain* J 3: 22; Ac 12: 19; 15: 35.

διατροφή, ῆς, ἡ pl. *food, sustenance* 1 Ti 6: 8.*

διαυγάζω *shine through* 2 Cor 4: 4 v.l. *Dawn, break* 2 Pt 1: 19.*

διαυγής, ές *transparent* Rv 21: 21.*

διαφανής, ές *transparent* Rv 21: 21 v.l.*

διαφέρω—1. trans. *carry through* Mk 11: 16; *spread* Ac 13: 49; *drive* or *carry about* 27: 27.— 2. intrans. *differ, be different from* w. gen. 1 Cor 15: 41; Gal 4: 1. *Be worth more than, be superior to* w. gen. Mt 6: 26; 10: 31; 12: 12; Lk 12: 7, 24. τὰ διαφέροντα *the things that really matter* Ro 2: 18; Phil 1: 10. Impers. *it makes a difference* Gal 2: 6.*

διαφεύγω *escape* Ac 27: 42.*

διαφημίζω *make known by word of mouth, spread the news about someone* Mt 9: 31. *Spread widely, disseminate* Mk 1: 45; Mt 28: 15.*

διαφθείρω *spoil, destroy* Lk 12: 33; 2 Cor 4: 16; Rv 8: 9; 11: 18a. *Ruin morally* 1 Ti 6: 5; Rv 11: 18b; 19: 2 v.l.*

διαφθορά, ᾶς, ἡ *destruction, corruption* Ac 2: 27, 31; 13: 34ff.*

διάφορος, ον *different* Ro 12: 6; Hb 9: 10; *outstanding, excellent* 1: 4; 8: 6.*

διαφυλάσσω *guard, protect* Lk 4: 10.*

διαχειρίζω mid. *lay violent hands on, kill, murder* Ac 5: 30; 26: 21.*

διαχλευάζω *mock, deride* Ac 2: 13.*

διαχωρίζω *separate* pass. *be separated, part, go away* Lk 9: 33.*

διγαμία, ας, ἡ *second marriage* Tit 1: 9 v.l.*

δίγαμος, ον *married for the second time* Tit 1: 9 v.l.*

διδακτικός, ή, όν *skilful in teaching* 1 Ti 3: 2; 2 Ti 2: 24.*

διδακτός, ή, όν *taught, instructed* δ. θεοῦ *taught by God* J 6: 45; *taught, imparted* 1 Cor 2: 13.*

διδασκαλία, ας, ἡ the *act of teaching, instruction* Ro 12: 7; 15: 4; 2 Ti 3: 16. *Teaching* = that which is taught Mk 7: 7; Col 2: 22; 1 Ti 1: 10; 4: 6; 2 Ti 3: 10; Tit 1: 9.

διδάσκαλος, ου, ὁ *teacher* Ro 2: 20; Hb 5: 12. As a term of honor and respect Mt 8: 19; Mk 10; 17; Lk 9: 38; J 3: 10. Of teachers in the Christian church Ac 13: 1; 1 Cor 12: 28f; Js 3: 1.

διδάσκω teach Mk 1: 21; Ac 15: 35; 1 Cor 11: 14; Col 3: 16; Rv 2: 14. ὑμᾶς διδάξει πάντα he will instruct you in everything J 14: 26.

διδαχή, ῆς, ἡ teaching as an activity, instruction Mk 4: 2; 1 Cor 14: 6; 2 Ti 4: 2. Teaching = what is taught Mt 16: 12; Mk 1: 27; J 7: 16f; Ro 16: 17; Rv 2: 14f, 24. Either meaning is possible in Mt 7: 28; Mk 11: 18; Lk 4: 32.

διδόασιν third pl. pres. ind. act. of δίδωμι.

δίδραχμον, ου, τό a double drachma, two-drachma piece a Greek silver coin about equal to a half shekel or normally 36 cents in our money Mt 17: 24.*

Δίδυμος, ου, ὁ Didymus; the name means 'twin'. J 11: 16; 20: 24; 21: 2.*

δίδωμι give Mt 4: 9; 7: 6, 11; Lk 17: 18; J 9: 24; Ac 20: 35; Rv 4: 9. The context often permits variations in translation, e.g. bring Lk 2: 24; grant Mt 13: 11; cause Ac 2: 19; 1 Cor 9: 12; put Lk 15: 22; 2 Cor 6: 3; Rv 17: 17; inflict 2 Th 1: 8; permit Ac 2: 27; Mk 10: 37; yield Js 5: 18; produce 1 Cor 14: 7f; entrust Mt 25: 15; J 6: 37, 39; pay Mk 12: 14; appoint Ac 13: 20; Eph 1: 22; give up, sacrifice Mk 10: 45; Lk 22: 19. λόγον δ. render account Ro 14: 12. δὸς ἐργασίαν take pains, make an effort Lk 12: 58.

διέβην 2 aor. act. ind. of διαβαίνω.

διεγείρω wake up, arouse lit. Mk 4: 39; Lk 8: 24; fig. J 6: 18; 2 Pt 1: 13.

διεῖλον 2 aor. act. ind. of διαιρέω.

διενέγκω aor. act. subj. of διαφέρω.

διενθυμέομαι ponder, reflect Ac 10: 19.*

διεξέρχομαι come out Ac 28: 3 v.l.*

διέξοδος, ου, ἡ lit. 'a way out through'; δ. τῶν ὁδῶν the place where a highway leaves the city, perhaps street-crossing Mt 22: 9.*

διερμηνεία, ας, ἡ explanation, interpretation, translation 1 Cor 12: 10 v.l.*

διερμηνευτής, οῦ, ὁ interpreter, translator 1 Cor 14: 28.*

διερμηνεύω translate Ac 9: 36. Explain, interpret Lk 24: 27; Ac 18: 6 v.l. Explain, interpret or translate 1 Cor 12: 30; 14: 5, 13, 27.*

διέρχομαι—1. go through Mt 12: 43; Mk 10: 25; Ac 13: 6; 1 Cor 10: 1; Hb 4: 14; pierce Lk 2: 35. Go about Ac 20: 25; go from place to place 8: 4; spread Lk 5: 15. Pass Ac 12: 10.—**2.** simply come, go Lk 2: 15; J 4: 15; Ac 9: 38; Ro 5: 12.

διερωτάω find by inquiry Ac 10: 17.*

διεστείλατο 1 aor. mid. ind. of διαστέλλω.

διέστη 2 aor. act. ind. of διΐστημι.

διεστραμμένος perf. pass. ptc. of διαστρέφω.

διετής, ές two years old Mt 2: 16.*

διετία, ας, ἡ a period of two years Ac 24: 27; 28: 30.*

διεφθάρη 2 aor. pass. ind. of διαφθείρω.

διηγέομαι tell, relate, describe Mk 9: 9; Lk 9: 10; Ac 8: 33; 12: 17; Hb 11: 32.

διήγησις, εως, ἡ narrative, account Lk 1: 1.*

διηγοῦ pres. imperative mid. of διηγέομαι.

διηνεκής, ές continuous εἰς τὸ δ. forever Hb 7: 3; 10: 14; for all time 10: 12; continually 10: 1.*

διθάλασσος, ον surrounded on both sides by the sea; the τόπος δ. Ac 27: 41 may be a sandbank or reef or headland.*

διϊκνέομαι pierce, penetrate Hb 4: 12.*

διΐστημι—1. intr. (2 aor.) *go away*, part Lk 24: 51; *pass* 22: 59.— 2. trans. (1 aor.) *drive on* with τὴν ναῦν supplied βραχὺ διαστήσαντες *after they had sailed a short distance farther* Ac 27: 28.*

διϊστορέω *examine carefully* Ac 17: 23 v.l.*

διϊσχυρίζομαι *insist, maintain firmly* Lk 22: 59; Ac 12: 15; 15: 2 v.l.*

δικάζω *judge, condemn* Lk 6: 37 v.l.*

δικαιοκρισία, ας, ἡ *righteous judgment* Ro 2: 5; 2 Th 1: 5 v.l.*

δίκαιος, αία, ον of men *upright, just, righteous* Mt 10: 41; 13: 43; Mk 6: 20; Ro 1: 17; 5: 7; Hb 12: 23; 1 J 3: 7; *law-abiding* 1 Ti 1: 9; *honest, good, just* Mt 1: 19. Of God and Christ *just, righteous* J 17: 25; Ac 7: 52; 2 Ti 4: 8; of Jesus *innocent* Lk 23: 47, cf. Mt 23: 35 and 27: 24 v.l. τὸ δίκαιον (*what is*) *right* Mt 20: 4; Lk 12: 57; Ac 4: 19; Col 4: 1; 2 Pt 1: 13.

δικαιοσύνη, ης, ἡ *righteousness, uprightness* Mt 5: 6; Ac 24: 25; Ro 9: 30; Phil 3: 6; Tit 3: 5; *religious requirement* Mt 3: 15. *Mercy, charitableness* Mt 6: 1; 2 Cor 9: 9f. *Justice* Ac 17: 31; Hb 11: 33. In Paul δ. θεοῦ, etc. is the *righteousness bestowed by God* Ro 1: 17; 3: 21f, 26; 5: 17 and the meaning approximates *salvation*. δ. approaches the sense *Christianity* Mt 5: 10; Hb 5: 13; 1 Pt 2: 24; 3: 14. ποιεῖν δ. *do what is right* 1 J 2: 29; Rv 22: 11.

δικαιόω—1. *justify, vindicate, treat as just* Mt 11: 19; Lk 10: 29; 16: 15. δ. τὸν θεόν *acknowledge God's justice* 7: 29. God *is proved to be right* Ro 3: 4; also Christ 1 Ti 3: 16.—2. pass., with reference to men *be acquitted, be pronounced and treated as righteous*, in theological language *be justified* = receive the divine gift of δικαιοσύνη Mt 12: 37; Ac 13: 39; Ro 2: 13; 5: 1, 9; Gal 2: 16f; Tit 3: 7; Js 2: 21, 24f. Act., of God's activity Ro 3: 26, 30; Gal 3: 8; for these and other passages *make upright* is possible. *Make free* or *pure* act. and pass. Ac 13: 38f; Ro 6: 7; 1 Cor 6: 11.

δικαίωμα, ατος, τό—1. *regulation, requirement, commandment* Lk 1: 6; Ro 1: 32; 2: 26; 8: 4; Hb 9: 1, 10.—2. *righteous deed* Ro 5: 18; Rv 15: 4; 19: 8. In Ro 5: 16 δ. = δικαίωσις *acquittal*.*

δικαίως adv. *justly, uprightly, rightly* Lk 23: 41; 1 Th 2: 10; Tit 2: 12; 1 Pt 2: 23; *as one ought* 1 Cor 15: 34.*

δικαίωσις, εως, ἡ *justification, vindication, acquittal* Ro 4: 25. δ. ζωῆς *acquittal that brings life* 5: 18.*

δικαστής, οῦ, ὁ *judge* Ac 7: 27, 35; Lk 12: 14 v.l.*

δίκη, ης, ἡ *penalty, punishment* 2 Th 1: 9; Jd 7; Ac 25: 15 v.l. *Justice* personified as a goddess Ac 28: 4.*

δίκτυον, ου, τό *net* Mk 1: 18f; J 21: 6, 8, 11.

δίλογος, ον *double-tongued, insincere* 1 Ti 3: 8.*

διό inferential conjunction (= δι' ὅ) *therefore, for this reason* Mt 27: 8; Lk 7: 7; Ac 27: 25, 34; Ro 15: 22; 2 Cor 5: 9.

διοδεύω *go* or *travel through* Ac 17: 1. *Go about* Lk 8: 1.*

Διονύσιος, ου, ὁ *Dionysius* Ac 17: 34.*

διόπερ inferential conjunction (= δι' ὅπερ) *therefore, for this very reason* 1 Cor 8: 13; 10: 14; 14: 13 v.l.*

διοπετής, ές *fallen from heaven* τὸ δ. *the image* (of Artemis) *fallen from heaven* Ac 19: 35.*

διόρθωμα, ατος, τό *reform* Ac 24: 2.*

διόρθωσις, εως, ἡ *improvement, reformation, new order* Hb 9: 10.*

διορύσσω *dig through, break in* Mt 6: 19f; 24: 43; Lk 12: 39.*

Διός gen. of Ζεύς.

Διόσκουροι, ων, οἱ *the Dioscuri* Castor and Pollux, twin sons of Zeus and Leda, patron deities of sailors, used as figureheads for ships Ac 28: 11.*

διότι (= δι' ὅτι) conjunction *because* Lk 2: 7; 1 Cor 15: 9; Hb 11: 5. *Therefore* Ac 13: 35; 20: 26. *For* Lk 1: 13; Ro 1: 19, 21; 1 Pt 1: 16, 24. *That* = ὅτι perh. Ro 8: 21.

Διοτρέφης, ους, ὁ *Diotrephes* 3 J 9.*

διπλοῦς, ῆ, οῦν *double, two-fold* 1 Ti 5: 17; Rv 18: 6. Comp. διπλότερος, neut. as adv. *twice as much* Mt 23: 15.*

διπλόω *to double* δ. τὰ διπλᾶ *pay back double* Rv 18: 6.*

δίς adv. *twice* Mk 14: 30, 72; Lk 18: 12; Jd 12. ἅπαξ καὶ δ. *once and again* = *several times* Phil 4: 16; 1 Th 2: 18.

δισμυριάς, άδος, ἡ *a double myriad* = 20,000 Rv 9: 16.*

διστάζω *doubt* Mt 14: 31; 28: 17.*

δίστομος, ον *double-edged* Hb 4: 12; Rv 1: 16; 2: 12; 19: 15 v.l.*

δισχίλιοι, αι, α *two thousand* Mk 5: 13.*

διϋλίζω *filter out, strain out* Mt 23: 24.*

διχάζω *cause a separation* δ. ἄνθρωπον κατὰ τ. πατρός *turn a man against his father* Mt 10: 35.*

διχοστασία, ας, ἡ *dissension* Ro 16: 17; Gal 5: 20; 1 Cor 3: 3 v.l.*

διχοτομέω *cut in two*, though in the context of Mt 24: 51 and Lk 12: 46 *punish with utmost severity* is a likely meaning.*

διψάω *thirst*—1. lit. *be thirsty, suffer from thirst* Mt 25: 35, 37;

J 4: 13, 15; 1 Cor 4: 11.—2. fig. *thirst* for the water of life J 4: 14; 7: 37; *thirst* or *long for* something Mt 5: 6.

δίψος, ους, τό *thirst* 2 Cor 11: 27.*

δίψυχος, ον *irresolute, doubting, hesitating* lit. *double-minded* Js 1: 8; 4: 8.*

διωγμός, οῦ, ὁ *persecution* (for religious reasons only) Mk 4: 17; Ac 8: 1; 13: 50; Ro 8: 35; 2 Ti 3: 11.

διώκτης, ου, ὁ *persecutor* 1 Ti 1: 13.*

διώκω—1. *persecute* Mt 5: 11f, 44; Lk 21: 12; J 5: 16; 1 Cor 4: 12; Gal 5: 11; 2 Ti 3: 12.— 2. *run after, pursue* lit. Lk 17: 23. Fig. *pursue, strive for, seek after* Ro 9: 30f; 14: 19; 1 Cor 14: 1; 2 Ti 2: 22. *Hasten, run, press on* Phil 3: 12, 14.—3. *drive away, drive out* Mt 23: 34.

δόγμα, ατος, τό *decree, commandment* Lk 2: 1; Ac 16: 4; 17: 7; *ordinance* Eph 2: 15; *requirement* Col 2: 14.*

δογματίζω *decree* pass. *submit to rules and regulations* Col 2: 20.*

δοκέω—1. trans. *think, believe, suppose, consider* Mt 3: 9; Lk 24: 37; 1 Cor 3: 18; Hb 10: 29; Js 4: 5; *be disposed* 1 Cor 11: 16. —2. intrans. *seem* Lk 10: 36; Ac 17: 18; 1 Cor 12: 22; Hb 12: 11. ἔδοξα ἐμαυτῷ *I was convinced* Ac 26: 9. *Be influential, have a reputation, be recognized* Mk 10: 42; Gal 2: 2, 6, 9.— 3. impers., w. dat. *it seems* (to me, etc.), hence *I think* or *believe* (etc.) Mt 17: 25; J 11: 56. κατὰ τὸ δοκοῦν αὐτοῖς *at their discretion* Hb 12: 10. Also *it seems best to me, I decide* Lk 1: 3; Ac 15: 22, 25, 28.

δοκιμάζω—1. *put to the test, examine* Lk 14: 19; 1 Cor 11: 28; Gal 6: 4; I Th 5: 21; 1 Ti 3: 10; *try to learn* Eph 5: 10; *discover* Ro 12: 2.—2. *prove* by testing

1 Pt 1: 7. *Accept as proved,
approve* 1 Cor 16: 3; 2 Cor 8: 8,
22; *see fit* Ro 1: 28. For Ro 2:
18 and Phil 1: 10 *discover* and
approve are both possible.

δοκιμασία, ας, ἡ *testing, examination* πειράζειν ἐν δ. *put to the
test* Hb 3: 9.*

δοκιμή, ῆς, ἡ lit. 'the quality of
being approved,' hence *character*
Ro 5: 4; 2 Cor 2: 9; 9: 13; Phil
2: 22; *test, ordeal* 2 Cor 8: 2;
proof 13: 3.*

δοκίμιον, ου, τό *testing* Js 1: 3;
genuineness, sterling quality 1 Pt
1: 7.*

δόκιμος, ον *approved, genuine* 2
Cor 10: 18; 13: 7; 2 Ti 2: 15;
Js 1: 12; *tried and true* Ro 16:
10; 1 Cor 11: 19; *respected,
esteemed* Ro 14: 18.*

δοκός, οῦ, ἡ *beam of wood* Mt 7:
3ff; Lk 6: 41f.*

δόλιος, ία, ον *deceitful, treacherous,
dishonest* 2 Cor 11: 13.*

δολιόω *deceive* Ro 3: 13.*

δόλος, ου, ὁ *deceit, cunning,
treachery* Mk 7: 22; 14: 1; J 1:
47; 2 Cor 12: 16.

δολόω *falsify, adulterate* 2 Cor 4: 2;
1 Cor 5: 6 v.l.*

δόμα, ατος, τό *gift* Mt 7: 11; Lk
11: 13; Eph 4: 8; Phil 4:
17.*

δόξα, ης, ἡ—**1.** *brightness, radiance,
splendor* Lk 9: 31f; Ac 22: 11;
1 Cor 15: 40f. *Glory, majesty*
as an attribute of God and
heavenly beings Ac 7: 2; Ro
1: 23; 1 Cor 2: 8; Phil 3: 21; Col
1: 11, 27; Hb 1: 3; Js 2: 1; Rv
15: 8; with added idea of *power*
Ro 6: 4. *Reflection* 1 Cor 11: 7.
Magnificence, splendor of kings,
etc. Mt 4: 8; 6: 29; Rv 21: 24,
26.—**2.** *fame, renown, honor* J
5: 41, 44; 8: 54; 12: 43; Ro 3: 23;
1 Th 2: 6, 20. *Praise* Lk 2: 14;
Ac 12:23; Ro 11: 36; 1 Cor 10: 31;
Phil 2: 11; Rv 19: 7.—**3.** *glorious
angelic beings* Jd 8; 2 Pt 2: 10;

majesties, illustrious persons is
also possible in these passages.

δοξάζω—**1.** *praise, honor, magnify*
Mt 5: 16; 6: 2; Lk 5: 25f; Ac
11: 18; Ro 11: 13; 1 Cor 12: 26;
1 Pt 4: 16.—**2.** *clothe in splendor,
glorify* J 8: 54; 13: 31f; 17: 1, 4;
21: 19; 2 Cor 3: 10; 1 Pt 1: 8;
of life after death J 12: 16,
23; Ac 3: 13; Ro 8: 30.

Δορκάς, άδος, ἡ *Dorcas* meaning
gazelle Ac 9: 36, 39.*

δόσις, εως, ἡ *gift* Js 1: 17. The act
of *giving* Mt 6: 1 v.l. δ. καὶ
λήμψις *giving and receiving,
debit and credit* Phil 4: 15.*

δότης, ου, ὁ *giver* 2 Cor 9: 7.*

δουλαγωγέω *enslave, bring into
subjection* fig. 1 Cor 9: 27.*

δουλεία, ας, ἡ *slavery* fig. Ro 8: 15,
21; Gal 4: 24; 5: 1; Hb 2:
15.*

δουλεύω *be a slave, be subjected* lit.
J 8: 33; Ac 7: 7; Gal 4: 25; fig.
Ro 7: 6. W. dat. *serve someone
as a slave, serve* Mt 6: 24; Lk
15: 29; 16: 13; Ro 14: 18; Gal
5: 13; Eph 6: 7; *be a slave* fig.
Ro 6: 6; 7: 25.

δούλη, ης, ἡ *female slave, bondmaid*
Lk 1: 38, 48; Ac 2: 18.*

δοῦλος, η, ον *slavish, servile* Ro 6:
19.*

δοῦλος, ου, ὁ *slave* lit. Lk 7: 2f;
J 8: 35; 1 Cor 7: 21ff; Gal 4: 1,
7; Phil 2: 7; Col 3: 11, 22. Fig.
Mt 20: 27; Ro 6: 16f, 20; 2 Cor
4: 5. To God or Christ Lk 2: 29;
Ac 4: 29; Ro 1: 1; Gal 1: 10;
Js 1: 1; Rv 2: 20. Of a king's
officials *subject* Mt 18: 23, 26ff.

δουλόω *make* someone *a slave,
enslave, subject* lit. Ac 7: 6; 2 Pt
2: 19. Fig. Ro 6: 18, 22; 1 Cor
7: 15; 9: 19; Gal 4: 3; Tit 2: 3.*

δοῦναι, δούς 2 aor. act. inf. and
ptc. of δίδωμι.

δοχή, ῆς, ἡ *reception, banquet* Lk
5: 29; 14: 13.*

δράκων, οντος, ὁ *dragon, serpent*
Rv 12: 3f, 7, 9; 20: 2.

δραμεῖν, -ών 2 aor. act. inf. and
    ptc. of τρέχω.
δράσσομαι *catch, seize* 1 Cor 3: 19.*
δραχμή, ῆς, ἡ *drachma* a Greek
    silver coin worth normally about
    18 cents, but with much greater
    purchasing power than at pre-
    sent Lk 15: 8f.*
δρέπανον, ου, τό *sickle* Mk 4: 29;
    Rv 14: 14ff.*
δρόμος, ου, ὁ *course, race* fig. 2 Ti
    4: 7; *course, career* Ac 13: 25; 20:
    24.*
Δρούσιλλα, ης, ἡ *Drusilla*,
    daughter of Herod Agrippa I,
    wife of Felix the procurator Ac
    24: 24, 27 v.l.*
δύναμαι *I can, am able* Mt 6: 24;
    Mk 3: 23; Lk 9: 40; Ac 4: 20;
    26: 32. δ. approaches the mean-
    ing *like* in J 6: 60. *Be able to do
    something* Mk 9: 22; Lk 12: 26;
    2 Cor 13: 8.
δύναμις, εως, ἡ *power, might,
    strength, force* Mt 14: 2; 22: 29;
    Ac 1: 8; Ro 1: 4; Col 1: 11; 2 Ti
    3: 5; Hb 7: 16; 2 Pt 1: 3.
    δ.=*God* Mk 14: 62. *Ability,
    capability* Mt 25: 15; 2 Cor 1: 8;
    meaning 1 Cor 14: 11. Specialized
    senses *deed of power, miracle*
    Mt 11: 20f; Mk 6: 5; 2 Cor 12:
    12; Hb 2: 4. *Force* in a military
    sense Mk 13: 25; Lk 21: 26.
    Power as a supernatural being or
    angel Ac 8: 10; Ro 8: 38; 1 Cor
    15: 24.
δυναμόω *strengthen* Col 1: 11;
    Hb 11: 34; Eph 6: 10 v.l.*
δυνάστης, ου, ὁ *ruler, sovereign*
    Lk 1: 52; 1 Ti 6: 15. *Court
    official* Ac 8: 27.*
δυνατέω *be strong* 2 Cor 13: 3; *be
    strong enough, be able* Ro 14: 4;
    2 Cor 9: 8.*
δυνατός, ή, όν *powerful, strong,
    mighty, able* Lk 1: 49; Ac 25: 5;
    Ro 4: 21; 2 Cor 10: 4; 13: 9;
    Js 3: 2. Neuter δυνατόν *possible*
    Mt 19: 26; 26: 39; Gal 4: 15.
    τὸ δ.=ἡ δύναμις Ro 9: 22.

δύνω *go down, set* of the sun Mk
    1: 32; Lk 4: 40.*
δύο gen. and acc. δύο, dat. δυσί
    two; εἰς δύο *in two* Mk 15: 38.
    ἀνὰ δ. *two apiece* Lk 9: 3; J
    2: 6; *two by two* Lk 10: 1. κατὰ δ.
    two at a time 1 Cor 14: 27. δύο
    δύο *two by two* Mk 6: 7.
δυσβάστακτος, ον *hard to bear* Lk
    11: 46; Mt 23: 4 v.l.*
δυσεντέριον, ου, τό *dysentery* Ac
    28: 8.*
δυσερμήνευτος, ον *hard to explain*
    Hb 5: 11.*
δυσί see δύο.
δύσις, εως, ἡ *west* lit. 'setting'
    short ending of Mark.*
δύσκολος, ον *hard, difficult* Mk 10:
    24.*
δυσκόλως adv. *hardly, with dif-
    ficulty* Mt 19: 23; Mk 10: 23;
    Lk 18: 24.*
δυσμή, ῆς, ἡ *west* lit. 'setting' Mt
    8: 11; Lk 13: 29. ἀπὸ δ. *in the
    west* Rv 21: 13. ἐπὶ δυσμῶν *in the
    west* Lk 12: 54. ἕως δ. *to the
    west* Mt 24: 27.*
δυσνόητος, ον *hard to understand*
    2 Pt 3: 16.*
δυσφημέω *slander, defame* 1 Cor
    4: 13.*
δυσφημία, ας, ἡ *slander, ill repute*
    2 Cor 6: 8.*
δύω 2 aor. subj. act. of δύνω.
δῶ, δώσῃ 3 sing. 2 aor. subj.
    act., 3 sing. 1 aor. subj. act. of
    δίδωμι.
δώδεκα indecl. *twelve* Mt 10: 1f, 5;
    Mk 5: 25, 42; Lk 2: 42; 1 Cor
    15: 5.
δωδέκατος, η, ον *twelfth* Rv 21:
    20.*
δωδεκάφυλον, ου, τό *the twelve
    tribes* Ac 26: 7.*
δῴη 2 aor. opt. act. of δίδωμι.
δώῃ 2 aor. subj. act. of δίδωμι.
δῶμα, ατος, τό *roof, housetop* Mt
    10: 27; Lk 5: 19; 17: 31; Ac 10:
    9.
δωρεά, ᾶς, ἡ *gift, bounty* J 4: 10;
    Ac 8: 20; Ro 5: 15, 17; Hb 6: 4.

δωρεάν acc. of δωρεά used as adv.—**1.** *as a gift, without payment, gratis* Mt 10: 8; Ro 3: 24; 2 Cor 11: 7; 2 Th 3: 8; Rv 21: 6; 22: 17.—**2.** *undeservedly, without reason* J 15: 25.—**3.** *in vain, to no purpose* Gal 2: 21.*

δωρέομαι *give, bestow* Mk 15: 45; 2 Pt 1: 3f.*

δώρημα, ατος, τό *gift* Ro 5: 16; Js 1: 17.*

δῶρον, ου, τό *gift* Mt 2: 11; Eph 2: 8; Rv 11: 10. Sacrificial *gift, offering* Mt 5: 23f; Mk 7: 11; Hb 5: 1; 11: 4. τὰ δῶρα *offering chest* Lk 21: 4.

δωροφορία, ας, ἡ *the bringing of a gift* Ro 15: 31 v.l.*

E

ε as numeral = *five, fifth* Ac 19: 9 v.l.*

ἔα exclamation denoting surprise or displeasure *ah!, ha!* Mk 1: 24 v.l.; Lk 4: 34; some connection with ἔα, imperative of ἐάω, *let alone!* seems possible in both passages.*

ἐάν conjunction *if:* in a present general condition, w. pres. or aor. subj., and present in apodosis (main clause) Mt 8: 2; Mk 3: 24; Lk 6: 33; J 5: 31; 1 Cor 8: 8. In a future more vivid condition, w. pres. or aor. subj. and future in apodosis Mt 6: 14; 9: 21; Mk 8: 3; Lk 4: 7; J 15: 10. With the indicative: fut. Lk 19: 40; Ac 8: 31; pres. 1 Th 3: 8. At times ἐάν closely approaches ὅταν *whenever, when* J 12: 32; 1 J 2: 28. ἐὰν καί *even if* Gal 6: 1. ἐὰν δὲ καί *but if* 1 Cor 7: 11. ἐὰν μή *if not, unless* Mt 10: 13; Mk 3: 27; J 4: 48; Ro 10: 15. ἐάν is frequently used in place of ἄν with relative words Mt 5: 19, 32; 8: 19; 1 Cor 16: 6; Rv 11: 6.

ἐάνπερ conj. *if indeed* Hb 6: 3.

ἑαυτοῦ, ῆς, οὗ pl. ἑαυτῶν—**1.** reflexive pronoun: of the third person *himself, herself, itself, themselves* Mt 18: 4; 27: 42; Mk 5: 5; J 19: 24. γίνεσθαι ἐν ἑ. or εἰς ἑ. ἔρχεσθαι *come to one's senses* Lk 15: 17; Ac 12: 11. ἀφ'

ἑαυτοῦ *by itself* J 15: 4.—Of the first and second persons plural *ourselves, yourselves* Mt 23: 31; 1 Cor 11: 31; perh. also for second pers. sing. J 18: 34.—**2.** reciprocal pronoun = ἀλλήλων *each other, one another* Mk 10: 26; J 12: 19; Eph 4: 32; Col 3: 13, 16; 1 Th 5: 13.—**3.** possessive pronoun = αὐτοῦ, etc. *his, her, their* Mt 8: 22; 21: 8; Lk 9: 60; 11: 21; 12: 36.

ἐάω *let, permit* Mt 24: 43; Ac 14: 16; 23: 32; 1 Cor 10: 13. *Let go, leave alone* Ac 5: 38 v.l.; Rv 2: 20 v.l.; *leave* Ac 27: 40. *Stop!* Lk 22: 51.

ἑβδομήκοντα, indecl. *seventy* Lk 10: 1, 17; Ac 7: 14.

ἑβδομηκοντάκις indecl. *seventy times* ἑβ. ἑπτά may be short for ἑβ. ἑπτάκις *seventy times seven times*, but it is more likely *seventy-seven times* (as Gen 4: 24) Mt 18: 22.*

ἕβδομος, η, ον *seventh* J 4: 52; Hb 4: 4; Jd 14; Rv 8: 1.

ἐβεβλήκει, ἐβέβλητο pluperf. act and pass. of βάλλω.

Ἔβερ, ὁ indecl. *Eber* Lk 3: 35.*

ἐβλήθην 1 aor. pass. ind. of βάλλω.

Ἑβραϊκός, ή, όν *Hebrew* Lk 23: 38 v.l.*

Ἑβραῖος, ου, ὁ *a Hebrew* 2 Cor 11: 22; Phil 3: 5; one speaking Aramaic Ac 6: 1.*

Ἑβραΐς, ίδος, ἡ *Hebrew* language, i.e. the Aramaic spoken at that time in Palestine Ac 21: 40; 22: 2; 26: 14.*

Ἑβραϊστί adv. *in Hebrew* or *Aramaic* J 5: 2; 19: 13, 17, 20; 20: 16; Rv 9: 11; 16: 16.*

ἐγγίζω *come near, approach* Mt 21: 1; 26: 45; Mk 1: 15; Lk 7: 12; 10: 9, 11; 18: 35; Ac 9: 3; Ro 13: 12; *draw near* Hb 7: 19; *come close* Phil 2: 30.

ἐγγράφω *write* (*in*), *record* lit. Lk 10: 20; fig. 2 Cor 3: 2 f.*

ἔγγυος, ον as noun ὁ ἔ. *guarantee* Hb 7: 22.*

ἐγγύς adv. followed by gen. or dat. *near, close to* Mt 26: 18; Lk 19: 11; J 3: 23; 19: 42; Ac 9: 38; Ro 10: 8; Eph 2: 13, 17; Phil 4: 5.

ἐγγύτερον comparative degree of ἐγγύς.

ἐγεγόνει pluperf. act. ind. of γίνομαι.

ἐγείρω—1. trans. *wake, rouse* Mt 8: 25. *Raise, help to rise* Mt 12: 11; Mk 1: 31; Ac 3: 7. *Raise* the dead Mt 10: 8; J 12: 1, 9, 17; 1 Cor 15: 15ff; Gal 1: 1. *Raise up, bring into being* Mt 3: 9; Ac 13: 22; *cause* Phil 1: 17. Passive: *awaken* Mt 1: 24; Ro 13: 11. *Be raised, rise* Lk 9: 7; 11: 8; J 2: 22; 1 Cor 15: 12. *Appear* Mt 11: 11; Mk 13: 22; J 7: 52.—2. intr., only in imperative *get up!, come!* Mk 2: 9, 11; 14: 42; Lk 5: 23f; J 5: 8; Eph 5: 14; Rv 11: 1.

ἔγερσις, εως, ἡ *resurrection* Mt 27: 53.*

ἐγκάθετος, ον *lying in wait*, as noun *spy* Lk 20: 20.*

ἐγκαίνια, ίων, τά *the festival of Rededication* J 10: 22, known also as Hanukkah and the Feast of Lights, beginning the 25th of Chislev (roughly = November–December) to commemorate the rededication of the temple by Judas Maccabaeus on that date in 165 BC.*

ἐγκαινίζω lit. 'renew'; *inaugurate, dedicate* Hb 9: 18; *open* 10: 20.*

ἐγκακέω *become weary, tired, lose heart, despair* Lk 18: 1; 2 Cor 4: 1, 16; Gal 6: 9; Eph 3: 13; 2 Th 3: 13.*

ἐγκαλέω *accuse, bring charges against* sometimes w. dat. Ac 19: 38; 23: 28; Ro 8: 33.

ἐγκαταλείπω—1. *leave behind* Ro 9: 29; *leave, allow to remain* Ac 2: 27, 31.—2. *forsake, abandon, desert* Mt 27: 46; Mk 15: 34; 2 Cor 4: 9; 2 Ti 4: 10, 16; Hb 10: 25; 13: 5.*

ἐγκατοικέω *live, dwell* (*among*) 2 Pt 2: 8.*

ἐγκαυχάομαι *boast, be proud* 2 Th 1: 4.*

ἐγκεντρίζω *graft* (*in*) Ro 11: 17, 19, 23f.*

ἐγκλείω *lock up* Lk 3: 20 v.l.*

ἔγκλημα, ατος, τό *charge, accusation* Ac 23: 29; 25: 16; 23: 24 v.l.*

ἐγκομβόομαι *clothe oneself with, put on* fig. 1 Pt 5: 5.*

ἐγκοπή, ῆς, ἡ *hindrance* 1 Cor 9: 12.*

ἐγκόπτω *hinder, thwart* Gal 5: 7; 1 Th 2: 18; 1 Pt 3: 7; *prevent* Ro 15: 22; *weary* or *detain* Ac 24: 4.*

ἐγκράτεια, ας, ἡ *self-control* Ac 24: 25; Gal 5: 23; 2 Pt 1: 6.*

ἐγκρατεύομαι *control oneself, exercise self-control* 1 Cor 7: 9; 9: 25.*

ἐγκρατής, ές *in full control of oneself, disciplined* Tit 1: 8.*

ἐγκρίνω *class* someone in a certain group 2 Cor 10: 12.*

ἐγκρύπτω *put*, lit. *hide* Mt 13: 33; Lk 13: 21 v.l.*

ἔγκυος, ον *pregnant* Lk 2: 5.*

ἔγνωκα, ἔγνων, ἔγνωσμαι perf. act., 2 aor. act., perf. mid. and pass. ind. of γινώσκω.

ἐγχρίω *rub* or *put on* Rv 3: 18.*

ἐγώ gen. ἐμοῦ (μου), dat. ἐμοί (μοι), acc. ἐμέ (με); pl. ἡμεῖς, ἡμῶν, ἡμῖν, ἡμᾶς. *I*; its use often serves to emphasize the first pers. of a verb Mt 5: 22, 28; Lk 21: 8; J 10: 7–14; sometimes no emphasis is felt Mk 12: 26; J 10: 34. Sing. and pl. sometimes used without distinction 1 Cor 1: 23; 4: 10. ἐγώ alone = *I* (*will*) or *yes* Mt 21: 29. The expression τί ἐμοὶ καὶ σοί; may be rendered *what have I to do with you? what have we in common? leave me alone! never mind!* Mk 5: 7; Lk 8: 28; J 2: 4; cf. Mt 8: 29; Mk 1: 24; Lk 4: 34.

ἐδαφίζω *dash to the ground, raze to the ground* Lk 19: 44.*

ἔδαφος, ους, τό *ground* Ac 22: 7.*

ἐδολιοῦσαν imperf. 3 pl. of δολιόω.

ἑδραῖος, (αία), αῖον *firm, steadfast* 1 Cor 7: 37; 15: 58; Col 1: 23.*

ἑδραίωμα, ατος, τό *foundation*, perh. *mainstay* 1 Ti 3: 15.*

ἔδραμον 2 aor. ind. act. of τρέχω.

ἔδυν 2 aor. ind. act. of δύνω.

Ἐζεκίας, ου, ὁ *Hezekiah* Mt 1: 9f; Lk 3: 23ff v.l.*

ἔζην imperf. act. of ζάω.

ἐθελοθρησκία, ας, ἡ *self-made religion*, perh. *would-be religion* Col 2: 23.*

ἐθέλω classical form for θέλω; not in N.T.

ἐθέμην, ἔθηκα 2 aor. mid. ind.; aor. act. ind. of τίθημι.

ἐθίζω *accustom* τὸ εἰθισμένον *the custom* Lk 2: 27.*

ἐθνάρχης, ου, ὁ *governor, ethnarch* 2 Cor 11: 32.*

ἐθνικός, ή, όν *Gentile, heathen*; in the N.T. only as noun ὁ ἐθνικός *the Gentile* in contrast to the Jew Mt 5: 47; 6: 7; 18: 17; 3 J 7.*

ἐθνικῶς adv. *like the heathen* Gal 2: 14.*

ἔθνος, ους, τό—**1.** *nation, people* Mt 24: 14; Lk 12: 30; Ac 8: 9; 10: 22; 13: 19.—**2.** τὰ ἔθνη *heathen, pagans, Gentiles* as contrasted with Jews Mt 6: 32;

10: 18; Ac 11: 1, 18; 14: 5; Ro 3: 29. *Gentiles* who are Christian Ro 16: 4; Gal 2: 12; Eph 3: 1.

ἔθος, ους, τό *habit, usage* Lk 22: 39; J 19: 40; Ac 25: 16; Hb 10: 25. *Custom, law* Lk 1: 9; Ac 6: 14; 21: 21; 28: 17.

ἔθου 2nd sing. 2 aor. mid. ind. of τίθημι.

ἔθρεψα 1 aor. act. ind. of τρέφω.

ἔθω obsolete pres. from which εἴωθα is formed.

εἰ—**1.** conditional particle *if:* with indicative in general conditions Mt 4: 3; 26: 33, 42; Lk 16: 11f; Ro 2: 17 or in contrary to fact conditions (see ἄν) Mt 11: 21; Lk 7: 39; J 9: 33. With subjunctive Rv 11: 5. With optative in a future less vivid (should–would) condition Ac 24: 19; 1 Pt 3: 14, 17; εἰ τύχοι *it may be, for example, perhaps* 1 Cor 14: 10; 15: 37. *If = since* Mt 6: 30; J 7: 23; Ro 6: 8. After verbs of emotion *that* Mk 15: 44a; Ac 26: 23; 1 J 3: 13. In strong assertions, with the apodosis omitted, εἰ has a negative effect (Hebraistic) εἰ δοθήσεται ... σημεῖον *if a sign shall be given* (something fearful will result), hence *a sign will certainly not be given* Mk 8: 12; cf. Hb 4: 3, 5.—**2.** interrogative particle: with direct questions, εἰ is left untranslated Mt 12: 10; Lk 13: 23; Ac 1: 6. With indirect questions *whether, if* Mt 26: 63; Mk 3: 2; Ac 17: 11. —**3.** with other particles εἰ δὲ μή *if not, otherwise* Mk 2: 21f; J 14: 2; Rv 2: 5, 16. εἰ καί *even if, even though* Lk 11: 8; 1 Cor 7: 21. εἰ μή *except, if not* Mt 5: 13; 11: 27; Ro 7: 7; Gal 1: 19 or *but* Mt 12: 4; Gal 1: 7. εἴ πως *if perhaps, if somehow* Ac 27: 12; Ro 1: 10.

εἰ μήν, more correctly **εἶ μήν** *surely, certainly* Hb 6: 14.*

εἶα, εἴασα 3rd sing. imperf. act.,

and 1st sing. 1 aor. act. ind. of
ἐάω.

εἰδέα, ας, ἡ appearance, perh. face
Mt 28: 3.*

εἰδέναι perf. act. inf. of οἶδα.

εἶδον used as 2 aor. of ὁράω; the
Hellenistic forms εἶδα, etc., are
often found in the N.T. see.—1.
lit. see, perceive Mt 2: 2, 9f;
3: 7; Mk 5: 14; J 1: 46; Ac 10:
17; Gal 6: 11; look at Mk 8: 33;
Lk 14: 18. ἰδὼν εἶδον I have
surely seen Ac 7: 34.—2. non-lit.
and fig. feel, become aware of
Mt 27: 54. Notice, note Mt 9: 2;
Ro 11: 22. Consider, deliberate
Ac 15: 6; 1 J 3: 1. See = experience Lk 2: 26; J 3: 3; 1 Pt 3:
10. Visit 1 Cor 16: 7; learn to
know Lk 9: 9; Ro 1: 11.

εἶδος, ους, τό form, outward
appearance Lk 3: 22; 9: 29; J
5: 37. Kind 1 Th 5: 22. Seeing,
sight 2 Cor 5: 7.*

εἰδῶ perf. subj. act. of οἶδα.

εἰδωλεῖον, ου, τό an idol's temple
1 Cor 8: 10.*

εἰδωλόθυτος, ον only as noun τὸ
εἰδωλόθυτον meat offered to an
idol Ac 15: 29; 21: 25; 1 Cor 8: 1,
4, 7, 10; 10: 19, 28 v.l.; Rv 2: 14,
20.*

εἰδωλολάτρης, ου, ὁ idolater 1 Cor
5: 10f; 6: 9; 10: 7; Eph 5: 5;
Rv 21: 8; 22: 15.*

εἰδωλολατρία, ας, ἡ idolatry 1 Cor
10: 14; Gal 5: 20; Col 3: 5; 1 Pt
4: 3.*

εἴδωλον, ου, τό idol as an image
Ac 7: 41; 1 Cor 12: 2; Rv 9: 20.
Idol as a false god Ac 15: 20;
Ro 2: 22; 1 Cor 8: 4, 7; 10: 19;
2 Cor 6: 16; 1 Th 1: 9; 1 J 5: 21.*

εἰδώς, υἶα, ός perf. act. ptc. of
οἶδα.

εἰθισμένος perf. pass. ptc. of
ἐθίζω.

εἰκῆ adv. without cause Col 2: 18;
Mt 5: 22 v.l. In vain, to no
avail Gal 3: 4; 4: 11. To no
purpose Ro 13: 4; 1 Cor 15: 2.*

εἴκοσι twenty Lk 14: 31; Ac 1: 15.

εἴκω yield Gal 2: 5.*

εἰκών, όνος, ἡ image, likeness Mk
12: 16; 1 Cor 11: 7; 15: 49; Rv
13: 14f. Form, appearance Ro
1: 23; 8: 29; Col 3: 10; Hb 10: 1.

εἴλατο 2 aor. mid. ind. of αἱρέομαι.

εἴληφα, εἴλημμαι perf. act. and
pass. ind. of λαμβάνω.

εἰλικρίνεια, ας, ἡ sincerity, purity
of motive 1 Cor 5: 8; 2 Cor 1: 12;
2: 17.*

εἰλικρινής, ές, gen. οὖς pure, unsullied, sincere Phil 1: 10; 2 Pt
3: 1.*

εἷλκον, εἵλκυσα imperf. and 1 aor.
act. ind. of ἕλκω.

εἱλκωμένος perf. pass. ptc. of
ἑλκόω.

εἰμί ptc. ὤν, οὖσα, ὄν; inf. εἶναι
be Mt 11: 29; 12: 11; Mk 3: 11;
Lk 16: 1, 19; J 3: 1. Exist Ro
4: 17; Hb 11: 6. Be present Mk
8: 1. Live Mt 23: 30; stay, reside
2: 13. Take place 24: 3. Mean 9:
13; 13: 38; 27: 46; 1 Cor 3: 7;
10: 19. Belong w. gen. 1: 12;
3: 4; w. ἐκ or ἐξ Lk 22: 3;
Col 4: 9. There is, there was, etc.
Lk 16: 1, 19; 1 Cor 8: 5; 12:
4ff. Impers. it is possible 1 Cor
11: 20; Hb 9: 5. W. dat. have
Lk 1: 7. With a participle as
periphrasis for a single verb
form Mk 1: 22; 2: 18; 4: 38; Lk
1: 20; 5: 10, 17; 2 Cor 9: 12.
ὁ ἦν, where ἦν is a substitute
for a past ptc. the one who was
Rv 1: 4, 8. ἡ οὖσα ἐκκλησία the
church there Ac 13: 1. Followed
by εἰς become Mk 10: 8; Ac 8:
23; 2 Cor 6: 18; serve (as something) 1 Cor 14: 22; Js 5: 3.
There are obviously many other
possible translations of εἰμί in
various contexts.

εἵνεκεν prep. w. gen. (see ἕνεκα)
on account of Lk 4: 18; 18: 29;
Ac 28: 20; 2 Cor 3: 10.*

εἶπα a form of εἶπον with endings
of the 1 aor.

εἴπερ *if indeed* Ro 3: 30; 8: 9, 17.
εἶπον used as 2 aor. of λέγω: *say,
speak* Mt 2: 8; 28: 7; Mk 12: 12;
Lk 8: 4; 19: 11; J 1: 15; 12: 27;
2 Cor 12: 6. *Order* Mk 5: 43; *tell*
8: 7; *call* J 10: 35; 15: 15; *foretell* Mt 28: 6; J 14: 28.
εἴπως see εἰ.
εἰργασάμην, εἰργασμένος 1 aor.
mid. ind., and perf. mid. and
pass. ptc. of ἐργάζομαι.
εἴρηκα perf. act. ind. of εἶπον.
εἰρηνεύω *live in peace, keep the
peace* Mk 9: 50; Ro 12: 18;
2 Cor 13: 11; 1 Th 5: 13.*
εἰρήνη, ης, ἡ *peace*—1. *peace, har-
mony, tranquility* Mt 10: 34; Lk
11: 21; Ac 9: 31; 24: 2; Ro 3: 17;
14: 19; 1 Cor 14: 33; Js 3: 18.—
2. *peace* in the Hebrew sense =
welfare, health Mk 5: 34; Ro 1:
7; 1 Cor 1: 3; 16: 11; 1 Th 1: 1;
Js 2: 16.—3. *peace* in a specif.
Christian sense, nearly = *messianic salvation* Lk 2: 14; J 16:
33: Ro 5: 1; Eph 6: 15; Phil
4: 7.
εἰρηνικός, ή, όν *peaceable, peaceful*
Hb 12: 11; Js 3: 17.*
εἰρηνοποιέω *make peace* Col 1: 20.*
εἰρηνοποιός, όν *making peace* as
noun ὁ εἰ. the *peace-maker* Mt
5: 9.*
εἰς prep. w. acc.—1. of place *into*
Mt 26: 18; Lk 2: 15; J 1: 9; Ac
17: 10; 2 Th 2: 4; *to* Mk 7: 31;
13: 14; J 8: 26; *toward* Lk 9: 16.
On, in Mt 5: 39; Lk 14: 10.
Among Mk 4: 7; Lk 10: 36. εἰς
is frequently used where ἐν
would be expected *in* Mk 10: 10;
13: 9; Lk 11: 7; J 1: 18; Ac 8:
40; 21: 13; Hb 11: 9.—2. of
time *to, up to, until* Mk 13: 13;
2 Ti 1: 12. *For, at, on, in* Mt 6:
34; Lk 1: 20; 12: 19; Ac 13: 42;
Phil 2: 16; Hb 7: 3.—3. generally
to, into, toward Mt 6: 13; J 13: 1;
Ro 1: 26; 5: 8; 2 Cor 11: 13f;
Hb 2: 10. *With reference to*
Ac 2: 25. *In response to* Mt 12:

41. *In* 18: 6. *Against* Lk 15:
18, 21. *For* Mt 5: 13; Lk 5: 4b;
9: 13; 1 Cor 16: 1; Rv 22: 2. *As*
Ac 10: 4; *serving as* Lk 2: 32.
Of 1 Pt 1: 11. *By* after a verb of
swearing Mt 5: 35; *by* or *with* in
the instrumental sense Ac 7: 53.
εἰς τριάκοντα *thirty-fold* Mk
4: 8. εἰς τοῦτο *for this reason* or
purpose J 18: 37; Ac 9: 21. εἰς
τό with inf. *so that* (result) Ro 1:
20; 2 Th 2: 10f but *in order to*
(purpose) Mt 20: 19; Mk 14: 55.
To be omitted in translation
ἐγένετο εἰς δένδρον Lk 13: 19.
εἷς, μία, ἕν gen. ἑνός, μιᾶς, ἑνός
numeral *one* Mt 5: 41; 19: 5;
Mk 8: 14; Ac 21: 7: Ro 5: 12;
12: 5. For emphasis *one and
the same* Lk 12: 52; Ro 3: 30;
1 Cor 12: 11; *only one, (a) single*
Mt 23: 15; Mk 12: 6; 10: 21;
Ro 3: 10; 1 Ti 3: 2; *alone* Mk 2:
7. Equivalent to the indefinite
τὶς *someone, anyone* Mt 18: 24;
Lk 24: 18; with τὶς *a certain
(one)* Mk 14: 47; J 11: 49;
equivalent to the indefinite
article *a, an* Mt 8: 19; Mk 12:
42; Rv 8: 13. Equivalent to
πρῶτος *first* Mt 28: 1; 1 Cor 16:
2; Tit 3: 10. (ὁ) εἷς . . . (ὁ) εἷς
(the) one . . . the other Mt 20: 21;
J 20: 12; Gal 4: 22. εἷς τὸν ἕνα
one another 1 Th 5: 11. καθ' ἕνα
one by one 1 Cor 14: 31. εἷς κατὰ
εἷς (the second εἷς is an undeclined nominative) *one after
the other* Mk 14: 19; J 8: 9.
εἰσάγω *bring* or *lead in, into* Lk
2: 27; 14: 21; J 18: 16; Ac 9: 8;
21: 28f, 37; Hb 1: 6.
εἰσακούω *hear, listen to, obey* Mt
6: 7; Lk 1: 13; Ac 10: 31;
1 Cor 14: 21; Hb 5: 7.*
εἰσδέχομαι *take in, receive, welcome* 2 Cor 6: 17.*
εἴσειμι *go (in, into)* Ac 3: 3; 21:
18, 26; Hb 9: 6.*
εἰσέρχομαι *come (in, into), go (in,
into), enter* Mt 19: 24; Mk 1: 21;

5: 12f; 11: 11; 15: 43; Lk 17: 7; J 18: 1; Ro 5: 12; *reach into* Hb 6: 19. Fig. *come (into)= share (in), come to enjoy* Mt 5: 20; 18: 8f; 26: 41; J 4: 38; Hb 3: 11, 18.

εἰσῄει 3 sing. imperf. act. of εἴσειμι.

εἴσιασι 3 pl. pres. ind. act. of εἴσειμι.

εἰσκαλέομαι *invite* in Ac 10: 23.*

εἴσοδος, ου, ἡ *entering, entrance, access* 1 Th 1: 9; 2: 1; Hb 10: 19; 2 Pt 1: 11; *coming* Ac 13: 24.*

εἰσπηδάω *leap* or *rush in* Ac 16: 29; 14: 14 v.l.*

εἰσπορεύομαι *go (in), come (in), enter* Mt 15: 17; Mk 1: 21; 4: 19; 5: 40; Lk 19: 30; Ac 8: 3.

εἰστήκει 3 sing. pluperf. act. of ἵστημι.

εἰστρέχω *run in* Ac 12: 14.*

εἰσφέρω *bring* or *lead (in)* Mt 6: 13; Lk 5: 18f; 11: 4; Ac 17: 20; 1 Ti 6: 7; Hb 13: 11; *drag in* Lk 12: 11.*

εἶτα adv. *then, next* Mk 4: 17; J 13: 5; 1 Cor 15: 7, 24; 1 Ti 2: 13; *furthermore* Hb 12: 9.

εἴτε = εἰ + τε; εἴτε . . . εἴτε *if . . . if, whether . . . or* Ro 12: 6–8; 1 Cor 3: 22; 12: 26; 2 Cor 1: 6; 1 Th 5: 10.

εἴτεν Ionic-Hellenistic form of εἶτα Mk 4: 28.*

εἶχαν, εἴχοσαν two forms of the 3 pl. imperf. act. of ἔχω.

εἴωθα perf. of an obsolete pres. ἔθω *be accustomed* Mt 27: 15; Mk 10: 1. τὸ εἰωθός *custom* Lk 4: 16; Ac 17: 2.*

εἴων 3 pl. imperf. act of ἐάω.

ἐκ; before vowels **ἐξ** prep. w. gen. *from, out of, away from.*—**1.** to denote separation Mt 2: 15; 26: 27; Mk 16: 3; J 12: 27; 17: 15; Ac 17: 33; Gal 3: 13; Rv 14: 13; *from among* Lk 20: 35; Ac 3: 23.—**2.** to denote the direction from which something comes *from, out from* Mt 17: 9; Mk 11: 20; Lk 5: 3; in answer to

the question where? *at, on* Mt 20: 21, 23; Ac 2: 25, 34.—**3.** to denote origin, cause, motive reason *from, of, by* Mt 1: 3, 5, 18; J 1: 13, 46; 1 Cor 7: 7; 2 Cor 5: 1; Gal 2: 15; 4: 4; Phil 3: 5. *Because of, by* Mk 7: 11; 2 Cor 2: 2; Rv 8: 11. *By reason of, as a result of, because of* Lk 12: 15; Ac 19: 25; Ro 4: 2; *with* Lk 16: 9. *Of, from* of source or material Mt 12: 34; J 19: 2; 1 Cor 9: 13; Rv 18: 12. *According to, in accordance with* Mt 12: 37; 2 Cor 8: 11, 13. ἐκ τούτου *for this reason, therefore* J 6: 66. οἱ ἐκ νόμου *partisans of the law* Ro 4: 14.—**4.** in periphrasis for the partitive gen. Mt 10: 29; 25: 2; Lk 11: 15, which may even function as subject of a sentence ἐκ τ. μαθητῶν *some of the disciples* J 16: 17; used with εἶναι = *belong to someone* or *something* Mt 26: 73; Ac 21: 8; 1 Cor 12: 15f. After verbs of filling *with* Lk 15: 16; J 12: 3; Rv 8: 5. For the gen. of price or value *for* Mt 20: 2; 27: 7; Ac 1: 18.—**5.** of time *from, from—on* Mt 19: 12; Mk 10: 20; J 9: 1, 32; *for* Lk 23: 8; *after* 2 Pt 2: 8.

ἕκαστος, η, ον *each, every* J 19: 23; Hb 3: 13; Rv 22: 2; perh. *both kinds* Lk 6: 44. As noun *each one, every one* Mt 16: 27; Lk 13: 15; 1 Cor 15: 38. εἷς ἕκαστος *every single one* Mt 26: 22; Lk 4: 40; 1 Cor 12: 18. For ἀνὰ εἷς ἕκαστος Rv 21: 21 see ἀνά 1.

ἑκάστοτε adv. *at any time, always* 2 Pt 1: 15.*

ἑκατόν indecl. *one hundred* Mt 13: 8, 23; Lk 15: 4; J 19: 39; Rv 7: 4.

ἑκατονταετής, ές *a hundred years old* Ro 4: 19.*

ἑκατονταπλασίων, ον *a hundred-fold* Mk 10: 30; Lk 8: 8; Mt 19: 29 v.l., Lk 18: 30 v.l.*

ἐκατοντάρχης, ου or ἐκατόνταρ-
χος, ου, ὁ centurion, captain
Mt 8: 13; Ac 27: 1, 6, 11, 31,
43 (all -ης), and Mt 8: 5, 8;
Ac 22: 25 (all -ος).

ἐκβαίνω go out, come (from) Hb
11: 15.*

ἐκβάλλω—1. drive out, expel lit.
throw out more or less forcibly
Mt 9: 25, 34; 21: 12, 39; 25: 30;
Lk 9: 40; 11: 20; J 2: 15; Ac
9: 40. Disdain, spurn Lk 6: 22;
repudiate Gal 4: 30; 3 J 10.—
2. without the connotation of
force: send out Lk 10: 2; release
Ac 16: 37; lead out Mk 1: 12;
J 10: 4.—3. take out, remove Mt
7: 4f; Mk 9: 47; Lk 10: 35; bring
out Mt 13: 52; evacuate 15: 17.
Leave out of consideration Rv 11:
2. Lead on Mt 12: 20.

ἔκβασις, εως, ἡ a way out 1 Cor
10: 13; end, perh. outcome,
result Hb 13: 7.*

ἐκβλαστάνω sprout up Mk 4: 5 v.l.*

ἐκβολή, ῆς, ἡ jettisoning, lit.
'throwing out' of a ship's cargo
Ac 27: 18.*

ἐκγαμίζω marry, give in marriage
as v.l. for γαμίζω in the following passages: Mt 22: 30; 24: 38;
Lk 17: 27; 20: 35; 1 Cor 7: 38.*

ἔκγονος, ον as noun ὁ, ἡ ἔκγονος
descendant specifically grand-
child 1 Ti 5: 4.*

ἐκδαπανάω spend completely, ex-
haust fig. 2 Cor 12: 15.*

ἐκδέχομαι wait for, expect J 5: 3
v.l.; Ac 17: 16; 1 Cor 11: 33; 16:
11; Js 5: 7; look foward to Hb
11: 10; followed by ἕως wait
until 10: 13.*

ἔκδηλος, ον quite evident, plain
2 Ti 3: 9.*

ἐκδημέω leave one's home or
country fig. leave, get away from
2 Cor 5: 8. Be in a strange land
fig. be away, be absent 5: 6, 9.*

ἐκδίδωμι mid. let out for hire, lease
Mt 21: 33, 41; Mk 12: 1; Lk
20: 9.*

ἐκδιηγέομαι tell (in detail) Ac
13: 41; 15: 3.*

ἐκδικέω—1. take vengeance for,
punish 2 Cor 10: 6; Rv 6: 10;
19: 2.—2. avenge someone, procure justice for someone Lk 18:
5. ἐ. με see to it that I get justice
18: 3. ἐ. ἑαυτόν take one's
revenge Ro 12: 19.*

ἐκδίκησις, εως, ἡ vengeance,
punishment Lk 21: 22; 2 Cor 7:
11; 2 Th 1: 8; 1 Pt 2: 14. ἐμοὶ
ἐ. vengeance belongs to me Ro
12: 19; Hb 10: 30. ἐ. ποιεῖν see
to it that justice is done Lk 18: 7f;
Ac 7: 24.*

ἔκδικος, ον avenging as noun the
avenger, the one who punishes
Ro 13: 4; 1 Th 4: 6.*

ἐκδιώκω persecute severely 1 Th
2: 15; Lk 11: 49 v.l.*

ἔκδοτος, ον given up, delivered up
Ac 2: 23.*

ἐκδοχή, ῆς, ἡ expectation Hb 10:
27.*

ἐκδύω strip, take off Mt 27: 28,
31; Mk 15: 20; Lk 10: 30; fig.
2 Cor 5: 4; verse 3 v.l.*

ἐκεῖ adv.—1. there, in that place
Mt 2: 13, 15; Mk 5: 11; Lk 12:
34. οἱ ἐκεῖ those who were there
Mt 26: 71. Pleonastic, to be
omitted in translation Rv 12: 6,
14.—2. there, to that place,
'thither' Mt 2: 22; Lk 21: 2; J
11: 8; Ro 15: 24.

ἐκεῖθεν adv. from there Mt 4: 21;
5: 26; 9: 9, 27.

ἐκεῖνος, η, ο demonstrative adj.
or pron. that person or thing,
that Mk 4: 11; Hb 12: 25; Js 4:
15. Equivalent to he, she, it
Mk 16: 10; J 5: 37; 14: 21, 26.
Emphatic Mt 17: 27; Tit 3: 7. As
adj. Mt 7: 25, 27; 10: 15; Mk
1: 9; 2 Th 1: 10; Rv 11: 13.
Adverbial gen. there Lk 19: 4.

ἐκεῖσε adv., in N.T. = ἐκεῖ 1 there,
at that place Ac 21: 3; 22: 5.*

ἐκέρασε 1 aor. act. ind. of
κεράννυμι.

ἐκζητέω seek out, search for Ac 15: 17; Ro 3: 11; Hb 11: 6; 12: 17; 1 Pt 1: 10. Charge with, require of Lk 11: 50f.*

ἐκζήτησις, εως, ἡ useless speculation 1 Ti 1: 4.*

ἐκθαμβέω pass. be amazed Mk 9: 15; be distressed 14: 33; be alarmed 16: 5f.*

ἔκθαμβος, ον utterly astonished Ac 3: 11.*

ἐκθαυμάζω wonder greatly Mk 12: 17.*

ἔκθετος, ον exposed, abandoned Ac 7: 19.*

ἐκκαθαίρω clean out, cleanse 1 Cor 5: 7; 2 Ti 2: 21.*

ἐκκαίω pass. be inflamed Ro 1: 27.*

ἐκκακέω lose heart as v.l. for ἐγκακέω in all these passages: Lk 18: 1; 2 Cor 4: 1, 16; Gal 6: 9; Eph 3: 13; 2 Th 3: 13.*

ἐκκεντέω pierce J 19: 37; Rv 1: 7.*

ἐκκέχυται perf. pass ind. of ἐκχέω.

ἐκκλάω break off Ro 11: 17, 19, 20.*

ἐκκλείω shut out, exclude Gal 4: 17; eliminate Ro 3: 27.*

ἐκκλησία, ας, ἡ—1. assembly regularly convened for political purposes Ac 19: 39; meeting generally 19: 32, 40.—2. congregation, assembly of the Israelites Ac 7: 38; Hb 2: 12.—3. the Christian church or congregation: as a church meeting 1 Cor 11: 18; 14: 4f; 3 J 6; as a group of Christians living in one place Mt 18: 17; Ac 5: 11; Ro 16: 1, 5; 1 Cor 1: 2; Gal 1: 22; Phlm 2; as the church universal, to which all believers belong Mt 16: 18; Ac 9: 31; 1 Cor 12: 28; Eph 1: 22; 3: 10. Church of God or Christ 1 Cor 10: 32; 1 Th 1: 1; 2: 14.

ἐκκλίνω turn away Ro 16: 17; 1 Pt 3: 11; turn aside Ro 3: 12.*

ἐκκολυμβάω swim away Ac 27: 42.*

ἐκκομίζω carry out Lk 7: 12.*

ἐκκοπή, ῆς, ἡ lit. cutting out v.l. for ἐγκοπή hindrance 1 Cor 9: 12.*

ἐκκόπήσῃ 2 sing. fut. pass. ind. of ἐκκόπτω.

ἐκκόπτω cut off or down Mt 3: 10; 5: 30; 7: 19; 18: 8; Lk 3: 9; 13: 7, 9; Ro 11: 24; fig. 11: 22. Remove 2 Cor 11: 12.*

ἐκκρεμάννυμι mid. hang on fig. Lk 19: 48.*

ἐκλαλέω tell Ac 23: 22.*

ἐκλάμπω shine (out) Mt 13: 43.*

ἐκλανθάνομαι forget (altogether) w. gen. Hb 12: 5.*

ἔκλαυσα 1 aor. act. ind. of κλαίω.

ἐκλέγομαι choose, select Mk 13: 20; Lk 9: 35; 10: 42; J 15: 16; Ac 15: 22, 25; Eph 1: 4; Js 2: 5. In Lk 6: 44 ἐκλ. is v.l. for συλλέγω.

ἐκλείπω fail Lk 22: 32; give out of money 16: 9 (the v.l. ὅταν ἐκλίπητε here means when you die); grow dark, perh. be eclipsed 23: 45; come to an end Hb 1: 12.*

ἐκλεκτός, ή, όν chosen, select Mt 22: 14; 24: 22, 24, 31; Lk 18: 7; 23: 35; Col 3: 12; I Ti 5: 21; 2 Ti 2: 10; 1 Pt 2: 9; 2 J 1, 13. Choice 1 Pt 2: 4, 6; ὁ ἐ. ἐν κυρίῳ the outstanding Christian Ro 16: 13.

ἐκλελεγμένος perf. pass. ptc. of ἐκλέγομαι.

ἐκλέλησμαι perf. pass. ind. of ἐκλανθάνομαι.

ἐκλήθην 1 aor. pass. ind. of καλέω.

ἐκλογή, ῆς, ἡ selection, choosing, election Ro 9: 11; 11: 5, 28; 1 Th 1: 4; 2 Pt 1: 10. σκεῦος ἐκλογῆς a chosen instrument Ac 9: 15. In passive sense those selected Ro 11: 7.*

ἐκλύω pass. become weary or slack, give out Mt 15: 32; Mk 8: 3; Gal 6: 9. Lose courage Hb 12: 3, 5.*

ἐκμάσσω wipe Lk 7: 38, 44; J 11: 2; 12: 3; dry 13: 5.*

ἐκμυκτηρίζω sneer at, ridicule Lk 16: 14; 23: 35.*

ἐκνεύω turn aside, withdraw J 5: 13.*

ἐκνήφω become sober fig. come to one's senses 1 Cor 15: 34.*

ἐκούσιος, ία, ιον voluntary, as a volunteer κατὰ ἑκούσιον of one's own free will Phlm 14.*

ἐκουσίως adv. willingly 1 Pt 5: 2. Without compulsion, i.e. deliberately, intentionally Hb 10: 26.*

ἔκπαλαι adv. for a long time, long ago 2 Pt 2: 3; 3: 5.*

ἐκπειράζω put to the test, try, tempt Mt 4: 7; Lk 4: 12; 10: 25; 1 Cor 10: 9.*

ἐκπέμπω send out or away Ac 13: 4; 17: 10.*

ἐκπέπτωκα perf. act. ind. of ἐκπίπτω.

ἐκπερισσῶς adv. excessively ἐ. λαλεῖν say with great emphasis Mk 14: 31.*

ἐκπεσεῖν 2 aor. act. inf. of ἐκπίπτω

ἐκπετάννυμι spread or hold out Ro 10: 21.*

ἐκπηδάω rush out Ac 14: 14; start up, get up quickly 10: 25 v.l.*

ἐκπίπτω—1. fall off or from Ac 12: 7; Js 1: 11; 1 Pt 1: 24; perh. Ac 27: 32, but see 2 below.— 2. drift off course, run aground Ac 27: 17, 26, 29, perh. 32 (see 1 above).—3. fig. lose w. gen. Gal 5: 4; 2 Pt 3: 17. Fail, weaken Ro 9: 6; 1 Cor 13: 8 v.l.*

ἐκπλεῦσαι 1 aor. act. inf. of ἐκπλέω.

ἐκπλέω sail away Ac 15: 39; 18: 18; 20: 6.*

ἐκπληρόω fulfill (completely) Ac 13: 33.*

ἐκπλήρωσις, εως, ἡ completion Ac 21: 26.*

ἐκπλήσσω pass. be amazed, overwhelmed Mt 19: 25; 22: 33; Mk 6: 2; Lk 2: 48; Ac 13: 12.

ἐκπνέω breathe one's last, expire Mk 15: 37, 39; Lk 23: 46.*

ἐκπορεύομαι come or go out, proceed Mt 17: 21; Mk 7: 15, 20; Lk 3: 7; J 15: 26; Rv 4: 5. Spread Lk 4: 37; project Rv 1: 16; flow out 22: 1.

ἐκπορνεύω indulge in immorality Jd 7.*

ἐκπτύω despise, disdain lit. 'spit out' Gal 4: 14.*

ἐκπυρόω set on fire, destroy by fire conjectural emendation for εὑρεθήσεται 2 Pt 3: 10.*

ἐκριζόω uproot, pull out by the roots Mt 13: 29; 15: 13; Lk 17: 6; Jd 12.*

ἐκρύβην 2 aor. pass. ind. of κρύπτω.

ἔκστασις, εως, ἡ—1. astonishment, bewilderment, terror Mk 5: 42; 16: 8; Lk 5: 26; Ac 3: 10.—2. trance, ecstasy Ac 10: 10; 11: 5; 22: 17.*

ἐκστρέφω turn aside, pervert Tit 3: 11.*

ἐκσῴζω bring safely v.l. for ἐξωθέω Ac 27: 39.*

ἐκταράσσω agitate, throw into confusion Ac 16: 20; 15: 24 v.l.*

ἐκτείνω stretch out, hold out, extend Mt 8: 3; 26: 51; Mk 3: 5; Lk 22: 53; J 21: 18; Ac 4: 30; 26: 1. Of an anchor run out 27: 30.

ἐκτελέω finish, bring to completion Lk 14: 29f.*

ἐκτένεια, ας, ἡ perseverance, earnestness Ac 26: 7; 12: 5 v.l.*

ἐκτενής, ές eager, earnest Ac 12: 5 v.l.; constant 1 Pt 4: 8.*

ἐκτενῶς adv. eagerly, fervently, constantly Ac 12: 5; 1 Pt 1: 22. Comparative ἐκτενέστερον prob. very fervently Lk 22: 44.*

ἐκτίθημι expose, abandon Ac 7: 21. Fig. explain, set forth 11: 4; 18: 26; 28: 23.*

ἐκτινάσσω shake off Mt 10: 14; Mk 6: 11; Ac 13: 51; Lk 9: 5 v.l.; shake out Ac 18: 6.*

ἔκτος, η, ον *sixth* Mt 20: 5; Mk 15: 33; Lk 1: 26, 36; J 4: 6; Rv 6: 12.

ἐκτός adv. *outside*—1. ἐκτὸς εἰ μή *unless, except* 1 Cor 14: 5; 15: 2; 1 Ti 5: 19. As noun τὸ ἐ. *the outside* Mt 23: 26.—2. as improper prep. w. gen. *outside* 1 Cor 6: 18; 2 Cor 12: 2; *except* Ac 26: 22; 1 Cor 15: 27.*

ἐκτρέπω mid. and pass. *turn, turn away* 1 Ti 1: 6; 5: 15; 2 Ti 4: 4; *avoid* 1 Ti 6: 20. For Hb 12: 13 *turn away* is possible, but *be dislocated* is perh. better.*

ἐκτρέφω *feed, nourish* Eph 5: 29; *bring up* 6: 4.*

ἔκτρομος, ον *trembling* Hb 12: 21 v.l.*

ἔκτρωμα, ατος, τό *untimely birth, miscarriage* 1 Cor 15: 8.*

ἐκφέρω *carry* or *bring out* Lk 15: 22; Ac 5: 6, 9f, 15; 1 Ti 6: 7; *lead out* Mk 8: 23. *Produce* Hb 6: 8.*

ἐκφεύγω *run away, seek safety in flight* Ac 19: 16. *Escape* Lk 21: 36; Ac 16: 27; Ro 2: 3; Hb 12: 25.

ἐκφοβέω *frighten, terrify* 2 Cor 10: 9.*

ἔκφοβος, ον *terrified* Mk 9: 6; Hb 12: 21.*

ἐκφύω *put forth*, lit. 'cause to grow' Mt 24: 32; Mk 13: 28.*

ἐκφωνέω *cry out* Lk 16: 24 v.l.*

ἐκχέαι 1 aor. act. inf. of ἐκχέω.

ἐκχέω or ἐκχύννω *pour out, shed, spill* Mt 9: 17; 23: 35; Mk 14: 24; J 2: 15; Ac 1: 18; Rv 16: 6; fig. *pour out* Ac 2: 17f, 33; Ro 5: 5; Tit 3: 6. Pass. *give oneself up, abandon oneself* Jd 11.

ἐκχωρέω *go out, go away* Lk 21: 21.*

ἐκψύχω *breathe one's last, die* Ac 5: 5, 10; 12: 23.*

ἑκών, οῦσα, όν *willing(ly), of one's own free will* Ro 8: 20; 1 Cor 9: 17.*

ἔλαθον 2 aor. act. ind. of λανθάνω.

ἐλαία, ας, ἡ *olive tree* Mt 21: 1; Ro 11: 17, 24; Rv 11: 4; *olive*, the fruit Js 3: 12.

ἔλαιον, ου, τό (*olive*) *oil* Mt 25: 3f, 8; Mk 6: 13; Lk 10: 34; Hb 1: 9; *olive orchard* Rv 6: 6.

ἐλαιών, ῶνος, ὁ *olive grove, olive orchard* Lk 19: 29; 21: 37; Ac 1: 12.*

ἐλάκησα 1 aor. act. ind. of λακάω.

Ἐλαμίτης, ου, ὁ *an Elamite*, from the region east of the lower Tigris valley Ac 2: 9.*

ἐλάσσων, ἔλασσον (the Attic ἐλάττων is found 1 Ti 5: 9; Hb 7: 7) used as comparative of μικρός: *smaller = younger* Ro 9: 12; *inferior* J 2: 10; Hb 7: 7; Mt 20: 28 v.l. Adv. ἔλαττον *less* 1 Ti 5: 9.*

ἐλαττονέω *have less* or *too little* 2 Cor 8: 15.*

ἐλαττόω *make inferior* Hb 2: 7, 9. Pass. *diminish* J 3: 30; *be worse off* or *in need* 2 Cor 12: 13 v.l.*

ἐλάττων see ἐλάσσων.

ἐλαύνω *drive* Lk 8: 29; Js 3: 4; 2 Pt 2: 17; *row* Mk 6: 48; J 6: 19.*

ἐλαφρία, ας, ἡ *vacillation, levity* τῇ ἐ. χρᾶσθαι *be vacillating, fickle* 2 Cor 1: 17.*

ἐλαφρός, ά, όν *light* in weight Mt 11: 30. τὸ ἐ. *insignificance, triviality* 2 Cor 4: 17.*

ἔλαχε 2 aor. act. ind. of λαγχάνω.

ἐλάχιστος, ίστη, ον used as superlative of μικρός: *smallest, least* 1 Cor 15: 9. Usually reduced in degree *very small, quite unimportant, insignificant* Mt 2: 6; Js 3: 4; *trivial* 1 Cor 6: 2; *least important, of little importance* Mt 25: 40, 45; 1 Cor 4: 3. With comparative ending added *very least* Eph 3: 8.

Ἐλεάζαρ, ὁ indecl. *Eleazar* Mt 1: 15.*

ἐλεάω an alternate form for ἐλεέω *have mercy on*, found in Ro 9: 16; Jd 22, 23.*

ἐλεγμός, οῦ, ὁ reproof, conviction or punishment 2 Ti 3: 16.*

ἔλεγξις, εως, ἡ rebuke, reproof 2 Pt 2: 16.*

ἔλεγχος, ου, ὁ proof, proving perh. inner conviction Hb 11: 1; reproof, correction 2 Ti 3: 16 v.l.*

ἐλέγχω—1. bring to light, expose, set forth J 3: 20; Eph 5: 11, 13; Tit 2: 15.—2. convict, convince, point out J 8: 46; Js 2: 9; Tit 1: 9, 13; Jd 15.—3. reprove, correct Mt 18: 15; Lk 3: 19; 1 Ti 5: 20; discipline, punish Hb 12: 5; Rv 3: 19.

ἐλεεινός, ή, όν miserable, pitiable 1 Cor 15: 19; Rv 3: 17.*

ἐλεέω have mercy or pity on someone, show mercy to someone Mt 5: 7; 9: 27; 18: 33; 20: 30f; 1 Cor 7: 25; Phil 2: 27; do acts of mercy Ro 12: 8.

ἐλεημοσύνη, ης, ἡ kind deed, then alms, charitable giving Mt 6: 2ff; Lk 11: 41; Ac 9: 36; 10: 2, 4, 31.

ἐλεήμων, ον, gen. ονος merciful, sympathetic Mt 5: 7; Hb 2: 17.*

ἐλέησον 1 aor. imperative act. of ἐλεέω.

ἔλεος, ους, τό mercy, compassion, pity Mt 23: 23; Lk 1: 72; Ro 15: 9; Gal 6: 16; Eph 2: 4; Hb 4: 16.

ἐλευθερία, ας, ἡ freedom, liberty Ro 8: 21; 1 Cor 10: 29; 2 Cor 3: 17; Gal 2: 4; 5: 1, 13; Js 1: 25; 2: 12; 1 Pt 2: 16; 2 Pt 2: 19.*

ἐλεύθερος, έρα, ον free, independent as adj. and noun (= a free man, etc.) Mt 17: 26; J 8: 33, 36; 1 Cor 7: 22, 39; Gal 4: 31; Rv 6: 15; 19: 18.

ἐλευθερόω free, set free J 8: 32, 36; Ro 6: 18, 22; 8: 2, 21; Gal 5: 1.*

ἔλευσις, εως, ἡ coming, advent Ac 7: 52; as v.l. in Lk 21: 7 and 23: 42.*

ἐλεύσομαι fut. mid. ind. of ἔρχομαι.

ἐλεφάντινος, η, ον made of ivory Rv 18: 12.*

ἐλήλακα perf. act. ind. of ἐλαύνω.

ἐλήλυθα perf. act. ind. of ἔρχομαι.

ἐλθεῖν 2 aor. act. inf. of ἔρχομαι.

Ἐλιακίμ, ὁ indecl. Eliakim Mt 1: 13; Lk 3: 30; 3: 23ff v.l.*

ἕλιγμα, ατος, τό package, roll J 19: 39 v.l.*

Ἐλιέζερ, ὁ indecl. Eliezer Lk 3: 29.*

Ἐλιούδ, ὁ indecl. Eliud Mt 1: 14f; Lk 3: 23ff v.l.*

Ἐλισάβετ, ἡ indecl. Elizabeth Lk 1: 5, 7, 13, 24, 36, 40f, 57; 1: 46 v.l.*

Ἐλισαῖος, ου, ὁ Elisha Lk 4: 27.*

ἑλίσσω roll up Hb 1: 12; Rv 6: 14.*

ἕλκος, ους, τό sore, abscess, ulcer Lk 16: 21; Rv 16: 2, 11.*

ἑλκόω pass. be covered with sores Lk 16: 20.*

ἑλκύω and ἕλκω drag, pull, draw J 18: 10; Ac 16: 19; 21: 30; haul J 21: 6, 11; hale Js 2: 6. Draw, attract J 6: 44; 12: 32.*

Ἑλλάς, άδος, ἡ Greece, Hellas Ac 20: 2.*

Ἕλλην, ηνος, ὁ a Greek, a Hellene Ro 1: 14. Gentile, pagan, heathen J 7: 35; Ac 11: 20; 20: 21; 1 Cor 1: 24; Gal 3: 28. Of proselytes J 12: 20; Ac 17: 4.

Ἑλληνικός, ή, όν Greek Lk 23: 38 v.l.; supply 'language' Rv 9: 11.*

Ἑλληνίς, ίδος, ἡ Gentile (lit. Greek) Ac 17: 12; Gentile woman Mk 7: 26.*

Ἑλληνιστής, οῦ, ὁ a Hellenist, a Greek-speaking Jew Ac 6: 1; 9: 29; 11: 20 v.l.*

Ἑλληνιστί adv. in the Greek language J 19: 20. Ἑ. γινώσκειν understand Greek Ac 21: 37.*

ἐλλογάω or ἐλλογέω charge (to someone's account) Ro 5: 13; Phlm 18.*

Ἐλμαδάμ, ὁ indecl. Elmadam Lk 3: 28.*

ἑλόμενος 2 aor. mid. ptc. of αἱρέω.

ἐλπίζω hope, hope for, expect, foresee Lk 6: 34; 23: 8; Ac 26: 7;

1 Cor 13: 7; 2 Cor 8: 5. *Put one's hope* (*in*) Mt 12: 21; J 5: 45; 2 Cor 1: 10; 1 Pt 1: 13.

ἐλπίς, ίδος, ἡ *hope, expectation, prospect* Ac 16: 19; 23: 6; Ro 4: 18; 8: 20, 24; 1 Cor 9: 10; 2 Cor 1: 7. *Christian hope* Ac 26: 6; Ro 5: 4f; 1 Cor 13: 13; Eph 2: 12; 1 Th 1: 3; 1 Pt 1: 3; (*object of*) *hope* 1 Th 2: 19; 1 Ti 1: 1; *hope, something hoped for* Ro 8: 24; Col 1: 5; Tit 2: 13; Hb 6: 18.

Ἐλύμας, α, ὁ *Elymas* Ac 13: 8.*

ἐλωΐ Aramaic *my God* Mk 15: 34; Mt 27: 46 v.l.*

ἔμαθον 2 aor. act. ind. of μανθάνω.

ἐμαυτοῦ, ῆς reflexive pron. of the first pers. *myself*—1. in the genitive *my own* 1 Cor 10: 33. ἀπ' or ἐξ ἐμαυτοῦ *on my own authority, of my own free will* J 5: 30; 10: 18; 12: 49; 14: 10.— 2. in the dative ἔδοξα ἐμαυτῷ *I once believed* Ac 26: 9. σύνοιδά τι ἐμαυτῷ *I am aware of something* 1 Cor 4: 4.—3. in the accusative *myself* Lk 7: 7; J 14: 21; 1 Cor 9: 19. ὑπ' ἐμαυτόν *under my authority* Mt 8: 9.

ἐμβαίνω *go in, step in* J 5: 4. *Get into, embark* Mt 8: 23; Mk 8: 10; Lk 8: 22, 37; J 6: 17, 24; Ac 21: 6.

ἐμβάλλω *throw* (into) Lk 12: 5.*

ἐμβαπτίζω *dip* (in, into) Mk 14: 20 v.l.*

ἐμβάπτω *dip* (in, into) Mt 26: 23; Mk 14: 20.*

ἐμβατεύω in N.T. only Col 2: 18 ἃ ἑόρακεν ἐμβατεύων, where the meaning is in dispute. The verb can mean *set foot upon, enter, go into detail*, etc. Among the possibilities for Col 2: 18 are *entering at length upon the tale of what he has seen* in a vision, or *who enters* (the sanctuary) *which he saw* (in ecstasy). Perhaps the text is not in order.*

ἐμβιβάζω *put in, put on board* Ac 27: 6.*

ἐμβλέπω *look at, fix one's gaze upon* often with dative Mk 10: 21, 27; Lk 20: 17; J 1: 36. With εἰς Mt 6: 26 (see below); Ac 1: 11 v.l. Perh. *be able to see* Mk 8: 25; Ac 22: 11. Perh. *consider* Mt 6: 26 (see above).

ἐμβριμάομαι w. dat. *scold, censure* Mk 14: 5; *warn sternly* Mt 9: 30; Mk 1: 43. ἐ. τῷ πνεύματι or ἐν ἑαυτῷ *be deeply moved* lit. 'groan' J 11: 33, 38.*

ἐμέ accusative sing. of ἐγώ.

ἔμεινα 1 aor. act. ind. of μένω.

ἐμέω *spit out* fig. Rv 3: 16.*

ἐμμαίνομαι *be enraged* Ac 26: 11.*

Ἐμμανουήλ, ὁ indecl. *Emmanuel* Mt 1: 23.*

Ἐμμαοῦς, ἡ *Emmaus* a village approximately seven miles from Jerusalem Lk 24: 13.*

ἐμμένω *stay* or *live* (*in*) Ac 28: 30. Fig. *persevere in, stand by, be true to* 14: 22; *abide by* Gal 3: 10; Hb 8: 9.*

ἐμμέσῳ v.l. for ἐν μέσῳ Rv 1: 13; 2: 1; 4: 6; 5: 6; 6: 6; 22: 2.*

Ἐμμώρ, ὁ indecl. *Hamor* Ac 7: 16.*

ἐμνήσθην 1 aor. pass. ind. of μιμνῄσκομαι.

ἐμοί dat. sing. of ἐγώ.

ἐμός, ή, όν possessive pron. *my, mine* without emphasis Mt 18: 20; J 15: 11; with emphasis *my own* Gal 6: 11; Phlm 19. εἰς τὴν ἐμὴν ἀνάμνησιν *in memory of me* 1 Cor 11: 24f. As noun τὸ ἐμόν *what is mine, my property* Mt 20: 15; 25: 27; J 16: 14f.

ἐμπαιγμονή, ῆς, ἡ *mocking* 2 Pt 3: 3.*

ἐμπαιγμός, οῦ, ὁ *scorn, mocking*, or *derisive torture* Hb 11: 36.*

ἐμπαίζω *ridicule, make fun of, mock* w. dat. Mt 27: 29, 31; Mk 10: 34; Lk 22: 63. *Deceive, trick* Mt 2: 16.

ἐμπαίκτης, ου, ὁ *mocker* 2 Pt 3: 3; Jd 18.*

ἐμπέμπω *send* (*in*) Lk 19: 14 v.l.*

ἐμπεπλησμένος perf. pass. ptc. of ἐμπίμπλημι.

ἐμπεριπατέω walk about, move 2 Cor 6: 16.*

ἐμπί(μ)πλημι or ἐμπι(μ)πλάω fill, satisfy Lk 1: 53; 6: 25; J 6: 12; Ac 14: 17; enjoy ὑμῶν your company Ro 15: 24.*

ἐμπί(μ)πρημι set on fire, burn Mt 22: 7. As v.l. in Ac 28: 6, for which see πίμπρημι.*

ἐμπίπτω fall (in, into) lit. Lk 6: 39. Fig. fall (into, among) 10: 36; 1 Ti 3: 6f; Hb 10: 31.

ἐμπλακείς 2 aor. pass. ptc. of ἐμπλέκομαι.

ἐμπλέκω pass. become entangled or involved in 2 Ti 2: 4; 2 Pt 2: 20.*

ἐμπλησθῶ 1 aor. pass. subj. of ἐμπί(μ)πλημι.

ἐμπλοκή, ῆς, ἡ braiding 1 Pt 3: 3.*

ἐμπνέω breathe w. gen. Ac 9: 1.*

ἐμπορεύομαι carry on business Js 4: 13. Exploit, lit. 'sell' 2 Pt 2: 3.*

ἐμπορία, ας, ἡ business, trade Mt 22: 5.*

ἐμπόριον, ου, τό market οἶκος ἐμπορίου market-house J 2: 16.*

ἔμπορος, ου, ὁ merchant, (wholesale) dealer Mt 13: 45; Rv 18: 3, 11, 15, 23.*

ἐμπρήθω alternate form for ἐμπίμπρημι.

ἔμπροσθεν—1. adv. in front, forward, ahead Lk 19: 4, 28; Rv 4: 6. τὰ ἔ. what lies ahead Phil 3: 13.—2. improper prep. w. gen. in front of, before Mt 5: 24; 27: 29; Lk 5: 19; Ac 18: 17. Before, in the presence of Mt 10: 32f; 27: 11; Gal 2: 14; 1 Th 1: 3; 2: 19. Before, in the sight of Mt 6: 1; Mk 2: 12; Lk 19: 27; J 12: 37; Ac 10: 4; in the face of Mt 23: 13. Of rank before, higher than J 1: 15, 30. For the simple gen. Mt 18: 14, or dat. 11: 26.

ἐμπτύω spit on or at w. dat. or εἰς and acc. Mt 27: 30; Mk 10: 34; 14: 65; Lk 18: 32.

ἐμφανής, ές visible Ac 10: 40; ἐ. ἐγενόμην I have been revealed (=revealed myself) Ro 10: 20.*

ἐμφανίζω—1. reveal J 14: 21f; pass. become visible, appear Mt 27: 53; Hb 9: 24.—2. make known, explain, inform, make a report Ac 23: 15, 22; 25: 15; Hb 11: 14; bring formal charges Ac 24: 1; 25: 2.*

ἔμφοβος, ον afraid, startled, terrified Lk 24: 5; Ac 24: 25; Rv 11: 13.

ἐμφυσάω breathe upon J 20: 22.*

ἔμφυτος, ον implanted Js 1: 21.*

ἐμφωνέω only as v.l. for φωνέω in Lk 16: 24.*

ἐν prep. w. dat., most common prep. in N.T., used with greatest variety of meanings, of which the following are typical:—I. of place: in Mt 3: 1; Lk 2: 49; Ac 5: 42; 1 Ti 3: 15. On Mt 5: 25; 6: 5; J 4: 20f; 2 Cor 3: 3. At, near Lk 13: 4; J 8: 20; Eph 1: 20. In the case of, to Mt 17: 12; Mk 14: 6; 1 Cor 4: 2, 6; 9: 15. In the presence of, before 1 Cor 2: 6; in the judgment of 14: 11. Among, in Mt 2: 6; Mk 8: 38; Gal 1: 14. With (denoting accompaniment or association, merging into instrument) Mt 16: 28; Lk 14: 31; 1 Cor 4: 21; 2 Cor 10: 14; Hb 9: 25; in the power of, under the influence of Mk 1: 23; 12: 36; 1 J 5: 19. The sense into, where εἰς would be expected, is rare, but see Lk 9: 46; Rv 11: 11. In of mystical relation J 10: 38; 14: 20; Ro 6: 11, 23; 16: 11; 1 Cor 1: 30; 3: 1; 4: 15; Gal 2: 20; Phil 4: 1f; 3: 1.—II. of time—1. of a period of time in the course of, within Mt 2: 1; 3: 1; 27: 40; J 2: 19f. ἐν τῷ μεταξύ meanwhile J 4: 31.—2. denoting a point of time when something occurs in, at Mt 8: 13; Mk 12: 23; J 11: 9, 10, 24; 1 Cor 15: 23, 52.—3. when, while, during Mt

13: 4, 25; 21: 22; Mk 15: 7; 12: 38; Eph 6: 20.—**III.** causal—**1.** expressing means or instrument *with, in, by* Mt 5: 13; 26: 52; Lk 1: 51; Ro 5: 9; Rv 17: 16; *with the help of* Mt 9: 34; Ac 17: 31. ἐν τῷ ἐλαύνειν *as they rowed* (temporal) or *because of the rowing* (instrumental) Mk 6: 48.—**2.** kind and manner ἐν δυνάμει *with power, powerfully* Mk 9: 1; Col 1: 29. ἐν ἐκτενείᾳ *earnestly* Ac 26: 7. ἐν παρρησίᾳ *freely, openly* J 7: 4.—**3.** cause or reason *because of, on account of* Mt 6: 7; J 16: 30; Ac 24: 16; Ro 1: 24.—**IV.** various other uses: *amounting to* Ac 7: 14. *Consisting in* Eph 2: 15. ἐν w. dat. stands for the ordinary dative Lk 2: 14; Ro 1: 19; Gal 1: 16; very rarely for the genitive Ro 5: 15. With ὄμνυμι *by* Mt 5: 34ff; Rv 10: 6; with ὁμολογεῖν omit ἐν in translation Lk 12: 8. ἐν ᾧ may mean *wherein* Ro 14: 22; *while, as long as* Mk 2: 19; Lk 5: 34; *whereby* Ro 14: 21; *because* 8: 3.

ἐναγκαλίζομαι *take in one's arms* Mk 9: 36; 10: 16.*

ἐνάλιος, ον *belonging to the sea* Js 3: 7.*

ἐνάλλομαι *leap upon* Ac 19: 16 v.l.*

ἐνανθρωπέω *take on human form* 1 J 4: 17 v.l.*

ἔναντι adv. used as improper prep. w. gen. *before, in the judgment of* Lk 1: 8; Ac 8: 21; 7: 10 v.l.*

ἐναντίον improper prep. w. gen. *before, in the presence (of)* Lk 20: 26; Ac 8: 32; Mk 2: 12 v.l. *In the sight* or *judgment (of)* Lk 1: 6; 24: 19; Ac 7: 10. Adv. with the article τοὐναντίον *on the other hand* 2 Cor 2: 7; Gal 2: 7; 1 Pt 3: 9.*

ἐναντιόομαι *oppose (oneself)* w. dat. Ac 13: 45 v.l.*

ἐναντίος, α, ον *opposite, against,* contrary Mt 14: 24; Mk 6: 48; Ac 27: 4; 28: 17; *hostile* 1 Th 2: 15. ἐναντία πράσσειν πρός *oppose* Ac 26: 9. ἐξ ἐναντίας *opposite* Mk 15: 39; ὁ ἐξ ἐ. *the opponent* Tit 2: 8.*

ἐναργής, ές *clear, evident, visible* Hb 4: 12 v.l.*

ἐνάρχομαι *begin, make a beginning* Gal 3: 3; Phil 1: 6.*

ἔνατος, η, ον *ninth* Rv 21: 20. ἐ. ὥρα *ninth hour* = 3 p.m. Mt 20: 5; Ac 10: 3, 30.

ἐναφίημι *let, permit* Mk 7: 12 v.l.*

ἐνγ- see ἐγγ-.

ἐνδεής, ές *poor, impoverished* Ac 4: 34.*

ἔνδειγμα, ατος, τό *evidence, plain indication* 2 Th 1: 5.*

ἐνδείκνυμι *show, demonstrate* Ro 9: 17, 22; Eph 2: 7; Hb 6: 10. *Do* 2 Ti 4: 14.

ἔνδειξις, εως, ἡ *proof* Ro 3: 25f; 2 Cor 8: 24. *Sign, omen* Phil 1: 28.*

ἕνδεκα indecl. *eleven* Mt 28: 16; Lk 24: 9, 33; Ac 1: 26; 2: 14.

ἑνδέκατος, η, ον *eleventh* Rv 21: 20. ἐ. ὥρα *eleventh hour* = 5 p.m. Mt 20: 9, cf. 20: 6.*

ἐνδέχομαι impers. *it is possible* Lk 13: 33.*

ἐνδημέω *be at home* fig. 2 Cor 5: 6, 8f.*

ἐνδιδύσκω *dress* with double acc. Mk 15: 17; mid. *dress oneself* Lk 16: 19; 8: 27 v.l.*

ἔνδικος, ον *just, deserved* Ro 3: 8; Hb 2: 2.*

ἐνδόμησις v.l. for ἐνδώμησις Rv 21: 18.*

ἐνδοξάζομαι *be glorified, honored* 2 Th 1: 10, 12.*

ἔνδοξος, ον *honored, distinguished* 1 Cor 4: 10. *Splendid* Lk 7: 25; 13: 17; *glorious* Eph 5: 27.*

ἔνδυμα, ατος, τό *garment, clothing* Mt 3: 4; 6: 25, 28; 7: 15; 22: 11f; 28: 3; Lk 12: 23.*

ἐνδυναμόω *strengthen* Phil 4: 13; 1 Ti 1: 12; 2 Ti 4: 17. Pass.

become strong Ac 9: 22; Ro 4: 20; Eph 6: 10; 2 Ti 2: 1.*

ἐνδύνω *go (in), creep (in)* 2 Ti 3: 6.*

ἔνδυσις, εως, ἡ *putting on* 1 Pt 3: 3.*

ἐνδύω act. *dress, clothe* lit. Lk 15: 22; with double acc. Mt 27: 31; Mk 15: 20. Mid. *clothe oneself in, put on, wear* lit. Mt 6: 25; Mk 6: 9; Lk 8: 27; Ac 12: 21; Ro 13: 12; Rv 19: 14; fig., mid. and pass. Lk 24: 49; Ro 13: 14; 1 Cor 15: 53f; Col 3: 12.

ἐνδώμησις, εως, ἡ *construction, material,* perh. *foundation* Rv 21: 18.*

ἐνεγκ- unaugmented stem of aor. of φέρω.

ἐνέδρα, ας, ἡ *plot, ambush* Ac 23: 16; 25: 3.*

ἐνεδρεύω *lie in wait (for), plot* Lk 11: 54; Ac 23: 21.*

ἔνεδρον, ου, τό a variant form for ἐνέδρα in Ac 23: 16 v.l.*

ἐνειλέω *wrap up in* Mk 15: 46.*

ἔνειμι ptc. τὰ ἐνόντα *what is inside, the contents* Lk 11: 41.*

ἕνεκα also **ἕνεκεν** and **εἵνεκεν** improper prep. w. gen. *because of, on account of* Mt 5: 10f; Ac 28: 20; Ro 14: 20; *for the sake of* Mt 16: 25; 19: 29. ἕ. τούτου *for this reason* 19: 5. τίνος ἕ.; *why?* Ac 19: 32. ἕ. τοῦ w. inf. *in order that* 2 Cor 7: 12.

ἐνεκεντρίσθην 1 aor. pass. ind. of ἐγκεντρίζω.

ἐνενήκοντα indecl. *ninety* Mt 18: 12f; Lk 15: 4, 7.*

ἐνεός, ά, όν *speechless* Ac 9: 7.*

ἐνεπαίχθην 1 aor. pass. ind. of ἐμπαίζω.

ἐνέπλησα 1 aor. act. ind. of ἐμπί(μ)πλημι.

ἐνέπρησε 1 aor. act. ind. of ἐμπί(μ)πρημι.

ἐνέργεια, ας, ἡ *working, operation, activity* Col 2: 12; 2 Th 2: 9. *Manifestation* Eph 1: 19; 3: 7; 4: 16; Col 1: 29; *power* Phil

3: 21. ἐ. πλάνης *a deluding influence* 2 Th 2: 11.

ἐνεργέω—1. intrans. *work, be at work, operate, be effective* act. Mk 6: 14; Gal 2: 8; Eph 2: 2. τὸ θέλειν καὶ τὸ ἐ. *the will and the action* Phil 2: 13b. Mid. *work, be at work* Ro 7: 5; 2 Cor 4: 12; Eph 3: 20; 1 Th 2: 13; *become effective* 2 Cor 1: 6. δέησις ἐ. *effective prayer* Js 5: 16.— 2. transitive *work, produce, effect* 1 Cor 12: 6; Eph 1: 11; 2: 2; Phil 2: 13a.

ἐνέργημα, ατος, τό *working, activity* 1 Cor 12: 6, 10.*

ἐνεργής, ές *effective, active, powerful* Phlm 6; Hb 4: 12. θύρα ἐ. *a door* (fig.) *for effective service* 1 Cor 16: 9.*

ἐνεστηκώς, ἐνεστώς first and second perf. act. participles of ἐνίστημι.

ἐνετειλάμην 1 aor. mid. ind. of ἐντέλλω.

ἐνέτυχον 2 aor. act. ind. of ἐντυγχάνω.

ἐνευλογέω *bless* Ac 3: 25; Gal 3: 8.*

ἐνεχθ- 1 aor. pass. ptc. of φέρω.

ἐνέχω *be hostile* Lk 11: 53; w. dat. *have a grudge against* someone, with χόλον 'anger' understood Mk 6: 19. Pass., w. dat. *be subject to, be loaded down with* Gal 5: 1; 2 Th 1: 4 v.l.*

ἐνθάδε adv. *here, to this place* J 4: 15f; Ac 25: 17. *Here, in this place* Lk 24: 41; Ac 10: 18; 16: 28; 17: 6; 25: 24.*

ἔνθεν adv. *from here* Mt 17: 20; Lk 16: 26.*

ἐνθυμέομαι *reflect (on), consider, think* Mt 1: 20; 9: 4; Ac 10: 19 v.l.*

ἐνθύμησις, εως, ἡ *thought, reflection, idea* Mt 9: 4; 12: 25; Ac 17: 29; Hb 4: 12.*

ἔνι (for ἔνεστι) *there is* 1 Cor 6: 5; Gal 3: 28; Col 3: 11; Js 1: 17.*

ἐνιαυτός, οῦ, ὁ *year* Lk 4: 19;

J 11: 49; Ac 11: 26; Hb 9: 7;
Rv 9: 15. Perh. certain *days of
the year* Gal 4: 10.

ἐνίστημι—1. *be present, have come*
2 Th 2: 2. The participles
ἐνεστηκώς and ἐνεστώς mean
present Ro 8: 38; Gal 1: 4; Hb
9: 9.—**2.** *impend, be imminent* 1
Cor 7: 26; 2 Ti 3: 1; but meaning
1 is possible for these passages.

ἐνισχύω intrans. *grow strong, regain one's strength* Ac 9: 19;
19: 20 v.l. Trans. *strengthen* Lk
22: 43.*

ἐνκ- see ἐγκ-.

ἐννέα indecl. *nine* Mt 18: 12f; Lk
15: 4, 7; 17: 17.*

ἐννεός see ἐνεός.

ἐννεύω *nod, make signs* Lk 1: 62.*

ἔννοια, ας, ἡ *thought, knowledge,
insight* Hb 4: 12; 1 Pt 4: 1.*

ἔννομος, ον *legal,* perh. *regular* Ac
19: 39. *Subject to the law,* perh.
true to the law 1 Cor 9: 21.*

ἐννόμως adv.=ἐν νόμῳ *subject to*
or *in possession of the law* Ro
2: 12 v.l.*

ἔννυχος, ον *at night* neut. pl.
ἔννυχα as adv. *while it was still
dark* Mk 1: 35.*

ἐνοικέω *live* or *dwell (in)* Ro 7: 17;
8: 11; 2 Cor 6: 16; Col 3: 16;
2 Ti 1: 5, 14; Lk 13: 4 v.l.*

ἐνορκίζω *adjure, cause to swear*
with double accusative 1 Th
5: 27.*

ἑνότης, ητος, ἡ *unity* Eph 4: 3,
13.*

ἐνοχλέω *trouble, annoy* Lk 6: 18;
cause trouble Hb 12: 15.*

ἔνοχος, ον (=ἐνεχόμενος 'caught
in') *subject to* Hb 2: 15. *Liable,
answerable, guilty* Mt 5: 21f;
Mk 3: 29; *guilty (of a sin
against)* 1 Cor 11: 27. *Deserving*
Mt 26: 66; Mk 14: 64; 3: 29 v.l.
γέγονεν πάντων ἔ. *has sinned
against all* Js 2: 10. ἔ. εἰς τ.
γέενναν *guilty enough (to go)
into hell* Mt 5: 22 c.*

ἐνπ- see ἐμπ-.

ἔνταλμα, ατος, τό *commandment,
precept* Mt 15: 9; Mk 7: 7; Col
2: 22.*

ἐνταφιάζω *prepare for burial, bury*
Mt 26: 12; J 19: 40.*

ἐνταφιασμός, οῦ, ὁ *preparation
for burial* or *burial itself* Mk 14:
8; J 12: 7.*

ἐντελεῖται fut. mid. ind. of ἐντέλλω.

ἐντέλλω mid. *command, order,
give orders* Mt 17: 9; 19: 7; J
14: 31; Ac 1: 2; 13: 47; Hb 11:
22; *ordain* 9: 20.

ἐντέταλμαι perf. mid. ind. of
ἐντέλλω.

ἐντεῦθεν adv. *from here* Lk 4: 9;
J 2: 16; 7: 3; 18: 36. ἐντεῦθεν
καὶ ἐντεῦθεν *on each side* 19:
18. *From this* Js 4: 1.

ἔντευξις, εως, ἡ *prayer* 1 Ti 2: 1;
4: 5.*

ἐντίθημι *put in, implant* Ac 18: 4
v.l.*

ἔντιμος, ον *honored, respected, distinguished* Lk 14: 8; *valuable,
precious* 7: 2; 1 Pt 2: 4, 6. ἔ.
ἔχειν *hold in esteem* Phil 2: 29.*

ἐντολή, ῆς, ἡ *command(ment),
order, decree* Mt 22: 36, 38, 40;
Mk 10: 19; J 11: 57; 13: 34;
Ro 13: 9; 1 Cor 7: 19; Col 4: 10;
1 Ti 6: 14; 2 Pt 2: 21. *Law* Lk
23: 56; Hb 7: 16.

ἐντόπιος, ία, ον *local, belonging to a
certain place, resident* Ac 21: 12.*

ἐντός improper prep. w. gen.
inside, within τὸ ἐντός *the inside*
Mt 23: 26. In Lk 17: 21 ἐ. ὑμῶν
may be *within you, in your
hearts* or *among you, in your
midst.*

ἐντραπῇ 2 aor. pass. subj. of
ἐντρέπω.

ἐντρέπω *make ashamed* 1 Cor 4:
14; pass. *be put to shame, be
ashamed* 2 Th 3: 14; Tit 2: 8.
W. middle sense *have respect* or
regard for Mt 21: 37; Lk 20: 13;
Hb 12: 9.

ἐντρέφω *bring up, rear, train*
1 Ti 4: 6.*

ἔντρομος, ον *trembling* Lk 8: 47
v.l.; Ac 7: 32; 16: 29; Hb 12:
21.*
ἐντροπή, ῆς, ἡ *shame, humiliation*
1 Cor 6: 5; 15: 34.*
ἐντρυφάω *revel, carouse* 2 Pt 2:
13.*
ἐντυγχάνω *approach, appeal, plead*
Ac 25: 24; Ro 8: 27, 34; 11: 2;
Hb 7: 25.*
ἐντυλίσσω *wrap* (*up*) Mt 27: 59;
Lk 23: 53; *fold up* J 20: 7.*
ἐντυπόω *carve, impress* 2 Cor 3:
7.*
ἐνυβρίζω *insult, outrage* Hb 10:
29.*
ἐνυπνιάζομαι *to dream, have
visions* Ac 2: 17; Jd 8.*
ἐνύπνιον, ου, τό *a dream* Ac 2:
17.*
ἐνφ- see ἐμφ-.
ἐνώπιον *improper prep.* w. gen.
—1. *before* Lk 1: 19; Ac 10: 30;
Rv 3: 8; 7: 15.—2. *in the sight
or presence of* Lk 23: 14; J 20:
30; Ac 10: 33; 1 Ti 6: 12; Rv 3:
5; 13: 13.—3. *in the opinion or
judgment of* Lk 16: 15; 2 Cor 8:
21.—4. Various uses: simply
to Ac 6: 5; 2 Cor 7: 12. *Among*
Lk 15: 10. *Against* 15: 18, 21.
By the authority of, on behalf of
Rv 13: 12, 14.
'Ενώς, ὁ indecl. *Enos* Lk 3: 38.*
ἐνωτίζομαι *give ear to, pay attention to* Ac 2: 14.*
'Ενώχ, ὁ indecl. *Enoch* Lk 3: 37;
Hb 11: 5; Jd 14; introduced by
conjecture 1 Pt 3: 19.*
ἐξ *prep.* see ἐκ.
ἕξ indecl. *six* Mt 17: 1; Lk 4: 25;
J 12: 1; Js 5: 17.
ἐξαγγέλλω *proclaim, report* 1 Pt
2: 9 and short ending of Mk.*
ἐξαγοράζω *redeem* (lit. 'buy back'),
deliver Gal 3: 13; 4: 5. Mid. ἐξ.
τ. καιρόν prob. *make the most
of the time* Eph 5: 16; Col 4: 5.*
ἐξάγω *lead out, bring out* Lk 24:
50; J 10: 3; Ac 7: 36, 40; 12: 17;
21: 38; Hb 8: 9.

ἐξαιρέω—1. act. *take out, tear out*
Mt 5: 29; 18: 9.—2. mid. *set
free, deliver, rescue* Ac 7: 10, 34;
12: 11; 23: 27; Gal 1: 4. For
Ac 26: 17 *deliver* or *select, choose
out.**
ἐξαίρω *remove, drive away* 1 Cor
5: 13; also 5: 2 v.l.*
ἐξαιτέω mid. *ask for, demand* Lk
22: 31.*
ἐξαίφνης adv. *suddenly, unex-
pectedly* Mk 13: 36; Lk 2: 13;
9: 39; Ac 9: 3; 22: 6.*
ἐξακολουθέω *follow, obey* 2 Pt 1:
16; 2: 2; *follow, pursue* 2: 15.*
ἐξακόσιοι, αι, α *six hundred* Rv
13: 18; 14: 20.*
ἐξαλείφω *wipe away* Rv 7: 17; 21:
4. *Wipe out, erase* 3: 5. *Remove,
obliterate, blot out* Ac 3: 19;
Col 2: 14.*
ἐξάλλομαι *leap up* Ac 3: 8; 14:
10 v.l.*
ἐξανάστασις, εως, ἡ *resurrection*
Phil 3: 11.*
ἐξανατέλλω *spring up* Mt 13: 5;
Mk 4: 5.*
ἐξανίστημι trans. *raise up* Mk 12:
19; Lk 20: 28. Intrans. *stand
up* Ac 15: 5.*
ἐξανοίγω *to open* (*fully*) Ac 12: 16
v.l.*
ἐξαπατάω *deceive, cheat* Ro 7: 11;
16: 18; 1 Cor 3: 18; 2 Cor 11: 3;
2 Th 2: 3; 1 Ti 2: 14.*
ἐξάπινα adv. *suddenly* Mk 9: 8.*
ἐξαπορέω pass. *be in great difficulty, despair* 2 Cor 4: 8. τοῦ
ζῆν *despair of living* 1: 8.*
ἐξαποστέλλω *send out, send away*
Lk 1: 53; 24: 49; Ac 7: 12;
17: 14; 22: 21; Gal 4: 4, 6.
ἐξάρατε, ἐξαρθῇ 1 aor. act. imperative, and 1 aor. pass. subj.
of ἐξαίρω.
ἐξαρτάω *be attached to, be an
adherent of* Mk 3: 21 v.l.*
ἐξαρτίζω *finish, complete* Ac 21: 5.
Equip, furnish 2 Ti 3: 17.*
ἐξαστράπτω *flash* or *gleam like
lightning* Lk 9: 29.*

ἐξαυτῆς adv. *at once, immediately, soon thereafter* Mk 6: 25; Ac 10: 33; 21: 32; Phil 2: 23.

ἐξεγείρω *awaken* pass. *wake up, awaken* Mk 6: 45 v.l. *Raise* from the dead 1 Cor 6: 14. *Cause to appear, bring into being* Ro 9: 17.*

ἐξέδετο 2 aor. ind. mid. of ἐκδίδωμι.

ἐξείλατο 2 aor. mid. ind. of ἐξαιρέω.

ἔξειμι (from εἶμι) *go out, go away* Ac 13: 42; 20: 7; 27: 43.

ἔξειμι from εἰμί, see ἔξεστιν.

ἐξεκαύθην 1 aor. pass. ind. of ἐκκαίω.

ἐξεκλάσθην 1 aor. pass. ind. of ἐκκλάω.

ἐξεκόπην 2 aor. pass. ind. of ἐκκόπτω.

ἐξεκρέμετο imperf. mid. ind. of ἐκκρεμάννυμι.

ἔξελε, ἐξελέσθαι 2 aor. imperative act., and inf. mid. of ἐξαιρέω.

ἐξελέγχω *convict* Jd 15 v.l.*

ἐξελέξω 2 sing. 1 aor. mid. of ἐκλέγω.

ἐξελήλυθα perf. act. ind. of ἐξέρχομαι.

ἐξέλκω *drag away* Js 1: 14.*

ἐξέμαξα 1 aor. act. ind of ἐκμάσσω.

ἐξενεγκ- aor. stem of ἐκφέρω.

ἐξέπεσα aor. act. ind. of ἐκπίπτω.

ἐξεπέτασα 1 aor. act. ind. of ἐκπετάννυμι.

ἐξεπλάγην 2 aor. pass. ind. of ἐκπλήσσω.

ἐξέπλει 3 sing. imperf. act. ind. of ἐκπλέω.

ἐξέπλευσα 1 aor. act. ind. of ἐκπλέω.

ἐξέπνευσα 1 aor. act. ind. of ἐκπνέω.

ἐξέραμα, ατος, τό *vomit, what has been vomited* 2 Pt 2: 22.*

ἐξεραυνάω Hellenistic for ἐξερευνάω *inquire carefully* 1 Pt 1: 10.*

ἐξέρχομαι *go out, come out, get out, go away* Mt 8: 28; 25: 1;

Mk 1: 35; 5: 2; J 13: 3; Ac 12: 9f; Js 3: 10; Rv 19: 21. *Be released* Lk 12: 59. *Appear* Mk 8: 11. *Proceed, be descended* Hb 7: 5. *Be gone* Ac 16: 19. ἐκ τ. κόσμου ἐ. *leave the world = die* 1 Cor 5: 10.

ἐξεστακέναι perf. act. inf. of ἐξίστημι.

ἔξεστι impersonal 3 sing. of the unused verb ἔξειμι; *it is permitted, it is possible* or *proper* Mt 12: 2; Mk 3: 4; Lk 6: 9; J 18: 31; Ac 22: 25; 1 Cor 6: 12. The neut. participle of ἐ. is ἐξόν; with ἐστί expressed or understood it = ἔξεστι Mt 12: 4; Ac 2: 29.

ἐξέστραπται perf. pass. ind. of ἐκστρέφω.

ἐξετάζω *inquire* Mt 10: 11. ἐ. περί τινος *make a careful search for someone* 2: 8. *Question, examine* J 21: 12.*

ἐξετράπην 2 aor. pass. ind. of ἐκτρέπω.

ἐξέφνης Hellenistic spelling of ἐξαίφνης.

ἐξέχεα, ἐξεχύθην 1 aor. act. and 1 aor. pass. ind. of ἐκχέω.

ἐξέχω *stand out, be prominent* Mt 20: 28 v.l.*

ἐξέψυξα 1 aor. act. ind. of ἐκψύχω.

ἐξηγέομαι *explain, interpret, tell, report, describe* Lk 24: 35; Ac 10: 8; 15: 12, 14; 21: 19. *Make known, bring news of* J 1: 18.*

ἐξῄειν imperf. act. ind. of ἔξειμι (1).

ἐξήκοντα indecl. *sixty* Mt 13: 8; Lk 24: 13; 1 Ti 5: 9; Rv 13: 18.

ἐξήρανε, ἐξηράνθη, ἐξήρανται 1 aor. act. and pass., perf. pass. ind. of ξηραίνω.

ἑξῆς adv. *next* Lk 9: 37; Ac 21: 1; 25: 17; 27: 18. ἐν τῷ ἑξῆς *(soon) afterward* Lk 7: 11.*

ἐξητήσατο 1 aor. mid. ind. of ἐξαιτέω.

ἐξηχέω pass. *be caused to sound forth, ring out* 1 Th 1: 8.*

ἕξις, εως, ἡ *practice, exercise* Hb 5: 14.*

**ἐξίστημι, ἐξιστάνω, ἐξιστάω—
1.** trans. *confuse, amaze, astound*
Lk 24: 22; Ac 8: 9, 11.—**2.**
intrans. (2 aor. and perf. act.;
all of the mid.) *be out of one's
senses* Mk 3: 21; 2 Cor 5: 13.
Be amazed or *astonished* Mt 12:
23; Mk 5: 42; Lk 2: 47; Ac 2:
7, 12.

ἐξιστῶν pres. act. participle of
ἐξίστημι (ἐξιστάω).

ἐξισχύω *be able, be strong enough,
be in a position* Eph 3: 18.*

ἔξοδος, ου, ἡ *going out* or *away; the
exodus* Hb 11: 22. Fig. *depart-
ure, death* Lk 9: 31; 2 Pt 1: 15.*

ἐξοίσουσι fut. act. ind. of ἐκφέρω.

ἐξολεθρεύω *destroy utterly, root
out* Ac 3: 23.*

ἐξομολογέω—1. act. *promise, consent* Lk 22: 6.—**2.** mid.—**a.**
confess, admit Mt 3: 6; Mk 1: 5;
Ac 19: 18; Js 5: 16.—**b.** *acknowledge* Phil 2: 11.—**c.** *praise* Mt
11: 25; Lk 10: 21; Ro 14: 11;
15: 9.*

ἐξόν see ἔξεστιν.

ἐξορκίζω *adjure, charge under oath*
Mt 26: 63. *Exorcize* Ac 19: 13 v.l.,
14 v.l.*

ἐξορκιστής, οῦ, ὁ *exorcist*, one who
drives out demons Ac 19: 13.*

ἐξορύσσω *dig out, tear out* Gal 4:
15; *dig through* Mk 2: 4.*

ἐξουδενέω and **ἐξουδενόω** *treat
with contempt* Mk 9: 12.*

ἐξουθενέω and **ἐξουθενόω—1.** *despise, disdain* Lk 18: 9; Ro 14: 3,
10; 1 Cor 16: 11; Gal 4: 14;
amount to nothing 2 Cor 10: 10.—
2. *reject with contempt* Ac 4: 11;
1 Th 5: 20; *treat with contempt*
Lk 23: 11.

ἐξουσία, ας, ἡ—1. *freedom of
choice, right* to act, decide, etc. J
10: 18; Ac 5: 4; Ro 9: 21; 1 Cor
9: 4ff, 12; 2 Th 3: 9; Hb 13: 10;
Rv 13: 5; 22: 14.—**2.** *ability,
capability, might, power* Mt 9: 8;
Mk 1: 22, 27; Lk 10: 19; Ac
8: 19; Rv 9: 19; 20: 6.—**3.**
authority, absolute power Mt
21: 23, 24, 27; 28: 18; Mk 2: 10;
Ac 26: 12.—**4.** power or authority exercised by rulers, etc., by
virtue of their office—**a.** *ruling
power, official power* Lk 7: 8; 20:
20; Rv 17: 12f.—**b.** *domain,
jurisdiction* Lk 4: 6; 23: 7;
Eph 2: 2; Col 1: 13.—**c.** bearers
of authority, *authorities, officials,
government* Lk 12: 11; Ro 13: 1,
2, 3; *spirit powers* 1 Cor 15: 24;
Eph 1: 21; 3: 10; Col 2: 15.—
5. *means of exercising power*,
prob. *a veil* 1 Cor 11: 10.

ἐξουσιάζω *have power* w. gen.
over someone Lk 22: 25; 1 Cor
7: 4. Pass. *be mastered* 6: 12.*

ἐξοχή, ῆς, ἡ *prominence* ἄνδρες οἱ
κατ᾽ ἐξοχήν *the most prominent
men* Ac 25: 23.*

ἐξυπνίζω *wake up, arouse* fig. J
11: 11.*

ἔξυπνος, ον *awake, aroused* Ac 16:
27.*

ἔξω—1. adv. *outside* Mt 12: 46f;
Mk 11: 4; Lk 1: 10; J 18: 16.
Out Mt 26: 75; Lk 14: 35; J 18:
29; Rv 3: 12. δεῦρο ἔξω *come
out!* J 11: 43. As a noun οἱ ἔξω
those who are outside Mk 4: 11;
1 Cor 5: 12f. As an adj. *outer,
outside* 2 Cor 4: 16; *foreign* Ac
26: 11.—**2.** improper prep. w.
gen. *outside* Hb 13: 11f; *out of,
out from* Mt 10: 14; Lk 4: 29;
Ac 4: 15; 14: 19.

ἔξωθεν—1. adv. *from the outside*
Mk 7: 18. *Outside* Mt 23: 27f;
2 Cor 7: 5. As noun οἱ ἔ. *those
on the outside* 1 Ti 3: 7. τὸ ἔ.
the outside Lk 11: 39f. As adj.
external 1 Pt 3: 3.—**2.** improper
prep. w. gen. *from outside* Mk
7: 15; *outside* Rv 14: 20.

ἐξωθέω *drive out, expel* Ac 7: 45.
Beach, run ashore 27: 39.*

ἐξῶσαι 1 aor. inf. act. of ἐξωθέω.

ἐξώτερος, α, ον comparative used
as superlative *farthest (out)* Mt
8: 12; 22: 13; 25: 30.*

ἔοικα be like, resemble w. dat. Js 1: 6, 23.*

ἑορτάζω celebrate a festival 1 Cor 5: 8.*

ἑορτή, ῆς, ἡ festival, feast Mt 26: 5; Mk 14: 2; Lk 2: 41f; 22: 1; J 7: 2, 8, 10f, 14; 13: 1; Col 2: 16.

ἐπαγγελία, ας, ἡ promise Ac 2: 39; 23: 21; Ro 4: 20; Gal 3: 16, 18, 29; Hb 7: 6; what was promised Ac 1: 4; 2: 33; Gal 3: 14.

ἐπαγγέλλομαι—1. promise, offer Mk 14: 11; Ro 4: 21; Gal 3: 19; Hb 6: 13; Js 1: 12.—2. profess, lay claim to 1 Ti 2: 10; 6: 21.

ἐπάγγελμα, ατος, τό promise 2 Pt 3: 13; the thing promised 1: 4.*

ἐπάγω bring on or upon Ac 5: 28; 2 Pt 2: 1, 5; stir up Ac 14: 2 v.l.*

ἐπαγωνίζομαι fight, contend Jd 3.*

ἐπαθροίζω collect besides or in addition pass. Lk 11: 29.*

'Επαίνετος, ου, ὁ Epaenetus Ro 16: 5.*

ἐπαινέω praise Lk 16: 8; Ro 15: 11; 1 Cor 11: 2, 17, 22.*

ἔπαινος, ου, ὁ praise, approval, recognition Ro 2: 29; 1 Cor 4: 5; Eph 1: 6, 12, 14; 1 Pt 2: 14; a thing worthy of praise Phil 4: 8.

ἐπαίρω lift up, hold up Mt 17: 8; Lk 6: 20; 21: 28; J 17: 1; Ac 14: 11; 1 Ti 2: 8. Pass. be taken up Ac 1: 9; fig. rise up, be in opposition 2 Cor 10: 5; be presumptuous, put on airs 2 Cor 11: 20.

ἐπαισχύνομαι be ashamed (of) Mk 8: 38; Lk 9: 26; Ro 1: 16; 6: 21; 2 Ti 1: 8, 12, 16; Hb 2: 11; 11: 16.*

ἐπαιτέω beg as a mendicant Lk 16: 3; 18: 35; Mk 10: 46 v.l.*

ἐπακολουθέω follow, come after 1 Ti 5: 24; 1 Pt 2: 21; devote oneself (to) 1 Ti 5: 10; accompany, authenticate Mk 16: 20.*

ἐπακούω hear, listen to w. gen. 2 Cor 6: 2.*

ἐπακροάομαι listen to w. gen. Ac 16: 25.*

ἐπάν conj. w. subjunctive when, as soon as Mt 2: 8; Lk 11: 22, 34.*

ἐπάναγκες adv. necessarily τὰ ἐ. the necessary things Ac 15: 28.*

ἐπανάγω lead or bring up intrans. —1. put out to sea Lk 5: 3f.— 2. return Mt 21: 18.*

ἐπαναμιμνῄσκω remind again Ro 15: 15.*

ἐπαναπαύομαι rest Lk 10: 6; find rest or support in, rely on Ro 2: 17.*

ἐπανέρχομαι return Lk 10: 35; 19: 15.*

ἐπανίστημι rise up in rebellion Mt 10: 21; Mk 13: 12.*

ἐπανόρθωσις, εως, ἡ correcting, improvement 2 Ti 3: 16.*

ἐπάνω adv. above, over Lk 11: 44; more than Mk 14: 5; 1 Cor 15: 6. As improper prep. w. gen. over, above, on Mt 2: 9; 5: 14; 23: 18, 20, 22; Lk 19: 17, 19; J 3: 31; Rv 20: 3. ἐ. αὐτῆς at her head Lk 4: 39.

ἐπάξας 1 aor. act. ptc. of ἐπάγω.

ἐπᾶραι, ἐπάρας, ἐπάρατε 1 aor. act. inf., ptc., imperative of ἐπαίρω.

ἐπάρατος, ον accursed J 7: 49.*

ἐπαρκέω help, aid w. dat. 1 Ti 5: 10, 16.*

ἐπαρχεία, ας, ἡ province Ac 23: 34; 25: 1 v.l.*

ἐπάρχειος, ον belonging to an eparch ἡ ἐπάρχειος the province Ac 25: 1.*

ἐπαρχικός, ή, όν pertaining to the eparch or prefect Phlm subscr.

ἔπαυλις, εως, ἡ farm, homestead, residence Ac 1: 20.*

ἐπαύριον adv. tomorrow τῇ ἐ. on the next day Mk 11: 12; J 1: 29, 35, 43; Ac 20: 7; 25: 6, 23. εἰς τὴν ἐ. Ac 4: 3 v.l.

'Επαφρᾶς, ᾶ, ὁ Epaphras Col 1: 7; 4: 12; Phlm 23.*

ἐπαφρίζω cause to splash up like foam Jd 13.*

'Επαφρόδιτος, ου, ὁ Epaphroditus Phil 2: 25; 4: 18.*

ἐπέβην 2 aor. act. ind. of ἐπιβαίνω.

ἐπεγείρω *rouse up* fig. *arouse, excite, stir up* Ac 13: 50; 14: 2.*

ἐπεί conj.—**1.** *when, after* Lk 7: 1 v.l.—**2.** *because, since, for* Mt 18: 32; Mk 15: 42; Lk 1: 34; J 19: 31; 1 Cor 14: 12; 2 Cor 13: 3; Hb 5: 2, 11; *for otherwise* Ro 3: 6; 1 Cor 14: 16; Hb 10: 2.

ἐπειδή conj.—**1.** *when, after* Lk 7: 1.—**2.** *since, since then, because* Lk 11: 6; Ac 15: 24; 1 Cor 14: 16; 15: 21.

ἐπειδήπερ conj. *inasmuch as, since* Lk 1: 1.*

ἐπεῖδον 2 aor. of ἐφοράω *fix one's glance upon, look at, concern oneself* (*with*) Lk 1: 25; Ac 4: 29.*

ἔπειμι (from εἶμι) ptc. ἐπιών, ἐπιοῦσα, ἐπιόν; τῇ ἐπιούσῃ ἡμέρᾳ *on the next day* Ac 7: 26; cf. 16: 11; 20: 15; 21: 18; 23: 11. τῷ ἐπιόντι σαββάτῳ Ac 18: 19 v.l.*

ἐπείπερ conj. *since indeed* Ro 3: 30 v.l.*

ἔπεισα 1 aor. act. ind. of πείθω.

ἐπεισαγωγή, ῆς, ἡ *bringing in, introduction* Hb 7: 19.*

ἐπεισέρχομαι *rush in suddenly* Lk 21: 35.*

ἔπειτα adv. *then, thereupon* Lk 16: 7; 1 Cor 12: 28; 15: 46; Gal 1: 21; 1 Th 4: 17; Hb 7: 2, 27; Js 3: 17.

ἐπέκεινα adv. *farther on, beyond* w. gen. Ac 7: 43.*

ἐπεκλήθην 1 aor. pass. ind. of ἐπικαλέω.

ἐπεκτείνομαι *stretch out, strain* w. dat. Phil 3: 13.*

ἐπελαθόμην 2 aor. mid. ind. of ἐπιλανθάνομαι.

ἐπενδύομαι *put on* (*in addition*) 2 Cor 5: 2, 4.*

ἐπενδύτης, ου, ὁ *outer garment, coat* J 21: 7.*

ἐπεποίθει pluperf. act. ind. of πείθω.

ἐπέρχομαι *come, come along, appear* Ac 14: 19. *Come on, approach*

Eph 2: 7. *Come upon* Lk 21: 26; Ac 8: 24; Js 5: 1; *from on high* Lk 1: 35; Ac 1: 8. *Come about* Ac 13: 40. *Attack* Lk 11: 22.*

ἐπερωτάω *ask* a question Mt 12: 10; 22: 46; Mk 9: 32; 10: 10; 12: 18; Lk 2: 46; Ac 5: 27; 1 Cor 14: 35. With two accusatives *ask someone about something* Mk 7: 17, but *ask someone for something* Mt 16: 1. *Inquire after* Ro 10: 20.

ἐπερώτημα, ατος, τό *request, appeal* or *pledge* 1 Pt 3: 21.*

ἔπεσα and ἔπεσον aor. act. ind. of πίπτω.

ἐπέστην 2 aor. act. ind. of ἐφίστημι.

ἐπετίθεσαν 3 pl. imperf. act. ind. of ἐπιτίθημι.

ἐπέτυχε 2 aor. act. ind. of ἐπιτυγχάνω.

ἐπέχω—**1.** trans. *hold fast* Phil 2: 16; Lk 4: 42 v.l.—**2.** intr. *hold toward, aim at; fix one's attention* Ac 3: 5; *take pains* 1 Ti 4: 16; *notice* Lk 14: 7. *Stop, stay* Ac 19: 22.*

ἐπήνεσα 1 aor. act. ind. of ἐπαινέω.

ἐπῆρα, ἐπήρθην 1 aor. act. and pass. ind. of ἐπαίρω.

ἐπηρεάζω *mistreat, abuse, revile* Lk 6: 28; 1 Pt 3: 16; Mt 5: 44 v.l.*

ἐπί prep. w. gen., dat. or acc.—
I. with the genitive—**1.** of place, lit. and fig. *on, upon* Mt 1: 11; Mk 4: 26; 6: 48f; Lk 17: 31, 34; 1 Cor 11: 10; Gal 3: 13. *At, near, by* Mt 21: 19; Lk 22: 30; J 21: 1; Ac 5: 23. *Before, in the presence of* Mk 13: 9; Ac 23: 30; 1 Cor 6: 1; 1 Ti 6: 13. *Over* of power, authority, control Lk 12: 42; Ac 6: 3; Ro 9: 5; Rv 5: 10; 17: 18; *in charge of* Ac 8: 27. *On the basis* or *evidence of* Mk 12: 14, 32; Ac 4: 27; 1 Ti 5: 19; Hb 7: 11.—**2.** of time *in the time of* Mt 1: 11; Mk 2: 26; Lk 3: 2; Ac 11: 28; Eph 1: 16;

Jd 18.—**II.** with the dative— **1.** of place, lit. and fig. *on, in, above* Mt 9: 16; 14: 8, 11; 16: 18; Mk 6: 39; Lk 23: 38; J 11: 38; Ac 3: 11; 27: 44. *Against* Lk 12: 52f. *At, near, by* Mk 13: 29; J 4: 6; Ac 3: 10; Rv 9: 14. *Over* of power, authority, control Mt 24: 47; Lk 12: 44. *To, in addition to* Lk 3: 20; 1 Cor 14: 16; 2 Cor 7: 13; Col 3: 14. *On, on the basis of* Lk 4: 4; 5: 5; Ac 3: 16; Ro 8: 20; Hb 8: 6. *At, because of, from, with* Mk 1: 22; Lk 1: 29; Ac 3: 10; 20: 38; Ro 16: 19; Phlm 7; Rv 12: 17; 18: 20. *About* J 12: 16; Hb 11: 4; Rv 22: 16. *For* Gal 5: 13; Eph 2: 10; 1 Th 4: 7; 2 Ti 2: 14.—**2.** of time *at, in, at the time of, during* 2 Cor 1: 4; Phil 1: 3; 2: 17; 1 Th 3: 7b; Hb 9: 15, 26. ἐπὶ τούτῳ *in the meanwhile* J 4: 27.— **III.** with the accusative—**1.** of place, lit. and fig., often with motion implied *across, over* Mt 14: 25, 28f; Lk 23: 44; Ac 11: 28. *On, upon* Mt 5: 45; 13: 5; Lk 6: 29; 23: 30; 1 Cor 14: 25; Rv 7: 11. *To, upon* Mt 22: 9; Ac 8: 26; Rv 7: 1. *To, up to, in the neighborhood of, on* Mt 3: 13; Mk 5: 21; Lk 22: 44; J 19: 33; 21: 20; *before* Lk 12: 58; Ac 25: 12. *To, toward* Mt 12: 49; 2 Pt 2: 22. *Against* with hostile intent Mt 10: 21; Mk 14: 48; Lk 11: 17f; Ac 13: 50. Simply *on, over* with no motion Mt 13: 2; Mk 4: 38; J 12: 15; 2 Cor 3: 15; Rv 4: 4. ἐπὶ τὸ αὐτό *at the same place, together* Lk 17: 35; Ac 1: 15, but *to the same place* with verbs of motion Mt 22: 34; 1 Cor 11: 20; 14: 23 and προσετίθει ἐπὶ τὸ αὐτό *he added to their number* Ac 2: 47. *Over* of power, rule, control Mt 25: 21, 23; Lk 1: 33; Ac 7: 10; Ro 5: 14; Rv 6: 8. *To, in addition to* Mt 6: 27; Lk 12: 25; Phil 2: 27. *On, upon, to, over*

Mt 12: 28; 27: 25; Lk 3: 2; 10: 6; J 1: 32f; Ac 2: 17f; 13: 11; Ro 2: 2, 9; 1 Pt 5: 7; Rv 11: 11. *In, on, for, toward* Mt 27: 43; Mk 9: 22; Ac 11: 17; Ro 4: 24; Eph 2: 7; Hb 6: 1; Rv 1: 7.— **2.** of time: time when *on, at* Lk 10: 35; Ac 3: 1; 4: 5. Of extension over a period *for, over a period of* Lk 4: 25; Ac 13: 31; 18: 20; 28: 6.

ἐπιβαίνω *go up* or *upon, mount, board* Mt 21: 5; Ac 27: 2; *go on board, embark* 21: 2. *Set foot (in)* Ac 20: 18; 25: 1.

ἐπιβάλλω—1. act., trans. *throw over* 1 Cor 7: 35. *Lay on, put on* Mt 9: 16; Mk 14: 46; Lk 9: 62; J 7: 44; Ac 21: 27.—**2.** act., intrans. *throw oneself, beat upon* Mk 4: 37. ἐπιβαλὼν ἔκλαιεν Mk 14: 72 most likely = *he began to weep* or *when he reflected on it, he wept.* *Fall to, belong to* Lk 15: 12.

ἐπιβαρέω *weigh down, burden* 1 Th 2: 9; 2 Th 3: 8. ἵνα μὴ ἐπιβαρῶ 2 Cor 2: 5 is probably 'in order not to heap up too great a burden of words' = *in order not to say too much.**

ἐπιβιβάζω *put on, cause to mount* Lk 10: 34; 19: 35; Ac 23: 24.*

ἐπιβλέπω *look at, consider, care about* Lk 1: 48; 9: 38; Js 2: 3.*

ἐπίβλημα, ατος, τό *a patch* Mt 9: 16; Mk 2: 21; Lk 5: 36.*

ἐπιβοάω *cry out loudly* Ac 25: 24 v.l.*

ἐπιβουλή, ῆς, ἡ *plot* Ac 9: 24; 20: 3, 19; 23: 30.*

ἐπιγαμβρεύω *marry as next of kin* Mt 22: 24.*

ἐπίγειος, ον *earthly* 1 Cor 15: 40; 2 Cor 5: 1; Phil 2: 10; 3: 19; Js 3: 15. τὰ ἐπίγεια *earthly things* J 3: 12.*

ἐπιγίνομαι *come up* Ac 28: 13; *come on* 27: 27 v.l.*

ἐπιγινώσκω—1. *know exactly, completely* Lk 1: 4; Ro 1: 32; 1 Cor 13: 12; Col 1: 6. *Know again,*

recognize Lk 24: 16, 31; Ac 12: 14.
Acknowledge Mt 17: 12; 1 Cor
16: 18.—**2.** *know* Mt 7: 16, 20;
Mk 6: 54; 1 Ti 4: 3. *Learn, find
out* Mk 6: 33; Lk 7: 37; Ac 28: 1.
Ascertain 23: 28; 24: 11. *Notice,
perceive, learn of* Mk 5: 30; Ac
9: 30. *Understand, know* Ac
25: 10; 2 Cor 1: 13f. *Learn to
know* 2 Pt 2: 21b.

ἐπίγνωσις, εως, ἡ *knowledge* Col 1:
9f; 1 Ti 2: 4; Tit 1: 1; Phlm 6;
Hb 10: 26; 2 Pt 1: 2; *consciousness* Ro 3: 20. ἔχειν ἐν ἐ.
recognize 1: 28.

ἐπιγραφή, ῆς, ἡ *inscription, superscription* Mt 22: 20; Mk 12: 16;
15: 26; Lk 20: 24; 23: 38.*

ἐπιγράφω *write on* or *in, inscribe*
Mk 15: 26; Ac 17: 23; Rv 21: 12;
fig. Hb 8: 10; 10: 16.*

ἔπιδε 2 aor. act. imperative of
ἐπεῖδον, which is in turn the 2
aor. of ἐφοράω.

ἐπιδείκνυμι *show, point out* Mt 16:
1; 22: 19; 24: 1; Lk 17: 14; Ac
9: 39. *Demonstrate, show* Ac
18: 28; Hb 6: 17.*

ἐπιδέχομαι *receive as a guest* 3 J
10; *accept, recognize* 3 J 9. *Take
along* Ac 15: 40 v.l.*

ἐπιδημέω *stay in a place as a
stranger* or *visitor, be in town* Ac
2: 10; 17: 21; 18: 27 v.l.*

ἐπιδιατάσσομαι *add a codicil to*
Gal 3: 15.*

ἐπιδίδωμι *give, hand over, deliver*
Mt 7: 9f; Lk 4: 17; 24: 30, 42;
Ac 15: 30; *give up* 27: 15.

ἐπιδιορθόω *correct* (*in addition*)
Tit 1: 5.*

ἐπιδύω *set* Eph 4: 26.*

ἐπιείκεια, ας, ἡ *gentleness, graciousness, clemency* Ac 24: 4;
2 Cor 10: 1.*

ἐπιεικής, ές *gentle, kind, yielding*
1 Ti 3: 3; Tit 3: 2; Js 3: 17; 1 Pt
2: 18. τὸ ἐπιεικές = ἡ ἐπιείκεια Phil
4: 5.*

ἐπιεικία another spelling for ἐπιείκεια.

ἐπιζητέω *search for, seek after*
Lk 4: 42; Ac 12: 19; *want to
know* 19: 39. *Wish* (*for*) Mt 6: 32;
Phil 4: 17; Hb 13: 14. *Demand,
desire* Mt 12: 39; 16: 4.

ἐπιθανάτιος, ον *condemned to
death* 1 Cor 4: 9.*

ἐπίθες 2 aor. act. imperative of
ἐπιτίθημι.

ἐπίθεσις, εως, ἡ *laying on* Ac 8:
18; 1 Ti 4: 14; 2 Ti 1: 6; Hb 6:
2.*

ἐπιθυμέω *desire, long for* w. gen. or
acc. Mt 5: 28; Ac 20: 33; Gal
5: 17; 1 Ti 3: 1; Hb 6: 11;
Rv 9: 6. ἐπιθυμίᾳ ἐπιθυμεῖν *eagerly
desire* Lk 22: 15.

ἐπιθυμητής, οῦ, ὁ *one who desires*
ἐ. κακῶν *desirous of evil* 1 Cor
10: 6.*

ἐπιθυμία, ας, ἡ *desire, longing* Mk
4: 19; Lk 22: 15; Gal 5: 24; Phil
1: 23; Col 3: 5; 1 Th 2: 17; 4: 5;
Js 1: 14f; *craving* Gal 5: 16. ἐ.
μιασμοῦ *defiling passion* 2 Pt
2: 10.

ἐπιθύω *offer a sacrifice* Ac 14: 13
v.l.*

ἐπικαθίζω *sit* or *sit down* (*on*) Mt
21: 7.*

ἐπικαλέω—1. act. and pass. *call,
name, give a name* or *surname
to* Mt 10: 25; Ac 1: 23; 12: 12;
Hb 11: 16. ἐφ' οὓς ἐπικέκληται
τὸ ὄνομα *upon whom the name
has been invoked* (to indicate
that the persons involved belong
to the one named) Ac 15: 17.—
2. mid. *call upon someone for
aid* Ac 2: 21; Ro 10: 12f; 1 Cor
1: 2; 2 Cor 1: 23; 2 Ti 2: 22; 1
Pt 1: 17. *Appeal to* Ac 25: 11f,
21, 25.

ἐπικάλυμμα, ατος, τό *covering,
veil* 1 Pt 2: 16.*

ἐπικαλύπτω *cover* Ro 4: 7.*

ἐπικατάρατος, ον *cursed* Gal 3:
10, 13; Lk 6: 5 v.l.*

ἐπίκειμαι—1. *lie upon* lit. J 11:
38; 21: 9; fig. Ac 27: 20; 1 Cor
9: 16.—**2.** *press around, press*

upon, be urgent Lk 5: 1; 23: 23. *Be imposed* Hb 9: 10.*

ἐπικέλλω *bring to shore, run aground* Ac 27: 41.*

ἐπικερδαίνω *gain in addition* Mt 25: 20 v.l.; 22 v.l.*

ἐπικεφάλαιον, ου, τό *poll tax* Mk 12: 14 v.l.*

ἐπικληθείς 1 aor. pass. ptc. of ἐπικαλέω.

'Επικούρειος, ου, ὁ *an Epicurean* Ac 17: 18.*

ἐπικουρία, ας, ἡ *help* Ac 26: 22.*

ἐπικράνθη 1 aor. pass. ind. of πικραίνω.

ἐπικράζω *shout threats* Ac 16: 39 v.l.*

ἐπικρίνω *decide, determine* Lk 23: 24.*

ἐπιλαμβάνομαι—1. *take hold of, grasp, catch* w. gen. or acc. Mt 14: 31; Mk 8: 23; Lk 9: 47; 14: 4; Ac 17: 19; 18: 17.—2. fig. *catch* Lk 20: 20, 26; *take hold of* 1 Ti 6: 12; *be concerned with, take an interest in, help* Hb 2: 16.

ἐπιλάμπω *shine out, shine forth* Ac 12: 7 v.l.*

ἐπιλανθάνομαι *forget* Mk 8: 14; Phil 3: 13; Js 1: 24. *Neglect, overlook* Lk 12: 6; Hb 13: 2, 16.

ἐπιλέγω pass. *be called* or *named* J 5: 2; mid. *choose, select* Ac 15: 40.*

ἐπιλείπω *leave behind*, hence *fail* in Hb 11: 32.*

ἐπιλείχω *lick* Lk 16: 21.*

ἐπιλελησμένος perf. mid. and pass. ptc. of ἐπιλανθάνομαι.

ἐπιλησμονή, ῆς, ἡ *forgetfulness* ἀκροατὴς ἐπιλησμονῆς *a forgetful hearer* Js 1: 25.*

ἐπίλοιπος, ον *left, remaining* 1 Pt 4: 2; Lk 24: 43 v.l.*

ἐπίλυσις, εως, ἡ *explanation, interpretation* 2 Pt 1: 20.*

ἐπιλύω *explain, interpret* Mk 4: 34; *decide, settle* pass. Ac 19: 39.*

ἐπιμαρτυρέω *bear witness* 1 Pt 5: 12.*

ἐπιμέλεια, ας, ἡ *care, attention* Ac 27: 3.*

ἐπιμελέομαι *care for, take care of* w. gen. Lk 10: 34f; 1 Ti 3: 5.*

ἐπιμελῶς adv. *carefully, diligently* Lk 15: 8.*

ἐπιμένω—1. *stay, remain* Ac 10: 48; 21: 4; 1 Cor 16: 8; Gal 1: 18. —2. *continue, persist (in), persevere* w. dat. Ro 6: 1; 11: 22; Col 1: 23. With participle following *keep on, persist in doing something* J 8: 7; Ac 12: 16.

ἐπινεύω *give consent* (by a nod) Ac 18: 20.*

ἐπίνοια, ας, ἡ *thought, intent* Ac 8: 22.*

ἐπιορκέω *swear falsely* or *break one's oath* Mt 5: 33.*

ἐπίορκος, ον *perjured* as noun *perjurer* 1 Ti 1: 10.*

ἐπιοῦσα, ης, ἡ *the next day* see ἔπειμι.

ἐπιούσιος, ον an extremely rare word of uncertain meaning; among the possibilities are *daily*; *necessary for existence*; *for the following day*; *for the future.* Found in the NT only Mt 6: 11; Lk 11: 3.*

ἐπιπίπτω—1. *fall upon, approach eagerly* often w. dat. Mk 3: 10; Ac 20: 10, 37.—2. *come upon* Lk 1: 12; Ac 8: 16; 10: 44; 19: 17; Ro 15: 3.

ἐπιπλήσσω *strike at, reprove, rebuke* 1 Ti 5: 1.*

ἐπιποθέω *long for, desire* Ro 1: 11; 2 Cor 9: 14; Phil 1: 8; 1 Th 3: 6; 1 Pt 2: 2.

ἐπιπόθησις, εως, ἡ *longing* 2 Cor 7: 7, 11.*

ἐπιπόθητος, ον *longed for* Phil 4: 1.*

ἐπιποθία, ας, ἡ *longing, desire* Ro 15: 23.*

ἐπιπορεύομαι *go* or *journey (to)* Lk 8: 4.*

ἐπι(ρ)ράπτω *sew (on)* Mk 2: 21.*

ἐπι(ρ)ρίπτω *throw, cast* Lk 19: 35; 1 Pt 5: 7.*

ἐπισείω urge on, incite Ac 14: 19 v.l.*

ἐπίσημος, ον prominent, outstanding Ro 16: 7. Notorious Mt 27: 16.*

ἐπισιτισμός, οῦ, ὁ food, something to eat Lk 9: 12.*

ἐπισκέπτομαι—1. look for, select Ac 6: 3.—2. go to see, visit Mt 25: 36; Ac 7: 23; 15: 36; look after Js 1: 27.—3. visit for the purpose of bringing salvation Lk 1: 68; 7: 16; be concerned about Ac 15: 14.

ἐπισκευάζομαι make preparations Ac 21: 15.*

ἐπισκηνόω take up one's abode 2 Cor 12: 9.*

ἐπισκιάζω cast a shadow, overshadow Mt 17: 5; Lk 1: 35; Ac 5: 15.

ἐπισκοπέω take care, see to it Hb 12: 15. Oversee, care for 1 Pt 5: 2 v.l.*

ἐπισκοπή, ῆς, ἡ—1. visitation: favorable Lk 19: 44; favorable or unfavorable 1 Pt 2: 12.—2. position or office as an overseer Ac 1: 20; office of a bishop 1 Ti 3: 1.*

ἐπίσκοπος, ου, ὁ overseer, guardian 1 Pt 2: 25. Superintendent, bishop Ac 20: 28; Phil 1: 1; 1 Ti 3: 2; Tit 1: 7.*

ἐπισπάομαι pull over the foreskin to conceal circumcision 1 Cor 7: 18.*

ἐπισπείρω sow (afterward) Mt 13: 25.*

ἐπίσταμαι understand Mk 14: 68; 1 Ti 6: 4. Know, be acquainted with Ac 15: 7; 19: 15; 26: 26; Hb 11: 8; Jd 10.

ἐπίστασις, εως, ἡ attack, onset Ac 24: 12. For 2 Cor 11: 28 pressure is probably best; other possibilities are attention, oversight, hindrance.*

ἐπιστάτης, ου, vocative ἐπιστάτα, ὁ master Lk 5: 5; 8: 24, 45; 9: 33, 49; 17: 13.*

ἐπιστέλλω inform or instruct by letter, write Ac 15: 20; 21: 25; Hb 13: 22.*

ἐπιστῇ, ἐπίστηθι 2 aor. subj. and imperative act. of ἐφίστημι.

ἐπιστήμη, ης, ἡ understanding, knowledge Phil 4: 8 v.l.*

ἐπιστήμων, ον, gen. ονος expert, learned, understanding Js 3: 13.*

ἐπιστηρίζω strengthen Ac 14: 22; 15: 32, 41; 11: 2 v.l.; 18: 23 v.l.*

ἐπιστολή, ῆς, ἡ letter, epistle Ac 9: 2; 23: 25; Ro 16: 22; 1 Cor 5: 9; 2 Cor 3: 1; 10: 9; 1 Th 5: 27.

ἐπιστομίζω stop the mouth of, silence Tit 1: 11.*

ἐπιστρέφω turn lit. and fig. Lk 1: 16; Js 5: 20; turn around Mk 5: 30; turn back, return Mt 10: 13; 12: 44. Be converted J 12: 40 v.l.

ἐπιστροφή, ῆς, ἡ conversion, lit. 'turning' Ac 15: 3.*

ἐπισυνάγω gather (together) Mt 23: 37; Mk 13: 27; Lk 17: 37.

ἐπισυναγωγή, ῆς, ἡ meeting Hb 10: 25; assembling 2 Th 2: 1.*

ἐπισυντρέχω run together Mk 9: 25.*

ἐπισυρράπτω for ἐπι(ρ)ράπτω (q.v.) Mk 2: 21 v.l.*

ἐπισύστασις, εως, ἡ uprising, disturbance, insurrection Ac 24: 12 v.l. 2 Cor 11: 28 v.l.*

ἐπισφαλής, ές unsafe, dangerous Ac 27: 9.*

ἐπισχύω insist Lk 23: 5.*

ἐπισωρεύω accumulate 2 Ti 4: 3.*

ἐπιταγή, ῆς, ἡ command, order 1 Cor 7: 25; authority Tit 2: 15. κατ' ἐπιταγήν by command Ro 16: 26; 1 Ti 1: 1; Tit 1: 3. κατ' ἐπιταγὴν λέγειν say as a command 1 Cor 7: 6; 2 Cor 8: 8.*

ἐπιτάσσω order, command with dat. Mk 1: 27; 6: 39; Lk 8: 25; Ac 23: 2; Phlm 8. Without dat. order, give orders Mk 6: 27; Lk 14: 22.

ἐπιτελέω—1. end, finish Ro 15: 28; 2 Cor 8: 6, 11.—2. complete,

perform, bring about 2 Cor 7: 1;
Hb 9: 6; *erect* 8: 5; *lay upon* 1
Pt 5: 9.

ἐπιτήδειος, εία, ον *necessary, suitable* Ac 24: 25 v.l. As noun τὰ ἐ.
what is necessary Js 2: 16.*

ἐπιτίθει pres: act. imperative of
ἐπιτίθημι.

ἐπιτίθημι *lay* or *put upon* Mt
9: 18; 27: 29, 37; Mk 8: 23;
J 9: 6, 15; Ac 19: 6; 1 Ti 5: 22.
Inflict Ac 16: 23. *Bring upon,
add* Rv 22: 18. *Give* Mk 3: 16f;
Ac 28: 10. *Set upon, attack* 18: 10.

ἐπιτιμάω *rebuke, censure, warn*
Mt 8: 26; 16: 20; Mk 8: 30;
10: 13; Lk 18: 15, 39; 23: 40.
In Jd 9 the meaning could be
rebuke or *punish*.

ἐπιτιμία, ας, ἡ *punishment* 2 Cor
2: 6.*

ἐπιτρέπω *allow, permit* w. dat.
Mt 8: 21; Mk 10: 4; Lk 9: 59,
61; Ac 27: 3; 1 Ti 2: 12; *give
permission* Mk 5: 13; J 19: 38;
1 Cor 16: 7; Hb 6: 3.

ἐπιτροπεύω *be procurator, governor*
Lk 3: 1 v.l.*

ἐπιτροπή, ῆς, ἡ *permission, full
power* Ac 26: 12.*

ἐπίτροπος, ου, ὁ *manager, foreman,
steward* Mt 20: 8 and perhaps
Lk 8: 3, where the mng. may
also be *governor, procurator.
Guardian* Gal 4: 2.*

ἐπιτυγχάνω *obtain, attain to, reach*
w. gen Hb 6: 15; 11: 33; w.
acc. Ro 11: 7; abs. Ac 13: 29
v.l.; Js 4: 2.*

ἐπιτυχεῖν 2 aor. inf. act. of ἐπιτυγχάνω.

ἐπιφαίνω act. and pass. *appear,
make an appearance, show oneself* Lk 1: 79; Ac 27: 20; Tit 2:
11; 3: 4.*

ἐπιφάνεια, ας, ἡ *appearing, appearance, epiphany* 2 Th 2: 8; 1 Ti
6: 14; 2 Ti 1: 10; 4: 1, 8; Tit
2: 13.*

ἐπιφανής, ές *splendid, glorious* Ac
2: 20.*

ἐπιφαύσκω *arise, appear, shine*
Eph 5: 14.*

ἐπιφαύσω fut. act. ind. of ἐπιφαύσκω.

ἐπιφέρω *bring over* or *upon* Ac 19:
12 v.l. *Bring, pronounce* Ac
25: 18 v.l.; Jd 9. *Inflict* Ro 3: 5.*

ἐπιφωνέω *cry out (loudly)* Lk 23: 21;
Ac 12: 22; 21: 34; 22: 24.*

ἐπιφώσκω *shine forth, dawn, break*
perhaps *draw on* Mt 28: 1;
Lk 23: 54.*

ἐπιχειρέω *set one's hand to,
attempt, try* Lk 1: 1; Ac 9: 29;
19: 13.*

ἐπιχείρησις, εως, ἡ *attempt, attack*
Ac 12: 3 v.l.*

ἐπιχέω *pour over, pour on* Lk 10:
34.*

ἐπιχορηγέω *furnish, provide* 2 Pt
1: 5. *Give, grant* 2 Cor 9: 10;
Gal 3: 5; 2 Pt 1: 11. *Support* Col
2: 19.*

ἐπιχορηγία, ας, ἡ *support* Eph
4: 16; Phil 1: 19.*

ἐπιχρίω *spread* or *smear* (*on*) J 9:
6 v.l.; *anoint* 9: 11.*

ἐπιψαύω *touch, grasp, attain to*
w. gen. Eph 5: 14 v.l.*

ἐπλήγην 2 aor. pass. of πλήσσω.

ἔπλησα 1 aor. act. ind. of πίμπλημι.

ἐποικοδομέω *build* (*on, upon*) fig.
1 Cor 3: 10, 12, 14; Eph 2: 20;
Col 2: 7; Jd 20; Ac 20: 32 v.l.;
1 Pt 2: 5 v.l.*

ἐποκέλλω *run aground* Ac 27: 41
v.l.*

ἐπονομάζω *call, name* Ro 2: 17.*

ἐποπτεύω *observe, see* 1 Pt 2: 12;
3: 2.*

ἐπόπτης, ου, ὁ *eyewitness* 2 Pt 1:
16.*

ἔπος, ους, τό *word* ὡς ἔ. ἐιπεῖν *so
to speak, one might almost say,*
perhaps *to use just the right word*
Hb 7: 9.*

ἐπουράνιος, ον *heavenly, celestial*
1 Cor 15: 40, 48f; Eph 1: 3,
20; Phil 2: 10; Hb 3: 1; 8: 5.

ἐπράθην 1 aor. pass. of πιπράσκω.

ἐπρίσθην 1 aor. pass. of πρίζω.

ἑπτά indecl. *seven* Mt 12: 45; Mk 8: 5f; Lk 20: 29; Ac 6: 3; Rv 1: 4, 11; 16: 1; 17: 9.

ἑπτάκις adv. *seven times* Mt 18: 21f; Lk 17: 4.*

ἑπτακισχίλιοι, αι, α *seven thousand* Ro 11: 4.*

ἑπταπλασίων, ον, gen. ονος *sevenfold* Lk 18: 30 v.l.*

ἐπύθετο 3 sing. 2 aor. ind. of πυνθάνομαι.

Ἔραστος, ου, ὁ *Erastus*—1. Ro 16: 23.—2. Ac 19: 22; 2 Ti 4: 20.*

ἐραυνάω *search, examine, investigate* J 5: 39; 7: 52; Ro 8: 27; 1 Cor 2: 10; 1 Pt 1: 11; Rv 2: 23.*

ἐργάζομαι—1. intr. *work, be active* Mt 21: 28; 25: 16; Ro 4: 4f; 1 Cor 4: 12; 9: 6; 1 Th 2: 9.— 2. trans. *do, accomplish, carry out* Mt 26: 10; J 3: 21; 6: 28; Ac 13: 41; Ro 2: 10; 13: 10; 1 Cor 16: 10; Gal 6: 10; 2 Th 3: 11. *Practise, perform* 1 Cor 9: 13. *Bring about, give rise to* 2 Cor 7: 10; Js 1: 20. *Work (on)* Rv 18: 17. *Work for, earn* or *prepare, assimilate* J 6: 27.

ἐργασία, ας, ἡ *practice, pursuit* Eph 4: 19. *Trade, business* Ac 19: 25. *Profit, gain* 16: 16, 19; 19: 24. δὸς ἐργασίαν *take pains* Lk 12: 58.*

ἐργάτης, ου, ὁ *workman, laborer* lit. Mt 9: 37f; 20: 1f, 8; Ac 19: 25; 1 Ti 5: 18; Js 5: 4. Fig. 2 Cor 11: 13; Phil 3: 2; 2 Ti 2: 15. *A doer, one who does* Lk 13: 27.

ἔργον, ου, τό *work*—1. *deed, action* Lk 24: 19; Col 3: 17; 2 Th 2: 17; Hb 4: 3, 4, 10; Js 2: 14ff. *Manifestation, practical proof, practice* Ro 2: 15; Eph 4: 12; 1 Th 1: 3; 2 Th 1: 11; Js 1: 4. *Deed, accomplishment* Mt 11: 2; Mk 14: 6; Lk 11: 48; J 3: 19, 20f; 6: 28f; 7: 3, 21; 10: 25, 37f; Ac 9: 36; Ro 3: 20, 28;

Col 1: 10; Hb 6: 1; Js 3: 13; Rv 15: 3.—2. *work, occupation, task* Mk 13: 34; J 17: 4; Ac 14: 26; 15: 38; 1 Cor 15: 58; 2 Ti 4: 5.—3. *work* in the passive sense, indicating what is produced by work Ac 7: 41; 1 Cor 3: 13, 14, 15; Hb 1: 10; 2 Pt 3: 10; 1 J 3: 8.—4. *thing, matter* Ac 5: 38; perhaps 1 Ti 3: 1.

ἐρεθίζω *arouse, provoke* in a good sense 2 Cor 9: 2; in a bad sense *irritate, embitter* Col 3: 21.*

ἐρείδω *jam fast* Ac 27: 41.*

ἐρεύγομαι *utter, proclaim* Mt 13: 35.*

ἐρευννάω classical form of ἐραυνάω.

ἐρημία, ας, ἡ *uninhabited region, desert* Mt 15: 33; Mk 8: 4; 2 Cor 11: 26; Hb 11: 38.*

ἔρημος, ον—1. as adj. *abandoned, empty, desolate* Mt 14: 13, 15; Mk 1: 35, 45; Ac 1: 20; *lonely* 8: 26. *Deserted, desolate* Gal 4: 27.—2. as noun ἡ ἔρημος *desert, grassland, wilderness* Mt 24: 26; Mk 1: 4; Lk 15: 4; J 11: 54; Ac 7: 30; 21: 38; Rv 12: 6, 14. *Lonely places* Lk 1: 80.

ἐρημόω *lay waste, depopulate* Mt 12: 25; Lk 11: 17; Rv 17: 16; 18: 19. *Ruin* Rv 18: 17.*

ἐρήμωσις, εως, ἡ *devastation, destruction* Mt 24: 15; Mk 13: 14; Lk 21: 20.*

ἐρίζω *quarrel, wrangle* Mt 12: 19.*

ἐριθεία, ας, ἡ *strife* or *selfish ambition* Ro 2: 8; 2 Cor 12: 20; Gal 5: 20; Phil 1: 17; 2: 3; Js 3: 14, 16.*

ἐριμμένος perf. pass. ptc. of ῥίπτω.

ἔριον, ου, τό *wool* Hb 9: 19; Rv 1: 14.*

ἔρις, ιδος, ἡ *strife, discord, contention* Ro 1: 29; 1 Cor 3: 3; Gal 5: 20; Phil 1: 15; Tit 3: 9. Pl. *quarrels* 1 Cor 1: 11.

ἐρίφιον, ου, τό *goat,* lit. 'kid' Mt 25: 33; Lk 15: 29 v.l.*

ἔριφος, ου, ὁ *kid* Lk 15: 29; *goat* Mt 25: 32.*

Ἑρμᾶς, ᾶ, ὁ *Hermas* Ro 16: 14.*

ἑρμηνεία, ας, ἡ *translation, interpretation* 1 Cor 12: 10; 14: 26.*

ἑρμηνευτής, οῦ, ὁ *translator* 1 Cor 14: 28 v.l.*

ἑρμηνεύω *explain, interpret* Lk 24: 27 v.l. *Translate* J 1: 38 v.l., 42; 9: 7; Hb 7: 2.*

Ἑρμῆς, οῦ, ὁ *Hermes*—1. the Greek god Ac 14: 12.—2. recipient of a greeting Ro 16: 14.*

Ἑρμογένης, ους, ὁ *Hermogenes* 2 Ti 1: 15.*

ἑρπετόν, οῦ, τό *reptile* Ac 10: 12; 11: 6; Ro 1: 23; Js 3: 7.*

ἐρρέθην 1 aor. pass. ind. of εἶπον.

ἔ(ρ)ρηξα 1 aor. act. ind. of ῥήγνυμι.

ἐ(ρ)ριμμένος perf. mid. and pass. ptc. of ῥίπτω.

ἔρρωσο perf. pass. imperative of ῥώννυμι.

ἐρυθρός, ά, όν *red* Ac 7: 36; Hb 11: 29.*

ἔρχομαι—1. *come*—a. in a literal sense Mt 8: 9; Mk 7: 1, 31; Lk 19: 5; J 10: 10; Ac 16: 37, 39; Ro 9: 9; 2 Cor 13: 1; Hb 6: 7; Rv 18: 10. *Appear, come before the public* Mt 21: 9; Mk 9: 11; Lk 3: 16; 7: 33; J 7: 27, 31; Ac 1: 11; 1 Cor 4: 5; 1 Ti 1: 15.— b. in a non-literal sense Mt 23: 35; Lk 15: 17; J 18: 4; Eph 5: 6. ἔ. ἐκ τ. θλίψεως *have suffered persecution* Rv 7: 14. ἔ. εἰς κρίσιν *submit to judgment* J 5: 24. εἰς προκοπήν *result in furthering* Phil 1: 12.—2. *go* Mt 16: 24; Mk 11: 13; Lk 15: 20; J 21: 3.

ἐρῶ fut. act. ind of εἶπον.

ἐρωτάω—1. *ask, ask a question* Mt 21: 24; Mk 4: 10; Lk 22: 68; J 8: 7.—2. *ask, request* Mt 15: 23; Lk 14: 32; J 14: 16; Ac 10: 48; Phil 4: 3; 2 Th 2: 1; *beseech* Lk 4: 38.

ἔσβεσα 1 aor. act. ind. of σβέννυμι.

ἐσθής, ῆτος, ἡ *clothing* Lk 23: 11; 24: 4; Ac 1: 10; 10: 30; 12: 21; Js 2: 2, 3. The dat. pl. ἐσθήσεσι (Ac 1: 10; Lk 24: 4 v.l.) is not from a separate form ἔσθησις, but is the result of doubling the dat. ending.*

ἐσθίω and ἔσθω *eat*—1. lit. Mt 15: 32; Mk 2: 26; 7: 28; Lk 22: 30; Ac 10: 14; Ro 14: 2; 1 Cor 10: 25, 27; 2 Th 3: 12; Rv 19: 18; *get sustenance* 1 Cor 9: 7.—2. fig. *consume, devour* Hb 10: 27; Js 5: 3.

ἐσήμανα 1 aor. act. ind. of σημαίνω.

ἐσκυλμένος perf. pass. ptc. of σκύλλω.

Ἐσλί, ὁ indecl. *Esli* Lk 3: 25.*

ἐσόμενος fut. ptc. of εἰμί.

ἔσοπτρον, ου, τό *mirror* 1 Cor 13: 12; Js 1: 23.*

ἐσπαρμένος perf. pass. ptc. of σπείρω.

ἑσπέρα, ας, ἡ *evening* Lk 24: 29; Ac 4: 3; 20: 15; 28: 23.*

ἑσπερινός, ή, όν *of or pertaining to the evening* φυλακή six to nine p.m. Lk 12: 38 v.l.*

Ἑσρώμ, ὁ indecl. *Hezron* Mt 1: 3; Lk 3: 33.*

ἑσσόομαι *be defeated, be overpowered, be worse off* 2 Cor 12: 13 v.l.*

ἑστάναι, ἑστώς perf. act. inf. and ptc. of ἵστημι.

ἐστρωμένος, ἔστρωσα perf. pass. ptc. and 1 aor. act. ind. of στρώννυμι.

ἔστωσαν 3 pl. imperative of εἰμί.

ἐσφάγην, ἐσφαγμένος, ἔσφαξα 2 aor. pass. ind., perf. pass. ptc., 1 aor. act. ind. of σφάζω.

ἔσχατος, η, ον *last.* Of place Lk 14: 9f. τὸ ἔσχατον *the end* Ac 1: 8; 13: 47. Of rank and succession *last, least, most insignificant* Mt 20: 16; Lk 13: 30; 1 Cor 4: 9. Of time *least, last* Mt 20: 8, 12, 14; J 6: 39f; 7: 37; Ac 2: 17; 1 Cor 15: 26, 45, 52; 2 Ti 3: 1; Js 5: 3; Rv 2: 19.

ἐσχάτως adv. *finally* ἐ. ἔχειν *be at the point of death* Mk 5: 23.*

ἔσω *in, into* Mt 26: 58; Mk 14: 54. *Inside, within* J 20: 26; Ac 5: 23; 1 Cor 5: 12; *inner* Ro 7: 22; 2 Cor 4: 16.

ἔσωθεν adv. *from inside* Mk 7: 21, 23; Lk 11: 7. *Inside, within* Mt 23: 25, 27f; 2 Cor 7: 5. τὸ ἔ. ὑμῶν *your inner nature* Lk 11: 39.

ἐσώτερος, α, ον *inner* Ac 16: 24. τὸ ἐσώτερον *what is inside* (=behind) Hb 6: 19.*

ἑταῖρος, ου, ὁ *comrade, companion, friend* Mt 11: 16 v.l.; 20: 13; 22: 12; 26: 50.*

ἐτάφην 2 aor. pass. ind. of θάπτω.

ἔτεκον 2 aor. act. ind. of τίκτω.

ἑτερόγλωσσος, ον *speaking a foreign language* 1 Cor 14: 21.*

ἑτεροδιδασκαλέω *teach a different* (i.e. *heretical*) *doctrine* 1 Ti 1: 3; 6: 3.*

ἑτεροζυγέω *be unevenly yoked, be mismated* 2 Cor 6: 14.*

ἕτερος, α, ον *other* of two Lk 5: 7; 7: 41; 18: 10; Ac 23: 6; 1 Cor 4: 6. Of more than two Mt 11: 3; 12: 45; J 19: 37; Ac 15: 35; Ro 2: 1, 21; 1 Cor 12: 9f; used interchangeably with ἄλλος Gal 1: 6f; 2 Cor 11: 4. *Next* Ac 20: 15. *Another, different* Mk 16: 12; Ro 7: 23; 1 Cor 15: 40.

ἑτέρως adv. *differently, otherwise* Phil 3: 15.*

ἐτέχθην 1 aor. pass. ind. of τίκτω.

ἔτι adv. *yet, still* Mt 12: 46; Lk 14: 32; 15: 20; Ro 9: 19; Gal 1: 10; Rv 9: 12. *Again* 2 Cor 1: 10; Hb 12: 26f; *further* Mk 14: 63; Hb 7: 11; *other* Mt 18: 16.

ἐτίθει 3 sing. imperf. act. ind. of τίθημι.

ἑτοιμάζω *put* or *keep in readiness, prepare* Mt 22: 4; 25: 34, 41; Mk 1: 3; Lk 22: 13; J 14: 2f; Rv 9: 7; 21: 2; *make preparations* Lk 9: 52.

ἑτοιμασία, ας, ἡ *readiness, preparation, equipment* Eph 6: 15.*

Ἕτοιμας v.l. for Ἐλύμας in Ac 13: 8.*

ἕτοιμος, η, ον *ready, prepared* Mt 22: 4; 25: 10; Mk 14: 15; J 7: 6; Ac 23: 15, 21; 2 Cor 9: 5; 1 Pt 1: 5. τὰ ἕτοιμα *what has been accomplished* 2 Cor 10: 16. ἐν ἑτοίμῳ ἔχειν *be ready* 10: 6.

ἑτοίμως adv. *readily* ἑ. ἔχειν *be ready, be willing* Ac 21: 13; 2 Cor 12: 14; 13: 1 v.l.; 1 Pt 4: 5.*

ἔτος, ους, τό *year* Mt 9: 20; Mk 5: 42; Lk 4: 25; Ac 7: 30; Gal 1: 18; Rv 20: 4. πεντήκοντα ἔτη ἔχειν *be fifty years old* J 8: 57. πρὸ ἐτῶν δεκατεσσάρων *fourteen years ago* 2 Cor 12: 2.

εὖ adv. *well* εὖ ποιεῖν *do good, show kindness* Mk 14: 7. εὖ πράσσειν *do well, act rightly* Ac 15: 29. ἵνα εὖ σοι γένηται *that you may prosper* Eph 6: 3. Used alone *well done! excellent!* Mt 25: 21, 23; Lk 19: 17 v.l.*

Εὕα, ας, ἡ *Eve* 2 Cor 11: 3; 1 Ti 2: 13.*

εὐαγγελίζω *bring* or *announce good news* Lk 1: 19; Rv 14: 6. *Proclaim, preach* (*the gospel*) Lk 4: 43; Ac 13: 32; Ro 15: 20; 1 Cor 15: 1; 2 Cor 10: 16; Gal 1: 11, 23; 1 Pt 1: 12. Pass. *have good news* (*the gospel*) *preached to one* Mt 11: 5; Hb 4: 2, 6.

εὐαγγέλιον, ου, τό *good news, gospel* Mt 4: 23; 26: 13; Mk 1:1, 14, 15; 8: 35; Ac 15: 7; Ro 1: 16; 1 Cor 9: 12, 18, 23; 2 Cor 4: 4; 11: 7; Eph 6: 15; Col 1: 5, 23; 1 Pt 4: 17.

εὐαγγελιστής, οῦ, ὁ *preacher of the gospel, evangelist* Ac 21: 8; Eph 4: 11; 2 Ti 4: 5.*

εὐαρεστέω *please, be pleasing* Hb 11: 5f; *be pleased, be satisfied* 13: 16.*

εὐάρεστος, ον *pleasing, acceptable* Ro 12: 1f; 2 Cor 5: 9; Eph 5: 10; Tit 2: 9; Hb 13: 21.

εὐαρέστως adv. *in an acceptable manner* Hb 12: 28.*

Εὔβουλος, ου, ὁ Eubulus 2 Ti 4: 21.*

εὖγε adv. well done! excellent! Lk 19: 17.*

εὐγενής, ές, gen. οὖς well-born, high-born 1 Cor 1: 26. ἄνθρωπος εὐ. nobleman Lk 19: 12. Noble-minded, high-minded Ac 17: 11.*

εὐγλωττία, ας, ἡ glibness, fluency of speech Ro 16: 18 v.l.*

εὐδία, ας, ἡ fair weather Mt 16: 2.*

εὐδοκέω consider good, consent, resolve Lk 12: 32; Ro 15: 26f; 2 Cor 5: 8; Col 1: 19; 1 Th 2: 8. Be well pleased, take delight Mt 3: 17; 12: 18; 1 Cor 10: 5; 2 Pt 1: 17. Delight in, approve, like 2 Cor 12: 10; 2 Th 2: 12; Hb 10: 6, 8.

εὐδοκία, ας, ἡ—1. good will Phil 1: 15; 2: 13; 2 Th 1: 11 (see 3 below).—2. favor, good pleasure Mt 11: 26; Lk 10: 21; Eph 1: 5, 9. ἐν ἀνθρώποις εὐδοκίας Lk 2: 14 may be among men of good will or among men with whom he is pleased.—3. wish, desire Ro 10: 1, perhaps 2 Th 1: 11.*

εὐεργεσία, ας, ἡ the doing of good, service 1 Ti 6: 2; good deed Ac 4: 9.*

εὐεργετέω do good (to), benefit Ac 10: 38.*

εὐεργέτης, ου, ὁ benefactor Lk 22: 25.*

εὔθετος, ον fit, suitable, usable Lk 9: 62; 14: 35; Hb 6: 7.*

εὐθέως adv. at once, immediately Mt 4: 20, 22; 14: 31; Lk 12: 36; J 6: 21; Ac 9: 18, 20, 34; Gal 1: 16; Rv 4: 2.

εὐθυδρομέω run a straight course Ac 16: 11; 21: 1.*

εὐθυμέω be cheerful Js 5: 13; cheer up, keep up one's courage Ac 27: 22, 25.*

εὔθυμος, ον cheerful, in good spirits, encouraged Ac 27: 36.*

εὐθύμως adv. cheerfully Ac 24: 10.*

εὐθύνω straighten, make straight

J 1: 23. Steer (straight) ὁ εὐθύνων the pilot Js 3: 4.*

εὐθύς, εῖα, ύ gen. έως straight. Lit. Mt 3: 3; Mk 1: 3; Lk 3: 4f; Ac 9: 11. Fig. Ac 13: 10; 2 Pt 2: 15; right, upright Ac 8: 21.*

εὐθύς adv. immediately, at once Mt 13: 20f; Mk 1: 10, 12; Lk 6: 49; J 13: 30, 32; Ac 10: 16. Perhaps then, so then Mk 1: 21, 23, 29.

εὐθύτης, ητος, ἡ righteousness, up-rightness, lit. 'straightness'. ῥάβ-δος τῆς εὐθύτητος the righteous scepter Hb 1: 8.*

εὐκαιρέω have (a favorable) time, leisure, opportunity Mk 6: 31; 1 Cor 16: 12; spend one's time Ac 17: 21.*

εὐκαιρία, ας, ἡ favorable oppor-tunity, the right moment Mt 26: 16; Lk 22: 6.*

εὔκαιρος, ον well-timed, suitable Mk 6: 21; εὐ. βοήθεια help in time of need Hb 4: 16.*

εὐκαίρως adv. conveniently Mk 14: 11; in season, when it is con-venient 2 Ti 4: 2. εὐ. ἔχειν have leisure Mk 6: 31 v.l.*

εὔκοπος, ον easy comparative εὐκοπώτερος: εὐκοπώτερόν ἐστιν it is easier Mt 9: 5; Mk 10: 25; Lk 16: 17; 18: 25.

εὐλάβεια, ας, ἡ awe, reverence, fear of God Hb 12: 28; piety 5: 7.*

εὐλαβέομαι be afraid, be concerned Ac 23: 10 v.l. For Hb 11: 7 take care and reverence, respect are also possible.*

εὐλαβής, ές devout Lk 2: 25; Ac 2: 5; 8: 2; 22: 12.*

εὐλογέω speak well of, praise, extol Lk 1: 64; 24: 53; Js 3: 9; give thanks and praise Mt 14: 19; Lk 24: 30; 1 Cor 14: 16. Bless Mt 25: 34; Lk 1: 42; 6: 28; 24: 50f; 1 Cor 4: 12; Eph 1: 3; Hb 7: 1, 6f. Bless, consecrate Mk 8: 7; 1 Cor 10: 16.

εὐλογητός, ή, όν blessed, praised Mk 14: 61; Lk 1: 68; Ro 9: 5; Eph 1: 3; 1 Pt 1: 3.

εὐλογία, ας, ἡ praise Rv 5: 12f.
Flattery, false eloquence Ro 16:
18. Blessing Ro 15: 29; Eph 1: 3;
Js 3: 10; Hb 6: 7. Consecration τὸ
ποτήριον τῆς εὐ. the consecrated
cup 1 Cor 10: 16. Bounty 2 Cor
9: 6, perhaps Hb 6: 7.

εὐμετάδοτος, ον generous 1 Ti
6: 18.*

Εὐνίκη, ης, ἡ Eunice 2 Ti 1: 5.*

εὐνοέω be well-disposed (to), make
friends (with) Mt 5: 25.*

εὔνοια, ας, ἡ good will, enthusiasm
Eph 6: 7.*

εὐνουχίζω emasculate, make a
eunuch of Mt 19: 12.*

εὐνοῦχος, ου, ὁ emasculated man,
eunuch Mt 19: 12; Ac 8: 27,
34, 36, 38f.*

εὐξαίμην 1 aor. mid. opt. of
εὔχομαι.

Εὐοδία, ας, ἡ Euodia Phil 4: 2.*

εὐοδόω get along well, prosper,
succeed Ro 1: 10; 3 J 2; gain 1
Cor 16: 2.*

εὐπάρεδρος, ον constant, devoted
1 Cor 7: 35.*

εὐπειθής, ές gen. οῦς obedient,
compliant Js 3: 17.*

εὐπερίσπαστος, ον easily dis-
tracting Hb 12: 1 v.l.*

εὐπερίστατος, ον easily ensnaring
Hb 12: 1.*

εὐποιΐα, ας, ἡ the doing of good
Hb 13: 16.*

εὐπορέω have plenty, be well off
καθὼς εὐπορεῖτό τις according
to his (financial) ability Ac 11:
29.*

εὐπορία, ας, ἡ prosperity Ac 19:
25.*

εὐπρέπεια, ας, ἡ beauty Js 1: 11.*

εὐπρόσδεκτος, ον acceptable, pleasant, welcome Ro 15: 16, 31;
2 Cor 6: 2; 8: 12; 1 Pt 2: 5.*

εὐπρόσεδρος, ον constant 1 Cor 7:
35 v.l.*

εὐπροσωπέω make a good showing
Gal 6: 12.*

εὐρακύλων, ωνος, ὁ the northeast
wind, Euraquilo Ac 27: 14.*

εὑρίσκω find, discover, come upon
Mt 7: 7f; Mk 14: 55; Lk 6: 7; 11:
24; J 7: 34, 36; Ac 13: 6, 28;
27: 6; Ro 7: 21; 2 Cor 12: 20;
Rv 20: 15. Find, obtain Lk 1: 30;
2 Ti 1: 18; Hb 4: 16; 9: 12. Pass.
be found, find oneself, be Ac 8:
40; Phil 3: 9; 1 Pt 2: 22;
prove to be Ro 7: 10.

εὐροκλύδων, ωνος, ὁ Euroclydon,
the southeast wind. Another form
is εὐρυκλύδων; both as variant
readings for εὐρακύλων in Ac
27: 14.*

εὐρύχωρος, ον broad, spacious Mt
7: 13.*

εὐσέβεια, ας, ἡ piety, godliness,
religion Ac 3: 12; 1 Ti 2: 2; 3:
16; 4: 7f; 6: 3, 5f, 11; 2 Ti 3: 5;
Tit 1: 1; 2 Pt 1: 3, 6f. Pl.
godly acts 2 Pt 3: 11.*

εὐσεβέω worship Ac 17: 23. Show
piety toward 1 Ti 5: 4.*

εὐσεβής, ές devout, godly, pious,
reverent Ac 10: 2, 7; 2 Pt 2: 9.*

εὐσεβῶς adv. in a godly manner
2 Ti 3: 12; Tit 2: 12.*

εὔσημος, ον easily recognizable,
clear, distinct 1 Cor 14: 9.*

εὔσπλαγχνος, ον tender-hearted,
compassionate Eph 4: 32; 1 Pt
3: 8.*

εὐσχημονέω behave in an affected
manner 1 Cor 13: 5 v.l.*

εὐσχημόνως adv. decently, be-
comingly, properly Ro 13: 13;
1 Cor 14: 40; 1 Th 4: 12.*

εὐσχημοσύνη, ης, ἡ propriety, de-
corum, presentability 1 Cor 12:
23.*

εὐσχήμων, ον, gen. ονος proper,
presentable 1 Cor 12: 24. Prominent, of high standing Mk 15:
43; Ac 13: 50; 17: 12, 34 v.l. τὸ
εὐ. good order 1 Cor 7: 35.*

εὐτόνως adv. powerfully, vigorously,
vehemently Lk 23: 10; Ac 18:
28.*

εὐτραπελία, ας, ἡ coarse jesting,
buffoonery Eph 5: 4.*

Εὔτυχος, ου, ὁ Eutychus Ac 20: 9.*

εὐφημία, ας, ἡ good report 2 Cor
6: 8.*

εὔφημος, ον praiseworthy, appealing Phil 4: 8.*

εὐφορέω bear good crops, be fruitful
Lk 12: 16.*

εὐφραίνω act. gladden, cheer 2 Cor
2: 2. Pass. be glad, enjoy oneself
rejoice Lk 15: 32; Ac 2: 26; 7:
41; Ro 15: 10; be merry Lk
12: 19.

Εὐφράτης, ου, ὁ the Euphrates
river Rv 9: 14; 16: 12.*

εὐφροσύνη, ης, ἡ joy, gladness,
cheerfulness Ac 2: 28; 14: 17.*

εὐχαριστέω give thanks, render or
return thanks Mt 26: 27; Mk 8:
6; Lk 17: 16; 18: 11; Ac 27: 35;
28: 15; Ro 1: 21; 1 Cor 14: 17f;
Col 1: 3, 12; 1 Th 1: 2; 2: 13.

εὐχαριστία, ας, ἡ thankfulness,
gratitude Ac 24: 3. The rendering
of thanks, thanksgiving 2 Cor
9: 11; Eph 5: 4; Col 2: 7; 1 Th
3: 9; Rv 4: 9. Prayer of thanksgiving 1 Cor 14: 16; 2 Cor 9: 12.
Lord's Supper, Eucharist 1 Cor
10: 16 v.l.

εὐχάριστος, ον thankful Col 3: 15.*

εὐχή, ῆς, ἡ—1. prayer ἡ εὐ. τῆς
πίστεως the prayer offered in
faith Js 5: 15.—2. oath, vow Ac
18: 18; 21: 23.*

εὔχομαι—1. pray (for) Ac 26: 29;
2 Cor 13: 7, 9; Js 5: 16 v.l.—
2. wish (for) Ac 27: 29; Ro 9: 3;
3 J 2.*

εὔχρηστος, ον useful, serviceable 2
Ti 2: 21; 4: 11; Phlm 11.*

εὐψυχέω be glad, have courage
Phil 2: 19.*

εὐωδία, ας, ἡ aroma, fragrance 2
Cor 2: 15; Eph 5: 2; Phil 4:
18.*

εὐώνυμος, ον left, as opposed to
'right' Mt 20: 21, 23; 25: 33,
41; Mk 15: 27; Ac 21: 3; Rv
10: 2.

εὐωχία, ας, ἡ banquet, feasting
Jd 12 v.l.*

ἔφαγον 2 aor. act. ind. of ἐσθίω.

ἐφάλλομαι leap (upon) Ac 19:
16.*

ἐφάπαξ adv.—1. at once, at one
time 1 Cor 15: 6.—2. once for all
Ro 6: 10; Hb 7: 27; 9: 12; 10:
10.*

Ἐφέσιος, ία, ιον Ephesian Ac 19:
28, 34f; 21: 29.

Ἔφεσος, ου, ἡ Ephesus a seaport
in w. Asia Minor, famous for the
worship of Artemis. Ac 18: 19,
21, 24; 19: 1, 17, 26; 1 Cor 15:
32; 16: 8.

ἐφευρετής, οῦ, ὁ inventor, contriver Ro 1: 30.*

ἐφημερία, ας, ἡ class or division
of priests Lk 1: 5, 8.*

ἐφήμερος, ον for the day, daily
Js 2: 15.*

ἔφθασα 1 aor. act. ind. of φθάνω.

ἐφικνέομαι come (to), reach 2 Cor
10: 13f.*

ἐφίστημι—1. pres. and aor. (2 aor.
act. ind ἐπέστην) stand by or
near, approach, appear Lk 4: 39;
10: 40; Ac 4: 1; 6: 12; 10: 17;
1 Th 5: 3. Attack Ac 17: 5.
ἐπίστηθι stand by, be ready 2 Ti
4: 2.—2. perf. (act. ind. ἐφέσ-
τηκα, ptc. ἐφεστώς) stand by, be
present Ac 22: 20; 28: 2. Be
imminent 2 Ti 4: 6.

Ἐφραίμ, ὁ indecl. Ephraim, a
city J 11: 54.*

ἔφυγον 2 aor. act. ind. of φεύγω.

ἐφφαθά Aramaic word be opened
Mk 7: 34.*

ἐχθές adv. yesterday J 4: 52; Ac.
16: 35 v.l.; 7: 28; of the past as
a whole Hb 13: 8.*

ἔχθρα, ας, ἡ enmity Lk 23: 12;
Ro 8: 7; Gal 5: 20; Eph 2: 14,
16. ἔ. τοῦ θεοῦ enmity toward
God Js 4: 4.*

ἐχθρός, ά, όν—1. as adj. hated,
hostile Mt 13: 28; Ro 11: 28.—
2. as noun ὁ ἐχθρός the (personal)
enemy Mt 5: 43f; Mk 12: 36; Lk
1: 74; 10: 19; Ro 5: 10; 12: 20;
1 Cor 15: 26; Gal 4: 16; Phil
3: 18; 2 Th 3: 15.

ἔχιδνα, ης, ἡ *viper* Mt 3: 7; 12: 34; 23: 33; Lk 3: 7; Ac 28: 3.*

ἔχρησα 1 aor. act. ind. of κίχρημι.

ἔχω—I. act. transitive—1. *have, hold* Mt 26: 7; Rv 1: 16; 5: 8. *Have on, wear* Mt 3: 4; J 18: 10; Rv 9: 9, 17. *Keep, preserve* Lk 19: 20; 1 Ti 3: 9; Rv 6: 9. *Seize* Mk 16: 8.—2. *have* as one's *own, possess* lit. and fig. Mt 18: 8f; 19: 22; Lk 11: 5; 15: 4; 19: 26; J 8: 41; Ac 2: 44; Ro 12: 4; 1 Cor 4: 7; 5: 1; 7: 2; Eph 5: 5; Col 4: 1; 1 J 2: 23; Rv 18: 19. Of all conditions of body and soul *have* Mt 11: 18; J 5: 42; Ac 28: 9; Ro 10: 2; 1 Cor 13: 1; Hb 10: 2, 19. *Have at hand, have at one's disposal* Mt 14: 17; Mk 8: 1; J 4: 11; Phil 2: 20; 1 J 2: 1. With indications of time and age πεντήκοντα ἔτη ἔχειν *be fifty years old* J 8: 57. πολὺν χρόνον ἔχειν *be for a long time* 5: 6. ἡλικίαν ἔχειν *be of age* 9: 21, 23. *Have = have* something over one, *be under* something ἀνάγκην ἔχειν *be under necessity* 1 Cor 7: 37; *be compelled* Lk 14: 18. χρείαν ἔ. *be in need* Eph 4: 28; *need* Lk 19: 31, 34. διακονίαν 2 Cor 4: 1. *Have within oneself* Mk 13: 17; J 5: 26; 2 Cor 1: 9; Phil 1: 7.—3. *have* or *include in itself, bring about, cause* Hb 10: 35; Js 1: 4; 2: 17; 1 J 4: 18.—4. *consider, look upon, view* Mt 14: 5; 21: 46; Mk 11: 32; Lk 14: 18f; Phil 2: 29.—5. ἔ. with inf. following *have the possibility, can, be able, be in a position* Mt 18: 25; Lk 12: 4; Ac 4: 14; 25: 26; Hb 6: 13; 2 Pt 1: 15. *One must* Lk 12: 50; 2 J 12.—6.

Special combinations: ἔ. ἐν ἐπιγνώσει *acknowledge* Ro 1: 28. ἐν ἐμοὶ οὐκ ἔχει οὐδέν *he has no hold on me* J 14: 30. ἔ. κατὰ πρόσωπον *meet face to face* Ac 25: 16. ἔ. ὁδόν *be situated* (a certain distance) *away* Ac 1: 12.—II. act., intrans., with an adverb *be, be situated* πῶς ἔχουσιν *how they are* Ac 15: 36. ἑτοίμως ἔχειν *be ready* 2 Cor 12: 14. κακῶς ἔ. *be sick* Mt 4: 24. καλῶς ἔ. *be well, healthy* Mk 16: 18. ἐσχάτως ἔχειν *be at the point of death* 5: 23. τὸ νῦν ἔχον *for the present* Ac 24: 25. Other expressions: Ac 7: 1; 12: 15; 1 Ti 5: 25.—III. mid. *hold oneself fast, cling to* τὰ ἐχόμενα σωτηρίας *things that belong to salvation* Hb 6: 9. ἐχόμενος *neighboring* Mk 1: 38. Of time immediately *following:* τῇ ἐχομένῃ ἡμέρᾳ *on the next day* Ac 21: 26; cf. 20: 15; Lk 13: 33.

ἐψεύσω 1 aor. mid. ind. of ψεύδομαι, 2 sing.

ἕως—1. temporal conjunction *till, until* Mt 2: 9; Mk 6: 10; Lk 21: 32; J 21: 22f; Ac 2: 35; 1 Cor 4: 5; 2 Th 2: 7; Hb 10: 13. *As long as, while* Mk 6: 45; Lk 17: 8; J 9: 4.—2. improper prep. w. gen.: of time *until, up to* Mt 11: 13; 27: 64; Mk 14: 25; Lk 23: 44; Ac 1: 22; 1 Cor 1: 8. ἕως οὖ *until* Mt 13: 33; Ac 21: 26; 25: 21. ἕως πότε *how long* Mk 9: 19; J 10: 24; Rv 6: 10. Of place *as far as, to* Lk 2: 15; Ac 1: 8; 2 Cor 12: 2. ἕως ἑπτάκις *as many as seven times* Mt 18: 21f. ἕως ἔσω *right into* Mk 14: 54. οὐκ ἔστιν ἕως ἑνός *there is not even one* Ro 3: 12.

Z

Ζαβουλών, ὁ indecl. *Zebulun* an Israelite tribe Mt 4: 13, 15; Rv 7: 8; Lk 4: 31 v.l.*

Ζακχαῖος, ου, ὁ *Zacchaeus* Lk 19: 2, 5, 8.*

Ζάρα, ὁ indecl. *Zerah* Mt 1: 3.*

ζαφθάνι the reading of ms. D for σαβαχθάνι in Mt 27: 46; Mk 15: 34.*

Ζαχαρίας, ου, ὁ *Zechariah*—**1.** father of John the Baptist Lk 1: 5, 12f, 18, 21, 40, 59, 67; 3: 2.—**2.** son of Barachiah Mt 23: 35; Lk 11: 51.—**3.** Z. the prophet, as v.l. for Jeremiah in Mt 27: 9.*

[ζάω] contracted **ζῶ** *live*—**1.** of natural life Mt 4: 4; Lk 24: 5; Ro 7: 1, 2, 3; 1 Cor 15: 45; Phil 1: 22. Of the conduct of life Lk 2: 36; Ac 26: 5; Ro 14: 7; 2 Cor 5: 15. *Be well, recover* Mk 5: 23. Of God Mt 26: 63; Hb 3: 12; ζῶ ἐγώ *as surely as I live* Ro 14: 11. τὸ ζῆν *life* 2 Cor 1: 8. Fig. J 4: 10f; Ac 7: 38; 1 Pt 1: 3; 2: 4.—**2.** of the supernatural life of the child of God Lk 10: 28; J 5: 25; Ro 1: 17; 2 Cor 13: 4; Gal 2: 20; 1 Th 5: 10.

ζβέννυμι alternate form of σβέννυμι.

Ζεβεδαῖος, ου, ὁ *Zebedee* father of the apostles James and John Mt 4: 21; Mk 10: 35; Lk 5: 10; J 21: 2.

ζεστός, ή, όν *hot* Rv 3: 15f.*

ζεύγνυμι *connect, join* (lit. with a yoke) Mk 10: 9 v.l.*

ζεῦγος, ους, τό *yoke*, of two animals united by a yoke Lk 14: 19. *Pair* 2: 24.*

ζευκτηρία, ας, ἡ *bands, ropes* that tied the rudders Ac 27: 40.*

Ζεύς, Διός, acc. **Δία, ὁ** *Zeus* king of the Greek gods Ac 14: 12, 13.*

ζέω *boil, seethe* fig. ζέων τῷ πνεύ-

ματι *with burning zeal* Ac 18: 25, but τῷ πνεύματι ζέοντες *maintain(ing) the spiritual glow* Ro 12: 11.*

ζῇ third sing. pres. act. ind. of [ζάω].

ζηλεύω *be eager, earnest* Rv 3: 19.*

ζῆλος, ου, ὁ and **ζῆλος, ους, τό**—**1.** in a good sense *zeal, ardor* Ro 10: 2; 2 Cor 7: 11; 9: 2; Phil 3: 6.—**2.** in a bad sense *jealousy, envy* Ac 5: 17; Ro 13: 13; 2 Cor 12: 20; Js 3: 14, 16.

ζηλόω—**1.** in a good sense *strive (for), desire* 1 Cor 12: 31; 14: 1, 39. *Be deeply concerned about* Gal 4: 17. *Show zeal* 4: 18.—**2.** in a bad sense *be filled with jealousy or envy (toward)* Ac 7: 9; 1 Cor 13: 4; Js 4: 2.

ζηλωτής, οῦ, ὁ *zealot, enthusiast, one who is eager* or *zealous for* w. gen. Ac 22: 3; 1 Cor 14: 12; Tit 2: 14; 1 Pt 3: 13. Of Simon as a former member of a Jewish faction Lk 6: 15; Ac 1: 13.

ζημία, ας, ἡ *damage, loss* Ac 27: 10, 21; Phil 3: 7, 8.*

ζημιόω *inflict injury* or *punishment.* Pass. *suffer damage* or *loss, forfeit* with acc. of respect or specification Mt 16: 26; Mk 8: 36; Phil 3: 8; without acc. 2 Cor 7: 9. *Be punished* 1 Cor 3: 15.

ζῆν pres. act. inf. of [ζάω].

Ζηνᾶς, acc. **-ᾶν, ὁ** *Zenas* Tit 3: 13.*

Ζήνων, ωνος, ὁ *Zeno* 2 Ti 4: 19 v.l.*

ζητέω—**1.** *seek, look for* Mt 13: 45; 18: 12; Mk 1: 37; Lk 19: 10; J 18: 4; Ac 10: 19, 21; 2 Ti 1: 17; *search for* Ac 17: 27. *Investigate, examine, consider, deliberate* Mk 11: 18; Lk 12: 29; J 8: 50; 16: 19.—**2.** somewhat removed from the idea of seeking; *try to obtain, desire to possess* Mt 6: 33; 26: 59; Lk 22: 6; J 5: 44; Ro 2: 7; Col 3: 1. *Strive for, aim (at), desire, wish* Mt 12: 46; Lk 17: 33; J 1: 38; Ac 16: 10; 1 Cor 13: 5; Gal 1: 10. *Ask for, request, demand* Mk 8: 11f; Lk 12: 48; J 4: 23; 2 Cor 13: 3. Pass. *it is required* 1 Cor 4: 2.

ζήτημα, ατος, τό *(controversial) question, issue* Ac 15: 2; 18: 15; 23: 29; 25: 19; 26: 3.*

ζήτησις, εως, ἡ *investigation, controversial question, controversy, discussion, debate* J 3: 25; Ac 15: 2, 7; 25: 20; 1 Ti 6: 4; 2 Ti 2: 23; Tit 3: 9.*

ζιζάνιον, ου, τό *darnel, cheat* a troublesome weed resembling wheat Mt 13: 25ff, 29f, 36, 38, 40.*

Ζμύρνα a variant of Σμύρνα.

Ζοροβαβέλ, ὁ, indecl. *Zerubbabel* (Ezra 2: 2; 3: 8) Mt 1: 12f; Lk 3: 27.*

ζόφος, ου, ὁ *darkness, gloom* Hb 12: 18; in the nether regions, *hell* 2 Pt 2: 17; 2: 4 v.l.; Jd 6, 13.*

ζυγός, οῦ, ὁ—1. *yoke* fig. Mt 11: 29f; Ac 15: 10; Gal 5: 1; 1 Ti 6: 1.—2. *balance, pair of scales* Rv 6: 5.*

ζύμη, ης, ἡ *yeast, leaven* lit. Mt 16: 12; Lk 13: 21; 1 Cor 5: 6;

Gal 5: 9. Fig. Mt 16: 6, 11; Lk 12: 1; 1 Cor 5: 7f.

ζυμόω *to ferment, leaven* Mt 13: 33; Lk 13: 21; 1 Cor 5: 6; Gal 5: 9.*

ζωγρέω *capture (alive)* Lk 5: 10; 2 Ti 2: 26.*

ζωή, ῆς, ἡ *life*—1. in the physical sense Lk 16: 25; Ac 17: 25; Ro 8: 38; 2 Cor 4: 10f; 1 Ti 4: 8; Js 4: 14.—2. of the supernatural life belonging to God, Christ and the believer Mt 25: 46; Mk 10: 17, 30; J 1: 4; 3: 15f; 5: 26; 6: 35; Ac 5: 20; Ro 6: 4; 8: 2; Eph 4: 18; Phil 2: 16; 1 Ti 6: 19; Js 1: 12; Rv 2: 7; 13: 8.

ζώνη, ης, ἡ *belt, girdle* Mt 3: 4; Mk 6: 8; Ac 21: 11; Rv 1: 13; 15: 6.

ζώννυμι or ζωννύω *gird* J 21: 18; Ac 12: 8.*

ζωογονέω *give life to, make alive* 1 Ti 6: 13. *Keep* or *preserve alive* Lk 17: 33; Ac 7: 19.*

ζῷον, ου, τό *animal* in the usual sense Hb 13: 11; 2 Pt 2: 12; Jd 10. *Living thing* or *being* Rv 4: 6–9; 6: 1, 3, 5–7; 19: 4.

ζωοποιέω *make alive, give life to* J 5: 21; 1 Cor 15: 22, 36, 45; 2 Cor 3: 6; 1 Pt 3: 18; *bring to life* Ro 4: 17.

ζῶσαι, ζώσω 1 aor. mid. imperative and fut. act. ind. of ζώννυμι.

H

ἤ particle—1. disjunctive *or* Mt 5: 17, 36; Mk 3: 4; Ro 8: 35; 14: 13; Rv 3: 15. ἤ—ἤ *either—or* Mt 6: 24; Lk 16: 13; 1 Cor 14: 6. In interrogative sentences Mt 26: 53; Lk 13: 4; 1 Cor 9: 7; Gal 1: 10.—2. denoting comparison *than* Mt 10: 15; 18: 8, 9, 13; Mk 10: 25; Lk 15: 7; Ac

17: 21; 1 Cor 9: 15; 14: 19. πρὶν ἤ *before* Mk 14: 30; Lk 2: 26; Ac 25: 16.

ἤ adv. *truly*, perhaps the correct accentuation in 1 Cor 9: 15.

ἤγαγον 2 aor. act. ind. of ἄγω.

ἡγεμονεύω *be leader, rule* of a governor Lk 2: 2 and a procurator 3: 1.*

ἡγεμονία, ας, ἡ *leadership, chief command* of the office of the Roman emperor Lk 3:1.*

ἡγεμών, όνος, ὁ *prince* Mt 2: 6. *Governor* Mt 10: 18; Mk 13: 9; 1 Pt 2: 14. *Procurator* Mt 27: 2, 11, 14f; Lk 20: 20; Ac 23: 24; 24: 1; 26: 30.

ἡγέομαι—1. *lead, guide* pres. participle ὁ ἡγούμενος *ruler, leader* Mt 2: 6; Lk 22: 26; Ac 7: 10; Hb 13: 7, 17, 24. ὁ ἡγούμενος τοῦ λόγου *the chief speaker* Ac 14: 12.—2. *think, consider, regard* Ac 26: 2; 2 Cor 9: 5; Phil 2: 3; 3: 8; Hb 10: 29; Js 1: 2.

ἠγέρθην 1 aor. pass. ind. of ἐγείρω.

ἡγνικώς, ἡγνισμένος perf. act. participle and perf. pass. participle of ἁγνίζω.

ᾔδειν pluperf. act. ind., first pers. sing., of οἶδα.

ἡδέως adv. *gladly* 2 Cor 11: 19. ἡ. ἀκούειν *like to hear* Mk 6: 20; 12: 37. Superlative ἥδιστα *very gladly* 2 Cor 12: 9, 15.*

ἤδη adv. *now, already, by this time* Mt 5: 28; 15: 32; 17: 12; Mk 4: 37; 6: 35; Lk 21: 30; J 3: 18; 4: 36. ἤδη καί *even now* Lk 3: 9. ἤδη ποτέ *now at length* Ro 1: 10; Phil 4: 10.

ἥδιστα see ἡδέως.

ἡδονή, ῆς, ἡ *pleasure, enjoyment* in an unfavorable sense Lk 8: 14; Tit 3: 3; Js 4: 1, 3; 2 Pt 2: 13.*

ἡδύοσμον, ου, τό *mint* (garden plant) Mt 23: 23; Lk 11: 42.*

ἤθελον imperfect act. of θέλω.

ἦθος, ους, τό *custom, usage, habit* 1 Cor 15: 33.*

ἠκαιρεῖσθε imperfect of ἀκαιρέομαι.

ἥκω *have come, be present* Mt 8: 11; Mk 8: 3; Lk 15: 27; J 4: 47; 8: 42; Hb 10: 37; Rv 15: 4; 18: 8.

ἡλάμην 1 aor. mid. ind. of ἅλλομαι.

ἠλεήθην, ἠλεημένος 1 aor. pass. ind., perf. pass. participle of ἐλεέω.

ἦλθα, ἦλθον aor. act. ind. of ἔρχομαι.

ἠλί (also spelled ἡλι, ἠλει, ἡλει) Hebrew *my God* Mt 27: 46.*

Ἡλί, ὁ indecl. *Heli* Lk 3: 23.*

Ἡλίας, ου, ὁ *Elijah* (1 Kings 17–20) Mt 11: 14; 17: 3f, 10ff; Mk 15: 35f; Lk 1: 17; 4: 25f; J 1: 21, 25; Js 5: 17. ἐν Ἡλίᾳ *in the story of Elijah* Ro 11: 2.

ἡλικία, ας, ἡ—1. *age, time of life* This sense is greatly to be preferred over 2 in Mt 6: 27 = Lk 12: 25. *Mature age* Eph 4: 13. *Years* Lk 2: 52. ἡλικίαν ἔχειν *be of age* J 9: 21, 23. παρὰ καιρὸν ἡλικίας *past the normal age* Hb 11: 11.—2. *bodily stature* Lk 19: 3. This mng. is also possible for Lk 2: 52 and Eph 4: 13 above, and some prefer it for Mt 6: 27 = Lk 12: 25.*

ἡλίκος, η, ον *how great, how large* Col 2: 1; Js 3: 5; Gal 6: 11 v.l.*

ἥλιος, ου, ὁ *the sun* Mt 13: 6, 43; Lk 21: 25; 23: 45; Ac 13: 11; 27: 20; 1 Cor 15: 41; Rv 7: 2, 16; 21: 23.

ἧλος, ου, ὁ *nail* J 20: 25.*

ἤλπικα perf. act. ind. of ἐλπίζω.

ἡμεῖς nom. pl. of ἐγώ.

ἡμέρα, ας, ἡ *day*—1. of the period of daylight Mt 4: 2; Mk 4: 27; Lk 4: 42; 9: 12; J 1: 39; 11: 9; 2 Pt 1: 19; Rv 8: 12. Fig. 1 Th 5: 5.—2. of civil or legal day, including the night Mt 6: 34; 28: 15; Mk 2: 1; Lk 17: 4; Ac 13: 31; Ro 8: 36; 1 Cor 10: 8; Hb 3: 13; Rv 1: 10; 9: 15.—3. of a day appointed for a special purpose Mt 10: 15; Lk 17: 24, 30; Ac 28: 23; 1 Cor 4: 3; 5: 5; Hb 10: 25; Rv 16: 14.—4. of a longer period *time* Mt 2: 1; Lk 21: 22; Ac 5: 36; 2 Cor 6: 2; 2 Ti 3: 1; Hb 5: 7; 8: 9.

ἡμέτερος, α, ον *our* Ac 2: 11; Ro 15: 4; 1 J 1: 3. τὸ ἡμ. *what is ours* Lk 16: 12.

ἦ μήν see ἦ.

ἡμιθανής, ές half dead Lk 10: 30.*

ἥμισυς, εια, υ half Lk 19: 8. τὸ ἥ. one half Mk 6: 23; Rv 11: 9, 11; 12: 14.*

ἡμίωρον, ου, τό a half hour Rv 8: 1.*

ἠμφιεσμένος perf. pass. participle of ἀμφιέννυμι.

ἤνεγκα aor. act. ind. of φέρω.

ἠνεῳγμένος, ἠνεῴχθην perf. mid. participle, 1 aor. pass. ind. of ἀνοίγω.

ἡνίκα particle denoting time when, at the time when with ἄν whenever 2 Cor 3: 15; with ἐάν when, every time that vs. 16.*

ἠνοίγην, ἠνοίχθην 2 aor. pass. ind., 1 aor. pass. ind. of ἀνοίγω.

ἠντληκώς perf. act. participle of ἀντλέω.

ἤπερ strengthened form of ἤ than J 12: 43.*

ἤπιος, α, ον gentle 1 Th 2: 7; 2 Ti 2: 24.*

ἠπίστησα, ἠπίστουν 1 aor. act. ind. and imperfect act. of ἀπιστέω.

Ἤρ, ὁ indecl. Er Lk 3: 28.*

ἦρα, ἤρθην 1 aor. act. ind., 1 aor. pass. ind. of αἴρω.

ἤρεμος, ον quiet, tranquil 1 Ti 2: 2.*

ἤρεσε 1 aor. act. ind. of ἀρέσκω.

Ἡρῴδης, ου, ὁ Herod—1. Herod I, the Great (41–4 BC) Mt 2: 1–22.—2. Herod Antipas, son of Herod I Mk 6: 14–22; Lk 3: 1, 19; 13: 31; 23: 7; Ac 4: 27.—3. Herod Agrippa I, grandson of Herod I Ac 12: 1, 6, 11, 19, 21.

Ἡρῳδιανοί, ῶν, οἱ the Herodians, partisans of Herod I and his family Mt 22: 16; Mk 3: 6; 8: 15 v.l.; 12: 13.*

Ἡρῳδιάς, άδος, ἡ Herodias, wife of Herod Antipas Mt 14: 3, 6; Mk 6: 17, 19, 22; Lk 3: 19.*

Ἡρῳδίων, ωνος, ὁ Herodion Ro 16: 11.*

Ἡσαΐας, ου, ὁ Isaiah the prophet and his book Mt 3: 3; 13: 14; Mk 1: 2; Lk 4: 17; J 12: 38f; Ac 8: 28; Ro 9: 27, 29.

Ἠσαῦ, ὁ indecl. Esau (Gen 27 and 28) Ro 9: 13; Hb 11: 20; 12: 16.*

ἦσθα imperfect act. of εἰμί, 2 pers. sing.

ἡσσώθην 1 aor. pass. ind. of ἐσσόομαι.

ἥσσων or ἥττων, ον, gen. ονος comparative without a positive lesser, inferior, weaker Mt 20: 28 v.l. εἰς τὸ ἧσσον for the worse 1 Cor 11: 17. The neut. as adv. less 2 Cor 12: 15.*

ἡσυχάζω be quiet, rest, abstain from work Lk 23: 56; 1 Th 4: 11; remain silent Lk 14: 4; Ac 11: 18; 21: 14; 22: 2 v.l.*

ἡσυχία, ας, ἡ quietness, rest 2 Th 3: 12. Silence 1 Ti 2: 11f; Ac 21: 40 v.l. παρέχειν ἡσυχίαν be quiet, silent Ac 22: 2.*

ἡσύχιος, ον quiet 1 Ti 2: 2; 1 Pt 3: 4.*

ἤτοι strengthened form of ἤ; ἤτοι—ἤ either—or Ro 6: 16.*

ἡττάομαι be defeated (by), succumb (to) 2 Pt 2: 19f; be inferior 2 Cor 12: 13 v.l.*

ἥττημα, ατος, τό defeat Ro 11: 12; 1 Cor 6: 7.*

ἤφιε imperfect of ἀφίημι, third sing.

ἠχέω sound, ring out 1 Cor 13: 1. Roar, thunder Lk 21: 25 v.l.*

ἤχθην 1 aor. pass. ind. of ἄγω.

ἦχος, ου, ὁ sound, tone, noise Ac 2: 2; Hb 12: 19. Report, news Lk 4: 37.*

ἦχος, ους, τό sound, tone, noise Lk 21: 25.*

ἠχώ, οῦς, ἡ sound. If the gen. in Lk 21: 25 is accented ἠχοῦς, the form comes from this nominative.

Θ

Θαδδαῖος, ου, ὁ *Thaddaeus* Mt 10: 3; Mk 3: 18.*

θάλασσα, ης, ἡ *sea* Mt 23: 15; Mk 9: 42; Ac 7: 36; 10: 6, 32; 2 Cor 11: 26; Rv 8: 8f. *Lake* Mt 4: 18; 8: 24; J 6: 1.

θάλπω *cherish, comfort* Eph 5: 29; 1 Th 2: 7.*

Θαμάρ, ἡ indecl. *Tamar* (Gen 38) Mt 1: 3.*

θαμβέω intrans. *be astounded* Ac 9: 6 v.l. Trans. pass. *be astounded amazed* Mk 1: 27; 10: 24, 32; Ac 3: 11 v.l.*

θάμβος, ους, τό and **θάμβος, ου, ὁ** *astonishment, fear* Lk 4: 36; 5: 9; Ac 3: 10.*

θανάσιμος, ον *deadly* Mk 16: 18.*

θανατηφόρος, ον *death-bringing* Js 3: 8.*

θάνατος, ου, ὁ *death*—**1.** of natural death Mt 10: 21; 20: 18; J 11: 4, 13; Ac 22: 4; Ro 5: 12,14,17; Phil 2: 27, 30; Hb 7: 23; Rv 18: 8.— **2.** fig., of spiritual death Mt 4: 16; J 8: 51; Ro 1: 32; 7: 10, 13; 1 J 5: 16f.

θανατόω *put to death* lit. Mt 10: 21; Mk 14: 55; Lk 21: 16; 2 Cor 6: 9. *Be in danger of death* Ro 8: 36. Fig. Ro 7: 4; 8: 13.

θάπτω *bury* Mt 8: 21f; Lk 9: 59f; Ac 5: 6, 9f; 1 Cor 15: 4.

Θάρα, ὁ indecl. *Terah*, father of Abraham Lk 3: 34.*

θαρρέω and **θαρσέω** *be confident, be courageous, cheerful* Mt 9: 2, 22; Mk 6: 50; Ac 23: 11; 2 Cor 5: 6; 7: 16; Hb 13: 6.

θάρσος, ους, τό *courage* Ac 28: 15.*

θαῦμα, ατος, τό *a wonder, marvel* 2 Cor 11: 14. ἐθαύμασα θαῦμα *I wondered in great amazement* Rv 17: 6.*

θαυμάζω *wonder, marvel, be astonished* Mt 8: 10; Mk 15: 5;

Lk 1: 21, 63; 11: 38; J 5: 20; Ac 2: 7; Gal 1: 6; Rv 17: 6. *Admire, wonder at* Lk 7: 9; J 5: 28; Ac 7: 31; 2 Th 1: 10. Pass. *wonder, be amazed* Rv 13: 3; 17: 8.

θαυμάσιος, α, ον *wonderful, remarkable* Mt 21: 15.*

θαυμαστός, ή, όν *wonderful, marvelous, remarkable* Mt 21: 42; Mk 12: 11; J 9: 30; 1 Pt 2: 9; Rv 15: 1, 3.*

θεά, ᾶς, ἡ *goddess* Ac 19: 27.*

θεάομαι *see, look at* Mt 11: 7; Mk 16: 11, 14; Lk 5: 27; J 1: 14, 32; 4: 35; Ac 21: 27; 1 J 1: 1; *come to see, visit* Ro 15: 24; *greet* Mt 22: 11. Pass. *be noticed* Mt 6: 1.

θεατρίζω *put to shame, expose publicly* Hb 10: 33.*

θέατρον, ου, τό *theater* Ac 19: 29, 31. *Play, spectacle* 1 Cor 4: 9.*

θεῖον, ου, τό *sulphur* Lk 17: 29; Rv 9: 17f; 14: 10; 19: 20; 20: 10; 21: 8.*

θεῖος, θεία, θεῖον *divine* 2 Pt 1: 3f. τὸ θεῖον *divine being, divinity* Ac 17: 29, 27 v.l.; Tit 1: 9 v.l.*

θειότης, ητος, ἡ *divinity, divine nature* Ro 1: 20.*

θείς 2 aor. act. participle of τίθημι.

θειώδης, ες *sulphurous* Rv 9: 17.*

Θέκλα, ης, ἡ *Thecla* 2 Ti 3: 11 v.l.*

θέλημα, ατος, τό *will* Mt 6: 10; Lk 12: 47; J 6: 38–40; Ac 21: 14; Ro 2: 18; 12: 2; 15: 32; Eph 1: 9; Hb 10: 10; 2 Pt 1: 21. *Desire* 1 Cor 7: 37. τὰ θελήματα τ. σαρκός *what the flesh desires* Eph 2: 3.

θέλησις, εως, ἡ *will* Hb 2: 4.*

θέλω—**1.** *wish* of desire, *wish to have, desire, want* Mt 20: 21;

Mk 10: 43; Lk 5: 39; J 9: 27; Ro
1: 13; Gal 4: 20. Js 2: 20. τί θέλω
how I wish Lk 12: 49. τί θέλετε
ποιήσω ὑμῖν; *what do you want
me to do for you?* Mt 20: 32.—
2. *wish, will* of purpose or resolve,
wish to do Mt 20: 14; Mk 3: 13;
J 6: 21, 67; Ac 18: 21; Ro 7: 15f,
19f; 2 Cor 8: 10; Col 1: 27; Rv
11: 5. οὐ θέλω *I will not* Mt
21: 30.—**3.** τί θέλει τοῦτο εἶναι
what does this mean? Ac 2: 12;
cf. 17: 20; Lk 15: 26 v.l.—
4. *take pleasure in, like* Mt 27: 43;
Mk 12: 38; Lk 20: 46; Col 2: 18.
—**5.** *maintain* 2 Pt 3: 5.

θεμέλιον, ου, τό *foundation* Ac 16:
26.*

θεμέλιος, ου, ὁ *foundation* lit.
Lk 6: 48f; 14: 29; Hb 11: 10;
foundation stone Rv 21: 14, 19.
Fig. Ro 15: 20; 1 Cor 3: 10–12;
Hb 6: 1; *treasure, reserve* 1 Ti
6: 19.

θεμελιόω *found* Mt 7: 25; Lk 6:
48 v.l.; Hb 1: 10. Fig. *establish,
strengthen* Eph 3: 17; Col 1: 23;
1 Pt 5: 10.*

θεοδίδακτος, ον *taught by God*
1 Th 4: 9.*

θεολόγος, ου, ὁ *one who speaks of
God* or *divine things* Rv inscr.
v.l.*

θεομαχέω *fight against God* Ac
23: 9 v.l.*

θεομάχος, ον *fighting against God*
Ac 5: 39.*

θεόπνευστος, ον *inspired by God*
2 Ti 3: 16.*

θεός, οῦ, ὁ and **ἡ** *God, god*—**1.** of
divine beings generally Ac 7:
43; 12: 22; 28: 6; 1 Cor 8: 4f; Gal
4: 8. ἡ θεός *the goddess* Ac 19:
37.—**2.** of Christ J 1: 1, 18; 20:
28; Tit 2: 13; Hb 1: 8f and God
the Father Mt 1: 23; Mk 13: 19;
Lk 2: 14; 20: 37; J 17: 3; Ro 1:
8; 8: 8; 15: 6, 13, 33; Gal 1: 4;
2: 6. τῷ θεῷ *in the sight of God,*
hence *very* Ac 7: 20. ὁ θεός as a
vocative *O God!* Lk 18: 11; Hb

1: 8.—**3.** fig. of persons J 10:
34f; of a thing Phil 3: 19.—
4. the devil is referred to as ὁ θ.
τοῦ αἰῶνος τούτου *the god of
this age* 2 Cor 4: 4.

θεοσέβεια, ας, ἡ *reverence for God,
piety, religion* 1 Ti 2: 10.*

θεοσεβής, ές *God-fearing, devout*
J 9: 31.*

θεοστυγής, ές *hating God,* perhaps *God-forsaken* Ro 1: 30.*

θεότης, ητος, ἡ *deity, divinity* Col
2: 9.*

Θεόφιλος, ου, ὁ *Theophilus* Lk
1: 3; Ac 1: 1.*

θεραπεία, ας, ἡ *serving, care* hence
healing Lk 9: 11; Rv 22: 2. ἡ
θ. = οἱ θεράποντες *servants* Lk
12: 42; Mt 24: 45 v.l.*

θεραπεύω *serve* Ac 17: 25. *Care
for,* then *heal, restore* Mt 4: 23f;
Mk 3: 2, 10; Lk 4: 23, 40; 14: 3;
Rv 13: 3.

θεράπων, οντος, ὁ *servant* Hb 3:
5.*

θερίζω *reap, harvest* lit. Mt 6: 26;
J 4: 36; Js 5: 4. Fig. Lk 19: 21f;
J 4: 37f; Gal 6: 7–9; Rv 14:
15f.

θερισμός, οῦ, ὁ *harvest* Mt 13: 30,
39; Mk 4: 29; J 4: 35a. Fig. Mt
9: 37f; Lk 10: 2; J 4: 35b; Rv
14: 15.*

θεριστής, οῦ, ὁ *reaper, harvester*
Mt 13: 30, 39.*

θερμαίνω mid. *warm oneself, keep
warm* Mk 14: 54, 67; J 18: 18,
25; Js 2: 16.*

θέρμη, ης, ἡ *heat* Ac 28: 3.*

θέρος, ους, τό *summer* Mt 24: 32;
Mk 13: 28; Lk 21: 30.*

θέσθε 2 aor. mid. imperative of
τίθημι, 2 pl.

Θεσσαλία, ας, ἡ *Thessaly,* a region
in northeast Greece Ac 17: 15
v.l.*

Θεσσαλονικεύς, έως, ὁ *Thessalo-
nian,* an inhabitant of Thessalonica Ac 20: 4; 27: 2; 1 Th 1: 1,
inscr.; 2 Th 1: 1, inscr.*

Θεσσαλονίκη, ης, ἡ *Thessalonica,*

a seaport city in Macedonia Ac
17: 1, 11, 13; Phil 4: 16; 2 Ti
4: 10.*

Θευδᾶς, ᾶ, ὁ *Theudas* Ac 5: 36.*

θεωρέω *see, look at, observe, per-*
ceive Mt 27: 55; Mk 12: 41; Lk
14: 29; J 12: 45; 14: 17; 20: 12;
Ac 7: 56; 9: 7; 17: 22; *view* Mt
28: 1; *catch sight of, notice* Mk
3: 11; *experience* J 8: 51.

θεωρία, ας, ἡ *spectacle, sight* Lk
23: 48.*

θήκη, ης, ἡ *sheath* J 18: 11.*

θηλάζω *give suck* Mt 24: 19; Mk
13: 17; Lk 21: 23. *Suck* Mt 21:
16; Lk 11: 27.*

θῆλυς, εια, υ *female* Mt 19: 4;
Mk 10: 6; Ro 1: 26, 27; Gal 3:
28.*

θήρα, ας, ἡ *net, trap* Ro 11: 9.*

θηρεύω *hunt, catch* fig. Lk 11:
54.*

θηριομαχέω *fight with wild animals*
probably fig. 1 Cor 15: 32.*

θηρίον, ου, τό (*wild*) *animal, beast*
lit. Mk 1: 13; Hb 12: 20; Js
3: 7; of animal-like beings Rv
11: 7; 13: 1ff; 20: 4, 10. Fig.
of persons, *beast, monster* Tit
1: 12.

θησαυρίζω *store up, gather, save*
lit. Mt 6: 19; Lk 12: 21; 1 Cor
16: 2; 2 Cor 12: 14; Js 5: 3. Fig.
Mt 6: 20; Ro 2: 5; *reserve* 2 Pt
3: 7.*

θησαυρός, οῦ, ὁ *treasure* lit. Mt 6:
19, 21; 13: 44; Lk 12: 34; Hb
11: 26. Fig. Mt 6: 20; Mk 10: 21;
Lk 6: 45; 2 Cor 4: 7; Col 2: 3.
Treasure box or *chest* Mt 2: 11;
storehouse 13: 52.

θιγγάνω *touch* Col 2: 21; Hb 11:
28; 12: 20.*

θλίβω *press upon, crowd* Mk 3: 9;
make narrow Mt 7: 14. *Oppress,*
afflict pass. 2 Cor 1: 6; 7: 5; 1 Th
3: 4; 1 Ti 5: 10; Hb 11: 37.

θλῖψις, εως, ἡ *oppression, affliction,*
tribulation Mt 24: 9, 21; Ac
11: 19; Ro 12: 12; 2 Cor 4: 17;
Col 1: 24; 2 Th 1: 6; Rv 2: 9, 22;

7: 14. *Difficult circumstances* 2
Cor 8: 13; Js 1: 27. *Trouble* 2 Cor
2: 4; Phil 1: 17.

θνήσκω *die* perf. τέθνηκα *have*
died, be dead lit. Mk 15: 44; Lk
8: 49; J 19: 33; Ac 14: 19. Fig.
1 Ti 5: 6.

θνητός, ή, όν *mortal* Ro 6: 12; 8:
11; 1 Cor 15: 53f; 2 Cor 4: 11;
5: 4.*

θορυβάζω *cause trouble* pass. *be*
distracted Lk 10: 41.*

θορυβέω *throw into disorder* Ac
17: 5; 21: 13 v.l. Pass. *be*
troubled, aroused, distressed Mt
9: 23; Mk 5: 39; 13: 7 v.l.; Ac
20: 10.*

θόρυβος, ου, ὁ *noise, clamor* Ac
21: 34; *turmoil, excitement, up-*
roar Mt 26: 5; 27: 24; Mk 5: 38;
14: 2; Ac 20: 1; 24: 18.*

θραυματίζω *break* Lk 4: 18 v.l.*

θραύω *break* perf. pass. participle τεθραυσμένοι *the down-*
trodden Lk 4: 18.*

θρέμμα, ατος, τό (*domesticated*)
animal, especially a sheep or
goat J 4: 12.*

θρηνέω *mourn* (*for*), *lament* Lk
23: 27; J 16: 20. *Sing a dirge* Mt
11: 17; Lk 7: 32.*

θρῆνος, ου, ὁ *dirge* Mt 2: 18 v.l.*

θρησκεία, ας, ἡ *religion, worship*
Ac 26: 5; Col 2: 18; Js 1: 26f.*

θρησκός, όν *religious* Js 1: 26.*

θριαμβεύω *lead in a triumphal*
procession Col 2: 15. This may
also be the mng. in 2 Cor 2: 14,
but in that passage the sense
may be *cause to triumph* or
exhibit in a public procession.

θρίξ, τριχός, ἡ *hair* Mt 3: 4; 5: 36;
Lk 21: 18; J 11: 2; 1 Pt 3: 3; Rv
9: 8.

θροέω pass. *be disturbed* or
frightened Mt 24: 6; Mk 13: 7;
2 Th 2: 2; Lk 24: 37 v.l.*

θρόμβος, ου, ὁ *drop* Lk 22: 44.*

θρόνος, ου, ὁ *throne* Mt 5: 34; 19:
28; 25: 31; Lk 1: 32, 52; Hb 4:
16; Rv 2: 13; 4: 4; 12: 5.

Dominion, sovereignty of a class of supernatural beings Col 1: 16.

θρύπτω *break in pieces* 1 Cor 11: 24 v.l.*

Θυάτειρα, ων, τά *Thyatira*, a city in Lydia in Asia Minor, noted for the purple cloth it produced Ac 16: 14; Rv 1: 11; 2: 18, 24.*

θυγάτηρ, τρός, ἡ *daughter* lit. Mt 10: 35, 37; Mk 5: 35; Lk 2: 36; Ac 7: 21; Hb 11: 24. Fig. Mk 5: 34; Lk 1: 5; 23: 28; J 12: 15; 2 Cor 6: 18.

θυγάτριον, ου, τό (*little*) *daughter* Mk 5: 23; 7: 25.*

θύελλα, ης, ἡ *storm, whirlwind* Hb 12: 18.*

θύϊνος, η, ον *from the citron tree* Rv 18: 12.*

θυμίαμα, ατος, τό *incense* Rv 5: 8; 8: 3f; 18: 13; *incense-burning, incense offering* Lk 1: 10f.*

θυμιατήριον, ου, τό *altar of incense* Hb 9: 4.*

θυμιάω *make an incense-offering* Lk 1: 9.*

θυμομαχέω *be very angry* Ac 12: 20.*

θυμός, οῦ, ὁ *anger, wrath, rage* Lk 4: 28; Ac 19: 28; Ro 2: 8; Gal 5: 20; Hb 11: 27; Rv 12: 12; 14: 10. *Passion* is *possible for* 14: 8.

θυμόω *make angry* pass. *become angry* Mt 2: 16.*

θύρα, ας, ἡ *door* lit. Mt 6: 6; Mk 1: 33; Lk 11: 7; J 20: 19, 26; Ac 5: 19; *entrance* Mk 15: 46; Rv 4: 1. Fig. Mt 24: 33; Lk 13: 24; J 10: 9; 1 Cor 16: 9; Js 5: 9; Rv 3: 20.

θυρεός, οῦ, ὁ a long, oblong *shield* Eph 6: 16.*

θυρίς, ίδος, ἡ *window* Ac 20: 9; 2 Cor 11: 33.*

θυρωρός, οῦ, ὁ and ἡ *doorkeeper* Mk 13: 34; J 10: 3; 18: 16f.*

θυσία, ας, ἡ *sacrifice, offering* lit. Mt 9: 13; Mk 12: 33; Ac 7: 41f; 1 Cor 10: 18; Hb 10: 1, 8, 12. Fig. Ro 12: 1; Phil 2: 17 (here *act of offering* is also possible); 4: 18; Hb 13: 15.

θυσιαστήριον, ου, τό *altar* lit. Mt 5: 23f; Lk 1: 11; 11: 51; Hb 7: 13; Js 2: 21; Rv 11: 1; 14: 18. Fig. Hb 13: 10.

θύω *sacrifice* Ac 14: 13, 18; 1 Cor 10: 20. *Slaughter, kill* Mt 22: 4; Lk 15: 23; J 10: 10; Ac 10: 13; 1 Cor 5: 7. *Celebrate* Mk 14: 12.

Θωμᾶς, ᾶ, ὁ (Aramaic = 'twin') *Thomas* Mt 10: 3; Mk 3: 18; Lk 6: 15; J 11: 16; 14: 5; 20: 24, 26–28; 21: 2; Ac 1: 13.*

θώραξ, ακος, ὁ *breastplate* lit. Rv 9: 9b, 17; fig. Eph 6: 14; 1 Th 5: 8. Probably *chest* Rv 9: 9a.*

I

'Ιάϊρος, ου, ὁ *Jaïrus* Mk 5: 22; Lk 8: 41.*

'Ιακώβ, ὁ indecl. *Jacob*—1. the patriarch, son of Isaac Mt 1: 2; Mk 12: 26; Lk 13: 28; J 4: 5f, 12; Ac 7: 8, 46; Ro 9: 13; 11: 26.—2. the father of Joseph, in the genealogy of Jesus Mt 1: 15f; Lk 3: 23 v.l.

'Ιάκωβος, ου, ὁ (Grecized form of the preceding) *James*—1. son of Zebedee, brother of John, member of the Twelve Mt 4: 21; Mk 3: 17; Lk 9: 28, 54; Ac 1: 13a; 12: 2.—2. son of Alphaeus Mt 10: 3; Mk 3: 18; Lk 6: 15; Ac 1: 13b. He is perhaps identical with—3. son of Mary Mt 27: 56; Mk 16: 1; Lk 24: 10; in Mk 15: 40 he is called 'I. ὁ μικρός James the small or the younger.—**4**. James, the Lord's brother Mt 13: 55; Mk 6: 3; 1 Cor 15: 7; Gal 1: 19; 2: 9, 12; Ac 12: 17; 15: 13; 21: 18; Js 1: 1.—**5**. James, father of an apostle named Judas Lk 6: 16a; Ac 1: 13c.—**6**. In Mk 2: 14 v.l. the tax-collector is called James (instead of Levi).

ἴαμα, ατος, τό healing 1 Cor 12: 9, 28, 30.*

Ἰαμβρῆς, ὁ Jambres an Egyptian sorcerer 2 Ti 3: 8.*

Ἰανναί, ὁ indecl. Jannai Lk 3: 24.*

Ἰάννης, ὁ Jannes an Egyptian sorcerer 2 Ti 3: 8.*

ἰάομαι heal, cure lit. Mt 8: 8, 13; Mk 5: 29; Lk 5: 17; 9: 11, 42; J 4: 47; 5: 13. Fig. restore Mt 13: 15; Lk 4: 18 v.l.; J 12: 40; Hb 12: 13.

Ἰάρετ, ὁ indecl. Jared Lk 3: 37.*

ἴασις, εως, ἡ healing, cure Lk 13: 32; Ac 4: 22, 30.*

ἴασπις, ιδος, ἡ jasper a precious stone found in various colors Rv 4: 3; 21: 11, 18f.*

Ἰάσων, ονος, ὁ Jason—**1**. Ac 17: 5-7, 9.—**2**. Ro 16: 21.—**3**. Ac 21: 16 v.l.*

ἰατρός, οῦ, ὁ physician Mt 9: 12; Mk 2: 17; 5: 26; Lk 4: 23; 5: 31; 8: 43 v.l.; Col 4: 14.*

Ἰαχίν, ὁ indecl. Jachin Lk 3: 23ff v.l.*

ιβ' numeral twelve Mk 6: 7 v.l.; Ac 1: 26 v.l.*

ἴδε imperative of εἶδον, stereotyped as a particle (you) see Mk 2: 24; 13: 1; J 3: 26; 5: 14; 11: 36; 12: 19; 18: 21; Gal 5: 2. Here is (are) Mt 25: 20; Mk 3: 34; 16: 6. There Mt 26: 65. You hear Mk 15: 4, cf. vs. 35.

ἰδέα, ας, ἡ appearance, aspect Lk 9: 29 v.l.*

ἴδιος, ία, ον one's own, private, peculiar to oneself Mt 25: 15; Lk 6: 41, 44; J 10: 3f; Ac 2: 8; 4: 32; Ro 10: 3; 1 Cor 3: 8; 4: 12; Tit 1: 3; 2: 5, 9; 2 Pt 1: 20; 2: 22. As noun οἱ ἴδιοι one's own people of fellow-Christians Ac 4: 23; 24: 23; relatives J 1: 11b; 1 Ti 5: 8. τὰ ἴδια home Lk 18: 28; J 1: 11a; 16: 32; Ac 21: 6, but property, supply J 8: 44 and one's own affairs 1 Th 4: 11; the sing. J 15: 19. ἰδίᾳ by oneself, privately 1 Cor 12: 11. κατ' ἰδίαν privately, by oneself Mt 14: 13; Mk 9: 2, 28; Lk 10: 23; Ac 23: 19; Gal 2: 2.

ἰδιώτης, ου, ὁ layman in contrast to an expert, untrained man Ac 4: 13. ἰ. τῷ λόγῳ unskilled in speaking 2 Cor 11: 6. Inquirer, catechumen of one seeking to know more about Christianity 1 Cor 14: 16, 23f.*

ἰδού aor. mid. imperative of εἶδον, used as a demonstrative particle when accented thus. Can be translated variously: (you) see, look, behold, or left untranslated Mt 2: 1, 13; 13: 3; Lk 1: 20; 22: 10; Ac 2: 7; Js 5: 9; Rv 9: 12; and yet Mt 7: 4; 2 Cor 6: 9; remember, consider Mt 10: 16; Lk 2: 48; Ac 9: 11; 2 Cor 7: 11; ἰ. δέκα κ. ὀκτὼ ἔτη eighteen long years Lk 13: 16. Here or there is (are) or was (were) or comes (came) Mt 3: 17; 12: ,10; Lk 7: 34, 37; 13: 11; J 19: 5; Ac 8: 27, 36; 2 Cor 6: 2; Rv 12: 3. ἰ. ἐγώ here I am Ac 9: 10.

Ἰδουμαία, ας, ἡ Idumaea (O.T. Edom) a mountainous district south of Judaea Mk 3: 8; Ac 2: 9 v.l.*

ἱδρώς, ῶτος, ὁ sweat, perspiration Lk 22: 44.*

Ἰεζάβελ, ἡ indecl. Jezebel (1 Kings 16: 31 and subsequent chapters), applied to a woman who endangered orthodox teaching Rv 2: 20.*

Ἱεράπολις, εως, ἡ Hierapolis, a city on the Lycus River in Asia Minor Col 4: 13.*

ἱερατεία, ας, ἡ *priestly office* Lk 1: 9; Hb 7: 5; *priesthood* Rv 5: 10 v.l.*

ἱεράτευμα, ατος, τό *priesthood* 1 Pt 2: 5, 9.*

ἱερατεύω *perform the service of a priest* Lk 1: 8.*

'Ιερεμίας, ου, ὁ *Jeremiah* the prophet Mt 2: 17; 16: 14; 27: 9.*

ἱερεύς, έως, ὁ *priest* Mt 8: 4; Mk 1: 44; Lk 10: 31; Ac 14: 13; Hb 7: 14f, 17, 20f, 23; 8: 4; Rv 20: 6.

'Ιεριχώ, ἡ indecl. *Jericho* a city in the Jordan valley just north of the Dead Sea Mt 20: 29; Mk 10: 46; Lk 10: 30; 18: 35; 19: 1; Hb 11: 30.*

ἱερόθυτος, ον *sacrificed to a deity* as noun τὸ ἱερόθυτον *meat sacrificed to idols* 1 Cor 10: 28.*

ἱερόν, οῦ, τό (neut. of the adj. ἱερός, used as a noun) *temple, sanctuary* Mt 12: 6; 21: 12; Mk 13: 3; Lk 22: 52; J 10: 23; Ac 19: 27.

ἱεροπρεπής, ές *worthy of reverence, holy* Tit 2: 3.*

ἱερός, ά, όν *holy* 2 Ti 3: 15; Col 4: 13 v.l. τὰ ἱερά *the holy things,* i.e. *services* 1 Cor 9: 13.*

'Ιεροσόλυμα, τά and ἡ, and 'Ιερουσαλήμ, ἡ indecl. *Jerusalem* the holy city Mt 2: 1, 3; Mk 3: 8; Lk 19: 28; J 2: 13; Ac 25: 1; Gal 4: 25; Hb 12: 22; Rv 21: 2.

'Ιεροσολυμίτης, ου, ὁ *an inhabitant of Jerusalem* Mk 1: 5; J 7:25.*

ἱεροσυλέω *rob temples* Ro 2: 22.*

ἱερόσυλος, ὁ *temple-robber* or simply *sacrilegious person* Ac 19: 37.*

ἱερουργέω *perform holy service, act as a priest* ἱ. τὸ εὐαγγέλιον *serve the gospel as a priest* Ro 15: 16.*

'Ιερουσαλήμ see 'Ιεροσόλυμα.

ἱερωσύνη, ης, ἡ *priestly office, priesthood* Hb 7: 11f, 24.*

'Ιεσσαί, ὁ indecl. *Jesse,* father of David (1 Sam 16) Mt 1: 5f; Lk 3: 32; Ac 13: 22; Ro 15: 12.*

'Ιεφθάε, ὁ indecl. *Jephthah* (Judges 11f) Hb 11: 32.*

'Ιεχονίας, ου, ὁ *Jechoniah* Mt 1: 11f; Lk 3: 23ff v.l.*

'Ιησοῦς, gen. οῦ, dat. οῦ, acc. οῦν, voc. οῦ, ὁ *Jesus,* Greek form of the Hebrew name Joshua or later Jeshua.—1. *Joshua,* successor to Moses Ac 7: 45; Hb 4: 8.—2. *Jesus,* son of Eliezer Lk 3: 29.—3. *Jesus Christ* Mt 1: 1, 21, 25 and often throughout the N.T.—4. *Jesus Barabbas* Mt 27: 16f v.l.—5. *Jesus* who is called Justus Col 4: 11.

ἱκανός, ή, όν—1. *sufficient, adequate, large enough* or simply *large, much. Large* Mk 10: 46; Ac 11: 24, 26. ἀργύρια *a large sum of money* Mt 28: 12. φῶς *a very bright light* Ac 22: 6. ἱκανὸν ἡ ἐπιτιμία *the punishment is severe enough* 2 Cor 2: 6. Of time *long, considerable* Lk 8: 27; 23: 8; Ac 14: 3; 27: 9; *many* Ac 9: 23, 43; Ro 15: 23. ἱκανόν ἐστιν *it is enough* Lk 22: 38. τὸ ἱκανὸν ποιεῖν *satisfy* Mk 15: 15. τὸ ἱκανόν *pledge, security, bond* Ac 17: 9. ἐφ' ἱκανόν *enough, as long as one wishes* Ac 20: 11.—2. *fit, appropriate, competent, able, worthy* Mt 3: 11; Lk 7: 6; 1 Cor 15: 9; 2 Cor 2: 16; 3: 5.

ἱκανότης, ητος, ἡ *fitness, capability, qualification* 2 Cor 3: 5.*

ἱκανόω *make sufficient, qualify, authorize* Col 1: 12; with double accusative 2 Cor 3: 6.*

ἱκετηρία, ας, ἡ *prayer, supplication* Hb 5: 7.*

ἱκμάς, άδος, ἡ *moisture* Lk 8: 6.*

'Ικόνιον, ου, τό *Iconium* a city in central Asia Minor Ac 13: 51; 14: 1, 19, 21; 16: 2; 2 Ti 3: 11.*

ἱλαρός, ά, όν *cheerful,* perhaps *kind, gracious* 2 Cor 9: 7.*

ἱλαρότης, ητος, ἡ *cheerfulness, graciousness* Ro 12: 8.*

ἱλάσκομαι—1. *propitiate, conciliate*

pass. *be propitiated, be merciful* Lk 18: 13.—**2.** *expiate* Hb 2: 17.*

ἱλασμός, οῦ, ὁ *expiation, propitiation, sin-offering* 1 J 2: 2; 4: 10.*

ἱλαστήριον, ου, τό *means of expiation, place of propitiation* Ro 3: 25; Hb 9: 5.*

ἵλεως, neut. ων (Attic second declension) *gracious, merciful* Hb 8: 12. ἵλεώς σοι *may God be gracious to you, God forbid* Mt 16: 22.*

'Ιλλυρικόν, οῦ, τό *Illyricum* a district across the Adriatic Sea from Italy Ro 15: 19.*

ἱμάς, άντος, ὁ leather *strap* or *thong* for sandals Mk 1: 7; Lk 3: 16; J 1: 27. In Ac 22: 25 ἵ. may mean *thong* or *whip.*.*

ἱματίζω *dress, clothe* Mk 5: 15; Lk 8: 35.*

ἱμάτιον, ου, τό *garment, clothing* in general Mt 9: 16; 27: 35; Mk 5: 28, 30; Lk 7: 25; Hb 1: 11f; 1 Pt 3: 3. *Cloak, robe* of outer clothing Mt 5: 40; 9: 20f; Lk 6: 29; 22: 36; J 19: 2; Ac 9: 39; 12: 8; 16: 22; Rv 19: 16.

ἱματισμός, οῦ, ὁ *clothing, apparel* Lk 7: 25; 9: 29; J 19: 24; Ac 20: 33; 1 Ti 2: 9.*

ἱμείρομαι *desire, long for* 1 Th 2: 8 v.l.*

ἵνα conjunction—**1.** denoting purpose, aim or goal *in order that, that* Mt 1: 22; Mk 4: 21; Lk 20: 10; J 5: 20; Ac 5: 15; Ro 14: 9; Gal 2: 4; Eph 6: 22; Rv 3: 9.—**2.** as a substitute for the infinitive, as used in Greek and English ἀρκετὸν τῷ μαθητῇ ἵνα γένηται *it is enough for the disciple to become* Mt 10: 25. τῷ θυρωρῷ ἐνετείλατο ἵνα γρηγορῇ *he gave orders to the door-keeper to be on the alert* Mk 13: 34. ἐδεήθην τῶν μαθητῶν ἵνα ἐκβάλωσιν αὐτό *I begged the disciples to cast it out* Lk 9: 40. Cf. Mt 7: 12; Mk 9: 30; 11: 16;

Lk 7: 6; J 6: 29; 16: 30; 1 Cor 1: 10; 4: 2; Rv 2: 21; 9: 5.— **3.** indicating result *so that* Lk 9: 45; J 9: 2; Gal 5: 17; Rv 9: 20. Sometimes purpose and result cannot be clearly differentiated Lk 11: 50; J 4: 36; Ro 3: 19; 8: 17.—**4.** as a periphrasis for the imperative ἵνα ἐπιθῇς τὰς χεῖρας αὐτῇ (please) *lay your hands on her* Mk 5: 23. ἡ δὲ γυνὴ ἵνα φοβῆται τὸν ἄνδρα *the wife is to respect her husband* Eph 5: 33. ἵνα ἀναπαήσονται *let them rest* Rv 14: 13. Cf. Mt 20: 33; Mk 10: 51; 2 Cor 8: 7; Gal 2: 10.

ἱνατί (ἵνα + τί) *why? for what reason?* Mt 9: 4; Lk 13: 7; Ac 4: 25; 1 Cor 10: 29.

'Ιόππη, ης, ἡ *Joppa*, modern Jaffa, a city on the s. coast of Palestine Ac 9: 36, 38, 42f; 10: 5, 8, 23, 32; 11: 5, 13.*

'Ιορδάνης, ου, ὁ *the Jordan*, chief river of Palestine Mt 3: 5f; 19: 1; Mk 10: 1; Lk 4: 1; J 3: 26; 10: 40.

ἰός, οῦ, ὁ *poison* Ro 3: 13; Js 3: 8. *Rust* Js 5: 3.*

'Ιουδαία, ας, ἡ *Judaea* the part of Palestine south of Samaria Mt 2: 1, 5, 22; 24: 16; Mk 1: 5; Lk 1: 65; 6: 17; Ac 1: 8; 12: 19; 28: 21; Ro 15: 31; Gal 1: 22. In a wider sense, the region occupied by the Jewish nation Mt 19: 1; Lk 1: 5; Ac 10: 37; 1 Th 2: 14.

ἰουδαΐζω *live as a Jew, according to Jewish customs* Gal 2: 14.*

'Ιουδαϊκός, ή, όν *Jewish* Tit 1: 14.*

'Ιουδαϊκῶς adv. *in a Jewish manner, according to Jewish customs* Gal 2: 14.*

'Ιουδαῖος, αία, αῖον *Jewish* Mk 1: 5; Ac 13: 6; 19: 13f; 21: 39. As noun ὁ 'Ι. *the Jew* Mt 2: 2; Mk 7: 3; Lk 23: 51; J 2: 18, 20; 9: 18, 22; 11: 8; Ac 2: 11; 18: 4; Ro 2: 9f, 17, 28f; 3: 1; Gal 2: 14. Of Jewish Christians Gal 2: 13.

'Ιουδαϊσμός, οῦ, ὁ *Judaism* Gal 1: 13f.*

'Ιούδας, α, ὁ *Judah* (Hebrew), *Judas* (Greek), *Jude* (see 8).— 1. *Judah*, son of Jacob, and the tribe named for him Mt 1: 2f; 2: 6; Lk 1: 39; Hb 7: 14; Rv 5: 5.—2. *Judas* in the genealogy of Jesus Lk 3: 30.—3. *Judas* of Galilee, a revolutionary Ac 5: 37.—4. *Judas* of Damascus, Paul's host Ac 9: 11.—5. *Judas*, an apostle, son (or brother) of James Lk 6: 16; J 14: 22; Ac 1: 13.—6. *Judas* Iscariot, betrayer of Jesus Mt 10: 4; 26: 14, 25, 47; 27: 3; Mk 3: 19; 14: 10, 43; Lk 6: 16; 22: 3, 47f; J 6: 71; 12: 4; 13: 2, 29; 18: 2f, 5; Ac 1: 16, 25.—7. *Judas* called Barsabbas, a Christian prophet Ac 15: 22, 27, 32 (34).—8. *Judas*, the brother of Jesus Mt 13: 55; Mk 6: 3. Probably the same man is meant by the *Jude* of Jd 1.

'Ιουλία, ας, ἡ *Julia* Ro 16: 15.*

'Ιούλιος, ου, ὁ *Julius* Ac 27: 1, 3.*

'Ιουνιᾶς, ᾶ ὁ *Junias* Ro 16: 7.*

'Ιοῦστος, ου, ὁ *Justus*, surname of—1. Joseph Barsabbas Ac 1: 23.—2. Titius Ac 18: 7.—3. Jesus, a Jewish Christian Col 4: 11.*

ἱππεύς, έως, ὁ *horseman, cavalry-man* Ac 23: 23, 32.*

ἱππικός, ή, όν *pertaining to a horseman* τὸ ἱ. *the cavalry* Rv 9: 16.*

ἵππος, ου, ὁ *horse, steed* Js 3: 3; Rv 6: 2, 4f, 8; 9: 7, 17; 18: 13; 19: 11, 14.

ἶρις, ιδος, ἡ *rainbow* Rv 10: 1. *Halo, radiance* 4: 3.*

'Ισαάκ, ὁ indecl. *Isaac* son of Abraham, father of Jacob Mt 8: 11; Mk 12: 26; Lk 3: 34; Ac 7: 8; Ro 9: 7, 10; Gal 4: 28; Hb 11: 17.

ἰσάγγελος, ον *like an angel* Lk 20: 36.*

ἴσασι 3rd pl. perf. act. ind. of οἶδα.

ἴσθι 2nd sing. imperative of εἰμί.

'Ισκαριώθ indecl. and 'Ισκαριώτης, ου, ὁ *Iscariot* surname of Judas the betrayer and of his father Mt 10: 4; 26: 14; Mk 14: 10; Lk 6: 16; 22: 3; J 6: 71; 13: 2, 26; 14: 22.

ἴσος, η, ον *equal* Mt 20: 12; J 5: 18; Rv 21: 16; *consistent* Mk 14: 56, 59. ἡ ἴ. *the same* Ac 11: 17; τὰ ἴσα *an equal amount* Lk 6: 34. ἴσα (used as adv.) εἶναι *be equal* Phil 2: 6.*

ἰσότης, ητος, ἡ *equality* 2 Cor 8: 14; ἐξ ἰσότητος *as a matter of equality* 8: 13. *Fairness* Col 4: 1.*

ἰσότιμος, ον *of the same kind*, lit. *equal in value* 2 Pt 1: 1.*

ἰσόψυχος, ον *of like soul* or *mind* Phil 2: 20.*

'Ισραήλ, ὁ indecl. *Israel*—1. the patriarch Jacob Mt 10: 6; Lk 1: 16; Ac 2: 36; Phil 3: 5; Hb 8: 10.—2. the nation of *Israel* Mt 2: 6; Mk 12: 29; Lk 2: 34; J 3: 10; Ac 4: 10; Ro 11: 2; Rv 7: 4.—3. of Christians as the true Israel Ro 9: 6b; Gal 6: 16.

'Ισραηλίτης, ου, ὁ *the Israelite* J 1: 47; Ro 11: 1; 2 Cor 11: 22. ἄνδρες 'Ισραηλῖται *men of Israel* Ac 2: 22; 5: 35; 21: 28.

'Ισσαχάρ, ὁ indecl. *Issachar* son of Jacob, and an Israelite tribe named after him Rv 7: 7.*

ἴστε 2nd pl. perf. act. ind. of οἶδα.

ἵστημι or ἱστάνω—1. trans. (pres., impf., fut., 1 aor. act.) *put, place, set, bring* Mt 25: 33; Mk 9: 36; Lk 4: 9; Ac 5: 27. *Put forward, propose* Ac 1: 23; 6: 13. *Establish, confirm* Ro 3: 31; 10: 3; Hb 10: 9. *Cause to stand* Ro 14: 4. *Set, fix* Ac 17: 31. *Set out* or *weigh out* Mt 26: 15.—2. intrans. (2 aor., perf., plpf. act.; fut. mid. and pass.; 1 aor. pass.) aor. and fut. *stand still, stop* Mt 20: 32; Mk 10: 49; Lk 6: 17; 8:

44; Ac 8: 38; Js 2: 3. *Come up, stand, appear* Mt 27: 11; Mk 13: 9; Lk 24: 36; Ac 10: 30; 11: 13. *Resist* Eph 6: 11, 13. *Stand firm, hold one's ground* Mt 12: 25f; Mk 3: 26; Ro 14: 4a; Eph 6: 14; Rv 6: 17. Perf. and plpf. *I stand, I stood* Mt 27: 47; Lk 23: 10; J 7: 37; Ac 1: 11. *Be, exist* Mt 12: 46f; 26: 73; Lk 18: 13; J 11: 56; Ac 7: 55f; 21: 40; Rv 18: 10. Fig. *stand, stand firm* Ro 11: 20; 1 Cor 7: 37; 2 Ti 2: 19. *Stand or be* Ro 5: 2; 1 Cor 15: 1; 2 Cor 1: 24.

ἱστίον, ου, τό *a sail* Ac 27: 16 v.l.*

ἱστορέω *visit* Gal 1: 18; Ac 17: 23 v.l.*

ἰσχυρός, ά, όν *strong, mighty, powerful* Mt 3: 11; Mk 3: 27; 1 Cor 1: 25; 4: 10; 10: 22; Rv 6: 15; 18: 8. *Severe* Lk 15: 14; *loud* Hb 5: 7; Rv 18: 2; 19: 6. *Effective* 2 Cor 10: 10.

ἰσχύς, ύος, ἡ *strength, power, might* Mk 12: 30, 33; Eph 1: 19; 2 Th 1: 9; 2 Pt 2: 11; Rv 5: 12.

ἰσχύω *be strong, powerful, able* Mt 8: 28; Mk 14: 37; Lk 14: 6, 29f; J 21: 6; Ac 15: 10. *Be strong enough* Lk 16: 3. *Be in good health* Mk 2: 17. *Win out, prevail* Ac 19: 16; Rv 12: 8. *Have meaning, be valid* Gal 5: 6; Hb 9: 17. ἰ. πολύ *be able to do much* Js 5: 16. εἰς οὐδέν *be good for nothing* Mt 5: 13.

ἴσως adv. *perhaps, probably* Lk 20: 13.*

'Ιταλία, ας, ἡ *Italy* Ac 18: 2; 27: 1, 6; Hb 13: 24; Hb subscription.*

'Ιταλικός, ή, όν *Italian* Ac 10: 1.*

'Ιτουραῖος, αία, αῖον ἡ 'Ι. χώρα *Ituraea* a region along the Lebanon and Anti-lebanon ranges, part of the tetrarchy of Philip Lk 3: 1.*

ἰχθύδιον, ου, τό *little fish* Mt 15: 34; Mk 8: 7.*

ἰχθύς, ύος, ὁ *fish* Mt 7: 10; 17: 27; Mk 6: 38, 41, 43; Lk 5: 6, 9; J 21: 6, 8, 11; 1 Cor 15: 39.

ἴχνος, ους, τό *footprint, footstep* fig. Ro 4: 12; 2 Cor 12: 18; 1 Pt 2: 21.*

'Ιωαθάμ, ὁ indecl. *Jotham* Mt 1: 9; Lk 3: 23ff v.l.*

'Ιωακίμ, ὁ indecl. *Jehoiakim* Mt 1: 11 v.l.; Lk 3: 23ff v.l.*

'Ιωανάν, ὁ indecl. *Joanan* Lk 3: 27.*

'Ιωάν(ν)α, ας, ἡ *Joanna* Lk 8: 3; 24: 10.*

'Ιωάν(ν)ης, ου, ὁ *John*—**1.** *John* the Baptist or Baptizer Mt 3: 1, 4, 13f; 11: 2, 4, 7, 11–13, 18; 21: 25f; Mk 1: 4; 6: 14, 16–18; Lk 16: 16; 20: 4, 6; J 1: 6, 15; 3: 23–27; Ac 1: 5, 22; 18: 25; 19: 3f.—**2.** *John*, son of Zebedee, brother of James, one of the 12 disciples Mt 4: 21; Mk 1: 19, 29; 5: 37; Lk 8: 51; Ac 3: 1, 3f, 11; 12: 2; Gal 2: 9.—**3.** *John* of the Apocalypse, equated by church tradition with 2, the son of Zebedee Rv 1: 1, 4, 9; 22: 8.—**4.** *John*, father of Peter J 1: 42; 21: 15–17.—**5.** *John* an otherwise unknown member of the high council Ac 4: 6.—**6.** *John* surnamed Mark Ac 12: 12, 25; 13: 5, 13; 15: 37.

'Ιωάς, ὁ indecl. *Joash*, king of Judah (2 Kings 14: 1) Mt 1: 8 v.l.; Lk 3: 23ff v.l.*

'Ιώβ, ὁ indecl. *Job*, hero of the book of the same name Js 5: 11.*

'Ιωβήδ, ὁ indecl. *Obed*, David's grandfather Mt 1: 5; Lk 3: 32.*

'Ιωδά, ὁ indecl. *Joda* Lk 3: 26.*

'Ιωήλ, ὁ indecl. *Joel*, the O.T. prophet Ac 2: 16.*

'Ιωνάθας, ου, ὁ *Jonathas* Ac 4: 6 v.l. instead of 'Ιωάννης.*

'Ιωνάμ, ὁ indecl. *Jonam* Lk 3: 30.*

'Ιωνᾶς, ᾶ, ὁ *Jonah*—**1.** the O.T. prophet Mt 12: 39–41; 16: 4; Lk

11: 29f, 32.—**2.** a Galilean fisherman, father of Simon Peter and Andrew Mt 16: 17 v.l. Also as v.l. in J 1: 42; 21: 15–17.*

'Ιωράμ, ὁ indecl. *Joram* or *Jehoram,* king of Judah (2 Kings 8: 16ff) Mt 1: 8; Lk 3: 23ff v.l.*

'Ιωρίμ, ὁ indecl. *Jorim* Lk 3: 29.*

'Ιωσαφάτ, ὁ indecl. *Jehoshaphat,* king of Judah (1 Kings 22: 41ff) Mt 1: 8; Lk 3: 23ff v.l.*

'Ιωσῆς, ῆ or **ῆτος, ὁ** *Joses*—**1.** a brother of Jesus Mk 6: 3; Mt 13: 55 v.l.—**2.** son of a woman named Mary and brother of James the younger Mk 15: 40, 47; Mt 27: 56 v.l.—**3.** a member of the early church better known as Barnabas Ac 4: 36 v.l.*

'Ιωσήφ, ὁ indecl. *Joseph*—**1.** the patriarch J 4: 5; Ac 7: 9, 13f, 18; Hb 11: 21f. In Rv 7: 8 the tribe of Joseph stands for the half-tribe Ephraim.—**2.** son of

Jonam Lk 3: 30—**3.** son of Mattathias Lk 3: 24.—**4.** husband of Mary the mother of Jesus Mt 1: 16, 18–20, 24; 2: 13, 19; Lk 1: 27; 2: 4, 16, 33 v.l.; 3: 23; 4: 22; J 1: 45; 6: 42.— **5.** a brother of Jesus Mt 13: 55.—**6.** *Joseph* of Arimathea Mt 27: 57, 59; Mk 15: 43, 45; Lk 23: 50; J 19: 38.—**7.** *Joseph,* surnamed Barnabas Ac 4: 36.— **8.** *Joseph,* surnamed Barsabbas, also called Justus 1: 23.—**9.** son of a certain Mary Mt 27: 56.*

'Ιωσήχ, ὁ indecl. *Josech* Lk 3: 26.*

'Ιωσίας, ου, ὁ *Josiah,* king of Judah (2 Kings 22) Mt 1: 10f; Lk 3: 23ff v.l.*

ἰῶτα, τό indecl. *iota,* smallest letter of the Greek alphabet, corresponding to yod, the smallest in the Aramaic alphabet Mt 5: 18.*

K

κάβος, ου, ὁ *the cab,* a dry measure equivalent to approximately two quarts Lk 16: 6 v.l.*

κἀγώ formed by crasis from καί plus ἐγώ, dat. κἀμοί, acc. κἀμέ *and I* Mt 11: 28; Lk 2: 48; J 1: 31, 33f; 6: 56; 2 Cor 12: 20; Gal 6: 14. *But I* J 12: 32; Ac 10: 28; Js 2: 18a. *I also, I too* Mt 2: 8; Lk 1: 3; J 5: 17; Ac 8: 19; 2 Cor 11: 21f. *I for my part, I in turn* Mt 10: 32f; Lk 11: 9; 22: 29; Rv 3: 10. *I in particular, I for instance* Ro 3: 7. κἀγώ = ἐγώ 1 Cor 7: 8; 10: 33; 11: 1; Eph 1: 15.

κάδος, ου, ὁ *jar, container* Lk 16: 6 v.l.*

καθά conj. or adv. *just as* Mt 6: 12 v.l.; 27: 10; Lk 1: 2 v.l.*

καθαίρεσις, εως, ἡ *tearing down,*

destruction 2 Cor 10: 4, 8; 13: 10.*

καθαιρέω—**1.** *take down, bring down* Mk 15: 36, 46; Lk 1: 52; 23: 53; Ac 13: 29.—**2.** *tear down, overpower, destroy* Lk 12: 18; Ac 13: 19; 2 Cor 10: 4; pass. *suffer the loss of* Ac 19: 27.*

καθαίρω *make clean;* of a vine *clear, prune* by removing superfluous wood J 15: 2.*

καθάπερ conj. or adv. *just as* Ro 3: 4; 11: 8; 1 Cor 10: 10; 2 Cor 3: 13, 18; 1 Th 2: 11. καθάπερ καί *as also* Ro 4: 6; 1 Th 3: 6, 12.

καθάπτω *take hold of, seize* Ac 28: 3.*

καθαριεῖ 3rd sing. of the Attic fut. of καθαρίζω.

καθαρίζω *make clean, cleanse, purify* lit. and fig. Mt 23: 25f;

Mk 7: 19; Ac 10: 15; 15: 9; 2 Cor 7: 1; Tit 2: 14; Hb 9: 22f; 10: 2; Js 4: 8. *Heal* Mt 8: 3.

καθαρισμός, οῦ, ὁ *purification* Mk 1: 44; Lk 2: 22; 5: 14; J 2: 6; 3: 25; Hb 1: 3; 2 Pt 1: 9.*

κάθαρμα, ατος τό *off-scouring, scapegoat* v.l. for περικάθαρμα (q.v.) in 1 Cor 4: 13.*

καθαρός, ά, όν *clean, pure* lit. and fig., ceremonially and morally Mt 5: 8; 23: 26; 27: 59; Lk 11: 41; J 13: 10; Ro 14: 20; Hb 10: 22; Js 1: 27; Rv 15: 6; 21: 18.

καθαρότης, ητος, ἡ *purity* Hb 9: 13.*

καθέδρα, ας, ἡ *chair, seat* Mt 21: 12; 23: 2; Mk 11: 15.*

καθέζομαι *sit* Mt 26: 55; Lk 2: 46; J 11: 20; Ac 6: 15; 20: 9; 3: 10 v.l. *Sit there* J 20: 12. *Sit down* 4: 6; 6: 3 v.l.*

καθεῖλον and **καθελεῖν** 2 aor. act. ind. and inf. of καθαιρέω.

καθεῖς = καθ' εἷς *individually* Ro 12: 5 v.l.*

καθεξῆς adv. *in order, one after the other* Lk 1: 3; Ac 3: 24; 11: 4; 18: 23; *afterward* Lk 8: 1.*

καθερίζω variant form of καθαρίζω.

καθεύδω *sleep* lit. Mt 8: 24; 13: 25; Mk 4: 27, 38; 14: 37, 40f. The fig. meaning *die, be dead* is possible in Mt 9: 24; Mk 5: 39; Lk 8: 52, and certain for 1 Th 5: 10. Of spiritual indifference Eph 5: 14; 1 Th 5: 6.

καθηγητής, οῦ, ὁ *teacher* Mt 23: 10.*

καθῆκα aor. act. ind. of καθίημι.

καθήκω *be proper* or *fitting* Ac 22: 22. τὰ μὴ καθήκοντα *what is improper* Ro 1: 28.*

κάθημαι *sit* Mt 26: 64; 27: 61; Mk 2: 6; 13: 3; Lk 10: 13; 18: 35; Ac 8: 28; 23: 3; Col 3: 1; Rv 6: 8, 16; *sit (there)* Lk 5: 17; J 2: 14; *be enthroned* Rv 18: 7. *Stay, live, reside* Lk 1: 79; 21: 35; Rv 14: 6. *Sit down* Mt 22:

44; 28: 2; Mk 4: 1; Ac 2: 34; Js 2: 3.

καθημέραν = καθ' (κατά) ἡμέραν.

καθημερινός, ή, όν *daily* Ac 6: 1.*

καθῆψα 1 aor. act. ind. of καθάπτω.

καθίζω—1. trans. *cause to sit down, seat, set* Ac 2: 30; Eph 1: 20. *Appoint* 1 Cor 6: 4.—2. intrans. *sit down* Mt 5: 1; 26: 36; Mk 9: 35; Lk 4: 20; Ac 8: 31; 13: 14; 1 Cor 10: 7; Hb 1: 3; *rest* Ac 2: 3. *Settle, stay, live* Lk 24: 49; Ac 18: 11.

καθίημι *let down* Lk 5: 19; Ac 9: 25; 10: 11; 11: 5.*

καθιστάνω see καθίστημι.

καθίστημι and **καθιστάνω**—1. *bring, conduct, take* Ac 17: 15.—2. *appoint, put in charge* Mt 24: 45, 47; Ac 6: 3; *ordain, appoint* Lk 12: 14; Ac 7: 10, 27; Tit 1: 5; Hb 5: 1.—3. *make, cause* 2 Pt 1: 8. Pass. *be made, become* Ro 5: 19; Js 4: 4.

καθό adv. = καθ' ὅ. *as* Ro 8: 26. *In so far as, to the degree that* 2 Cor 8: 12; 1 Pt 4: 13.*

καθολικός, ή, όν *general, universal, catholic* Js inscription v.l.*

καθόλου adv. *entirely, completely* μὴ κ. *not at all* Ac 4: 18.*

καθοπλίζω mid. *arm* or *equip oneself* Lk 11: 21.*

καθοράω *perceive* Ro 1: 20.*

καθότι *as, to the degree that* Ac 2: 45; 4: 35. *Because, in view of the fact that* Lk 1: 7; 19: 9; Ac 2: 24; 17: 31.*

κάθου pres. imperative 2 sing. of κάθημαι.

καθώς adv. *as, just as* Mt 21: 6; 28: 6; Mk 1: 2; Lk 11: 30; 24: 24; J 1: 23; Ac 15: 8; Ro 1: 17; 1 Cor 15: 49; 2 Cor 1: 5; 1 Ti 1: 3; 1 J 3: 2. *As, to the degree that* Mk 4: 33; Ac 11: 29; 1 Cor 12: 11, 18; 1 Pt 4: 10. *Since, in so far as* J 17: 2; Ro 1: 28; Eph 1: 4; Phil 1: 7. *When* Ac 7: 17. *How, that* Ac 15: 14; 3 J 3.

καθώσπερ adv. *just as* Hb 5: 4;
2 Cor 3: 18 v.l.*

καί conjunction—**1.** *and* Mt 13:
55; 23: 32; Lk 2: 47; 3: 14; Ro
7: 12; Ac 5: 29; Hb 1: 1.
When Mt 26: 45; Mk 15: 25;
J 2: 13; Hb 8: 8. *That* = ὅτι Mk
6: 14. καὶ ἐγένετο . . . καί *and
it came about* . . . *that* Mt 9: 10;
Mk 2: 15; Lk 5: 1, 12, 17.
But Mt 12: 43; Lk 13: 7; Ro
1: 13; 1 Th 2: 18. *And so, that is,
namely* Mt 8: 33; J 1: 16; Ro
1: 5; 1 Cor 3: 5. καί . . . καί
both . . . *and, not only* . . . *but also*
Mt 10: 28; Mk 4: 41; 9: 13; J
7: 28; Ac 26: 29; 1 Cor 1: 22;
Phil 4: 16. Sometimes καί may
be left untranslated as πολλὰ . . .
κ. ἄλλα σημεῖα *many other signs*
J 20: 30; cf. Lk 3: 18; Ac 25:
7.—**2.** used rather as an adverb
also, likewise Mt 5: 39f; 12: 45;
Mk 8: 7. *Even* Mt 5: 46f; Mk 1:
27; Ac 5: 39; 2 Cor 1: 8; Phlm
21; Hb 7: 25; Jd 23. ὁ καί with
double names *who is also called*
Ac 13: 9.

Καϊάφας, α, ὁ *Caiaphas,* high
priest 18–36 A.D.: Mt 26: 3, 57;
Lk 3: 2; J 11: 49; 18: 13f, 24,
28; Ac 4: 6.*

καίγε = καί + γε

Κάϊν, ὁ indecl. *Cain,* son of Adam
Hb 11: 4; 1 J 3: 12; Jd 11.*

Καϊνάμ, ὁ indecl. *Cainan*—**1.** son
of Arphaxad Lk 3: 36.—**2.** son
of Enos 3: 37.*

καινός, ή, όν *new* Mt 13: 52; 27:
60; Mk 2: 21f; Lk 22: 20; J 13:
34; 2 Cor 3: 6; 5: 17; Hb 9: 15;
Rv 2: 17; 5: 9; 21: 1, 5; *strange*
Mk 1: 27. Comparative τι καινό-
τερον *something quite new* Ac
17: 21.

καινότης, ητος, ἡ *newness* κ. ζωῆς
a new life Ro 6: 4; cf. 7: 6.*

καινοφωνία see κενοφωνία.

καίπερ conjunction *although* Phil
3: 4; Hb 5: 8; 7: 5; 12: 17; 2 Pt
1: 12.*

καιρός, οῦ, ὁ *time,* i.e. *point of time*
as well as *period of time*—**1.** generally Lk 21: 36; Ac 14: 17; 2
Cor 6: 2; Eph 6: 18; 2 Ti 3: 1;
present (time) Ro 3: 26; 13: 11.
κατὰ καιρόν *from time to time*
J 5: 4.—**2.** *the right, proper,
favorable time* Mt 24: 45; Mk
12: 2; Lk 20: 10; J 7: 6, 8; Ac
24: 25. *Opportunity* Gal 6: 10;
Col 4: 5; Hb 11: 15.—**3.** *definite,
fixed time* Mt 13: 30; 26: 18; Mk
11: 13; Lk 8: 13; 19: 44; Gal 4:
10; 6: 9; 2 Ti 4: 6.—**4.** *the time
of crisis, the last times* Mt 8: 29;
16: 3; Mk 10: 30; 13: 33; Lk
21: 8; 1 Cor 7: 29; Eph 1: 10;
Rv 1: 3.

Καῖσαρ, ος, ὁ *Caesar, emperor* Mk
12: 14, 16f; Lk 2: 1; 3: 1; 23: 2;
J 19: 12; Ac 17: 7; 25: 10–12;
Phil 4: 22.

Καισάρεια, ας, ἡ *Caesarea*—**1.**
Καισάρεια ἡ Φιλίππου *Caesarea
Philippi,* a city at the foot of Mt.
Hermon, in the tetrarchy of
Philip Mt 16: 13; Mk 8: 27.—
2. *Caesarea* 'by the sea,' south
of Mt. Carmel, seat of the Roman procurators and capital of
Palestine Ac 8: 40; 10: 1, 24;
18: 22; 21: 8, 16; 25: 1, 4, 6,
13.

καίτοι particle *and yet* Ac 14: 17;
Hb 4: 3.*

καίτοιγε or καίτοι γε particle *and
yet* J 4: 2; Ac 14: 17 v.l.*

καίω—**1.** *light* something, *have* or
keep something *burning* lit. Mt
5: 15; Lk 12: 35; J 5: 35; Hb
12: 18; Rv 8: 8, 10; 21: 8.
Fig. Lk 24: 32.—**2.** pass. *be
burned* J 15: 6; 1 Cor 13: 3.

κἀκεῖ = καὶ ἐκεῖ adv. *and there*
Mt 5: 23; 10: 11; 28: 10; J 11:
54; Ac 14: 7; 27: 6. *There also*
Mk 1: 38 v.l.; Ac 17: 13.

κἀκεῖθεν = καὶ ἐκεῖθεν adv. *and
from there* Mk 9: 30; Lk 11: 53;
Ac 7: 4; 16: 12; 27: 4; 28: 15.
And then Ac 13: 21.

κἀκεῖνος, η, ο = καὶ ἐκεῖνος *and that one, and he* Lk 11: 7; J 10: 16; Ac 18: 19; *and he, and it* or *that* Mt 15: 18; Mk 16: 11; J 7: 29. *That one also, also he, he too* Mk 12: 4f; Lk 20: 11; J 6: 57; Ac 15: 11; 1 Cor 10: 6; 2 Ti 2: 12.

κακία, ας, ἡ *badness, faultiness* in the sense *depravity, wickedness, vice* Ac 8: 22; 1 Cor 14: 20; Js 1: 21; 1 Pt 2: 16. *Malice, ill-will, malignity* Ro 1: 29; Col 3: 8; 1 Pt 2: 1. *Trouble, misfortune* Mt 6: 34.

κακοήθεια, ας, ἡ *malice, malignity, craftiness* Ro 1: 29.*

κακολογέω *speak evil of, revile, insult* Mt 15: 4; Mk 7: 10; 9: 39; Ac 19: 9.*

κακοπάθεια, ας, ἡ and κακοπαθία, ας, ἡ *perseverance, strenuous effort* Js 5: 10.*

κακοπαθέω *suffer misfortune* 2 Ti 2: 9; Js 5: 13. *Bear hardship patiently* 2 Ti 4: 5.*

κακοπαθία see κακοπάθεια.

κακοποιέω *do wrong, be an evil-doer* or *a criminal* 1 Pt 3: 17; 3 J 11. In Mk 3: 4 = Lk 6: 9 the meaning may be as above or *harm, injure.*

κακοποιός, όν *doing evil*, as noun *evil-doer, criminal* 1 Pt 2: 12, 14; 4: 15; J 18: 30 v.l.*

κακός, ή, όν *bad, evil* Mt 21: 41; 24: 48; 27: 23; Mk 7: 21; J 18: 23; Ro 7: 19, 21; 1 Cor 15: 33; Rv 2: 2. *Evil, wrong, harmful*, as noun *harm* Ac 9: 13; 16: 28; 28: 5; Ro 12: 17; 13: 10; 14: 20; Js 3: 8; 1 Pt 3: 9.

κακοῦργος, ον as noun ὁ κ. *criminal, evil-doer* Lk 23: 32f, 39; 2 Ti 2: 9.*

κακουχέω *maltreat, torment* Hb 11: 37; 13: 3.*

κακόω *harm, mistreat* Ac 7: 6, 19; 12: 1; 18: 10; 1 Pt 3: 13. *Make angry, embitter* Ac 14: 2.*

κακῶς adv. *badly, wrongly, wickedly* J 18: 23; Ac 23: 5; Js

4: 3. *Severely* Mt 15: 22; 17: 15 v.l. κ. ἔχειν *be ill, sick* Mt 4: 24; Mk 6: 55; Lk 5: 31.

κάκωσις, εως, ἡ *mistreatment, oppression* Ac 7: 34.*

καλάμη, ης, ἡ *straw*, perhaps *stubble* 1 Cor 3: 12.*

κάλαμος, ου, ὁ *reed* Mt 11: 7; 12: 20; Lk 7: 24. *Stalk, staff* Mt 27: 29f, 48; Mk 15: 19, 36. *Measuring rod* Rv 11: 1; 21: 15f. *Reed pen* 3 J 13.*

καλέω *call, name, address as* Mt 22: 43, 45; 23: 7f,10; Lk 1: 59f; 2: 4; 10: 39; Ac 14: 12; Ro 9: 26; 1 Pt 3: 6. Almost equivalent to the verb 'to be' Mt 2: 23; Lk 1: 32, 35f; 1 Cor 15: 9; Hb 3: 13. *Invite* Mt 22: 3, 9; J 2: 2; 1 Cor 10: 27; Rv 19: 9; *call together* Mt 20: 8; 25: 14; Lk 19: 13. *Summon* Mt 2: 7, 15; Mk 3: 31; Ac 4: 18; 24: 2. Fig., of God or Christ *call* to eternal salvation, repentance, etc. Mk 2: 17; 1 Cor 1: 9; Gal 5: 8, 13; Eph 4: 1; 1 Ti 6: 12; Hb 9: 15; 1 Pt 5: 10.

καλλιέλαιος, ου, ἡ *the cultivated olive tree* Ro 11: 24.*

κάλλιον comparative degree of καλῶς.

καλοδιδάσκαλος, ον *teaching what is good* Tit 2: 3.*

Καλοὶ λιμένες, Καλῶν λιμένων, οἱ *Fair Havens* a bay on the south coast of Crete, near the city of Lasaea Ac 27: 8.*

καλοκἀγαθία, ας, ἡ *nobility of character, excellence* Js 5: 10 v.l.*

καλοποιέω *do what is right* or *good* 2 Th 3: 13.*

καλός, ή, όν *beautiful* Lk 21: 5. *Good, useful, free from defects, fine* Mt 7: 17ff; 13: 8, 23, 48; Mk 4: 8, 20; Lk 14: 34; J 2: 10. *Morally good, noble, praiseworthy* Mt 5: 16; Mk 14: 6; Ro 7: 18, 21; Gal 6: 9; Hb 5: 14; 10: 24; 13: 18; Js 2: 7; 4: 17; 1 Pt

4: 10. καλόν (ἐστιν) *it is good,
pleasant, advantageous* Mt 18:
8f; Mk 9: 5; 1 Cor 7: 26a;
morally good Mk 7: 27; 1 Cor 7:
1, 8, 26b; Hb 13: 9. καλόν ἐστιν
αὐτῷ μᾶλλον *it is better for him*
Mk 9: 42. καλὸν ἦν αὐτῷ *it
would have been better for him*
Mt 26: 24.

κάλυμμα, ατος, τό *veil, covering*
lit. 2 Cor 3: 13. Fig. 3: 14, 15, 16.*

καλύπτω *cover, hide, conceal* lit.
Mt 8: 24; Lk 8: 16; 23: 30. Fig.
Js 5: 20; 1 Pt 4: 8; 2 Cor 4: 3.

καλῶς adv. *well* Mk 7: 37; Lk 6:
48; Gal 5: 7; *rightly* Mk 7: 6;
as exclamation *well said* Mk
12: 32; Ro 11: 20; used ironi-
cally 2 Cor 11: 4. κ. ποιεῖν *do
good* Mt 12: 12; Lk 6: 27, but
do what is right 1 Cor 7: 37f;
Js 2: 8, 19. κ. ἔχειν *be in good
health* Mk 16: 18. Comparative
κάλλιον Ac 25: 10.

κάμέ = καὶ ἐμέ.

κάμηλος, ου, ὁ and ἡ *camel* Mt
3: 4; 23: 24; Mk 10: 25; Lk
18: 25.

κάμητε 2 pl. 2 aor. subj. act. of
κάμνω.

κάμιλος, ου, ὁ *rope, ship's cable* as
v.l. in Mt 19: 24; Mk 10: 25;
Lk 18: 25.*

κάμινος, ου, ἡ *oven, furnace* Mt
13: 42, 50; Rv 1: 15; 9: 2.*

καμμύω *close (the eyes)* Mt 13: 15;
Ac 28: 27.*

κάμνω *be weary* Hb 12: 3. *Be
ill* Js 5: 15.*

κάμοί = καὶ ἐμοί.

κάμπτω *bend, bow* Ro 11: 4; 14:
11; Eph 3: 14; Phil 2: 10.*

κἄν = καὶ ἐάν *and if* Mk 16: 18;
Lk 12: 38; J 8: 55; Js 5: 15.
Even if Mt 21: 21; J 8: 14; Hb
12: 20. *(Even) if only, at least* Ac
5: 15; 2 Cor 11: 16.

Κανά, ἡ indecl. *Cana,* a city in
Galilee J 2: 1, 11; 4: 46; 21: 2.*

Καναναῖος, ου, ὁ *Cananaean* surname of the second Simon

among the 12; it means *enthusiast, zealot* Mt 10: 4; Mk 3: 18.*

Κανανίτης, ου, ὁ *Canaanite, man
from Cana,* as v.l. in Mt 10: 4; Mk
3: 18.*

Κανδάκη, ης, ἡ *Candace,* title of
the queen of Ethiopia Ac 8: 27.*

κανών, όνος, ὁ—1. *rule, standard*
Gal 6: 16.—2. *sphere* of action,
province, limits 2 Cor 10: 13, 15f.

Καπερναούμ see Καφαρναούμ.

καπηλεύω *trade in, peddle, huck-
ster* 2 Cor 2: 17.*

καπνός, οῦ, ὁ *smoke* Ac 2: 19;
Rv 9: 2f, 17f; 15: 8.

Καππαδοκία, ας, ἡ *Cappadocia,*
a province in the interior of
Asia Minor Ac 2: 9; 1 Pt 1: 1.*

καραδοκία, ας, ἡ *eager expectation*
Phil 1: 20 v.l.*

καρδία, ας, ἡ *heart* as the seat of
physical life Ac 14: 17. Mainly
as the center and source of the
whole inner life Mt 18: 35; Lk
16: 15; 2 Cor 5: 12; 1 Th 2: 4;
1 Pt 1: 22; 3: 4. Of the emotions
J 16: 6, 22; Ro 1: 24; Hb 10:
22. Of the will Ac 11: 23; Ro
2: 5, 15; 2 Pt 2: 14. καρδία may
sometimes be translated *mind*
Lk 24: 25; Ac 7: 23; Ro 1: 21;
2 Cor 9: 7, and approaches the
sense *conscience* 1 J 3: 20f. ἐν
τῇ κ. *to oneself* Mt 24: 48; Ro
10: 6; Rv 18: 7. Fig. καρδία in
the sense *interior, center* Mt
12: 40.

καρδιογνώστης, ου, ὁ *knower of
hearts* Ac 1: 24; 15: 8.*

Κάρπος, ου, ὁ *Carpus,* a Christian
2 Ti 4: 13.*

καρπός, οῦ, ὁ *fruit*—1. lit. Mt 12:
33; 21: 34; Mk 11: 14; Lk 13:
6f; Js 5: 7, 18; Rv 22: 2.
Crop(s) Mk 4: 29; Lk 12: 17; J
4: 36. Of offspring Lk 1: 42;
Ac 2: 30.—2. fig. *fruit* in the
sense *result, outcome, deed* Mt
7: 16, 20; J 15: 5, 8, 16; Gal 5:
22; Eph 5: 9; Phil 1: 11; Js 3:
18; Hb 12: 11. In the sense

advantage, gain Ro 1: 13; Phil 1: 22; 4: 17.

καρποφορέω *bear fruit* or *crops*—**1.** lit. Mk 4: 28.—**2.** fig. Mt 13: 23; Mk 4: 20; Lk 8: 15; Ro 7: 4f; Col 1: 6, 10.*

καρποφόρος, ον *fruitbearing, fruitful* Ac 14: 17; J 15: 2 v.l.*

καρτερέω *endure, persevere* Hb 11: 27.*

κάρφος, ους, τό *speck, chip,* a small piece of straw, chaff, wood, etc. Mt 7: 3ff; Lk 6: 41f.*

κατά prep. w. gen. and acc.—**I.** with the genitive—**1.** of place *down (from)* Mk 5: 13; *throughout* Lk 23: 5; Ac 9: 31, 42; 10: 37.—**2.** fig. *by* Mt 26: 63; Hb 6: 13, 16. *Against* Mt 5: 11; 10: 35; Mk 14: 55; Lk 11: 23; J 19: 11; Ac 25: 3, 15, 27; Ro 8: 31; 1 Cor 4: 6; Gal 5: 17; Rv 2, 4, 14, 20. —**II.** with the accusative—**1.** of place—**a.** of extension in space *along* Ac 25: 3; 27: 5. *Through* Lk 8: 39. *Throughout* Ac 11: 1. *Over* 8: 1. *Among* 21: 21.—**b.** of direction *toward* Ac 8: 26; Phil 3: 14. *Up to* Lk 10: 32; *to* Ac 16: 7. κατὰ πρόσωπον *to the face* Gal 2: 11.—**c.** serving to isolate or separate *by* Ac 28: 16; Js 2: 17; *to* Ro 14: 22. κατὰ μόνας *alone, by oneself* Mk 4: 10; Lk 9: 18.—**d.** as a distributive κατὰ πόλιν *in every city* Ac 15: 21; 20: 23; Tit 1: 5. Cf. Lk 8: 1; Ac 15: 36.—**2.** of time *at* Ro 9: 9; *in* Hb 1: 10; 3: 8; *during* Mt 1: 20; 2: 12; *about* Ac 16: 25. Distributively κ. ἔτος *every year* Lk 2: 41; cf. Mt 26: 55; Ac 2: 46f; 17: 17; 2 Cor 11: 28; Rv 22: 2.—**3.** distributively (apart from place and time as above) κ. δύο ἤ τρεῖς *two or three at a time* 1 Cor 14: 27. κ. ἕνα *one after the other* 14: 31. Cf. Mk 6: 40; Ac 21: 19. κ. ὄνομα *by name* J 10: 3; 3 J

15.—**4.** of goal or purpose *for (the purpose of)* J 2: 6; *to* 2 Cor 11: 21.—**5.** of the norm, of similarity, homogeneity—**a.** to introduce the norm which governs something *according to, in accordance with* Mt 2: 16; Lk 2: 22; 22: 22; J 19: 7; Ro 8: 28; 1 Cor 3: 8; 15: 3; Hb 7: 5. *As a result of, on the basis of* Mt 19: 3; Gal 2: 2; Phil 4: 11; Phlm 14.—**b.** of equality, similarity, example (*just*) *as, similar(ly) to* Mt 23: 3; Gal 4: 28. κατὰ τὰ αὐτά *in (just) the same way* Lk 6: 23, 26; 17: 30. κατὰ τὸ αὐτό *together* Ac 14: 1. καθ' ὃν τρόπον *just as* 15: 11; 27: 25. Frequently the κατά-phrase is equivalent to an adverb: κ. συγκυρίαν *by chance* Lk 10: 31. κ. κράτος *powerfully* Ac 19: 20. κ. λόγον *reasonably* 18: 14.— **6.** denoting relationship to something *with respect to, in relation to* Ac 17: 22; Ro 1: 3f; 9: 3, 5; Col 3: 20, 22; Hb 2: 17.—**7.** sometimes the κατά-phrase can function as an adj., a possessive pronoun, or the genitive of a noun. Adj.: κατὰ φύσιν *natural* Ro 11: 21. κατὰ σαρκα *earthly* Eph 6: 5. Poss. pron.: καθ' ὑμᾶς *your* Ac 17: 28. κατ' ἐμέ *my* Ro 1: 15. Gen. of a noun κ. Ἰουδαίους *of the Jews* Ac 26: 3. κ. πίστιν *of faith* Hb 11: 7. Cf. the title εὐαγγέλιον κατὰ Ματθαῖον, etc.

κατάβα 2 aor. act. imperative, 2 sing. of καταβαίνω.

καταβαίνω *come down, go down, climb down* Mt 8: 1; Mk 1: 10; 9: 9; 15: 30, 32; Lk 19: 5f; Ac 25: 7; J 2: 12; 4: 47, 49, 51; Ro 10: 7; Eph 4: 10; Js 1: 17; Rv 12: 12. *Get out* Mt 14: 29. *Fall* 7: 25, 27. Fig. *be brought down* 11: 23.

καταβάλλω act. and pass. *throw down, strike down* 2 Cor 4: 9; Rv

12: 10 v.l. Mid. *found, lay (a foundation)* fig. Hb 6: 1.*

καταβαρέω *burden, be a burden to* 2 Cor 12: 16.*

καταβαρύνω *weigh down, burden* pass. *be heavy* Mk 14: 40.*

κατάβασις, εως, ἡ *slope, declivity* Lk 19: 37.*

καταβάτω 2 aor. imperative act., 3rd sing., of καταβαίνω.

καταβῇ 2 aor. subj. act., 3rd sing., of καταβαίνω.

καταβιβάζω *bring down, make come down* Mt 11: 23 v.l.; Lk 10: 15 v.l.; Ac 19: 33 v.l.*

καταβοάω *cry out, bring charges, complain* Ac 18: 13 vl.*

καταβολή, ῆς, ἡ *foundation, beginning* Mt 25: 34; Lk 11: 50; J 17: 24; Eph 1: 4; Hb 11: 11; Rv 17: 8.

καταβραβεύω *decide against* (as umpire), *rob of a prize, condemn* Col 2: 18.*

καταγαγεῖν 2 aor. act. inf. of κατάγω.

καταγγελεύς, έως, ὁ *proclaimer, preacher* Ac 17: 18.*

καταγγέλλω *proclaim* Ac 13: 5; 16: 21; 17: 23; Ro 1: 8; 1 Cor 9: 14; 11: 26; Phil 1: 17f.

καταγελάω *laugh at, ridicule* w. gen. Mt 9: 24; Mk 5: 40; Lk 8: 53.*

καταγινώσκω *condemn* w. gen. Gal 2: 11; 1 J 3: 20f; Mk 7: 2 v.l.*

κατάγνυμι *break* Mt 12: 20; J 19: 31–33.*

καταγράφω *write* J 8: 6, also vs. 8 v.l.*

κατάγω *lead* or *bring down* Ac 9: 30; 22: 30; 23: 15, 20, 28; Ro 10: 6. Act. *bring boats to land* Lk 5: 11; pass. *put in* at a harbor Ac 27: 3; 28: 12; 21: 3 v.l.*

καταγωνίζομαι *conquer, defeat, overcome* Hb 11: 33.*

καταδέω *bind up* Lk 10: 34.*

κατάδηλος, ον *very clear, quite plain* Hb 7: 15.*

καταδικάζω *condemn* Mt 12: 7, 37; Lk 6: 37; Js 5: 6.*

καταδίκη, ης, ἡ *condemnation, sentence of condemnation* Ac 25: 15.*

καταδιώκω *search for, hunt for* Mk 1: 36.*

καταδουλόω *enslave, reduce to slavery* fig. 2 Cor 11: 20; Gal 2: 4.*

καταδυναστεύω *oppress, exploit, dominate* w. gen. Ac 10: 38; Js 2: 6.*

κατάθεμα, ατος, τό *accursed thing* Rv 22: 3.*

καταθεματίζω *curse* Mt 26: 74.*

καταισχύνω *dishonor, disfigure* 1 Cor 11: 4f. *Put to shame* 1 Cor 1: 27; pass. *be put to shame, be humiliated* Lk 13: 17; 2 Cor 7: 14; 9: 4; 1 Pt 3: 16; Mt 20: 28 v.l. *Humiliate* 1 Cor 11: 22. *Disappoint* Ro 5: 5; pass. 9: 33; 10: 11; 1 Pt 2: 6.*

κατακαήσομαι 2 fut. pass. ind. of κατακαίω.

κατακαίω *burn up, burn down, consume by fire* Mt 3: 12; 13: 30, 40; Ac 19: 19; Hb 13: 11; Rv 8: 7; 18: 8; 2 Pt 3: 10 v.l.

κατακαλύπτω mid. *cover oneself with a veil* 1 Cor 11: 6f.*

κατακαῦσαι, κατακαύσει 1 aor. act. inf., fut. act. ind. 3rd sing. of κατακαίω.

κατακαυχάομαι *boast (against)* Ro 11: 18; Js 3: 14; 4: 16 v.l. *Triumph over* w. gen. Js 2: 13.*

κατάκειμαι *lie down* of sick people Mk 1: 30; 2: 4; cf. 5: 40 v.l.; Lk 5: 25; J 5: 3, 6; Ac 9: 33; 28: 8. *Recline* on a couch at table, *dine* Mk 2: 15; 14: 3; Lk 5: 29; 7: 37; 1 Cor 8: 10.*

κατακλάω *break in pieces* Mk 6: 41; Lk 9: 16.*

κατακλείω *shut up, lock up* Lk 3: 20; Ac 26: 10.*

κατακληροδοτέω *parcel out by lot* Ac 13: 19 v.l.*

κατακληρονομέω *give (over) as an inheritance* Ac 13: 19.*

110   κατακλίνω–καταναρκάω

κατακλίνω act. *cause to lie down
or sit down* to eat Lk 9: 14f.
Pass. *recline at table* Lk 7: 36;
14: 8; 24: 30.*

κατακλύζω *flood, inundate* pass.
2 Pt 3: 6.*

κατακλυσμός, οῦ, ὁ *flood, deluge*
Mt 24: 38f; Lk 17: 27; 2 Pt 2:
5.*

κατακολουθέω *follow* w. dat. Lk
23: 55; Ac 16: 17.*

κατακόπτω *cut, bruise, beat* Mk
5: 5.*

κατακρημνίζω *throw down (from)
a cliff* Lk 4: 29.*

κατάκριμα, ατος, τό *punishment,
doom* Ro 5: 16, 18; 8: 1.*

κατακρίνω *condemn* Mt 27: 3;
Mk 10: 33; Lk 11: 31f; Ro 2: 1;
8: 3, 34; Hb 11: 7; 2 Pt 2: 6.

κατάκρισις, εως, ἡ *condemnation*
2 Cor 3: 9; 7: 3.*

κατακύπτω *bend down* J 8: 8.*

κατακυριεύω *become master, gain
dominion over, subdue* w. gen. Ac
19: 16. *Be master, lord it (over),
rule* w. gen. Mt 20: 25; Mk 10:
42; 1 Pt 5: 3.*

καταλαλέω *speak against, speak
evil of, slander* w. gen. Js 4: 11;
1 Pt 2: 12; 3: 16.*

καταλαλιά, ᾶς, ἡ *evil speech,
slander, defamation* 2 Cor 12: 20;
1 Pt 2: 1.*

κατάλαλος, ον *slanderous* subst. ὁ
κ. *the slanderer* Ro 1: 30.*

καταλαμβάνω—1.—a. act. and
pass. *seize, win, attain, make one's
own* Ro 9: 30; 1 Cor 9: 24; Phil
3: 12f; ending of Mk in the
Freer Gospels 3. For J 1: 5
there are two sets of possibilities:
grasp, comprehend and *overcome,
put out, master.—**b.** *seize with
hostile intent, overtake, come
upon* Mk 9: 18; J 12: 35; 6: 17
v.l.; 1 Th 5: 4.—**c.** *catch, detect*
J 8: 3f.—**2.** mid. *grasp, find,
understand* Ac 4: 13; 10: 34;
25: 25; Eph 3: 18.*

καταλέγω *select, enroll* 1 Ti 5: 9.*

κατάλειμμα, ατος, τό *remnant* Ro
9: 27 v.l.*

καταλείπω *leave (behind)* Mt 16:
4; 19: 5; 21: 17; Mk 12: 19, 21;
Lk 15: 4; 20: 31; Ac 18: 19;
24: 27; Hb 11: 27. *Abandon, give
up* Mk 14: 52; Lk 5: 28. *Neglect*
Ac 6: 2. *Keep* Ro 11: 4. Pass.
remain behind J 8: 9; 1 Th 3: 1;
be open Hb 4: 1.

καταλελειμμένος perf. pass. participle of καταλείπω.

καταλιθάζω *stone to death* Lk 20:
6.*

καταλιπών 2 aor. act. participle
of καταλείπω.

καταλλαγή, ῆς, ἡ *reconciliation* Ro
5: 11; 11: 15; 2 Cor 5: 18f.*

καταλλάσσω *reconcile* Ro 5: 10;
1 Cor 7: 11; 2 Cor 5: 18–20; Ac
12: 22 v.l.*

κατάλοιπος, ον *left, remaining* οἱ
κ. *the rest* Ac 15: 17.*

κατάλυμα, ατος, τό *inn* Lk 2: 7.
Guest room, dining room Mk 14:
14; Lk 22: 11.*

καταλύω—1. trans.—**a.** *throw
down, detach* Mk 13: 2.—**b.** *destroy,
demolish, dismantle* lit. Mt 27:
40; Mk 14: 58; Ac 6: 14. Fig.
Ro 14: 20; 2 Cor 5: 1; Gal 2:
18.—**c.** *do away with, annul,
make invalid* Mt 5: 17; Lk 23: 2
v.l. *Ruin, bring to an end* Ac 5:
38; *stop* 5: 39.—**2.** intrans. *halt,
rest, find lodging* Lk 9: 12; 19: 7.

καταμανθάνω *observe (well), notice*
Mt 6: 28.*

καταμαρτυρέω *bear witness against,
testify against* Mt 26: 62; 27: 13;
Mk 14: 60.*

καταμένω *stay, live* Ac 1: 13; 1
Cor 16: 6.*

καταμόνας = κατὰ μόνας.

καταντάθεμα v.l. for κατάθεμα in
Rv 22: 3, with the same meaning.

καταναθεματίζω *curse* Mt 26: 74
v.l.*

καταναλίσκω *consume* Hb 12: 29.*

καταναρκάω *burden, be a burden
to* w. gen. 2 Cor 11: 9; 12: 13f.*

κατανεύω *signal* by means of a nod Lk 5: 7.*

κατανοέω *notice, observe* Mt 7: 3; Lk 6: 41; Ac 27: 39. *Look at, consider, contemplate* Lk 12: 24, 27; Ac 7: 31f; Js 1: 23f. *Consider, notice* in a spiritual sense Lk 20: 23; Hb 3: 1.

καταντάω *come (to), arrive (at)* Ac 16: 1; 18: 19; 28: 13; 1 Cor 10: 11; 14: 36. *Attain (to)* Ac 26: 7; Eph 4: 13; Phil 3: 11.

κατάνυξις, εως, ἡ *stupefaction, stupor* Ro 11: 8.*

κατανύσσομαι *be pierced, stabbed* fig. Ac 2: 37.*

καταξιόω *consider worthy* pass. Lk 20: 35; 21: 36 v.l.; Ac 5: 41; 2 Th 1: 5.*

καταπατέω *trample under foot* lit. Mt 5: 13; 7: 6; Lk 8: 5; 12: 1. Fig. *treat with disdain* Hb 10: 29.*

κατάπαυσις, εως, ἡ *rest* Ac 7: 49. *Place of rest* Hb 3: 11, 18; 4: 1, 3, 5, 10f.*

καταπαύω—1. trans. *(cause to) stop, restrain* Ac 14: 18. *Bring to a place of rest* Hb 4: 8.—2. intrans. *stop, rest* 4: 4, 10.*

καταπέτασμα, ατος, τό *curtain* Mt 27: 51; Mk 15: 38; Lk 23: 45; Hb 6: 19; 9: 3; 10: 20.*

καταπίῃ 2 aor. subj. act., 3 sing. of καταπίνω.

καταπίνω *swallow up*—1. lit. though more or less transferred Mt 23: 24; Rv 12: 16. *Devour* 1 Pt 5: 8. Pass. *be drowned* Hb 11: 29; *be overwhelmed* 2 Cor 2: 7.—2. fig. *swallow up* 1 Cor 15: 54; 2 Cor 5: 4.*

καταπίπτω *fall (down)* Lk 8: 6; Ac 26: 14; 28: 6.*

καταπλέω *sail (toward,* lit. *down)* Lk 8: 26.*

καταποθῇ 1 aor. pass. subj., 3 sing. of καταπίνω.

καταπονέω *subdue, wear out, oppress* pres. pass. participle 2 Pt 2: 7; Ac 4: 2 v.l. As noun *one who is oppressed* Ac 7: 24.*

καταποντίζω *throw into the sea,* pass. *be sunk, be drowned* Mt 18: 6; *sink* 14: 30.*

κατάρα, ας, ἡ *a curse, an imprecation* Gal 3: 10, 13; Hb 6: 8; Js 3: 10; 2 Pt 2: 14.*

καταράομαι *to curse* Mt 25: 41; Mk 11: 21; Lk 6: 28; Ro 12: 14; Js 3: 9.*

καταργέω—1. *make ineffective, powerless* lit. *use up, waste* Lk 13: 7. Fig. *make ineffective, nullify* Ro 3: 3; 4: 14; 1 Cor 1: 28; Gal 3: 17; *make invalid* Ro 3: 31; Eph 2: 15.—2. *abolish, set aside, do away with, bring to an end* Ro 6: 6; 1 Cor 6: 13; 13: 11; 15: 24, 26; 2 Th 2: 8; 2 Ti 1: 10; Hb 2: 14. Pass. *cease, pass away* 1 Cor 2: 6; 13: 8, 10; 2 Cor 3: 7, 11, 13f; Gal 5: 11.—3. καταργοῦμαι ἀπό τινος *be released from, have nothing more to do with* Ro 7: 2, 6; *be estranged* Gal 5: 4.*

καταριθμέω *count* pass. *belong to* Ac 1: 17.*

καταρτίζω—1. *put in order, restore* 2 Cor 13: 11; Gal 6: 1; *mend* Mt 4: 21; Mk 1: 19. *Complete, make complete* 1 Cor 1: 10; 1 Th 3: 10; Hb 13: 21; 1 Pt 5: 10. κατηρτισμένος *fully trained* Lk 6: 40.—2. *prepare, make, create* Mt 21: 16; Ro 9: 22; Hb 10: 5; 11: 3.*

κατάρτισις, εως, ἡ *being made complete* 2 Cor 13: 9.*

καταρτισμός, οῦ, ὁ *equipping* or *training* Eph 4: 12.*

κατασείω *shake, wave* Ac 19: 33. *Motion, signal* 12: 17; 13: 16; 21: 40.*

κατασκάπτω *tear down, raze to the ground* Ro 11: 3; Ac 15: 16 v.l.*

κατασκευάζω *make ready, prepare* Mk 1: 2; Lk 1: 17. *Build, construct, create* Hb 3: 3f; 11: 7; 1 Pt 3: 20. *Furnish, equip* Hb 9: 2, 6.

κατασκηνοῖν pres. act. inf. of κατασκηνόω.

κατασκηνόω live, dwell Ac 2: 26. Nest Mt 13: 32; Mk 4: 32; Lk 13: 19.*

κατασκήνωσις, εως, ἡ a place to live, a nest Mt 8: 20; Lk 9: 58.*

κατασκιάζω overshadow Hb 9: 5.*

κατασκοπέω spy out, lie in wait for Gal 2: 4.*

κατάσκοπος, ου, ὁ a spy Hb 11: 31; Js 2: 25 v.l.*

κατασοφίζομαι take advantage of by trickery Ac 7: 19.*

καταστείλας 1 aor. act. participle of καταστέλλω.

καταστέλλω restrain, quiet Ac 19: 35f.*

κατάστημα, ατος, τό behavior, demeanor Tit 2: 3.*

καταστολή, ῆς, ἡ deportment 1 Ti 2: 9.*

καταστρέφω upset, overturn Mt 21: 12; Mk 11: 15; J 2: 15 v.l. τὰ κατεστραμμένα ruins Ac 15: 16.*

καταστρηνιάω become wanton against 1 Ti 5: 11.*

καταστροφή, ῆς, ἡ ruin, destruction 2 Ti 2: 14; 2 Pt 2: 6.*

καταστρώννυμι lay low, kill pass. 1 Cor 10: 5.*

κατασύρω drag (away by force) Lk 12: 58.*

κατασφάζω or -σφάττω slaughter, strike down Lk 19: 27.*

κατασφραγίζω seal (up) Rv 5: 1.*

κατάσχεσις, εως, ἡ possession, taking into possession Ac 7: 5, 45; 13: 33 v.l. Holding back, restraining, delay 20: 16 v.l.*

κατάσχωμεν 2 aor. act. subj., 1 pl., of κατέχω.

κατατίθημι—1. lay, place Mk 15: 46.—2. mid. with χάρις as object, grant or do a favor Ac 24: 27; 25: 9.*

κατατομή, ῆς, ἡ mutilation Phil 3: 2.*

κατατοξεύω shoot down Hb 12: 20 v.l.*

κατατρέχω run down Ac 21: 32.*

καταυγάζω shine upon, illuminate 2 Cor 4: 4 v.l.*

καταφαγεῖν 2 aor. act. inf. of κατεσθίω.

καταφέρω cast a vote against Ac 26: 10; bring charges 25: 7. Pass. sink into sleep 20: 9a; overwhelmed by sleep 20: 9b.*

καταφεύγω flee Ac 14: 6. Take refuge Hb 6: 18.*

καταφθείρω destroy 2 Pt 2: 12 v.l. Ruin, corrupt, deprave 2 Ti 3: 8.*

καταφιλέω kiss Mt 26: 49; Mk 14: 45; Lk 7: 38, 45; 15: 20; Ac 20: 37.*

καταφρονέω—1. look down on, despise, scorn w. gen. Mt 6: 24; 18: 10; Lk 16: 13; 1 Cor 11: 22; 1 Ti 4: 12; 2 Pt 2: 10; Tit 2: 15 v.l. Entertain wrong ideas about Ro 2: 4; 1 Ti 6: 2.—2. care nothing for, disregard, be unafraid of Hb 12: 2.*

καταφρονητής, οῦ, ὁ despiser, scoffer Ac 13: 41.*

καταφωνέω v.l. for ἐπιφωνέω with the same meaning Ac 22: 24.*

καταχέω pour out or down over w. gen. Mt 26: 7; Mk 14: 3.*

καταχθόνιος, ον under the earth, subterranean Phil 2: 10.*

καταχράομαι use 1 Cor 7: 31; make full use of 9: 18.*

καταψηφίζομαι be enrolled Ac 1: 26 v.l.*

καταψύχω cool (off) Lk 16: 24.*

κατεάγην, κατέαξα 2 aor. pass. and 1 aor. act. ind. of κατάγνυμι.

κατείδωλος, ον full of idols Ac 17: 16.*

κατειλημμένος perf. mid. and pass. participle of καταλαμβάνω.

κατεκάην 2 aor. pass. ind. of κατακαίω.

κατέναντι adv. opposite Lk 19: 30. As improper prep. w. gen. op-

posite Mk 13: 3; *in the presence of* Mt 27: 24; *before* Ro 4: 17; 2 Cor 2: 17; 12: 19.

κατενεχθείς 1 aor. pass. participle of καταφέρω.

κατενύγην 2 aor. pass. ind. of κατανύσσομαι.

κατενώπιον adv. as improper prep. w. gen. *in the presence of* Jd 24; *before* Eph 1: 4; Col 1: 22.*

κατεξουσιάζω *exercise authority over* w. gen. Mt 20: 25; Mk 10: 42.*

κατεπόθην 1 aor. pass. ind. of καταπίνω.

κατεργάζομαι—**1.** *achieve, accomplish, do* Ro 1: 27; 7: 15, 17f, 20; 1 Cor 5: 3; 1 Pt 4: 3; perhaps Eph 6: 13 (see 3 below). —**2.** *bring about, produce, create* Ro 4: 15; 7: 8, 13; 2 Cor 7: 10f; 9: 11; Js 1: 3. *Work out* Phil 2: 12. *Prepare* 2 Cor 5: 5.—**3.** *subdue, conquer* perhaps Eph 6: 13 (see 1 above).

κατέρχομαι *come down* Lk 4: 31; 9: 37; Ac 8: 5; 15: 1, 30; 21: 10; Js 3: 15. Of ships *arrive, put in* Ac 18: 22; 27: 5.

κατεσθίω and **κατέσθω** *eat up, consume, devour* lit. Mt 13: 4; Rv 10: 9f; 12: 4. Fig. *destroy, consume* Mk 12: 40; Lk 15: 30; J 2: 17; 2 Cor 11: 20; Gal 5: 15; Rv 11: 5; 20: 9.

κατεστρώθην 1 aor. pass. ind. of καταστρώννυμι.

κατευθύνω *lead, direct* Lk 1: 79; 1 Th 3: 11; 2 Th 3: 5.*

κατευλογέω *bless* Mk 10: 16.*

κατέφαγον 2 aor. act. ind. of κατεσθίω.

κατεφθαρμένος perf. pass. participle of καταφθείρω.

κατεφίσταμαι *rise up against* w. dat. Ac 18: 12.*

κατεφθαρμένος perf. pass. participle of καταφθείρω.

κατέχω—**1.** trans.—**a.** *hold back, hinder* Lk 4: 42; *keep* Phlm 13;

suppress Ro 1: 18; *restrain, check* 2 Th 2: 6f.—**b.** *hold fast* 1 Cor 11: 2; 15: 2; 1 Th 5: 21; Hb 3: 6; 10: 23; *possess* 1 Cor 7: 30; 2 Cor 6: 10; *occupy* Lk 14: 9.—**c.** pass. *be bound* Ro 7: 6; J 5: 4 v.l.—**2.** intrans. of a ship, *head for, steer toward* Ac 27: 40.

κατηγορείτωσαν pres. act. imperative, 3 pl., of κατηγορέω.

κατηγορέω *accuse* Mt 12: 10; 27: 12; Mk 15: 3f; Lk 23: 2, 10, 14; J 5: 45; Ac 24: 2, 8, 13, 19; 25: 5; Ro 2: 15; Rv 12: 10.

κατηγορία, ας, ἡ *accusation* J 18: 29; 1 Ti 5: 19; Tit 1: 6; Lk 6: 7 v.l.*

κατήγορος, ου, ὁ *accuser* Ac 23: 30, 35; 24: 8 v.l.; 25: 16, 18; Rv 12: 10 v.l.*

κατήγωρ, ορος, ὁ *accuser* Rv 12: 10.*

κατηραμένος perf. pass. participle of καταράομαι.

κατηράσω 1 aor. mid. ind., 2 sing., of καταράομαι.

κατήργηκα perf. act. ind. of καταργέω.

κατήφεια, ας, ἡ *gloominess, dejection* Js 4: 9.*

κατηχέω *inform* Ac 21: 21, 24. *Teach, instruct* Lk 1: 4; Ac 18: 25; Ro 2: 18; 1 Cor 14: 19; Gal 6: 6.*

κατήχθημεν 1 aor. pass. ind., 1 pl. of κατάγω.

κατ' ἰδίαν see ἴδιος.

κατιόω pass. *become rusty, tarnished, corroded* Js 5: 3.*

κατισχύω *be dominant, prevail* Lk 23: 23; *be able* 21: 36. *Win a victory over* w. gen. Mt 16: 18.*

κατοικέω—**1.** intrans. *live, dwell, settle* Mt 2: 23; 12: 45; Ac 1: 20; 2: 5; 7: 2, 4a, 48; 17: 24, 26; 22: 12; Eph 3: 17; Col 2: 9; Hb 11: 9; 2 Pt 3: 13; Rv 3: 10; 17: 8.—**2.** trans. *inhabit, dwell in* Mt 23: 21; Lk 13: 4; Ac 1: 19; 2: 14; Rv 17: 2.

κατοίκησις, εως, ἡ living quarters, dwelling Mk 5: 3.*

κατοικητήριον, ου, τό dwelling-place Eph 2: 22; Rv 18: 2.*

κατοικία, ας, ἡ habitation Ac 17: 26.*

κατοικίζω cause to dwell Js 4: 5.*

κατοπτρίζω mid. look at as in a mirror, contemplate 2 Cor 3: 18.*

κατόρθωμα, ατος, τό success, prosperity, good order Ac 24: 2 v.l.*

κάτω adv.—1. below Mk 14: 66; Ac 2: 19; under Mt 2: 16 v.l. τὰ κάτω this world J 8: 23.—2. downwards, down Mt 4: 6; Lk 4: 9; J 8: 6; Ac 20: 9. ἕως κάτω to bottom Mk 15: 38.

κατώτερος, α, ον lower Eph 4: 9.*

κατωτέρω adv. lower, under Mt 2: 16.*

Καῦδα see Κλαῦδα.

καῦμα, ατος, τό burning, heat Rv 7: 16; 16: 9.*

καυματίζω burn Mt 13: 6; Mk 4: 6; Rv 16: 8f.*

καυματόω be scorched by the heat Mt 13: 6 v.l.*

καῦσις, εως, ἡ burning Hb 6: 8.*

καυσόω pass. be consumed by heat, burn up 2 Pt 3: 10, 12.*

καυστηριάζω brand with a red-hot iron, sear pass., fig. 1 Ti 4: 2.*

καύσων, ωνος, ὁ heat, burning (sun) Mt 20: 12; a hot day Lk 12: 55; scorching heat Js 1: 11.*

καυτηριάζω v.l. for καυστηριάζω.

καυχάομαι—1. intrans. boast, glory, pride oneself Ro 2: 17, 23; 1 Cor 1: 31; 4: 7; 13: 3 v.l.; 2 Cor 10: 13, 15–17; 12: 5; Gal 6: 13f; Phil 3: 3; Js 1: 9; 4: 16.—2. trans. boast about 2 Cor 7: 14; 9: 2; 10: 8; 11: 16, 30.

καύχημα, ατος, τό—1. boast, object of boasting, something to boast about Ro 4: 2; 1 Cor 5: 6; 9: 15f; Gal 6: 4; Phil 1: 26; Hb 3: 6; pride 2 Cor 1: 14; Phil 2: 16.—2. boast, what is said in boasting 2 Cor 5: 12; 9: 3.*

καύχησις, εως, ἡ boasting, pride

Ro 3: 27; 15: 17; 1 Cor 15: 31; 2 Cor 7: 4, 14; 8: 24; 11: 10, 17; Js 4: 16; 1 Th 2: 19. Object of boasting, reason for boasting 2 Cor 1: 12.*

Καφαρναούμ, ἡ indecl. Capernaum, a city on the Sea of Galilee Mt 4: 13; 8: 5; 11: 23; 17: 24; Mk 1: 21; 2: 1; 9: 33; Lk 4: 23, 31; 7: 1; 10: 15; J 2: 12; 4: 46; 6: 17, 24, 59.*

Κεγχρεαί, ῶν, αἱ Cenchreae, the seaport of Corinth Ac 18: 18; Ro 16: 1; subscription.*

κέδρος, ου, ἡ cedar tree J 18: 1 v.l.*

Κεδρών, ὁ indecl. Kidron, a valley near Jerusalem J 18: 1.*

κεῖμαι lie, recline—1. lit. Mt 5: 14; Lk 2: 12, 16; 23: 53; J 20: 5f, 12; 2 Cor 3: 15; stand J 2: 6; Rv 4: 2; be stored up Lk 12: 19; be laid Mt 3: 10; 1 Cor 3: 11; be laid out Rv 21: 16.—2. fig. be appointed, set, destined Lk 2: 34; Phil 1: 16; 1 Th 3: 3. Be given, be valid 1 Ti 1: 9. Find oneself, be 1 J 5: 19.

κειρία, ας, ἡ bandage, graveclothes J 11: 44.*

κείρω shear Ac 8: 32. Mid. have one's hair cut 18: 18; 1 Cor 11: 6.*

κεκαθαρμένος perf. pass. participle of καθαίρω.

κεκάθικα perf. act. ind. of καθίζω.

κεκαυμένος perf. pass. participle of καίω.

κεκερασμένος perf. pass. participle of κεράννυμι.

κέκληκα perf. act. ind. of καλέω.

κέκλικα perf. act. ind. of κλίνω.

κέκμηκα perf. act. ind. of κάμνω.

κεκορεσμένος perf. pass. participle of κορέννυμι.

κέλευσμα, ατος, τό signal, (cry of) command 1 Th 4: 16.*

κελεύω command, order, urge Mt 8: 18; 14: 19, 28; 18: 25; 27: 58; Lk 18: 40; Ac 4: 15; 8: 38; 12: 19; 16: 22; 21: 34; 23: 10; 25: 23.

κενεμβατεύω *step on emptiness,*
make a misstep in rope-walking,
conjectural v.l. in Col 2: 18.*

κενοδοξία, ας, ἡ *empty conceit* Phil
2: 3.*

κενόδοξος, ον *conceited, boastful*
Gal 5: 26.*

κενός, ή, όν *empty*—**1.** lit. *empty-*
handed Mk 12: 3; Lk 1: 53;
20: 10f.—**2.** fig. *empty* in the
sense *without any basis, without*
truth or *power* 1 Cor 15: 14;
Eph 5: 6; Col 2: 8. In the sense
without effect, without reaching
its goal, (in) vain Ac 4: 25; 1 Cor
15: 10; 1 Th 2: 1. *Foolish,*
senseless Js 2: 20. εἰς κενόν *in*
vain 2 Cor 6: 1; Gal 2: 2; Phil
2: 16; 1 Th 3: 5.

κενοφωνία, ας, ἡ *chatter, empty*
talk 1 Ti 6: 20; 2 Ti 2: 16.*

κενόω *to empty* Phil 2: 7. *Destroy,*
render void or *invalid* 1 Cor 9: 15;
pass. Ro 4: 14; 1 Cor 1: 17; *lose*
its justification 2 Cor 9: 3.*

κέντρον, ου, τό *the sting* of an
animal Rv 9: 10; fig. 1 Cor 15:
55f. *A goad,* a pointed stick Ac
26: 14; 9: 5 v.l.*

κεντυρίων, ωνος, ὁ (Latin loanword) *centurion* a Roman army
officer, roughly equivalent to
our captain Mk 15: 39, 44f.*

Κενχρεαί see Κεγχρεαί.

κενῶς adv. *in vain, to no purpose*
Js 4: 5.*

κεραία, ας, ἡ *projection, hook* as
part of a letter, *serif,* lit. 'horn'
Mt 5: 18; Lk 16: 17.*

κεραμεύς, έως, ὁ *potter* Mt 27:
7, 10; Ro 9: 21.*

κεραμικός, ή, όν *belonging to the*
potter or *made of clay* Rv 2:
27.*

κεράμιον, ου, τό *earthenware vessel,*
jar Mk 14: 13; Lk 22: 10.*

κέραμος, ου, ὁ *a roof tile* made of
clay Lk 5: 19.*

κεράννυμι *mix* Rv 18: 6; *pour*
14: 10.*

κέρας, ατος, τό *horn* lit. Rv 5: 6;

17: 3, 7, 12, 16; *corners* of the
altar 9: 13. Fig., for might,
power Lk 1: 69.

κεράτιον, ου, τό *carob pod* Lk 15:
16.*

κερδαίνω—**1.** *to gain* lit. Mt 16: 26;
25: 16f, 20, 22; Mk 8: 36; Lk 9:
25; *make a profit* Js 4: 13. Fig.
Mt 18: 15; 1 Cor 9: 19–22; Phil
3: 8; pass. 1 Pt 3: 1.—**2.** *avoid*
Ac 27: 21.*

κερδάνω aor. subj. act. of κερδαίνω.

κερδήσω fut. act. ind. of κερδαίνω.

κέρδος, ους, τό *a gain* Phil 1: 21;
3: 7; Tit 1: 11.*

κερέα another spelling of κεραία.

κέρμα, ατος, τό *coin,* small *change*
J 2: 15.*

κερματιστής, οῦ, ὁ *money-changer*
J 2: 14.*

κεφάλαιον, ου, τό—**1.** *main thing,*
main point Hb 8: 1.—**2.** financial
capital, sum of money Ac 22:
28.*

κεφαλαιόω in the text of Mk 12:
4 is better spelled κεφαλιόω; see
the latter entry.

κεφαλή, ῆς, ἡ *head*—**1.** lit. Mt 5:
36; 8: 20; 27: 29f; Mk 6: 24f,
27f; 15: 29; Lk 21: 28; J 13: 9;
Ac 21: 24; Ro 12: 20; 1 Cor 11:
4f, 7, 10; Rv 10: 1; 17: 3, 7, 9;
18: 19; 19: 12.—**2.** fig.—**a.** *head*
denoting one of superior rank
1 Cor 11: 3; Eph 1: 22; 4: 15;
5: 23; Col 1: 18; 2: 10.—**b.** *head*
as *extremity, end* κ. γωνίας
cornerstone Mt 21: 42; Mk 12: 10;
Lk 20: 17; Ac 4: 11; 1 Pt 2: 7.
Capital or *frontier city* Ac 16: 12
v.l.

κεφαλιόω *strike on the head* Mk
12: 4 v.l.*

κεφαλίς, ίδος, ἡ *roll* of a book
Hb 10: 7.*

κέχρημαι perf. mid. and pass.
ind. of χράομαι.

κηδεύω *take care of, bury* a corpse
Mk 6: 29 v.l.*

κημόω *to muzzle* 1 Cor 9: 9.*

κῆνσος, ου, ὁ (Latin loanword:

census) *tax, poll-tax* Mt 17: 25;
22: 17, 19; Mk 12: 14.*

κῆπος, ου, ὁ *garden* Lk 13: 19;
J 18: 1, 26; 19: 41.*

κηπουρός, οῦ, ὁ *gardener* J 20:
15.*

κηρίον, ου, τό *wax, honey-comb* Lk
24: 42 v.l.*

κήρυγμα, ατος, τό *proclamation,
preaching* Mt 12: 41; Lk 11: 32;
Ro 16: 25; 1 Cor 1: 21; 2: 4;
15: 14; 2 Ti 4: 17; Tit 1: 3.*

κῆρυξ, υκος, ὁ *preacher,* lit. 'herald'
1 Ti 2: 7; 2 Ti 1: 11; 2 Pt 2: 5.*

κηρύσσω—1. *proclaim aloud, announce, mention publicly,* lit.
'to herald' Mk 1: 45; 5: 20; 7:
36; Lk 8: 39; Rv 5: 2.—**2.** *proclaim, preach* a message that is
religious in nature Mt 10: 27;
Mk 1: 4, 39; 13: 10; Lk 9: 2;
12: 3; 24: 47; Ac 15: 21; Ro 2:
21; 1 Cor 9: 27; 15: 12; 2 Cor
4: 5; Gal 2: 2; 5: 11; 1 Th 2: 9;
2 Ti 4: 2.

κῆτυς, ους, τό *sea-monster* Mt 12:
40.*

Κηφᾶς, ᾶ, ὁ (Aramaic = 'rock')
Cephas, surname of Simon J 1:
42; 1 Cor 1: 12; 3: 22; 9: 5;
15: 5; Gal 1: 18; 2: 9, 11, 14.*

κιβώριον, ου, τό *ciborium, the
seed-vessel of the Egyptian bean,*
also a *vessel* of similar shape Ac
19: 24 v.l.*

κιβωτός, οῦ, ἡ *box, chest, the
ark* of Noah Mt 24: 38; Lk
17: 27; Hb 11: 7; 1 Pt 3: 20.
The ark in the Holy of Holies Hb
9: 4; Rv 11: 19.*

κιθάρα, ας, ἡ *lyre, harp* 1 Cor 14:
7; Rv 5: 8; 14: 2; 15: 2.*

κιθαρίζω *play the lyre* or *harp* 1 Cor
14: 7; Rv 14: 2.*

κιθαρῳδός, οῦ, ὁ *lyre-player, har-
pist* Rv 14: 2; 18: 22.*

Κιλικία, ας, ἡ *Cilicia* a province
in the southeast corner of Asia
Minor; Tarsus is its capital Ac
6: 9; 15: 23, 41; 21: 39; 22: 3;
23: 34; 27: 5; Gal 1: 21.*

Κίλιξ, ικος, ὁ *a Cilician* Ac 23: 34
v.l.*

κινδυνεύω *be in danger, run a risk*
Lk 8: 23; Ac 19: 27, 40; 1 Cor
15: 30.*

κίνδυνος, ου, ὁ *danger, risk* Ro 8:
35; 2 Cor 11: 26.*

κινέω *move, move away, remove* Mt
23: 4; Rv 2: 5; 6: 14. *Shake* Mt
27: 39; Mk 15: 29. *Arouse* Ac
21: 30; 14: 7 v.l. *Cause, bring
about* 24: 5. Pass. *be moved, move*
Ac 17: 28.*

κίνησις, εως, ἡ *motion* J 5: 3
v.l.*

κιννάμωμον, ου, τό *cinnamon* Rv
18: 13.*

Κίς, ὁ indecl. *Kish,* father of Saul
Ac 13: 21.*

κίχρημι *lend* Lk 11: 5.*

κλάδος, ου, ὁ *branch* Mt 13: 32;
21: 8; 24: 32; Mk 4: 32; 13: 28;
Lk 13: 19. Fig. Ro 11: 16–19,
21.*

κλαίω *weep, cry* Mk 14: 72; Lk 7:
13, 32, 38; 19: 41; 22: 62; J 20:
11, 13, 15; Ac 9: 39; 1 Cor
7: 30; Js 4: 9; Rv 5: 5; 18: 9.
Weep for, bewail Mt 2: 18; Rv
18: 9 v.l.

κλάσις, εως, ἡ *breaking* Lk 24: 35;
Ac 2: 42; Phlm subscr.*

κλάσμα, ατος, τό *fragment, piece,
crumb* Mt 14: 20; 15: 37; Mk
6: 43; 8: 8, 19f; Lk 9: 17; J 6:
12f.*

Κλαῦδα *Clauda,* a small island
south of Crete Ac 27: 16.*

Κλαυδία, ας, ἡ *Claudia* 2 Ti 4: 21.*

Κλαύδιος, ου, ὁ *Claudius—1.* Roman emperor 41–54 AD Ac 11:
28; 18: 2.—**2.** Claudius Lysias,
Roman official in Jerusalem 23:
26.*

κλαυθμός, οῦ, ὁ *weeping, crying*
Mt 2: 18; 13: 42, 50; 25: 30;
Ac 20: 37.

κλαύσω fut. act. ind. of κλαίω.

κλάω *break* Mt 14: 19; 26: 26;
Mk 8: 6, 19; Lk 24: 30; Ac 20:
7, 11; 1 Cor 11: 24.

κλείς, κλειδός, ἡ *key* Mt 16: 19;
Lk 11: 52; Rv 1: 18; 3: 7; 9: 1;
20: 1.*

κλείω *shut, lock, close* lit. and fig.
Mt 6: 6; 23: 13; 25: 10; Lk 11:
7; J 20: 19, 26; Ac 21: 30; 1 J
3: 17; Rv 3: 7f; 11: 6; 20: 3;
21: 25. Pass. Ac 5: 23; Lk 4:
25.*

κλέμμα, ατος, τό *stealing, theft*
Rv 9: 21; Mk 7: 22 v.l.*

Κλεοπᾶς, ᾶ, ὁ *Cleopas* Lk 24: 18.*

κλέος, ους, τό *fame, credit* 1 Pt
2: 20.*

κλέπτης, ου, ὁ *thief* Mt 6: 19f;
J 10: 1, 8, 10; 1 Cor 6: 10;
1 Pt 4: 15; Rv 3: 3.

κλέπτω *steal* Mt 6: 19f; 27: 64;
Mk 10: 19; Ro 2: 21; Eph 4:
28.

κληθήσομαι 1 fut. pass. ind. of
καλέω.

κλῆμα, ατος, τό *branch*, especially
of a vine J 15: 2, 4–6.*

Κλήμης, εντος, ὁ *Clement* Phil
4: 3.*

κληρονομέω—**1.** *inherit, be an heir*
Gal 4: 30.—**2.** *acquire, obtain,
come into possession of* Mt 5: 5;
25: 34; 1 Cor 6: 9f; 15: 50; Gal
5: 21. *Receive, share in* Mt 19:
29; Mk 10: 17; Lk 10: 25; Hb
1: 4, 14; 12: 17; Rv 21: 7.

κληρονομία, ας, ἡ—**1.** *inheritance*
Mt 21: 38; Mk 12: 7; Lk 12: 13;
20: 14. *Possession, property* Ac
7: 5; 13: 33 v.l.; Hb 11: 8. *The
heirs* Ro 11: 1 v.l.—**2.** in a
specifically Christian usage *salvation* Ac 20: 32; Gal 3: 18; Col
3: 24; Eph 1: 14, 18; Hb 9: 15;
1 Pt 1: 4; *share* Eph 5: 5.*

κληρονόμος, ου, ὁ *heir*—**1.** lit.
Mt 21: 38; Mk 12: 7; Lk 20: 14;
Gal 4: 1.—**2.** fig. Ro 4: 13f; 8:
17; Gal 3: 29; 4: 7; Tit 3: 7; Hb
1: 2; 6: 17; 11: 7; Js 2: 5.*

κλῆρος, ου, ὁ—**1.** *lot* (i.e. a pebble,
small stick, etc., thrown or
drawn to arrive at a decision)
Mt 27: 35; Mk 15: 24; Lk 23:
34; J 19: 24; Ac 1: 26.—**2.** *that
which is assigned by lot, portion,
share, place* Ac 1: 17, 25 v.l.;
8: 21; 26: 18; Col 1: 12. κλῆρος
in 1 Pt 5: 3 means a *portion* of a
congregation.*

κληρόω act. *appoint by lot* pass.
be appointed by lot ἐν ᾧ ἐκληρώ-
θημεν *in whom our lot is cast* Eph
1: 11.*

κλῆσις, εως, ἡ—**1.** *call, calling,
invitation* Ro 11: 29; 1 Cor 1: 26;
Eph 4: 1, 4; Phil 3: 14; 2 Th
1: 11; 2 Ti 1: 9; Hb 3: 1; 2 Pt
1: 10; Lk 11: 42 v.l. ἡ ἐλπὶς τῆς
κ. αὐτοῦ *the hope to which he
calls* Eph 1: 18.—**2.** *station* in
life, *position, vocation* 1 Cor 7:
20.*

κλητός, ἡ, όν *called, invited* Mt 20:
16 v.l.; 22: 14; Ro 1: 1, 7; 8: 28;
1 Cor 1: 1f, 24; Jd 1; Rv 17: 14.
κλητοὶ 'Ιησοῦ Χριστοῦ *called by
Jesus Christ* Ro 1: 6.*

κλίβανος, ου, ὁ *oven, furnace* Mt
6: 30; Lk 12: 28.*

κλίμα, ατος, τό *district*, pl. *region*
Ro 15: 23; 2 Cor 11: 10; Gal
1: 21.*

κλινάριον, ου, τό *bed* Ac 5: 15.*

κλίνη, ης, ἡ *bed, couch* Mk 4: 21;
7: 30; Lk 8: 16; 17: 34; *dining
couch* Mk 7: 4 v.l. *Pallet,
stretcher* Mt 9: 2, 6; Lk 5: 18.
Sickbed Rv 2: 22.*

κλινίδιον, ου, τό *bed = pallet,
stretcher* Lk 5: 19, 24.*

κλίνω—**1.** trans. *incline, bend,
bow* Lk 24: 5; J 19: 30. *Lay
(down)* Mt 8: 20; Lk 9: 58. *Turn
to flight* Hb 11: 34.—**2.** intrans.
decline, be far spent Lk 9: 12; 24:
29.*

κλισία, ας, ἡ *a group of people
eating together* Lk 9: 14.*

κλοπή, ῆς, ἡ *theft, stealing* Mt 15:
19; Mk 7: 21.*

κλύδων, ωνος, ὁ (*a succession of*)
waves Lk 8: 24; *surf* Js 1: 6.*

κλυδωνίζομαι *be tossed here and
there by waves* fig. Eph 4: 14.*

Κλωπᾶς, ᾶ, ὁ *Clopas* J 19: 25.*

κνήθω *itch* pass. *feel an itching* fig. 2 Ti 4: 3.*

Κνίδος, ου, ἡ *Cnidus*, a peninsula with a city of the same name on the coast of Caria in s.w. Asia Minor Ac 27: 7.*

κοδράντης, ου, ὁ (Latin loanword: quadrans) *quadrans, penny*, a Roman coin worth less than one cent Mt 5: 26; Mk 12: 42; Lk 12: 59 v.l.*

κοιλία, ας, ἡ *body-cavity, belly*— 1. *stomach, belly* Mt 15: 17; Mk 7: 19; Lk 15: 16; Ro 16: 18; 1 Cor 6: 13; Phil 3: 19; Rv 10: 9f; *belly* Mt 12: 40.—2. *womb, uterus* Lk 1: 41, 44; 23: 29; J 3: 4. ἐκ κοιλίας etc. *from birth* Lk 1: 15; Ac 14: 8; Gal 1: 15.— 3. κ. is sometimes equivalent to *heart* J 7: 38.

κοιμάω pass. *sleep, fall asleep*—1. lit. Mt 28: 13; Lk 22: 45; J 11: 12; Ac 12: 6.—2. fig., of death, *fall asleep, die, pass away* Mt 27: 52; J 11: 11; Ac 7: 60; 13: 36; 1 Cor 7: 39; 11: 30; 15: 6, 18, 20, 51; 1 Th 4: 13–15; 2 Pt 3: 4.*

κοίμησις, εως, ἡ *sleep* J 11: 13.*

κοινός, ή, όν *common*—1. *communal, common* Ac 2: 44; 4: 32; Tit 1: 4; Jd 3.—2. *common, ordinary, ceremonially unclean, impure* Mk 7: 2, 5; Ac 10: 14, 28; 11: 8; Ro 14: 14; Hb 10: 29; Rv 21: 27.*

κοινόω *make common* or *impure, defile* ceremonially Mt 15: 11, 18, 20; Mk 7: 15, 18, 20, 23; Hb 9: 13. *Profane, desecrate* Ac 21: 28. *Consider* or *declare unclean* Ac 10: 15; 11: 9.

κοινωνέω—1. *share in, have a share in* w. gen. Hb 2: 14. W. dat. Ro 12: 13; 15: 27; 1 Ti 5: 22; 1 Pt 4: 13; 2 J 11.—2. *give a share* Gal 6: 6; Phil 4: 15.— 3. κ. is found in the same sense as κοινόω *make impure* as v.l. in Mt 15: 11, 18, 20.*

κοινωνία, ας, ἡ—1. *association, communion, fellowship, close relationship* Ac 2: 42; Ro 15: 26; 1 Cor 1: 9; 2 Cor 6: 14; 13: 13; Gal 2: 9; Phil 1: 5; 2: 1; 1 J 1: 3, 6f.—2. *generosity, fellow-feeling* 2 Cor 9: 13; Hb 13: 16; perhaps Phil 2: 1.—3. *sign of fellowship, gift* perhaps Ro 15: 26 and 1 Cor 10: 16.—4. *participation, sharing* 2 Cor 8: 4; Phil 3: 10; Phlm 6; perhaps 1 Cor 1: 9; 10: 16; 2 Cor 13: 13.*

κοινωνικός, ή, όν *sharing* what is one's own, *liberal, generous* 1 Ti 6: 18.*

κοινωνός, οῦ, ὁ and ἡ *companion, partner, sharer* often w. gen. or dat. Mt 23: 30; Lk 5: 10; 1 Cor 10: 18, 20; 2 Cor 1: 7; 8: 23; Phlm 17; Hb 10: 33; 1 Pt 5: 1; 2 Pt 1: 4.*

κοίτη, ης, ἡ—1. *bed* Lk 11: 7; *marriage-bed* Hb 13: 4.—2. euphemistically for *sexual intercourse* pl. *sexual excesses* Ro 13: 13. *Conception* of a child 9: 10.*

κοιτών, ῶνος, ὁ *bedroom* ὁ ἐπὶ τοῦ κοιτῶνος *the chamberlain* Ac 12: 20.*

κόκκινος, η, ον *red, scarlet* Mt 27: 28; Hb 9: 19; Rv 17: 3; *scarlet cloth* or *garment* 17: 4; 18: 12, 16.*

κόκκος, ου, ὁ *seed, grain* Mt 13: 31; 17: 20; Mk 4: 31; Lk 13: 19; 17: 6; J 12: 24; 1 Cor 15: 37.*

κολάζω *punish* Ac 4: 21; 2 Pt 2: 9.*

κολακεία, ας, ἡ *flattery* 1 Th 2: 5.*

κόλασις, εως, ἡ *punishment* Mt 25: 46; 1 J 4: 18.*

Κολασσαεύς, έως, ὁ *a Colossian* only as v.l. in the title of Col.

Κολασσαί v.l. for Κολοσσαί Col 1: 2.

κολαφίζω *strike with the fist, beat*— 1. lit. Mt 26: 67; Mk 14: 65; 1 Pt 2: 20; *be roughly treated* 1 Cor 4: 11.—2. fig., of attacks of illness 2 Cor 12: 7.*

κολλάω *join closely together, unite* pass. *cling* Lk 10: 11. *Join oneself to, join, cling to, associate with* Mt 19: 5; Ac 5: 13; 8: 29; 9: 26; 10: 28; Ro 12: 9; 1 Cor 6: 16f. *Become a follower of* Ac 17: 34. *Hire oneself out to* Lk 15: 15. *Touch, reach* Rv 18: 5.*

κολλούριον, ου, τό *eye-salve* Rv 3: 18.*

κολλυβιστής, οῦ, ὁ *money-changer* Mt 21: 12; Mk 11: 15; J 2: 15.*

κολλύριον a variant spelling of κολλούριον.

κολοβόω *shorten, curtail* Mt 24: 22; Mk 13: 20.*

Κολοσσαεύς, έως, ὁ *the Colossian* title of Col. *

Κολοσσαί, ῶν, αἱ *Colossae*, a city in Phrygia, in w. Asia Minor Col 1: 2; Phlm subscr. v.l.*

κόλπος, ου, ὁ—1. *bosom, breast, chest* ἀνακεῖσθαι ἐν τῷ κόλπῳ τινός *recline* (at a meal) with one's head *on someone's breast* J 13: 23. Similarly Lk 16: 22f; J 1: 18.—**2.** *the fold of a garment,* formed as it falls from the chest over the girdle, used as a pocket Lk 6: 38.—**3.** *bay, gulf* of the sea Ac 27: 39.*

κολυμβάω *swim,* lit. 'dive' Ac 27: 43.*

κολυμβήθρα, ας, ἡ *pool, swimming-pool* J 5: 2, 4, 7; 9: 7.*

κολωνία, ας, ἡ (Latin loanword: colonia) *colony* Ac 16: 12.*

κομάω *wear long hair, let one's hair grow long* 1 Cor 11: 14f.*

κόμη, ης, ἡ *hair* 1 Cor 11: 15.*

κομιοῦμαι, κομιεῖται fut. mid. ind., 1 sing. and 3 sing., of κομίζω.

κομίζω—1. act. *bring* Lk 7: 37.—**2.** mid. *carry off, get, receive, obtain* 2 Cor 5: 10; Eph 6: 8; Col 3: 25; Hb 10: 36; 11: 13, 39; 1 Pt 1: 9; 5: 4; 2 Pt 2: 13. *Get back, recover* Mt 25: 27; Hb 11: 19.*

κομψότερον adv. *better* κ. ἔσχεν he *began to improve* J 4: 52.*

κονιάω *to whitewash* Mt 23: 27; Ac 23: 3.*

κονιορτός, οῦ, ὁ *dust* Mt 10: 14; Lk 9: 5; 10: 11; Ac 13: 51; 22: 23.*

κοπάζω *abate,* of wind *fall* Mt 14: 32; Mk 4: 39; 6: 51.*

κοπετός, οῦ, ὁ *mourning, lamentation* Ac 8: 2.*

κοπή, ῆς, ἡ *cutting down, defeat* Hb 7: 1.*

κοπιάω—1. *become weary, tired* Mt 11: 28; J 4: 6; Rv 2: 3.—**2.** *work hard, toil, strive, struggle* Mt 6: 28; J 4: 38b; Ac 20: 35; Ro 16: 6, 12; 1 Cor 4: 12; Phil 2: 16; Col 1: 29; 1 Ti 5: 17. *Labor for* J 4: 38a.

κόπος, ου, ὁ—1. *trouble, difficulty* Mk 14: 6; Lk 11: 7; Gal 6: 17.—**2.** *work, labor, toil* J 4: 38; 1 Cor 15: 58; 2 Cor 6: 5; 11: 23, 27; 1 Th 1: 3; 3: 5; 2 Th 3: 8; Rv 14: 13.

κοπρία, ας, ἡ *dung-heap, rubbish-heap* Lk 14: 35.*

κόπριον, ου, τό *dung, manure* Lk 13: 8.*

κόπρος, ου, ἡ *dung, manure* Lk 13: 8 v.l.*

κόπτω—1. act., *cut (off)* Mt 21: 8; Mk 11: 8.—**2.** mid., *beat* one's breast, *mourn* Mt 11: 17; 24: 30; Lk 8: 52; 23: 27; Rv 1: 7; 18: 9.*

κόραξ, ακος, ὁ *crow, raven* Lk 12: 24.*

κοράσιον, ου, τό *girl* Mt 9: 24f; 14: 11; Mk 5: 41f; 6: 22, 28.*

κορβᾶν indecl. (Hebrew word) *corban,* a *gift* consecrated to God Mk 7: 11.*

κορβανᾶς, ᾶ, ὁ (Hebrew) *temple treasury* Mt 27: 6.*

Κόρε, ὁ indecl. *Korah* (Numbers 16) Jd 11.*

κορέννυμι *satiate, fill* pass. *have enough* Ac 27: 38; 1 Cor 4: 8.*

Κορίνθιος, ου, ὁ *the Corinthian* Ac 18: 8, 27 v.l.; 2 Cor 6: 11; titles of 1 and 2 Cor; Ro subscr.*

Κόρινθος, ου, ἡ *Corinth,* an important commercial city on the isthmus joining central and southern Greece. Ac 18: 1, 27 v.l.; 19: 1; 1 Cor 1: 2; 2 Cor 1: 1, 23; 2 Ti 4: 20; Ro and 1 Th subscr.*

Κορνήλιος, ου, ὁ *Cornelius* Ac 10: 1, 3, 17, 22, 24f, 30f.*

κόρος, ου, ὁ *cor,* a dry *measure* amounting to between ten and twelve bushels Lk 16: 7.*

κοσμέω—1. *put in order* Mt 12: 44; Lk 11: 25; *trim* Mt 25: 7.— **2.** *adorn, decorate* lit. Mt 23: 29; Lk 21: 5; 1 Ti 2: 9; Rv 21: 2, 19; perhaps Mt 12: 44; Lk 11: 25. Fig. *make beautiful* or *attractive* 1 Pt 3: 5; *adorn, do credit to* Tit 2: 10.*

κοσμικός, ή, όν *earthly* Hb 9: 1. *Worldly* Tit 2: 12.*

κόσμιος, (ία), ον *respectable, honorable* 1 Ti 3: 2; *modest* 2: 9.*

κοσμίως adv. *modestly* 1 Ti 2: 9 v.l.*

κοσμοκράτωρ, ορος, ὁ *world-ruler* Eph 6: 12.*

κόσμος, ου, ὁ—1. *adornment, adorning* 1 Pt 3: 3.—**2.** *world,* in many senses—**a.** *the world* in its most inclusive sense, *the* (*orderly*) *universe* Mt 25: 34; J 17: 5; Ac 17: 24; Ro 1: 20; 1 Cor 8: 4; Phil 2: 15; Hb 4: 3.—**b.** *the world* as the earth, the planet on which we live Mt 4: 8; Mk 14: 9; Lk 12: 30; J 10: 36; 11: 9, 27; 16: 21, 28; 18: 36; 1 Ti 6: 7; 1 Pt 5: 9; Rv 11: 15.—**c.** *the world* as mankind in general Mt 18: 7; J 1: 29; 3: 16; 4: 42; 6: 33, 51; 8: 12; 12: 19; 17: 6; 18: 20; Ro 3: 6, 19; 1 Cor 4: 13; 2 Pt 2: 5.—**d.** *the world* as the scene of earthly possessions, joys, sufferings, etc. Mt 16: 26; Mk 8: 36; Lk 9: 25; 1 Cor 7: 31a, 33f; 1 J 2: 15f; 3: 17.— **e.** *the world* is sometimes spoken of as that which is at enmity

with God, lost in sin, ruined, depraved J 7: 7; 8: 23; 12: 31; 15: 18f; 16: 33; 17: 25; 18: 36; 1 Cor 2: 12; 3: 19; 11: 32; 2 Cor 5: 19; Gal 6: 14; Js 1: 27; 1 J 4: 17; 5: 4f, 19.—**f.** *the world* as *totality, sum total* Js 3: 6.

Κούαρτος, ου, ὁ *Quartus* Ro 16: 23; 1 Cor subscr.*

κοῦμ Aramaic word meaning *stand up* Mk 5: 41.*

κουμι an alternate form of κοῦμ.

κουστωδία, ας, ἡ (Latin loanword: custodia) *a guard* composed of soldiers Mt 27: 65f; 28: 11.*

κουφίζω *make light, lighten* Ac 27: 38.*

κόφινος, ου, ὁ a large, heavy *basket* Mt 14: 20; 16: 9; Mk 6: 43; 8: 19; Lk 9: 17; 13: 8 v.l.; J 6: 13.*

κράβαττος, ου, ὁ *mattress, pallet,* the poor man's *bed* Mk 2: 4, 9, 11f; 6: 55; J 5: 8–11; Ac 5: 15; 9: 33.*

κράζω—1. *cry out, scream* wordlessly Mt 14: 26; 27: 50; Mk 5: 5; 9: 26; Lk 9: 39; Ac 7: 57; Rv 12: 2.—**2.** *call, call out, cry*—**a.** lit. Mt 15: 23; 20: 30f; Mk 10: 48; 15: 14; Lk 18: 39; J 7: 28; Ac 7: 60; 16: 17; 19: 32; 24: 21; Rv 6: 10.—**b.** fig. Lk 19: 40; Ro 8: 15; 9: 27; Gal 4: 6; Js 5: 4.

κραιπάλη, ης, ἡ *dissipation* Lk 21: 34.*

κρανίον, ου, τό *skull* κρανίου τόπος *the place that is called* (*a*) *skull* Mt 27: 33; Mk 15: 22; J 19: 17; cf. Lk 23: 33.*

κράσπεδον, ου, τό—1. *edge, border, hem* of a garment Mt 9: 20; 14: 36; Mk 6: 56; Lk 8: 44; meaning 2 is also possible for all these passages.—**2.** *tassel* (Deut 22: 12) Mt 23: 5.*

κραταιός, ά, όν *powerful, mighty* 1 Pt 5: 6.*

κραταιόω *strengthen* pass. *become*

or *be strong* Lk 1: 80; 2: 40; 1 Cor 16: 13; Eph 3: 16.*

κρατέω—1. *take into one's possession* or *custody*—a. *arrest, apprehend* Mt 26: 4, 48, 50, 55, 57; Mk 3: 21; 6: 17; Ac 24: 6; Rv 20: 2.—b. *take hold of, grasp, seize* w. acc. or gen. Mt 12: 11; 22: 6; 28: 9; Mk 1: 31; 9: 27; Lk 8: 54. *Attain* Ac 27: 13.— **2.** *hold* Ac 3: 11 ; Rv 2: 1. *Hold back, restrain* 7: 1; pass. *be prevented* Lk 24: 16. *Hold fast* Mk 7: 3f, 8; Ac 2: 24; Col 2: 19; Rv 2: 13–15. *Keep* Mk 9: 10. *Retain* J 20: 23.

κράτιστος, η, ον *most noble, most excellent* used in addressing a person of high rank Ac 23: 26; 24: 3; 26: 25. In polite address, with no official connotation Lk 1: 3.*

κράτος, ους, τό *power, might, sovereignty* Ac 19: 20; Eph 1: 19; 6: 10; Col 1: 11; 1 Ti 6: 16; Hb 2: 14; Rv 1: 6. *Mighty deed* Lk 1: 51.

κραυγάζω *cry (out), cry loudly* Mt 12: 19; Lk 4: 41; J 11: 43; 12: 13; 18: 40; 19: 6, 12, 15; Ac 22: 23.*

κραυγή, ῆς, ἡ *shout(ing), clamor* Mt 25: 6; Lk 1: 42; Ac 23: 9; Eph 4: 31; Hb 5: 7. *Crying* Rv 21: 4.*

κρέας, κρέως and **κρέατος, τό** *meat* Ro 14: 21; 1 Cor 8: 13.*

κρείσσων and **κρείττων, ον,** gen. **ονος** *better*—**1.** in the sense *more prominent, higher in rank, preferable* Hb 1: 4; 7: 7, 19, 22; 11: 16, 35, 40.—**2.** in the sense *more useful, more advantageous* 1 Cor 7: 9; 11: 17; Phil 1: 23; Hb 6: 9; 1 Pt 3: 17; 2 Pt 2: 21.—**3.** as adv. *better* 1 Cor 7: 38; Hb 12: 24.

κρέμαμαι see κρεμάννυμι 2.

κρεμάννυμι—1. trans. *hang (up)* Ac 5: 30; 10: 39. Pass. Mt 18: 6; Lk 23: 39.—**2.** intrans. mid. κρέμαμαι *hang* lit. Ac 28: 4; Gal 3: 13. Fig. *depend* Mt 22: 40.*

κρεπάλη a different spelling for κραιπάλη.

κρημνός, οῦ, ὁ *steep slope* or *bank, cliff* Mt 8: 32; Mk 5: 13; Lk 8: 33.*

Κρής, ητός, ὁ pl. Κρῆτες *a Cretan* Ac 2: 11; Tit 1: 12; Tit subscr.*

Κρήσκης, εντος, ὁ *Crescens* 2 Ti 4: 10.*

Κρήτη, ης, ἡ *Crete,* a large island at the south end of the Aegean Sea Ac 27: 7, 12f, 21; Tit 1: 5.*

κριθή, ῆς, ἡ *barley* Rv 6: 6.*

κριθήσομαι fut. pass. ind. of κρίνω.

κρίθινος, η, ον *made of barley flour* J 6: 9, 13.*

κρίμα, ατος, τό *lawsuit* 1 Cor 6: 7. *Decision, decree* Ro 11: 33. *Judging, judgment* Mt 7: 2; Ac 24: 25; Hb 6: 2; 1 Pt 4: 17; *authority to judge* Rv 20: 4. *Verdict* Ro 5: 16. Mostly *condemnation, punishment* Mk 12: 40; Lk 24: 20; Ro 2: 2f; 3: 8; 1 Cor 11: 29, 34; 1 Ti 5: 12; 2 Pt 2: 3; Rv 17: 1.

κρίνον, ου, τό *lily* Mt 6: 28; Lk 12: 27.*

κρίνω—1. *separate, distinguish,* then *select, prefer* Ro 14: 5a; in 14: 5b κ. probably means *hold in esteem.* —**2.** *judge, think, consider, look upon* Lk 7: 43; Ac 4: 19; 13: 46; 16: 15; 26: 8; 1 Cor 11: 13; 2 Cor 5: 14.— **3.** *reach a decision, decide, propose, intend* Ac 3: 13; 16: 4; 20: 16; 21: 25; 27: 1; 1 Cor 2: 2; 5: 3; 7: 37; Ro 14: 13.—**4.** as legal term, of human or divine courts *judge, decide, hale before a court, condemn, hand over for punishment* Mt 5: 40; 7: 1b, 2b; Lk 19: 22; J 5: 30; 7: 51; 18: 31; Ac 13: 27; 17: 31; 23: 3; 25: 9; 26: 6; Ro 2: 16, 27; 1 Cor 5: 12f; 6: 2f, 6; 2 Ti 4: 1; Js 2: 12; 1 Pt 1: 17; Rv 6: 10; 20: 12f. *Condemn, punish* J 3: 17f; 12: 47f; 16: 11; Ro 2: 12; 1 Cor

11: 31f; Hb 10: 30; Rv 18: 8.—
5. *judge, pass judgment on, express an opinion about* Mt 7: 1a, 2a; Lk 6: 37a; J 7: 24; 8: 15. In an unfavorable sense *criticize, find fault with, condemn* Ro 2: 1, 3; 14: 3f, 10, 13a, 22; 1 Cor 4: 5; 10: 29; Col 2: 16; Js 4: 11f.

κρίσις, εως, ἡ—**1.** *judging, judgment* Mt 10: 15; Lk 10: 14; J 5: 30; 2 Th 1: 5; Hb 9: 27; 2 Pt 2: 9; Jd 6. κρίσιν ποιεῖν *act as judge* J 5: 27. *Condemnation, punishment* Mt 23: 33; J 5: 24, 29; Hb 10: 27; Js 5: 12; Rv 18: 10; 19: 2.—**2.** *board of judges, local court* Mt 5: 21f.—**3.** *right* in the sense of *justice, righteousness* Mt 12: 18, 20; 23: 23; Lk 11: 42. This meaning is also possible for J 7: 24; 12: 31; Ac 8: 33 and others.

Κρίσπος, ου, ὁ *Crispus* Ac 18: 8; 1 Cor 1: 14; 2 Ti 4: 10 v.l.*

κριτήριον, ου, τό—**1.** *lawcourt, tribunal* Js 2: 6.—**2.** *lawsuit, legal action* is probable for 1 Cor 6: 2, 4, though meaning 1 is possible.*

κριτής, οῦ, ὁ *judge* Mt 5: 25; 12: 27; Lk 18: 2, 6; Ac 10: 42; 24: 10; 2 Ti 4: 8; Hb 12: 23; Js 2: 4; 4: 11f. A leader of the people in the period of the Judges Ac 13: 20.

κριτικός, ή, όν *able to discern* or *judge* Hb 4: 12.*

κρούω *knock* (*at*) Mt 7: 7f; Lk 11: 9f; 12: 36; 13: 25; Ac 12: 13, 16; Rv 3: 20.*

κρυβῆναι 2 aor. pass. inf. of κρύπτω.

κρύπτη, ης, ἡ *a dark and hidden place, a cellar* Lk 11: 33.*

κρυπτός, ή, όν *hidden, secret* as adj. Mt 10: 26; Mk 4: 22; Lk 12: 2; 1 Pt 3: 4. As noun *a hidden thing* Lk 8: 17; Ro 2: 16; 1 Cor 4: 5; 14: 25. τὰ κ. τῆς αἰσχύνης *the things that are hidden out of a sense of shame* 2 Cor 4: 2. *A*

hidden place J 7: 4; 18: 20. ἐν τῷ κ. *in secret* Mt 6: 4, 6, 18 v.l., but *inwardly* Ro 2: 29. ὡς ἐν κ. *privately, as it were* J 7: 10.

κρύπτω *hide, conceal, cover* lit. Mt 13: 44; 25: 18, 25; Lk 13: 21; J 12: 36; Rv 6: 15f. Fig. Mt 11: 25; Lk 18: 34; J 19: 38; Col 3: 3; 1 Ti 5: 25.

κρυσταλλίζω *shine like crystal, be as transparent as crystal* Rv 21: 11.*

κρύσταλλος, ου, ὁ *rock-crystal* Rv 4: 6; 22: 1.*

κρυφαῖος, αία, αῖον *hidden* ἐν τῷ κ. *in secret* Mt 6: 18.*

κρυφῇ adv. *in secret* Eph 5: 12.*

κρύφιος, ία, ιον *hidden, secret* Mt 6: 18 v.l.*

κτάομαι *procure for oneself, acquire, get* Mt 10: 9; Lk 18: 12; 21: 19; Ac 1: 18; 8: 20; 22: 28; 1 Th 4: 4.*

κτῆμα, ατος, τό *property, possession* Mt 19: 22; Mk 10: 22; Ac 2: 45. *Field, piece of ground* 5: 1.*

κτῆνος, ους, τό *animal, domesticated animal* 1 Cor 15: 39; used for riding Lk 10: 34; Ac 23: 24. Pl. *cattle* Rv 18: 13.*

κτήτωρ, ορος, ὁ *owner* Ac 4: 34.*

κτίζω *create* Mt 19: 4; Mk 13: 19; 1 Cor 11: 9; Eph 2: 10, 15; 4: 24; 1 Ti 4: 3; Rv 10: 6.

κτίσις, εως, ἡ—**1.** *creation*—**a.** the act of creation Ro 1: 20.—**b.** *creation* in the sense *that which is created, creature* Mk 10: 6; 13: 19; Ro 1: 25; 8: 19–22, 39; 2 Cor 5: 17; Col 1: 15, 23; Hb 4: 13; 2 Pt 3: 4.—**2.** *institution* 1 Pt 2: 13.

κτίσμα, ατος, τό *that which is created* (by God), *creature* 1 Ti 4: 4; Js 1: 18; Rv 5: 13; 8: 9.*

κτίστης, ου, ὁ *Creator* of God 1 Pt 4: 19.*

κυβεία, ας, ἡ *craftiness, trickery,* lit. 'dice-playing' Eph 4: 14.*

κυβέρνησις, εως, ἡ *administration* 1 Cor 12: 28.*

κυβερνήτης, ου, ὁ *steersman, pilot* Ac 27: 11; Rv 18: 17.*

κυβία a different spelling for κυβεία.

κυκλεύω *surround* Rv 20: 9; J 10: 24 v.l.*

κυκλόθεν adv. *all around, from all sides* Rv 4: 8. As improper prep. w. gen. *around* 4: 3f.*

κυκλόω *surround, encircle* Lk 21: 20; J 10: 24; Ac 14: 20. *Go around, circle round* pass. Hb 11: 30.*

κύκλῳ dat. of κύκλος fixed as an adv. *around, all around,* lit. *in a circle* Mk 3: 34; 6: 6; Ro 15: 19. Used as an adj. *nearby* Mk 6: 36; *around here* Lk 9: 12. Improper prep. w. gen. *around* Rv 4: 6; 5: 11; 7: 11.*

κύλισμα, ματος, τό v.l. for κυλισμός.

κυλισμός, οῦ, ὁ *rolling, wallowing* 2 Pt 2: 22.*

κυλίω act. *roll* Lk 23: 53 v.l. Pass. *roll (oneself)* Mk 9: 20.*

κυλλός, ή, όν *crippled, deformed* Mt 18: 8; Mk 9: 43. As noun *cripple* Mt 15: 30f.*

κῦμα, ατος, τό *wave* lit. Mt 8: 24; 14: 24; Mk 4: 37; Ac 27: 41 v.l. Fig. Jd 13.*

κύμβαλον, ου, τό *cymbal* 1 Cor 13: 1.*

κύμινον, ου, τό *cummin* Mt 23: 23.*

κυνάριον, ου, τό *little dog* or simply *dog* Mt 15: 26f; Mk 7: 27f.*

Κύπριος, ου, ὁ *a Cyprian, an inhabitant of Cyprus* Ac 4: 36; 11: 20; 21: 16.*

Κύπρος, ου, ἡ *Cyprus* an island south of Asia Minor Ac 11: 19; 13: 4; 15: 39; 21: 3; 27: 4.*

κύπτω *bend (oneself) down* Mk 1: 7; J 8: 6, 8 v.l.*

Κυρεῖνος variant spelling of Κυρήνιος.

Κυρηναῖος, ου, ὁ *a Cyrenian* Mt 27: 32; Mk 15: 21; Lk 23: 26; Ac 6: 9; 11: 20; 13: 1.*

Κυρήνη, ης, ἡ *Cyrene,* an important Greek city in N. Africa, west of Egypt Ac 2: 10.*

Κυρήνιος and Κυρίνιος, ου, ὁ *Quirinius* (P. Sulpicius Q.) imperial governor of Syria Lk 2: 2.*

κυρία, ας, ἡ *lady, mistress* in 2 J verses 1 and 5 may refer to an individual or, more likely, to a congregation.*

κυριακός, ή, όν *belonging to the Lord, the Lord's* 1 Cor 11: 20. κ. ἡμέρα *the Lord's Day, Sunday* Rv 1: 10.*

κυριεύω *be lord* or *master, rule, lord it (over), control* w. gen. Lk 22: 25; Ac 19: 16 v.l.; Ro 6: 9, 14; 7: 1; 14: 9; 2 Cor 1: 24; 1 Ti 6: 15.*

κύριος, ου, ὁ *lord, Lord, master—* **1.** *generally—***a.** *owner, master* Mt 6: 24; 20: 8; 24: 48; Lk 12: 46; 19: 33; J 13: 16; Ro 14: 4; Gal 4: 1; *lord, master,* one who has full control of something Mt 9: 38; Mk 2: 28.—**b.** as a respectful designation of any person of high position *lord* 1 Pt 3: 6. Often equivalent to our *sir* Mt 21: 29; 25: 11; 27: 63; J 12: 21; Ac 16: 30; Rv 7: 14.—**2.** in religious usage—**a.** as a designation of God Mt 5: 33; 11: 25; Mk 5: 19; 12: 29f; Lk 1: 11, 15, 17, 32; 2: 15, 22; Ac 7: 31; 8: 24; 2 Th 3: 3; 1 Ti 6: 15; Hb 8: 2; Js 1: 7; 2 Pt 2: 9.— **b.** as a designation of a (deified) ruler Ac 25: 26.—**c.** as a designation of Jesus Christ, raising him above the human level Mt 8: 2, 6, 8; Mk 11: 3; Lk 7: 13; 10: 1, 39, 41; 12: 41; J 4: 11, 15, 19, 49; 20: 2, 18, 20, 28; Ac 2: 36; 9: 10f, 42; 10: 36; Ro 1: 4; 10: 9; 12: 11; 16: 12; 1 Cor 4: 17; 6: 13f, 17; 11: 23; Eph 6: 8; Col 1: 10; Phlm 25; Hb 2: 3; 7: 14; 1 Pt 1: 3; Rv 22: 20.—**d.** In many places it is not clear whether God or Christ is meant, e.g. Ac 9: 31; 1 Cor 4: 19; 7: 17; 2 Cor 8: 21; Col 3: 22b; 1 Th 4: 6; 2 Th 3: 16.— e. of other supernatural beings Ac 10: 4; 1 Cor 8: 5.

κυριότης, ητος, ἡ—1. *ruling power, lordship, dominion* 2 Pt 2: 10; Jd 8.—2. a special class of angelic powers, *bearers of the ruling power, dominions* Eph 1: 21; Col 1: 16.*

κυρόω—1. *confirm, ratify, validate* Gal 3: 15.—2. *conclude, decide in favor of,* perhaps *reaffirm* 2 Cor 2: 8.*

κυσί dat. pl. of κύων.

κύων, κυνός, ὁ *dog* lit. Mt 7: 6; Lk 16: 21; 2 Pt 2: 22. Fig. Phil 3: 2; Rv 22: 15.*

κῶλον, ου, τό pl. *dead body, corpse,* lit. 'limbs' Hb 3: 17.*

κωλύω—1. *hinder, prevent, forbid* Mt 19: 14; Mk 9: 38f; Lk 9: 49f;

Ac 8: 36; 11: 17; 27: 43; Ro 1: 13; 1 Cor 14: 39; 1 Th 2: 16; 2 Pt 2: 16.—2. *refuse, deny, withhold, keep back* Lk 6: 29; Ac 10: 47.

κώμη, ης, ἡ *village, small town* Mt 9: 35; Mk 6: 36, 56; 8: 23, 26; Lk 13: 22; 17: 12; J 11: 1, 30.

κωμόπολις, εως, ἡ *market-town* Mk 1: 38.*

κῶμος, ου, ὁ *carousing, revelry* Ro 13: 13; Gal 5: 21; 1 Pt 4: 3.*

κώνωψ, ωπος, ὁ *gnat, mosquito* Mt 23: 24.*

Κώς, Κῶ, ἡ acc. Κῶ *Cos,* an island in the Aegean Sea Ac 21: 1.*

Κωσάμ, ὁ indecl. *Cosam* Lk 3: 28.*

κωφός, ή, όν—1. *dumb, mute* Mt 9: 32f; 12: 22; 15: 30f; Lk 1: 22; 11: 14.—2. *deaf* Mt 11: 5; Mk 7: 32, 37; 9: 25; Lk 7: 22.*

Λ

λ' numeral = 30 Lk 3: 23 v.l.

λάβε 2 aor. act. imperative of λαμβάνω.

λαγχάνω—1. *receive, obtain* (by lot, or by divine will) Ac 1: 17; 1 Pt 1: 1.—2. *be appointed* or *chosen by lot* Lk 1: 9.—3. *cast lots* J 19: 24.*

Λάζαρος, ου, ὁ *Lazarus*—1. brother of Mary and Martha J 11: 1f, 5, 11, 14, 43; 12: 1f, 9f, 17.— 2. name of a beggar in the parable Lk 16: 20, 23ff.*

λαθεῖν 2 aor. act. inf. of λανθάνω.

λάθρᾳ adv. *secretly* Mt 1: 19; 2: 7; Mk 5: 33 v.l.; J 11: 28; Ac 16: 37.*

λαῖλαψ, απος, ἡ *whirlwind, hurricane* 2 Pt 2: 17. λ. ἀνέμου a fierce gust of wind Mk 4: 37; Lk 8: 23.*

λακάω *burst open* Ac 1: 18.*

λακτίζω *kick* Ac 26: 14; 9: 5 v.l.*

λαλέω—1. *sound, give forth sounds* or *tones* of inanimate things Hb 11: 4; 12: 24; Rv 4: 1; 10: 4.— 2. *speak* Mt 12: 34, 46f; 13: 3; Mk 1: 34; Lk 1: 19, 55; Ac 13: 45; 18: 9; 1 Cor 13: 11; 14: 29; Hb 2: 5; Rv 13: 11. *Be able to speak* Mk 7: 35, 37; Lk 1: 20, 64. *Proclaim, say* Mt 12: 36; Mk 2: 2; J 3: 34; 16: 25a; 1 Cor 2: 6f.

λαλιά, ᾶς, ἡ *speech, speaking* J 4: 42. *Form of speech, way of speaking* Mt 26: 73; J 8: 43.*

λαμά (Hebrew) *lama = why?* Mt 27: 46 v.l.; Mk 15: 34.*

λαμβάνω—1. in a more or less active sense *take, take hold of, grasp* Mt 26: 26a; Mk 12: 19–21; 15: 23; J 19: 30; Js 5: 10; Rv

5: 8f. *Seize* Mt 21: 35, 39; Lk
5: 26; 9: 39; 1 Cor 10: 13. *Catch*
Lk 5: 5. *Draw* Mt 26: 52. *Put on*
J 13: 12; Phil 2: 7. *Take up,
receive* Mt 13: 20; J 6: 21; 12:
48; 13: 20; 19: 27. *Collect* Mt
17: 24; 21: 34; Mk 12: 2; Hb
7: 8f. *Choose, select* Hb 5: 1.
Sometimes the participle can
be translated *with* λαβὼν τὴν
σπεῖραν ἔρχεται *he came with a
detachment* J 18: 3.—**2.** in a more
or less passive sense *receive, get,
obtain* Mk 10: 30; 12: 40; Lk
11: 10; Ac 1: 20; 10: 43; 20:
35; 1 Cor 4: 7; 9: 24f; Js 1: 12;
Rv 22: 17. As a periphrasis for
the pass. οἰκοδομὴν λ. *be edified*
1 Cor 14: 5. Cf. J 7: 23; Ro 5:
11.

Λάμεχ, ὁ indecl. *Lamech* Lk 3:
36.*

λαμπάς, άδος, ἡ *torch* J 18: 3;
Rv 4: 5; 8: 10. *Lamp* Mt 25: 1,
3f, 7f; Ac 20: 8.*

λαμπρός, ά, όν *bright, shining,
radiant* Lk 23: 11; Ac 10: 30;
Js 2: 2f; Rv 15: 6; 19: 8; 22: 16.
Clear, transparent Rv 22: 1.
τὰ λαμπρά *splendor* 18: 14.*

λαμπρότης, ητος, ἡ *brightness* Ac
26: 13.*

λαμπρῶς adv. *splendidly, sump-
tuously* Lk 16: 19.*

λάμπω *shine* lit. Mt 5: 15; Ac 12:
7; *gleam* Mt 17: 2; *flash* Lk
17: 24; *shine forth* 2 Cor 4: 6a.
Fig. Mt 5: 16; 2 Cor 4: 6b.*

λανθάνω *escape notice, be hidden*
Mk 7: 24; Lk 8: 47; Ac 26: 26;
Hb 13: 2; 2 Pt 3: 5, 8.*

λαξευτός, ή, όν *hewn in the rock* Lk
23: 53.*

Λαοδίκεια, ας, ἡ *Laodicea,* a city
in Phrygia in Asia Minor Col 2:
1; 4: 13, 15f; subscr. of 1 and 2
Ti; Rv 1: 11; 3: 14.*

Λαοδικεύς, έως, ὁ *a Laodicean* Col
4: 16.*

λαός, οῦ, ὁ *people* Mt 26: 5; Lk
7: 29; 19: 48; Ac 3: 23; 4: 10,

25; 15: 14; Ro 9: 25; Hb 2:
17; 4: 9; 1 Pt 2: 9; Jd 5; Rv
5: 9; 17: 15; *populace* Mt 27:
64.

λάρυγξ, γγος, ὁ *throat, gullet* Ro
3: 13.*

Λασαία, ας, or **Λασέα, ας, ἡ**
Lasaea, a city on the south
coast of Crete. Ac 27: 8.*

λάσκω a form erroneously thought
to be the source of ἐλάκησεν
Ac 1: 18, which is 1 aor. act.
ind. of λακάω.

λατομέω *hew out of the rock* Mt
27: 60; Mk 15: 46; Lk 23: 53
v.l.*

λατρεία, ας, ἡ religious *service,
worship (of God)* J 16: 2; Ro 9: 4;
12: 1; Hb 9: 1; pl. *rites* 9: 6.*

λατρεύω *serve* by carrying out
religious duties, w. dat. Mt 4:
10; Lk 1: 74; Ac 7: 7, 42; 26: 7;
Ro 1: 9; 2 Ti 1: 3; Hb 9: 9, 14;
Rv 7: 15.

λάχανον, ου, τό *garden herb, vege-
table* Mt 13: 32; Mk 4: 32; Lk
11: 42; Ro 14: 2.*

λαχοῦσιν dat. pl., 2 aor. act.
participle of λαγχάνω.

λάχωμεν 2 aor. subj. act., 1 pl.
of λαγχάνω.

Λεββαῖος, ου, ὁ *Lebbaeus* Mt 10: 3
v.l. and Mk 3: 18 v.l.*

λεγιών, ῶνος, ἡ (Latin loanword:
legio) *legion,* a detachment of
6,000 Roman soldiers Mt 26:
53; Mk 5: 9, 15 (masc. because
the demon is masc.); Lk 8: 30.*

λέγω *say*—**1.** generally, *say, tell,
give expression to* orally, but also
in writing Mt 1: 20; 9: 34; 21:
45; Mk 1: 15; Lk 13: 6, 24; J
2: 3; 18: 34; Ac 14: 11; Ro 10:
16, 20; Hb 8: 8; 11: 32. *Mean*
Mk 14: 71; 1 Cor 10: 29;
Gal 3: 17. *Bring charges* Ac
23: 30.—**2.** more specifically,
of special forms of saying, etc.
Ask Mt 9: 14; Mk 14: 14.
Answer Mt 4: 10; 19: 8; J 1: 21.
Order, command, direct Mk 13:

37; Lk 6: 46; J 2: 7f; Rv 10: 9. *Assure, assert* Mt 11: 22; Mk 11: 24; Lk 9: 27. *Maintain, declare, proclaim* Mt 22: 23; Mk 15: 2; Ro 15: 8; 1 Cor 15: 12; Gal 4: 1. *Speak, report, tell of* Mk 7: 36; Lk 9: 31; Ac 1: 3; Eph 5: 12. *Call, name* Mt 27: 33b; Mk 10: 18; 12: 37; J 5: 18; 20: 16; Col 4: 11; Rv 2: 20.

λεῖμμα, ατος, τό *remnant* Ro 11: 5.*

λεῖος, α, ον *smooth, level* Lk 3: 5.*

λείπω mid. and pass., and intrans. act. *fall short, lack* Lk 18: 22; Tit 1: 5; 3: 13; Js 1: 4. *Be in need* or *want of* Js 1: 5; 2: 15.*

λειτουργέω *perform a* (religious) *service* Hb 10: 11; Tit 1: 9 v.l. Fig. Ac 13: 2. *Serve* Ro 15: 27.*

λειτουργία, ας, ἡ *service* of a ritual or other religious nature Lk 1: 23; 2 Cor 9: 12; Phil 2: 17, 30; Hb 8: 6; 9: 21.*

λειτουργικός, ή, όν *engaged in holy service* Hb 1: 14.*

λειτουργός, οῦ, ὁ *servant, minister* with religious connotation Ro 13: 6; 15: 16; Phil 2: 25; Hb 1: 7; 8: 2.*

λείχω *lick* Lk 16: 21 v.l.*

Λέκτρα, ας, ἡ *Lectra* 2 Ti 4: 19 v.l.*

λεμά (Aramaic) *lema = why?* Mt 27: 46.*

λέντιον, ου, τό (Latin loanword: linteum) linen *towel* J 13: 4f.*

λεπίς, ίδος, ἡ *scale* Ac 9: 18.*

λέπρα, ας, ἡ *leprosy* Mt 8: 3; Mk 1: 42; Lk 5: 12f.*

λεπρός, ά, όν *leprous* Lk 17: 12. As noun *leper* Mt 10: 8; 11: 5; Mk 1: 40; 14: 3; Lk 4: 27.

λεπτός, ή, όν *small, thin.* As noun τὸ λεπτόν *small copper coin* worth a fraction of a cent Mk 12: 42; Lk 12: 59; 21: 2.*

Λευί, ὁ indecl. and **Λευίς,** gen. Λευί, acc. Λευίν *Levi*—**1.** son of Jacob Hb 7: 5, 9; Rv 7: 7.—

2. son of Melchi Lk 3: 24.—**3.** son of Symeon 3: 29.—**4.** the tax-collector, a disciple of Jesus Mk 2: 14; Lk 5: 27, 29. Called Matthew Mt 9: 9.*

Λευίτης, ου, ὁ *a Levite*, one of a group that performed the lowlier services in the temple ritual Lk 10: 32; J 1: 19; Ac 4: 36.*

Λευιτικός, ή, όν *Levitical* Hb 7: 11.*

λευκαίνω *whiten, make white* lit. Mk 9: 3; fig. Rv 7: 14.*

λευκοβύσσινος v.l. for βύσσινον λευκόν *white linen* Rv 19: 14b.*

λευκός, ή, όν—**1.** *bright, shining, gleaming* Mt 17: 2; Lk 9: 29.— **2.** *white* Mt 5: 36; Mk 9: 3; 16: 5; Lk 9: 29; J 4: 35; Ac 1: 10; Rv 1: 14; 2: 17; 6: 2; 7: 9, 13; 19: 11, 14; 20: 11.

λέων, οντος, ὁ *lion* lit. Hb 11: 33; 1 Pt 5: 8; Rv 4: 7; 9: 8, 17; 10: 3; 13: 2. Fig. 2 Ti 4: 17; Rv 5: 5.*

λήθη, ης, ἡ *forgetfulness* λήθην λαμβάνειν *forget* 2 Pt 1: 9.*

λῆμψις, εως, ἡ *receiving, credit* Phil 4: 15.*

λήμψομαι fut. mid. ind. of λαμβάνω.

ληνός, οῦ, ἡ *wine-press* Mt 21: 33; Rv 14: 19f; 19: 15.*

λῆρος, ου, ὁ *idle talk, nonsense* Lk 24: 11.*

ληστής, οῦ, ὁ—**1.** *robber, highwayman, bandit* Mt 27: 38; Mk 11: 17; 15: 27; Lk 10: 30, 36; J 10: 1, 8; 2 Cor 11: 26.—**2.** *revolutionary, insurrectionist* J 18: 40 and probably Mt 26: 55; Mk 14: 48; Lk 22: 52.

λῆψις variant form of λῆμψις.

λίαν adv. *very (much), exceedingly* Mt 2: 16; 8: 28; 27: 14; Mk 1: 35; 16: 2; Lk 23: 8; 2 J 4; *vehemently* 2 Ti 4: 15.

λίβα acc. sing. of λίψ.

λίβανος, ου, ὁ *frankincense*, an aromatic resinous gum Mt 2: 11; Rv 18: 13.*

λιβανωτός, οῦ, ὁ censer Rv 8: 3,
5.*

Λιβερτῖνος, ου, ὁ freedman Ac
6: 9.*

Λιβύη, ης, ἡ Libya, a district in
N. Africa near Cyrene Ac 2:
10.*

Λιβυστῖνος, ου, ὁ Libyan v.l. for
Λιβερτῖνος in Ac 6: 9.*

λιθάζω to stone J 8: 5; 10: 31–33;
11: 8; Ac 5: 26; 14: 19; 2 Cor
11: 25; Hb 11: 37.*

λίθινος, ίνη, ον (made of) stone J 2:
6; 2 Cor 3: 3; Rv 9: 20.*

λιθοβολέω throw stones at Mt 21:
35; Mk 12: 4 v.l.; Ac 14: 5.
Stone (to death) Mt 23: 37; Lk
13: 34; J 8: 5 v.l.; Ac 7: 58f;
Hb 12: 20.*

λίθος, ου, ὁ stone lit. Mt 3: 9;
24: 2; Mk 5: 5; 15: 46; Lk 4: 3,
11; 21: 5; J 8: 7, 59; Ac 17: 29;
Rv 17: 4; 18: 21; 21: 11, 19.
Fig. Lk 20: 17f; Ac 4: 11; Ro
9: 32f; 1 Pt 2: 4–8.

λιθόστρωτος, ον paved with blocks
of stone, as noun stone pavement
or mosaic J 19: 13.*

λικμάω crush Mt 21: 44; Lk 20:
18.*

λιμήν, ένος, ὁ harbor Ac 27: 12.
For the place name Καλοὶ
λιμένες 27: 8 see this as a
separate entry.*

λίμμα a different spelling for
λεῖμμα.

λίμνη, ης, ἡ lake Lk 5: 1f; Rv
20: 14f; 21: 8.

λιμός, οῦ, ὁ and ἡ—1. hunger Lk
15: 17; Ro 8: 35; 2 Cor 11: 27.—
2. famine Mk 13: 8; Lk 4: 25;
15: 14; Ac 7: 11; Rv 6: 8.

λίνον, ου, τό flax, linen, then
something made of them: lamp-
wick Mt 12: 20; linen garment Rv
15: 6.*

Λίνος, ον, ὁ Linus 2 Ti 4: 21.*

λιπαρός, ά, όν bright, costly, rich
as noun τὰ λιπαρά luxury Rv
18: 14.*

λίτρα, ας, ἡ (Latin loanword:

libra) a (Roman) pound (12
ounces; 327.45 grams) J 12: 3;
19: 39.*

λίψ, λιβός, ὁ the southwest Ac
27: 12.*

λογεία, ας, ἡ collection of money
1 Cor 16: 1f.*

λογίζομαι—1. reckon, calculate—
a. count, take into account Ro
4: 8; 1 Cor 13: 5; 2 Cor 5: 19;
2 Ti 4: 16. Credit Ro 4: 3f, 5f, 9,
11; 2 Cor 12: 6; Js 2: 23.—
b. evaluate, estimate, look upon as,
consider Ac 19: 27; Ro 2: 26; 9:
8; 1 Cor 4: 1; 2 Cor 10: 2b.
Class Lk 22: 37.—2. think (about),
consider, let one's mind dwell on
J 11: 50; 2 Cor 10: 11; Hb 11:
19. Propose 2 Cor 10: 2a. Reason,
make plans 1 Cor 13: 11.—
3. think, believe, be of the opinion
Ro 2: 3; 3: 28; 14: 14; 2 Cor 11:
5; Phil 3: 13; 1 Pt 5: 12.

λογικός, ή, όν spiritual, lit.
rational Ro 12: 1; 1 Pt 2: 2.*

λόγιον, ου, τό saying pl. sayings,
oracles Ac 7: 38; Ro 3: 2; Hb
5: 12; 1 Pt 4: 11.*

λόγιος, ία, ιον eloquent or learned
Ac 18: 24.*

λογισμός, οῦ, ὁ thought Ro 2: 15;
reasoning, sophistry 2 Cor 10:
4.*

λογομαχέω dispute about words
2 Ti 2: 14.*

λογομαχία, ας, ἡ word-battle, dispute about words 1 Ti 6: 4;
Tit 3: 9 v.l.*

λόγος, ου, ὁ—1. word—a. generally
Mt 12: 37; 13: 19–23; 22: 46;
Mk 7: 13; Lk 5: 1; 24: 19; Ac
15: 27; Ro 9: 6; 2 Cor 11: 6;
Eph 5: 6; Phil 2: 16; Col 3: 17;
1 Ti 1: 15; Tit 2: 5; 1 Pt 1: 23;
Rv 6: 9. εἰπέ λόγῳ say the word
Mt 8: 8.—b. subject under discussion, matter, thing Mt 5: 32;
Mk 9: 10; Ac 8: 21; 15: 6; complaint 19: 38.—c. statement, as-
sertion, declaration Mt 12: 32;
15: 12; 19: 11, 22; 22: 15; Mk

5: 36; 7: 29; Lk 1: 29; J 4: 39, 50; 19: 8; Ac 6: 5; 1 Th 4: 15.— **d.** The translation of λ. will often vary according to the context: *what you say* Mt 5: 37. *Question* 21: 24. *Prayer* Mk 14: 39. *Preaching* 1 Ti 5: 17. *Prophecy* J 2: 22. *Command* Lk 4: 36. *Report, story* 5: 15; J 21: 23; Ac 11: 22. *Proverb* J 4: 37. *Proclamation, instruction, teaching, message* Lk 4: 32; J 4: 41; Ac 10: 44; 1 Cor 1: 17. *A speech* Ac 15: 32; 20: 2.—**2.** The *Word* or *Logos*, the personified 'Word' (of God) J 1: 1, 14; 1 J 1: 1; Rv 19: 13.—**3.** *computation, reckoning*—**a.** *account(s), reckoning* Mt 12: 36; Lk 16: 2; Ac 19: 40; Ro 14: 12; 1 Pt 3: 15; 4: 5.—**b.** *settlement* (of an account) Mt 18: 23; 25: 19; Phil 4: 15, 17.—**c.** *reason, motive* Ac 10: 29; 18: 14; perhaps Mt 5: 32 (see **1b** above).—**d.** πρὸς ὃν ἡμῖν ὁ λόγος *with whom we have to reckon* Hb 4: 13.

λόγχη, ης, ἡ *spear, lance* J 19: 34; Mt 27: 49 v.l.*

λοιδορέω *revile, abuse* J 9: 28; Ac 23: 4; 1 Cor 4: 12; 1 Pt 2: 23.*

λοιδορία, ας, ἡ *reviling, reproach, verbal abuse* 1 Ti 5: 14; 1 Pt 3: 9.*

λοίδορος, ου, ὁ *reviler, abusive person* 1 Cor 5: 11; 6: 10.*

λοιμός, οῦ, ὁ *pestilence* Lk 21: 11; Mt 24: 7 v.l. Fig. *a plague-spot* Ac 24: 5.*

λοιπός, ή, όν *remaining*—**1.** *left* Rv 8: 13; 9: 20; 11: 13.—**2.** *other*, sometimes in pl. *the rest* Ac 2: 37; Ro 1: 13; 1 Cor 9: 5; Gal 2: 13; Phil 4: 3. As noun Mt 22: 6; Lk 8: 10; 12: 26; Ac 5: 13; Ro 11: 7; 2 Cor 13: 2; 1 Th 4: 13; 5: 6; Rv 3: 2; 19: 21.—**3.** adverbial uses (τὸ) λοιπόν *from now on, in the future, henceforth* 1 Cor 7: 29; 2 Ti 4: 8; Hb 10: 13; *finally* Ac 27: 20;

perhaps *still* Mk 14: 41. τὸ λοιπόν can also mean *as far as the rest is concerned, beyond that, in addition, finally* 1 Cor 1: 16; 2 Cor 13: 11; Phil 4: 8; 1 Th 4: 1. *Furthermore* 1 Cor 4: 2. τοῦ λοιποῦ *from now on, in the future* Gal 6: 17; *finally* Eph 6: 10.

Λουκᾶς, ᾶ, ὁ *Luke* Col 4: 14; Phlm 24; 2 Ti 4: 11; title of third gospel; 2 Cor subscr.*

Λούκιος, ου, ὁ *Lucius*—**1.** from Cyrene, at Antioch Ac 13: 1.—**2.** sender of a greeting Ro 16: 21.*

λουτρόν, οῦ, τό *bath, washing* of baptism Eph 5: 26; Tit 3: 5.*

λούω *wash, bathe*—**1.** act., lit. Ac 9: 37; 16: 33; Rv 1: 5 v.l.—**2.** mid. *I wash myself* or *for myself* J 13: 10; Hb 10: 22; 2 Pt 2: 22.*

Λύδδα, gen. ας or ης, acc. **Λύδδα, ἡ** *Lydda,* a city about 10½ miles southeast of Joppa Ac 9: 32, 35, 38.*

Λυδία, ας, ἡ *Lydia* Ac 16: 14, 40.*

Λυκαονία, ας, ἡ *Lycaonia,* a province in the interior of Asia Minor, in which were located the cities of Lystra, Iconium and Derbe. Ac 14: 6.*

Λυκαονιστί adv. *in (the) Lycaonian* (language) Ac 14: 11.*

Λυκία, ας, ἡ *Lycia,* a projection on the south coast of Asia Minor Ac 27: 5.*

λύκος, ου, ὁ *wolf* lit. Mt 10: 16; Lk 10: 3; J 10: 12. Fig. Mt 7: 15; Ac 20: 29.*

λυμαίνω *harm, damage, ruin, destroy*; imperfect ἐλυμαίνετο *he was trying to destroy* Ac 8: 3.*

λυπέω *grieve, pain*—**1.** act. 2 Cor 2: 2, 5; 7: 8; Eph 4: 30.—**2.** pass. *become sad, sorrowful, distressed* Mt 14: 9; 18: 31; J 16: 20; 21: 17; 2 Cor 2: 4; 1 Pt 1: 6. *Be sad, be distressed, grieve* Mk 10: 22; 14: 19; Ro 14: 15; 2 Cor 6: 10; 1 Th 4: 13.

λύπη, ης, ἡ *grief, sorrow, pain, affliction* Lk 22: 45; J 16: 6, 20-22; Ro 9: 2; 2 Cor 2: 1, 3, 7; 7: 10; 9: 7; Phil 2: 27; Hb 12: 11; 1 Pt 2: 19.*

Λυσανίας, ου, ὁ *Lysanias* Lk 3: 1.*

Λυσίας, ου, ὁ (*Claudius*) *Lysias* Ac 23: 26; 24: 7, 22.*

λύσις, εως, ἡ *divorce* 1 Cor 7: 27.*

λυσιτελέω *be advantageous* impersonal *it is better* Lk 17: 2.*

Λύστρα acc. Λύστραν; dat. Λύστροις, ἡ or τά, *Lystra* a city in Lycaonia in Asia Minor Ac 14: 6, 8, 21; 16: 1f; 27: 5 v.l.; 2 Ti 3: 11.*

λύτρον, ου, τό *price of release, ransom* Mt 20: 28; Mk 10: 45.*

λυτρόω *free by paying a ransom, redeem* fig. 1 Pt 1: 18. *Set free, redeem, rescue* Lk 24: 21; Tit 2: 14; Ac 28: 19 v.l.*

λύτρωσις, εως, ἡ *ransoming, releasing, redemption* Lk 1: 68; 2: 38; Hb 9: 12.*

λυτρωτής, οῦ, ὁ *redeemer* Ac 7: 35.*

λυχνία, ας, ἡ *lampstand* Mk 4: 21; Lk 8: 16; Hb 9: 2; Rv 1: 12f, 20; 11: 4.

λύχνος, ου, ὁ *lamp* lit. Mt 5: 15; Mk 4: 21; Lk 11: 33, 36; 15: 8; J 5: 35; Rv 18: 23; 22: 5. Fig. Mt 6: 22; Rv 21: 23.

λύω—1. *loose, untie, set free* lit. Mt 21: 2; Mk 1: 7; Lk 13: 15; J 11: 44; Ac 7: 33; 22: 30; Rv 9: 14f; 20: 3; *break* 5: 2. Fig. *untie, free, release* Mk 7: 35; Lk 13: 16; 1 Cor 7: 27; Rv 1: 5; *permit* Mt 16: 19; 18: 18.—2. *break up, tear down* J 2: 19; Ac 13: 43; 27: 41; Eph 2: 14; 2 Pt 3: 10–12.—3. *destroy, bring to an end, abolish, do away with* Ac 2: 24; 1 J 3: 8; *repeal, annul, abolish* Mt 5: 19; J 5: 18; 7: 23; 10: 35.

Λωΐς, ΐδος, ἡ *Lois* 2 Ti 1: 5.*

Λώτ, ὁ indecl. *Lot* (Gen 11: 27) Lk 17: 28f, 32; 2 Pt 2: 7.*

M

μ' numeral =*forty* Ac 10: 41 v.l.*

Μάαθ, ὁ indecl. *Maath* Lk 3: 26.*

Μαγαδάν, ἡ indecl. *Magadan* a place on Lake Gennesaret Mt 15: 39; Mk 8: 10 v.l.*

Μαγδαληνή, ῆς, ἡ *Magdalene, woman from Magdala*, a town on the west side of Lake Gennesaret Mt 27: 56, 61; 28: 1; Mk 15: 40, 47; 16: 1, 9; Lk 8: 2; 24: 10; J 19: 25; 20: 1, 18.*

Μαγεδών see Ἁρμαγεδ(δ)ών.

μαγεία, ας, ἡ *magic* Ac 8: 11.*

μαγεύω *practice magic* Ac 8: 9.*

μαγία a different spelling for μαγεία.

μάγος, ου, ὁ—1. *a Magus*, pl. *Magi*, a wise man or astrologer Mt 2: 1, 7, 16.—2. *magician* Ac 13: 6, 8.*

Μαγώγ, ὁ indecl. *Magog* (Ezekiel 38: 2–39: 16) Rv 20: 8.*

Μαδιάμ, ὁ indecl. *Midian*, a people in Arabia Ac 7: 29.*

μαζός, οῦ, ὁ *breast* Rv 1: 13 v.l.*

μαθεῖν 2 aor. act. inf. of μανθάνω.

μαθητεύω—1. intrans. act. and pass. deponent *be* or *become a pupil* or *disciple* Mt 13: 52; 27: 57; 27: 57 v.l.—2. trans. act. *make a disciple of, teach* Mt 28: 19; Ac 14: 21.*

μαθητής, οῦ, ὁ *learner, pupil, disciple*—1. *pupil, apprentice* Mt 10: 24f; Lk 6: 40.—2. *disciple, adherent* Mt 10: 1; 22: 16; Mk 2: 18; 5: 31; Lk 6: 17; 8: 9; J 1: 35, 37; 6: 66; Ac 9: 1; practically =*Christian* Ac 6: 1f, 7; 13: 52.

μαθήτρια, ας, ἡ a (woman) disciple, Christian woman Ac 9: 36.*

Μαθθάθ see Ματθάτ.

Μαθθαῖος see Ματθαῖος.

Μαθθάν see Ματθάν.

Μαθθάτ see Ματθάτ.

Μαθθίας see Ματθίας.

Μαθουσάλα,. ὁ indecl. Methuselah Lk 3: 37.*

Μαϊνάν see Μεννά.

μαίνομαι be mad, be out of one's mind J 10: 20; Ac 12: 15; 26: 24f; 1 Cor 14: 23.*

μακαρίζω call or consider blessed, happy, fortunate Lk 1: 48; Js 5: 11.*

μακάριος, ία, ιον blessed, fortunate, happy Mt 11: 6; 13: 16; Lk 11: 27; 23: 29; J 13: 17; Ac 26: 2; 1 Cor 7: 40; 1 Ti 6: 15; Js 1: 25; 1 Pt 3: 14. μακάριος ὁ blessed is he who Mt 5: 3ff; Lk 6: 20ff; J 20: 29; Rv 1: 3; 22: 7, 14.

μακαρισμός, οῦ, ὁ blessing Ro 4: 6, 9; Gal 4: 15.*

Μακεδονία, ας, ἡ Macedonia Ac 16: 9f, 12; 19: 21f; Ro 15: 26; 1 Cor 16: 5; 2 Cor 2: 13; 8: 1; Phil 4: 15; 1 Ti 1: 3.

Μακεδών, όνος, ὁ a Macedonian Ac 16: 9; 19: 29; 27: 2; 2 Cor 9: 2, 4.*

μάκελλον, ου, τό meat market, food market 1 Cor 10: 25.*

μακράν far (away) adv. Mt 8: 30; Mk 12: 34; Lk 15: 20; J 21: 8; Ac 17: 27; Eph 2: 13, 17. As prep. w. gen. Lk 7: 6 v.l.

μακρόθεν adv. from far away, from a distance, at a distance, sometimes with ἀπό Mt 26: 58; 27: 55; Mk 11: 13; 14: 54; Lk 18: 13; 22: 54; Rv 18: 10, 15, 17. Far away Mk 8: 3.

μακροθυμέω have patience, wait Hb 6: 15; Js 5: 7f. Be patient, forbearing Mt 18: 26, 29; 1 Cor 13: 4; 1 Th 5: 14; 2 Pt 3: 9. μακροθυμεῖ ἐπ' αὐτοῖς; Lk 18: 7 is probably will he delay long over them?*

μακροθυμία, ας, ἡ patience, steadfastness, endurance, forbearance Ro 2: 4; 9: 22; 2 Cor 6: 6; Gal 5: 22; Eph 4: 2; Col 1: 11; 3: 12; 1 Ti 1: 16; 2 Ti 3: 10; 4: 2; Hb 6: 12; Js 5: 10; 1 Pt 3: 20; 2 Pt 3: 15.*

μακροθύμως adv. patiently Ac 26: 3.*

μακρός, ά, όν long Mt 23: 14 v.l.; Mk 12: 40; Lk 20: 47. Far away, distant Lk 15: 13; 19: 12.*

μακροχρόνιος, ον long-lived Eph 6: 3.*

μαλακία, ας, ἡ ailment, sickness, lit. 'softness' Mt 4: 23; 9: 35; 10: 1.*

μαλακός, ή, όν soft Mt 11: 8; Lk 7: 25; effeminate, homosexual 1 Cor 6: 9.*

Μαλελεήλ, ὁ indecl. Maleleel Lk 3: 37.*

μάλιστα adv. especially, above all, particularly, (very) greatly Ac 20: 38; 26: 3; Gal 6: 10; Phil 4: 22; 1 Ti 5: 8, 17; 2 Ti 4: 13; Phlm 16.

μᾶλλον adv. more, rather—1. more, to a greater degree Mk 9: 42; 10: 48; 1 Cor 12: 22; 14: 18; Phil 1: 9, 12; 3: 4; now more than ever Lk 5: 15; Ac 5: 14; 2 Cor 7: 7. Superfluous, with other comparative expressions Mt 6: 26; Phil 1: 23.—2. for a better reason—a. rather, sooner 1 Cor 7: 21; Phil 2: 12; 1 Ti 6: 2; Hb 12: 9.—b. more (surely), more (certainly) Mt 6: 30; 7: 11; Lk 11: 13; Ro 5: 9f, 15, 17; 1 Cor 9: 12; Phlm 16; Hb 9: 14.—3. rather in the sense instead Mt 10: 6, 28; 25: 9; Mk 15: 11; J 3: 19; Ro 8: 34; 1 Cor 5: 2; 2 Cor 12: 9; Eph 4: 28; Phlm 9; Hb 12: 13.

Μάλχος, ου, ὁ Malchus J 18: 10.*

μάμμη, ης, ἡ grandmother 2 Ti 1: 5.*

μαμωνᾶς, ᾶ, ὁ (Aramaic) wealth, property Lk 16: 9, 11. Personified, 'Mammon' Mt 6: 24; Lk 16: 13.*

Μαναήν, ὁ indecl. *Manaen* Ac 13: 1.*

Μανασσῆς, ῆ, acc. ῆ, ὁ *Manasseh* —1. an Israelite tribe Rv 7: 6.— 2. Hebrew king Mt 1: 10; Lk 3: 23ff v.l.*

μανθάνω *learn* Mt 11: 29; Mk 13: 28; J 7: 15; Ro 16: 17; 1 Cor 14: 31, 35; Phil 4: 11; Col 1: 7; 1 Ti 2: 11; Hb 5: 8; *find out* Ac 23: 27; Gal 3: 2. μαθεῖν in Rv 14: 3 may mean *hear*, but *learn* and *understand* are also possible.

μανία, ας, ἡ *madness, delirium,* also in weakened sense *eccentricity, queerness* Ac 26: 24.*

μάννα, τό indecl. *manna* (Exodus 16: 32ff) J 6: 31, 49; Hb 9: 4; fig. Rv 2: 17.*

μαντεύομαι *prophesy, divine, give an oracle* Ac 16: 16.*

μαραίνω *quench, destroy,* pass. *die out, fade, disappear, wither* Js 1: 11.*

μαρὰν ἀθᾶ (Aramaic) (our) *Lord has come,* better separated μαρ-άνα θᾶ (our) *Lord, come!* 1 Cor 16: 22.*

μαργαρίτης, ου, ὁ *pearl* Mt 7: 6; 13: 45f; 1 Ti 2: 9; Rv 17: 4; 18: 12, 16; 21: 21.*

Μάρθα, ας, ἡ *Martha* Lk 10: 38, 40f; J 11: 1, 5, 19ff, 24, 30, 39; 12: 2.*

Μαρία, ας, ἡ and Μαριάμ, indecl. *Mary*—1. the mother of Jesus Christ Mt 1: 16, 18, 20; 2: 11; 13: 55; Mk 6: 3; Lk 1: 27–56 passim; 2: 5, 16, 19, 34; Ac 1: 14.*—2. *Mary Magdalene* (see Μαγδαληνή) Mt 27: 56, 61; 28: 1; Mk 15: 40, 47; 16: 1, 9; Lk 8: 2; 24: 10; J 19: 25; 20: 1, 11, 16, 18.*—3. the 'other' *Mary*, mother of James and Joses Mt 27: 56, 61; 28: 1; Mk 15: 40, 47; 16: 1; Lk 24: 10.* She could be identical with—4. *Mary*, the wife of Clopas J 19: 25.*—

5. *Mary*, sister of Martha and Lazarus Lk 10: 39, 42; J 11: 1–45 passim; 12: 3.*—6. *Mary*, mother of John Mark Ac 12: 12.* —7. *Mary*, recipient of a greeting Ro 16: 6.*

Μᾶρκος, ου, ὁ *Mark*, surname of John, son of Mary of Jerusalem Ac 12: 12, 25; 15: 37, 39; Col 4: 10; Phlm 24; 2 Ti 4: 11; 1 Pt 5: 13; title of the second gospel.*

μάρμαρος, ου, ὁ *marble* as precious material Rv 18: 12.*

μαρτυρέω—1. act.—a. *bear witness, be a witness, testify* Mt 23: 31; J 1: 7f, 15 ; 5: 33; 8: 13f, 18; 15: 27; Ac 22: 5; 26: 5; 2 Cor 8: 3; Gal 4: 15; Hb 11: 4; Rv 22: 18.— b. *bear witness to, declare, confirm* J 3: 11, 32; 1 J 1: 2; 5: 10; Rv 1: 2; 22: 20.—c. *testify favorably, speak well (of), approve (of)* w. dat. Lk 4: 22; J 3: 26; Ac 13: 22; 14: 3; 3 J 12b. —d. *be a witness (unto death), be martyred* 1 Ti 6: 13.—2. pass.— a. *be witnessed, have witness borne* Ro 3: 21; Hb 7: 8, 17.— b. *be well spoken of, be approved* Ac 6: 3; 10: 22; 16: 2; 22: 12; Hb 11: 2, 4f, 39; 3 J 12a.

μαρτυρία, ας, ἡ *testimony* Mk 14: 55f, 59; J 1: 7, 19; 3: 11; 8: 13f, 17; 19: 35; Ac 22: 18; Tit 1: 13; Rv 1: 2, 9; 6: 9; 11: 7; 12: 11, 17; 20: 4. *Standing* 1 Ti 3: 7.

μαρτύριον, ου, τό *testimony, proof* Mt 10: 18; 24: 14; Mk 1: 44; 6: 11; 13: 9; Lk 21: 13; Ac 4: 33; 7: 44; 2 Cor 1: 12; 2 Th 1: 10; 1 Ti 2: 6; Hb 3: 5; Js 5: 3.

μαρτύρομαι *testify, bear witness* Ac 20: 26; 26: 22; Gal 5: 3. *Affirm, insist, implore* Eph 4: 17; 1 Th 2: 12.*

μάρτυς, μάρτυρος, ὁ *witness*—1. lit., in the legal sense Mt 18: 16; Mk 14: 63; Ac 6: 13; 7: 58; Hb 10: 28.—2. fig., of anyone in a non-legal sense Lk 11: 48; Ac 1: 8, 22; 26: 16; Ro 1: 9; 2

Cor 1: 23; 1 Ti 6: 12; Hb 12: 1; 1 Pt 5: 1; Rv 11: 3.—3. *one who witnessed unto death, a martyr* Ac 22: 20; Rv 1: 5; 2: 13; 3: 14; 17: 6.

μασάομαι *bite* Rv 16: 10.*

μασθός v.l. for μαστός.

μαστιγόω *whip, flog, scourge* lit. Mt 10: 17; 20: 19; 23: 34; Mk 10: 34; Lk 18: 33; J 19: 1. Fig. *punish, chastise* Hb 12: 6.*

μαστίζω *scourge* Ac 22: 25.*

μάστιξ, ιγος, ἡ *whip, lash* lit. Ac 22: 24; Hb 11: 36. Fig. *torment, suffering, illness* Mk 3: 10; 5: 29, 34; Lk 7: 21.*

μαστός, οῦ, ὁ *breast* Lk 11: 27; 23: 29; Rv 1: 13.*

ματαιολογία, ας, ἡ *empty, fruitless talk* 1 Ti 1: 6.*

ματαιολόγος, ον *talking idly* as noun *an idle talker* Tit 1: 10.*

μάταιος, αία, αιον *idle, empty, worthless, foolish* 1 Cor 3: 20; 15: 17; Tit 3: 9; Js 1: 26; 1 Pt 1: 18. τὰ μάταια *idols* Ac 14: 15.*

ματαιότης, ητος, ἡ *emptiness, futility, frustration, transitoriness* Ro 8: 20; Eph 4: 17; 2 Pt 2: 18.*

ματαιόω *render futile* pass. *be given over to worthlessness, think about worthless things* Ro 1: 21.*

μάτην adv. *in vain, to no end* Mt 15: 9; Mk 7: 7.*

Ματθαῖος, ου, ὁ *Matthew* Mt 9: 9; 10: 3; Mk 3: 18; Lk 6: 15; Ac 1: 13; title of the first gospel.*

Ματθάν, ὁ indecl. *Matthan* Mt 1: 15; Lk 3: 23 ff v.l.*

Ματθάτ, ὁ indecl. *Matthat*—1. Lk 3: 24.—2. 3: 29.*

Ματθίας, ου, ὁ *Matthias* Ac 1: 23, 26.*

Ματταθά, ὁ indecl. *Mattatha* Lk 3: 31.*

Ματταθίας, ου, ὁ *Mattathias*—1. Lk 3: 25.—2. 3: 26.*

μάχαιρα, ης, ἡ *sword, saber* lit. Mt 26: 52; Mk 14: 43, 47f; Lk 21: 24; 22: 36, 38, 49; J 18:

10f; Ac 16: 27; Hb 4: 12; 11: 34, 37; Rv 13: 10, 14. Fig. Mt 10: 34; Ro 8: 35; 13: 4; Eph 6: 17.

μάχη, ης, ἡ pl. *fighting, quarrels, strife, disputes* 2 Cor 7: 5; 2 Ti 2: 23; Tit 3: 9; Js 4: 1.*

μάχομαι *to fight* lit. Ac 7: 26. Fig. *be quarrelsome* 2 Ti 2: 24; *dispute* J 6: 52; Js 4: 2.*

μέ acc. of ἐγώ.

μεγαλαυχέω *become proud, boast* Js 3: 5 v.l.*

μεγαλεῖος, α, ον *magnificent, splendid* as noun τὰ μ. *the mighty deeds* Ac 2: 11; cf. Lk 1: 49 v.l.*

μεγαλειότης, ητος, ἡ *grandeur, sublimity, majesty* Lk 9: 43; Ac 19: 27; 2 Pt 1: 16.*

μεγαλοπρεπής, ές *magnificent, sublime, majestic* 2 Pt 1: 17.*

μεγαλύνω *make large* or *long, magnify*—1. lit. Mt 23: 5; Lk 1: 58; pass. *increase, grow* 2 Cor 10: 15.—2. fig. *exalt, glorify, praise, extol* Lk 1: 46; Ac 5: 13; 10: 46; pass. Ac 19: 17; Phil 1: 20.*

μεγάλως adv. *greatly* Phil 4: 10; *heartily* Ac 15: 4 v.l.*

μεγαλωσύνη, ης, ἡ *majesty* Jd 25; as a periphrasis for God *Majesty* Hb 1: 3; 8: 1.*

μέγας, μεγάλη, μέγα *large, great*—1. lit. Mk 4: 32; 5: 11; 16: 4; Lk 14: 16; 22: 12; 2 Ti 2: 20; Rv 8: 8, 10; 12: 3; 14: 19. *Long* Rv 6: 4; 20: 1. *Wide* 1 Cor 16: 9.—2. fig.—a. of measure, intensity Mt 8: 26; 28: 2; Mk 5: 7; Lk 2: 9f; 21: 11; J 6: 18; Ac 4: 33; 11: 28; Hb 10: 35; 11: 24; Rv 11: 18; 15: 3. *Loud* Mt 27: 46; Mk 15: 37; Lk 19: 37; Ac 7: 57; 23: 9; Rv 5: 2. *Bright* Mt 4: 16. *Intense* Rv 16: 9. *Severe* Ac 8: 1.—b. of rank and dignity *great*, etc. Mt 20: 25; Mk 10: 43; Lk 7: 16; J 19: 31; Ac 2: 20; 19: 27f, 34f; Eph 5: 32; Tit 2: 13; Hb 4: 14. μεγάλα *proud words* Rv 13: 5.—For μείζων and μέγιστος see them as separate entries.

μέγεθος, ους, τό *greatness* Eph 1: 19.*

μεγιστάν, ᾶνος, ὁ *great man, courtier, magnate* Mk 6: 21; Rv 6: 15; 18: 23.*

μέγιστος superlative of μέγας *very great* 2 Pt 1: 4.*

μεθερμηνεύω *translate* Mt 1: 23; Mk 5: 41; 15: 22, 34; J 1: 38, 42; Ac 4: 36; 13: 8.*

μέθη, ης, ἡ *drunkenness* Lk 21: 34; Ro 13: 13; Gal 5: 21.*

μεθίστημι or **μεθιστάνω** *remove* Ac 13: 22; 1 Cor 13: 2; *transfer* Col 1: 13; pass. *be discharged* Lk 16: 4. *Turn away, mislead* Ac 19: 26.*

μεθοδεία, ας, ἡ *scheming, craftiness* Eph 4: 14; pl. *wiles, stratagems* 6: 11, 12 v.l.*

μεθόριον, ου, τό *boundary*, pl. *region* Mk 7: 24 v.l.*

μεθύσκω *cause to become intoxicated* pass. *become intoxicated, get drunk* Lk 12: 45; Eph 5: 18; 1 Th 5: 7; Rv 17: 2; *drink freely, be drunk* J 2: 10.*

μέθυσος, ου, ὁ *drunkard* 1 Cor 5: 11; 6: 10.*

μεθύω *be drunk* lit. Mt 24: 49; Ac 2: 15; 1 Cor 11: 21; 1 Th 5: 7; fig. Rv 17: 6.*

μείγνυμι or **μειγνύω** *mix, mingle* Mt 27: 34; Lk 13: 1; Rv 8: 7; 15: 2.*

μειζότερος, α, ον comparative of μέγας *greater* 3 J 4.*

μείζων, ον comparative of μέγας *greater* Mt 11: 11; 12: 6; Lk 22: 26f; J 4: 12; 14: 28; 1 Cor 12: 31; 14: 5; Hb 6: 13; 1 J 3: 20; 4: 4. ὁ μ. *the older* Ro 9: 12. μεῖζον as adv. *all the more* Mt 20: 31. μείζων as superlative *greatest* Mt 18: 1, 4; Mk 9: 34; 1 Cor 13: 13.

μέλαν, τό, see μέλας.

μέλας, μέλαινα, μέλαν gen. **ανος,** αἴνης, **ανος** *black* Mt 5: 36; Rv 6: 5, 12. Neut. τὸ μέλαν, νος *ink* 2 Cor 3: 3; 2 J 12; 3 J 13.*

Μελεά, ὁ indecl. *Melea* Lk 3: 31.*

μέλει third pers. sing. of μέλω, used mostly impersonally, but sometimes personally; w. dat. *it is a care* or *concern to someone*, i.e. *someone cares* Mt 22: 16; Mk 4: 38; 12: 14; Lk 10: 40; J 10: 13; 12: 6; 1 Cor 9: 9; 1 Pt 5: 7. Personal Ac 18: 17. μή σοι μελέτω *never mind* 1 Cor 7: 21.*

μελετάω *practice, cultivate* 1 Ti 4: 15. *Think about, meditate upon* Ac 4: 25; *rack one's brains* Mk 13: 11 v.l.*

μέλι, ιτος, τό *honey* Mt 3: 4; Mk 1: 6; Rv 10: 9f.*

μελίσσιος, ιον *pertaining to the bee* μ. κηρίον *honeycomb* Lk 24: 42 v.l. The other v.l. ἀπὸ μελισσίου κηρίον belongs to **μελισσ(ε)ῖον, ου, τό** *beehive*.*

Μελίτη, ης, ἡ *Malta* an island south of Sicily Ac 28: 1.*

Μελιτήνη v.l. for Μελίτη.

μέλλω—1. *be about to, be on the point of* Mk 13: 4; Lk 7: 2; 19: 4; 22: 23; Ac 12: 6; 16: 27; Ro 8: 18; 1 Ti 1: 16; 1 Pt 5: 1; Rv 3: 2, 16.—**2.** *be destined, must* Mt 17: 12, 22; J 11: 51; Ac 26: 22; Gal 3: 23; Hb 1: 14; Rv 1: 19.—**3.** *intend* Mt 2: 13; Lk 10: 1; J 6: 15, 71; 7: 35; Ac 17: 31; 20: 3, 7, 13.—**4.** the participle often means *future, to come* Mt 12: 32; Ro 8: 38; Eph 1: 21; Col 2: 17; 1 Ti 6: 19; Hb 2: 5; 13: 14.—**5.** *delay* Ac 22: 16.

μέλος, ους, τό *member, part, limb* lit. Mt 5: 29f; Ro 7: 5, 23; 12: 4; 1 Cor 12: 18–20; Js 3: 5. Fig. Ro 12: 5; 1 Cor 6: 15a; 12: 27; Eph 5: 30.

Μελχί, ὁ indecl. *Melchi*—**1.** Lk 3: 24.—**2.** 3: 28.*

Μελχισέδεκ, ὁ indecl. *Melchizedek* (Gen 14: 18) Hb 5: 6, 10; 6: 20; 7: 1, 10f, 15, 17.*

μεμβράνα, ης, ἡ (Latin loanword: membrana) *parchment,* used for making books 2 Ti 4: 13.*

μέμνημαι perf. mid. and pass. ind. of μιμνήσκομαι.

μέμφομαι *find fault with, blame* Ro 9: 19; Hb 8: 8; Mk 7: 2 v.l.*

μεμψίμοιρος, ον *fault-finding, complaining* Jd 16.*

μέμψις, εως, ἡ *reason for complaint* Col 3: 13 v.l.*

μέν affirmative particle—1. used correlatively with other particles —a. frequently indicating a (strong) contrast between two clauses. μὲν . . . δέ, μὲν . . . ἀλλά may be translated *to be sure . . . but* or *on the one hand . . . on the other hand,* though this scheme will not always fit Mt 3: 11; 9: 37; Mk 9: 12; 14: 21; J 19: 32; Ro 14: 20; 1 Cor 14: 17.— b. When used with conjunctions μέν is often left untranslated Lk 13: 9; 1 Cor 11: 7; Hb 11: 15. μέν may sometimes be left untranslated even when unaccompanied by a conjunction Lk 11: 48; 1 Cor 1: 12, 18, 23; Phil 3: 1.—c. When it is used with the definite article ὁ μὲν . . . ὁ δέ or the relative pronoun ὃς μέν . . . ὃς δέ the combination means *the one . . . the other,* but pl. *some . . . others* Mt 21: 35; 25: 15; Lk 23: 33; Ac 14: 4; 17: 32; 27: 44; Ro 14: 5; Gal 4: 23; Eph 4: 11; Phil 1: 16; Jd 22. ὁ μὲν οὕτως, ὁ δὲ οὕτως *one in one way, one in another* 1 Cor 7: 7.—2. Sometimes the second clause of the contrast is omitted altogether, though it can be supplied from the context 1 Cor 6: 7; 2 Cor 12: 12; Col 2: 23.

Μεννά, ὁ indecl. *Menna* Lk 3: 31.*

μενοῦν Lk 11: 28; Ro 9: 20 v.l.; Phil 3: 8 v.l. and μενοῦνγε (μενοῦν γε) particles *rather, on*

the contrary Lk 11: 28. *Indeed* Ro 10: 18. ἀλλὰ μενοῦνγε *more than that* Phil 3: 8. μενοῦνγε σὺ τίς εἶ; *on the contrary, who are you?* Ro 9: 20.*

μέντοι particle—1. *really, actually* Js 2: 8.—2. *though, to be sure, indeed* J 4: 27; 7: 13; 20: 5; 21: 4. *Nevertheless* 2 Ti 2: 19. ὅμως μ. *yet, despite that* J 12: 42. *But* Jd 8.*

μένω—1. intrans. *remain, stay* J 7: 9; 12: 24; 15: 4b; Ac 27: 31; 1 Cor 7: 11, 40; Hb 7: 3. *Live, dwell* Lk 8: 27; J 1: 38; Ac 28: 16. *Continue, abide* J 6: 56; 12: 46; 14: 10; 15: 4f, 9f; 1 J 2: 24; 3: 15; 4: 13; 2 J 9. *Last, persist, continue to live* or *exist* Mt 11: 23; J 9: 41; 21: 22f; 1 Cor 13: 13; 15: 6; 2 Cor 3: 11; Phil 1: 25; Hb 13: 1, 14; Rv 17: 10.— 2. trans. *wait for, await* Ac 20: 5, 23.

μερίζω *divide, separate*—1. *divide* act. and pass., fig. Mt 12: 25f; Mk 3: 24–26; 1 Cor 1: 13; 7: 34; mid. *share* Lk 12: 13.— 2. *distribute* Mk 6: 41; *assign, apportion* Ro 12: 3; 1 Cor 7: 17; 2 Cor 10: 13; Hb 7: 2.*

μέριμνα, ης, ἡ *anxiety, worry, care* Mt 13: 22; Mk 4: 19; Lk 8: 14; 21: 34; 2 Cor 11: 28; 1 Pt 5: 7.*

μεριμνάω—1. *have anxiety, be anxious, be (unduly) concerned* Mt 6: 25, 27f, 31, 34a; 10: 19; Lk 10: 41; 12: 11, 22, 25f; Phil 4: 6.—2. *care for, be concerned about* Mt 6: 34b v.l.; 1 Cor 7: 32–34; 12: 25; Phil 2: 20.*

μερίς, ίδος, ἡ—1. *part, district* Ac 16: 12.—2. *share* Ac 8: 21; Col 1: 12; *portion* Lk 10: 42. τίς μερὶς πιστῷ μετὰ ἀπίστου; *what has a believer in common with an unbeliever?* 2 Cor 6: 15.*

μερισμός, οῦ, ὁ *separation* Hb 4: 12. *Distribution, apportionment* 2: 4.*

μεριστής, οῦ, ὁ *arbitrator, divider* Lk 12: 14.*

μέρος, ους, τό—1. *part* Lk 11: 36; 15: 12; Ac 5: 2; Eph 4: 16; Rv 16: 19. Specialized uses: *side* J 21: 6; *piece* Lk 24: 42; *party* Ac 23: 6, 9; *line of business* 19: 27; *matter, affair* 2 Cor 3: 10; 9: 3; pl. *region, district* Mt 2: 22; 15: 21; Ac 2: 10; 19: 1.—With prepositions: ἀνὰ μέρος *one after the other* 1 Cor 14: 27.—ἀπὸ μέρους *in part* Ro 11: 25; 15: 15; 2 Cor 1: 14; 2: 5; *for a while* Ro 15: 24.—ἐκ μέρους *individually* 1 Cor 12: 27; *in part* 13: 9f, 12.—ἐν μέρει *in the matter of* Col 2: 16.—κατὰ μέρος *in detail* Hb 9: 5.—μέρος τι as adverbial acc. *in part, partly* 1 Cor 11: 18.—2. *share* Rv 20: 6; 22: 19. *Place* Mt 24: 51; Lk 12: 46; J 13: 8; Rv 21: 8.

μεσάζω *be in* or *at the middle* J 7: 14 v.l.*

μεσημβρία, ας, ἡ *midday, noon* Ac 22: 6. κατὰ μεσημβρίαν 8: 26 may be *about noon*, but is more likely used of place *toward the south.**

μεσιτεύω *mediate, guarantee* Hb 6: 17.*

μεσίτης, ου, ὁ *mediator, arbitrator* Gal 3: 19f; 1 Ti 2: 5; Hb 8: 6; 9: 15; 12: 24.*

μεσονύκτιον, ου, τό *midnight* Mk 13: 35; Lk 11: 5; Ac 16: 25; 20: 7.*

Μεσοποταμία, ας, ἡ *Mesopotamia*, country between the Tigris and Euphrates rivers Ac 2: 9; 7: 2.*

μέσος, η, ον *middle, in the middle*—1. as adj. Mt 25: 6; Lk 23: 45; J 19: 18; Ac 1: 18; 26: 13. μέσος αὐτῶν *among them* Lk 22: 55; cf. J 1: 26.—2. (τὸ) μέσον as noun *the middle:* ἀνὰ μέσον w. gen. *among* Mt 13: 25; *within* Mk 7: 31; *between* 1 Cor 6: 5 (the expression is incomplete); *on the center* Rv 7: 17.—ἐν (τῷ) μέσῳ *before* Mt 14: 6; Mk 6: 47;

J 8: 3; Ac 4: 7, but *in the middle* J 8: 9; *within* Lk 21: 21; *among* 22: 27.—ἐκ μέσου *from among* Col 2: 14.—With other prepositions Mk 3: 3; 14: 60; Lk 4: 30, 35.—3. the neut. μέσον serves as an adv., used as an improper prep. w. gen. *in the middle* or *midst of* Mt 14: 24 v.l.; Phil 2: 15.

μεσότοιχον, ου, τό *dividing wall* Eph 2: 14.*

μεσουράνημα, ατος, τό *zenith, midheaven* Rv 8: 13; 14: 6; 19: 17.*

μεσόω *be at the mid-point* J 7: 14.*

Μεσσίας, ου, ὁ (Hebrew) *the Messiah* = *the Anointed One*, translated into Greek as Χριστός J 1: 41; 4: 25.*

μεστός, ή, όν *full* lit. J 19: 29; 21: 11. Fig. Mt 23: 28; Ro 1: 29; 15: 14; Js 3: 8, 17; 2 Pt 2: 14.*

μεστόω *fill* pass. *be filled* Ac 2: 13.*

μετά prep.—1. w. genitive *with*— a. generally Mk 3: 5; 10: 30; Ac 13: 17; 2 Cor 7: 15; 8: 4; Eph 6: 7; 1 Ti 2: 9; 1 Pt 3: 16.— b. *with, in company with* Mt 2: 3; 8: 11; 20: 20; 26: 18, 38, 40; Mk 11: 11; Lk 22: 59; J 11: 54; Gal 2: 1; 4: 25; 2 Ti 4: 11; 1 J 2: 19; Rv 22: 12.—c. *among* Mt 24: 51; Mk 1: 13; 14: 54; Lk 22: 37; 24: 5; J 6: 43; Rv 1: 7.—d. *be with* someone, to aid or help Lk 1: 28; J 3: 2; Ac 11: 21; 1 Cor 16: 24; 2 Cor 13: 11; Gal 6: 18.—e. *with* of hostile or friendly association Lk 23: 12; J 16: 19; Ro 12: 18; 1 Cor 6: 6; 1 J 1: 3a, 7; Rv 2: 16; 11: 7.— 2. w. accusative *after* Mt 17: 1; 25: 19; 26: 32; Mk 1: 14; 8: 31; 13: 24; Ac 20: 29; 27: 14. *Behind* Hb 9: 3.

μετάβα 2 aor. act. imperative, 2 sing., of μεταβαίνω.

μεταβαίνω—1. lit. *go* or *pass over* (*from one place to another*) Mt 8: 34; 17: 20; J 7: 3; 13: 1; Ac 18: 7; *change one's residence, move*

Lk 10: 7.—**2.** fig. *pass, move* J 5: 24; 1 J 3: 14.

μεταβάλλω mid. *change one's mind* Ac 28: 6.*

μετάβηθι 2 aor. act. imperative, 2 sing. of μεταβαίνω.

μετάγω *guide, steer* Js 3: 3f; pass. *be brought back* Ac 7: 16 v.l.*

μεταδίδωμι *impart, share, give* Lk 3: 11; Ro 1: 11; 12: 8; Eph 4: 28; 1 Th 2: 8.*

μετάθεσις, θέσεως, ἡ *removal* Hb 12: 27. *Taking up* or *translation* 11: 5. *Change, transformation* 7: 12.*

μεταίρω *go away* Mt 13: 53; 19: 1.*

μετακαλέω mid. *call to oneself, summon* Ac 7: 14; 10: 32; 20: 17; 24: 25.*

μετακινέω *shift, remove* fig. Col 1: 23.*

μεταλαμβάνω *receive one's share, share in, receive* Ac 2: 46; 27: 33f; 2 Ti 2: 6; Hb 6: 7; 12: 10. καιρὸν μ. *find time* Ac 24: 25.*

μετάλημψις, εως, ἡ *sharing, receiving* 1 Ti 4: 3.*

μεταλλάσσω *exchange* Ro 1: 25f.*

μεταμέλομαι *regret, repent* Mt 21: 30, 32; 27: 3; 2 Cor 7: 8; Hb 7: 21.*

μεταμορφόω pass. *be changed in form, be transformed* Ro 12: 2; 2 Cor 3: 18. *Be transfigured* Mt 17: 2; Mk 9: 2.*

μετανοέω *feel remorse, repent,* lit. 'change one's mind' Mt 11: 21; 12: 41; Mk 1: 15; Lk 11: 32; 13: 3, 5; Ac 3: 19; 8: 22; 2 Cor 12: 21; Rv 9: 20f; 16: 9.

μετάνοια, ας, ἡ *remorse, repentance, turning about,* lit. 'change of mind' Mt 3: 8, 11; Mk 1: 4; Lk 15: 7; Ac 5: 31; 20: 21; 26: 20; 2 Cor 7: 9f; Hb 6: 1; 12: 17.

μεταξύ adv.—**1.** used as adv. *between* ἐν τῷ μεταξύ *in the meanwhile* J 4: 31. *Afterward, next* Ac 13: 42.—**2.** as improper prep. w. gen. *between* Mt 18: 15;

23: 35; Lk 16: 26; Ac 12: 6; 15: 9; *among* Ro 2: 15.

μεταπέμπω mid. and pass. *send for, summon* Ac 10: 5, 22, 29; 24: 24, 26.

μετάπεμψαι 1 aor. mid. imperative, 2 sing. of μεταπέμπω.

μεταστρέφω *change* Ac 2: 20; Js 4: 9 v.l. *Pervert* Gal 1: 7.*

μετασχηματίζω *change (the form of), transform* Phil 3: 21. Mid. *change* or *disguise oneself* 2 Cor 11: 13–15. The act. in 1 Cor 4: 6 *means something like apply.**

μετατίθημι *change (the position of)* —**1.** lit. *bring back* Ac 7: 16. *Be taken up, translated* Hb 11: 5.— **2.** non-literally *change, alter* Hb 7: 12. *Pervert* Jd 4. Mid. *turn away* Gal 1: 6.*

μετατρέπω *turn around* pass. *be turned* Js 4: 9.*

μεταφυτεύω *transplant* Lk 17: 6 v.l.*

μετέβη 2 aor. act. ind., 3 sing. of μεταβαίνω.

μετέπειτα adv. *afterwards* Hb 12: 17.*

μετέχω *share (in), have a share (of), participate (in)* w. gen. 1 Cor 10: 21; Hb 2: 14; *belong to* 7: 13. *Eat, drink, enjoy* 1 Cor 9: 10, 12; 10: 17, 30; Hb 5: 13. *Have* Lk 1: 34 v.l.*

μετεωρίζομαι *be anxious, worry* Lk 12: 29.*

μετῆρα 1 aor. act. ind. of μεταίρω.

μετοικεσία, ας, ἡ *deportation, captivity* Mt 1: 11f, 17.*

μετοικίζω *remove (to another place of habitation)* Ac 7: 4. *Deport* 7: 43.*

μετοχή, ῆς, ἡ *sharing, participation* 2 Cor 6: 14.*

μέτοχος, ον *sharing* or *participating in* w. gen. Hb 3: 1, 14; 6: 4; 12: 8. As noun ὁ μ. *the partner, companion* Lk 5: 7; Hb 1: 9.*

μετρέω *measure*—**1.** *take the dimensions of, measure*—**a.** lit.

Rv 11: 1f; 21: 15–17.—**b.** fig.
2 Cor 10: 12.—**2.** *give out, deal
out, apportion* Mt 7: 2; Mk 4: 24;
Lk 6: 38.*

μετρητής, οῦ, ὁ a liquid *measure*
amounting to about nine gallons
J 2: 6.*

μετριοπαθέω *moderate one's feelings, deal gently* w. dat. Hb 5: 2.*

μετρίως adv. *moderately* Ac 20:
12.*

μέτρον, ου, τό *measure* Mk 4: 24;
Ro 12: 3; 2 Cor 10: 13; Eph 4: 7,
13, 16; Rv 21: 15. οὐκ ἐκ μέτρου
not from a measure, that is,
without measure J 3: 34.

μέτωπον, ου, τό *forehead* Lk 23:
48 v.l.; Rv 7: 3; 14: 1, 9; 22: 4.

μέχρι or **μέχρις** *until*—**1.** prep. w.
gen. Mt 11: 23; 28: 15; Lk 16:
16; Ac 10: 30; 20: 7; Hb 3: 6, 14;
9: 10; *as far as* Ro 15: 19; *to the
point of* 2 Ti 2: 9; Hb 12: 4;
unto Phil 2: 8, 30.—**2.** conjunction *until* Mk 13: 30; Gal 4:
19; Eph 4: 13.

μή negative particle *not*—**1.** as a
neg. particle Mt 5: 20; 18: 25;
24: 22; Mk 3: 9; Lk 20: 27;
J 20: 17; Ac 23: 8; Ro 5: 13;
14: 21; 2 Cor 3: 7; Gal 5: 26;
6: 14; Eph 4: 26; Col 2: 21;
1 Pt 3: 10.—**2.** as a conjunction,
that . . . (not), lest Mk 13: 5, 36;
Gal 6: 1; Col 2: 8; Hb 12: 15.—
3. as an interrogative particle
when a negative answer is
expected μή τινος ὑστερήσατε;
*you did not lack anything, did
you?* Lk 22: 35; cf. Mt 7: 9f;
J 3: 4; Ac 7: 28; 1 Cor 1: 13.—
4. οὐ μή strengthens the negation, *never, certainly not,* etc.
Mt 5: 18, 20, 26; 16: 22; Lk 6:
37; J 13: 8; 18: 11; 1 Cor 8: 13;
Hb 13: 5. On the other hand, in
the combination μή οὐ, μή is an
interrogative word and οὐ negatives the word; an affirmative
answer is expected Ro 10: 18f;
1 Cor 9: 4f.

μήγε = μή + γε.

μηδαμῶς adv. *by no means,
certainly not* Ac 10: 14; 11: 8.*

μηδέ negative particle *and not, but
not* Mt 22: 29; Mk 6: 11; J 14:
27; Ro 9: 11; 1 Cor 5: 8;
1 Pt 3: 14. *Not even* Mk 2: 2; 3:
20; 8: 26; 1 Cor 5: 11; Eph 5: 3.

μηδείς, μηδεμία, μηδέν or **μηθείς,**
etc.—**1.** adj. *no* Ac 13: 28;
25: 17; 28: 18; 1 Cor 1: 7;
1 Ti 5: 14; Hb 10: 2; with
another negative *no . . . at all*
2 Cor 6: 3; 13: 7; 1 Pt 3: 6.—
2. substantive μηδείς *nobody*
Mt 8: 4; Mk 7: 36; Ac 9: 7;
11: 19; Ro 12: 17; 1 Cor 10: 24;
Rv 3: 11. μηδέν *nothing* Mk 1:
44; Lk 9: 3; Ac 8: 24; Ro 13: 8;
1 Cor 10: 25; Gal 6: 3; *not . . .
at all, in no way* Mk 5: 26; Lk 4:
35; Ac 4: 21; Phil 4: 6; Js 1: 6.

μηδέποτε adv. *never* 2 Ti 3: 7.*

μηδέπω adv. *not yet* Hb 11: 7.*

Μῆδος, ου, ὁ a *Mede,* inhabitant of
Media Ac 2: 9.*

μηθαμῶς see μηδαμῶς.

μηθέν see μηδείς.

μηκέτι adv. *no longer, not from
now on* Mk 1: 45; 11: 14; J 5: 14;
Ac 13: 34; 25: 24; Ro 6: 6;
2 Cor 5: 15; 1 Pt 4: 2.

μῆκος, ους, τό *length* Eph 3: 18;
Rv 21: 16.*

μηκύνω *make long,* pass. *become
long, grow (long)* Mk 4: 27.*

μηλωτή, ῆς, ἡ *sheepskin* Hb 11: 37.*

μήν particle; see εἰ μήν as a
separate entry.

μήν, μηνός, ὁ *month* Lk 1: 24, 26,
56; Ac 7: 20; 18: 11; Js 5: 17;
Rv 9: 5; 13: 5; 22: 2. *New moon*
(festival) Gal 4: 10.

μηνύω *make known, reveal* Lk 20:
37; Ac 23: 30; *report* J 11: 57;
inform 1 Cor 10: 28.*

μὴ οὐ see μή 4.

μήποτε—**1.** negative particle *never*
Hb 9: 17.—**2.** conjunction *that
. . . not, lest* Lk 21: 34; Hb 3: 12;
4: 1; *(in order) that . . . not*

Mt 5: 25; Mk 4: 12; Ac 5: 39; Hb 2: 1.—**3**. interrogative particle *whether, perhaps* J 7: 26; 2 Ti 2: 25.

μήπου or **μή που** conj. *lest* or *that* . . . *somewhere* Ac 27: 29.*

μήπω adv. *not yet* Ro 9: 11; Hb 9: 8.*

μήπως or **μή πως** conj.—**1**. denoting purpose, etc. *so that* . . . *(perhaps) not, lest somehow, that perhaps* 1 Cor 8: 9; 9: 27; 2 Cor 2: 7; 9: 4; Gal 4: 11; 1 Th 3: 5.—**2**. introducing an indirect question *that perhaps* Gal 2: 2.

μηρός, οῦ, ὁ *thigh* Rv 19: 16.*

μήτε negative copula *and not,* after μή *not* . . . *and not, neither* . . . *nor,* etc. Lk 7: 33; 9: 3; Ac 23: 8, 12, 21; Hb 7: 3; Js 5: 12; Rv 7: 1, 3.

μήτηρ, τρός, ἡ *mother* lit. Mt 1: 18; 2: 11, 13f, 20f; 10: 37; 12: 46; Mk 5: 40; 6: 24, 28; 2 Ti 1: 5. Fig. Mt 12: 49f; J 19: 27; Gal 4: 26; Rv 17: 5.

μήτι interrogative particle in questions that expect a negative answer, often left untranslated, but cf. μήτι συλλέγουσιν *surely they do not gather* . . . *do they?* Mt 7: 16; also cf. 26: 22, 25; Mk 14: 19; J 18: 35; Ac 10: 47; 2 Cor 12: 18. *Perhaps* Mt 12: 23; J 4: 29.

μήτιγε=μήτι γε *not to speak of, let alone* 1 Cor 6: 3.*

μήτρα, ας, ἡ *womb* Lk 2: 23; Ro 4: 19.*

μητραλῴας or **μητρολῴας, ου, ὁ** *one who murders his mother, a matricide* 1 Ti 1: 9.*

μητρόπολις, εως, ἡ *capital city* 1 Ti subscr.*

μιαίνω *stain, defile* fig., of ceremonial or moral defilement J 18: 28; Tit 1: 15; Hb 12: 15; Jd 8; Ac 5: 38 v.l.*

μιανθῶ 1 aor. pass. subjunctive of μιαίνω.

μίασμα, ατος, τό *shameful deed, misdeed, crime* 2 Pt 2: 20.*

μιασμός, οῦ, ὁ *pollution, corruption* 2 Pt 2: 10.*

μίγμα, ατος, τό *mixture, compound* J 19: 39.*

μίγνυμι see μείγνυμι.

μικρός, ά, όν *small* Mt 13: 32; Lk 12: 32; Js 3: 5; Rv 3: 8. *Small* or *young* Mk 15: 40. *Little one, child* Mt 18: 6, 10, 14; cf. Ac 8: 10; Rv 11: 18. *Humble* Mk 9: 42; ὁ μικρότερος *the one of least importance* Mt 11: 11. *Short* J 7: 33. *Little* 1 Cor 5: 6. The neut. (τὸ) μικρόν: μικρόν τι *a little* 2 Cor 11: 1, 16. (ἔτι) μικρὸν καί *soon* J 16: 16–19. μικρόν alone *a short distance* Mt 26: 39; *a short time* Mk 14: 70; J 13: 33.

Μίλητος, ου, ἡ *Miletus,* a seaport city on the west coast of Asia Minor, 35 miles south of Ephesus Ac 20: 15, 17; 2 Ti 4: 20.*

μίλιον, ου, τό (Latin loanword: mille) a Roman *mile,* about 4,854 feet or 1478.5 meters Mt 5: 41.*

μιμέομαι *imitate, emulate, follow* 2 Th 3: 7, 9; Hb 13: 7; 3 J 11.*

μιμητής, οῦ, ὁ *imitator* 1 Cor 4: 16; 11: 1; Eph 5: 1; 1 Th 1: 6; 2: 14; Hb 6: 12; 1 Pt 3: 13 v.l.*

μιμνῄσκομαι—**1**. reflexive *remind oneself, recall to mind, remember* w. gen. Mt 5: 23; 27: 63; Lk 24: 6, 8; J 2: 17, 22; Ac 11: 16; 1 Cor 11: 2; 2 Ti 1: 4. *Remember* in the sense *think of, be concerned about* Lk 1: 72; 23: 42; Hb 2: 6; 8: 12.—**2**. pass. *be mentioned* or *be called to remembrance* Ac 10: 31; Rv 16: 19.

μισέω *hate, detest, abhor* Mt 5: 43; 24: 10; Mk 13: 13; Lk 1: 71; 14: 26; J 3: 20; 15: 18f, 23f, 25; Ro 7: 15; 9: 13; Eph 5: 29; Hb 1: 9; Jd 23; Rv 2: 6; 18: 2.

μισθαποδοσία, ας, ἡ *reward* Hb 10:

35; 11: 26; *punishment, penalty*
2: 2.*

μισθαποδότης, ου, ὁ *rewarder*
Hb 11: 6.*

μίσθιος, ου, ὁ *day laborer, hired man* Lk 15: 17, 19, 21 v.l.*

μισθός, οῦ, ὁ *pay, wages* lit. Mt 20: 8; Lk 10: 7; J 4: 36; Ac 1: 18; 1 Ti 5: 18; 2 Pt 2: 13, 15. Personified Js 5: 4. μισθοῦ *for pay* Jd 11. Fig. *reward* Mt 5: 46; 6: 2, 5, 16; Mk 9: 41; Lk 6: 23, 35; Ro 4: 4; 1 Cor 3: 8, 14; Rv 11: 18; *reward or punishment* 22: 12.

μισθόω mid. *hire, engage* Mt 20:1, 7.*

μίσθωμα, ατος, τό in Ac 28: 30 the word means either *expense* or *rented lodging.**

μισθωτός, οῦ, ὁ *hired man* Mk 1: 20; J 10: 12f.*

Μιτυλήνη, ης, ἡ *Mitylene,* chief city of the island of Lesbos, off the northwest coast of Asia Minor Ac 20: 14.*

Μιχαήλ, ὁ indecl. *Michael,* an archangel Jd 9; Rv 12: 7.*

μνᾶ, μνᾶς, ἡ (Semitic loanword) *mina,* a Greek monetary unit = 100 drachmas; the Attic mina was worth about eighteen to twenty dollars in normal times Lk 19: 13, 16, 18, 20, 24f.*

μνάομαι *woo or court for one's bride;* perf. participle μεμνησμένη *engaged, betrothed* Lk 1: 27 v.l.*

Μνάσων, ωνος, ὁ *Mnason* Ac 21: 16.*

μνεία, ας, ἡ—1. *remembrance, memory* Ro 12: 13 v.l.; 2 Ti 1: 3; μνείαν ἔχειν *think kindly* 1 Th 3: 6.—**2.** *mention* Ro 1: 9; Eph 1: 16; Phil 1: 3; 1 Th 1: 2; Phlm 4.*

μνῆμα, ατος, τό *grave, tomb* Mk 15: 46; 16: 2; Lk 8: 27; 24: 1; Ac 2: 29; Rv 11: 9.

μνημεῖον, ου, τό *monument, memorial* Lk 11: 47. *Grave, tomb* Mt 23: 29; 27: 52f; Mk 5:

2; 6: 29; 16: 3, 5, 8; Lk 11: 44; 24: 2, 9, 12; J 11: 17, 31, 38; 20: 1–4, 6, 8, 11; Ac 13: 29.

μνήμη, ης, ἡ *remembrance, memory* μνήμην ποιεῖσθαι *recall to mind* 2 Pt 1: 15.*

μνημονεύω *remember, keep in mind, think of, mention* w. gen. or acc. Mt 16: 9; Lk 17: 32; J 15: 20; Ac 20: 31, 35; Gal 2: 10; 1 Th 1: 3; 2 Ti 2: 8; Hb 13: 7; Rv 2: 5.

μνημόσυνον, ου, τό *memory, remembrance* Mt 26: 13; Mk 14: 9. *Memorial offering* Ac 10: 4.*

μνηστεύω *woo and win, betroth* pass. *be betrothed, become engaged* Mt 1: 16 v.l., 18; Lk 1: 27; 2: 5.*

μογγιλάλος, ον *speaking in a hoarse* or *hollow voice* Mk 7: 32 v.l.*

μογιλάλος, ον *speaking with difficulty* or *mute* Mk 7: 32, 33 v.l.*

μόγις adv. *scarcely, with difficulty* Lk 9: 39 v.l.; 23: 53 v.l.; Ac 14: 18 v.l.; Ro 5: 7 v.l.*

μόδιος, ίου, ὁ *a peck-measure,* a grain measure containing about 8.75 liters, almost exactly one peck Mt 5: 15; Mk 4: 21; Lk 11: 33.*

μοί dat. of ἐγώ.

μοιχαλίς, ίδος, ἡ *adulteress* lit. Ro 7: 3; 2 Pt 2: 14. Fig. Js 4: 4; as adj. *adulterous* Mt 12: 39; 16: 4; Mk 8: 38.*

μοιχάω *cause to commit adultery* pass. *commit adultery* Mt 5: 32 in text and v.l.; 19: 9 in text and v.l.; Mk 10: 11f.*

μοιχεία, ας, ἡ *adultery* Mt 15: 19; Mk 7: 22; J 8: 3.*

μοιχεύω *commit adultery* Mt 5: 27f, 32; Lk 16: 18; J 8: 4; Ro 2: 22; Rv 2: 22.

μοιχός, οῦ, ὁ *adulterer* lit. Lk 18: 11; 1 Cor 6: 9; Hb 13: 4; fig. Js 4: 4 v.l.*

μόλις adv. *scarcely, with difficulty* Lk 9: 39; Ac 14: 18; 23: 29 v.l.;

27: 7f, 16; 1 Pt 4: 18; *not readily,*
only rarely or *hardly* Ro 5: 7.*

Μολόχ, ὁ indecl. *Moloch,* the
Canaanite-Phoenician god of
sky and sun Ac 7: 43.*

μολύνω *stain, defile, make impure,*
soil 1 Cor 8: 7; Rv 3: 4; 14: 4;
Ac 5: 38 v.l.*

μολυσμός, οῦ, ὁ *defilement* 2 Cor 7:
1.*

μομφή, ῆς, ἡ *blame, (cause for)*
complaint Col 3: 13.*

μονή, ῆς, ἡ *staying, tarrying* μονὴν
ποιεῖσθαι *live, stay* J 14: 23.
Dwelling(-place), room, abode
14: 2.*

μονογενής, ές *only* Lk 7: 12;
8: 42; 9: 38; Hb 11: 17. *Only,*
unique or *only-begotten, begotten*
of the Only One J 1: 14, 18; 3: 16,
18; 1 J 4: 9.*

μόνον see μόνος 2.

μόνος, η, ον *only, alone*—**1.** adj.
Mt 4: 4; 14: 23; Mk 9: 8; Lk 9:
36; 24: 12, 18; J 8: 9; 17: 3;
Ro 16: 27; 1 Th 3: 1; 1 Ti 1: 17;
Hb 9: 7; Rv 15: 4; *alone,*
deserted, helpless J 8: 29; 16: 32.
—**2.** adv., the neut. μόνον Mt 9:
21; Lk 8: 50; J 11: 52; Ac 19:
26; Ro 4: 12, 16; Gal 1: 23;
5: 13; Hb 9: 10; Js 1: 22.—
3. κατὰ μόνας *alone* Mk 4: 10;
Lk 9: 18.

μονόφθαλμος, ον *one-eyed* Mt 18:
9; Mk 9: 47.*

μονόω *make solitary* pass. *be left*
alone 1 Ti 5: 5.*

μορφή, ῆς, ἡ *form, outward appear-*
ance, shape Mk 16: 12; Phil 2:
6f.*

μορφόω *to form, shape* pass. *take*
on form, be formed Gal 4: 19.*

μόρφωσις, εως, ἡ—**1.** *embodi-*
ment, formulation Ro 2: 20.—
2. *outward form, appearance*
2 Ti 3: 5.*

μοσχοποιέω *make a calf* Ac 7: 41.*

μόσχος, ου, ὁ *calf, young bull* or *ox*
Lk 15: 23, 27, 30; Hb 9: 12, 19;
Rv 4: 7.*

μοῦ gen. of ἐγώ.

μουσικός, ή, όν *pertaining to*
music ὁ μουσικός as noun *the*
musician Rv 18: 22.*

μόχθος, ου, ὁ *labor, exertion,*
hardship 2 Cor 11: 27; 1 Th 2:
9: 2 Th 3: 8.*

μυελός, οῦ, ὁ *marrow* Hb 4:
12.*

μυέω *initiate (into the mysteries)*
pass. *be initiated, learn the*
secret Phil 4: 12.*

μῦθος, ου, ὁ *tale, fable, myth* 1 Ti 1:
4; 4: 7; 2 Ti 4: 4; Tit 1: 14;
2 Pt 1: 16.*

μυκάομαι *roar* Rv 10: 3.*

μυκτηρίζω *treat with contempt,*
mock Gal 6: 7.*

μυλικός, ή, όν *belonging to a mill*
Mk 9: 42 v.l.; Lk 17: 2; Rv 18:
21 v.l.*

μύλινος, η, ον *belonging to a mill*
Rv 18: 21.*

μύλος, ου, ὁ—**1.** *mill* Mt 24: 41;
Rv 18: 22.—**2.** *millstone* Mt 18:
6; Mk 9: 42; Rv 18: 21 v.l.*

μυλών, ῶνος, ὁ *mill-house* Mt 24:
41 v.l.*

μυλωνικός, ή, όν *belonging to the*
mill-house Mk 9: 42 v.l.*

Μύρα, ων, τά *Myra,* a city on the
south coast of Asia Minor Ac 27:
5; 21: 1 v.l.*

μυριάς, άδος, ἡ *myriad* (ten
thousand) lit., as a number Ac
19: 19. A very large number, not
exactly defined, pl. *myriads*
Lk 12: 1; Ac 21: 20; Hb 12: 22;
Jd 14; Rv 5: 11; 9: 16.*

μυρίζω *anoint* Mk 14: 8.*

μύριοι, αι, α *ten thousand* Mt 18:
24.*

μύριος, α, ον *innumerable, count-*
less 1 Cor 4: 15; 14: 19.*

μύρον, ου, τό (Semitic loanword)
ointment, perfume Mk 14: 3–5;
J 11: 2; 12: 3, 5; Rv 18: 13.*

Μύρρα a variant form of Μύρα.

Μυσία, ας, ἡ *Mysia* a province in
the northwest of Asia Minor
Ac 16: 7f.*

μυστήριον, ου, τό secret, secret
teaching, mystery Mk 4: 11;
Ro 11: 25; 1 Cor 2: 7; 13: 2;
15: 51; Eph 3: 3f, 9; Col 1: 26f;
4: 3; Rv 10: 7. Secret truths
1 Cor 14: 2. Allegorical significance Rv 1: 20; 17: 7. τὸ τ.
εὐσεβείας μ. the Christian religion 1 Ti 3: 16.
μυωπάζω be short-sighted fig. 2 Pt
1: 9.*
μώλωψ, ωπος, ὁ welt, bruise,
wound 1 Pt 2: 24.*
μωμάομαι mid. dep. find fault
with, blame 2 Cor 8: 20; pass.
have fault found with it 6: 3.*
μῶμος, ου, ὁ blemish 2 Pt 2: 13.*
μωραίνω—1. show to be foolish

1 Cor 1: 20; pass. become foolish
Ro 1: 22.—2. make tasteless
pass. become tasteless, insipid
Mt 5: 13; Lk 14: 34.*
μωρία, ας, ἡ foolishness 1 Cor 1: 18,
21, 23; 2: 14; 3: 19.*
μωρολογία, ας, ἡ foolish, silly
talk Eph 5: 4.*
μωρός, ά, όν foolish, stupid Mt 7:
26; 25: 2f, 8; 1 Cor 1: 25, 27;
4: 10; 2 Ti 2: 23. μωρέ you fool
Mt 5: 22.
Μωσῆς variant form of Μωϋσῆς.
Μωϋσῆς, έως, ὁ Moses Mt 19: 7f;
22: 24; Mk 1: 44; Lk 20: 37;
J 1: 17; 7: 19, 22f; Ac 7: 20ff;
26: 22; 2 Cor 3: 7, 13; Hb 3: 5;
Jd 9. Books of Moses 2 Cor 3: 15.

N

Ναασσών, ὁ indecl. Nahshon Mt 1:
4; Lk 3: 32.*
Ναγγαί, ὁ indecl. Naggai Lk 3:
25.*
Ναζαρά, Ναζαρέτ, Ναζαρέθ, ἡ
indecl. Nazareth, a village in
Galilee, home of Jesus' parents
Mt 2: 23; 4: 13; 21: 11; Mk 1: 9;
Lk 1: 26; 2: 4, 39, 51; 4: 16;
J 1: 45f; Ac 10: 38.*
Ναζαρηνός, ή, όν coming from
Nazareth only as noun ὁ N. the
Nazarene Mk 1: 24; 10: 47; 14:
67; 16: 6; Lk 4: 34; 24: 19;
J 18: 5 v.l.*
Ναζωραῖος, ου, ὁ Nazorean, Naza-
rene Mt 2: 23; 26: 69 v.l., 71;
Lk 18: 37; J 18: 5, 7; 19: 19;
Ac 2: 22; 3: 6; 4: 10; 6: 14;
22: 8; 24: 5; 26: 9.*
Ναθάμ, ὁ indecl. Nathan Lk 3: 31.*
Ναθαναήλ, ὁ indecl. Nathanael, a
disciple of Jesus J 1: 45–49;
21: 2.*
ναί affirmative particle yes, yes
indeed Mt 5: 37; 11: 9, 26; 17:
25; Lk 7: 26; 12: 5; J 11: 27;

21: 15f; Ac 22: 27; 2 Cor 1:
17–20; Phlm 20; Js 5: 12.
Certainly, indeed Mt 15: 27;
Mk 7: 28; Rv 14: 13; surely
22: 20.
Ναιμάν, ὁ indecl. Naaman (2
Kings 5: 1ff) Lk 4: 27.*
Ναΐν, ἡ indecl. Nain, a city in
Galilee Lk 7: 11.*
ναός, οῦ, ὁ temple lit. Mt 23: 17,
35; Mk 14: 58; 15: 38; Lk 1:
21f; J 2: 20; Ac 17: 24; 19: 24
(here perhaps shrine); Rv 11:
2, 19; 15: 6, 8; 21: 22. Fig.
J 2: 19–21; 1 Cor 3: 16, 17;
6: 19.
Ναούμ, ὁ indecl. Nahum Lk 3: 25.*
νάρδος, ου, ἡ oil of (spike)nard,
extracted from the root of the
nard plant, used as perfume
Mk 14: 3; J 12: 3.*
Νάρκισσος, ου, ὁ Narcissus Ro 16:
11.*
ναυαγέω suffer shipwreck lit. 2 Cor
11: 25; fig. 1 Ti 1: 19.*
ναύκληρος, ου, ὁ ship-owner or
captain Ac 27: 11.*

ναῦς, acc. ναῦν, ἡ *ship* Ac 27: 41.*

ναύτης, ου, ὁ *sailor* Ac 27: 27, 30; Rv 18: 17.*

Ναχώρ, ὁ indecl. *Nahor* Lk 3: 34.*

νεανίας, ου, ὁ *young man* Ac 7: 58; 20: 9; 23: 17, 18 v.l., 22 v.l.*

νεανίσκος, ου, ὁ *young man* Mt 19: 20, 22; Mk 14: 51; Lk 7: 14; Ac 23: 18, 22; 1 J 2: 13f.

Νεάπολις see νέος, end.

Νεεμάν variant spelling of Ναιμάν.

νεκρός, ά, όν *dead*—1. adj., lit. Mt 28: 4; Mk 9: 26; Ac 5: 10; 28: 6; Rv 1: 17f. Fig. Ro 6: 11; Eph 2: 1, 5; Hb 6: 1; Js 2: 17, 26; Rv 3: 1.—2. as noun ὁ νεκρός *the dead person, corpse* lit. Mt 10: 8; 17: 9; 22: 32; Mk 9: 9f; Lk 7: 15; J 2: 22; 21: 14; Ac 10: 42; 13: 30; Ro 10: 7; 14: 9; 1 Cor 15: 20f; Col 2: 12; 2 Ti 4: 1; Hb 13: 20; Rv 16: 3. Fig. Mt 8: 22; Eph 5: 14.

νεκρόω *put to death* Col 3: 5. Pass. *be worn out, as good as dead* Ro 4: 19; Hb 11: 12.*

νέκρωσις, εως, ἡ—1. *death, putting to death* 2 Cor 4: 10.—2. *deadness, mortification* Ro 4: 19; *deadening* Mk 3: 5 v.l.*

νενικήκατε perf. act. ind., 2 pl., of νικάω.

νενομοθέτητο unaugmented pluperf. pass., 3 sing., of νομοθετέω.

νεομηνία, ας, ἡ *new moon* festival, *first of the month* Col 2: 16.*

νέος, α, ον comparative νεώτερος —1. adj. *new, fresh* Lk 5: 37–39; 1 Cor 5: 7; Col 3: 10; Hb 12: 24. *Young,* comp. *younger* Lk 15: 12f; 1 Ti 5: 11.—2. as noun (οἱ) νέοι *the young people,* fem. Tit 2: 4. Comp., with little comp. force Ac 5: 6; 1 Ti 5: 1, 2; 1 Pt 5: 5, but equal to superlative Lk 22: 26.—3. Νέα πόλις *Neapolis* (New City), the harbor of Philippi in Macedonia Ac 16: 11.

νεοσσός another form of νοσσός.

νεότης, τητος, ἡ *youth* Mk 10: 20; Lk 18: 21; Ac 26: 4; 1 Ti 4: 12.

νεόφυτος, ον *newly converted,* lit. 'newly planted' 1 Ti 3: 6.*

Νέρων, ωνος, ὁ *Nero,* Roman emperor 54–68 A.D. 2 Ti subscr.*

νεύω *nod* as a signal J 13: 24; Ac 24: 10.*

νεφέλη, ης, ἡ *cloud* Mt 17: 5; Mk 13: 26; Lk 12: 54; Ac 1: 9; 1 Cor 10: 1f; Jd 12; Rv 14: 14–16.

Νεφθαλίμ, ὁ indecl. *Naphtali,* a Hebrew tribe and its ancestor Mt 4: 13, 15; Lk 4: 31 v.l.; Rv 7: 6.*

νέφος, ους, τό *cloud,* fig. *host* Hb 12: 1.*

νεφρός, οῦ, ὁ *kidney,* fig. of the inner life *mind* Rv 2: 23.*

νεωκόρος, ου, ὁ lit. *temple-keeper,* in Ac 19: 35 *guardian of the temple.**

νεωτερικός, ή, όν *youthful* 2 Ti 2: 22.*

νεώτερος see νέος.

νή particle of strong affirmation *by* w. acc. 1 Cor 15: 31.*

νήθω *spin* Mt 6: 28; Lk 12: 27.*

νηπιάζω *be (as) a child* 1 Cor 14: 20.*

νήπιος, ία, ιον *infant, minor*—1. lit. of very young children: *child* Mt 21: 16; 1 Cor 13: 11 (five times). Fig. *immature* Ro 2: 20; 1 Cor 3: 1; Eph 4: 14; Hb 5: 13. *Childlike, innocent* Mt 11: 25; Lk 10: 21.—2. *minor, not yet of age* Gal 4: 1, 3; 1 Th 2: 7 as important v.l.*

Νηρεύς, έως, ὁ *Nereus* Ro 16: 15.*

Νηρί, ὁ indecl. *Neri* Lk 3: 27.*

νησίον, ου, τό *little island* Ac 27: 16.*

νῆσος, ου, ἡ *island* Ac 13: 6; 27: 26; 28: 1, 7, 9, 11; Rv 1: 9; 6: 14; 16: 20.*

νηστεία, ας, ἡ *fasting, abstention from food*—1. of necessity, *hunger* 2 Cor 6: 5; 11: 27.—2. as a religious rite Mt 17: 21; Mk 9:

29 v.l.; Lk 2: 37; Ac 14: 23; 27: 9; 1 Cor 7: 5 v.l.*

νηστεύω to fast as a religious rite Mt 4: 2; 6: 16–18; Mk 2: 18–20; Lk 18: 12; Ac 13: 2f.

νῆστις, ὁ, ἡ gen. ιος or ιδος, acc. pl. νήστεις not eating, hungry Mt 15: 32; Mk 8: 3.*

νηφαλέος, α, ον variant form of νηφάλιος.

νηφάλιος, ία, ον temperate in the use of wine, sober 1 Ti 3: 2, 11; Tit 2: 2.*

νήφω be sober, be well-balanced, self-controlled 1 Th 5: 6, 8; 2 Ti 4: 5; 1 Pt 1: 13; 4: 7; 5: 8.*

νήψατε 1 aor. act. imperative, 2 pl., of νήφω.

Νίγερ, ὁ (Latin loanword: Niger) Niger (dark-complexioned) surname of Simeon Ac 13: 1.*

Νικάνωρ, ορος, ὁ Nicanor Ac 6: 5.*

νικάω—1. intrans. be victor, prevail, conquer Rv 2: 7, 11, 17, 26; 6: 2; 15: 2; 21: 7; in a legal action Ro 3: 4.—2. trans. conquer, overcome, vanquish Lk 11: 22; J 16: 33; Ro 12: 21b; 1 J 5: 4f; Rv 11: 7. Pass., let oneself be overcome Ro 12: 21a.

νίκη, ης, ἡ victory 1 J 5: 4.*

Νικόδημος, ου, ὁ Nicodemus J 3: 1, 4, 9; 7: 50; 19: 39.*

Νικολαΐτης, ου, ὁ Nicolaitan, a follower of Nicolaus, an otherwise unknown founder of a sect Rv 2: 6, 15.*

Νικόλαος, ου, ὁ Nicolaus Ac 6: 5.*

Νικόπολις, εως, ἡ Nicopolis; most probably the city bearing this name in Epirus (northwest of Greece) Tit 3: 12; subscriptions of 1 Ti and Tit.*

νῖκος, ους, τό victory Mt 12: 20; 1 Cor 15: 54f, 57.*

νικοῦντι = νικῶντι.

Νινευή, ἡ indecl. Nineveh, capital of the later Assyrian empire Lk 11: 32 v.l.*

Νινευίτης, ου, ὁ Ninevite, in-

habitant of Nineveh Mt 12: 41; Lk 11: 30, 32.*

νιπτήρ, ῆρος, ὁ (wash-) basin J 13: 5.*

νίπτω wash act. J 13: 5f, 8, 12, 14; 1 Ti 5: 10. Mid. wash oneself J 9: 7b, 11, 15; 13: 10; bathe 9: 7a; wash (for oneself) Mt 6: 17; 15: 2; Mk 7: 3; J 13: 10 (if εἰ μὴ τ. πόδας is accepted).*

νίψαι 1 aor. mid. imperative, 2 sing., of νίπτω.

νοέω—1. perceive, understand, gain an insight into Mt 16: 9, 11; Mk 7: 18; J 12: 40; Ro 1: 20; 1 Ti 1: 7; Hb 11: 3.—2. consider, take note of, think over Mk 13: 14; 2 Ti 2: 7.—3. think, imagine Eph 3: 20.

νόημα, ατος, τό—1. thought, mind 2 Cor 3: 14; 4: 4; 11: 3; Phil 4: 7.—2. purpose, design, plot 2 Cor 2: 11; 10: 5.*

νόθος, η, ον born out of wedlock, illegitimate Hb 12: 8.*

νομή, ῆς, ἡ—1. pasture J 10: 9.— 2. fig. spreading νομὴν ἕξει it will spread 2 Ti 2: 17.*

νομίζω—1. have in common use, pass. be the custom Ac 16: 13 v.l. —2. think, believe, suppose, consider Mt 5: 17; 10: 34; Lk 2: 44; Ac 7: 25; 8: 20; 16: 13, 27; 1 Cor 7: 26, 36.

νομικός, ή, όν pertaining to the law Tit 3: 9. ὁ νομικός legal expert, jurist, lawyer Mt 22: 35; Lk 7: 30; 10: 25; 11: 45f, 52, 53 v.l.; 14: 3; Tit 3: 13.*

νομίμως adv. in accordance with rules 2 Ti 2: 5. Lawfully 1 Ti 1: 8.*

νόμισμα, ατος, τό coin Mt 22: 19.*

νομοδιδάσκαλος, ου, ὁ teacher of the law Lk 5: 17; Ac 5: 34; 1 Ti 1: 7.*

νομοθεσία, ας, ἡ legislation, law Ro 9: 4.*

νομοθετέω function as lawgiver pass. receive law(s) Hb 7: 11. Be enacted 8: 6.*

νομοθέτης, ου, ὁ *lawgiver* Js 4: 12.*

νόμος, ου, ὁ *law*—1. *rule, principle, norm* Ro 7: 21, 23; 8: 2b; Hb 7: 16.—2. of any kind of law Ro 3: 27; perhaps 7: 1f.—3. of the Mosaic law Mt 22: 36; Lk 2: 22; 16: 17; J 7: 23, 51; 18: 31; Ac 13: 38; 18: 13; 21: 24; Ro 2: 25; 3: 19; 4: 14; 7: 2; Gal 3: 12f, 17, 19; 5: 23; 1 Ti 1: 9; Hb 7: 19. Almost equivalent to (*Jewish*) *religion* Ac 23: 29. Specifically of the written law, the Pentateuch Mt 7: 12; 12: 5; Lk 2: 23; 24: 44; 1 Cor 9: 9; Gal 3: 10; 4: 21b. Of the scriptures generally Mt 5: 18; J 10: 34; Ro 3: 19. —4. of Christianity as a 'new law' Ro 3: 27b; 8: 2a; Gal 6: 2; Js 1: 25; 2: 8f, 12.

νοσέω *be sick, ailing* fig. 1 Ti 6: 4.*

νόσημα, ατος, τό *disease* J 5: 4 v.l.*

νόσος, ου, ἡ *disease, illness* Mt 8: 17; 9: 35; Mk 1: 34; Lk 7: 21; 9: 1; Ac 19: 12.

νοσσιά, ᾶς, ἡ *brood* Lk 13: 34.*

νοσσίον, ου, τό *the young* of a bird Mt 23: 37.*

νοσσός, οῦ, ὁ *the young* of a bird Lk 2: 24.*

νοσφίζω mid. *put aside for oneself, misappropriate* Ac 5: 2f; Tit 2: 10.*

νότος, ου, ὁ *south* or *southwest wind* Lk 12: 55; Ac 27: 13; 28: 13. *South* Lk 13: 29; Rv 21: 13. A country in the *south* Mt 12: 42; Lk 11: 31.*

νουθεσία, ας, ἡ *admonition, instruction, warning* 1 Cor 10: 11; Eph 6: 4; Tit 3: 10.*

νουθετέω *admonish, warn, instruct* Ac 20: 31; Ro 15: 14; 1 Cor 4: 14; Col 1: 28; 3: 16; 1 Th 5: 12, 14; 2 Th 3: 15; Tit 1: 11 v.l.*

νουμηνία contract form of νεομηνία.

νουνεχῶς adv. *wisely, thoughtfully* Mk 12: 34.*

νοῦς, gen. νοός, dat. νοΐ, acc. νοῦν, ὁ—1. *the understanding, the mind* as the faculty of thinking Lk 24: 45; 1 Cor 14: 14, 15, 19; Phil 4: 7; Rv 13: 18; 17: 9; *composure* 2 Th 2: 2; *intellect* Ro 7: 23, 25.—2. *mind, attitude, way of thinking* Ro 1: 28; 12: 2; 1 Cor 1: 10; Eph 4: 17, 23; Col 2: 18; 1 Ti 6: 5; 2 Ti 3: 8; Tit 1: 15.—3. *mind* as the result of thinking, *thought* Ro 11: 34; 14: 5; 1 Cor 2: 16 (in the latter passage νοῦς is practically equivalent to πνεῦμα, verse 14f).*

Νυμφᾶν is an accusative form in Col 4: 15; it is not clear whether it is from the feminine name Νύμφα, ας, *Nympha*, or from the masculine name Νυμφᾶς, ᾶ, *Nymphas*.*

νύμφη, ης, ἡ—1. *bride* Mt 25: 1 v.l.; J 3: 29; Rv 18: 23; 21: 2, 9; 22: 17.—2. *daughter-in-law* Mt 10: 35; Lk 12: 53.*

νυμφίος, ου, ὁ *bridegroom* Mt 25: 1, 5f, 10; Mk 2: 19f; J 2: 9; 3: 29; Rv 18: 23.

νυμφών, ῶνος, ὁ—1. *wedding hall* Mt 22: 10.—2. *bridal chamber* οἱ υἱοὶ τοῦ νυμφῶνος *the bridegroom's attendants* Mt 9: 15; Mk 2: 19; Lk 5: 34.*

νῦν adv. *now*—1. lit., of time Mt 27: 42f; Lk 16: 25; 22: 36; J 9: 21; 13: 31; Ac 12: 11; 16: 36; Ro 5: 11; 8: 1; 1 Cor 3: 2; Eph 5: 8; 1 Pt 2: 10, 25. *Just now* J 11: 8; Ac 7: 52; Phil 1: 20.—2. *as things now stand* Ac 15: 10; 1 Th 3: 8. νῦν δέ sometimes contrasts the real state of affairs with something unreal *but, as a matter of fact* Lk 19: 42; J 8: 40; 9: 41; 1 Cor 5: 11; 12: 18, 20; Hb 11: 16; Js 4: 16.—3. used with the article: ὁ, ἡ, τὸ νῦν *the present* as adj. Ro 3: 26; 8: 18; 2 Cor 8: 14; Gal 4: 25; 1 Ti 4: 8; 2 Ti 4: 10; Tit 2: 12; 2 Pt 3: 7. As noun

τὸ **νῦν** the present time, now
Mt 24: 21; Lk 1: 48; 5: 10;
Ac 18: 6; Ro 8: 22; Phil 1: 5.
As adv. τὰ **νῦν** as far as the
present situation is concerned =
now Ac 4: 29; 17: 30; 27: 22. τὸ
νῦν ἔχον for the present Ac 24:
25.

νυνί adv., emphatic form of **νῦν**
now—**1**. lit., of time Ac 22: 1;
24: 13; Ro 3: 21; 15: 23, 25;
2 Cor 8: 22; Eph 2: 13; Col 3: 8;
Phlm 9.—**2**. with the idea of
time weakened or entirely absent
νυνὶ δέ but now, but, as a matter
of fact Ro 7: 17; 1 Cor 5: 11 v.l.;
13: 13; 15: 20; Hb 9: 26.

νύξ, νυκτός, ἡ night—**1**. lit. Mt 4:
2; 14: 25; 28: 13; Mk 5: 5;
14: 30; Lk 5: 5; 21: 37; J 13:
30; 19: 39; Ac 16: 33; 20: 31;
23: 11; Rv 8: 12.—**2**. Fig. J 9:
4; Ro 13: 12; 1 Th 5: 5.

νύσσω prick, stab, pierce J 19: 34;
Mt 27: 49 v.l. Nudge Ac 12:
7 v.l.*

νυστάζω nod, become drowsy, doze
lit. Mt 25:5; fig. be sleepy, idle
2 Pt 2: 3.*

νυχθήμερον, ου, τό a day and a
night = 24 hours 2 Cor 11: 25.*

Νῶε, ὁ indecl. Noah Mt 24: 37f;
Lk 3: 36; 17: 26f; Hb 11: 7;
1 Pt 3: 20; 2 Pt 2: 5.*

νωθρός, ά, όν lazy, sluggish Hb 6:
12. ν. ταῖς ἀκοαῖς hard of
hearing 5: 11.*

νῶτος, ου, ὁ back Ro 11: 10.*

Ξ

ξαίνω comb, card wool Mt 6:28 v.l.*
ξενία, ας, ἡ hospitality, or more
likely guest room Ac 28: 23;
Phlm 22.*
ξενίζω—**1**. receive as a guest,
entertain Ac 10: 23; 28: 7;
Hb 13: 2. Pass. be entertained,
stay Ac 10: 6, 18, 32; 21: 16;
1 Cor 16: 19 v.l.—**2**. surprise,
astonish Ac 17: 20. Pass. be
surprised, wonder 1 Pt 4: 4, 12.*
ξενοδοχέω show hospitality 1 Ti 5:
10.*
ξένος, η, ον—**1**. adj. strange,
foreign Ac 17: 18; Hb 13: 9;
surprising, unheard of 1 Pt 4:
12. ξ. τῶν διαθηκῶν estranged
from the covenants Eph 2: 12.—
2. as noun ὁ ξένος the stranger,
alien Mt 25: 35, 38, 43f; 27: 7;
Ac 17: 21; Eph 2: 19; Hb 11: 13;
3 J 5. Host, one who extends
hospitality Ro 16: 23.*
ξέστης, ου, ὁ pitcher, jug Mk 7: 4,
8 v.l.*

ξηραίνω dry, dry out Js 1: 11.
Become dry, dry up, wither
Mt 21: 19f; Mk 3: 1, 3 v.l.;
4: 6; 5: 29; J 15: 6; 1 Pt 1: 24;
Rv 14: 15; 16: 12; become stiff
Mk 9: 18.
ξηρός, ά, όν dry, dried (up) Lk 23:
31; Hb 11: 29; dry land Mt 23:
15. Withered, paralysed Mk 3: 3;
J 5: 3.
ξύλινος, η, ον wooden 2 Ti 2: 20;
Rv 9: 20.*
ξύλον, ου, τό—**1**. wood 1 Cor 3: 12;
Rv 18: 12.—**2**. of objects made
of wood: stocks Ac 16: 24.
Club, cudgel Mt 26: 47, 55;
Mk 14: 43, 48; Lk 22: 52. Cross
Ac 5: 30; 10: 39; 13: 29; Gal 3:
13; 1 Pt 2: 24.—**3**. tree Lk
23: 31; Rv 2: 7; 22: 2, 14,
19.*
ξυν—alternate form of συν-.
ξυράω, ξυρέω, ξύρω mid. have
oneself shaved Ac 21: 24; 1 Cor
11: 5f.*

O

ὁ, ἡ, τό pl. οἱ, αἱ, τά the definite article, the—**1.** as a demonstrative pronoun this one, that one τοῦ γὰρ καὶ γένος ἐσμέν for we are also his (lit. 'this One's') offspring Ac 17: 28.—ὁ μὲν ... ὁ δέ the one ... the other, pl. οἱ μὲν ... οἱ δέ some ... others Ac 14: 4; 17: 32; 1 Cor 7: 7; Hb 7: 5f, 20f. ὁ δέ, οἱ δέ but he, but they Mt 2: 9, 14; 4: 4; 9: 31. —**2.** as definite article, the, in a great variety of uses. It will suffice to say here that the definite article is omitted in translation in the following expressions—**a.** when it is used between a demonstrative adjective (οὗτος, this; ἐκεῖνος, that) and a noun, or when this adj. follows its noun Mt 15: 8; Mk 7: 6; 14: 71; Lk 14: 30; J 9: 24.—**b.** when it is placed before the nominative of a noun, thus making it a vocative ὁ πατήρ (O) father Mt 11: 26; cf. 7: 23; Lk 8: 54; 18: 11, 13; J 19: 3.—**c.** when the neuter of the article is used with an infinitive τὸ φαγεῖν to eat, eating Mt 15: 20; cf. Mk 12: 33; Ro 7: 18; 2 Cor 8: 10f. In the genitive case with a variety of uses, including purpose Mt 13: 3; Lk 1: 77; Ro 6: 6; Phil 3: 10 or result Mt 21: 32; Ac 7: 19; Ro 7: 3.—**d.** when it precedes personal names Mt 27: 21; Mk 1: 14.

ὀγδοήκοντα indecl. eighty Lk 2: 37; 16: 7.*

ὄγδοος, η, ον the eighth Lk 1: 59; Ac 7: 8; 2 Pt 2: 5; Rv 17: 11; 21: 20.*

ὄγκος, ου, ὁ weight, burden, impediment Hb 12: 1.*

ὅδε, ἥδε, τόδε this (one) Lk 10: 39; Ac 21: 11; Rv 2: 1, 8, 12, 18; 3: 1, 7, 14. εἰς τήνδε τὴν πόλιν into such and such a city Js 4: 13.*

ὁδεύω travel Lk 10: 33.*

ὁδηγέω lead, guide lit. Mt 15: 14; Lk 6: 39; Rv 7: 17. Fig. lead, guide, instruct J 16: 13; Ac 8: 31.*

ὁδηγός, οῦ, ὁ leader, guide Mt 15: 14; 23: 16, 24; Ac 1: 16; Ro 2: 19.*

ὁδοιπορέω travel, be on the way Ac 10: 9.*

ὁδοιπορία, ας, ἡ walking, journey J 4: 6; 2 Cor 11: 26.*

ὁδοποιέω make a path Mk 2: 23 v.l.*

ὁδός, οῦ, ἡ way—**1.** lit.—**a.** as a place: way, road, highway Mt 2: 12; 3: 3; Mk 10: 46; Lk 8: 5; Ac 8: 26, 36. ὁδόν w. gen. toward Mt 4: 15.—**b.** as an action: way, journey Mt 10: 10; Mk 8: 3; Lk 12: 58; 24: 35; Ac 9: 27. σαββάτου ὁδός a Sabbath day's journey Ac 1: 12. —**2.** fig.—**a.** way Mt 7: 13f; 10: 5; Lk 1: 79; J 14: 6; Ac 2: 28; 16: 17; Ro 3: 17.—**b.** way of life or acting, conduct Mt 21: 32; Lk 20: 21; Ro 11: 33; Js 5: 20; Hb 3: 10; 2 Pt 2: 21; Rv 15: 3. —**c.** the Way or teaching, of Christianity Ac 9: 2; 19: 9, 23; 22: 4; 24: 14, 22; 1 Cor 4: 17; 2 Pt 2: 2.

ὀδούς, ὀδόντος, ὁ tooth Mt 5: 38; 8: 12; 13: 42, 50; Mk 9: 18; Lk 13: 28; Ac 7: 54; Rv 9: 8.

ὀδυνάω cause pain pass. feel pain Lk 16: 24f; Ac 20: 38; be anxious Lk 2: 48.*

ὀδύνη, ης, ἡ pain, grief Ro 9: 2; 1 Ti 6: 10; Mt 24: 8 v.l.*

ὀδυρμός, οῦ, ὁ lamentation, mourning Mt 2: 18; 2 Cor 7: 7.*

'Οζίας, ου, ὁ Uzziah, Hebrew king Mt 1: 8f; Lk 3: 23ff v.l.*

ὄζω smell, give off an unpleasant odor J 11: 39.*

ὅθεν adv. from where, whence Mt 12: 44; 25: 24, 26; Lk 11: 24; Ac 14: 26; 28: 13. From which fact 1 J 2: 18. For which reason, therefore, hence Mt 14: 7; Ac 26: 19; Hb 2: 17; 3: 1; 11: 19.

ὀθόνη, ης, ἡ linen cloth, sheet Ac 10: 11; 11: 5.*

ὀθόνιον, ου, τό linen cloth, bandage J 19: 40; 20: 5ff; Lk 24: 12 v.l.*

οἶδα—1. know (about) Mt 6: 32; 20: 22; 25: 13; Mk 1: 34; 6: 20; Lk 4: 41; 11: 44; J 4: 25; 9: 25; Ac 2: 22; 3: 16; Ro 8: 27; 1 Cor 13: 2; 16: 15; 2 Cor 12: 2; Gal 4: 8; Col 4: 6; 1 Ti 1: 8; 2 Pt 1: 12. ἴστε Js 1: 19 can be either indicative you know or imperative know!—2. be (intimately) acquainted with, stand in a close relation to Mt 26: 72, 74; Lk 22: 57; J 8: 19; 2 Cor 5: 16; 2 Th 1: 8; Tit 1: 16.—3. know or understand how, can, be able Mt 7: 11; 27: 65; Lk 12: 56; Phil 4: 12; 1 Th 4: 4; 1 Ti 3: 5; Js 4: 17.—4. understand, recognize, come to know Mt 26: 70; Mk 4: 13; 12: 15; Lk 22: 60; J 6: 61; 16: 18; 1 Cor 2: 11; Eph 1: 18.—5. various other uses: remember 1 Cor 1: 16. Respect or take an interest in 1 Th 5: 12.

οἰκεῖος, (α), ον belonging to the house οἱ οἰκεῖοι members of the household Gal 6: 10; Eph 2: 19; 1 Ti 5: 8.*

οἰκετεία, ας, ἡ the slaves in a household Mt 24: 45.*

οἰκέτης, ου, ὁ house slave, domestic, slave generally Lk 16: 13; Ac 10: 7; Ro 14: 4; 1 Pt 2: 18.*

οἰκέω intrans. live, dwell, have one's habitation Ro 7: 18, 20; 8: 9, 11; 1 Cor 3: 16; 7: 12f. Trans. inhabit, dwell in 1 Ti 6: 16.—On οἰκουμένη see it as a separate entry.*

οἴκημα, ατος, τό room, euphemistically for prison Ac 12: 7.*

οἰκητήριον, ου, τό dwelling, habitation lit. Jd 6; fig. 2 Cor 5: 2.*

οἰκία, ας, ἡ—1. house lit. Mt 7: 24–27; 9: 28; 19: 29; Mk 1: 29; 6: 10; 13: 34f; Lk 18:29; 20: 47; J 8: 35; 12: 3; Ac 4: 34; 10: 6; 1 Cor 11: 22. Fig. J 14: 2; 2 Cor 5: 1.—2. household, family Mt 12: 25; Mk 3: 25; 6: 4; J 4: 53; 1 Cor 16: 15.—3. a kind of middle position between meanings 1 and 2 is held by Mt 10: 12f and Phil 4: 22; in the latter passage οἰκία refers to the servants and slaves in the emperor's court.

οἰκιακός, οῦ, ὁ member of a household Mt 10: 25, 36.*

οἰκοδεσποτέω manage one's household, keep house 1 Ti 5: 14.*

οἰκοδεσπότης, ου, ὁ the master of the house Mt 10: 25; 13: 52; 20: 1; 21: 33; 24: 43; Mk 14: 14; Lk 13: 25; 22: 11.

οἰκοδομέω build—1. lit. build, erect Mt 7: 24, 26; 23: 29; Mk 12: 1; Lk 6: 48; 12: 18; 1 Pt 2: 7. Build up again, restore Mt 27: 40; Mk 15: 29.—2. fig. Mt 16: 18; Ro 15: 20; Gal 2: 18; 1 Pt 2: 5.—3. also in a non-literal sense, with little consciousness of the basic meaning build up, edify, benefit, strengthen Ac 9: 31; 20: 32; 1 Cor 8: 1, 10; 10: 23; 14: 4, 17; 1 Th 5: 11.

οἰκοδομή, ῆς, ἡ—1. lit. building, edifice Mt 24: 1; Mk 13: 1f.— 2. fig. building 1 Cor 3: 9; 2 Cor 5: 1; Eph 2: 21. In the sense edifying, edification, building up 1 Cor 14: 3, 12; 2 Cor 12: 19; 13: 10; Ro 15: 2; Eph 4: 12, 16.

οἰκοδομία, ας, ἡ edification 1 Ti 1: 4 v.l.*

οἰκοδόμος, ου, ὁ builder Ac 4: 11.*

οἰκονομέω be manager Lk 16: 2.*

οἰκονομία, ας, ἡ management of a

household, *administration, office*
Lk 16: 2–4; Col 1: 25; *commis-
sion* 1 Cor 9: 17; *stewardship*
Eph 3: 2. *Plan* of salvation
1: 10; 3: 9. *Training* in the way
of salvation 1 Ti 1: 4.*

οἰκονόμος, ου, ὁ (*house-*) *steward,
manager*—**1.** lit. Lk 12: 42;
16: 1, 3, 8; 1 Cor 4: 2; Gal 4: 2.
ὁ οἰκ. τῆς πόλεως the *city
treasurer* Ro 16: 23.—**2.** fig.
administrator 1 Cor 4: 1; Tit 1:
7; 1 Pt 4: 10.*

οἶκος, ου, ὁ—**1.** *house, home*—
a. lit. Mt 9: 7; 11: 8; 21: 13;
Mk 2: 1; 5: 38; 8: 3; Lk 6: 4;
11: 17; 15: 6; Ac 2: 2; 7: 47, 49;
Ro 16: 5; Phlm 2. κατ' οἶκον *in
the various private homes* Ac 2:
46; 5: 42. οἶκος = *city* Mt 23: 38;
Lk 13: 35.—**b.** fig. 1 Pt 2: 5;
perhaps 1 Ti 3: 15; 1 Pt 4: 17.
Dwelling, habitation Mt 12: 44;
Lk 11: 24.—**2.** *household, family*
Lk 10: 5; 19: 9; Ac 10: 2; 16: 31;
1 Cor 1: 16; 1 Ti 3: 4f; 2 Ti 1: 16;
4: 19; Tit 1: 11; Hb 3: 2–6.—
3. *house = descendants, nation*
Mt 10: 6; 15: 24; Lk 1: 27, 69;
2: 4; Ac 2: 36; 7: 42; Hb 8: 8,
10.—**4.** *property, possessions* Ac
7: 10.

οἰκουμένη, ης, ἡ lit. 'inhabited,'
with γῆ supplied—**1.** *the inhabited earth, the world* Mt 24:
14; Lk 4: 5; 21: 26; Ac 11: 28;
Ro 10: 18; Hb 1: 6; Rv 3: 10;
16: 14. *World* in the sense
humankind Lk 2: 1; Ac 17: 31;
19: 27; Rv 12: 9.—**2.** *the Roman
Empire* Ac 24: 5; *its inhabitants*
17: 6.—**3.** ἡ οἰκ. ἡ μέλλουσα *the
world to come* Hb 2: 5.*

οἰκουργός, όν *working at home,
domestic* Tit 2: 5.*

οἰκουρός, όν *staying at home,
domestic* Tit 2: 5 v.l.*

οἰκτείρω a different spelling for
οἰκτίρω.

οἰκτιρμός, οῦ, ὁ *pity, mercy,
compassion* Ro 12: 1; 2 Cor 1:

3; Col 3: 12; Phil 2: 1; Hb 10:
28.*

οἰκτίρμων, ον *merciful, compassionate* Lk 6: 36; Js 5: 11.*

οἰκτίρω *have compassion on* Ro 9:
15.*

οἶμαι see οἴομαι.

οἰνοπότης, ου, ὁ *wine-drinker,
drunkard* Mt 11: 19; Lk 7: 34.*

οἶνος, ου, ὁ *wine*—**1.** lit. Mt 9: 17;
Mk 15: 23; Lk 1: 15; 7: 33;
10: 34; J 2: 3, 9f; Ro 14: 21;
Eph 5: 18; 1 Ti 3: 8; 5: 23;
Tit 2: 3; Rv 18: 13.—**2.** fig.
Rv 14: 8, 10; 18: 3; 19: 15.—
3. *vineyard* 6: 6.

οἰνοφλυγία, ας, ἡ *drunkenness*
1 Pt 4: 3.*

οἴομαι contracted **οἶμαι** *think,
suppose, expect* J 21: 25; Phil 1:
17; Js 1: 7.*

οἷος, α, ον relative pron. *of what
sort,* (*such*) *as* Mt 24: 21; Mk 9:
3; 13: 19; 2 Cor 12: 20; 2 Ti 3:
11; Rv 16: 18. οἷος . . . τοιοῦτος
1 Cor 15: 48; cf. 2 Cor 10: 11.
Which Phil 1: 30. οὐχ οἷον ὅτι
it is by no means as if Ro 9: 6.
οἵῳ δηποτοῦν κατείχετο νοσήματι
no matter what disease he had
J 5: 4 v.l.

οἰοσδηποτοῦν see οἷος.

οἴσω fut. act. ind. of φέρω.

ὀκνέω *hesitate, delay* Ac 9: 38.*

ὀκνηρός, ά, όν *idle, lazy, indolent*
Mt 25: 26; Ro 12: 11. *Troublesome* Phil 3: 1.*

ὀκταήμερος, ον *on the eighth day*
Phil 3: 5.*

ὀκτώ *eight* Lk 2: 21; 13: 16; J 20:
26; 1 Pt 3: 20.

ὀλεθρευτής, ὀλεθρεύω different
spellings for ὀλοθρευτής, ὀλοθρεύω.

ὀλέθριος, ον *deadly, destructive*
2 Th 1: 9 v.l.*

ὄλεθρος, ου, ὁ *destruction, ruin,
death* 1 Cor 5: 5; 1 Th 5: 3;
2 Th 1: 9; 1 Ti 6: 9.*

ὀλιγοπιστία, ας, ἡ *littleness* or
poverty of faith Mt 17: 20.*

ὀλιγόπιστος, ον of little faith or trust Mt 6: 30; 8: 26; 14: 31; 16: 8; Lk 12: 28.*

ὀλίγος, η, ον—1. plural few, a few Mt 9: 37; 22: 14; 25: 21, 23; Mk 8: 7; Lk 12: 48; 13: 23; Ac 17: 4; Hb 12: 10; 1 Pt 5: 12; Rv 2: 14; 3: 4.—2. singular little, small, short Lk 7: 47; Ac 12: 18; 15: 2; 19: 24; 2 Cor 8: 15; 1 Ti 5: 23; Rv 12: 12.—3. the neut. ὀλίγον in adverbial expressions a little Mk 1: 19; 6: 31; Lk 5: 3; 7: 47b; 1 Pt 1: 6; 5: 10; Rv 17: 10. ἐν ὀλίγῳ in brief Eph 3: 3, but in a short time Ac 26: 28, cf. verse 29. πρὸς ὀλίγον for a short time Js 4: 14, but for (a) little 1 Ti 4: 8.

ὀλιγόψυχος, ον faint-hearted, discouraged 1 Th 5: 14.*

ὀλιγωρέω think lightly of, make light of w. gen. Hb 12: 5.*

ὀλίγως adv. scarcely, barely 2 Pt 2: 18.*

ὀλοθρευτής, οῦ, ὁ the destroyer 1 Cor 10: 10.*

ὀλοθρεύω destroy Hb 11: 28.*

ὁλοκαύτωμα, ατος, τό whole burnt offering Mk 12: 33; Hb 10: 6, 8.*

ὁλοκληρία, ας, ἡ wholeness, completeness, soundness Ac 3: 16.*

ὁλόκληρος, ον whole, complete, intact 1 Th 5: 23; Js 1: 4.*

ὀλολύζω cry out Js 5: 1.*

ὅλος, η, ον whole, entire, complete Mt 14: 35; 16: 26; Mk 6: 55; Lk 5: 5; 13: 21; J 4: 53; 7: 23; Ac 11: 26; Ro 1: 8; 8: 36; Tit 1: 11; 1 J 5: 19; all Ac 21: 31. δι' ὅλου throughout J 19: 23.

ὁλοτελής, ές complete; in 1 Th 5: 23 wholly.*

'Ολυμπᾶς, ᾶ, ὁ Olympas Ro 16: 15.*

ὄλυνθος, ου, ὁ late or summer fig Rv 6: 13.*

ὅλως adv. generally speaking, actually, everywhere 1 Cor 5: 1; 6: 7; w. neg. not at all Mt 5: 34; 1 Cor 15: 29.*

ὄμβρος, ου, ὁ rain-storm Lk 12: 54.*

ὁμείρομαι have a kindly feeling for, long for w. gen. 1 Th 2: 8.*

ὁμίλεω talk, converse Lk 24: 14f; Ac 20: 11; 24: 26.*

ὁμιλία, ας, ἡ association, company 1 Cor 15: 33.*

ὅμιλος, ου, ὁ crowd, throng Rv 18: 17 v.l.*

ὁμίχλη, ης, ἡ mist, fog 2 Pt 2: 17.*

ὄμμα, ατος, τό eye Mt 20: 34; Mk 8: 23.*

ὀμνύω swear, take an oath; the person or thing by which one swears may be expressed by: the simple acc. Js 5: 12; ἐν with the dat. Mt 5: 34, 36; Rv 10: 6; κατά with the gen. Hb 6: 13. In other constructions Mk 6: 23; Lk 1: 73; Ac 2: 30; Hb 3: 18.

ὁμοθυμαδόν adv. with one mind or purpose or impulse Ac 1: 14; 4: 24; 8: 6; 15: 25; 19: 29; Ro 15: 6; together Ac 5: 12.

ὁμοιάζω be like, resemble w. dat., only as v.l. in Mt 23: 27, 26: 73 and Mk 14: 70.*

ὁμοιοπαθής, ές with the same nature w. dat. as someone Ac 14: 15; Js 5: 17.*

ὅμοιος, οία, οιον of the same nature, like, similar with the person or thing compared in the dative: Mt 11: 16; 13: 31, 33, 44f; Lk 6: 47–49; J 8: 55; 9: 9; Ac 17: 29; Gal 5: 21; 1 J 3: 2; Rv 4: 3, 6f; 21: 11, 18. With the genitive J 8: 55 v.l. In an extraordinary construction with the accusative Rv 1: 13; 14: 14. In a special sense as powerful as, equally important, equal to w. dat. Mt 22: 39; Mk 12: 31 v.l.; Rv 13: 4; 18: 18.

ὁμοιότης, ητος, ἡ likeness, similarity καθ' ὁμοιότητα in (quite) the same way Hb 4: 15; 7: 15.*

ὁμοιόω—1. make like pass. become like, be like Mt 7: 24, 26; 22: 2; Ac 14: 11; Ro 9: 29; Hb 2: 17.

—**2.** compare Mt 11: 16; Mk 4: 30; Lk 7: 31; 13: 20.

ὁμοίωμα, ατος, τό—1. likeness Ro 5: 14; 6: 5; 8: 3; Phil 2: 7. —**2.** image, copy Ro 1: 23.— **3.** form, appearance Rv 9: 7.*

ὁμοίως adv. likewise, so, similarly, in the same way Mt 22: 26; Mk 4: 16; Lk 3: 11; 5: 10; 13: 3; Ro 1: 27; 1 Cor 7: 3f; 1 Pt 3: 1, 7; Jd 8. Also J 5: 19; 6: 11; 21: 13.

ὁμοίωσις, εως, ἡ likeness Js 3: 9.*

ὁμολογέω—1. promise, assure Mt 14: 7; Ac 7: 17.—**2.** agree, admit Hb 11: 13.—**3.** confess J 1: 20; Ac 24:14; 1 J 1: 9.— **4.** declare (publicly), acknowledge, confess Lk 12: 8; J 9: 22; Ac 23: 8; Ro 10: 9; 1 Ti 6: 12; 1 J 4: 2f, 15; Rv 3: 5; say plainly Mt 7: 23; claim Tit 1: 16.— **5.** praise, w. dat. Hb 13: 15.

ὁμολογία, ας, ἡ confessing 2 Cor 9: 13. Confession, acknowledgment 1 Ti 6: 12f; Hb 3: 1; 4: 14; 10: 23.*

ὁμολογουμένως adv. confessedly, undeniably, most certainly 1 Ti 3: 16.*

ὁμόσε adv. together Ac 20: 18 v.l.*

ὁμότεχνος, ον practicing the same trade Ac 18: 3.*

ὁμοῦ adv. together J 4: 36; 20: 4; 21: 2; Ac 2: 1.*

ὁμόφρων, ον like-minded 1 Pt 3: 8.*

ὅμως adv. all the same, nevertheless, yet J 12: 42. This may also be the sense in 1 Cor 14: 7 and Gal 3: 15, but likewise, also is possible.*

ὀναίμην 2 aor. opt. mid. of ὀνίνημι.

ὄναρ, τό (found only in nom. and acc. sing.) dream κατ' ὄναρ in a dream Mt 1: 20; 2: 12f, 19, 22; 27: 19.*

ὀνάριον, ου, τό (little) donkey J 12: 14.*

ὀνειδίζω reproach, revile, heap insults upon Mt 5: 11; 27: 44; Mk 15: 32; Js 1: 5; 1 Pt 4: 14; reproach justifiably Mt 11: 20; Mk 16: 14.

ὀνειδισμός, οῦ, ὁ reproach, reviling, disgrace, insult Ro 15: 3; 1 Ti 3: 7; Hb 10: 33; 11: 26; 13: 13.*

ὄνειδος, ους, τό disgrace Lk 1: 25.*

Ὀνήσιμος, ου, ὁ Onesimus, slave of Philemon Col 4: 9; Phlm 10; subscr. of Col and of Phlm.*

Ὀνησίφορος, ου, ὁ Onesiphorus 2 Ti 1: 16; 4: 19.*

ὀνικός, ή, όν pertaining to a donkey μύλος ὀν. a millstone worked by donkey-power Mt 18: 6; Mk 9: 42; Lk 17: 2 v.l.*

ὀνίνημι mid., 2 aor. opt. ὀναίμην as a formula may I have joy or benefit Phlm 20.*

ὄνομα, ατος, τό—1. name—a. generally Mt 10: 2; Mk 14: 32; Lk 8: 30, 41; 10: 20; Hb 1: 4; Rv 9: 11. ὀνόματι by name, named Mt 27:32; Lk 5: 27; Ac 5: 1, 34.—b. in combination with God or Jesus Mt 6: 9; Lk 1: 49; Ro 2: 24; 2 Th 1: 12; Hb 2: 12; 13: 15; Rv 2: 13; 11: 18. The following uses with prepositions are noteworthy: ἐν τῷ ὀνόματι with or at the mention of the name Mk 9: 38; Lk 10: 17; Ac 4: 7, 10; 10: 48; Phil 2: 10; Js 5: 14, but at the command of, commissioned by Mt 21: 9; J 5: 43; 12: 13.—ἐπὶ τῷ ὀνόματι when the name is mentioned, using the name Mt 24: 5; Mk 9: 39; Lk 24: 47; Ac 2: 38; 4: 17f. πρὸς τὸ ὄνομα in opposition to the name Ac 26: 9.—**2.** title, category ὁ δεχόμενος προφήτην εἰς ὄνομα προφήτου whoever receives a prophet within the category 'prophet,' i.e. as a prophet Mt 10: 41a; cf. 41b, 42; Mk 9: 41. For the sake of 1 Pt 4: 14. In the capacity 4: 16.—**3.** person Ac 1: 15; 18: 15; Rv 3: 4; 11: 13. —**4.** reputation, fame Mk 6: 14; Rv 3: 1.

ὀνομάζω give a name, call, name
Mk 3: 14 v.l.; Lk 6: 13f; 2: 21
v.l.; 1 Cor 5: 11; Eph 3: 15. Use
a name or word Ac 19: 13; Eph 1:
21; 5: 3; 2 Ti 2: 19. Pass. be
named, in the sense be known
Ro 15: 20; 1 Cor 5: 1 v.l.*

ὄνος, ου, ὁ and ἡ donkey (male or
female), ass, she-ass Mt 21: 2,
5, 7; Lk 13: 15; 14: 5 v.l.;
J 12: 15.*

ὄντως adv. really, certainly, in
truth Mk 11: 32; Lk 23: 47; 24:
34; J 8: 36; 1 Cor 14: 25;
Gal 3: 21. As adj. real 1 Ti 5:
3, 5, 16; 6: 19; 2 Pt 2: 18 v.l.*

ὄξος, ους, τό sour wine, wine
vinegar Mt 27: 48; Mk 15: 36;
Lk 23: 36; J 19: 29f.*

ὀξύς, εῖα, ύ—1. sharp Rv 1: 16;
2: 12; 14: 14, 17f; 19: 15.—
2. quick, swift Ro 3: 15.*

ὀπή, ῆς, ἡ opening, hole Hb 11: 38;
Js 3: 11.*

ὄπισθεν adv.—1. as adv. from
behind Mt 9: 20; Mk 5: 27;
Lk 8: 44. Behind Rv 4: 6; on the
back 5: 1.—2. as improper prep.
w. gen. behind, after Mt 15: 23;
Lk 23: 26; Rv 1: 10 v.l.*

ὀπίσω adv.—1. as adv. behind
Lk 7: 38. τὰ ὀπίσω what lies
behind Phil 3: 13. εἰς τὰ ὀπ.
back J 18: 6; 20: 14; backwards
Lk 9: 62.—2. as improper prep.
w. gen. after Mt 3: 11; 16: 24;
Mk 8: 34; Lk 9: 23; 14: 27;
J 1: 15, 27, 30; Jd 7; Rv 12: 15.
δεῦτε ὀπ. μου come, follow me
Mk 1: 17.

ὁπλίζω equip, arm mid., fig. arm
oneself with w. acc. 1 Pt 4: 1.*

ὅπλον, ου, τό weapon—1. lit.
J 18: 3; Ro 6: 13 (here tool is
possible).—2. fig. Ro 13: 12;
2 Cor 6: 7; 10: 4.*

ὁποῖος, οἵα, οἷον correlative pron.
of what sort, as Ac 26: 29; 1 Cor
3: 13; Gal 2: 6; 1 Th 1: 9; Js 1:
24.*

ὁπότε particle when Lk 6: 3.*

ὅπου particle where Mt 6: 19f;
26: 57; Mk 9: 48; J 1: 28;
6: 62; 8: 21f; Ro 15: 20; Col 3:
11; Hb 9: 16; Js 3: 16; Rv 2:
13; in so far as 1 Cor 3: 3. ὅπου
ἄν or ἐάν wherever, whenever
Mt 26: 13; Lk 9: 57; Rv 14: 4.

ὀπτάνομαι appear Ac 1: 3.*

ὀπτασία, ας, ἡ a vision Lk 1: 22;
24: 23; Ac 26: 19; 2 Cor 12: 1.*

ὀπτός, ή, όν broiled Lk 24: 42.*

ὀπώρα, ας, ἡ fruit Rv 18: 14.*

ὅπως conjunction indicating purpose, etc. (in order) that Mt 5: 45;
23: 35; Lk 2: 35; 16: 26, 28;
Ac 9: 17, 24; 15: 17; 2 Cor 8: 11;
Hb 9: 15. After verbs of asking
that Mt 8: 34; 9: 38; Ac 25: 3;
Js 5: 16.

ὅραμα, ατος, τό vision Mt 17: 9;
Ac 7: 31; 10: 3, 17, 19; 18: 9.

ὅρασις, εως, ἡ appearance Rv 4: 3.
Vision Ac 2: 17; Rv 9: 17.*

ὁρατός, ή, όν visible Col 1: 16.*

ὁράω—1. trans.—a. see, catch
sight of, notice Mt 24: 30; 28: 7,
10; Mk 14: 62; Lk 1: 22; J 1: 18;
8: 38, 57; 16: 16f, 19, 22;
Ac 2: 17; 22: 15; 1 Cor 9: 1;
Col 2: 1, 18; 1 J 1: 1–3; 3: 2; visit
Hb 13: 23. Pass. become visible,
appear Ac 2: 3; 7: 2; 16: 9;
1 Ti 3: 16; Rv 11: 19.—b. experience, witness Lk 3: 6; 17:
22; J 1: 50; 3: 36.—c. mentally
and spiritually see, perceive,
look at Ac 8: 23; Ro 15: 21;
Hb 2: 8; Js 2: 24.—2. intrans.
look J 19: 37. See to, take care
Mt 16: 6; 27: 4, 24; Lk 12: 15;
Ac 18: 15; Hb 8: 5; Rv 19: 10.

ὀργή, ῆς, ἡ anger, wrath, indignation Mk 3: 5; J 3: 36; Ro 12: 19;
13: 4f; Eph 4: 31; 1 Ti 2: 8;
Hb 3: 11; Js 1: 19. Judgment
Lk 21: 23; Ro 5: 9; Eph 2: 3;
Col 3: 6; Rv 6: 16f; 14: 10;
punishment Ro 3: 5.

ὀργίζω pass. be angry Mt 5: 22;
18: 34; 22: 7; Lk 15: 28; Eph 4:
26; Rv 12: 17.

ὀργίλος, η, ον inclined to anger, quick-tempered Tit 1: 7.*

ὀργυιά, ᾶς, ἡ fathom = six feet Ac 27: 28.*

ὀρέγω mid. aspire to, strive for, desire, long for w. gen. 1 Ti 3: 1; 6: 10; Hb 11: 16.*

ὀρεινός, ή, όν hilly ἡ ὀρεινή the hill country Lk 1: 39, 65.*

ὄρεξις, εως, ἡ desire Ro 1: 27.*

ὀρθοποδέω act rightly, be straight-forward Gal 2: 14, though progress, advance are also possible.*

ὀρθός, ή, όν straight Hb 12: 13; upright Ac 14: 10.*

ὀρθοτομέω guide along a straight path 2 Ti 2: 15.*

ὀρθρίζω be up or get up very early in the morning Lk 21: 38.*

ὀρθρινός, ή, όν early in the morning Lk 24: 22.*

ὄρθριος, ία, ιον early in the morning Lk 24: 22 v.l.*

ὄρθρος, ου, ὁ dawn, early morning Lk 24: 1; J 8: 2; Ac 5: 21.*

ὀρθῶς adv. rightly, correctly Lk 7: 43; 10: 28; 20: 21; normally Mk 7: 35.*

ὁρίζω determine, fix, set Ac 2: 23; 11: 29; 17: 26; Hb 4: 7. τὸ ὡρισμένον Lk 22: 22. Appoint, designate, declare Ac 10: 42; 17: 31; Ro 1: 4.*

ὅριον, ου, τό boundary pl. boundaries = region, district Mt 2: 16; 4: 13; 8: 34; 15: 22, 39; 19: 1; Mk 5: 17; 7: 24, 31; 10: 1; Ac 13: 50.*

ὁρκίζω adjure, implore Mk 5: 7; Ac 19: 13; Mt 26: 63 v.l.; 1 Th 5: 27 v.l.*

ὅρκος, ου, ὁ oath Mt 5: 33; 14: 7, 9; 26: 72; Mk 6: 26; Lk 1: 73; Ac 2: 30; Hb 6: 16f; Js 5: 12.*

ὁρκωμοσία, ας, ἡ oath, taking an oath Hb 7: 20f, 28.*

ὁρμάω set out, rush (headlong) Mt 8: 32; Mk 5: 13; Lk 8: 33; Ac 7: 57; 19: 29.*

ὁρμή, ῆς, ἡ impulse, inclination, desire Ac 14: 5; Js 3: 4.*

ὅρμημα, ατος, τό violent rush Rv 18: 21.*

ὄρνεον, ου, τό bird Rv 18: 2; 19: 17, 21.*

ὄρνιξ v.l. for ὄρνις Lk 13: 34.*

ὄρνις, ιθος, ὁ and ἡ bird, specifically cock or hen Mt 23: 37; Lk 13: 34.*

ὁροθεσία, ας, ἡ fixed boundary Ac 17: 26.*

ὄρος, ους, τό mountain, hill Mt 5: 1, 14; 17: 1; 28: 16; Mk 5: 5, 11; 14: 26; Lk 3: 5; J 4: 20f; Ac 7: 30, 38; 1 Cor 13: 2; Hb 11: 38; 12: 22; Rv 6: 15f; 8: 8.

ὅρος, ου, ὁ limit ending of Mk in the Freer manuscript 7.*

ὀρύσσω dig (up) Mt 25: 18. Dig out, prepare by digging 21: 33; Mk 12: 1. Dig (a hole) Mt 25: 18 v.l.*

ὀρφανός, ή, όν orphaned lit. deprived of one's parents as noun orphan Mk 12: 40 v.l.; Js 1: 27. Fig. J 14: 18.*

ὀρχέομαι dance Mt 11: 17; 14: 6; Mk 6: 22; Lk 7: 32.*

ὅς, ἥ, ὅ relative pronoun who, which, what, that usually agreeing with its antecedent in gender and number; its case is determined by the construction within its own clause Mt 2: 9; Lk 9: 9; J 1: 47; Ac 13: 6; 17: 3; Ro 2: 29. At times, however, the relative is attracted or assimilated to the case of its antecedent Mt 18: 19; 24: 50b; Lk 2: 20; J 7: 31; Ac 1: 22; 3: 25; 1 Cor 6: 19.—With prepositions: ἀντί: ἀνθ' ὧν because Lk 1: 20; 19: 44; Ac 12: 23; 2 Th 2: 10, but therefore Lk 12: 3. εἰς: εἰς ὅ to this end 2 Th 1: 11. ἐπί: ἐφ' ᾧ because Ro 5: 12; 2 Cor 5: 4; Phil 3: 12, but for 4: 10. χάριν: οὗ χάριν therefore Lk 7: 47.—At times there is a demonstrative pronoun 'concealed' within the relative pronoun, so that it means *the one who*, etc. Mt 10: 27, 38; Mk 9: 40; 15: 12; J 5: 21; 18: 26; Ro 6: 16; 1 Cor 10: 30; Gal 1: 8. In still other instances the relative pronoun functions as a demonstrative ὅς δέ *but he* (lit. *that one*) Mk 15: 23; J 5: 11. ὅς μὲν . . . ὅς δέ *the one . . . the other*, etc. Mt 22: 5; Lk 23: 33; Ac 27: 44; Ro 14: 5; 1 Cor 11: 21; 2 Cor 2: 16; Jd 22f. ὃ μὲν . . . ὃ δέ *this . . . that* Ro 9: 21. ἃ μὲν . . . ἃ δέ *some . . . others* 2 Ti 2: 20.

ὁσάκις adv. *as often as* 1 Cor 11: 25f; Rv 11: 6.*

ὅσγε = ὅς γε.

ὅσιος, ία, ον *devout, pleasing to God, holy* 1 Ti 2: 8; Tit 1: 8. Of God or Christ *holy* Ac 2: 27; 13: 35; Hb 7: 26; Rv 15: 4; 16: 5. τὰ ὅσια *sure decrees* Ac 13: 34.*

ὁσιότης, τητος, ἡ *holiness* of life Lk 1: 75; Eph 4: 24.*

ὁσίως adv. *in a holy manner* 1 Th 2: 10.*

ὀσμή, ῆς, ἡ *fragrance, odor* lit. J 12: 3. Fig. 2 Cor 2: 14, 16; Eph 5: 2; Phil 4: 18.*

ὅσος, η, ον *as great, how great; as far, how far; as long, how long; as much, how much* correlative with πόσος, τοσοῦτος.—**1.** of space and time: τὸ μῆκος αὐτῆς (τοσοῦτόν ἐστιν), ὅσον τὸ πλάτος *its length is as great as its breadth* Rv 21: 16. ἐφ' ὅσ. χρόνον *as long as* Ro 7: 1; 1 Cor 7: 39; Gal 4: 1; also ἐφ' ὅσον Mt 9: 15; 2 Pt 1: 13 and ὅσον χρόνον Mk 2: 19 with the same meaning. ἔτι μικρὸν ὅσον ὅσον *in a very little while* Hb 10: 37. ὅσον ὅσον *a short distance* Lk 5: 3 v.l.—**2.** of quantity and number *how much (many)*, *as much (many)* as ὅσον ἤθελον *as*

much as they wanted J 6: 11. With πάντες (ἅπαντες) *all who* Lk 4: 40; J 10: 8; Ac 3: 24; 5: 36f, πάντα ὅσα *everything that* Mt 13: 46; Mk 11: 24; Lk 18: 12, 22. Even without πάντες, ὅσοι has the meaning *all that* or *who* J 1: 12; Ac 9: 13, 39; Ac 10: 45; Ro 8: 14; Gal 6: 12, 16; Phil 4: 8. ὅσοι alone *all those who* Mt 14: 36; Mk 6: 56; Ac 4: 6, 34; Ro 2: 12. ὅσα *everything that, whatever* Mt 17: 12; Mk 5: 19f; Lk 8: 39; Ac 14: 27; 2 Ti 1: 18. —**3.** of measure and degree: ὅσον . . ., μᾶλλον περισσότερον *as much as . . ., so much the more* Mk 7: 36. πλείονος . . ., καθ' ὅσον πλείονα *as much more . . . as* Hb 3: 3. τοσούτῳ . . . ὅσῳ (*by*) *as much . . . as* 1: 4. ὅσα . . . τοσοῦτον *to the degree that . . . to the same degree* Rv 18: 7.

ὅσπερ a slightly strengthened form of ὅς.

ὀστέον, ου, contracted **ὀστοῦν, οῦ, τό** *bone* Mt 23: 27; Lk 24: 39; J 19: 36; Hb 11: 22; Eph 5: 30 v.l.*

ὅστις, ἥτις, ὅ τι *whoever, whatever, every one who, everything that* Mt 5: 39, 41; 13: 12; 23: 12; Lk 14: 27; Ro 11: 4; Gal 5: 4, 10; Js 2: 10. Often equivalent to ὅς, ἥ, ὅ *who* Mt 27: 62; Mk 15: 7; Lk 2: 4; 8: 26; Ac 16: 12; 21: 4; 23: 14, 21, 33; Hb 9: 2, 9, though at times ὅστις emphasizes a characteristic quality οἵτινες μετήλλαξαν *since indeed they had exchanged* Ro 1: 25; cf. 2: 15; 6: 2. οἵτινες οὐκ ἔγνωσαν *who, to be sure, have not learned* Rv 2: 24.

ὀστράκινος, η, ον *made of earth* or *clay, earthen(ware)* 2 Cor 4: 7; 2 Ti 2: 20.*

ὄσφρησις, εως, ἡ *sense of smell* 1 Cor 12: 17.*

ὀσφῦς, ύος, ἡ—**1.** *waist* Mt 3: 4;

Mk 1: 6; Lk 12: 35; Eph 6: 14;
1 Pt 1: 13.—**2.** *loins* as the place
of the reproductive organs Ac 2:
30; Hb 7: 5, 10.*

ὅταν temporal particle *at the time
that, whenever, when* Mt 5: 11;
24: 15; 26: 29; Mk 3: 11; J 8:
28; 2 Cor 12: 10; 1 Th 5: 3;
Rv 4: 9. *Whenever, as often as,
every time that* Mt 6: 2, 5f, 16;
Mk 13: 11; 14: 7; Lk 12: 11;
14: 12f.

ὅτε temporal particle *when, while,
as long as* Mt 9: 25; 21: 34;
Mk 1: 32; 14: 12; 15: 41; Lk 13:
35; 17: 22; J 4: 21, 23; Ac 12: 6;
Ro 13: 11; 1 Cor 13: 11; Gal 1:
15; Hb 9: 17.

ὅτι conjunction—**1.** *that*, introducing an indirect statement,
etc. Mt 26: 54; 28: 7; Mk 11:
32; Ac 20: 26; 27: 10; 1 Cor 1:
15; 16: 15; 2 Cor 1: 23; 1 J 4:
9, 10, 13. *So that* expressing
result J 7: 35; 14: 22; 1 Ti 6: 7;
Hb 2: 6. τί ὅτι; *what* (is it) *that,
why?* Lk 2: 49; Ac 5: 4, 9;
Mk 2: 16 v.l. οὐχ ὅτι *not that,
not as if* J 6: 46; 7: 22; 2 Cor 1:
24; Phil 3: 12; 2 Th 3: 9.—
2. introducing direct discourse.
In this case it is not to be translated into English, but to be
represented by quotation marks:
ὁμολογήσω αὐτοῖς ὅτι οὐδέποτε
ἔγνων ὑμᾶς *I will declare to
them, 'I never knew you'* Mt 7:
23. Cf. Mt 26: 72–75; Mk 1: 37;
2: 16; Lk 1: 25, 61; J 1: 20, 32;
Ac 15: 1; Ro 3: 8; 1 J 4: 20.—
3. as a causal conjunction
because, since Mt 5: 3ff; Mk 5: 9;
Lk 10: 13; J 1: 30, 50a; 20: 29;
Ro 6: 15; 9: 32; 1 Cor 12: 15f.
For Mt 7: 13; Lk 9: 12; J 1:
16f; 1 Cor 1: 25; 4: 9; 2 Cor 4: 6;
7: 8, 14.

ὅτου gen. sing. masc. and neut. of
ὅστις.

οὖ the genitive of ὅς, functioning
as an adv. *where* Mt 2: 9; 18:

20; Lk 4: 16f; 10: 1; 23: 53;
Ac 1: 13; 16: 13; Ro 4: 15;
5: 20; 2 Cor 3: 17; *to which*
Mt 28: 16; Lk 24: 28.

οὐ (before consonants), **οὐκ** (before
a vowel with smooth breathing),
οὐχ (before a vowel with rough
breathing) negative adv.—**1.** οὔ
with an accent means *no* Mt 5:
37; 13: 29; J 1: 21; 7: 12; 21: 5;
2 Cor 1: 17; Js 5: 12.—**2.** οὐ as
an enclitic means *not* in a wide
variety of uses, examples of
which may be found in the
following passages: Mt 1: 25;
7: 21; Mk 4: 25; Ac 12: 9;
13: 10; 17: 4, 12; Ro 7: 7;
1 Cor 15: 51; 2 Cor 2: 11;
Hb 12: 25.—οὐ is regularly used
with the indicative, but it is
found with the participle in the
following passages Mt 22: 11;
Lk 6: 42; Gal 4: 8, 27; Hb 11: 1,
35; 1 Pt 2: 10.—**3.** οὐ is used in
direct questions when an affirmative answer is expected οὐκ
ἀκούεις; *you hear, do you not?*
Mt 27: 13. Cf. 6: 26, 30; 17: 24;
Mk 6: 3; Lk 11: 40; J 6: 70;
Ac 9: 21.—**4.** in combination
with other negatives—**a.**
strengthening the negation Mt
22: 16; Mk 5: 37; especially Lk
23: 53; J 6: 63; 15: 5; Ac 8: 39;
2 Cor 11: 9. For οὐ μή see μή 4.—
b. destroying the force of the
negation. In questions, if the
verb is already negatived (by
οὐ), the negation can be invali-
dated by μή used as an interrogative particle (see μή 3); the
stage is thus set for an affirmative answer: μὴ οὐκ ἤκουσαν
*surely they have heard, have they
not?* Ro 10: 18, cf. 19. μὴ οἰκίας
οὐκ ἔχετε; *you have houses, do
you not?* 1 Cor 11: 22; cf. 9: 4f.

οὐά interjection *aha!* as an expression of scornful wonder
Mk 15: 29. Cf. Mt 11: 26 v.l.*

οὐαί interjection *woe, alas!* Mt 11:

21; Mk 14: 21; Lk 6: 24f; 17: 1;
21: 23; Jd 11; Rv 12: 12; 18: 10,
16, 19. As noun 1 Cor 9: 16;
Rv 9: 12; 11: 14.

οὐδαμῶς adv. *by no means* Mt 2:
6.*

οὐδέ negative conjunction—**1.** *and
not, nor* Mt 6: 20, 26, 28; Mk 8:
17; Lk 6: 43f; J 8: 42; Ac 4: 12,
34; Rv 5: 3.—**2.** *also not, not
either, neither* Mt 6: 15; Mk 16:
13; Lk 16: 31; 23: 15; J 15: 4;
Ro 4: 15; 1 Cor 15: 13, 16.—
3. *not even* Mt 6: 29; 24: 36;
Lk 12: 26; 18: 13; J 1: 3; 21: 25;
Ac 19: 2; 1 Cor 5: 1; 14: 21;
Hb 8: 4.

οὐδείς, οὐδεμία, οὐδέν—**1.** as an
adj. *no* Lk 4: 24; 16: 13; J 16:
29; 18: 38; Ac 25: 18; 27: 22;
1 Cor 8: 4a; Phil 4: 15.—**2.** as a
substantive—**a.** οὐδείς *no one,
nobody* Mt 6: 24; Mk 7: 24;
Lk 5: 36f, 39; 23: 53; J 1: 18;
13: 28; 16: 5; Ac 5: 13.—
b. οὐδέν *nothing* Mt 5: 13;
17: 20; Mk 7: 15; 14: 60f; Lk 18:
34; J 3: 27; Ac 18: 17; 1 Cor 9:
15a.—The acc. οὐδέν *in no
respect, in no way* Ac 15: 9;
25: 10; 1 Cor 13: 3; 2 Cor 12:
11a; Gal 4: 1, 12.—In the sense
worthless, meaningless, invalid
Mt 23: 16, 18; J 8: 54; Ac 21:
24; 1 Cor 7: 19; 2 Cor 12: 11b.

οὐδέποτε adv. *never* Mt 7: 23; 21:
16, 42; 26: 33; Mk 2: 12; Lk 15:
29; J 7: 46; Ac 10: 14; 1 Cor 13:
8; Hb 10: 1, 11.

οὐδέπω adv. *not yet* J 7: 39; 20: 9.
οὐ . . . οὐδεὶς οὐδέπω *no one
ever* Lk 23: 53 v.l. οὐδέπω οὐδείς
J 19: 41; cf. Ac 8: 16.*

οὐθείς a late Greek form for
οὐδείς.

οὐκέτι adv. *no more, no longer, no
further*—**1.** lit., of time Mt 19: 6;
Mk 9: 8; Lk 15: 19, 21; J 4: 42;
6: 66; 14: 19; *never again* Ro 6:
9a; Ac 20: 25, 38; 2 Cor 1: 23.
οὐκέτι οὐ μή *never again* Mk 14:

25; Rv 18: 14.—**2.** in a non-
temporal use *then not* Ro 11: 6a;
14: 15; Gal 3: 18. Likewise
νυνὶ οὐκέτι Ro 7: 17.

οὐκοῦν adv., introducing a question *so, then* J 18: 37.*

Οὐλαμμαούς v.l. for 'Εμμαοῦς in
Lk 24: 13, influenced by the
earlier name of Bethel in the
LXX of Gen 28: 19.*

οὐ μή see μή 4.

οὖν particle, never found at the
beginning of a clause; its
sense is inferential and trans-
itional. Its meaning varies with
the context, and sometimes οὖν
may be left untranslated.—
1. inferential *therefore, consequently, accordingly, then* Mt 1:
17; 3: 8; 12: 12, 26; 13: 28;
Mk 10: 9; Lk 11: 35; 22: 70;
J 6: 13; Ac 5: 41; 21: 22;
Ro 3: 9; 5: 1; 1 Cor 3: 5; 4: 16;
Hb 4: 16; 3 J 8.—**2.** In historical
narrative οὖν serves—**a.** to
resume a subject *so, as has been
said* Lk 3: 7 (connecting with
verse 3). Cf. 19: 12; J 4: 6, 28;
Ac 8: 25; 12: 5; 1 Cor 8: 4;
11: 20.—**b.** to indicate a transition to something new *now,
then* J 1: 22; 2: 18, 20; 7: 25,
28, 33, 35, 40; Ac 25: 1.—**c.** to
indicate a response *in reply, in
turn* is possible in J 4: 9, 48;
6: 53 and elsewhere.—**3.** Other
possible meanings are *certainly,
really*, etc. Mt 3: 10; J 20: 30;
1 Cor 3: 5 and *but, however* J 9:
18; Ac 23: 21; 25: 4; 28: 5;
Ro 10: 14.

οὔπω adv. of time *not yet* Mt 24: 6;
J 2: 4; 6: 17; 8: 20, 57; 1 Cor 3:
2; Phil 3: 13; Hb 2: 8; Rv 17:
10, 12. οὐδεὶς οὔπω *no one ever*
Mk 11: 2; Lk 23: 53.

οὐρά, ᾶς, ἡ *tail* Rv 9: 10, 19; 12:
4.*

οὐράνιος, ον *heavenly, coming
from* or *living in heaven* Mt 5:
48; 6: 14, 26, 32; 15: 13; 18: 35;

23: 9; Lk 2: 13; Ac 26: 19;
1 Cor 15: 47 v.l.*

οὐρανόθεν adv. of place *from heaven* Ac 14: 17; 26: 13.*

οὐρανός, οῦ, ὁ *heaven* Mt 5: 16, 18, 45; 23: 22; Mk 1: 10; 13: 31; Lk 2: 15; J 3: 13, 31; Ac 7: 55f; Hb 12: 23; Col 1: 5; Rv 3: 12; more than one heaven 2 Cor 12: 2; Eph 4: 10; Hb 1: 10. *Sky* Mt 11: 23; 16: 2f; Lk 4: 25; 10: 18; 17: 29; Ac 2: 19; Rv 16: 21. Fig., synonymous with God Mt 3: 2; 21: 25; 22: 2; Lk 15: 18, 21.

Οὐρβανός, οῦ, ὁ *Urbanus* Ro 16:9.*

Οὐρίας, ου, ὁ *Uriah* (2 Sam 11; 12: 24) Mt 1: 6.*

οὖς, ὠτός, τό *ear*—**1.** lit. Mk 7: 33; Lk 12: 3; 22: 50; Ac 7: 57; 1 Cor 2: 9; Js 5: 4; 1 Pt 3: 12.— **2.** transferred to mental and spiritual understanding τοῖς ὠσὶ βαρέως ἀκούειν *be hard of hearing* = comprehend slowly or not at all Mt 13: 15. Cf. 11: 15; Mk 8: 18; Lk 9: 44; Ac 7: 51; Rv 2: 7, 11.

οὐσία, ας, ἡ *property, wealth* Lk 15: 12f.*

οὖτε adv. *and not.* οὖτε . . . οὖτε *neither . . . nor* Mt 6: 20; 12: 32; Mk 12: 25; Lk 20: 35; Ac 25: 8; Ro 8: 38f; 1 Th 2: 5f; Rv 9: 20. οὖτε ἄντλημα ἔχεις *you have no bucket* J 4: 11; cf. 3 J 10.

οὖτος, αὖτη, τοῦτο demonstrative pronoun, used as adjective and as substantive *this.*—**1.** as substantive Mt 3: 17; 26: 26, 28; Lk 5: 21; J 6: 29, 39f; Ac 7: 35; 9: 21; 25: 25; 1 Cor 1: 12; Gal 4: 24; Eph 3: 14; Hb 2: 14; Js 1: 23; 1 Pt 5: 12. *This one, he,* etc. Mt 3: 3; Lk 1: 32; J 1: 2, 41; Ac 21: 24; 1 Cor 2: 2; 2 Ti 3: 5f, 8; Hb 8: 3. *This (very) one* J 9: 9; Ac 4: 10; 9: 20; 1 J 5: 6; 2 Pt 2: 17. καὶ τοῦτο *and at that, and especially* Ro 13: 11;

1 Cor 6: 6, 8; Eph 2: 8. τοῦτο μὲν . . . τοῦτο δὲ *sometimes . . . sometimes, not only . . . but also* Hb 10: 33.—**2.** as an adj., coming before the substantive with the article between ἐν τούτῳ τῷ αἰῶνι *in this age* Mt 12: 32. Cf. 16: 18; Lk 7: 44; J 4: 15; Ac 1: 11; Hb 7: 1; Rv 20: 14. Following a substantive that has the article ἐκ τῶν λίθων τούτων *from these stones* Mt 3: 9. Cf. 5: 19; Mk 12: 16; Lk 11: 31; 21: 3; Ro 15: 28; 1 Cor 11: 26; Eph 3: 8; Rv 2: 24. —When the article is lacking, either the demonstrative or the noun belongs to the predicate τρίτην ταύτην ἡμέραν *this is the third day* Lk 24: 21. Cf. 1: 36; J 2: 11; 4: 54; 2 Cor 13: 1.

οὖτω and **οὖτως** adv. *in this manner, thus, so* Mt 5: 16, 19; 12: 40; Mk 7: 18; 10: 43; 14: 59; Lk 11: 30; 24: 24; J 3: 8; 11: 48; 21: 1; Ac 8: 32; Ro 1: 15; 12: 4f; Gal 3: 3; Rv 16: 18. *As follows* Mt 2: 5. *Without further ado, simply* J 4: 6, perhaps 13: 25. ὁ μὲν οὖτως, ὁ δὲ οὖτως *the one in one way, the other in another* 1 Cor 7: 7.

οὐχ see οὐ.

οὐχί (strengthened form of οὐ) negative adv.—**1.** *not* J 13: 10f; 14: 22; 1 Cor 5: 2; 6: 1; 10: 29. —**2.** *no, by no means* Lk 1: 60; 12: 51; 13: 3, 5; 16: 30; J 9: 9; Ro 3: 27.—**3.** interrogative word in questions that expect an affirmative answer *not* Mt 5: 46; 6: 25; 10: 29; Lk 6: 39; 12: 6; 17: 8; J 11: 9; Ro 3: 29.

ὀφειλέτης, ου, ὁ *debtor*—**1.** lit. Mt 18: 24.—**2.** fig. *one who is obligated* ὀφειλέτην εἶναι *be under obligation* Ro 1: 14; 8: 12; 15: 27; Gal 5: 3. *One who is guilty* of a misdeed, *one who is culpable* or *at fault* Mt 6: 12; *sinner* Lk 13: 4.*

ὀφειλή, ῆς, ἡ *debt*—1. lit. Mt 18: 32.—2. fig. *obligation, duty, one's due* 1 Cor 7: 3. Pl., of taxes, etc. Ro 13: 7.*

ὀφείλημα, ατος, τό *debt, what is owed, one's due* Ro 4: 4. *Debt*= sin Mt 6: 12.*

ὀφείλω *owe, be indebted*—1. lit., of financial debts Mt 18: 28, 30, 34; Lk 7: 41; 16: 5, 7; Phlm 18.— 2. fig.—a. generally *owe, be indebted* Ro 13: 8.—*Be obligated, one must, one ought* Lk 17: 10; J 19: 7; Ac 17: 29; Ro 15: 1; 1 Cor 9: 10; 11: 7; 2 Cor 12: 11, 14; 2 Th 1: 3.—b. ὀφείλει *he is obligated, bound* (by his oath) Mt 23: 16, 18. *Commit a sin* Lk 11: 4.

ὄφελον (2 aor. act. participle of ὀφείλω) a fixed form, functioning as a particle to introduce unattainable wishes *O that, would that* 1 Cor 4: 8; 2 Cor 11: 1; Gal 5: 12; Rv 3: 15.*

ὄφελος, ους, τό *benefit, good* 1 Cor 15: 32; Js 2: 14, 16.*

ὀφθαλμοδουλία, ας, ἡ *eye-service*, service performed merely to attract attention Eph 6: 6; Col 3: 22.*

ὀφθαλμός, οῦ, ὁ *eye*—1. lit. Mt 6: 23; 7: 3ff; Mk 9: 47; Lk 11: 34; 1 Cor 2: 9; 12: 16f; 15: 52; Hb 4: 13; 1 J 1: 1; 2: 16; Rv 4: 6, 8; 19: 12.—2. transferred to mental and spiritual understanding: Mt 13: 16; Mk 8: 18; Lk 19: 42; Ro 11: 8; Gal 3: 1; Eph 1: 18.

ὀφθείς, ὀφθήσομαι 1 aor. pass. participle, fut. pass. ind. of ὁράω.

ὄφις, εως, ὁ *snake, serpent*—1. lit. Mt 7: 10; 10: 16; Mk 16: 18; Lk 10: 19; 11: 11; J 3: 14; 1 Cor 10: 9; Rv 9: 19.—2. fig. and symbolic Mt 23: 33; 2 Cor 11: 3; Rv 12: 9, 14f; 20: 2.*

ὀφρῦς, ύος, ἡ lit. *eyebrow*, then *brow, edge* of a cliff or hill Lk 4: 29.*

ὀχετός, οῦ, ὁ *drain, sewer* Mk 7: 19 v.l.*

ὀχλέω *trouble, disturb* pass. Ac 5: 16; Lk 6: 18 v.l.*

ὀχλοποιέω *form a mob* Ac 17: 5.*

ὄχλος, ου, ὁ—1. *crowd, throng*, (*multitude*) Mt 9: 23, 25; 21: 8; Mk 2: 4, 13; 6: 34; Lk 5: 1; 12: 13; 19: 3; Ac 8: 6; 14: 11, 13, 18f; 21: 27; Rv 17: 15.— 2. *the* (*common*) *people, populace* Mt 14: 5; 15: 10; 21: 26, 46; Mk 11: 18; 12: 12; Ac 24: 12; *rabble* J 7: 49.—3. *large number* Lk 5: 29; 6: 17; Ac 1: 15; 6: 7.

Ὀχοζίας, ου, ὁ *Ahaziah* (2 Kings 8: 24) Mt 1: 8 v.l.; Lk 3: 23ff v.l.*

ὀχύρωμα, ατος, τό *stronghold, fortress* 2 Cor 10: 4.*

ὀψάριον, ου, τό *fish* J 6: 9, 11; 21: 9f, 13.*

ὀψέ adv. *late* (*in the day*), *in the evening* Mk 11: 11, 19; 13: 35. As improper prep. w. gen. *after* Mt 28: 1.*

ὀψία, ας, ἡ see ὄψιος 2.

ὄψιμος, ον *late* in the season ὑετὸς ὄψιμος *the late* (i.e. spring) *rain* Js 5: 7 v.l. The text has the substantive (ὁ) ὄψιμος in the same meaning.*

ὄψιος, α, ον *late*—1. adj. Mk 11: 11 v.l.—2. as substantive ἡ ὀψία *evening* Mt 8: 16; 14: 15, 23; 16: 2; 27: 57; Mk 1: 32; 4: 35; 15: 42; J 6: 16; 20: 19.

ὄψις, εως, ἡ—1. *outward appearance, aspect* J 7: 24.—2. *face* J 11: 44. Either *appearance* or *face* is possible for Rv 1: 16.*

ὀψώνιον, ου, τό *wages, pay, salary, compensation* Lk 3: 14; Ro 6: 23; 1 Cor 9: 7; 2 Cor 11: 8.*

Π

παγιδεύω *entrap* fig. Mt 22: 15.*

παγίς, ίδος, ἡ *trap, snare* lit. Lk 21: 35. Fig. Ro 11: 9; 1 Ti 3: 7; 6: 9; 2 Ti 2: 26.*

πάγος see Ἄρειος πάγος.

παθεῖν, παθών 2 aor. inf. and participle of πάσχω.

πάθημα, ατος, τό—1. *suffering, misfortune* Ro 8: 18; 2 Cor 1: 5–7; Phil 3: 10; Col 1: 24; 2 Ti 3: 11; Hb 2: 9f; 10: 32; 1 Pt 4: 13; 5: 1, 9. τὰ εἰς Χριστὸν παθήματα *the sufferings of Christ* 1: 11.—2. *passion* Ro 7: 5; Gal 5: 24.*

παθητός, ή, όν *subject to suffering* Ac 26: 23.*

πάθος, ους, τό *passion*, especially of a sexual nature Ro 1: 26; Col 3: 5; 1 Th 4: 5.*

παιδαγωγός, οῦ, ὁ *attendant (slave), custodian, guide*, lit. 'boy-leader', whose duty it was to superintend the conduct of the boys in the family to which he was attached 1 Cor 4: 15; Gal 3: 24f.*

παιδάριον, ου, τό *little boy, boy, child* Mt 11: 16 v.l. For J 6: 9 *youth* or *young slave* are also possible.*

παιδεία, ας, ἡ *training, discipline* Eph 6: 4; 2 Ti 3: 16; Hb 12: 5, 7, 8, 11.*

παιδευτής, οῦ, ὁ *instructor, teacher* Ro 2: 20; *one who disciplines, a corrector* Hb 12: 9.*

παιδεύω—1. *instruct, train, educate* Ac 7: 22; 22: 3.—2. *correct, give guidance to* 2 Ti 2: 25; Tit 2: 12.—3. *discipline* with punishment 1 Cor 11: 32; 2 Cor 6: 9; 1 Ti 1: 20; Hb 12: 6f, 10; Rv 3: 19. *Whip, scourge* Lk 23: 16, 22.*

παιδιόθεν adv. *from childhood* Mk 9: 21.*

παιδίον, ου, τό—1. *very young child, infant* Mt 2: 8f, 11; Lk 1: 59, 66; 2: 17; J 16: 21; Hb 11: 23.—2. *child* Mt 14: 21; 18: 2, 4f; Mk 5: 39–41; 9: 24, 36f; Lk 18: 17; J 4: 49.—3. fig. *child* Mt 18: 3; J 21: 5; 1 Cor 14: 20; Hb 2: 13f; 1 J 2: 18.

παιδίσκη, ης, ἡ *maid, servant-girl, female slave* Mt 26: 69; Mk 14: 66, 69; Lk 12: 45; 22: 56; J 18: 17; Ac 12: 13; 16: 16, 19 v.l.; Gal 4: 22f, 30f.*

παιδόθεν adv. *from childhood* Mk 9: 21 v.l.*

παίζω *play, amuse oneself, dance* 1 Cor 10: 7.*

παῖς, παιδός, ὁ or ἡ *child*—1. ὁ παῖς—a. with reference to a relation between two human beings *boy, youth* Mt 2: 16; 17: 18; 21: 15; Mk 9: 21 v.l.; Lk 2: 43; 9: 42; Ac 20: 12. *Son* J 4: 51; *son* is also possible for Mt 8: 6, 8, 13, but even more probable is *servant, slave* Lk 7: 7; 12: 45; 15: 26. *Courtier, attendant* Mt 14: 2.—b. in relation to God: of men as God's *servants, slaves* Lk 1: 54, 69; Ac 4: 25.—Of Christ: *servant* Mt 12: 18. For Ac 3: 13, 26; 4: 27, 30 either *servant* or *son* is possible.— 2. ἡ παῖς *girl* Lk 8: 51, 54.*

παίω *strike, hit, wound* Mt 26: 68; Mk 14: 47; Lk 22: 64; J 18: 10; *sting* Rv 9: 5.*

Πακατιανός, ή, όν *Pacatian, in Pacatia* a later name for the part of Phrygia in which Laodicea was located 1 Ti subscription.*

πάλαι adv. *long ago* Mt 11: 21; Lk 10: 13; Hb 1: 1; Jd 4; *former* 2 Pt 1: 9. *For a long time* 2 Cor 12: 19. *Already* Mk 15: 44.

παλαιός, ά, όν *old* Mt 13: 52; Mk 2: 21f; Lk 5: 39; Ro 6: 6;

1 Cor 5: 7f; 2 Cor 3: 14; Eph 4: 22; Col 3: 9; 1 J 2: 7.

παλαιότης, ητος, ἡ *age, obsoleteness* Ro 7: 6.*

παλαιόω act. *declare* or *treat as obsolete* Hb 8: 13a. Pass. *become old* Lk 12: 33; Hb 1: 11; 8: 13b.*

πάλη, ης, ἡ *struggle* fig. Eph 6: 12.*

παλιγγενεσία, ας, ἡ *rebirth, regeneration* Mt 19: 28; Tit 3: 5.*

πάλιν adv.—**1.** *back* Mk 5: 21; 14: 39; J 6: 15; 11: 7; Ac 18: 21; 2 Cor 1: 16; Gal 1: 17; 4: 9; Phil 1: 26.—**2.** *again, once more, anew* Mt 4: 8; 20: 5; 26: 42; 27: 50; Mk 2: 13; Lk 23: 20; Ac 17: 32; Ro 8: 15; 1 Cor 7: 5; Gal 2: 18.—**3.** *furthermore, thereupon* Mt 5: 33; 19: 24; Lk 13: 20; J 12: 39; 19: 37; Ro 15: 10–12; Hb 1: 5; 2: 13.—**4.** *on the other hand, in turn* Mt 4: 7; Lk 6: 43; 1 Cor 12: 21; 2 Cor 10: 7.—**5.** πάλιν in Mk 15: 13; J 18: 40 may be *back*; several other possibilities exist.

παλινγενεσία see παλιγγενεσία.

παμπληθεί adv. *all together* Lk 23: 18.*

πάμπολυς, παμπόλλη, πάμπολυ *very great* Mk 8: 1 v.l.*

Παμφυλία, ας, ἡ *Pamphylia*, a province along the Mediterranean seacoast of Asia Minor Ac 2: 10; 13: 13; 14: 24; 15: 38; 16: 6 v.l.; 27: 5.*

πανδοκεῖον see πανδοχεῖον.

πανδοκεύς see πανδοχεύς.

πανδοχεῖον, ου, τό *inn* Lk 10: 34.*

πανδοχεύς, έως, ὁ *inn-keeper* Lk 10: 35.*

πανήγυρις, εως, ἡ *festal gathering* Hb 12: 22.*

πανοικεί or **πανοικί** *with one's whole household* Ac 16: 34.*

πανοπλία, ας, ἡ *full armor* of a heavy-armed soldier, *panoply* lit. Lk 11: 22. Fig. Eph 6: 11, 13.*

πανουργία, ας, ἡ *cunning, craftiness, trickery* Lk 20: 23; 1 Cor 3:

19; 2 Cor 4: 2; 11: 3; Eph 4: 14.*

πανοῦργος, ον *clever, crafty, sly* 2 Cor 12: 16.*

πανπληθεί see παμπληθεί.

πανταχῇ adv. *everywhere* Ac 21: 28.*

πανταχόθεν adv. *from every direction* Mk 1: 45 v.l.*

πανταχοῦ adv. *everywhere* Mk 16: 20; Lk 9: 6; Ac 17: 30; 24: 3; 28: 22; 1 Cor 4: 17. *In all directions* Mk 1: 28.*

παντελής, ές *complete, perfect, absolute*; εἰς τὸ παντελές can mean *completely, wholly* or *forever, for all time* in Hb 7: 25. In Lk 13: 11 it may mean *fully* or *at all*.*

πάντη adv. *in every way* Ac 24: 3.*

πάντοθεν adv. *from all directions* Mk 1: 45; Lk 19: 43; *on all sides, entirely* Hb 9: 4.*

παντοκράτωρ, ορος, ὁ *the Almighty, All-Powerful, Omnipotent (One)* only of God 2 Cor 6: 18; Rv 1: 8; 4: 8; 11: 17; 15: 3; 16: 7, 14; 19: 6, 15; 21: 22.*

πάντοτε adv. *always, at all times* Mt 26: 11; Lk 15: 31; J 7: 6; Ro 1: 10; 1 Cor 1: 4; 2 Cor 2: 14; Hb 7: 25.

πάντως adv.—**1.** *by all means, certainly, probably, doubtless* Lk 4: 23; Ac 18: 21 v.l.; 21: 22; 28: 4; 1 Cor 9: 10.—**2.** *at least* or *by any and all means* 1 Cor 9: 22.—**3.** with a neg. *not at all* Ro 3: 9; 1 Cor 16: 12; *by no means* 5: 10.*

παρά prep. with three cases—**1.** w. gen. *from (the side of)* Mt 18: 19; Mk 12: 2; 14: 43; Lk 2: 1; J 6: 46; 8: 26, 40; 16: 27; Ac 9: 2, 14; Gal 1: 12; Eph 6: 8; 2 Ti 3: 14; Js 1: 5; Rv 3: 18. παρὰ κυρίου *at the Lord's command* Lk 1: 45. παρὰ θεοῦ *by God* J 1: 6. τὰ παρ' αὐτῆς *her property, what she had* Mk 5: 26; τὰ παρ' αὐτῶν *their gifts, what they give* Lk 10: 7. οἱ παρ' αὐτοῦ *his family, his relatives* Mk 3: 21.—**2.** w. dat. *at or by the side of, beside, near, with* Mt 6: 1; 22: 25; Lk 2: 52; 9: 47; 11: 37; J 14: 25; 19: 25; Ac 9: 43; 21: 7, 16; Ro 2: 11; 1 Cor 16: 2; Eph 6: 9; Col 4: 16. *For* Mt 19: 26. *In the sight or judgment of* Ro 2: 13; 12: 16; 1 Pt 2: 4, 20. —**3.** w. acc.—**a.** of space *to* (*the side of*) Mt 15: 29; Mk 2: 13; Ac 16: 13. *By, along* Mt 4: 18; Mk 4: 1; Ac 10: 6, 32. *Near, at* Lk 7: 38; 17: 16; Ac 5: 2; 22: 3. *On* Mt 13: 4, 19; Mk 4: 15; Lk 18: 35; Hb 11: 12.—**b.** in a comparative sense: *in comparison to, more than, beyond* Lk 3: 13; 13: 2, 4; Ro 14: 5; Hb 2: 7, 9; 9: 23; 12: 24. *Instead of, rather than, to the exclusion of* Lk 18: 14; Ro 1: 25; Hb 1: 9. *Beyond* 2 Cor 8: 3.—**c.** other uses: *because of* 1 Cor 12: 15f. *Against, contrary to* Ac 18: 13; Ro 1: 26; 4: 18; 11: 24; 16: 17; Gal 1: 8f. *Less* 2 Cor 11: 24.

παραβαίνω—**1.** *turn aside* Ac 1: 25.—**2.** *transgress, break* Mt 15: 2f; 2 J 9 v.l.*

παραβάλλω—**1.** *compare* Mk 4: 30 v.l.—**2.** *come near* (*by ship*) Ac 20: 15.*

παράβασις, εως, ἡ *overstepping, transgression, violation* Ro 2: 23; 4: 15; 5: 14; Gal 3: 19; 1 Ti 2: 14; Hb 2: 2; 9: 15.*

παραβάτης, ου, ὁ *transgressor* Ro 2: 25, 27; Gal 2: 18; Js 2: 9, 11.*

παραβιάζομαι *urge strongly, prevail upon* Lk 24: 29; Ac 16: 15.*

παραβολεύομαι *expose to danger, risk* w. dat. Phil 2: 30.*

παραβολή, ῆς, ἡ—**1.** *symbol, type, figure* Hb 9: 9; 11: 19.—**2.** *parable, illustration* Mt 13: 18, 24, 31, 33, 53; Mk 4: 2, 11, 30, 34; Lk 8: 9; 13: 6; 18: 1.

παραβουλεύομαι *be careless, have no concern* Phil 2: 30 v.l.*

παραγγελία, ας, ἡ *order, command*

Ac 5: 28; 16: 24. *Instruction* 1 Th 4: 2; 1 Ti 1: 5, 18.*

παραγγέλλω *give orders, command, instruct, direct* Mt 10: 5; Mk 6: 8; 8: 6; Ac 15: 5; 16: 18, 23; 23: 22; 1 Cor 11: 17; 1 Th 4: 11; 2 Th 3: 4; 1 Ti 6: 13.

παραγίνομαι—**1.** *come, arrive, be present* Mt 2: 1; 3: 13; Lk 11: 6; 22: 52; Ac 9: 26, 39; 20: 18; 24: 17, 24; 1 Cor 16: 3.—**2.** *appear, make a public appearance* Mt 3: 1; Lk 12: 51; Hb 9: 11.—**3.** *stand by, come to the aid of* 2 Ti 4: 16.

παράγω *pass by* Mt 20: 30; Mk 1: 16; 2: 14; 15: 21; J 9: 1. *Go away* Mt 9: 9, 27; J 8: 59 v.l. *Pass away* act. 1 Cor 7: 31; passive 1 J 2: 8, 17.*

παραδεδώκεισαν pluperf. act. ind., 3 pl., of παραδίδωμι, without augment.

παραδειγματίζω *hold up to contempt* Hb 6: 6; *expose, make an example of* Mt 1: 19 v.l.*

παράδεισος, ου, ὁ *paradise*, a place of blessedness above the earth Lk 23: 43; 2 Cor 12: 4; Rv 2: 7.*

παραδέχομαι *receive, accept, acknowledge* (*as correct*) Mk 4: 20; Ac 15: 4; 16: 21; 22: 18; 1 Ti 5: 19. *Receive favorably* = love Hb 12: 6.*

παραδιατριβή, ῆς, ἡ *useless occupation* 1 Ti 6: 5 v.l.*

παραδίδωμι—**1.** *hand over, give* (*over*)*, deliver, give up* Mt 10: 19; 25: 20, 22; 26: 2, 15; Mk 13: 11f; 15: 15; Lk 4: 6; 21: 12; 22: 22; J 19: 11, 30; Ac 3: 13; 12: 4; 28: 17; Ro 1: 24, 26, 28; 1 Cor 5: 5; 13: 3; Eph 4: 19. *Risk* Ac 15: 26. ὁ παραδιδούς *the betrayer* Mt 26: 25, 46, 48; Lk 22: 21; J 18: 2, 5.—**2.** *give over, commend, commit* Ac 14: 26; 15: 40; 1 Pt 2: 23.—**3.** *hand down, pass on, transmit, relate, teach* oral or written tradition

παράδοξος–παραλαμβάνω 161

Mk 7: 13; Lk 1: 2; Ac 6: 14; 16: 4; 2 Pt 2: 21; Jd 3.—**4.** *allow, permit* Mk 4: 29.

παράδοξος, ον *strange, wonderful, remarkable* Lk 5: 26.*

παράδοσις, εως, ἡ *tradition* Mt 15: 2f, 6; Mk 7: 3, 5, 8f, 13: 1 Cor 11: 2; Gal 1: 14; Col 2: 8; 2 Th 2: 15; 3: 6.*

παραδῶ 2 aor. act. sub., 3 sing. of παραδίδωμι.

παραζηλόω *provoke to jealousy* Ro 10: 19; 11: 11, 14; 1 Cor 10: 22.*

παραθαλάσσιος, ία, ον *(located) by the sea* or *lake* Mt 4: 13; Lk 4: 31 v.l.*

παραθεωρέω *overlook, neglect* Ac 6: 1.*

παραθήκη, ης, ἡ *deposit, property entrusted to another* fig. 1 Ti 6: 20; 2 Ti 1: 12, 14.*

παράθου, παραθῶσιν 2 aor. mid. imperative, 2 sing., and 2 aor. act. subj., 3 pl. of παρατίθημι.

παραινέω *advise, recommend, urge* Ac 27: 9, 22; Lk 3: 18 v.l.*

παραιτέομαι—**1.** *ask for, request, intercede for* Mk 15: 6. *Excuse* ἔχε με παρῃτημένον *consider me excused* Lk 14: 18b, 19; cf. 18a.—**2.** *decline*—**a.** *reject, refuse* 1 Ti 5: 11; Tit 3: 10; Hb 12: 25.—**b.** *reject, avoid* Ac 25: 11; 1 Ti 4: 7; 2 Ti 2: 23.—**c.** *beg* Hb 12: 19.*

παρακαθέζομαι *sit beside* Lk 10: 39.*

παρακαθίζω *sit down beside* Lk 10: 39 v.l.*

παρακαλέω—**1.** *call to one's side, summon, invite* Lk 8: 41; Ac 8: 31; 9: 38; 16: 9, 15. *Summon to one's aid, call upon for help* Mt 26: 53; 2 Cor 12: 8.—**2.** *appeal to, urge, exhort, encourage* Ac 14: 22; 16: 40; 20: 1f; Ro 12: 1, 8; 1 Cor 4: 16; 2 Cor 10: 1; 1 Th 5: 11; Hb 3: 13; 1 Pt 5: 1.—**3.** *request, implore, appeal to, entreat* Mt 8: 5; Mk 1: 40; Lk 7: 4; 8: 31f;

Ac 19: 31; 2 Cor 12: 18; Phlm 9.—**4.** *comfort, encourage, cheer up* Mt 5: 4; Lk 16: 25; 2 Cor 1: 4; 7: 6; Eph 6: 22; 1 Th 3: 2; 4: 18; Tit 1: 9.—**5.** in some passages π. may mean *try to console* or *conciliate* Ac 16: 39; 1 Cor 4: 13; 1 Th 2: 12 and possibly others.

παρακαλύπτω *hide, conceal* Lk 9: 45.*

παρακαταθήκη, ης, ἡ *deposit* v.l. in 1 Ti 6: 20 and 2 Ti 1: 14.*

παράκειμαι *be at hand, ready* Ro 7: 18, 21.*

παρακέκλημαι, παρακληθῶ perf. mid. and pass. ind., 1 aor. pass. subj. of παρακαλέω.

παράκλησις, εως, ἡ—**1.** *encouragement, exhortation* Ac 13: 15; Ro 12: 8; 1 Cor 14: 3; Phil 2: 1; 1 Th 2: 3; 1 Ti 4: 13; Hb 6: 18; 12: 5; 13: 22.—**2.** *appeal, request* 2 Cor 8: 4, 17.—**3.** *comfort, consolation* Lk 2: 25; 6: 24; Ac 4: 36; 9: 31; 15: 31; Ro 15: 4f; 2 Cor 1: 3–7; 7: 4, 7, 13; Phil 2: 1; 2 Th 2: 16; Phlm 7.*

παράκλητος, ου, ὁ *Helper, Intercessor* J 14: 16, 26; 15: 26; 16: 7; 1 J 2: 1.*

παρακοή, ῆς, ἡ *unwillingness to hear, disobedience* Ro 5: 19; 2 Cor 10: 6; Hb 2: 2.*

παρακολουθέω *follow* fig.—**1.** *follow, accompany, attend* Mk 16: 17.—**2.** *understand, make one's own* or *follow faithfully* w. dat. 1 Ti 4: 6; 2 Ti 3: 10.—**3.** *follow, trace, investigate* w. dat. Lk 1: 3.*

παρακούω *overhear* Mk 5: 36. *Refuse to listen to* w. gen. Mt 18: 17.*

παρακύπτω *bend over* lit. Lk 24: 12; J 20: 5; *bend over and look* 20:11. Fig. *look, glance* Js 1: 25; 1 Pt 1: 12.*

παραλαμβάνω—**1.** *take (to oneself), take with* or *along* Mt 1: 20, 24; 2: 13f, 20f; 12: 45; 24: 40f; Mk 4: 36; Lk 9: 28; 11: 26;

J 14: 3; Ac 15: 39; 21: 24, 26, 32. *Take into custody, arrest* Ac 16: 35 v.l.—**2.** *take over, receive* Mk 7: 4; 1 Cor 11: 23; 15: 3; Gal 1: 9; Col 4: 17; 1 Th 4: 1; Hb 12: 28.—**3.** *receive with favor, accept* J 1: 11; 1 Cor 15: 1; Phil 4: 9.

παραλέγομαι *sail past, coast along* Ac 27: 8, 13.*

παραληµφθήσοµαι 1 fut. pass. ind. of παραλαμβάνω.

παράλιος, ον (*located*) *by the sea* ἡ παράλιος (χώρα) *the sea-coast* (*district*) Lk 6: 17.*

παραλλαγή, ῆς, ἡ *change, variation* Js 1: 17.*

παραλογίζοµαι *deceive, delude* Col 2: 4; Js 1: 22.*

παραλυτικός, ή, όν *lame* only as noun (ὁ) π. *the lame person, the paralytic* Mt 4: 24; 8: 6; 9: 2, 6; Mk 2: 3–5, 9f; Lk 5: 24 v.l.; J 5: 3 v.l.*

παράλυτος, ον *lame* as noun ὁ π. *the paralytic* Mk 2: 9 v.l.*

παραλύω *undo, weaken, disable, paralyze* Lk 5: 18; Ac 9: 33; Hb 12: 12. ὁ παραλελυµένος *the paralytic* Lk 5: 24; Ac 8: 7.*

παραµένω *remain, stay* (at someone's side) 1 Cor 16: 6 v.l. *Continue* Phil 1: 25; Hb 7: 23; Js 1: 25.*

παραµυθέοµαι *encourage, cheer up* 1 Th 2: 12; 5: 14. *Console, comfort* J 11: 19, 31.*

παραµυθία, ας, ἡ *comfort, consolation* 1 Cor 14: 3.*

παραµύθιον, ου, τό *solace* Phil 2: 1.*

παράνοια, ας, ἡ *madness, foolishness* 2 Pt 2: 16 v.l.*

παρανοµέω *act contrary to the law* Ac 23: 3.*

παρανοµία, ας, ἡ *lawlessness, evildoing* 2 Pt 2: 16.*

παραπικραίνω *be disobedient, rebellious* Hb 3: 16.*

παραπικρασµός, οῦ, ὁ *embitterment,* then *revolt, rebellion* Hb 3: 8, 15.*

παραπίπτω *fall away, commit apostasy* Hb 6: 6.*

παραπλεῦσαι 1 aor. act. inf. of παραπλέω.

παραπλέω *sail past* w. acc. Ac 20: 16.*

παραπλήσιος, ία, ιον *coming near, resembling, similar.* The neut. παραπλήσιον as adv. ἠσθένησεν παραπλήσιον θανάτῳ *he was so ill that he nearly died* Phil 2: 27.*

παραπλησίως adv. *in just the same way* Hb 2: 14.*

παραπορεύοµαι *go* or *pass by* Mt 27: 39; Mk 11: 20; 15: 29. Simply *go* Mk 2: 23; 9: 30.*

παράπτωµα, ατος, τό *false step, transgression, sin* Mt 6: 14f; Mk 11: 25f; Ro 4: 25; 5: 15–18, 20; 2 Cor 5: 19; Gal 6: 1; Eph 1: 7; 2: 5.

παραρρέω *flow by, slip away* fig. *drift away* Hb 2: 1.*

παραρυῶµεν 2 aor. pass. subj., 1 pl. of παραρρέω.

παράσηµος, ον *distinguished, marked* παρασήµῳ Διοσκούροις *marked by the Dioscuri,* i.e. with the D. as figure-head Ac 28: 11.*

παρασκευάζω *prepare* act. Ac 10: 10; 1 Pt 2: 8 v.l. Mid. *prepare* (*oneself*) 1 Cor 14: 8; perf. *be ready* 2 Cor 9: 2f.*

παρασκευή, ῆς, ἡ *preparation,* i.e. *day of preparation* for a festival, *Friday* Mt 27: 62; Mk 15: 42; Lk 23: 54; J 19: 14, 31, 42.*

παραστάτις, ιδος, ἡ *a* (female) *helper* Ro 16: 2 v.l.*

παρασχών 2 aor. act. participle of παρέχω.

παρατείνω *extend, prolong* Ac 20: 7.*

παρατηρέω *watch closely, observe carefully*—**1.** *watch* (*maliciously*), *lie in wait for* Mk 3: 2; Lk 6: 7; 14: 1. *Watch one's opportunity* 20: 20. *Watch, guard* Ac 9: 24.— **2.** *observe* religiously Gal 4: 10.*

παρατήρησις, εως, ἡ *observation* Lk 17: 20.*

παρατίθημι *place beside, place before*—1. act. *set before* Mk 6: 41; 8: 6f; Lk 9: 16; 10: 8; 11: 6; Ac 16: 34; 1 Cor 10: 27. *Put before* Mt 13: 24, 31.— 2. mid. *give over, entrust, commend* Lk 12: 48; 23: 46; Ac 14: 23; 20: 32; 1 Ti 1: 18; 2 Ti 2: 2; 1 Pt 4: 19. *Demonstrate, point out* Ac 17: 3; 28: 23 v.l.*

παρατυγχάνω *happen to be there* Ac 17: 17.*

παραυτίκα adv. *immediately, for the present* as adj. *momentary* 2 Cor 4: 17.*

παραφέρω *take* or *carry away* Hb 13: 9; Jd 12. *Take away, remove* Mk 14: 36; Lk 22: 42.*

παραφρονέω *be beside oneself* 2 Cor 11: 23.*

παραφρονία, ας, ἡ *madness, insanity* 2 Pt 2: 16.*

παραφροσύνη, ης, ἡ *madness, insanity* 2 Pt 2: 16 v.l.*

παραχειμάζω *spend the winter* Ac 27: 12; 28: 11; 1 Cor 16: 6; Tit 3: 12.*

παραχειμασία, ας, ἡ *wintering* Ac 27: 12.*

παραχράομαι *misuse* 1 Cor 7: 31 v.l.

παραχρῆμα adv. *at once, immediately* Mt 21: 19f; Lk 1: 64; 13: 13; Ac 3: 7; 13: 11.

πάρδαλις, εως, ἡ *leopard* Rv 13: 2.*

παρέβην 2 aor. act. ind. of παραβαίνω.

παρεδίδοσαν and παρεδίδουν imperfect act. ind., 3 pl. of παραδίδωμι.

παρεδρεύω *sit beside, serve regularly* 1 Cor 9: 13.*

παρεῖδον 2 aor. act. ind. of παροράω.

παρειμένος perf. pass. participle of παρίημι.

πάρειμι—1. *be present* J 7: 6; 11: 28; Ac 10: 33; 24: 19; 1 Cor 5: 3; Gal 4: 18, 20; Col 1: 6; Rv 17: 8.—The pres. 'be here' can take on the perfect sense *have come* Mt 26: 50; Lk 13: 1; Ac 10: 21; 12: 20; 17: 6.—τὸ παρόν *the present* Hb 12: 11.—2. πάρεστίν τί μοι *something is at my disposal, I have something* 2 Pt 1: 9, 12. τὰ παρόντα *one's possessions* Hb 13: 5.

παρεισάγω *bring in secretly* or *maliciously* 2 Pt 2: 1.*

παρείσακτος, ον *secretly brought in, smuggled in* Gal 2: 4.*

παρεισδύ(ν)ω *slip in stealthily, sneak in* Jd 4.*

παρεισενέγκας aor. act. participle of παρεισφέρω.

παρεισέρχομαι *slip in, come in* as a side issue Ro 5: 20. *Slip in, sneak in* Gal 2: 4.*

παρεισφέρω *apply, bring to bear* 2 Pt 1: 5.*

παρεῖχαν imperf. act., 3 pl. of παρέχω.

παρεκτός adv.—1. used as adv. *besides, outside* 2 Cor 11: 28.— 2. as improper prep. w. gen. *apart from, except for* Mt 5: 32; 19: 9 v.l.; Ac 26: 29.*

παρελάβοσαν 2 aor. act. ind., 3 pl. of παραλαμβάνω.

παρεμβάλλω *put* or *throw up* Lk 19: 43.*

παρεμβολή, ῆς, ἡ—1. a (fortified) *camp* Hb 13: 11, 12 v.l., 13; Rv 20: 9.—2. *barracks, headquarters* Ac 21: 34, 37; 22: 24; 23: 10, 16, 32; 28: 16 v.l.—3. *army, battle line* Hb 11: 34.*

παρένεγκε aor. imperative act. of παραφέρω.

παρενοχλέω *cause difficulty (for), trouble, annoy* w. dat. Ac 15: 19.*

παρεπίδημος, ον *sojourning* as noun ὁ π. *stranger, exile* Hb 11: 13; 1 Pt 1: 1; 2: 11.*

παρέρχομαι—1. *go by, pass by*— a. lit. Mt 8: 28; Mk 6: 48; Lk 18: 37. *Pass* Mt 14: 15; Ac 27: 9; 1 Pt 4: 3.—b. fig. *pass away, come to an end, disappear* Mt

5: 18a; Mk 13: 31; Lk 21: 32; 2 Cor 5: 17; Js 1: 10; 2 Pt 3: 10; in the sense *lose force, become invalid* Mt 5: 18b; Lk 21: 33b. *Pass by, neglect, disobey* Lk 11: 42; 15: 29. *Pass* Mt 26: 39, 42; Mk 14: 35.—**2.** *go through, pass through* Ac 16: 8; 17: 15 v.l.—**3.** *come to, come here, come* Lk 12: 37; 17: 7; Ac 24: 7 v.l.

πάρεσις, εως, ἡ *passing over, letting go unpunished* Ro 3: 25.*

παρέχω—1. act.—**a.** *give up, offer, present* Lk 6: 29.—**b.** *grant, show* Ac 17: 31; 22: 2; 28: 2; 1 Ti 6: 17.—**c.** *cause, bring about* Mt 26: 10; Mk 14: 6; Lk 11: 7; 18: 5; Ac 16: 16; Gal 6: 17; 1 Ti 1: 4.—**2.** mid. ἑαυτόν τι π. *show oneself to be something* Tit 2: 7. *Grant* Lk 7: 4; Col 4: 1. *Get for oneself* Ac 19: 24.*

παρηγορία, ας, ἡ *comfort* Col 4: 11.*

παρηκολουθηκώς perf. act. participle of παρακολουθέω.

παρθενία, ας, ἡ *virginity* Lk 2: 36.*

παρθένος, ου, ἡ—1. *virgin* Mt 1: 23; 25: 1, 7, 11; Lk 1: 27; Ac 21: 9; 1 Cor 7: 25, 28, 34, 36–38; 2 Cor 11: 2.—**2.** *chaste man* Rv 14: 4.*

Πάρθοι, ων, οἱ *Parthians* (Parthia was east of the Euphrates) Ac 2: 9.*

παρίημι *leave undone, neglect* Lk 11: 42. *Slacken, weaken* perf. pass. participle παρειμένος *weakened, listless, drooping* Hb 12: 12.*

παριστάνω see παρίστημι.

παρίστημι and **παριστάνω—1.** trans.—**a.** *place beside, put at someone's disposal* Mt 26: 53; Ac 23: 24; Ro 6: 13, 16, 19.—**b.** *present* Lk 2: 22; Ac 1: 3; 9: 41; 23: 33; 2 Cor 11: 2. *Offer, present* Ro 12: 1.—**c.** *make, render* Eph 5: 27; Col 1: 22, 28; 2 Ti 2: 15. *Prove, demonstrate*

Ac 24: 13.—**2.** intrans. (all mid. forms, also perf., pluperf., 2 aor. act.)—**a.** pres., fut., aor. *approach, stand before* w. dat. Ac 9: 39; 27: 23f; Ro 14: 10. *Stand by, help, come to the aid of* Ro 16: 2; 2 Ti 4: 17.—**b.** perf. and pluperf. *stand, be present* Mk 15: 39; Lk 1: 19; J 18: 22; 19: 26. *Have come* Mk 4: 29.

Παρμενᾶς, ᾶ, ὁ acc. -ᾶν *Parmenas* Ac 6: 5.*

πάροδος, ου, ἡ *passing by* 1 Cor 16: 7.*

παροικέω *live as a stranger* Lk 24: 18 v.l. followed by ἐν. *Migrate* Hb 11: 9. Simply *inhabit, live in* Lk 24: 18.*

παροικία, ας, ἡ *the stay* or *sojourn* of one who is not a citizen *in a strange place* lit. Ac 13: 17. Fig. 1 Pt 1: 17.*

πάροικος, ον *strange* Ac 7: 6. ὁ π. as noun *stranger, alien* 7: 29; Eph 2: 19; 1 Pt 2: 11.*

παροιμία, ας, ἡ *proverb* 2 Pt 2: 22. *Dark saying, figure* of speech J 10: 6; 16: 25, 29.*

πάροινος, ον *drunken, addicted to wine* 1 Ti 3: 3; Tit 1: 7.*

παροίχομαι *pass by, be gone* Ac 14: 16.*

παρομοιάζω *be like* Mt 23: 27.*

παρόμοιος, (α), ον *like, similar* Mk 7: 8 v.l., 13.*

παρόν,τό see πάρειμι 2.

παροξύνω *urge on, provoke to wrath, irritate* pass. *become irritated, angry* 1 Cor 13: 5. *Be aroused* Ac 17: 16.*

παροξυσμός, οῦ, ὁ *stirring up, encouraging* Hb 10: 24. *Irritation, sharp disagreement* Ac 15: 39.*

παροράω *overlook, take no notice of* Ac 17: 30 v.l.*

παροργίζω *make angry* Ro 10: 19; Eph 6: 4; Col 3: 21 v.l.*

παροργισμός, οῦ, ὁ *angry mood, anger* Eph 4: 26.*

παροργιῶ fut. act. ind. of παροργίζω.

παροτρύνω *arouse, incite* Ac 13: 50.*

παρουσία, ας, ἡ—**1**. *presence* 1 Cor 16: 17; 2 Cor 10: 10; Phil 2: 12. —**2**. *coming, advent*—**a**. of human beings 2 Cor 7: 6f; Phil 1: 26.—**b**. of Christ and his Messianic Advent at the end of this age Mt 24: 3, 27, 37, 39; 1 Cor 1: 8 v.l.; 15: 23; 1 Th 2: 19; 3: 13; 4: 15; 5: 23; 2 Th 2: 1, 8f; Js 5: 7f; 2 Pt 1: 16; 3: 4, 12; 1 J 2: 28.—**c**. of the Antichrist 2 Th 2: 9.*

παροψίς, ίδος, ἡ *dish* Mt 23: 25, 26 v.l.*

παρρησία, ας, ἡ—**1**. *outspokenness, frankness, plainness of speech* J 16: 29; Ac 2: 29; 2 Cor 3: 12. παρρησίᾳ *plainly, openly* Mk 8: 32; J 7: 13; 10: 24; 11: 14; 16: 25, 29 v.l.—**2**. *openness to the public* παρρησίᾳ *in public, publicly* J 7: 26; 11: 54; 18: 20. Similarly J 7: 4; Ac 14: 19 v.l.; 28: 31; Phil 1: 20; Col 2: 15.— **3**. *courage, confidence, boldness, fearlessness* Ac 2: 29; 4: 13, 29, 31; 6: 10 v.l.; 16: 4 v.l.; 2 Cor 7: 4; Eph 6: 19; Phlm 8. *Joyousness, confidence* Eph 3: 12; 1 Ti 3: 13; Hb 3: 6; 4: 16; 10: 19, 35; 1 J 2: 28; 3: 21; 4: 17; 5: 14.*

παρρησιάζομαι—**1**. *speak freely, openly, fearlessly, express oneself freely* Ac 9: 27f; 13: 46; 14: 3; 18: 26; 19: 8; 26: 26; Eph 6: 20.—**2**. *have the courage, venture* 1 Th 2: 2.*

παρῳχημένος perf. participle of παροίχομαι.

πᾶς, πᾶσα, πᾶν gen. παντός, πάσης, παντός—**1**. adj., used with a noun—**a**. with the noun in the sing. without the article *every, each* πᾶν δένδρον *every tree* Mt 3: 10; Lk 3: 9. Similarly Mt 15: 13; Lk 3: 5; J 1: 9; Ac 5: 42; Ro 3: 4; 1 Cor 15: 24; Hb 3: 4; Rv 1: 7a. *All* Mk 13:

20; Lk 3: 6; Hb 12: 11.— *Every kind of, all sorts of* Mt 4: 23; 23: 27; Ac 2: 5; 7: 22; Ro 1: 18; 1 Cor 6: 18; Eph 1: 3, 8; Tit 1: 16; Js 1: 17.—*Every, any and every, just any* Mt 4: 4; 18: 19; 19: 3; 2 Cor 1: 4b; Eph 4: 14; 1 J 4: 1.—*Full, greatest, all* Ac 4: 29; 5: 23; 23: 1; 2 Cor 12: 12; Eph 6: 18c; 1 Ti 3: 4; 5: 2; Js 1: 2.—Before proper names *all, the whole* Mt 2: 3; Ac 17: 26b; Ro 11: 26.—**b**. with a noun in the pl., without the article πάντες ἄνθρωποι *all men, everyone* Ac 22: 15; Ro 5: 18; 12: 17f; 1 Cor 15: 19; Tit 2: 11. Cf. Hb 1: 6.—**c**. with a noun in the sing. with the article *the whole, all (the)* πᾶσα ἡ Ἰουδαία καὶ πᾶσα ἡ περίχωρος *all Judaea and the whole region around* Mt 3: 5. Cf. 8: 32, 34; 27: 25, 45; Mk 5: 33; 16: 15; Ac 3: 9, 11; Ro 8: 22; 9: 17; 1 Cor 13: 2b, c; Hb 9: 19b, c.—*All* 2 Cor 1: 4a; 7: 4; Phil 1: 3; 1 Th 3: 7; 1 Pt 5: 7.—πᾶς with the article is often used with a participle *every one who, whoever* Mt 5: 22; cf. 7: 8, 26; Lk 19: 26; J 3: 8, 15f, 20; Ac 13: 39; Ro 2: 1, 10; Hb 5: 13. πᾶν τό *everything that* Mt 15: 17; Mk 7: 18; 1 Cor 10: 25, 27; 1 J 5: 4. Also πᾶς ὅς, etc. *every one who* Mt 7: 24; 19: 29; Lk 14: 33; J 6: 37, 39; Ro 14: 23.—**d**. with a noun, pronoun, participle, etc. in the plural, with the article *all* Mt 1: 17; 4: 24; 25: 7; Mk 4: 13, 31f; Lk 2: 47; J 10: 8; Ac 1: 18; 2: 7, 14, 32; 16: 32; Ro 1: 7f; 9: 6; 1 Cor 12: 26; Phil 1: 4, 7f; Hb 11: 13, 39; Rv 7: 11; 13: 8.— **e**. πᾶς stands between article and noun: sing. *the whole* Ac 20: 18; Gal 5: 14; pl. *all the* Ac 21: 21; 27: 37; Ro 16: 15; Gal 1: 2.— **2**. substantive—**a**. without the article πᾶς *everyone* Lk 16: 16.

διὰ παντός *always, continually* Mt 18: 10; Mk 5: 5. ἐν παντί *in every respect, in everything* 1 Cor 1: 5; 2 Cor 7: 5, 11, 16; 1 Th 5: 18.—πάντες, πᾶσαι *all, everyone* Mt 10: 22; Mk 1: 37; Lk 1: 63; Ro 5: 12.—πάντα *all things, everything* Mt 11: 27; 18: 26; J 1: 3; 3: 35; 1 Cor 2: 10; 3: 21. πάντα as accusative of specification *in all respects, in every way, altogether* Ac 20: 35; 1 Cor 9: 25b. Cf. 2 Cor 2: 9.—**b.** with the article: οἱ πάντες *all (of them)* Ro 11: 32a, b; 1 Cor 9: 22; Phil 2: 21. (*We, they*) *all* Mk 14: 64; 1 Cor 10: 17; Eph 4: 13.—τὰ πάντα *all things, the universe* Ro 11: 36; 1 Cor 8: 6; Eph 1: 10; 3: 9; Hb 1: 3; 2: 10; Rv 4: 11. *All this* 2 Cor 4: 15; Col 3: 8. As accusative of specification *in all respects* Eph 4: 15.

πάσχα, τό indecl. *the Passover*—**1.** a Jewish festival Mt 26: 2; Mk 14: 1; Lk 2: 41; 22: 1; J 2: 13, 23; 6: 4; 11: 55; 12: 1; 13: 1; 18: 39; 19: 14; Ac 12: 4.— **2.** *the Paschal lamb* Mt 26: 17; Mk 14: 12, 14; Lk 22: 7, 11, 15; J 18: 28. Fig. 1 Cor 5: 7.— **3.** *the Passover meal* Mt 26: 18f; Mk 14: 16; Lk 22: 8, 13; Hb 11: 28.*

πάσχω—**1.** *have an experience* Gal 3: 4; cf. Mt 17: 15 v.l.—**2.** *suffer, endure*—**a.** *suffer*, sometimes *suffer death* Mt 17: 12; Lk 22: 15; 24: 46; Ac 1: 3; 17: 3; 1 Cor 12: 26; Phil 1: 29; 2 Th 1: 5; Hb 2: 18; 9: 26; 1 Pt 2: 19–21, 23; 3: 14, 17; 4: 19. *Undergo punishment* 1 Pt 4: 15.—**b.** *endure, undergo* Mt 27: 19; Mk 8: 31; 9: 12; Lk 9: 22; 17: 25; Ac 9: 16; 28: 5; 2 Cor 1: 6; 1 Th 2: 14; 2 Ti 1: 12; Hb 5: 8; Rv 2: 10.

Πάταρα, ων, τά *Patara* a city in Lycia, on the southwest coast of Asia Minor Ac 21: 1.*

πατάσσω *strike, hit* Mt 26: 51; Lk 22: 49f; Ac 12: 7, 23; Rv 11: 6; 19: 15. *Strike down, slay* Mt 26: 31; Mk 14: 27; Ac 7: 24.*

πατέω *tread (on)*—**1.** trans. *tread* Rv 14: 20; 19: 15. *Tread on, trample* Lk 21: 24; Rv 11: 2.— **2.** intrans. *walk, tread* Lk 10: 19.*

πατήρ, πατρός, ὁ *father*—**1.** lit.— **a.** of the immediate ancestor Mt 2: 22; 10: 21; Mk 5: 40; 15: 21; J 4: 53; Ac 7: 14; 1 Cor 5: 1; Hb 12: 9a. Plural *parents* 11: 23.—**b.** *forefather, ancestor, progenitor* Mt 3: 9; 23: 30, 32; Mk 11: 10; Lk 1: 73; 16: 24; J 4: 20; 8: 39, 53, 56; Ac 3: 13, 25; Ro 9: 10; Hb 1: 1.—**2.** fig., of spiritual fatherhood, or used in respectful address, etc. Ac 7: 2a; Ro 4: 11, 12a; 1 Cor 4: 15; 10: 1; 2 Pt 3: 4.—**3.** of God—**a.** as Father of mankind Mt 6: 4, 6, 9, 14f, 18, 26, 32; Lk 6: 36; J 8: 41f; 20: 17c; Ro 1: 7; 2 Cor 1: 2, 3b; Col 1: 2; Tit 1: 4.— **b.** as Father of Jesus Christ Mt 7: 21; 15: 13; 20: 23; Mk 8: 38; 14: 36; Lk 2: 49; J 4: 21, 23; 5: 17, 19–23, 43; 6: 40; Ro 15: 6; 2 Cor 11: 31; Eph 1: 3; Rv 2: 28.—**c.** Often God is simply called (ὁ) πατήρ (*the*) *Father* Gal 1: 1; Eph 1: 17; 2: 18; 3: 14; Phil 2: 11; 1 J 1: 2; 2: 1, 15.— **4.** of Satan J 8: 44.

Πάτμος, ου, ὁ *Patmos*, a small, rocky island in the Aegean Sea Rv 1: 9.*

πατραλῴας a variant form of πατρολῴας.

πατριά, ᾶς, ἡ *family, clan* Lk 2: 4; Eph 3: 15. *People, nation* Ac 3: 25.*

πατριάρχης, ου, ὁ *father of a nation, patriarch* Ac 7: 8f; Hb 7: 4. *Ancestor* Ac 2: 29.*

πατρικός, ή, όν *derived from or handed down by one's father, paternal* Gal 1: 14.*

πατρίς, ίδος, ἡ—1. *fatherland, homeland* J 4: 44; fig. Hb 11: 14.—2. *home town, one's own part of the country* Mt 13: 54, 57; Mk 6: 1, 4; Lk 2: 3 v.l.; 4: 23f; Ac 18: 25 v.l., 27 v.l.*

Πατροβᾶς, ᾶ, ὁ *Patrobas* Ro 16: 14.*

πατρολῴας, ου, ὁ *one who kills one's father, a parricide* 1 Ti 1: 9.*

πατροπαράδοτος, ον *inherited from one's father* or *forefathers* 1 Pt 1: 18.*

πατρῷος, α, ον *paternal, belonging to one's father* or *forefathers* Ac 22: 3; 28: 17. ὁ π. θεός *the God of my forefathers* 24: 14.*

Παῦλος, ου, ὁ *Paul,* a Roman name—1. Sergius Paulus, see Σέργιος.—2. Paul, an apostle of Jesus Christ Ac chapters 9 and 13–28 passim; Ro 1: 1; 1 Cor 1: 1, 12f; 3: 4f, 22; 16: 21; 2 Cor 1: 1; 10: 1; Gal 1: 1; 5: 2; Eph 1: 1; 3: 1; Phil 1: 1; Col 1: 1, 23; 4: 18; 1 Th 1: 1; 2: 18; 2 Th 1: 1; 3: 17; 1 Ti 1: 1; 2 Ti 1: 1; Tit 1: 1; Phlm 1, 9, 19; 2 Pt 3: 15.*

παύω—1. act. *stop, cause to stop, hinder, keep* 1 Pt 3: 10.—2. mid. *stop* (oneself), *cease* Lk 5: 4; 8: 24; Ac 5: 42; 20: 1, 31; 21: 32; 1 Cor 13: 8; Col 1: 9; Hb 10: 2. *Cease from* w. gen. 1 Pt 4: 1.

Πάφος, ου, ἡ *Paphos* a city on the west coast of Cyprus Ac 13: 6, 13.*

παχύνω *make fat* fig., pass. *become dull* Mt 13: 15; Ac 28: 27.*

πέδη, ης, ἡ *fetter, shackle* Mk 5: 4; Lk 8: 29.*

πεδινός, ή, όν *flat, level* Lk 6: 17.*

πεζεύω *travel by land* or *on foot* Ac 20: 13.*

πεζῇ adv. *by land,* lit. 'on foot' Mt 14: 13; Mk 6: 33.*

πεζός, ή, όν *going by land* Mt 14: 13 v.l.*

πειθαρχέω *obey* w. dat. Ac 5: 29, 32; *follow the advice of* 27: 21. *Be obedient* Tit 3: 1.*

πειθός, ή, όν *persuasive* 1 Cor 2: 4.*

πειθώ, οῦς, ἡ dat. πειθοῖ; ἐν πειθοῖ σοφίας *with the persuasiveness of wisdom* 1 Cor 2: 4 v.l.*

πείθω—1. act., except for 2 perf. and pluperf.—a. *convince* Ac 18: 4; 19: 8, 26; 28: 23.—b. *persuade, appeal to* Mt 27: 20; Ac 13: 43; 2 Cor 5: 11. The difficult passage Ac 26: 28 ἐν ὀλίγῳ με πείθεις Χριστιανὸν ποιῆσαι may be rendered *you are in a hurry to persuade me and make a Christian of me.*—c. *win over, strive to please* Ac 12: 20; 14: 19; Gal 1: 10.—d. *conciliate, set at ease* 1 J 3: 19. *Conciliate, satisfy* Mt 28: 14.—2. The 2 perf. πέποιθα and pluperf. ἐπεποίθειν have pres. and past meaning—a. *depend on, trust in, put one's confidence in* w. dat. Mt 27: 43; Lk 11: 22; 18: 9; 2 Cor 1: 9; 2: 3; Phil 1: 14; 3: 3f; 2 Th 3: 4; Phlm 21; Hb 2: 13.—b. *be convinced, be sure, certain* Ro 2: 19; 2 Cor 10: 7; Phil 1: 6, 25.—3. pass., except for the perf.—a. *be persuaded, be convinced, come to believe, believe* Lk 16: 31; Ac 17: 4; 21: 14; 26: 26; 28: 24.—b. *obey, follow* w. dat. Ro 2: 8; Gal 5: 7; Hb 13: 17; Js 3: 3.—c. Some passages stand between meanings a and b and allow either translation Ac 5: 36f, 39; 23: 21; 27: 11.—4. perf. pass. πέπεισμαι *be convinced, be certain* Lk 20: 6; Ro 8: 38; 15: 14; 2 Ti 1: 5, 12; Hb 6: 9.

Πειλᾶτος a variant spelling of Πιλᾶτος.

πεῖν 2 aor. act. inf. of πίνω.

πεινάω *hunger, be hungry* lit. Mt 4: 2; 12: 1, 3; 25: 35, 37, 42, 44;

Mk 11: 12; Lk 6: 3, 25; 1 Cor 11: 21, 34; Phil 4: 12; Rv 7: 16. Fig. Mt 5: 6; J 6: 35.

πεῖρα, ας, ἡ *attempt, trial* Hb 11: 29. *Experience* 11: 36.*

πειράζω—1. *try, attempt* Ac 9: 26; 16: 7; 24: 6.—2. *try, make trial of, put to the test*—a. generally Mt 16: 1; 22: 18, 35; Mk 10: 2; J 6: 6; 1 Cor 10: 13; 2 Cor 13: 5; Hb 2: 18; 11: 17; Rv 2: 2; 3: 10. Of making trial of God Ac 5: 9; 15: 10; 1 Cor 10: 9; Hb 3: 9.—b. *tempt, entice to sin* Mt 4: 1, 3; Mk 1: 13; Lk 4: 2; Gal 6: 1; 1 Th 3: 5; Js 1: 13f; Rv 2: 10.

πειρασμός, οῦ, ὁ—1. *test, trial* 1 Pt 4: 12. Of testing God Hb 3: 8.—2. *temptation, enticement to sin* Mt 6: 13; 26: 41; Mk 14: 38; Lk 8: 13; 11: 4; 22: 40, 46; Ac 15: 26 v.l.; 1 Ti 6: 9; 2 Pt 2: 9; Rv 3: 10; *way of tempting* Lk 4: 13.

πειράω mid. πειράομαι *try, attempt, endeavor* Ac 26: 21; 9: 26 v.l. πεπειραμένος κατὰ πάντα *who was experienced in all respects* Hb 4: 15 v.l.*

πεισμονή, ῆς, ἡ *persuasion* Gal 5: 8.*

πέλαγος, ους, τό *the open sea, the depths (of the sea)* Mt 18: 6. *Sea* Ac 27: 5.*

πελεκίζω *behead* Rv 20: 4.*

πεμπταῖος, α, ον *on the fifth day* Ac 20: 6 v.l.*

πέμπτος, η, ον *fifth* Rv 6: 9; 9: 1; 16: 10; 21: 20.*

πέμπω *send* Mt 2: 8; 14: 10; Mk 5: 12; Lk 4: 26; 7: 19; 20: 11f; J 1: 22; 5: 23f, 30, 37; 15: 26; Ac 10: 5, 32f; 20: 17; Ro 8: 3; Eph 6: 22; Phil 4: 16; Tit 3: 12; 1 Pt 2: 14; Rv 1: 11; 11: 10.

πένης, ητος, ὁ *poor man* 2 Cor 9: 9.*

πενθερά, ᾶς, ἡ *mother-in-law* Mt 8: 14; 10: 35; Mk 1: 30; Lk 4: 38; 12: 53.*

πενθερός, οῦ, ὁ *father-in-law* J 18: 13.*

πενθέω—1. intrans. *be sad, grieve, mourn* Mt 5: 4; 9: 15; Mk 16: 10; Lk 6: 25; 1 Cor 5: 2; Js 4: 9; Rv 18: 11, 15, 19.—2. trans. *mourn over* 2 Cor 12: 21.*

πένθος, ους, τό *grief, sadness, mourning* Js 4: 9; Rv 18: 7f; 21: 4.*

πενιχρός, ά, όν *poor, needy* Lk 21: 2.*

πεντάκις adv. *five times* 2 Cor 11: 24.*

πεντακισχίλιοι, αι, α *five thousand* Mt 14: 21; 16: 9; Mk 6: 44; 8: 19; Lk 9: 14; J 6: 10.*

πεντακόσιοι, αι, α *five hundred* Lk 7: 41; 1 Cor 15: 6.*

πέντε indecl. *five* Mt 14: 17, 19; 16: 9.

πεντεκαιδέκατος, η, ον *fifteenth* Lk 3: 1.*

πεντήκοντα indecl. *fifty* Mk 6: 40; Lk 7: 41; 9: 14; 16: 6; J 8: 57; 21: 11; Ac 13: 20.*

πεντηκοστή, ῆς, ἡ *Pentecost*, lit. 'fiftieth', i.e. the festival celebrated on the fiftieth day after Passover Ac 2: 1; 20: 16; 1 Cor 16: 8.*

πεπιστεύκεισαν pluperf. act. ind., 3 pl. of πιστεύω, without augment.

πέποιθα 2 perf. act. ind. of πείθω.

πεποιήκεισαν pluperf. act. ind., 3 pl., of ποιέω, without augment.

πεποίθησις, εως, ἡ *trust, confidence* 2 Cor 1: 15; 3: 4; 8: 22; 10: 2; Eph 3: 12; Phil 3: 4.*

πέπονθα 2 perf. act. ind. of πάσχω.

πέπρακα and πεπραμένος 1 perf. act. ind. and pass. participle of πιπράσκω.

πέπτωκα 1 perf. act. ind. of πίπτω.

πέπωκα 1 perf. act. ind. of πίνω.

περ enclitic particle, with intensive and extensive force, strengthening the word to which it is added; see διόπερ, ἐάνπερ, εἴπερ, ἐπειδήπερ, ἐπείπερ, ἤπερ, καθάπερ, καίπερ, ὅσπερ, ὥσπερ, ὡσπερεί.

Πέραια, ας, ἡ *Peraea*, part of Palestine east of the Jordan Lk 6: 17 v.l.*

περαιτέρω adv. *further, beyond* Ac 19: 39.*

πέραν adv. *on the other side*—**1.** subst. τὸ πέραν *the shore* or *land on the other side* Mt 8: 18, 28; Mk 6: 45; 8: 13.—**2.** as improper prep. w. gen. *to the other side* J 6: 1, 17; 10: 40. *On the other side* Mt 19: 1; Mk 5: 1; J 1: 28; 6: 22, 25. πέραν τοῦ 'Ιορδάνου *on the other side* (= east of) *the Jordan*, i.e. *Peraea* Mt 4: 15, 25; Mk 3: 8; 10: 1.

πέρας, ατος, τό *end, limit, boundary* Mt 12: 42; Lk 11: 31; Ro 10: 18; Hb 6: 16; Ac 13: 33 v.l.*

Πέργαμος, ου, ἡ or **Πέργαμον, ου τό** *Pergamus* or *Pergamum*, an important city in northwest Asia Minor Rv 1: 11; 2: 12.*

Πέργη, ης, ἡ *Perga* a city in Pamphylia, near the south central coast of Asia Minor Ac 13: 13f; 14: 25.*

περί prep. w. gen. and acc.— **1.** with the genitive *about, concerning* Mt 18: 19; 22: 42; Lk 2: 17; 9: 9; J 8: 13f, 18; Ac 17: 32; 24: 24; 1 Cor 7: 1; 2 Cor 9: 1; Jd 3.—*On account of, because of* Lk 3: 15; 19: 37; 24: 4; J 8: 26; 10: 33.—*With regard to, with reference to* Ac 15: 2; 1 Cor 7: 37; Col 4: 10; Hb 11: 20.— *For* Lk 6: 28; Ac 12: 5; Ro 8: 3; Col 1: 3; 2 Th 1: 11; 3: 1; Hb 10: 18, 26; 13: 18; 1 Pt 3: 18.— **2.** with the accusative *around, about, near* Mt 8: 18; 18: 6; 20: 3, 5f, 9; Mk 1: 6; 3: 34; 4: 10; Lk 13: 8; Ac 10: 3; 28: 7. οἱ περὶ Παῦλον *Paul and his companions* Ac 13: 13.—*With* Lk 10: 40f; Ac 19: 25.—*With*

regard or *respect to* 1 Ti 6: 21; 2 Ti 2: 18; Tit 2: 7. —τὰ περὶ ἐμέ *how I am getting along* Phil 2: 23.

περιάγω—**1.** trans. *lead around, have* someone *with oneself* or *accompanying oneself* 1 Cor 9: 5.—**2.** intrans. *go around, go about* Mt 4: 23; 9: 35; 23: 15; Mk 6: 6; Ac 13: 11.*

περιαιρέω *take away* (*from around*), *remove* 2 Cor 3: 16; Hb 10: 11. *Cast off* or *slip* an anchor Ac 27: 40. Pass. *be abandoned* 27: 20.—28: 13 v.l.*

περιάπτω *kindle* Lk 22: 55.*

περιαστράπτω trans. *shine around* Ac 9: 3; 22: 6 v.l. Intrans. *shine* 22: 6.*

περιβάλλω *throw, lay* or *put around* Lk 19: 43 v.l. *Put on* an article of clothing Mt 6: 31; Mk 14: 51; Lk 12: 27; J 19: 2; Ac 12: 8; Rv 19: 8. περιβέβλημαί τι *have put something on, wear* Mk 16: 5; Rv 7: 9, 13; 11: 3.

περιβλέπω *look around* (*at*) Mk 3: 5, 34; 5: 32; 9: 8; 10: 23; 11: 11; Lk 6: 10.*

περιβόλαιον, ου, τό *covering, wrap, cloak: cloak* Hb 1: 12; *covering* 1 Cor 11: 15.*

περιδέω *bind* or *wrap around* J 11: 44.*

περιεδέδετο pluperf. pass. ind., 3 sing., of περιδέω.

περιεζωσμένος perf. pass. participle of περιζώννυμι.

περιελεῖν, -ών 2 aor. act. inf. and participle of περιαιρέω.

περιεργάζομαι *be a busybody* 2 Th 3: 11.*

περίεργος, ον *meddlesome, curious* as noun *a busybody* 1 Ti 5: 13. τὰ περίεργα *magic* Ac 19: 19.*

περιέρχομαι *go from place to place* Ac 19: 13; *wander about* Hb 11: 37; cf. Ac 13: 6 v.l. π. τὰς οἰκίας *go about from house to house* 1 Ti 5: 13. *Sail around* Ac 28: 13.*

περιέτεμον 2 aor. act. ind. of περιτέμνω.

περιέχω—1. seize, come upon lit. 'encircle' Lk 5: 9.—2. contain trans. Ac 15: 23 v.l.; 23: 25 v.l. Intrans. περιέχει it stands or says 1 Pt 2: 6.*

περιζώννυμι and περιζωννύω gird about—1. act., with double acc. gird someone (about) with something pass. Lk 12: 35; Rv 1: 13; 15: 6.—2. mid. gird oneself Lk 12: 37; 17: 8; Ac 12: 8 v.l. Fig. Eph 6: 14.*

περιζωσάμενος 1 aor. mid. participle of περιζώννυμι.

περιῃρεῖτο imperfect pass. 3 sing. of περιαιρέω.

περίθεσις, εως, ἡ putting on 1 Pt 3: 3.*

περιΐστημι—1. stand around J 11: 42; Ac 25: 7.—2. avoid, shun 2 Ti 2: 16; Tit 3: 9.*

περικάθαρμα, ατος, τό refuse, offscouring, scapegoat 1 Cor 4: 13.*

περικαθίζω sit around Lk 22: 55 v.l.*

περικαλύπτω conceal, cover Mk 14: 65; Lk 22: 64; Hb 9: 4.*

περίκειμαι—1. lie or be placed around Mk 9: 42; Lk 17: 2. Surround Hb 12: 1.—2. περίκειμαί τι wear something, have something on Ac 28: 20. Fig. be subject to Hb 5: 2.*

περικεφαλαία, ας, ἡ helmet fig. Eph 6: 17; 1 Th 5: 8.*

περικρατής, ές having power, being in command περικρατεῖς γενέσθαι τῆς σκάφης to get the boat under control Ac 27: 16.*

περικρύβω hide, conceal Lk 1: 24.*

περικυκλόω surround, encircle Lk 19: 43.*

περιλάμπω shine around Lk 2: 9; Ac 26: 13.*

περιλείπομαι remain, be left behind 1 Th 4: 15, 17.*

περιλείχω lick all around, lick off Lk 16: 21 v.l.*

περίλυπος, ον very sad, deeply grieved Mt 26: 38; Mk 6: 26; 14: 34; Lk 18: 23.*

περιμένω wait for Ac 1: 4; wait 10: 24 v.l.*

πέριξ adv. (all) around Ac 5: 16.*

περιοικέω live in the neighborhood of Lk 1: 65.*

περίοικος, ον living around οἱ π. the neighbors Lk 1: 58.*

περιούσιος, ον chosen, special Tit 2: 14.*

περιοχή, ῆς, ἡ in Ac 8: 32 can mean either content, wording or portion.*

περιπατέω go about, walk around— 1. lit. walk around, go about, walk, go Mt 9: 5; 14: 25f, 29; Mk 11: 27; 12: 38; Lk 11: 44; 24: 17; J 6: 19, 66; 7: 1; 10: 23; 21: 18; Rv 2: 1; 3: 4; 16: 15.— 2. fig. walk in the sense live, conduct oneself Mk 7: 5; J 8: 12; Ac 21: 21; Ro 6: 4; 8: 4; 1 Cor 7: 17; Gal 5: 16; Eph 4: 1; Col 3: 7; 2 Th 3: 6, 11; 1 J 2: 6.

περιπείρω pierce through fig. 1 Ti 6: 10.*

περιπίπτω fall in with, encounter w. dat., lit. fall into the hands of Lk 10: 30; strike Ac 27: 41. Fig. become involved in Js 1: 2.*

περιποιέω mid.—1. save, preserve Lk 17: 33.—2. acquire, obtain, gain for oneself Ac 20: 28; 1 Ti 3: 13.*

περιποίησις, εως, ἡ saving Hb 10: 39. Gaining 1 Th 5: 9; 2 Th 2: 14. Possession, property Eph 1: 14; 1 Pt 2: 9.*

περι(ρ)ραίνω sprinkle (all around) Rv 19: 13 v.l.*

περι(ρ)ρήγνυμι tear off Ac 16: 22.*

περισπάω be or become distracted, overburdened Lk 10: 40.*

περισσεία, ας, ἡ surplus, abundance Ro 5: 17; 2 Cor 8: 2; 10: 15: Js 1: 21.*

περίσσευμα, ατος, τό—1. abundance, fulness Mt 12: 34; Lk 6: 45; 2 Cor 8: 14.—2. what remains, scraps Mk 8: 8.*

περισσεύω—1. intrans.—a. of things *be more than enough, be left over* Mt 14: 20; 15: 37; Lk 9: 17; J 6: 12f.—*Be present in abundance* Mt 5: 20; Mk 12: 44; Lk 21: 4; Ro 5: 15; 2 Cor 1: 5; Phil 1: 26.—*Be extremely rich* or *abundant, overflow* Ro 3: 7; 2 Cor 3: 9; 8: 2; 9: 12.— *Grow* Ac 16: 5; Phil 1: 9.— **b.** of persons *have an abundance, abound, be rich* w. gen. *of* or *in something* Ro 15: 13; 1 Cor 8: 8; 2 Cor 9: 8b; Phil 4: 12, 18.—*Be outstanding, be prominent, excel* 1 Cor 14: 12; 15: 58; 2 Cor 8: 7; Col 2: 7. *Progress* 1 Th 4: 1, 10.— **2.** trans. *cause to abound, make extremely rich* Mt 13: 12; 25: 29; Lk 15: 17; 2 Cor 4: 15; 9: 8a; Eph 1: 8; 1 Th 3: 12.

περισσός, ή, όν *exceeding the usual number* or *size*—**1.** *extraordinary, remarkable* Mt 5: 47. τὸ περισσόν *the advantage* Ro 3: 1.— **2.** *abundant, profuse* J 10: 10. *Superfluous, unnecessary* 2 Cor 9: 1.—**3.** in the comparative sense τὸ περισσὸν τούτων *whatever is more than this* Mt 5: 37.— ἐκ περισσοῦ *extremely* Mk 6: 51.*

περισσότερος, τέρα, ον *greater, more*—**1.** with a subst. Mk 12: 40; Lk 20: 47; 1 Cor 12: 23f; 2 Cor 2: 7.—**2.** *even more* Lk 12: 48; 1 Cor 15: 10. Cf. Mt 11: 9; Mk 12: 33; Lk 7: 26; 12: 4; 2 Cor 10: 8.—**3.** the neut. sing. as adv. *even more* Hb 6: 17; 7: 15. *So much more* Mk 7: 36.

περισσοτέρως adv.—**1.** *(even) more* Mk 15: 14 v.l.; *to a much greater degree* 2 Cor 11: 23; Gal 1: 14; cf. 2 Cor 12: 15. *So much (the) more* Phil 1: 14; Hb 2: 1; 13: 19.—**2.** *especially* 2 Cor 1: 12; 2: 4; 7: 13, 15; 1 Th 2: 17.*

περισσῶς adv. *exceedingly, beyond measure, very* Ac 26: 11.—*More,* *even more* Mt 27: 23; Mk 10: 26; 15: 14.*

περιστερά, ᾶς, ἡ *pigeon, dove* Mt 3: 16; 10: 16; Mk 11: 15; Lk 3: 22; J 1: 32; 2 : 14, 16.

περιτέμνω *circumcise*—**1.** lit. Lk 1: 59; 2: 21; J 7: 22; Ac 7: 8; 15: 1, 5; 16: 3; 21: 21; 1 Cor 7: 18; Gal 2: 3; 5: 2f; 6: 12f.— **2.** fig. of baptism Col 2: 11.*

περιτίθημι *put* or *place around, on* Mt 21: 33; 27: 28, 48; Mk 12: 1; 15: 17, 36; J 19: 29. Fig. *grant, show* 1 Cor 12: 23.*

περιτομή, ῆς, ἡ *circumcision*— **1.** lit. J 7: 22f; Ac 7: 8; Ro 2: 25f, 28; 1 Cor 7: 19; Gal 5: 11; 6: 15.—**2.** fig., of spiritual circumcision Ro 2: 29; Col 2: 11.— **3.** *those who are circumcised,* lit., of *Jews* Ac 10: 45; Ro 3: 30; Gal 2: 7–9; Col 3: 11. Fig., of Christians Phil 3: 3.

περιτρέπω *turn* Ac 26: 24.*

περιτρέχω *run about, go about in* Mk 6: 55.*

περιφέρω *carry about, carry here and there* Mk 6: 55; 2 Cor 4: 10. Fig., pass. Eph 4: 14; Hb 13: 9 v.l.*

περιφρονέω *look down on, despise* w. gen. Tit 2: 15.*

περίχωρος, ον *neighboring* as subst. ἡ περίχωρος (γῆ) *the region around, neighborhood* with its inhabitants Mt 3: 5; 14: 35; Lk 4: 14, 37; 8: 37; Ac 14: 6.

περίψημα, ατος, τό *dirt, offscouring* fig. 1 Cor. 4: 13.*

περπερεύομαι *boast, brag* 1 Cor 13: 4.*

Περσίς, ίδος, ἡ *Persis* Ro 16: 12.*

πέρυσι adv. *last year, a year ago* ἀπὸ πέρυσι *a year ago, since last year* 2 Cor 8: 10; 9: 2.*

πεσεῖν, πεσών, πεσοῦμαι 2 aor. act. inf. and participle, fut. mid. indic. of πίπτω.

πετάομαι a variant form of πέτομαι *fly,* found only as a v.l. in Rv 4: 7; 8: 13; 14: 6; 19: 17.*

πετεινόν, οῦ, τό *bird* Mt 6: 26; 13: 32; Mk 4: 4; Lk 12: 24; 13: 19; Ac 10: 12; Ro 1: 23; Js 3: 7.

πέτομαι *fly* Rv 4: 7; 8: 13.

πέτρα, ας, ἡ *rock* lit. Mt 7: 24f; 27: 51, 60; Lk 8: 6, 13; Ro 9: 33; 1 Cor 10: 4; 1 Pt 2: 8; Rv 6: 15f. Fig. Mt 16: 18.

Πέτρος, ου, ὁ *Peter*, surname of the head of the twelve disciples; his name was originally Simon. The following passages illustrate some of the main points in his career; Mt 16: 16, 18; Mk 1: 16, 21, 30; 3: 16; 5: 37; 9: 5; 16: 7; Ac 15: 7; Gal 2: 9; 1 Pt 1: 1; 2 Pt 1: 1.

πετρώδης, ες *rocky*, *stony* τὸ πετρῶδες and τὰ πετρώδη *rocky ground* Mt 13: 5, 20; Mk 4: 5, 16.*

πεφίμωσο perf. pass. imperative, 2 sing., of φιμόω.

πήγανον, ου, τό *rue* (ruta graveolens), a garden herb Lk 11: 42.*

πηγή, ῆς, ἡ *spring* of water, *fountain*—1. lit. Mk 5: 29; Js 3: 11; 2 Pt 2: 17; Rv 8: 10; 14: 7; 16: 4. *Well* J 4: 6.—2. symbolic J 4: 14; Rv 7: 17; 21: 6.*

πήγνυμι *set up* Hb 8: 2.*

πηδάλιον, ου, τό *steering paddle*, *rudder* Ac 27: 40; Js 3: 4.*

πηλίκος, η, ον pron. *how large?* Gal 6: 11. *How great* Hb 7: 4.*

πηλός, οῦ, ὁ *clay* Ro 9: 21. *Mud* J 9: 6, 11, 14f.*

πήρα, ας, ἡ *knapsack, traveler's bag* Mt 10: 10; Mk 6: 8; Lk 9: 3; 10: 4; 22: 35f.*

πηρόω *disable, maim* only as v.l. in the following passages: Mk 8: 17; J 12: 40; Ac 5: 3; Ro 11: 7.*

πήρωσις, εως, ἡ *shortsightedness, blindness* fig. Mk 3: 5 v.l.*

πῆχυς, εως, ὁ *cubit*, a measure of length, about 18 inches or .462 of a meter J 21: 8; Rv 21: 17. In Mt 6: 27 and Lk 12: 25 π.

is best understood as referring to time, e.g. *hour*; see ἡλικία 1.*

πιάζω *take (hold of)* Ac 3: 7. *Seize, arrest, take into custody* J 7: 30, 32, 44; 8: 20; 10: 39; 11: 57; Ac 12: 4; 2 Cor 11: 32. *Catch* J 21: 3, 10; Rv 19: 20.*

πίε, πιεῖν, πίεσαι 2 aor. act. imperative, infinitive, fut. mid. (2 sing.) ind. of πίνω.

πιέζω *press down* pass. Lk 6: 38.*

πιθανολογία, ας, ἡ *persuasive speech, plausible* (but false) *argument* Col 2: 4.*

πιθός another spelling for πειθός.

πικραίνω *make bitter* lit. Rv 8: 11; 10: 9f. Fig. *embitter* Col 3: 19.*

πικρία, ας, ἡ *bitterness* lit. Ac 8: 23; Hb 12: 15. Fig. *bitterness, animosity, anger* Ro 3: 14; Eph 4: 31.*

πικρός, ά, όν *bitter* lit. Js 3: 11; fig. 3: 14.*

πικρῶς adv. *bitterly* Mt 26: 75; Lk 22: 62.*

Πιλᾶτος, ου, ὁ Pontius *Pilate*, Roman procurator of Judaea 26–36 AD. Mt 27: 2ff; Mk 15: 1ff; Lk 3: 1; 13: 1; 23: 1ff; J 18: 29ff; 19: 1ff; Ac 3: 13; 4: 27; 13: 28, 29 v.l.; 1 Ti 6: 13.*

πίμπλημι *fill* lit. Mt 22: 10; 27: 48; Lk 1: 15, 41, 67; 5: 7, 26; 6: 11; Ac 3: 10; 4: 8, 31; 9: 17; 13: 9, 45; 19: 29. Fig. *be fulfilled* Lk 21: 22; *come to an end* Lk 1: 23, 57; 2: 6, 21f.

πίμπρημι in Ac 28: 6 may mean either *burn with fever* or *become distended, swell up*.*

πινακίδιον, ου, τό *little* (wooden) *tablet* for writing notes Lk 1: 63.*

πινακίς, ίδος, ἡ *little* (wooden) *writing tablet* Lk 1: 63 v.l.*

πίναξ, ακος, ἡ *platter, dish* Mt 14: 8, 11; Mk 6: 25, 28; Lk 11: 39.*

πίνω *drink*—1. lit. Mt 6: 25, 31; 11: 18; Mk 16: 18; Lk 1: 15;

J 6: 53f, 56; 1 Cor 10: 21.—
2. fig. Mk 10: 38f; J 7: 37; Hb
6: 7; Rv 14: 10.

πιότης, τητος, ἡ *fatness, richness*
Ro 11: 17.*

πιπράσκω *sell* Mt 13: 46; 18: 25;
26: 9; Ac 2: 45; 4: 34; 5: 4.
Fig. Ro 7: 14.

πίπτω *fall*—**1.** lit. Mt 15: 27; Mk
9: 20; Lk 8: 7; 21: 24; Ac 20: 9;
Rv 1: 17. *Fall down* as a sign
of devotion Mt 2: 11; 18: 26,
29; Rv 5: 14. *Fall to pieces,
collapse* Mt 7: 25, 27; Lk 13: 4;
Hb 11: 30; Rv 11: 13.—**2.** fig.
Ac 1: 26; 13: 11; Rv 7: 16.
Fail, become invalid Lk 16: 17;
1 Cor 13: 8. *Be destroyed* Rv 14:
8; 18: 2. In a moral or religious
sense *go astray, be ruined, fall* Ro
11: 11, 22; Hb 4: 11; 1 Cor 10:
12; Rv 2: 5.

Πισιδία, ας, ἡ *Pisidia*, a region in
central Asia Minor Ac 14: 24;
13: 14 v.l.*

Πισίδιος, ία, ιον *Pisidian* Ac 13:
14.*

πιστεύω—**1.** *believe, believe in, be
convinced of, give credence to*
Mt 21; 25, 32; Mk 16: 14; Lk 1:
20; J 2: 22; 8: 24; Ac 8: 37b;
Ro 4: 18; 1 Cor 13: 7; Gal 3: 6;
2 Th 1: 10b.—**2.** *believe (in),
trust* in a special sense, with God
or Christ as object: J 6: 30,
36, 47, 64; 14: 1, 12, 29; 16: 9;
Ac 5: 14; 16: 34; Ro 4: 5, 24;
1 Cor 14: 22; Gal 2: 16; 3: 22;
1 Ti 3: 16; Hb 4: 3; 1 Pt 2: 7.
Have confidence Mt 8: 13; 9: 28;
21: 22; Mk 9: 23f; 2 Cor 4:
13.—**3.** *entrust* Lk 16: 11; J
2: 24. Pass. Ro 3: 2; 1 Cor 9: 17;
Gal 2: 7.—**4.** *trust oneself* Ro 14: 2.

πιστικός, ή, όν may mean *genuine,
unadulterated*, or it may designate a certain kind of nard, e.g.
pistachio Mk 14: 3; J 12: 3.*

πίστις, εως, ἡ *faith, trust*—**1.** *that
which causes trust and faith
faithfulness, reliability* Mt 23:

23; Ro 3: 3; Gal 5: 22; Tit 2: 10.
Solemn promise, oath 1 Ti 5: 12;
proof, pledge Ac 17: 31.—**2.** *trust,
confidence, faith* in the active
sense = 'believing', in religious
usage, directed toward God and
Christ Mt 9: 2, 22, 29; 17: 20;
Mk 11: 22; Lk 18: 42; Ac 14: 9;
26: 18; Ro 4: 5, 9, 11–13; Gal
2: 16; Eph 1: 15; Col 2: 12; Hb
12: 2; Js 1: 6; 1 Pt 1: 21.—
Faith as true piety, genuine
religion, Christianity Lk 18: 8;
Ac 14: 27; Ro 1: 5, 8, 12, 17;
4: 5–20; 1 Cor 2: 5; 13: 13; 2
Cor 1: 24; Gal 3: 7–26; Hb 6:
12; Js 1: 3; 1 Pt 1: 5, 7, 9.
Conviction Ro 14: 22f. Faith
defined Hb 11: 1. A special kind
of faith Lk 17: 5f; 1 Cor 12:
9.—**3.** That which is believed,
body of faith or *belief, doctrine*
Ro 1: 5; Gal 1: 23; Jd 3, 20;
various other passages may be
classed here, e.g. Ro 12: 6; 1 Ti
1: 19; 2 Ti 2: 18; 4: 7 and others.

πιστός, ή, όν—**1.** *trustworthy,
faithful, dependable, inspiring
trust* or *faith* Mt 25: 21, 23; Lk
16: 10–12; 1 Cor 1: 9; 7: 25;
Col 4: 7; 1 Ti 1: 12, 15; 2 Ti
2: 2, 13; Tit 3: 8; Hb 2: 17; 10:
23; Rv 2: 13.—**2.** *trusting,
cherishing faith* or *trust*, also
believing, faithful J 20: 27; Ac
16: 15; Gal 3: 9; Eph 1: 1. Of
Christian *believers* Ac 10: 45;
16: 1; 1 Ti 4: 3, 12; 6: 2.

πιστόω *feel confidence, be convinced*
2 Ti 3: 14.*

πλανάω—**1.** *lead astray, cause to
wander* fig. *mislead, deceive* Mt
24: 4f, 11; J 7: 12; 1 J 1: 8; Rv
2: 20; 20: 3, 8, 10.—**2.** *go astray,
be misled* or *deluded, wander
about* lit. and fig. Mt 18: 12f;
Lk 21: 8; 1 Cor 15: 33; 2 Ti
3: 13; Tit 3: 3; Hb 11: 38; Js
5: 19; 1 Pt 2: 25; 2 Pt 2: 15; Rv
18: 23. *Be mistaken, deceive oneself* Mk 12: 24, 27; Gal 6: 7.

πλάνη, ης, ἡ *wandering* from the path of truth, *error, delusion, deception* Mt 27: 64; Ro 1: 27; Eph 4: 14; 2 Th 2: 11; Js 5: 20; Jd 11.

πλάνης, ητος, ὁ v.l. in Jd 13 for πλανήτης, with the same meaning.*

πλανήτης, ου, ὁ *wanderer* ἀστέρες πλανῆται *wandering stars* Jd 13.*

πλάνος, ον *leading astray, deceitful* 1 Ti 4: 1. ὁ πλάνος as noun *deceiver, impostor* Mt 27: 63; 2 Cor 6: 8; 2 J 7.*

πλάξ, πλακός, ἡ *flat stone, tablet, table* 2 Cor 3: 3; Hb 9: 4.*

πλάσμα, ατος, τό *that which is formed* or *molded* Ro 9: 20.*

πλάσσω *form, mold* Ro 9: 20; 1 Ti 2: 13.*

πλαστός, ή, όν *made up, fabricated, false* 2 Pt 2: 3.*

πλατεῖα, ας, ἡ *wide road, street* Mt 6: 5; 12: 19; Mk 6: 56; Lk 10: 10; Ac 5: 15; Rv 11: 8; 22: 2.

πλάτος, ους, τό *breadth, width* Eph 3: 18; Rv 20: 9; 21: 16.*

πλατύνω *make broad, enlarge* lit. Mt 23: 5. Fig. 2 Cor 6: 11, 13.*

πλατύς, εῖα, ύ *broad, wide* Mt 7: 13.*

πλέγμα, ατος, τό *anything woven* or *braided* of hair 1 Ti 2: 9.*

πλείων, πλειόνως, πλεῖστος see πολύς.

πλέκω *weave, plait* Mt 27: 29; Mk 15: 17; J 19: 2.*

πλέον see πολύς.

πλεονάζω—1. intrans. *be* or *become more, be present in abundance, grow, increase* Ro 5: 20; 6: 1; 2 Cor 4: 15; Phil 4: 17; 2 Th 1: 3; 2 Pt 1: 8. *Have more than is necessary* 2 Cor 8: 15.—2. trans. *cause to increase* 1 Th 3: 12.*

πλεονεκτέω *take advantage of, outwit, defraud, cheat* 2 Cor 2: 11; 7: 2; 12: 17f; 1 Th 4: 6.*

πλεονέκτης, ου, ὁ *one who is greedy, a covetous person* 1 Cor 5: 10f; 6: 10; Eph 5: 5.*

πλεονεξία, ας, ἡ *greediness, insatiableness, avarice, covetousness* Mk 7: 22; Lk 12: 15; Ro 1: 29; 2 Cor 9: 5; Eph 4: 19; 5: 3; Col 3: 5; 1 Th 2: 5; 2 Pt 2: 3, 14.*

πλευρά, ᾶς, ἡ *side* Mt 27: 49 v.l.; J 19: 34; 20: 20, 25, 27; Ac 12: 7.*

πλέω *travel by sea, sail* Lk 8: 23; Ac 21: 3; 27: 2, 6, 24; Rv 18: 17.*

πληγή, ῆς, ἡ *blow, stroke*—1. lit. Lk 12: 48; Ac 16: 23; 2 Cor 11: 23.—2. *wound, bruise* Ac 16: 33; Rv 13: 12, 14.—3. *plague, misfortune* Rv 9: 18, 20; 18: 4, 8; 22: 18.

πλῆθος, ους, τό—1. *quantity* or *number* Hb 11: 12.—2. *large number, multitude*—a. of things w. gen. Lk 5: 6; *bundle* Ac 28: 3; *host* Js 5: 20.—b. of persons— α. *crowd, throng, host* Mk 3: 7f; Lk 2: 13; 6: 17; Ac 5: 14; 21: 36.— β. *a meeting, assembly* Lk 23: 1; Ac 23: 7.—γ. *people, populace, population* Lk 8: 37; Ac 2: 6; 5: 16; 14: 4; 25: 24.—δ. *community, church, fellowship* Lk 1: 10; 19: 37; Ac 4: 32; 6: 5; 15: 12, 30; 19: 9.

πληθύνω—1. trans., act. and pass. Mt 24: 12; Ac 6: 7; 9: 31; 12: 24; 2 Cor 9: 10; Hb 6: 14; 1 Pt 1: 2.—2. intrans. *grow, increase* Ac 6: 1.

πλήκτης, ου, ὁ *pugnacious man, bully* 1 Ti 3: 3; Tit 1: 7.*

πλήμμυρα, ης, ἡ *high water, flood* Lk 6: 48.*

πλήν—1. adv., used as a conjunction *only, nevertheless, however, but* Mt 11: 22, 24; 26: 39; Lk 6: 24, 35; 11: 41; 22: 21f, 42; 23: 28.—*Only, in any case, however, but* 1 Cor 11: 11; Eph 5: 33; Phil 3: 16; 4: 14; Rv 2: 25.—πλήν ὅτι *except that* Ac

20: 23.—**2.** improper prep. w. gen. *except* Mk 12: 32; Ac 8: 1; 15: 28; 20: 23; 27: 22.

πλήρης, ες—1. *filled, full* Mt 15: 37; Mk 8: 19; Lk 4: 1; 5: 12; J 1: 14; Ac 7: 55; 9: 36; 11: 24; 13: 10.—**2.** *complete, full, in full* 2 J 8. πλήρης σῖτος *fully ripened grain* Mk 4: 28.

πληροφορέω—1. *fill (completely), fulfill* 2 Ti 4: 5, 17; *accomplish* Lk 1: 1.—**2.** *convince fully* pass. Ro 4: 21; 14: 5; Col 4: 12.*

πληροφορία, ας, ἡ *full assurance, certainty* Col 2: 2; 1 Th 1: 5; Hb 6: 11; 10: 22. For the passages from Col and Hb and Ro 15: 29 v.l. *fulness* is also possible.*

πληρόω—1. *fill, make full* Mt 13: 48; Lk 3: 5; J 12: 3; 16: 6; Ac 2: 2, 28; 5: 28; Ro 1: 29; Eph 5: 18; Phil 4: 18; 2 Ti 1: 4.—**2.** *of time fill up, complete, reach its end* pass. Mk 1: 15; J 7: 8; Ac 7: 23, 30; 9: 23; 24: 27.—**3.** *bring to completion, finish* something already begun J 3: 29; 17: 13; 2 Cor 10: 6; Phil 2: 2; Col 1: 25. Gal 5: 14 may be classed here or under 4 below.— **4.** *fulfill* a prophecy, promise, etc. Mt 1: 22; 5: 17; 13: 35; 26: 54, 56; Mk 14: 49; Lk 9: 31; 22: 16; J 18: 9, 32; 19: 24, 36; Ro 13: 8; Gal 5: 14 (see 3 above); Col 4: 17.—**5.** *complete, finish, bring to an end* Lk 7: 1; 21: 24; Ac 12: 25; 13: 25; 14: 26; 19: 21.

πλήρωμα, ατος, τό—1. *that which fills*—**a.** *that which fills (up), content or contents.* ἡ γῆ καὶ πλ. αὐτῆς *the earth and everything that is in it* 1 Cor 10: 26. κλάσματα δώδεκα κοφίνων πληρώματα (*enough*) *pieces to fill twelve baskets* Mk 6: 43; cf. 8: 20.— **b.** *that which makes something full or complete, supplement, complement* lit. *patch* Mt 9: 16;

Mk 2: 21. Perhaps *complement* for Eph 1: 23, though meaning 2 is more likely.—**2.** *that which is full of something*; in this case Eph 1: 23 would mean (*that*) *which is full of him who.*—**3.** *that which is brought to fulness or completion*— **a.** *full number* Ro 11: 25. The word in Ro 11: 12 may belong here or under 4 below.—**b.** *sum total, fulness, abundance* Ro 15: 29. πᾶν τὸ πλ. τῆς θεότητος *the full measure of deity* Col 2: 9; cf. 1: 19.—J 1: 16; Eph 3: 19. For Eph 4: 13 see μέτρον and ἡλικία.—**4.** *fulfilling, fulfilment* Ro 13: 10; perhaps 11: 12 (see 3a above).—**5.** *the state of being full, fulness* of time Gal 4: 4; Eph 1: 10.*

πλήσας, πλησθείς 1 aor. participles, act. and pass., of πίμπλημι.

πλησίον adv. *near, close by*— **1.** as noun (ὁ) πλησίον *the neighbor, the one who is near or close by, the fellow man* Mt 5: 43; Mk 12: 31, 33; Lk 10: 27, 29, 36; Ac 7: 27; Ro 13: 9f; 15: 2; Gal 5: 14; Js 4: 12.—**2.** as improper prep. w. gen. *near, close to* J 4: 5.

πλησμονή, ῆς, ἡ *gratification, indulgence* Col 2: 23.*

πλήσσω *strike* pass. Rv 8: 12.*

πλοιάριον, ου, τό diminutive of πλοῖον, though the diminutive sense is not always present: *small ship, boat, skiff* Mk 3: 9 (cf. 4: 1); 4: 36 v.l.; Lk 5: 2; J 6: 22–24; 21: 8.*

πλοῖον, ου, τό *ship* of rather large seafaring vessels Ac 20: 13, 38; 21: 2 f, 6; 27: 2–44; Js 3: 4; Rv 8: 9; 18: 19. *Boat* of fishing vessels on Lake Gennesaret Mt 4: 21f; 9: 1; Mk 1: 19f; 6: 51, 54; J 6: 19, 21f; 21: 3.

πλοκή, ῆς, ἡ *braiding, braid* 1 Pt 3: 3 v.l.*

πλόος, contracted **πλοῦς,** gen.

πλοός, acc. πλοῦν, ὁ *voyage, navigation* Ac 21: 7; 27: 9f.*

πλούσιος, ία, ιον *rich, wealthy*—**1.** lit. Mt 19: 23f; 27: 57; Mk 12: 41; Lk 12: 16; 16: 1, 19; 18: 23; 19: 2. As noun *rich man* Lk 16: 21f; 21: 1; Js 1: 10f; 2: 6; 5: 1; Rv 6: 15.—**2.** fig. 2 Cor 8: 9; Eph 2: 4; Js 2: 5; Rv 2: 9.

πλουσίως adv. *richly, abundantly* Col 3: 16; 1 Ti 6: 17; Tit 3: 6; 2 Pt 1: 11.*

πλουτέω *be rich*; aor. *become rich*; perf. *have become rich*—**1.** lit. Lk 1: 53; 1 Ti 6: 9; Rv 18: 3, 15, 19.—**2.** fig. Lk 12: 21; Ro 10: 12; 1 Cor 4: 8; 2 Cor 8: 9; 1 Ti 6: 18; Rv 3: 17f.*

πλουτίζω *make rich* fig. 1 Cor 1: 5; 2 Cor 6: 10; 9: 11.*

πλοῦτος, ου, ὁ or in nom. and acc. only πλοῦτος, τό *wealth, riches* —**1.** lit. Mt 13: 22; Mk 4: 19; Lk 8: 14; 1 Ti 6: 17; Js 5: 2; Rv 18: 17.—**2.** fig. *a wealth, abundance* Ro 9: 23; 11: 12, 33; 2 Cor 8: 2; Eph 1: 7, 18; 3: 8, 16; Phil 4: 19; Hb 11: 26; Rv 5: 12.

πλύνω *wash* lit. and symbolically Lk 5: 1; Rv 7: 14; 22: 14.*

πνεῦμα, ατος, τό—**1.** *blowing, breathing*—**a.** *wind* J 3: 8a; Hb 1: 7.—**b.** *the breathing out of air, breath* 2 Th 2: 8.—**2.** *breath, (life-) spirit, soul,* that which gives life to the body Mt 27: 50; Lk 8: 55; 23: 46; J 19: 30; Ac 7: 59; Js 2: 26; Hb 12: 23; 1 Pt 3: 19; Rv 11: 11.—**3.** *spirit* as part of the human personality—**a.** the immaterial part 1 Cor 5: 3–5; 7: 34; 2 Cor 7: 1; Col 2: 5; 1 Th 5: 23; Hb 4: 12.— **b.** the representative part of the inner life Mt 5: 3; 26: 41; Mk 2: 8; 8: 12; Lk 1: 47; J 4: 23; 11: 33; 13: 21; Ro 1: 9; 2 Cor 2: 13. One's *very self* Ro 8: 16; Phil 4: 23.—**c.** *spiritual state, state of mind, disposition* 1 Cor 4: 21; Gal 6: 1; Eph 4: 23; 1 Pt 3: 4.—

4. *a spirit* as an independent being, that cannot be perceived by the physical senses—**a.** God himself J 4: 24a.—**b.** lesser good *spirits* or *spirit-beings* Ac 23: 8f; Hb 1: 14; 12: 9; Rv 1: 4; 5: 6.— *Ghost* Lk 24: 37, 39.—**c.** evil *spirits* Mk 1: 23, 26f; Lk 11: 24, 26; Ac 5: 16; 16: 18; 19: 15f; Rv 18: 2.—**5.** *the Spirit* as that which differentiates God from everything that is not God— **a.** the Spirit of God or Christ Mt 3: 16; Lk 4: 18; Ac 5: 9; 16: 7; Ro 8: 9f; 1 Cor 2: 11b, 12b, 14; Gal 4: 6; Eph 3: 16; 1 Pt 1: 11.—**b.** *(the) Holy Spirit* Mt 3: 11; 12: 32; Mk 1: 8, 10, 12; 3: 29; Lk 2: 26; 10: 21; 12: 10; J 1: 32f; 3: 34; 14: 17; 16: 13; Ac 1: 8, 16; 8: 15, 17, 19; 19: 2; Ro 2: 29; 5: 5; 8: 2; 1 Cor 3: 17; 6: 19; Gal 3: 2f, 5, 14; 5: 16, 22, 25; Eph 4: 30; Col 1: 8; 1 Th 1: 6; Hb 10: 15; 2 Pt 1: 21.—Clearly as an independent personality Mt 28: 19; cf. 2 Cor 13: 13.—**c.** of a *spirit* that is not from God 1 Cor 12: 10; 2 Cor 11: 4; 2 Th 2: 2; 1 J 4: 1–3.

πνευματικός, ή, όν *pertaining to the spirit, spiritual*—**1.** *caused by* or *filled with the* (divine) *Spirit, pertaining* or *corresponding to the* (divine) *Spirit.*—**a.** as adj. Ro 1: 11; 7: 14; 1 Cor 10: 3f; 15: 44; Eph 1: 3; 5: 19; Col 1: 9; 3: 16; 1 Pt 2: 5. ὁ πνευματικὸς (ἄνθρωπος) in 1 Cor 2: 15 means *the spiritual man,* one whose natural ψυχή (cf. verse 14) has been replaced by the divine πνεῦμα. Cf. also 1 Cor 15: 47 v.l.—**b.** subst. τὰ πνευματικά *spiritual things* or *matters* Ro 15: 27; 1 Cor 2: 13; 9: 11; 15: 46. *Spiritual gifts* 1 Cor 12: 1; 14: 1. ὁ πνευματικός *the one who possesses the Spirit* 1 Cor 3: 1; 14: 37; Gal 6: 1.—**2.** *pertaining* *to* (evil) *spirits* subst. *spirit-forces* Eph 6: 12.*

πνευματικῶς adv. *spiritually, in a manner consistent with the* (divine) *Spirit* 1 Cor 2: 14; 2: 13 v.l. *In a spiritual* (allegorical) *way* Rv 11: 8.*

πνέω *blow,* of wind Mt 7: 25, 27; Lk 12: 55; J 3: 8; 6: 18; Ac 27: 15 v.l.; 27: 40; Rv 7: 1.*

πνίγω *choke, strangle* Mt 13: 7; 18: 28. *Drown* Mk 5: 13.*

πνικτός, ή, όν *strangled, choked to death* of animals killed for food without having the blood drained from them Ac 15: 20, 29; 21: 25.*

πνοή, ῆς, ἡ *wind* Ac 2: 2. *Breath* 17: 25.*

ποδαπός an older form of ποταπός.

ποδήρης, ες *reaching to the feet* as noun ὁ π. *the robe reaching to the feet* Rv 1: 13.*

πόθεν adv. *from where, from which, whence?*—**1.** *from what place? from where?* Mt 15: 33; Mk 8: 4; Lk 13: 25, 27; J 3: 8; 9: 29f; 19: 9; Rv 2: 5.—**2.** *from what source? brought about* or *given by whom? born of whom?* Mt 13: 27, 54, 56; Lk 20: 7; J 2: 9; 7: 27; Js 4: 1.—**3.** *how, why, in what way?* Mk 12: 37; Lk 1: 43; J 1: 48; 6: 5.

ποία, ας, ἡ *grass, herb.* This meaning was formerly assumed by some for Js 4: 14; the form is better taken as the feminine of ποῖος.*

ποιέω **I.** act.—**1.** *do, make*—**a.** of external things *make, manufacture, produce* J 18: 18; Ac 7: 40; 9: 39; Ro 9: 21; Hb 8: 5. *Create* Mk 10: 6; Ac 7: 50; 17: 24; Rv 14: 7.—**b.** *do, cause, accomplish,* also *keep, carry out, practice,* etc. Mt 7: 22; Mk 1: 17; 2: 23; 11: 3; Lk 19: 18; J 2: 23; 3: 21; 8: 39, 41; 12: 16; Ac 3: 12; 24: 12; Ro 13: 3f; 1 Cor 6: 18;

2 Ti 4: 5.—*Do with* Mt 27: 22. *Establish* Eph 2: 15. *Give* Lk 14: 12, 16. *Celebrate* Hb 11: 28. *Yield, bear* Mt 3: 10; Rv 22: 2. *Claim, pretend* J 19: 7, 12. *Exercise* Rv 13: 12a.—**c.** specialized expressions: *get, gain* Lk 12: 33; 16: 9; J 4: 1.— *Assume, suppose* Mt 12: 33.— *Take* outside Ac 5: 34.—*Spend, stay* Ac 15: 33; 18: 23; 20: 3; 2 Cor 11: 25; Js 4: 13.—**2.** *do, act, proceed* Mt 12: 12; 20: 5; Mk 15: 8; Lk 2: 27; 16: 8; Ac 10: 33. *Work, be active* Mt 20: 12a; Rv 13: 5.—**II.** mid. *make* or *do something for oneself* or *of oneself* Lk 5: 33; J 14: 23; Ro 1: 9; Phil 1: 4; 2 Pt 1: 10. *Form* Ac 23: 13. σπουδήν π. *be eager* Jd 3.

ποίημα, ατος, τό *what is made, creation* Ro 1: 20; Eph 2: 10.*

ποίησις, εως, ἡ *doing, working* Js 1: 25.*

ποιητής, οῦ, ὁ *one who does, a doer* Ro 2: 13; Js 1: 22f, 25; 4: 11. *Poet* Ac 17: 28.*

ποικίλος, η, ον *of various kinds, diversified, manifold* Mk 1: 34; 2 Ti 3: 6; Hb 13: 9; Js 1: 2; 1 Pt 4: 10.

ποιμαίνω *herd, tend,* (*lead to*) *pasture*—**1.** lit. 1 Cor 9: 7; *tend sheep* Lk 17: 7.—**2.** fig.—**a.** in the sense 'lead', 'guide', 'rule' Mt 2: 6; J 21: 16; Ac 20: 28; 1 Pt 5: 2; Rv 2: 27; 12: 5; 19: 15.—**b.** *care for, look after* Jd 12; Rv 7: 17.*

ποιμήν, ένος, ὁ *shepherd*—**1.** lit. Mt 9: 36; 25: 32; Mk 6: 34; 14: 27; Lk 2: 8, 15, 18, 20; as a symbol Mt 26: 31; J 10: 2, 11f, 14, 16.—**2.** fig. Hb 13: 20; 1 Pt 2: 25. *Pastor* Eph 4: 11.*

ποίμνη, ης, ἡ *flock* lit. Lk 2: 8; 1 Cor 9: 7; as a symbol Mt 26: 31; J 10: 16.*

ποίμνιον, ου, τό *flock* fig. Lk 12: 32; Ac 20: 28f; 1 Pt 5: 2f.*

ποῖος, α, ον—1. *of what kind?* Lk
6: 32–34; J 12: 33; 21: 19; Ac
7: 49; Ro 3: 27; 1 Cor 15: 35;
Js 4: 14; 1 Pt 1: 11.—2. *which,
what?* Mt 19: 18; 21: 23f, 27;
22: 36; Mk 11: 28; Lk 5: 19;
12: 39; J 10: 32; Ac 23: 34;
Rv 3: 3.

πολεμέω *make war, fight* lit. Rv
2: 16; 12: 7; 19: 11. Fig. Js 4: 2.

πόλεμος, ου, ὁ—1. lit. *armed conflict*—a. *war* Mt 24: 6; Lk 14:
31; Hb 11: 34; Rv 11: 7; 13:
7.—b. *battle, fight* 1 Cor 14: 8;
Rv 9: 7, 9; 16: 14.—2. fig. *strife,
conflict, quarrel* Js 4: 1.

πόλις, εως, ἡ *city, city state* Mt
8: 33; Lk 10: 8, 10; J 4: 8, 28,
30. *Capital city, main city* Ac
8: 5; Lk 8: 27. The heavenly
city, the New Jerusalem Hb 11:
10, 16; Rv 21: 2, 10, 14–16,
18f.—Fig., *city* for its inhabitants Mt 8: 34; Mk 1: 33; Lk 4:
43; Ac 14: 21; 21: 30.

πολιτάρχης, ου, ὁ *civic magistrate,
politarch*, five or six of whom
formed the city council in
Thessalonica Ac 17: 6, 8.*

πολιτεία, ας, ἡ *citizenship* Ac 22:
28, but *commonwealth, state* Eph
2: 12.*

πολίτευμα, ατος, τό *commonwealth, state* Phil 3: 20.*

πολιτεύομαι *live, conduct oneself,
lead one's life* Ac 23: 1; Phil 1:
27.*

πολίτης, ου, ὁ *citizen* Lk 15: 15;
Ac 21: 39. *Fellow-citizen* Lk
19: 14; Hb 8: 11.*

πολλά see πολύς.

πολλάκις adv. *many times, often,
frequently* Mt 17: 15; Mk 5: 4;
Ac 26: 11; Ro 1: 13; 2 Cor 8: 22;
Hb 6: 7; 9: 25f.

πολλαπλασίων, ον, gen. ονος neut.
pl. *many times as much* Mt 19:
29; Lk 18: 30.*

πολυεύσπλαγχνος, ον *rich in compassion* Js 5: 11 v.l.*

πολύλαλος, ον *talkative, garrulous*;

it has been suspected that πολύ-
λαλοι was once read for πολλοί
in Js 3: 1.*

πολυλογία, ας, ἡ *much speaking,
wordiness* Mt 6: 7; Lk 11: 2 v.l.*

πολυμερῶς adv. *in many ways*
Hb 1: 1.*

πολυπλήθεια, ας, ἡ *large crowd*
Ac 14: 7 v.l.*

πολυποίκιλος, ον (very) *many-
sided* Eph 3: 10.*

πολύς, πολλή, πολύ gen. πολλοῦ,
ῆς, οῦ—I. positive degree of
comparison *much, many*—1.
adj.—a. with a noun, etc., in the
plural *many, numerous, large,
great* Mt 4: 25; 7: 13, 22; Mk
6: 13; Lk 15: 13; J 20: 30; Ac 1:
3; 24: 10; Ro 4: 17f; 1 Cor 8: 5;
Hb 2: 10; Rv 5: 11. κτήματα
πολλά *a great deal of property* Mk
10: 22. πολλοὶ χρόνοι *long
periods of time* Lk 8: 29.—b. with
a noun in the singular *much,
large, great, strong, severe* Mt
20: 29; Ac 6: 7; 11: 21; 18: 10;
23: 10; 27: 21; Ro 9: 22; Eph
2: 4; 1 Th 2: 2. *Long* J 5: 6;
Ac 15: 32. ὥρα πολλή *late hour*
Mk 6: 35.—2. substantively—
a. πολλοί *many* persons Mk
2: 2; 10: 45; Lk 1: 1, 14, 16;
Gal 3: 16; 2 Cor 12: 21; 2 Pt 2:
2. οἱ πολλοί *the many* Mk 6: 2;
Ro 12: 5; 1 Cor 10: 33; *the
majority, most* Mt 24: 12; Hb
12: 15; *the crowd* 2 Cor 2: 17.—
b. πολλά *many things, much, at
length* Mt 13: 3; Mk 4: 2; Lk
9: 22; 2 Cor 8: 22a.—πολλά in
the acc. as adv. *greatly, earnestly,
strictly, loudly, often*, etc. Mk
5: 38, 43; 6: 20; 1 Cor 16: 12,
19; Js 3: 2; *hard* Ro 16: 6, 12.—
c. πολύ *much* Mt 6: 30; Lk 12:
48; Ac 28: 6; Ro 3: 2; Phil 2:
12; Hb 12: 9, 25. πολλοῦ gen.
of price *for a large sum of money*
Mt 26: 9. πολύ acc. as adv.
greatly, very much Mk 12: 27;
Lk 7: 47b.—II. comparative

degree πλείων, neut. πλεῖον or πλέον, genitive of all genders πλείονος; nom. pl. masc. and fem. πλείονες, contracted πλείους; neut. πλείονα, contracted πλείω; *more.*—1. adj. Mt 21: 36; J 4: 1; 7: 31; 15: 2; Ac 2: 40; 4: 22; Hb 3: 3; Rv 2: 19; *longer* Ac 18: 20; *many* 13: 31.— 2. subst.—a. (οἱ) πλείονες, (οἱ) πλείους the *majority, most* Ac 19: 32; 27: 12; 1 Cor 10: 5; 15: 6.—(*Even) more* J 4: 41; Ac 28: 23.—b. πλεῖον, πλέον *more* τὸ πλεῖον the *greater sum*, etc. Mt 6: 25; Mk 12: 43; Lk 7: 43; 9: 13.—Acc. as adv. *more, to a greater degree* Mt 5: 20; Lk 7: 42; J 21: 15.—III. superlative πλεῖστος, η, ον *most*—1. adj. *most of* Mt 11: 20. *Very great, very large* Mt 21: 8; Mk 4: 1.— 2. subst. οἱ πλεῖστοι the *majority, most* Ac 19: 32 v.l. Neut. acc. as adv. τὸ πλεῖστον *at the most* 1 Cor 14: 27.

πολύσπλαγχνος, ον *compassionate, merciful* Js 5: 11.*

πολυτελής, ές (*very) expensive, costly* Mk 14: 3; 1 Ti 2: 9; 1 Pt 3: 4.*

πολύτιμος, ον *very precious, valuable* Mt 13: 46; 26: 7 v.l.; J 12: 3: 1 Pt 1: 7.*

πολυτρόπως adv. *in various ways* Hb 1: 1.*

πόμα, ατος, τό *a drink* Hb 9: 10. Symbolically 1 Cor 10: 4; 12: 13 v.l.*

πονηρία, ας, ἡ *wickedness, baseness, maliciousness, sinfulness* Mt 22: 18; Lk 11: 39; Ac 3: 26; Ro 1: 29; 1 Cor 5: 8; Eph 6: 12; pl. *malicious acts* Mk 7: 22.*

πονηρός, ά, όν—1. adj.—a. in the physical sense *in poor condition, sick* Mt 6: 23; Lk 11: 34 (for other possibilities see ὀφθαλμός). *Painful, serious* Rv 16: 2. *Bad, spoiled* Mt 7: 17f.—b. in the ethical sense *wicked, evil, bad,*

vicious, degenerate Mt 12: 35; 16: 4; Lk 19: 22; J 3: 19; Ac 19: 15f; Gal 1: 4; 2 Ti 4: 18; Hb 3: 12; 10: 22; Js 2: 4. *Arrogant* Js 4: 16.—2. subst.— a. *wicked* or *evil-intentioned person, evil-doer* Mt 5: 39, 45; Lk 6: 35; 1 Cor 5: 13.—ὁ πονηρός *the evil one* = the devil Mt 13: 19; J 17: 15; Eph 6: 16; 1 J 3: 12; 5: 18f. The genitives in Mt 5: 37 and 6: 13 may be masculine *the evil one,* or neut. *evil.*—τὸ πονηρόν (*that which is) evil* Mt 5: 11; Mk 7: 23; Lk 6: 45c; Ac 25: 18; Ro 12: 9 (see Mt 5: 37 and 6: 13 above).

πόνος, ου, ὁ (*hard) labor, toil* Col 4: 13. *Pain, distress, affliction* Rv 16: 10f; 21: 4.*

Ποντικός, ή, όν *from Pontus* (see Πόντος) Ac 18: 2.*

Πόντιος, ου, ὁ *Pontius* the tribal (middle) name of Pilate Mt 27: 2 v.l.; Lk 3: 1; Ac 4: 27; 1 Ti 6: 13.*

πόντος, ου, ὁ *the* (high) *sea* Rv 18:17 v.l.*

Πόντος, ου, ὁ *Pontus,* a district in northeast Asia Minor Ac 2: 9; 1 Pt 1: 1.*

Πόπλιος, ου, ὁ *Publius,* a Roman personal name Ac 28: 7f.*

πορεία, ας, ἡ *journey, trip* Lk 13: 22; Js 1: 11; for the latter passage *way of life, conduct* is also possible.*

πορεύω only as mid. and pass. **πορεύομαι** *go, proceed, travel*— 1. lit. Mt 2: 20; 22: 15; 25: 41; Lk 7: 50; 9: 56; Ac 8: 39; 20: 1, 22; 25: 12; Ro 15: 24f; 1 Cor 10: 27; 16: 6; *I am about to go* J 14: 12, 28.—2. fig.—a. as a euphemism *go to one's death, die* Lk 22: 22.—b. π. ὀπίσω *follow,* i.e. indulge, w. gen. 2 Pt 2: 10.— c. *conduct oneself, live, walk* Lk 1: 6; Ac 9: 31; 14: 16; 1 Pt 4: 3; 2 Pt 3: 3; Jd 11, 16, 18.— d. *pass by* Lk 8: 14.

πορθέω *pillage, destroy, annihilate* Ac 9: 21; Gal 1: 13, 23.*

πορία a variant spelling for πορεία.

πορισμός, οῦ, ὁ *means of gain* 1 Ti 6: 5, 6.*

Πόρκιος, ου, ὁ *Porcius* tribal name of Festus Ac 24: 27.*

πορνεία, ας, ἡ *unchastity, prostitution, fornication,* of every kind of unlawful sexual intercourse.—**1.** lit. Mt 5: 32; 19: 9; Mk 7: 21; J 8: 41; Ac 15: 20; 1 Cor 6: 13, 18; 7: 2; 2 Cor 12: 21; Gal 5: 19; Col 3: 5.—**2.** fig., of idolatry, *immorality* Rv 2: 21; 14: 8; 17: 2, 4; 19: 2.

πορνεύω *to prostitute, practice prostitution* or *sexual immorality* in general—**1.** lit. Mk 10: 19 v.l.; 1 Cor 6: 18; 10: 8; Rv 2: 14, 20.—**2.** fig., of idolatry Rv 17: 2; 18: 3, 9.*

πόρνη, ης, ἡ *prostitute, harlot.*— **1.** lit. Mt 21: 31f; Lk 15: 30; 1 Cor 6: 15f; Hb 11: 31; Js 2: 25.—**2.** fig. Rv 17: 1, 5, 15f; 19: 2.*

πόρνος, ου, ὁ *one who practices sexual immorality, a fornicator* 1 Cor 5: 9–11; Eph 5: 5; 1 Ti 1: 10; Hb 12: 16; Rv 22: 15.

πόρρω adv. *far (away)* Mt 15: 8; Mk 7: 6; Lk 14: 32.—As comparative degree we have in the text of Lk 24: 28 πορρώτερον and as v.l. πορρωτέρω *farther.*

πόρρωθεν adv. *from a distance* Hb 11: 13. *At a distance* Lk 17: 12.*

πορρώτερον and πορρωτέρω see πόρρω.

πορφύρα, ας, ἡ *purple (cloth)* Lk 16: 19; *purple (garment)* Rv 18: 12; cf. 17: 4 v.l. Of the reddish *purple cloak* of the Roman soldier Mk 15: 17, 20.*

πορφυρόπωλις, ιδος, ἡ *a (woman) dealer in purple cloth* Ac 16: 14.*

πορφυροῦς, ᾶ, οῦν *purple* J 19: 2, 5. *Purple clothing* Rv 17: 4; 18: 16.*

ποσάκις adv. *how many times? how often?* Mt 18: 21; 23: 37; Lk 13: 34.*

πόσις, εως, ἡ *(the act of) drinking* Ro 14: 17; Col 2: 16. *A drink* J 6: 55.*

πόσος, η, ον pron.—**1.** *how great(?)* Mt 6: 23; 7: 11; Mk 9: 21; Lk 11: 13; Ro 11: 12, 24; 2 Cor 7: 11; Hb 10: 29.—**2.** *how much, how many(?)* Mt 27: 13; Mk 6: 38; Lk 15: 17; 16: 5, 7; Ac 21: 20.

ποταμός, οῦ, ὁ *river, stream* Mt 3: 6; Lk 6: 48f; J 7: 38; Ac 16: 13; 2 Cor 11: 26; Rv 9: 14; 22: 1f. *Mountain* or *winter torrent* Mt 7: 25, 27.

ποταμοφόρητος, ον *swept away by a river* Rv 12: 15.*

ποταπός, ή, όν *of what sort* or *kind* Mt 8: 27; Lk 1: 29; 7: 39; 2 Pt 3: 11. *How great* Mk 13: 1; *how glorious* 1 J 3: 1.*

ποταπῶς adv. *in what way, how* Ac 20: 18 v.l.*

πότε adv. *when(?)* Mt 25: 37–39, 44; Mk 13: 4, 35; Lk 17: 20; J 6: 25. ἕως π. *how long?* Mt 17: 17; Lk 9: 41; J 10: 24; Rv 6: 10.

ποτέ enclitic particle *at some time or other,* of the past *once, formerly* J 9: 13; Ro 7: 9; 11: 30; 1 Cor 9: 7; Gal 1: 13, 23; Eph 2: 2f; of the fut. *once* Lk 22: 32. ἤδη ποτέ *now at last* Ro 1: 10; Phil 4: 10.

πότερον interrogative word *whether* J 7: 17.*

ποτήριον, ου, τό *cup, drinking-vessel*—**1.** lit. Mt 10: 42; 26: 27; Mk 7: 4; 9: 41; 14: 23; Lk 11: 39; 22: 17, 20a; 1 Cor 10: 16, 21; 11: 25a, 27f; Rv 17: 4. The cup stands, by metonymy, for what it contains Lk 22: 20b; 1 Cor 11: 25b, 26.—**2.** fig., of undergoing a violent death Mt 20: 22f; 26: 39, 42 v.l.; Mk 10: 38f; 14: 36; Lk 22: 42; J 18: 11; Rv 14: 10; 16: 19; 18: 6.

ποτίζω—1. of persons *give to drink, cause someone to drink* Mt 10: 42; 25: 35; Mk 15: 36; 1 Cor 3: 2; 12: 13; Rv 14: 8.—2. of animals and plants Lk 13: 15; 1 Cor 3: 6–8.

Ποτίολοι, ων, οἱ *Puteoli*, a city on the Gulf of Naples in Italy Ac 28: 13.*

πότος, ου, ὁ *drinking party, carousal* 1 Pt 4: 3.*

ποῦ adv.—1. *where(?), at which place(?)* Mt 2: 2, 4; 8: 20; Mk 14: 12, 14; 15: 47; Lk 17: 17, 37; J 20: 2, 13, 15; Ro 3: 27; 1 Cor 1: 20; 2 Pt 3: 4; Rv 2: 13. —2. *where(?), whither(?), to what place(?)* J 3: 8; 7: 35; 8: 14; 13: 36; Hb 11: 8.

πού enclitic adv. *somewhere* Hb 2: 6; 4: 4. *About, approximately* Ro 4: 19.*

Πούδης, εντος, ὁ *Pudens*, a Roman personal name 2 Ti 4: 21.*

πούς, ποδός, ὁ *foot*—1. lit. Mt 7: 6; Lk 7: 46; 8: 35; 24: 39f; J 13: 5f; 20: 12; Ac 4: 35, 37; 5: 10; Eph 6: 15; Rv 3: 9; 19: 10. *Leg* Rv 10: 1. The *foot* as a measure of length Ac 7: 5.— 2. fig. Mt 5: 35; 22: 44; Lk 1: 79; Ro 3: 15; 16: 20; 1 Cor 15: 25, 27; Hb 1: 13.

πρᾶγμα, ατος, τό—1. *deed, thing, event, occurrence* Lk 1: 1; Ac 5: 4; Hb 6: 18; *matter* 2 Cor 7: 11.—2. *undertaking, occupation, task* Ro 16: 2; 1 Th 4: 6.—3. *thing, affair* Mt 18: 19; Hb 10: 1; 11: 1; Js 3: 16.—4. *lawsuit* 1 Cor 6: 1.*

πραγματεία, ας, ἡ *affair, undertaking* 2 Ti 2: 4.*

πραγματεύομαι *conduct* or *be engaged in a business* Lk 19: 13.*

πραθείς, πραθῆναι 1 aor. pass. participle and inf. of πιπράσκω.

πραιτώριον, ου, τό (Latin loanword: praetorium) *the praetorium, governor's official residence* Mt 27: 27; Mk 15: 16; J 18: 28,

33; 19: 9; Ac 23: 35. This may also be the meaning in Phil 1: 13, but here *praetorian guard* is also possible.*

πράκτωρ, ορος, ὁ *bailiff, constable* Lk 12: 58.*

πρᾶξις, εως, ἡ—1. *activity, function* Mt 16: 27; Ro 12: 4.—2. *act, action, deed* generally in the title of Ac. *Evil* or *disgraceful deed* Lk 23: 51; Ac 19: 18; Ro 8: 13; Col 3: 9.*

πρᾶος variant of πραΰς.

πραότης variant form of πραΰτης.

πρασιά, ᾶς, ἡ *garden plot* fig. πρασιαὶ πρασιαί *group by group* Mk 6: 40.*

πράσσω—1. trans.—a. *do, accomplish* Ac 5: 35; 26: 20, 26; 2 Cor 5: 10. *Do, commit* Lk 22: 23; 23: 15; Ac 16: 28; 19: 36; Ro 2: 1–3; 7: 19; 1 Cor 5: 2. *Practice, busy oneself with, mind* Ac 19: 19; 1 Th 4: 11; *observe* Ro 2: 25.—b. *collect* taxes, etc. Lk 3: 13; 19: 23.—2. intrans.— a. *act* Ac 3: 17; 17: 7; perhaps 15: 29.—b. *be, be situated* Eph 6: 21; perhaps Ac 15: 29.

πραϋπάθεια, ας, ἡ *gentleness* 1 Ti 6: 11.*

πραΰς, πραεῖα, πραΰ *gentle, humble, considerate* Mt 5: 5; 11: 29; 21: 5; 1 Pt 3: 4.*

πραΰτης, ητος, ἡ and πραότης, ητος, ἡ *gentleness, humility, courtesy, considerateness* 1 Cor 4: 21; 2 Cor 10: 1; Gal 5: 23; 6: 1; Eph 4: 2; Col 3: 12; 2 Ti 2: 25; Tit 3: 2; Js 1: 21; 3: 13; 1 Pt 3: 15.*

πρέπω *be fitting, be seemly* or *suitable* Mt 3: 15; 1 Cor 11: 13; 1 Ti 2: 10; Tit 2: 1; Hb 7: 26. Impersonal constr. w. dat. *it is fitting for someone* Eph 5: 3; Hb 2: 10.*

πρεσβεία, ας, ἡ *embassy, ambassador(s)* Lk 14: 32; 19: 14.*

πρεσβευτής, οῦ, ὁ see πρεσβύτης.

πρεσβεύω *be an ambassador, travel*

or *work as an ambassador* 2 Cor
5: 20; Eph 6: 20.*

πρεσβυτέριον, ου, τό *council of
elders*—**1.** *the Sanhedrin*, the
highest Jewish council in Jerusalem Lk 22: 66; Ac 22: 5.—
2. *the presbytery*, a Christian
church council, including all the
elders 1 Ti 4: 14.*

πρεσβύτερος, α, ον—**1.** of age
older, often subst. *old(er) person*
Lk 15: 25; J 8: 9; Ac 2: 17; 1 Ti
5: 1f. Of a period of time οἱ π.
the men of old, our ancestors Mt
15: 2; Mk 7: 3, 5; Hb 11: 2.—
2. as a designation of an official
elder, presbyter—**a.** among the
Jews Mt 16: 21; 27: 41; Mk 14:
43, 53; Lk 7: 3; 9: 22; Ac 4:
23; 6: 12.—**b.** among the Christians Ac 11: 30; 14: 23; 15: 2, 4,
6, 22f; 16: 4; 20: 17; 21: 18;
1 Ti 5: 17, 19; Tit 1: 5; Js 5: 14;
1 Pt 5: 1; 5: 5; 2 J 1; 3 J 1; Rv
4: 4, 10; 5: 5–14; 7: 11, 13;
11: 16; 14: 3; 19: 4.

πρεσβύτης, ου, ὁ *old man* Lk 1:
18; Tit 2: 2; Phlm 9. In the last-
named passage some prefer the
emendation πρεσβευτής *ambassador*.*

πρεσβῦτις, ιδος, ἡ *old(er) woman,
elderly lady* Tit 2: 3.*

πρηνής, ές gen. **οῦς** *head first,
headlong* Ac 1: 18. *Swollen, distended* is also possible.*

πρίζω or **πρίω** *saw (in two)* Hb
11: 37.*

πρίν—**1.** conjunction *before* Mt
1: 18; 26: 34, 75; Lk 2: 26; 22:
61; J 8: 58; 14: 29; Ac 7: 2.—
2. improper prep. w. gen. *before*
Mt 26: 34 v.l.; J 8: 58 v.l.

Πρίσκα and its diminutive **Πρίσ-
κιλλα, ης, ἡ** *Prisca, Priscilla*,
wife of Aquila. The form Πρίσ-
κιλλα Ac 18: 2, 18, 26; Πρίσκα
Ro 16: 3; 1 Cor 16: 19; 2 Ti
4: 19.*

πρίω see πρίζω.

πρό prep. w. gen. *before*—**1.**

of place *before, in front of,
at* Mt 11: 10; Lk 9: 52; Ac
12: 6; 14: 13; Js 5: 9.—
2. of time Mt 6: 8; 24: 38; Lk
11: 38; J 11: 55; Ac 23: 15;
Ro 16: 7; 1 Cor 4: 5; Gal 1: 17;
Eph 1: 4; Col 1: 17; 2 Ti 4: 21.—
3. of precedence Js 5: 12; 1 Pt
4: 8.

προάγω—**1.** trans. *lead forward,
lead* or *bring out* Ac 12: 6; 16:
30; 17: 5; 25: 26.—**2.** intrans.
go before, lead the way, precede—
a. in place Mt 2: 9; Mk 11: 9;
walk ahead of Mk 10: 32.—**b.** in
time *go* or *come before* Mt 14:
22; Mk 6: 45; 14: 28; 1 Ti 1: 18;
5: 24; Hb 7: 18; *get in before* Mt
21: 31.

προαιρέω mid. *choose (for oneself),
determine, decide* 2 Cor 9: 7.*

προαιτιάομαι *accuse, bring an
accusation beforehand* Ro 3: 9.*

προακούω *hear beforehand* Col 1:
5.*

προαμαρτάνω *sin beforehand* 2
Cor 12: 21; 13: 2.*

προαύλιον, ου, τό *forecourt, gateway* Mk 14: 68.*

προβαίνω *go ahead, go on* lit. Mt
4: 21; Mk 1: 19. Fig. *be advanced*
Lk 1: 7, 18; 2: 36.*

προβάλλω *put forward, cause to
come forward* Ac 19: 33. *Put out*
Lk 21: 30.*

προβάς 2 aor. act. participle of
προβαίνω.

προβατικός, ή, όν *pertaining to
sheep* ἡ προβατική *the sheep gate*
J 5: 2.*

προβάτιον, ου, τό *lamb* or *sheep*
J 21: 16f.*

πρόβατον, ου, τό *sheep*—**1.** lit.
Mt 7: 15; 12: 11f; Mk 14: 27;
Lk 15: 4, 6; J 2: 14f; Ro 8: 36;
Rv 18: 13.—**2.** symbolically and
allegorically Mt 25: 32f; J 10: 1–
16, 26f; Hb 13: 20; 1 Pt 2: 25.

προβεβηκώς perf. act. participle
of προβαίνω.

προβιβάζω *put forward, cause to*

come forward Mt 14: 8; Ac 19: 33 v.l.*

προβλέπω see beforehand mid. select, provide Hb 11: 40.*

προγίνομαι happen or be done before Ro 3: 25.*

προγινώσκω know beforehand or in advance, have foreknowledge (of) 1 Pt 1: 20; 2 Pt 3: 17. Choose beforehand Ro 8: 29; 11: 2. Know from time past Ac 26: 5.*

πρόγνωσις, εως, ἡ foreknowledge Ac 2: 23; 1 Pt 1: 2.*

πρόγονος, ον born early οἱ πρόγονοι parents, forefathers, ancestors 1 Ti 5: 4; 2 Ti 1: 3.*

προγράφω write before(hand) Ro 15: 4; Eph 3: 3; mark out Jd 4. Show forth or portray publicly, proclaim or placard in public Gal 3: 1.*

πρόδηλος, ον clear, evident, known to all 1 Ti 5: 24f; Hb 7: 14.*

προδίδωμι give in advance Ro 11: 35. Hand over, betray Mk 14: 10 v.l.*

προδότης, ου, ὁ traitor, betrayer Lk 6: 16; Ac 7: 52; 2 Ti 3: 4.*

πρόδρομος, ον going before subst. forerunner Hb 6: 20.*

προεῖδον 2 aor. act. ind. of προοράω.

προεῖπον foretell, tell beforehand —1. of prophetic utterances Mt 24: 25; Mk 13: 23; Ac 1: 16; Ro 9: 29; 2 Cor 13: 2; Gal 5: 21; 2 Pt 3: 2; Jd 17.—2. have said before or previously, have already said or mentioned 2 Cor 7: 3; Gal 1: 9; 1 Th 4: 6; Hb 4: 7; 10: 15 v.l.*

προείρηκα, προείρημαι perf. ind. act. and mid. of προεῖπον.

προέλαβον 2 aor. act. ind. of προλαμβάνω.

προελπίζω hope before, be the first to hope Eph 1: 12.*

προενάρχομαι begin (beforehand) 2 Cor 8: 6, 10.*

προεπαγγέλλω mid. and pass.

promise beforehand, previously Ro 1: 2; 2 Cor 9: 5.*

προέρχομαι—1. go forward, advance, proceed Mt 26: 39; Mk 14: 35; Ac 12: 10.—2. go before as forerunner or leader Lk 1: 17; 22: 47.—3. come or go before someone, go on before or ahead Mk 6: 33; Ac 20: 5, 13; 2 Cor 9: 5. Come out Ac 12: 13 v.l.*

προετοιμάζω prepare beforehand Ro 9: 23; Eph 2: 10.*

προευαγγελίζομαι proclaim good news in advance Gal 3: 8.*

προέχω in Ro 3: 9 προεχόμεθα if mid. can mean have an advantage or protect oneself. If it is pass., be excelled.*

προηγέομαι go before; in Ro 12: 10 outdo or consider better, esteem more highly.*

πρόθεσις, εως, ἡ—1. setting forth, putting out, presentation οἱ ἄρτοι τῆς προθέσεως loaves of presentation, sacred bread Mt 12: 4; Mk 2: 26; Lk 6: 4; cf. Hb 9: 2.—2. plan, purpose, resolve, will Ac 11: 23; 27: 13; Ro 8: 28; 9: 11; Eph 1: 11; 3: 11; 2 Ti 1: 9; 3: 10.*

προθεσμία, ας, ἡ appointed day, fixed or limited time Gal 4: 2.*

προθυμία, ας, ἡ willingness, readiness, good will Ac 17: 11; 2 Cor 8: 11f, 19; 9: 2.*

πρόθυμος, ον ready, willing, eager Mt 26: 41; Mk 14: 38. τὸ πρόθυμον desire, eagerness Ro 1: 15.*

προθύμως adv. willingly, eagerly, freely 1 Pt 5: 2.*

προϊδών 2 aor. act. participle of προοράω.

πρόϊμος, ον early as subst. early rain Js 5: 7.*

προϊνός a variant spelling of πρωϊνός.

προΐστημι—1. be at the head (of), rule, direct w. gen. 1 Ti 3: 4f, 12; 5: 17. Perhaps Ro 12: 8; 1 Th 5: 12.—2. be concerned about,

184   προκαλέω–πρός

care for, give aid perhaps Ro 12:
8; 1 Th 5: 12. Busy oneself with,
engage in w. gen. Tit 3: 8, 14.*
προκαλέω mid. provoke, challenge
Gal 5: 26.*
προκαταγγέλλω announce beforehand, foretell Ac 3: 18, 24 v.l.;
7: 52; 2 Cor 9: 5 v.l.*
προκαταρτίζω get ready or arrange
for in advance 2 Cor 9: 5.*
προκατέχω gain possession of or
occupy previously προκατέχομεν
περισσόν; do we have a previous
advantage? Ro 3: 9 v.l.*
πρόκειμαι be set before—1. be
exposed to public view Jd 7.—
2. lie before, be present, be set
before 2 Cor 8: 12; Hb 6: 18; 12:
1f.*
προκηρύσσω proclaim beforehand
Ac 13: 24; pass. 3: 20 v.l.*
προκοπή, ῆς, ἡ progress, advance-
ment Phil 1: 12, 25; 1 Ti 4: 15.*
προκόπτω go forward, make progress, advance, go on Lk 2: 52;
Gal 1: 14; 2 Ti 2: 16; 3: 9, 13.
Be advanced, be far gone Ro 13:
12.*
πρόκριμα, ατος, τό prejudgment,
discrimination 1 Ti 5: 21.*
προκυρόω ratify previously Gal
3: 17.*
προλαμβάνω take before(hand). Do
something before the usual time
προέλαβεν μυρίσαι she had
anointed beforehand Mk 14: 8.
Simply take 1 Cor 11: 21. Detect,
overtake, surprise Gal 6: 1.*
προλέγω tell beforehand or in
advance 2 Cor 13: 2; Gal 5: 21;
1 Th 3: 4.*
προλημφθῇ 1 aor. pass. subj., 3
sing., of προλαμβάνω.
προμαρτύρομαι bear witness to beforehand, predict 1 Pt 1: 11.*
προμελετάω practice beforehand,
prepare Lk 21: 14.*
προμεριμνάω concern oneself or be
anxious beforehand Mk 13: 11.*
προνοέω think of beforehand, take
care—1. care for, provide for

w. gen. 1 Ti 5: 8.—2. take into
consideration, have regard for
w. gen. Ro 12: 17; 2 Cor 8: 21.*
πρόνοια, ας, ἡ foresight, care, pro-
vision Ac 24: 2; Ro 13: 14.*
πρόοιδα know beforehand or previously Ac 2: 31 v.l.*
προοράω—1. see previously Ac 21:
29.—2. foresee, see in advance Ac
2: 31; Gal 3: 8.—3. mid. see
before one, have before one's eyes
Ac 2: 25.*
προορίζω decide upon beforehand,
predestine Ac 4: 28; Ro 8: 29f;
1 Cor 2: 7; Eph 1: 5, 11.*
προπάσχω suffer previously 1 Th
2: 2.*
προπάτωρ, ορος, ὁ forefather Ro
4: 1.*
προπέμπω—1. accompany, escort
Ac 20: 38; 21: 5.—2. help on
one's journey, send on one's way
Ac 15: 3; Ro 15: 24; 1 Cor
16: 6, 11; 2 Cor 1: 16; Tit 3:
13; 3 J 6.*
προπετής, ές gen. οὖς rash, reck-
less, thoughtless Ac 19: 36; 2 Ti
3: 4.*
προπορεύομαι go on before w. gen.
Lk 1: 76; Ac 7: 40.*
πρός prep. w. gen., dat. or acc.—
I. with the genitive to the advantage of, necessary for Ac 27: 34.—
II. with the dative near, at, by
Mk 5: 11; Lk 19: 37; J 18: 16;
20: 11f; around Rv 1: 13.—III.
with the accusative—1. of place
toward(s), to Mt 26: 57; Mk 1: 33;
Lk 16: 26; J 11: 15; Ac 25: 21;
Ro 10: 1; 1 Cor 12: 2; Eph 2: 18;
with Ac 3: 25.—2. of time toward
Lk 24: 29. For Lk 8: 13; J 5:
35; 1 Cor 7: 5; Gal 2: 5a; Hb
12: 10; Js 4: 14.—3. of a goal for,
for the purpose of, in order (to), on
behalf of Mt 23: 5; Mk 13: 22;
Ac 3: 10; 27: 12; Ro 3: 26;
1 Cor 7: 35a; 2 Cor 1: 20; Eph
4: 29; 1 Pt 4: 12. Of result so
that, etc. J 4: 35; 1 Cor 14: 26;
1 J 5: 16f.—4. denoting a

hostile or friendly relationship—**a.** hostile *against, with*
Ac 11: 2; 24: 19; 1 Cor 6: 1;
Eph 6: 12; Col 3: 13; Rv 13:
6.—**b.** friendly Ro 5: 1; 2 Cor
6: 14f; 7: 4; Gal 6: 10; Phlm 5;
1 J 3: 21; 2 Ti 2: 24.—**5.** to
indicate a connection—**a.** *with
reference to* Mt 19: 8; Mk 12: 12;
Lk 12: 41; 18: 1; J 13: 28; Ac
24: 16; Hb1: 7f.—**b.** *as far as—is
concerned, with regard to* Ro 15:
17; 2 Cor 4: 2; Hb 6: 11. τὰ πρός
τι *that which belongs to something*
or *is necessary for something* Lk
14: 32; Ac 28: 10; 2 Pt 1: 3.—
c. elliptically τί πρὸς ἡμᾶς;
what is that to us? Mt 27: 4. τί
πρὸς σέ; *how does it concern you?*
J 21: 22f.—**d.** *in accordance with*
Lk 12: 47; 2 Cor 5: 10; Gal 2:
14; Eph 3: 4. *In comparison
with* Ro 8: 18.—**6.** adverbial
expression πρὸς φθόνον *jealously*
Js 4: 5.—**7.** (*in company*) *with*
Mt 13: 56; Mk 14: 49; J 1: 1f;
Gal 1: 18; 4: 18, 20; Phil 1:
26; 1 Th 3: 4; 2 Th 3: 10; Phlm
13; 1 J 1: 2. πρὸς ἑαυτούς
among or *to themselves* Mk 9: 10;
cf. Lk 18: 11.

προσάββατον, ου, τό *the day before
the Sabbath*, i.e. *Friday* Mk 15:
42.*

προσαγορεύω *call, name, designate*
pass. Hb 5: 10.*

προσάγω—1. trans. *bring* (*forward*)
lit. Lk 9: 41; Ac 12: 6 v.l.; 16:
20; pass. Mt 18: 24. Fig. 1 Pt
3: 18.—**2.** intrans. *come near,
approach* Ac 27: 27.*

προσαγωγή, ῆς, ἡ *approach, access*
Ro 5: 2; Eph 2: 18; 3: 12.*

προσαιτέω *beg* J 9: 8; Mk 10: 46
v.l.; Lk 18: 35 v.l.*

προσαίτης, ου, ὁ *beggar* Mk 10:
46; J 9: 8.*

προσαναβαίνω *go up, move up*
Lk 14: 10.*

προσαναλαμβάνω *take in besides,
welcome* Ac 28: 2 v.l.*

προσαναλίσκω or **προσαναλόω**
spend lavishly (*in addition*) Lk
8: 43 v.l.*

προσαναπληρόω *fill up* or *reple-
nish besides* 2 Cor 9: 12; 11: 9.*

προσανατίθημι mid. *add* or *con-
tribute* Gal 2: 6. *Consult with*
w. dat. 1: 16.*

προσανεθέμην 2 aor. mid. ind. of
προσανατίθημι.

προσανέχω *rise up toward* w. dat.
Ac 27: 27 v.l.*

προσαπειλέω *threaten further* or *in
addition* Ac 4: 21.*

προσαχέω *resound* of the surf Ac
27: 27 v.l.*

προσδαπανάω *spend in addition*
Lk 10: 35.*

προσδέομαι *need* w. gen. Ac 17: 25.*

προσδέχομαι—1. *take up, receive,
welcome* Lk 15: 2; Ro 16: 2;
Phil 2: 29. *Receive willingly,
put up with* Hb 10: 34; *accept* Ac
24: 15; Hb 11: 35.—**2.** *wait for,
expect* Mk 15: 43; Lk 2: 25, 38;
12: 36; 23: 51; Ac 23: 21;
Tit 2: 13; Jd 21: Lk 1: 21 v.l.;
Ac 10: 24 v.l.*

προσδίδωμι *give* (over) Lk 24: 30
v.l.*

προσδοκάω *wait for, look for,
expect* Mt 11: 3; 24: 50; Lk 7:
19f; 12: 46; Ac 10: 24; 27: 33;
2 Pt 3: 12–14.

προσδοκία, ας, ἡ *expectation* Lk 21:
26; Ac 12: 11.*

προσδραμών 2 aor. act. participle
of προστρέχω.

προσεάω *permit to go farther* Ac
27: 7.*

προσεγγίζω *approach, come near*
Mk 2: 4 v.l.; Ac 10: 25 v.l.;
27: 27 v.l.*

προσεδρεύω *serve, wait upon* w.
dat. 1 Cor 9: 13 v.l.*

προσενήνοχα perf. act. ind. of
προσφέρω.

προσεργάζομαι *make more, earn in
addition* Lk 19: 16.*

προσέρχομαι *come* or *go to, approach—1.* lit. Mt 4: 3, 11; 5: 1

9: 14; 24: 1; Mk 6: 35; Lk 23: 52; J 12: 21; Ac 9: 1; Hb 12: 18, 22.—**2.** fig.—**a.** of coming to a deity Hb 4: 16; 7: 25; 10: 1, 22; 11: 6; 1 Pt 2: 3.—**b.** *agree with, accede to* 1 Ti 6: 3.

προσευχή, ῆς, ἡ—1. *prayer* Mt 17: 21; Mk 9: 29; Lk 6: 12; Ac 3: 1; Ro 12: 12; Phil 4: 6; Rv 8: 3f.—**2.** *place of prayer, chapel* Ac 16: 13, 16.

προσεύχομαι *pray* Mt 5: 44; 6: 5–7; Mk 1: 35; 14: 38; Lk 1: 10; 20: 47; Ac 6: 6; Ro 8: 26; 1 Cor 11: 4f, 13; 14: 14a, 15; Hb 13: 18; Js 5: 16f.

προσέχω—1. act. *turn one's mind to—***a.** *pay attention to, give heed to, follow* w. dat. Ac 8: 6, 10f; 16: 14; 1 Ti 1: 4; 4: 1; Tit 1: 14; Hb 2: 1; 2 Pt 1: 19.—**b.** *be concerned about, care for, pay attention to* w. dat. Ac 20: 28. προσέχειν ἑαυτῷ *be careful, be on one's guard* Lk 12: 1; 17: 3; Ac 5: 35; cf. Mt 7: 15; 10: 17.—**c.** *occupy oneself with, devote* or *apply oneself to* w. dat. 1 Ti 4: 13; Hb 7: 13; *be addicted* 1 Ti 3: 8.—**2.** mid. *cling to* w. dat. 1 Ti 6: 3 v.l.

προσηλόω *nail (fast)* Col 2: 14.*

προσήλυτος, ου, ὁ *proselyte, convert* Mt 23: 15; Ac 2: 11; 6: 5; 13: 43.*

πρόσθες 2 aor. act. imperative, 2 sing. of προστίθημι.

πρόσθεσις, εως, ἡ only as v.l. for πρόθεσις *presentation*, with the same meaning Mt 12: 4; Mk 2: 26; Lk 6: 4.*

πρόσκαιρος, ον *lasting only for a time, temporary, transitory* Mt 13: 21; Mk 4: 17; 2 Cor 4: 18; Hb 11: 25.*

προσκαλέω mid. *summon—***1.** lit. *summon, call to oneself, invite* Mt 10: 1; Mk 3: 13, 23; Lk 15: 26; Ac 5: 40; 23: 17f, 23; Js 5: 14.—**2.** fig. Ac 2: 39; 13: 2; 16: 10.

προσκαρτερέω *adhere to, persist in*

—1. w. dat. *attach oneself to, wait on, be faithful to* Ac 8: 13; 10: 7; *stand ready* Mk 3: 9.—**2.** w. dat.—**a.** *busy oneself with, be busily engaged in, be devoted to* Ac 1: 14; 6: 4; Ro 12: 12; Col 4: 2.—With εἴς τι Ro 13: 6.—**b.** *hold fast to, continue* or *persevere in* Ac 2: 42.—**3.** *spend much time* with ἐν Ac 2: 46.*

προσκαρτέρησις, εως, ἡ *perseverance, patience* Eph 6: 18.*

προσκεφάλαιον, ου, τό *pillow, cushion* Mk 4: 38.*

προσκληρόω *allot, assign* pass. *be attached to, join* w. dat. Ac 17: 4.*

πρόσκλησις, εως, ἡ *summons, invitation* 1 Ti 5: 21 v.l.*

προσκλίνω pass. intrans. *incline toward* w. dat. *attach oneself to, join* Ac 5: 36.*

πρόσκλισις, εως, ἡ *partiality* 1 Ti 5: 21.*

προσκολλάω pass. fig. *adhere closely to, be devoted to, join* Eph 5: 31; Mt 19: 5 v.l.; Mk 10: 7 v.l.; Ac 5: 36 v.l.*

πρόσκομμα, ατος, τό *stumbling, offense—***1.** *stumbling* λίθος προσκόμματος *a stone that causes men to stumble* Ro 9: 32f; 1 Pt 2: 8. διὰ προσκόμματος *with offense* Ro 14: 20.—**2.** *the opportunity to take offense, obstacle, hindrance* Ro 14: 13; 1 Cor 8: 9.*

προσκοπή, ῆς, ἡ *an occasion for taking offense* 2 Cor 6: 3.*

προσκόπτω—1. lit.—**a.** trans. *strike* Mt 4: 6; Lk 4: 11.—**b.** intrans. *stumble* J 11: 9f. *Beat against* Mt 7: 27.—**2.** fig. *take offense at, feel repugnance for, reject* Ro 9: 32; 14: 21; 1 Pt 2: 8.*

προσκυλίω *roll (up to)* Mt 27: 60; Mk 15: 46; Lk 23: 53 v.l.*

προσκυνέω *(fall down and) worship, do obeisance to, prostrate oneself before, do reverence to, welcome respectfully* depending on the object—**1.** to human beings Mt 18: 26; Ac 10: 25; Rv 3: 9.—**2.** to God Mt 4: 10; J 4: 20f, 23f; 12: 20; Ac 24: 11; 1 Cor 14: 25; Hb 11: 21; Rv 4: 10; 14: 7; 19: 4.—**2.** to idols Ac 7: 43.—**3.** to the devil and Satanic beings Mt 4: 9; Lk 4: 7; Rv 9: 20; 13: 4; 14: 9, 11.— **4.** to angels Rv 22: 8.—**5.** to Christ Mt 2: 2, 8, 11; 8: 2; 9: 18; 14: 33; 20: 20; 15: 25; 28: 9, 17; Mk 5: 6; 15: 19; Lk 24: 52 v.l.

προσκυνητής, οῦ, ὁ *worshiper* J 4: 23.*

προσλαλέω *speak to* or *with* Ac 13: 43; 28: 20.*

προσλαμβάνω—**1.** act. *take, partake* w. gen. Ac 27: 34 v.l.— **2.** mid.—**a.** *take aside* Mt 16: 22; Mk 8: 32; Ac 18: 26.— **b.** *receive* or *accept in one's society, home* or *circle of acquaintances* Ro 14: 1; 15: 7a. Of God or Christ *accepting* the believer 14: 3; 15: 7b.—Ac 28: 2; Phlm 12 v.l., 17.—**c.** *take along* Ac 17: 5.—**d.** *take* 27: 33, 36.*

προσλέγω *answer, reply* ending of Mk in the Freer ms. 6.*

πρόσλημψις or **πρόσληψις, εως, ἡ** *acceptance* Ro 11: 15.*

προσμένω—**1.** *remain* or *stay with* w. dat., lit. Mt 15: 32; Mk 8: 2. Fig. Ac 11: 23. *Continue in* Ac 13: 43; 11: 23 v.l.; 1 Ti 5: 5.— **2.** *remain longer, further* Ac 18: 18; 1 Ti 1: 3.*

προσορμίζω pass. *come into (the) harbor, come to anchor* Mk 6: 53.*

προσοφείλω *owe besides* Phlm 19.*

προσοχθίζω *be angry, offended, provoked* w. dat. Hb 3: 10, 17.*

προσπαίω *strike* or *beat against* w. dat.; the aor. προσέπαισαν is a conjectural emendation for προσέπεσαν in Mt 7: 25.*

πρόσπεινος, ον *hungry* Ac 10: 10.*

προσπήγνυμι *fix* or *fasten to, nail to (the cross)* Ac 2: 23.*

προσπίπτω—**1.** *fall down before* or *at the feet of* w. dat. Mk 3: 11; 5: 33; 7: 25; Lk 5: 8; 8: 28, 47; Ac 16: 29.—**2.** *fall upon, strike against* w. dat. Mt 7: 25.*

προσποιέω mid.—**1.** *make* or *act as though, pretend* Lk 24: 28.— **2.** *take notice* J 8: 6 v.l.*

προσπορεύομαι *come up to, approach* Mk 10: 35.*

προσρήσσω w. dat. *burst upon* Lk 6: 48; cf. 49; Mt 7: 27 v.l.*

προστάσσω *command, order, prescribe* Mt 1: 24; 8: 4; 21: 6 v.l.; Mk 1: 44; Lk 5: 14; Ac 10: 33, 48; 17: 26.*

προστάτις, ιδος, ἡ *protectress, patroness, helper* Ro 16: 2.*

προστεταγμένος perf. pass. participle of προστάσσω.

προστίθημι—**1.** *add, put to*—**a.** generally Mt 6: 27; Mk 4: 24; Lk 3: 20; 12: 25; Ac 2: 41, 47 v.l.; 5: 14; 13: 36; Gal 3: 19; Hb 12: 19; pass. *be brought* Ac 11: 24.—**b.** in accordance with Hebrew usage π. is used as a paraphrase for *again, further,* etc. προσθεὶς εἶπεν παραβολήν *again he told a parable,* or *he proceeded to tell a parable* Lk 19: 11. Cf. 20: 11f; Ac 12: 3; Mk 14: 25 v.l.—**2.** *provide, give, grant, do* Mt 6: 33; Lk 12: 31; 17: 5.*

προστρέχω *run up (to)* Mk 9: 15; 10: 17; Ac 8: 30; J 20: 16 v.l.*

προσφάγιον, ου, τό *fish* J 21: 5.*

πρόσφατος, ον *new* Hb 10: 20.*

προσφάτως adv. *recently* Ac 18: 2.*

προσφέρω—**1.** act. and pass. *bring (to)* Mt 4: 24; 9: 2, 32; 17: 16; 19: 13; 25: 20; Mk 2: 4; Lk 18: 15; 23: 14, 36; J 19: 29; Ac 8: 18.—**2.** *bring, offer, present* —**a.** lit. Mt 2: 11; 5: 23f; Mk 1: 44; Ac 7: 42; Hb 5: 1, 3; 8: 3f; 9: 7, 9, 14, 25, 28; 11: 4, 17.

—**b.** fig. J 16: 2; Hb 5: 7.—
3. pass. *meet, deal with* Hb 12: 7.

προσφιλής, ές *pleasing, agreeable, lovely* Phil 4: 8.*

προσφορά, ας, ή—**1.** *presenting, offering, sacrificing* Ac 24: 17; Hb 10: 10, 14, 18.—**2.** *that which is brought, gift, offering* Ac 21: 26; Ro 15: 16; Eph 5: 2; Hb 10: 5, 8.*

προσφωνέω—**1.** *call out, address* w. dat. Mt 11: 16; Lk 7: 32; 23: 20; Ac 22: 2; cf. 21: 40; Lk 23: 20 v.l.—**2.** *call to oneself* Lk 6: 13; 13: 12; Ac 11: 2 v.l.*

προσχαίρω *be glad* Mk 9: 15 v.l.*

πρόσχυσις, εως, ή *pouring, sprinkling* Hb 11: 28.*

προσψαύω *touch* w. dat. Lk 11: 46.*

προσωπολημπτέω *show partiality* Js 2: 9.*

προσωπολήμπτης, ου, ὁ *one who shows partiality* Ac 10: 34.*

προσωπολημψία, ας, ή *partiality* Ro 2: 11; Eph 6: 9; Col 3: 25; Js 2: 1.*

πρόσωπον, ου, τό—**1.** *face, countenance*—**a.** lit. Mt 6: 16f; 26: 67; Mk 14: 65; Lk 9: 29; Ac 6: 15; 1 Cor 14: 25; 2 Cor 3: 7, 13, 18; Js 1: 23; Rv 4: 7; 9: 7; 10: 1.—**b.** fig., in more or less symbolic expressions Mt 18: 10; Lk 9: 51, 53; 24: 5; 1 Cor 13: 12; Ac 20: 25, 38; Gal 1: 22; Hb 9: 24; 1 Pt 3: 12; Rv 22: 4. προσώπῳ *outwardly* 1 Th 2: 17. θαυμάζειν πρόσωπον *flatter* Jd 16. λαμβάνειν πρόσωπον *show partiality* or *favoritism* Lk 20: 21; cf. Gal 2: 6.—**c.** governed by prepositions, where π. may sometimes be translated *presence* or omitted altogether Mt 11: 10; Lk 2: 31; Ac 3: 13, 20; 5: 41; 13: 24; 2 Th 1: 9. εἰς πρ. *before* 2 Cor 8: 24. κατὰ πρ. *face to face* Ac 25: 16; 2 Cor 10: 1; *to one's face* Gal 2: 11.— **d.** *appearance* Mt 16: 3; Lk

12: 56; 2 Cor 5: 12; Js 1: 11.— **e.** *face = surface* Lk 21: 35; Ac 17: 26.—**2.** *person* ἐκ πολλῶν προσώπων *by many persons* 2 Cor 1: 11.

προτάσσω *fix, determine, allot (beforehand)* Ac 17: 26 v.l.*

προτείνω *stretch out, spread out* Ac 22: 25.*

πρότερος, α, ον—**1.** adj. *earlier, former* Eph 4: 22.—**2.** neut. πρότερον as adv. *earlier, formerly, in former times*—**a.** without the article J 7: 50, 51 v.l.; 2 Cor 1: 15; 1 Ti 1: 13 v.l.; Hb 4: 6; 7: 27.—**b.** with the art.— as adj. *former* Hb 10: 32; 1 Pt 1: 14.—As adv. τὸ πρ. *before, once, formerly* J 6: 62; 9: 8; 1 Ti 1: 13. For Gal 4: 13 *the first time* and *once* are both possible.*

προτίθημι mid.—**1.** *display publicly* Ro 3: 25.—**2.** *plan, purpose, intend* 1: 13; Eph 1: 9.*

προτρέπω *urge (on), encourage, persuade* Ac 18: 27.*

προτρέχω *run ahead* Lk 19: 4; J 20: 4; Ac 10: 25 v.l.*

προϋπάρχω *be, exist before* προϋπῆρχεν μαγεύων *he had practiced magic* Ac 8: 9.—Lk 23: 12.*

πρόφασις, εως, ή—**1.** *real motive, valid excuse* J 15: 22.—**2.** *falsely alleged motive, pretext, excuse* Mt 23: 14 v.l.; Mk 12: 40; Lk 20: 47; Ac 27: 30; Phil 1: 18; 1 Th 2: 5.*

προφέρω *bring out, produce* Lk 6: 45.*

προφητεία, ας, ή *prophecy*—**1.** *prophetic activity* Rv 11: 6.—**2.** *the gift of prophecy* Ro 12: 6; 1 Cor 12: 10; 13: 2, 8; 14: 22; 1 Th 5: 20; Rv 19: 10.—**3.** *the utterance of the prophet, prophecy* Mt 13: 14; 1 Cor 14: 6; 1 Th 5: 20; 1 Ti 1: 18; 4: 14; 2 Pt 1: 20f; Rv 1: 3; 22: 7, 10, 18f.*

προφητεύω *prophesy*—**1.** *proclaim a divine revelation* Mt 7: 22;

Ac 2: 17f; 19: 6; 21: 9; 1 Cor 11: 4f; 13: 9; 14: 1, 3–5, 24, 31, 39; Rv 11: 3.—**2.** *prophetically reveal* Mt 26: 68; Mk 14: 65; Lk 22: 64.—**3.** *foretell the future, prophesy* Mt 11: 13; 15: 7; Mk 7: 6; Lk 1: 67; J 11: 51; 1 Pt 1: 10; Jd 14; Rv 10: 11.*

προφήτης, ου, ὁ *prophet*—**1.** in the Old Testament Mt 2: 17, 23; 3: 3; 5: 17; 11: 13; 12: 39; 27: 9; Mk 1: 2; 6: 15; Lk 13: 28; 24: 44; J 1: 23; Ac 2: 16; 7: 48; 8: 28, 30; 13: 20; Ro 1: 2; 3: 21; Hb 11: 32; 1 Pt 1: 10; 2 Pt 2: 16.—**2.** John the Baptist is called a prophet or greater than a prophet: Mt 11: 9; 14: 5; 21: 26; Mk 11: 32; Lk 1: 76; 7: 26; 20: 6.—**3.** Jesus is called a prophet Mt 13: 57; 16: 14; 21: 11, 46; Mk 6: 4, 15; 8: 28; Lk 4: 24; 7: 16, 39; 9: 8, 19; 24: 19; J 4: 19, 44; 6: 14; 7: 40, 52; 9: 17; cf. 1: 21, 25.—Ac 3: 22f; 7: 37.—**4.** generally, of men who proclaim a divine message Mt 11: 9; 13: 57; 23: 30, 34, 37; Lk 10: 24; 11: 49; 13: 33f; Ac 7: 52; Rv 11: 10.—**5.** of Christian prophets Ac 11: 27; 13: 1; 15: 32; 21: 10; 1 Cor 12: 28f; 14: 29, 32, 37; Eph 2: 20; 3: 5; 4: 11; Rv 11: 18; 16: 6; 18: 20, 24; Rv 22: 6, 9.—**6.** of a pagan Tit 1: 12.

προφητικός, ή, όν *prophetic* Ro 16: 26; 2 Pt 1: 19.*

προφῆτις, ιδος, ἡ *prophetess* Lk 2: 36; Rv 2: 20.*

προφθάνω *come before, anticipate* Mt 17: 25.*

προχειρίζω mid. *choose for oneself, select, appoint* Ac 22: 14; 26: 16. Pass. 3: 20.*

προχειροτονέω *choose or appoint beforehand* Ac 10: 41.*

Πρόχορος, ου, ὁ *Prochorus* Ac 6: 5.*

πρύμνα, ης, ἡ *the stern (of a ship)* Mk 4: 38; Ac 27: 29, 41.*

πρωΐ adv. *early, early in the morning* Mt 16: 3; 20: 1; Mk 1: 35; 16: 2, 9; J 18: 28; 20: 1; Ac 28: 23. In Mk 13: 35 π. refers to the fourth and last watch of the night, 3–6 a.m.

πρωΐα, ας, ἡ *(early) morning* Mt 27: 1; 21: 18 v.l.; J 21: 4; 18: 28 v.l.*

πρώϊμος a variant spelling of πρόϊμος.

πρωϊνός, ή, όν *early, belonging to the morning* ὁ ἀστὴρ ὁ πρ. *the morning star*, Venus Rv 2: 28; 22: 16.*

πρῷρα, ης, ἡ *the forepart* or *prow of a ship* Ac 27: 30, 41.*

πρωτεύω *be first, have first place* Col 1: 18.*

πρωτοκαθεδρία, ας, ἡ *place of honor, best seat* Mt 23: 6; Mk 12: 39; Lk 11: 43; 20: 46.*

πρωτοκλισία, ας, ἡ *the place of honor* at a dinner Mt 23: 6; Mk 12: 39; Lk 14: 7f; 20: 46.*

πρωτόμαρτυς, υρος, ὁ *first martyr* Ac 22: 20 v.l.*

πρῶτος, η, ον—**1.** first.—**a.** *first, earliest, earlier* Mt 12: 45; 21: 28; Mk 12: 20; Lk 2: 2; 20: 29; J 1: 15,30 (both = *earlier*); 5: 4; 20: 4; Ac 1: 1; 20: 18; 26: 23; Phil 1: 5; 2 Ti 4: 16; Hb 9: 15; 10: 9; Rv 1: 17.—**b.** *first, foremost, most important, most prominent* Mt 20: 27; Mk 6: 21; 12: 28; Lk 13: 30; Ac 25: 2; 1 Cor 15: 3; Eph 6: 2; 1 Ti 1: 15.—**c.** *outer, anterior* Hb 9: 2, 6, 8.—**2.** the neut. πρῶτον as adv.—**a.** of time or sequence *first, in the first place, before, earlier, to begin with* Mt 5: 24; 8: 21; Mk 4: 28; 13: 10; Lk 12: 1; J 15: 18; 18: 13; Ac 7: 12; Ro 1: 8; 15: 24; 1 Cor 12: 28; 15: 46.—**b.** of degree *in the first place, above all, especially* Mt 6: 33; Ac 3: 26; Ro 1: 16; 2: 9f; 2 Cor 8: 5; 1 Ti 2: 1; 2 Pt 1: 20.

πρωτοστάτης, ου, ὁ leader, ring-
leader Ac 24: 5.*

πρωτοτόκια, ων, τά the birthright
of the oldest son, right of primo-
geniture Hb 12: 16.*

πρωτότοκος, ον first-born—1. lit.
Mt 1: 25 v.l.; Lk 2: 7; Hb 11:
28.—2. fig. of Christ Ro 8: 29;
Col 1: 15, 18; Hb 1: 6; Rv 1: 5;
2: 8 v.l.—Of men Hb 12: 23.*

πρώτως adv. for the first time Ac
11: 26.*

πταίω stumble, trip, then also make
a mistake, sin Ro 11: 11; Js
2: 10; 3: 2; be ruined or lost is
also possible for 2 Pt 1: 10.*

πτέρνα, ης, ἡ heel J 13: 18.*

πτερύγιον, ου, τό end, edge, pin-
nacle, summit Mt 4: 5; Lk 4:
9.*

πτέρυξ, υγος, ἡ wing Mt 23: 37;
Lk 13: 34; Rv 4: 8; 9: 9; 12:
14.*

πτηνός, (ἡ), όν feathered, winged
τά πτηνά the birds 1 Cor 15:
39.*

πτοέω terrify pass. be terrified,
be alarmed, frightened, startled
Lk 12: 4 v.l.; 21: 9; 24: 37.*

πτόησις, εως, ἡ terrifying, inti-
midation or fear, terror; either
meaning is possible in 1 Pt 3: 6.*

Πτολεμαΐς, ΐδος, ἡ Ptolemais, a
seaport city in Phoenicia Ac 21:
7.*

πτύξας 1 aor. act. participle of
πτύσσω.

πτύον, ου, τό winnowing shovel Mt
3: 12; Lk 3: 17.*

πτύρω frighten pass. let oneself be
intimidated Phil 1: 28.*

πτύσμα, ατος, τό saliva, spit(tle)
J 9: 6.*

πτύσσω fold or roll up Lk 4: 20.*

πτύω to spit Mk 7: 33; 8: 23;
J 9: 6.*

πτῶμα, ατος, τό (dead) body,
corpse Mt 14: 12; 24: 28; Mk
6: 29; 15: 45; Rv 11: 8f.*

πτῶσις, εως, ἡ falling, fall Mt
7: 27; Lk 2: 34.*

πτωχεία, ας, ἡ (extreme) poverty
2 Cor 8: 2, 9; Rv 2: 9.*

πτωχεύω be (extremely) poor 2 Cor
8: 9.*

πτωχός, ή, όν—1. poor in this
world's goods, lit. begging,
which sometimes plays a part in
the word's meaning in the NT:
Mk 12: 42f. As a noun Mk 10:
21; 14: 7; Lk 6: 20; 14: 13, 21;
16: 20, 22; J 12: 6, 8; Ro 15: 26;
2 Cor 6: 10; Gal 2: 10; Js 2: 2f,
5f.—Poor, oppressed Mt 11: 5;
Lk 4: 18; 7: 22.—Fig. Mt 5: 3;
Rv 3: 17.—2. poor, miserable,
beggarly, impotent Gal 4: 9;
1 Cor 15: 10 v.l.

πυγμή, ῆς, ἡ fist. In Mk 7: 3
πυγμῇ with the fist is variously
interpreted.

πυθόμενος 2 aor. mid. participle
of πυνθάνομαι.

πύθων, ωνος, ὁ a spirit of
divination πνεῦμα πύθωνα a spirit
of divination or prophecy Ac 16:
16.*

πυκνός, ή, όν frequent, numerous
1 Ti 5: 23. Neut. pl. πυκνά as
adv. often, frequently Mk 7: 3
v.l. (for πυγμῇ); Lk 5: 33.—Neut.
of the comparative πυκνότερον
as adv. rather frequently Ac 24:
26.*

πυκτεύω fight with fists, box symbolically 1 Cor 9: 26.*

πύλη, ης, ἡ gate—1. lit. Mt 16: 18;
Lk 7: 12; Ac 3: 10; 9: 24; 12:
10; 16: 13; Hb 13: 12.—2. fig.
and symbolically Mt 7: 13f;
Lk 13: 24 v.l.*

πυλών, ῶνος, ὁ—1. gate, especially
of a palace or temple Lk 16:
20; Ac 14: 13; Rv 21: 12f, 15,
21, 25; 22: 14.—2. gateway,
portal, vestibule Ac 10: 17; 12:
13f.—3. gateway, entrance separated from the house by a court
Mt 26: 71.*

πυνθάνομαι—1. inquire, ask, seek
to learn Mt 2: 4; Lk 15: 26;
18: 36; J 4: 52; Ac 4: 7; 10: 18,

29; 21: 33; 23: 19f.—**2.** *learn by inquiry* Ac 23: 34.*

πῦρ, ός, τό *fire*—**1.** lit. Mt 5: 22; 13: 40, 42, 50; 17: 15; Lk 17: 29; Ac 2: 3; 7: 30; 28: 5; 1 Cor 3: 15; Js 5: 3; Hb 12: 18; 2 Pt 3: 7; Rv 1: 14; 4: 5; 8: 7; 17: 16; 19: 20.—**2.** fig. Mk 9: 49; Lk 12: 49; Js 3: 6.

πυρά, ᾶς, ἡ *fire, pile of combustible* or *burning material* Ac 28: 2f; Lk 22: 55 v.l.*

πύργος, ου, ὁ *tower* Mt 21: 33; Mk 12: 1; Lk 13: 4; for 14: 28 either *tower* or *farm building* is possible.*

πυρέσσω *suffer with a fever* Mt 8: 14; Mk 1: 30.*

πυρετός, οῦ, ὁ *fever* Mt 8: 15; Mk 1: 31; Lk 4: 38f; J 4: 52; Ac 28: 8.*

πύρινος, η, ον *fiery, the color of fire* Rv 9: 17.*

πυρόω *set on fire, burn up* pass.— **1.** *burn*—**a.** lit. 2 Pt 3: 12; symbolically Eph 6: 16.— **b.** fig. *burn, be inflamed* 1 Cor 7: 9; 2 Cor 11: 29.—**2.** *make red hot, heat thoroughly* Rv 1: 15; 3: 18.*

πυρράζω *be (fiery) red* Mt 16: 2f.*

πυρρός, ά, όν *red (as fire)* Rv 6: 4; 12: 3.*

Πύρρος, ου, ὁ *Pyrrhus* Ac 20: 4.*

πύρωσις, εως, ἡ lit., the process of *burning* Rv 18: 9, 18. *Fiery ordeal* 1 Pt 4: 12.*

πωλέω *sell* Mt 10: 29; 13: 44; 25: 9; Mk 10: 21; 11: 15; Lk 17: 28; 18: 22; 22: 36; Ac 5: 1; 1 Cor 10: 25; Rv 13: 17.

πῶλος, ου, ὁ *colt, young donkey* Mt 21: 2, 5, 7; Mk 11: 2, 4f, 7; Lk 19: 30, 33, 35; J 12: 15. The meaning *horse* is possible for the passages in Mk and Lk.*

πώποτε adv. *ever, at any time* Lk 19: 30; J 1: 18; 5: 37; 6: 35; 8: 33; 1 J 4: 12.*

πωρόω *make dull* or *obtuse* or *blind*, lit. 'harden' Mk 6: 52; 8: 17; J 12: 40; Ro 11: 7; 2 Cor 3: 14.*

πώρωσις, εως, ἡ *dullness, insensibility, obstinacy* Mk 3: 5; Ro 11: 25; Eph 4: 18.*

πῶς interrogative particle *how? in what way?* Mt 23: 33; 26: 54; Mk 11: 18; Lk 1: 34; Ro 4: 10; 10: 14f; 1 Cor 7: 32–34; Eph 5: 15; Rv 3: 3.—*With what right? in what sense?* Mt 22: 12, 43; Mk 12: 35; J 12: 34.—*How is it (possible) that?* Mt 16: 11; Mk 4: 40; J 4: 9; Ac 2: 8; Gal 4: 9.—*How (could or should)?* =*by no means* Mt 12: 26, 29, 34; Ro 3: 6; 1 Cor 14: 7, 9, 16; 2 Cor 3: 8; Hb 2: 3.—In exclamations *how!* Mk 10: 23f; Lk 12: 50; 18: 24; J 11: 36.

πώς enclitic particle *somehow, in some way, perhaps* in combination with εἰ Ac 27: 12; Ro 1: 10 (see εἰ, end). See also μήπως.

Ρ

Ῥαάβ, ἡ indecl. *Rahab* (Josh 2 and 6: 17, 25) Hb 11: 31; Js 2: 25.*

ῥαββί (Hebrew = *my lord*) *rabbi*, a form of address, then an honorary title for outstanding teachers of the law: generally Mt 23: 7f. Of John the Baptist J

3: 26. Otherwise always of Jesus Mt 26: 25, 49; Mk 9: 5; 10: 51 v.l.; 11: 21; 14: 45; J 1: 38 (translated *teacher*), 49; 3: 2; 4: 31; 6: 25; 9: 2; 11: 8.*

ῥαββουνί (Hebrew, heightened form of ῥαββί) *my Lord, my*

Master as a form of address to Jesus in Mk 10: 51; J 20: 16.*

ῥαβδίζω *beat with a rod* Ac 16: 22; 2 Cor 11: 25.*

ῥάβδος, ου, ἡ *rod, staff, stick* Mt 10: 10; Mk 6: 8; Lk 9: 3; 1 Cor 4: 21; Hb 1: 8; 9: 4; 11: 21; Rv 2: 27; 11: 1; 12: 5; 19: 15.*

ῥαβδοῦχος, ου, ὁ the Roman *lictor,* roughly equivalent to *constable, policeman* Ac 16: 35, 38.*

ῥαβιθά. In Mk 5: 41 codex D reads ραββι ταβιτα; this is meant for ῥαβιθά *girl* (see ταλιθά).*

'Ραγαύ, ὁ indecl. *Reu* Lk 3: 35.*

ῥᾳδιούργημα, ατος, τό *knavery, crime* Ac 18: 14.*

ῥᾳδιουργία, ας, ἡ *wickedness, unscrupulousness* Ac 13: 10.*

ῥαίνω *sprinkle* pass. Rv 19: 13 v.l.*

ῥακά a term of abuse; among the most likely meanings are *empty-head, numbskull, fool* Mt 5: 22.*

ῥάκος, ους, τό *piece of cloth, patch* Mt 9: 16; Mk 2: 21.*

'Ραμά, ἡ indecl. *Rama,* a city about six miles north of Jerusalem Mt 2: 18.*

ῥαντίζω—1. (be)*sprinkle* for purposes of purification Hb 9: 13, 19, 21; Rv 19: 13 v.l.—2. mid. *cleanse, purify: wash oneself* Mk 7: 4; *purify for oneself* Hb 10: 22.*

ῥαντισμός, οῦ, ὁ *sprinkling* Hb 12: 24; 1 Pt 1: 2.*

ῥαπίζω *strike, slap* Mt 5: 39; 26: 67.*

ῥάπισμα, ατος, τό *blow, slap* Mk 14: 65; J 18: 22; 19: 3.*

ῥάσσω *strike, dash, throw down* Mk 9: 18 v.l.*

ῥαφίς, ίδος, ἡ *needle* Mt 19: 24; Mk 10: 25; Lk 18: 25 v.l.*

ῥαχά a variant form of ῥακά.

'Ραχάβ, ἡ indecl. *Rahab* Mt 1: 5.*

'Ραχήλ, ἡ, indecl. *Rachel,* Jacob's wife Mt 2: 18.*

'Ρεβέκκα, ας, ἡ *Rebecca,* wife of Isaac Ro 9: 10.*

ῥέδη, ης, ἡ *a* (four-wheeled) *carriage* Rv 18: 13.*

'Ρεμφάν, 'Ρεφάν variant forms of 'Ρομφά.

ῥεριμμένος perf. mid. and pass. participle of ῥίπτω.

ῥεύσω fut. act. ind. of ῥέω.

ῥέω *flow* symbolically J 7: 38.*

'Ρήγιον, ου, τό *Rhegium* a city at the 'toe' of Italy Ac 28: 13.*

ῥῆγμα, ατος, τό *wreck, ruin, collapse* Lk 6: 49.*

ῥήγνυμι and its by-form ῥήσσω—1. *tear* (*in pieces*), *break, burst* Mt 7: 6; 9: 17; Mk 2: 22; Lk 5: 6 v.l., 37.—2. *break out, break forth* Gal 4: 27.*

ῥηθείς 1 aor. pass. participle of εἶπον.

ῥῆμα, ατος, τό—1. *that which is said, word, saying, expression* Mt 12: 36; Mk 9: 32; Lk 2: 17, 50; J 5: 47; 6: 68; Ac 2: 14; 28: 25; Ro 10: 8, 17; 2 Cor 12: 4; Eph 6: 17; Hb 1: 3; 12: 19; Jd 17. *Threat* Ac 6: 13.—2. *thing, object, matter, event* Mt 18: 16; Lk 1: 37, 65; 2: 15, 19, 51; Ac 5: 32; 10: 37; 13: 42; 2 Cor 13: 1.

ῥῆξον 1 aor. act. imperative of ῥήγνυμι.

ῥήξω fut. act. ind. of ῥήγνυμι.

'Ρησά, ὁ indecl. *Rhesa* Lk 3: 27.*

ῥήσσω—1. by-form of ῥήγνυμι.—2. the epic ῥήσσω (cf. προσρήσσω) *throw down, dash to the ground* Mk 9: 18; Lk 9: 42.*

ῥήτωρ, ορος, ὁ *orator, advocate, attorney* Ac 24: 1.*

ῥητῶς adv. *expressly, explicitly* 1 Ti 4: 1.*

ῥίζα, ης, ἡ—1. *root*—a. lit. Mt 3: 10; 13: 6; Mk 4: 6; 11: 20; Lk 3: 9.—b. fig. Mt 13: 21; Mk 4: 17; Lk 8: 13; Ro 11: 16–18; 1 Ti 6: 10; Hb 12: 15.—2. *shoot, scion* Ro 15: 12; Rv 5: 5; 22: 16.*

ῥιζόω *cause to take root* fig., pass. *be* or *become firmly rooted* Eph 3: 17; Col 2: 7.*

ῥιπή, ῆς, ἡ *rapid movement, twinkling* 1 Cor 15: 52.*

ῥιπίζω *blow here and there, toss* pass. Js 1: 6.*

ῥίπτω and ῥιπτέω—1. *throw* Mt 27: 5; Lk 17: 2; Ac 27: 19, 29; *throw off* 22: 23; *throw down* Lk 4: 35.—2. *put* or *lay down* Mt 15: 30. Perf. pass. participle ἐρριμμένοι *lying down* 9: 36.*

'Ροβοάμ, ὁ indecl. *Rehoboam*, son and successor of Solomon Mt 1: 7; Lk 3: 23 ff v.l.*

'Ρόδη, ης, ἡ *Rhoda* a maidservant Ac 12: 13.*

'Ρόδος, ου, ἡ *Rhodes*, an island off the southwest point of Asia Minor Ac 21: 1.*

ῥοιζηδόν adv. *with a roar, with great suddenness* 2 Pt 3: 10.*

'Ρομφά, ὁ indecl. *Rephan, Rompha* a pagan deity Ac 7: 43.*

ῥομφαία, ας, ἡ *sword* Lk 2: 35; Rv 1: 16; 2: 12, 16; 6: 8; 19: 15, 21; Lk 21: 24 v.l.*

ῥοπή, ῆς, ἡ *downward movement, twinkling* 1 Cor 15: 52 v.l.*

'Ρουβήν, ὁ indecl. *Reuben* (Gen 29: 32) Rv 7: 5.*

'Ρούθ, ἡ indecl. *Ruth* Mt 1: 5.*

'Ροῦφος, ου, ὁ *Rufus*—1. son of Simon of Cyrene Mk 15: 21.— 2. recipient of a greeting Ro 16: 13.*

ῥύμη, ης, ἡ *(narrow) street, lane, alley* Mt 6: 2; Lk 14: 21; Ac 9: 11; 12: 10.*

ῥύομαι *save, rescue, deliver* Mt 6: 13; 27: 43; Lk 1: 74; 11: 4 v.l.; Ac 5: 15 v.l.; Ro 7: 24;

11: 26; 15: 31; 2 Cor 1: 10; Col 1: 13; 1 Th 1: 10; 2 Th 3: 2; 2 Ti 3: 11; 4: 17f; 2 Pt 2: 7, 9.*

ῥυπαίνω *befoul, soil* fig. *defile, pollute* pass. Rv 22: 11.*

ῥυπαρεύω *befoul, defile* Rv 22: 11 v.l.*

ῥυπαρία, ας, ἡ *dirt* fig. *moral uncleanness, sordid avarice* Js 1: 21.*

ῥυπαρός, ά, όν *dirty* lit. Js 2: 2. Fig. *unclean, defiled* Rv 22: 11.*

ῥύπος, ου, ὁ *dirt* 1 Pt 3: 21.*

ῥυπόω *defile, pollute* Rv 22: 11 v.l.*

ῥῦσαι 1 aor. mid. imperative of ῥύομαι.

ῥύσις, εως, ἡ *flowing, flow* Mk 5: 25; Lk 8: 43f.*

ῥυτίς, ίδος, ἡ *wrinkle* Eph 5: 27.*

'Ρωμαϊκός, ή, όν *Roman, Latin* Lk 23: 38 v.l.*

'Ρωμαῖος, α, ον *Roman* ὁ 'Ρ. subst. the *Roman*, the *Roman citizen* J 11: 48; Ac 2: 10; 16: 21, 37f; 22: 25–27, 29; 23: 27; 25: 16; 28: 17; Phlm subscr. *Roman Christians* Ro inscr.*

'Ρωμαϊστί adv. *in (the) Latin (language)* J 19: 20; subscr. after Mk in minuscule 13 et al.*

'Ρώμη, ης, ἡ *Rome* Ac 18: 2; 19: 21; 23: 11; 28: 14, 16; Ro 1: 7, 15; 2 Ti 1: 17; 1 Pt 5: 13 v.l.; subscriptions of Gal, Eph, Phil, Col, 2 Th, 2 Ti, Phlm, Hb.*

ῥώννυμι *be strong* perf. pass. imperative ἔρρωσο, ἔρρωσθε *farewell, goodbye* Ac 15: 29; 23: 30 v.l.*

Σ

σαβαχθάνι (Aramaic) *thou hast forsaken me* Mt 27: 46; Mk 15: 34.*

Σαβαώθ indecl. (Hebrew) *Sabaoth*, i.e. *armies, hosts* Ro 9: 29; Js 5: 4.*

σαββατισμός, οῦ, ὁ *Sabbath rest, Sabbath observance* fig. Hb 4: 9.*

σάββατον, ου, τό—1. *Sabbath*, the seventh day of the week,

held sacred by the Jews—**a.** sing.
Mt 12: 8; Mk 2: 27f; Lk 6: 7,
9; J 5: 9f, 18; Ac 1: 12; 13: 27,
44.—**b.** pl., of more than one
Sabbath Ac 17: 2.—τὰ σάββατα
for a single Sabbath day Mt
28: 1a; Mk 1: 21; 2: 23f; Lk 4:
16; 13: 10; Ac 16: 13.—**2.** *week*—
a. sing. Mk 16: 2 v.l., 9; Lk 18:
12; 1 Cor 16: 2.—**b.** pl., of a
single week Mt 28: 1b; Mk 16: 2;
Lk 24: 1; J 20: 1, 19; Ac 20: 7;
1 Cor 16: 2 v.l.

σαγήνη, ης, ἡ a large *dragnet* Mt
13: 47.*

Σαδδουκαῖος, ου, ὁ *the Sadducee*,
member of a Jewish party Mt
3: 7; 16: 1, 6, 11f; 22: 23, 34;
Mk 12: 18; Lk 20: 27; Ac 4: 1;
5: 17; 23: 6–8.*

Σαδώκ, ὁ indecl. *Zadok* Mt 1: 14;
Lk 3: 23ff v.l.*

σαίνω *fawn upon, flatter*, lit.,
of dogs 'wag the tail.' The pass.
in 1 Th 3: 3 may be rendered *be
shaken* or *disturbed*; less likely,
*be deceived.**

σάκκος, ου, ὁ *sack, sackcloth* Mt
11: 21; Lk 10: 13; Rv 6: 12;
11: 3.*

Σαλά, ὁ indecl. *Shelah*—**1.** Lk 3:
32.—**2.** 3: 35.*

Σαλαθιήλ, ὁ indecl. *Shealtiel, Sala-
thiel* father of Zerubbabel Mt 1:
12; Lk 3: 27.*

Σαλαμίς, ῖνος, ἡ *Salamis*, a city
on the east coast of Cyprus Ac
13: 5.*

σαλεύω *shake, cause to move to and
fro, cause to waver* or *totter*—
1. lit. Mt 11: 7; 24: 29; Mk 13:
25; Lk 6: 38, 48; 7: 24; 21: 26;
Ac 4: 31; 16: 26; Hb 12: 26; Rv
6: 13 v.l.—**2.** fig. Ac 2: 25; 2 Th
2: 2; Hb 12: 27. *Upset* Ac 17: 13.*

Σαλήμ, ἡ *Salem* (Hebrew = peace)
Hb 7: 1f.*

Σαλίμ, τό indecl. *Salim*, a locality
in Samaria J 3: 23.*

Σαλμών, ὁ indecl. *Salmon* Mt 1:
4f; Lk 3: 32 v.l.*

Σαλμώνη, ης, ἡ *Salmone*, a pro-
montory on the northeast corner
of Crete Ac 27: 7.*

σάλος, ου, ὁ *rolling* or *tossing
motion, waves* in a rough sea
Lk 21: 25.*

σάλπιγξ, ιγγος, ἡ *trumpet*—**1.** the
instrument itself 1 Cor 14: 8; Hb
12: 19; Rv 1: 10; 4: 1; 8: 2, 6,
13; 9: 14; Mt 24: 31 v.l.—
2. the sound made by the instrument, *trumpet-call*, (*sound of the*)
trumpet Mt 24: 31; 1 Cor 15:
52; 1 Th 4: 16.*

σαλπίζω *sound the trumpet, trumpet* (*forth*) Mt 6: 2; 1 Cor 15: 52;
Rv 8: 6–8, 10, 12f; 9: 1, 13; 10:
7; 11: 15.*

σαλπιστής, οῦ, ὁ *trumpeter* Rv
18: 22.*

Σαλώμη, ης, ἡ *Salome*, a Galilean
woman who followed Jesus Mk
15: 40; 16: 1; see also Mt 27: 56.
Salome was also the name of the
daughter of Herodias who is
mentioned but not named in Mk
6: 22ff; Mt 14: 6ff.*

Σαλωμών a variant of Σολομών Ac
7: 47.*

Σαμάρεια, ας, ἡ *Samaria*, the
province in west central Palestine Lk 17: 11; J 4: 4f, 7; Ac 1:
8; 8: 1, 5, 9, 14; 9: 31; 15:
3.*

Σαμαρία a different spelling for
Σαμάρεια.

Σαμαρίτης, ου, ὁ *Samaritan* Mt
10: 5; Lk 9: 52; 10: 33; 17: 16;
J 4: 9, 39f; 8: 48; Ac 8: 25.*

Σαμαρῖτις, ιδος, ἡ adj. and subst.
Samaritan (fem.) ἡ γυνὴ ἡ Σ. *the
Samaritan woman* J 4: 9.*

Σαμοθράκη, ης, ἡ *Samothrace*, an
island in the northern Aegean
Sea Ac 16: 11*

Σάμος, ου, ἡ *Samos*, an island off
the west coast of Asia Minor Ac
20: 15.*

Σαμουήλ, ὁ indecl. *Samuel* (1
Samuel chapters 1–25) Ac 3: 24;
13: 20; Hb 11: 32.*

Σαμφουρειν indecl. J 11: 54
v.l. = Sepphoris.*

Σαμψών, ὁ indecl. *Samson* (Judges
13–16) Hb 11: 32.*

σανδάλιον, ου, τό *sandal* Mk 6: 9;
Ac 12: 8.*

σανίς, ίδος, ἡ *board, plank* Ac
27: 44.*

Σαούλ, ὁ indecl. *Saul*—1. first
king of Israel Ac 13: 21.—
2. Jewish name of the Apostle
Paul Ac 9: 4, 17; 22: 7, 13; 26:
14. See Σαῦλος.*

σαπρός, ά, όν *decayed, rotten*—
1. lit. Mt 7: 17f; 12: 33; Lk
6: 43. *Decayed* or *unusable* Mt
13: 48.—2. fig. *bad, evil, un-
wholesome* Eph 4: 29.*

Σάπφιρα, gen. ης, dat. ῃ, ἡ *Sapphira*, wife of Ananias Ac 5: 1.*

σάπφιρος, ου, ἡ *the sapphire* Rv
21: 19.*

σαργάνη, ης, ἡ *basket, rope-basket*
2 Cor 11: 33.*

Σάρδεις, εων, αἱ *Sardis*, the capital
city of Lydia, in western Asia
Minor Rv 1: 11; 3: 1, 4.*

σάρδινος, ου, ὁ late form of σάρδιον
Rv 4: 3 v.l. See σάρδιον.*

σάρδιον, ου, τό *carnelian, sard(ius)*,
a reddish precious stone Rv
4: 3; 21: 20.*

σαρδόνυξ, υχος, ὁ *sardonyx*, a
variety of agate Rv 21: 20.*

Σάρεπτα, ων, τά *Zarephath*, a city
on the Phoenician coast Lk
4: 26.*

σαρκικός, ή, όν *fleshly, in the
manner of the flesh.*—1. *belonging
to the order of earthly things,
material* Ro 15: 27; 1 Cor 9:
11.—2. *belonging to the realm
of the flesh*, i.e. weak, sinful,
transitory 1 Cor 3: 3; 2 Cor 1:
12; 10: 4; 1 Pt 2: 11. Also as
v.l. in Ro 7: 14; 1 Cor 3: 1; Hb
7: 16.*

σάρκινος, η, ον—1. *fleshy, (made)
of flesh* 2 Cor 3: 3.—2. *fleshly,
belonging to the realm of the flesh,*
i.e. weak, sinful, transitory Ro

7: 14; 1 Cor 3: 1; Hb 7: 16;
2 Cor 1: 12 v.l.*

σάρξ, σαρκός, ἡ *flesh*—1. lit. Lk
24: 39; J 6: 51–56; Ro 2: 28; 1
Cor 15: 39; 2 Cor 12: 7; Gal 6:
13; Js 5: 3; Rv 19: 18, 21.—
2. *the body* Mk 10: 8; Ac 2: 26,
31; Gal 4: 13; Eph 5: 29; Col
2: 5; Hb 9: 10; 10: 20; 1 Pt 4:
1.—3. *a man of flesh and blood,
a person* Mt 16: 17; 24: 22;
Lk 3: 6; J 1: 14; Ro 3: 20; Gal
1: 16; 2: 16.—4. *human* or
mortal nature, earthly descent Ro
1: 3; 4: 1; 9: 3, 5, 8; 1 Cor 10:
18; Hb 2: 14; 12: 9.—5. *corpo-
reality, physical limitation(s),
life here on earth* 1 Cor 7: 28; Gal
2: 20; Phil 1: 22, 24; Col 1: 22,
24; 1 Pt 4: 2.—6. *the external* or
outward side of life, that which is
natural or earthly J 8: 15; 1 Cor
1: 26; 2 Cor 5: 16; 11: 18; Eph
6: 5; Phil 3: 3f. ἐν σαρκί *as a
man* Phlm 16.—7. the *flesh*,
especially in Paul's thought, is
often the willing instrument of
sin Mk 14: 38; J 3: 6; Ro 6: 19;
7: 5, 18, 25; 8: 3–9, 12f; 2 Cor
1: 17; Gal 5: 13, 16f, 19, 24;
Eph 2: 3; Col 2: 11, 18; Jd
23.—8. the *flesh* is the source of
the sexual urge, with no sug-
gestion of sinfulness J 1: 13.

Σαρούχ variant form of Σερούχ.

σαρόω *sweep (clean)* Mt 12: 44;
Lk 11: 25; 15: 8.*

Σάρρα, ας, ἡ *Sarah*, wife of Abraham Ro 4: 19; 9: 9; Hb 11: 11;
1 Pt 3: 6.*

Σαρων, ωνος, ὁ (the accent cannot
be determined) *Sharon*, a plain
along the north coast of Palestine
Ac 9: 35.*

σατάν, ὁ indecl. and σατανᾶς, ᾶ, ὁ
the Adversary, Satan, the enemy
of God and his people Mt 4: 10;
12: 26; Mk 1: 13; 3: 23, 26;
4: 15; Lk 10: 18; 11: 18; 13:
16; 22: 3, 31; J 13: 27; Ac 5: 3;
26: 18; Ro 16: 20; 1 Cor 5: 5;

7: 5; 2 Cor 2: 11; 11: 14; 12: 7; 1 Th 2: 18; 2 Th 2: 9; 1 Ti 1: 20; 5: 15; Rv 2: 9, 13, 24; 3: 9; 12: 9; 20: 2, 7.—In Mt 16: 23; Mk 8: 33 Peter is called Satan by Jesus because he is tempting the Master to abandon his role as Savior.*

σάτον, ου, τό *seah*, a Hebrew *measure* for grain, about a peck and a half Mt 13: 33; Lk 13: 21.*

Σαῦλος, ου, ὁ *Saul*, Grecized form of the Jewish name of the Apostle Paul (see Σαούλ) Ac 7: 58; 8: 1, 3; 9: 1, 8, 11, 22, 24; 11: 25, 30; 12: 25; 13: 1f, 7, 9; 22: 7 v.l.; 26: 14 v.l.*

σβέννυμι *extinguish, put out*— 1. lit. Mt 12: 20; 25: 8; Mk 9: 44, 46, 48; Eph 6: 16; Hb 11: 34.— 2. fig. *quench, stifle, suppress* 1 Th 5: 19.*

σβέσαι 1 aor. act. inf. of σβέννυμι.

σέ acc. of σύ.

σεαυτοῦ, ῆς reflexive pron., only in gen., dat. and acc. *yourself*— 1. gen. J 1: 22; 2 Ti 4: 11.—2. dat. Ac 9: 34; 16: 28; Ro 2: 5.— 3. acc. Mt 4: 6; Mk 1: 44; Lk 5: 14; Ro 2: 21; Gal 6: 1.

σεβάζομαι *worship* pass. in act. meaning Ro 1: 25.*

σέβασμα, ατος, τό *an object of worship, sanctuary* Ac 17: 23; 2 Th 2: 4.*

σεβαστός, ή, όν *revered, worthy of reverence, august*, as a translation of Lat. *Augustus*, designating the Roman emperor ὁ Σεβαστός *His Majesty the Emperor* Ac 25: 21, 25. σπεῖρα Σεβαστή *imperial cohort* 27: 1.*

σέβω mid. *worship* Mt 15: 9; Mk 7: 7; Ac 18: 13; 19: 27. σεβόμενοι τὸν θεόν *God-fearers, worshippers of God*, pagans who attended the synagogue but did not assume all the obligations of the Jewish law Ac 16: 14; 18: 7; cf. 13: 43, 50; 17: 4, 17.*

σειρά, ᾶς, ἡ *chain* 2 Pt 2: 4 v.l.*

σειρός a variant spelling for σιρός.

σεισμός, οῦ, ὁ *shaking*: of a *storm* at sea Mt 8: 24. *Earthquake* 24: 7; 27: 54; 28: 2; Mk 13: 8; Lk 21: 11; Ac 16: 26; Rv 6: 12; 8: 5; 11: 13, 19; 16: 18.*

σείω *shake, cause to quake, agitate* —1. lit. Hb 12: 26. Pass. Mt 27: 51; Rv 6: 13.—2. fig. *stir up* pass. *be stirred* Mt 21: 10. *Tremble* 28: 4.*

Σεκοῦνδος, ου, ὁ (a Latin name) *Secundus* Ac 20: 4.*

Σελεύκεια, ας, ἡ *Seleucia*, the port city of Antioch in Syria Ac 13: 4.*

σελήνη, ης, ἡ *moon* Mk 13: 24; Lk 21: 25; Ac 2: 20; 1 Cor 15: 41; Rv 8: 12; 21: 23.

σεληνιάζομαι *be moon-struck* Mt 4: 24; 17: 15.*

Σεμεΐν, ὁ indecl. *Semein* Lk 3: 26.*

σεμίδαλις, εως, ἡ *fine flour* Rv 18: 13.*

σεμνός, ή, όν *worthy of respect, dignified, serious* 1 Ti 3: 8, 11; Tit 2: 2. *Honorable, worthy, holy* Phil 4: 8.*

σεμνότης, τητος, ἡ *reverence, dignity, seriousness, probity* 1 Ti 2: 2; 3: 4; Tit 2: 7.*

Σέργιος, ου, ὁ *Sergius*, a Roman tribal name Ac 13: 7.*

Σερούχ, ὁ indecl. *Serug* Lk 3: 35.*

σέσωκα 1 perf. act. ind. of σῴζω.

Σήθ, ὁ indecl. *Seth* (Gen 4: 25f) Lk 3: 38.*

Σήμ, ὁ indecl. *Shem* (Gen 5: 32) Lk 3: 36.*

σημαίνω—1. *make known, report, communicate* Ac 25: 27; Rv 1: 1.—2. *indicate (beforehand), foretell* J 12: 33; 18: 32; 21: 19; Ac 11: 28.*

σημᾶναι 1 aor. act. inf. of σημαίνω.

σημεῖον, ου, τό *sign*—1. *the sign* or *(distinguishing) mark* by which something is known, *token, indication* Mt 16: 3; 24: 3, 30; Mk 13: 4; Lk 2: 12, 34; 11: 29f; 21: 7; Ro 4: 11; 1 Cor 14: 22; 2 Th 3: 17. *Signal* Mt 26: 48.— **2.** *a sign* consisting of a *miracle* or *wonder*—**a.** *miracle* of divine origin Mt 12: 38f; 16: 1, 4; Mk 8: 11f; 16: 17, 20; Lk 11: 16, 29; 23: 8; J 2: 11, 18; 3: 2; 4: 48; 6: 2, 14; 7: 31; 9: 16; Ac 2: 22, 43; 4: 16, 22; 14: 3; Ro 15: 19; 1 Cor 1: 22; 2 Cor 12: 12a; Hb 2: 4.—**b.** *miracle* of a demonic nature Mk 13: 22; 2 Th 2: 9; Rv 13: 13f; 16: 14; 19: 20.—**c.** *portent* Lk 21: 11, 25; Ac 2: 19; Rv 12: 1, 3; 15: 1.

σημειόω mid. *mark, take special notice of* 2 Th 3: 14.*

σήμερον adv. *today* Mt 6: 11, 30; 16: 3; Lk 23: 43; Ac 4: 9; Js 4: 13. ἡ σήμερον ἡμέρα *today, this very day* Mt 28: 15; Ac 20: 26; Ro 11: 8; 2 Cor 3: 14.

σημικίνθιον another spelling for σιμικίνθιον.

σήπω *cause to rot* 2 perf. σέσηπα *rot, decay* Js 5: 2.*

σηρικός another spelling for σιρικός.

σής, σητός, ὁ *the moth,* whose larvae eat clothing Mt 6: 19f; Lk 12: 33.*

σητόβρωτος, ον *motheaten* Js 5: 2.*

σθενόω *strengthen* 1 Pt 5: 10.*

σιαγών, όνος, ἡ *cheek* Mt 5: 39; Lk 6: 29.*

σιαίνομαι *be disturbed* or *annoyed* 1 Th 3: 3 v.l.*

σιγάτωσαν pres. act. imperative, 3 pl., of σιγάω.

σιγάω—**1.** intrans. *be silent, keep still*—**a.** *say nothing, keep silent* Lk 20: 26; Ac 15: 12; 1 Cor 14: 28, 30, 34.—**b.** *stop speaking, become silent* Lk 18: 39; Ac 15: 13; 1 Cor 14: 30.—**c.** *hold one's tongue* Lk 9: 36.—**2.** trans. *keep secret, conceal* pass. Ro 16: 25.*

σιγή, ῆς, ἡ *silence* Ac 21: 40; Rv 8: 1.*

σίδηρος, ου, ὁ *iron* Rv 18: 12.*

σιδηροῦς, ᾶ, οῦν (*made of*) *iron* Ac 12: 10; Rv 2: 27; 9:9; 12: 5; 19: 15.*

Σιδών, ῶνος, ἡ *Sidon,* an ancient royal city in Phoenicia Mt 11: 21f; Mk 3: 8; 7: 24, 31; Lk 6: 17; Ac 27: 3.

Σιδώνιος, ία, ιον *Sidonian, from Sidon* Ac 12: 20. ἡ Σιδωνία *the country around Sidon* Lk 4: 26.*

σικάριος, ου, ὁ (Latin loanword: sicarius) *dagger man, assassin* Ac 21: 38.*

σίκερα, τό indecl. *strong drink* Lk 1: 15.*

Σίλας, α or **Σιλᾶς, ᾶ, ὁ** *Silas,* friend and companion of Paul, mentioned 13 times between Ac 15: 22 and 18: 5.—The same person as Σιλουανός.*

Σιλουανός, οῦ, ὁ *Silvanus* 2 Cor 1: 19; 1 Th 1: 1; 2 Th 1: 1; 1 Pt 5: 12.—The same person as Σίλας.*

Σιλωάμ, ὁ indecl. *Siloam,* a system of water supply in Jerusalem Lk 13: 4; J 9: 7, 11.*

Σιμαίας, ου, ὁ *Simaias* 2 Ti 4: 19 v.l.*

σιμικίνθιον, ου, τό (Latin loanword: semicinctium) *an apron,* such as is used by workmen Ac 19: 12.*

Σίμων, ωνος, ὁ *Simon*—**1.** *Simon* Peter = Cephas Mt 4: 18; Mk 1: 16; Lk 4: 38 and often. See Πέτρος.—**2.** *Simon,* another of the 12 disciples, called ὁ Καναναῖος Mt 10: 4; Mk 3: 18 or (ὁ) ζηλωτής Lk 6: 15; Ac 1: 13. —**3.** name of a brother of Jesus Mt 13: 55; Mk 6:3.—**4.** *Simon* of Cyrene, who carried Jesus' cross Mt 27: 32; Mk 15: 21; Lk 23: 26.—**5.** father of Judas Iscariot J 6: 71; 12: 4 v.l.; 13: 2, 26.—**6.** *Simon* the leper Mt 26: 6; Mk 14: 3.—**7.** *Simon* the

Pharisee Lk 7: 40, 43f.—**8.** *Simon* the tanner in Joppa Ac 9: 43; 10: 6, 17, 32b.—**9.** *Simon* the magician Ac 8: 9, 13, 18, 24.

Σινά indecl. *Sinai* a mountain on the peninsula of the same name Ac 7: 30, 38; Gal 4: 24f.*

σίναπι, εως, τό *mustard* Mt 13: 31; 17: 20; Mk 4: 31; Lk 13: 19; 17: 6.*

σινδών, όνος, ἡ *linen cloth* or *sheet* Mt 27: 59; Mk 15: 46; Lk 23: 53; *sheet* or *tunic* Mk 14: 51f.*

σινιάζω *shake in a sieve, sift* fig. Lk 22: 31.*

σιρικός, ή, όν *silk(en)* subst. τὸ σιρικόν *silk* cloth or garments Rv 18: 12.*

σιρός, οῦ, ὁ *pit, cave* 2 Pt 2: 4.*

σιτευτός, ή, όν *fattened* Lk 15: 23, 27, 30.*

σιτίον, ου, τό pl. *food* (*made from grain*) Ac 7: 12.*

σιτιστός, ή, όν *fattened* subst. τὰ σιτιστά *cattle that have been fattened* Mt 22: 4.*

σιτομέτριον, ου, τό *a measured allowance of grain* or *food, a ration* Lk 12: 42.*

σῖτος, ου, ὁ *wheat, grain* in general Mt 3: 12; 13: 25, 29; Mk 4: 28; Lk 16: 7; 22: 31; J 12: 24; 1 Cor 15: 37; Rv 6: 6. The form τὰ σῖτα Ac 7: 12 v.l.

Σιχάρ a variant of Συχάρ.

Σιών, ἡ indecl. *Zion*—**1.** Mount *Zion*, a hill within the city of Jerusalem Hb 12: 22; Rv 14: 1. —**2.** in poetic usage: the daughter of Zion, of Jerusalem and its inhabitants Mt 21: 5; J 12: 15.— Of the people of Israel Ro 9: 33; 11: 26.—Of the New Jerusalem of Christianity 1 Pt 2: 6.*

σιωπάω *be silent*—**1.** *keep silent, say nothing* Mt 26: 63; Mk 3: 4; 9: 34; 14: 61; Ac 18: 9.— **2.** *stop speaking, be* or *become quiet* Mt 20: 31; Mk 10: 48; Lk 18: 39 v.l.; 19: 40. *Lose the ability*

to speak Lk 1: 20.—Symbolically Mk 4: 39.*

σιωπῇ adv. *quietly, privately* J 11: 28 v.l.*

σκανδαλίζω—**1.** *cause to be caught* or *to fall,* i.e. *cause to sin*— **a.** someone Mt 5: 29f; Mk 9: 42f, 45, 47; 1 Cor 8: 13. Pass. *be led into sin* perhaps 2 Cor 11: 29 (see below). *Be led into sin, fall away* Mt 13: 21; 24: 10; J 16: 1.—**b.** σκανδαλί-ζεσθαι ἔν τινι *be led into sin* or *repelled by someone, take offense at someone* Mt 11: 6; 26: 31, 33; Mk 6: 3.—**2.** *give offense to, anger, shock* Mt 17: 27; J 6: 61. Pass. Mt 15: 12. τίς σκανδαλί-ζεται; perhaps *who has any reason to take offense?* 2 Cor 11: 29 (see 1a above).

σκάνδαλον, ου, τό—**1.** *trap,* sym-bolically Ro 11: 9.—**2.** *temptation to sin, enticement* Mt 16: 23; 18: 7; Lk 17: 1; Ro 14: 13; 16: 17; Rv 2: 14.—**3.** *that which gives offense* or *causes revulsion, that which arouses opposition, an object of anger* or *disapproval, a stain,* etc. Mt 13: 41; 1 Cor 1: 23; Gal 5: 11; 1 J 2: 10. πέτρα σκανδάλου *a stone that causes men to fall* Ro 9: 33; 1 Pt 2: 8.*

σκάπτω *dig* Lk 6: 48; 13: 8; 16: 3.*

Σκαριώθ is the reading of ms. D in Mk 3: 19; J 6: 71 and **Σκαριώτης** is the reading of the same ms. in Mt 10: 4; 26: 14; Mk 14: 10 for 'Ισκαριώθ or 'Ισκαριώτης.*

σκάφη, ης, ἡ (*small*) *boat, skiff* Ac 27: 16, 30, 32.*

σκέλος, ους, τό *leg* J 19: 31–33.*

σκέπασμα, ατος, τό *covering, shelter, clothing, house* 1 Ti 6: 8.*

Σκευᾶς, ᾶ, ὁ *Sceva* Ac 19: 14.*

σκευή, ῆς, ἡ *equipment, ship's gear* Ac 27: 19.*

σκεῦος, ους, τό—1. lit.—a. generally *thing, object* Mk 11: 16; Ac 10: 11, 16; 11: 5; Hb 9: 21; Rv 18: 12. Pl. *property* Mt 12: 29; Mk 3: 27; Lk 17: 31. Perhaps *kedge* or *driving-anchor* Ac 27: 17.—b. *vessel, jar, dish*, etc. Lk 8: 16; J 19: 29; Ro 9: 21; 2 Ti 2: 20f; Rv 2: 27.—2. fig., often of the human body, *vessel*, etc. Ro 9: 22f; 2 Cor 4: 7; 1 Pt 3: 7. σκεῦος ἐκλογῆς *a chosen instrument* Ac 9: 15. τὸ ἑαυτοῦ σκεῦος 1 Th 4: 4 may refer either to *one's own body* or *one's own wife.**

σκηνή, ῆς, ἡ *tent, booth* Mt 17: 4; Mk 9: 5; Lk 9: 33; Hb 11: 9.— The *Tent of Testimony* or *Tabernacle* Ac 7: 44; Hb 8: 2, 5; 9: 2f, 6 (cf. 7), 8, 11, 21; 13: 10; Rv 15: 5. Of another sanctuary Ac 7: 43.—*Dwelling* generally Lk 16: 9; Ac 15: 16; Rv 13: 6; 21: 3.*

σκηνοπηγία, ας, ἡ *the building of tents* or *booths*, hence *the Festival of Booths* or *Tabernacles, Succoth*, celebrated in autumn J 5: 1 v.l.; 7: 2.*

σκηνοποιός, οῦ, ὁ *tent-maker* Ac 18: 3.*

σκῆνος, ους, τό *tent, lodging* fig. 2 Cor 5: 1, 4.*

σκηνόω *live, dwell* J 1: 14; Rv 7: 15; 12: 12; 13: 6; 21: 3.*

σκήνωμα, ατος, τό *dwelling-place, lodging* Ac 7: 46; 2 Pt 1: 13f.*

σκιά, ᾶς, ἡ—1. *shade, shadow* lit. Mk 4: 32; Ac 5: 15. Fig. Mt 4: 16; Lk 1: 79; 1 J 2: 8 v.l.— 2. *shadow, foreshadowing* Col 2: 17; Hb 8: 5; 10: 1.*

σκιρτάω *leap, spring about* Lk 1: 41, 44; 6: 23.*

σκληροκαρδία, ας, ἡ *hardness of heart, obstinacy* Mt 19: 8; Mk 10: 5; 16: 14.*

σκληρός, ά, όν *hard* (to the touch) fig. *hard, harsh, unpleasant* J 6: 60; Jd 15; *rough, strong* Js 3: 4; *strict, harsh, cruel* Mt 25:

24. σκληρόν σοι *it is hard for you* Ac 9: 5 v.l.; 26: 14.*

σκληρότης, ητος, ἡ *hardness* (of heart), *stubbornness* Ro 2: 5.*

σκληροτράχηλος, ον *stiff-necked, stubborn* Ac 7: 51.*

σκληρύνω *harden*, fig. *make stubborn* Ac 19: 9; Ro 9: 18; Hb 3: 8, 13, 15; 4: 7.*

σκολιός, ά, όν *crooked* lit. Lk 3: 5. Fig. *crooked, unscrupulous, dishonest* Ac 2: 40; Phil 2: 15; 1 Pt 2: 18.*

σκόλοψ, οπος, ὁ *thorn, splinter* 2 Cor 12: 7.*

σκοπέω *look* (out) *for, notice, keep one's eyes on, consider* Lk 11: 35; Ro 16: 17; 2 Cor 4: 18; Gal 6: 1; Phil 2: 4; 3: 17.*

σκοπός, οῦ, ὁ *goal, mark* Phil 3: 14.*

σκορπίζω *scatter, disperse* Mt 12: 30; Lk 11: 23; J 10: 12; 16: 32. *Distribute* 2 Cor 9: 9.*

σκορπίος, ου, ὁ *scorpion* Lk 10: 19; 11: 12; Rv 9: 3, 5, 10.*

σκοτεινός, ή, όν *dark* Mt 6: 23; Lk 11: 34, 36.*

σκοτία, ας, ἡ *darkness, gloom* lit. or fig. Mt 4: 16; 10: 27; Lk 12: 3; J 1: 5; 6: 17; 8: 12; 12: 35, 46; 20: 1; 1 J 1: 5; 2: 8f, 11.*

σκοτίζομαι pass. *be* or *become dark, be darkened* lit. or fig. Mt 24: 29; Mk 13: 24; Lk 23: 45 v.l.; Ro 1: 21; 11: 10; Rv 8: 12; Eph 4: 18 v.l.*

σκότος, ους, τό *darkness, gloom*— 1. lit. Mt 8: 12; 25: 30; Mk 15: 33; Ac 13: 11; 2 Pt 2: 17.— 2. fig. Mt 6: 23; Lk 1: 79; J 3: 19; Ac 26: 18; Ro 13: 12; 1 Cor 4: 5; 2 Cor 6: 14; Col 1: 13.

σκοτόω pass. *be* or *become darkened* lit. or fig. Eph 4: 18; Rv 9: 2; 16: 10.*

σκύβαλον, ου, τό *refuse, rubbish, dirt, dung* Phil 3: 8.*

Σκύθης, ου, ὁ *the Scythian*, living in what is now southern Russia Col 3: 11.*

σκυθρωπός, (ή), όν *with a sad,
gloomy* or *sullen look* Mt 6: 16;
Lk 24: 17.*

σκύλλου pres. pass. imperative,
2 sing., of σκύλλω.

σκύλλω *trouble, bother, annoy* Mk
5: 35; Lk 8: 49. Pass. *be weary* or
harassed Mt 9: 36; *trouble oneself* Lk 7: 6.*

σκῦλον, ου, τό pl. *booty, spoils* Lk
11: 22.*

σκωληκόβρωτος, ον *eaten by worms*
Ac 12: 23.*

σκώληξ, ηκος, ὁ *worm* Mk 9: 44
v.l., 46 v.l., 48.*

σμαράγδινος, η, ον (*of*) *emerald*
Rv 4: 3.*

σμάραγδος, ου, ὁ *emerald* Rv 21:
19.*

σμῆγμα, ατος, τό *ointment, salve*
J 19: 39 v.l.*

σμῖγμα, ατος, τό v.l. for μῖγμα J
19: 39.*

σμύρνα, ης, ἡ *myrrh* an aromatic
resinous gum Mt 2: 11; J 19: 39.*

Σμύρνα, ης, ἡ *Smyrna* a large city
on the west coast of Asia Minor
Rv 1: 11; 2: 8.*

Σμυρναῖος, α, ον *coming from
Smyrna* ὁ Σ. *the Smyrnaean* Rv
2: 8 v.l.*

σμυρνίζω *treat* or *flavor with
myrrh* Mk 15: 23.*

Σόδομα, ων, τά *Sodom* (Gen 19:
24) Mt 11: 23f; Lk 17: 29; Ro 9:
29; 2 Pt 2: 6; Rv 11: 8.

σοί dat. sing of σύ.

Σολομών, ῶνος, ὁ and Σολομῶν,
ῶντος, ὁ *Solomon*, son and
successor of David Mt 1: 6f; 6:
29; Lk 11: 31; J 10: 23; Ac 3:
11; 7: 47.

σορός, οῦ, ἡ *coffin, bier* Lk 7: 14.*

σός, σή, σόν *your, yours* (sing.);
in older and formal usage *thy,
thine* Mt 7: 3, 22; Mk 2: 18; J
4: 42; 18: 35; Ac 5: 4; 1 Cor 8:
11; Phlm 14. οἱ σοί *your own
people* Mk 5: 19. τὸ σόν, τὰ σά
what is yours Mt 20: 14; Lk 6:
30; J 17: 10.

σοῦ gen. sing. of σύ.

σουδάριον, ου, τό (Latin loanword : sudarium) *face-cloth, hand-
kerchief* Lk 19: 20; J 11: 44;
20: 7; Ac 19: 12.*

Σουσάννα, ης or ας, ἡ *Susanna*
Lk 8: 3.*

σοφία, ας, ἡ *wisdom*—1. the
wisdom found among men, whether natural or imparted by
God Mt 12: 42; Ac 6: 3, 10;
7: 10, 22; 1 Cor 1: 19f; 2: 13;
Col 1: 28; Js 3: 13, 15, 17; 2 Pt
3: 15.—2. *wisdom* of Christ and
of God Mk 6: 2; Lk 2: 40, 52;
1 Cor 1: 21a, 24, 30; Col 2: 3.—
3. *Wisdom* may be personified
in Mt 11: 19; Lk 7: 35; 11: 49.

σοφίζω *make wise, teach* 2 Ti 3:
15. *Reason out, devise craftily*
pass. 2 Pt 1: 16.*

σοφός, ή, όν—1. *clever, skilful,
experienced* 1 Cor 3: 10; 6: 5.—
2. *wise, learned* of wisdom from
a natural or divine source Mt
23: 34; Lk 10: 21; Ro 1: 14, 22;
1 Cor 1: 19f, 26f; 3: 18; Eph
5: 15; Js 3: 13.—3. God is called
wise in the absolute sense Ro 16:
27; 1 Cor 1: 25.

Σπανία, ας, ἡ *Spain* Ro 15: 24, 28.*

σπαράσσω *tear, pull to and fro,
convulse* Mk 1: 26; 9: 20 v.l.,
26; Lk 9: 39.*

σπαργανόω *wrap* (*up*) *in* (*swadd-
ling*) *cloths* Lk 2: 7, 12.*

σπαρείς 2 aor. pass. participle of
σπείρω.

σπαταλάω *live luxuriously* or
indulgently 1 Ti 5: 6; Js 5: 5.*

σπάω mid. *draw* Mk 14: 47; Ac
16: 27.*

σπεῖρα, ης, ἡ *cohort* (normally
about 600 soldiers) Mt 27: 27;
J 18: 3; Ac 10: 1; 27: 1.

σπείρω *sow* seed—1. lit. Mt 6: 26;
13: 22, 24, 27, 39; Mk 4: 3, 31;
Lk 8: 5; 1 Cor 15: 36f.—2. fig.
Mt 25: 24, 26; Mk 4: 14; J 4:
36f; 1 Cor 15: 42–44; Gal 6: 7;
Js 3: 18.

σπεκουλάτωρ, ορος, ὁ (Latin loanword: speculator) *executioner* Mk 6: 27.*

σπένδω *offer a libation* or *drink-offering* pass. and fig. *be offered up* Phil 2: 17; 2 Ti 4: 6.*

σπέρμα, ατος, τό *seed*—**1.** lit. Mt 13: 24, 27, 37f; Mk 4: 31; J 7: 42; 1 Cor 15: 38; 2 Cor 9: 10; Hb 11: 11.—**2.** fig. *survivors* Ro 9: 29. *Descendants, children, posterity* Mt 22: 24; Mk 12: 20, 22; Lk 1: 55; J 8: 33, 37; Ac 13: 23; Ro 9: 7f; 11: 1; Gal 3: 16, 19; Hb 2: 16. *Nature* 1 J 3: 9.

σπερμολόγος, ον *picking up seeds*, subst. *a rook*, fig. *gossip, chatterer, rag-picker* Ac 17: 18.*

σπεύδω—**1.** intrans. *hurry, make haste* Lk 2: 16; 19: 5f; Ac 20: 16; 22: 18.—**2.** trans. *hasten or strive for* 2 Pt 3: 12.*

σπήλαιον, ου, τό *cave, den* Mk 11: 17; J 11: 38; Hb 11: 38; Rv 6: 15.

σπιλάς, άδος, ἡ either *a rock washed by the sea, a (hidden) reef* or *spot, stain* symbolically Jd 12.*

σπίλος, ου, ὁ *spot* fig. *stain, blemish* Eph 5: 27; 2 Pt 2: 13.*

σπιλόω *stain, defile* fig. Js 3: 6; Jd 23.*

σπλαγχνίζομαι *have pity, feel sympathy* Mt 14: 14; 18: 27; Mk 1: 41; 6: 34; 8: 2; Lk 7: 13; 15: 20.

σπλάγχνον, ου, τό pl.—**1.** lit. *inward parts, entrails* Ac 1: 18.—**2.** fig., of the seat of the emotions, in our usage *heart* Lk 1: 78; 2 Cor 6: 12; 7: 15; Phil 2: 1; Col 3: 12; Phlm 7, 20; 1 J 3: 17. *Love, affection* Phil 1: 8; *object of affection, beloved* Phlm 12.*

σπόγγος, ου, ὁ *sponge* Mt 27: 48; Mk 15: 36; J 19: 29.*

σποδός, οῦ, ἡ *ashes* Mt 11: 21; Lk 10: 13; Hb 9: 13.*

σπορά, ᾶς, ἡ *seed* 1 Pt 1: 23.*

σπόριμος, ον *sown*, subst. τὰ σπόριμα *standing grain, grain fields* Mt 12: 1; Mk 2: 23; Lk 6: 1.*

σπόρος, ου, ὁ *seed* Mk 4: 26f; Lk 8: 5, 11; 2 Cor 9: 10.*

σπουδάζω—**1.** *hasten, hurry* 2 Ti 4: 9, 21; Tit 3: 12, though meaning 2 is acceptable in these passages.—**2.** *be zealous or eager, take pains, make every effort* Gal 2: 10; Eph 4: 3; 1 Th 2: 17; 2 Ti 2: 15; Hb 4: 11; 2 Pt 1: 10, 15; 3: 14.*

σπουδαῖος, α, ον *eager, zealous, earnest* 2 Cor 8: 22a; comp. σπουδαιότερος *very earnest, more zealous* 8: 17, 22b. Cf. 2 Ti 1: 17 v.l.*

σπουδαίως adv.—**1.** *with haste* comp. σπουδαιοτέρως *with special urgency* Phil 2: 28.—**2.** *diligently, earnestly, zealously* 2 Ti 1: 17; Tit 3: 13; *strongly* Lk 7: 4. Comp. *very eagerly* σπουδαιότερον and σπουδαιοτέρως both as v.l. in 2 Ti 1: 17.*

σπουδή, ῆς, ἡ—**1.** *haste, speed* Mk 6: 25; Lk 1: 39.—**2.** *eagerness, earnestness, diligence, zeal* Ro 12: 8, 11; 2 Cor 7: 11; 8: 7f; Hb 6: 11; 2 Pt 1: 5; Jd 3. *Good will, devotion* 2 Cor 7: 12; 8: 16.*

σπυρίς, ίδος, ἡ *basket, hamper* Mt 15: 37; 16: 10; Mk 8: 8, 20; Ac 9: 25.*

στάδιον, ου, τό—**1.** *stade as a measure of distance* = about 607 English feet. Mt 14: 24; Lk 24: 13; J 6: 19; 11: 18; Rv 14: 20; 21: 16.—**2.** *arena, stadium* 1 Cor 9: 24.*

στάμνος, ου, ὁ or ἡ *jar* Hb 9: 4.*

στασιαστής, οῦ, ὁ *rebel, revolutionary* Mk 15: 7.*

στάσις, εως, ἡ—**1.** *existence, continuance* Hb 9: 8.—**2.** *uprising, riot, revolt, rebellion* Mk 15: 7; Lk 23: 19, 25; Ac 19: 40.—

3. *strife, discord, dissension* Ac 15: 2; 24: 5; *dispute* 23: 7, 10.*

στατήρ, ῆρος, ὁ *the stater,* a silver coin = four drachmas, normally about 80 cents Mt 17: 27; 26: 15 v.l.*

σταυρός, οῦ, ὁ *the cross*—**1.** lit. Mt 27: 32; 40, 42; Mk 15: 21, 30, 32; Lk 23: 26; J 19: 17, 19, 25, 31; Phil 2: 8; Hb 12: 2.— **2.** symbolically, of suffering and death Mt 10: 38; 16: 24; Mk 8: 34; 10: 21 v.l.; Lk 9: 23; 14: 27.—**3.** the *cross* of Christ as one of the most important elements in Christian teaching 1 Cor 1: 17f; Gal 5: 11; 6: 12, 14; Eph 2: 16; Phil 2: 8; 3: 18; Col 1: 20; 2: 14.*

σταυρόω *nail to the cross, crucify*— **1.** lit. Mk 15: 13ff, 20, 24f, 27; 16: 6; J 19: 6, 10, 15f; Ac 2: 36; 4: 10; 1 Cor 2: 8; 2 Cor 13: 4; Rv 11: 8.—**2.** fig. Gal 5: 24; 6: 14.

σταφυλή, ῆς, ἡ (*a bunch of*) *grapes* Mt 7: 16; Lk 6: 44; Rv 14: 18.*

στάχυς, υος, ὁ *head* or *ear* (*of grain*) Mt 12: 1; Mk 2: 23; 4: 28; Lk 6: 1.*

Στάχυς, υος, ὁ *Stachys* Ro 16: 9.*

στέγη, ης, ἡ *roof* Mt 8: 8; Mk 2: 4; Lk 7: 6.*

στέγω—**1.** *cover, pass over in silence* perhaps 1 Cor 13: 7, though meaning 2 is also possible.—**2.** *bear, stand, endure* 1 Cor 9: 12; perhaps 13: 7 (see 1 above); 1 Th 3: 1, 5.*

στεῖρα, ας, ἡ (*a*) *barren* (*woman*), *one incapable of bearing children* Lk 1: 7, 36; 23: 29; Gal 4: 27.*

στέλλω mid.—**1.** *keep away, stand aloof* 2 Th 3: 6.—**2.** *avoid, try to avoid* 2 Cor 8: 20.*

στέμμα, ατος, τό *wreath* or *garland* Ac 14: 13.*

στεναγμός, οῦ, ὁ *sigh, groan, groaning* Ac 7: 34; Ro 8: 26.*

στενάζω *sigh, groan* Mk 7: 34; Ro 8: 23; 2 Cor 5: 2, 4; Hb 13: 17; *complain* Js 5: 9.*

στενός, ή, όν *narrow* Mt 7: 13f; Lk 13: 24.*

στενοχωρέω *crowd, cramp, confine, restrict* pass., fig. 2 Cor 6: 12; *be crushed* 4: 8.*

στενοχωρία, ας, ἡ fig. *distress, difficulty, anguish, trouble* Ro 2: 9; 8: 35; 2 Cor 6: 4; 12: 10.*

στερεός, ά, όν—**1.** lit. *firm, solid, strong* 2 Ti 2: 19; Hb 5: 12, 14.— **2.** fig. *steadfast, firm* 1 Pt 5: 9.*

στερεόω *make strong, make firm*— **1.** lit. Ac 3: 7, 16.—**2.** fig. 16: 5.*

στερέωμα, ατος, τό *firmness, steadfastness* Col 2: 5.*

Στεφανᾶς, ᾶ, ὁ *Stephanas,* a Corinthian Christian 1 Cor 1: 16; 16: 15, 17; subscr.*

Στέφανος, ου, ὁ *Stephen,* first Christian martyr Ac 6: 5, 8f; 7: 1 v.l., 59; 8: 2; 11: 19; 22: 20.*

στέφανος, ου, ὁ *wreath, crown*— **1.** lit. Mt 27: 29; Mk 15: 17; J 19: 2, 5; 1 Cor 9: 25; Rv 4: 4, 10; 6: 2; 9: 7; 12: 1; 14: 14.— **2.** fig.—**a.** *prize, reward* 2 Ti 4: 8; Js 1: 12; 1 Pt 5: 4; Rv 2: 10; 3: 11.—**b.** *adornment, pride* Phil 4: 1; 1 Th 2: 19.*

στεφανόω *crown, wreathe* lit. 2 Ti 2: 5. Fig. *honor, reward, crown* Hb 2: 7, 9.*

στῆθος, ους, τό *chest, breast* Lk 18: 13; 23: 48; J 13: 25; 21: 20; Rv 15: 6.*

στήκω—**1.** lit. *stand* Mk 3: 31; 11: 25; J 1: 26; (8: 44 is best taken as a form of ἵστημι); Rv 12: 4 v.l.—**2.** fig. *stand firm, be steadfast* Ro 14: 4; 1 Cor 16: 13; Gal 5: 1; Phil 1: 27; 4: 1; 1 Th 3: 8; 2 Th 2: 15.*

στηριγμός, οῦ, ὁ *firmness* 2 Pt 3: 17.*

στηρίζω *set up, fix* (*firmly*), *establish, support*—**1.** lit. Lk 16: 26; *set* 9: 51.—**2.** fig. *confirm, estab-*

lish, strengthen Lk 22: 32; Ac
18: 23; Ro 1: 11; 16: 25; 1 Th
3: 2, 13; 2 Th 2: 17; 3: 3; Js
5: 8; 1 Pt 5: 10; 2 Pt 1: 12; Rv
3: 2.*

στιβάς, άδος, ἡ *leaves, leafy
branches* Mk 11: 8.*

στίγμα, ατος, τό *mark, brand* Gal
6: 17.*

στιγμή, ῆς, ἡ *moment* Lk 4: 5.*

στίλβω *shine, be radiant* Mk 9:
3.*

στοά, ᾶς, ἡ *(roofed) colonnade* or
cloister, portico J 5: 2; 10: 23;
Ac 3: 11; 5: 12.*

στοιβάς a variant spelling of
στιβάς.

Στοϊκός, ή, όν *Stoic* Ac 17: 18.*

στοιχεῖον, ου, τό pl.—1. *elements
(of learning), fundamental principles, letters of the alphabet,
ABC's* Hb 5: 12. This meaning
is also possible in passages from
Gal and Col under 3 below.—
2. *elemental substances, elements*
from which everything is made
2 Pt 3: 10, 12.—3. *elemental
spirits* may be the meaning in
Gal 4: 3, 9; Col 2: 8, 20, but
meaning 1 above is also possible.*

στοιχέω *hold to, agree with, follow*
w. dat. Ac 21: 24; Ro 4: 12;
Gal 5: 25; 6: 16; Phil 3: 16.*

στολή, ῆς, ἡ *robe,* especially a *long,
flowing robe* Mk 12: 38; Lk 15:
22; Rv 6: 11; 7: 9; 22: 14.

στόμα, ατος, τό—1. *mouth* Mt 4:
4; 12: 34; 15: 11, 17f; Lk 1: 64;
4: 22; 21: 15; Ac 8: 32; 2 Cor
13: 1; Col 3: 8; Hb 11: 33; Js 3:
3, 10; Rv 9: 17–19; 14: 5.—
2. *edge* of a sword Lk 21: 24;
Hb 11: 34.

στόμαχος, ου, ὁ *stomach* 1 Ti 5:
23.*

στρατεία, ας, ἡ *campaign* fig.
warfare 2 Cor 10: 4; *fight* 1 Ti 1:
18.*

στράτευμα, ατος, τό *army* Rv 19:
14, 19. Of a smaller detachment

Ac 23: 10, 27. τὰ στρατεύματα
the troops Mt 22: 7; Lk 23: 11;
Rv 9: 16.*

στρατεύομαι *do military service,
serve in the army*—1. lit. Lk 3:
14; 1 Cor 9: 7; 2 Ti 2: 4.—
2. fig. 2 Cor 10: 3; 1 Ti 1: 18;
Js 4: 1; 1 Pt 2: 11.*

στρατηγός, οῦ, ὁ—1. *praetor, chief
magistrate* at Philippi Ac 16: 20,
22, 35f, 38.—2. *captain* Lk 22:
4, 52; Ac 4: 1; 5: 24, 26.*

στρατιά, ᾶς, ἡ *army* Lk 2: 13;
host Ac 7: 42. Equivalent to
στρατεία *warfare* 2 Cor 10: 4
v.l.*

στρατιώτης, ου, ὁ *soldier* lit.
Mt 8: 9; 27: 27; 28: 12; Mk 15:
16; Lk 7: 8; J 19: 2; Ac 10: 7.
Fig. 2 Ti 2: 3.

στρατολογέω *gather an army,
enlist soldiers* 2 Ti 2: 4.*

στρατοπεδάρχης or στρατοπέδ-
αρχος, ου, ὁ *military commander, commandant of a camp*
Ac 28: 16 v.l.*

στρατόπεδον, ου, τό *army, body of
troops* Lk 21: 20.*

στραφείς 2 aor. pass. participle of
στρέφω.

στρεβλόω *twist, distort* 2 Pt 3: 16.*

στρέφω—1. act.—1. trans. *turn*
Mt 5: 39; perhaps Ac 7: 42 (see
1b below). *Turn, change* Rv 11:
6. *Bring back, return* Mt 27: 3.—
b. intrans. *turn (away)* perhaps
Ac 7: 42 (see 1a above).—
2. pass.—a. *turn around, turn
toward* lit. Mt 7: 6; 9: 22; Lk 22:
61; 23: 28; J 1: 38. Fig. Ac 7:
39; 13: 46.—b. *turn, change*
inwardly, *be converted* Mt 18: 3;
J 12: 40.

στρέψον 1 aor. act. imperative,
2 sing., of στρέφω.

στρηνιάω *live in luxury, live
sensually* Rv 18: 7, 9.*

στρῆνος, ους, τό *sensuality, luxury*
Rv 18: 3.*

στρουθίον, ου, τό *sparrow* Mt 10:
29, 31; Lk 12: 6f.*

στρωννύω = στρώννυμι spread (out) Mt 21: 8; Mk 11: 8. The perf. pass. participle ἐστρωμένον Mk 14: 15; Lk 22: 12 may mean paved or furnished. στρῶσον σεαυτῷ make your own bed Ac 9: 34.*

στρῶσον 1 aor. act. imperative, 2 sing., of στρωννύω.

στυγητός, ή, όν hated, hateful Tit 3: 3.*

στυγνάζω—1. be shocked, appalled perhaps Mk 10: 22 (see 2 below). —2. be or become gloomy, dark, sad perhaps Mk 10: 22 (see 1 above). Of the sky Mt 16: 3.*

στῦλος, ου, ὁ pillar, column lit. Rv 10: 1. Fig. Gal 2: 9; 1 Ti 3: 15; Rv 3: 12.*

Στωϊκός a different spelling for Στοϊκός.

σύ, gen. σοῦ (σου), dat. σοί (σοι), acc. σέ (σε); pl. ὑμεῖς, ὑμῶν, ὑμῖν, ὑμᾶς you (older and more formal sing. thou).—1. the nominative Mt 2: 6; 3: 14; 11: 3; J 4: 9; Ac 1: 24; 2 Cor 13: 9; Js 2: 18. For emphasis Mt 16: 16, 18; Mk 14: 30, 68; Lk 1: 42; Ro 11: 17; Gal 6: 1.—2. The accented forms are used in the oblique cases of the sing. for emphasis or contrast Lk 2: 35; Ro 11: 18; Phil 4: 3; also with prepositions Mt 6: 23; Lk 1: 35. —3. σου and ὑμῶν your Mt 1: 20; 4: 6; 9: 6; Lk 7: 48; Ro 1: 8; Phil 1: 19; 1 Ti 4: 12.

συγγένεια, ας, ἡ relationship, kinship, the relatives Lk 1: 61; Ac 7: 3, 14.*

συγγενεῦσιν irregular dat. pl. of συγγενής.

συγγενής, ές related, akin to subst. relative Mk 6: 4; Lk 1: 36 v.l., 58; 2: 44; 14: 12; 21: 16; J 18: 26; Ac 10: 24; fellow-countryman, fellow-citizen Ro 9: 3; 16: 7, 11, 21.*

συγγενίς, ίδος, ἡ (female) relative, kinswoman Lk 1: 36.*

συγγνώμη, ης, ἡ concession 1 Cor 7: 6.*

συγκάθημαι sit (with) Mk 14: 54; Ac 26: 30.*

συγκαθίζω—1. trans. cause to sit down with Eph 2: 6.—2. intrans. sit down with others Lk 22: 55.*

συγκακοπαθέω suffer together with someone 2 Ti 2: 3; cf. 1: 8.*

συγκακουχέομαι suffer or be mistreated with Hb 11: 25.*

συγκαλέω call together—1. act. Mk 15: 16; Lk 15: 6, 9; Ac 5: 21. —2. mid. call to one's side, summon Lk 9: 1; 15: 6 v.l., 9 v.l.; 23: 13; Ac 5: 21 v.l.; 10: 24; 13: 7 v.l.; 28: 17.*

συγκαλύπτω cover (completely), conceal Lk 12: 2.*

συγκάμπτω (cause to) bend Ro 11: 10.*

συγκαταβαίνω go down with someone Ac 25: 5.*

συγκατάθεσις, εως, ἡ agreement 2 Cor 6: 16.*

συγκατανεύω agree, consent by a nod Ac 18: 27 v.l.*

συγκατατίθημι mid. agree with, consent to Lk 23: 51; Ac 4: 18 v.l.; 15: 12 v.l.*

συγκαταψηφίζομαι pass. be chosen together with, be added Ac 1: 26.*

σύγκειμαι recline together Mt 9: 10 v.l.*

συγκεκερασμένος or συγκεκραμένος perf. pass. participle of συγκεράννυμι.

συγκεράννυμι mix (together), blend, unite fig. compose 1 Cor 12: 24; unite Hb 4: 2.*

συγκεχυμένος perf. pass. participle of συγχέω.

συγκινέω arouse Ac 6: 12.*

συγκλείω close up together, hem in, enclose—1. lit. Lk 5: 6.— 2. fig. confine, imprison Ro 11: 32; Gal 3: 22f.*

συγκληρονόμος, ον inheriting together with or jointly Eph 3: 6. subst. fellow-heir Ro 8: 17; Hb 11: 9; 1 Pt 3: 7.*

συγκοινωνέω *participate in with* someone, *be connected with* Eph 5: 11; Phil 4: 14; Rv 18: 4.*

συγκοινωνός, οῦ, ὁ *participant, partner* Ro 11: 17; 1 Cor 9: 23; Phil 1: 7; Rv 1: 9.*

συγκομίζω *bury* Ac 8: 2.*

συγκρίνω *compare* 2 Cor 10: 12. For 1 Cor 2: 13 *compare, bring together,* and *explain, interpret* are all possible.*

συγκύπτω *be bent over* Lk 13: 11.*

συγκυρία, ας, ἡ *coincidence, chance* Lk 10: 31.*

συγχαίρω—1. *rejoice with, feel joy with* Lk 1: 58 (see 2 below); 15: 6, 9; 1 Cor 12: 26; 13: 6; Phil 2: 17f (see 2 below).— 2. *congratulate* w. dat. is also possible for Lk 1: 58; Phil 2: 17f (see 1 above).*

συγχέω and συγχύν(ν)ω *confuse, confound, trouble, stir up* Ac 9: 22; 19: 29 v.l., 32; 21: 27, 31; pass. *be amazed, excited* 2: 6.*

συγχράομαι *have dealings with, associate on friendly terms with* J 4: 9.*

συγχύ(ν)νω see συγχέω.

σύγχυσις, εως, ἡ *confusion, tumult* Ac 19: 29.*

συγχωρέω *permit* Ac 21: 39 v.l.*

συζάω *live with* Ro 6: 8; 2 Cor 7: 3; 2 Ti 2: 11.*

συζεύγνυμι *join together* Mt 19: 6; Mk 10: 9.*

συζητέω—1. *discuss, carry on a discussion* Mk 1: 27; 9: 10; Lk 24: 15.—2. *dispute, debate, argue* w. dat. Mk 8: 11; 9: 14, 16; 12: 28; Lk 22: 23; Ac 6: 9; 9: 29.*

συζήτησις, εως, ἡ *dispute, discussion* Ac 15: 2 v.l., 7 v.l.; 28: 29 v.l.*

συζητητής, οῦ, ὁ *disputant, debater* 1 Cor 1: 20.*

σύζυγος, ου, ὁ *comrade,* lit. 'yoke-fellow' Phil 4: 3.*

συζωοποιέω *make alive together with* someone Eph 2: 5; Col 2: 13.*

συκάμινος, ου, ἡ *the mulberry tree* Lk 17: 6.*

συκῆ, ῆς, ἡ *the fig tree* Mt 21: 19–21; 24: 32; Mk 11: 13, 20f; Lk 13: 6f; J 1: 48, 50; Js 3: 12.

συκομορέα, ας, ἡ *the fig-mulberry tree, sycamore fig* Lk 19: 4.*

σῦκον, ου, τό *the fig, ripe fig* Mt 7: 16; Mk 11: 13; Lk 6: 44; Js 3: 12.*

συκοφαντέω—1. *accuse falsely, annoy, harass, oppress* Lk 3: 14.—2. *extort* Lk 19: 8.*

συλαγωγέω *carry off as captive* fig. Col 2: 8.*

συλάω *rob* fig. 2 Cor 11: 8.*

συλλαλέω *talk* or *converse with, discuss with* Mt 17: 3; Mk 9: 4; Lk 4: 36; 9: 30; 22: 4; Ac 18: 12 v.l.; 25: 12.*

συλλαμβάνω—1. act. and fut. mid.—a. *seize, grasp, apprehend, arrest* Mt 26: 55; Mk 14: 48; Lk 22: 54; J 18: 12; Ac 1: 16; 12: 3; 23: 27. *Catch* Lk 5: 9.— b. *conceive, become pregnant* Lk 1: 24, 31, 36; 2: 21. Fig. Js 1: 15.—2. mid.—a. *seize, arrest* Ac 26: 21.—b. *come to the aid of, help, assist* w. dat. Lk 5: 7; Phil 4: 3.*

συλλέγω *collect, gather (in), pick* Mt 7: 16; 13: 28–30, 40f, 48; Lk 6: 44.*

συλλογίζομαι *reason, discuss, debate* Lk 20: 5.*

συλλυπέω *hurt* or *grieve with* pass. *be grieved with, feel sympathy* Mk 3: 5.*

συμβαίνω *meet, happen, come about* Mk 10: 32; Ac 20: 19; 21: 35; 1 Cor 10: 11; 1 Pt 4: 12; 2 Pt 2: 22. τὸ συμβεβηκός *what has happened* Ac 3: 10; cf. Lk 24: 14.*

συμβάλλω—1. act.—a. trans. *converse, confer* Ac 4: 15; 17: 18.— *Consider, ponder* Lk 2: 19.—b. intrans. *meet, fall in with* Ac 20: 14.—*Engage, fight* w. dat. Lk 14: 31.—*Quarrel, dispute* w. dat. 11:

53 v.l.—2. mid. *help, be of assistance* Ac 18: 27*

συμβασιλεύω *rule* (as *king*) with (*someone*) 1 Cor 4: 8; 2 Ti 2: 12.*

συμβιβάζω—1. *bring together, unite*—a. lit. *hold together* pass. Eph 4: 16; Col 2: 19.—b. fig. *unite, knit together* pass. Col 2: 2.—2. *conclude, infer* Ac 16: 10.—3. *demonstrate, prove* 9: 22.—4. *instruct, teach, advise* 19: 33; 1 Cor 2: 16.*

συμβουλεύω—1. act. *advise, give advice to* J 18: 14; Rv 3: 18.—2. mid. *consult, plot* Mt 26: 4; J 11: 53 v.l.; Ac 9: 23.*

συμβούλιον, ου, τό—1. *plan, purpose* σ. λαμβάνειν or διδόναι *form a plan, consult, plot* Mt 12: 14; 22: 15; 27: 1, 7; 28: 12; Mk 3: 6. σ. ἑτοιμάζειν *reach a decision* 15: 1.—2. *council* as a body Ac 25: 12.*

σύμβουλος, ου, ὁ *adviser, counsellor* Ro 11: 34.*

Συμεών, ὁ indecl. *Symeon, Simeon,* a Semitic name.—1. *son of Jacob,* ancestor of the tribe of Simeon Rv 7: 7.—2. Lk 3: 30.—3. a devout old man 2: 25, 34.—4. *Simeon* surnamed Niger Ac 13: 1.—5. The original name of Peter (Σίμων) is occasionally, written in this way Ac 15: 14; 2 Pt 1: 1.*

συμμαθητής, οῦ, ὁ *fellow-disciple* J 11: 16.*

συμμαρτυρέω *confirm, testify in support of* someone or something Ro 2: 15; 8: 16; 9: 1; Rv 22: 18 v.l.*

συμμερίζομαι *share with* 1 Cor 9: 13.*

συμμέτοχος, ον *sharing with* someone Eph 3: 6; 5: 7.*

συμμιμητής, οῦ, ὁ *fellow-imitator* Phil 3: 17.*

συμμορφίζω *invest with the same form* pass. *be conformed to, take on the same form as* Phil 3: 10.*

σύμμορφος, ον *having the same form, similar in form* Ro 8: 29; Phil 3: 21.*

συμμορφόω *give the same form* Phil 3: 10 v.l.*

συμπαθέω *sympathize with, have sympathy with* Hb 4: 15; 10: 34.*

συμπαθής, ές *sympathetic* 1 Pt 3: 8.*

συμπαραγίνομαι *come together* Lk 23: 48. *Come to the aid of* w. dat. 2 Ti 4: 16 v. l.*

συμπαρακαλέω *encourage together* Ro 1: 12.*

συμπαραλαμβάνω *take along* (*with oneself*) Ac 12: 25; 15: 37f; Gal 2: 1.*

συμπαραμένω *stay with* someone *to help* Phil 1: 25 v.l.*

συμπάρειμι *be present with* Ac 25: 24.*

συμπάσχω *suffer with, suffer the same thing as* Ro 8: 17; 1 Cor 12: 26.*

συμπέμπω *send with* 2 Cor 8: 18, 22.*

συμπεριέχω *surround, stand around* (*together*) Lk 12: 1 v.l.*

συμπεριλαμβάνω *throw one's arms around, embrace* Ac 20: 10.*

συμπίνω *drink with* Ac 10: 41.*

συμπίπτω *fall together, collapse* Lk 6: 49.*

συμπληρόω *fill completely,* pass. *become quite full*—1. *be swamped* Lk 8: 23.—2. fig. *be fulfilled, approach, come* Lk 9: 51; Ac 2: 1.*

συμπνίγω—1. (*crowd together and*) *choke* Mt 13: 22; Mk 4: 7, 19; Lk 8: 14.—2. *crowd around, press upon* Lk 8: 42; 12: 1 v.l.*

συμπολίτης, ου, ὁ *fellow-citizen* Eph 2: 19.*

συμπορεύομαι—1. *go* (*along*) *with* Lk 7: 11; 14: 25; 24: 15.—2. *come together, flock* Mk 10: 1.*

συμποσία, ας, ἡ *a common meal* Mk 6: 39 v.l.*

συμπόσιον, ου, τό *a party,* or *group* of people eating συμπόσια συμπόσια *in parties* Mk 6: 39.*

συμπρεσβύτερος, ου, ὁ *fellow-elder, fellow-presbyter* 1 Pt 5: 1.*

συμφέρω—1. *bring together* Ac 19: 19.—2. *help, confer a benefit, be advantageous* or *profitable* or *useful*—a. impersonal construction συμφέρει (*it*) *is good*, etc. Mt 5: 29; 19: 10; J 11: 50; 18: 14; 1 Cor 6: 12; 2 Cor 8: 10. b. the participle συμφέρων *profitable*, etc. τὰ συμφέροντα *what is good for you* Ac 20: 20; cf. 2 Cor 12: 1. τὸ συμφέρον *profit, advantage* 1 Cor 10: 33 v.l.; 12: 7; Hb 12: 10.

σύμφημι *agree with* Ro 7: 16.*

σύμφορος, ον *beneficial, advantageous* τὸ σύμφορον *benefit, advantage* 1 Cor 7: 35; 10: 33.*

συμφορτίζω *burden together with others* Phil 3: 10 v.l.*

συμφυείς 2 aor. pass. participle of συμφύω.

συμφυλέτης, ου, ὁ *fellow-countryman, compatriot* 1 Th 2: 14.*

σύμφυτος, ον *grown together* Ro 6: 5.*

συμφύω *grow up with* Lk 8: 7.*

συμφωνέω *agree* Mt 18: 19; Ac 5: 9; 15: 15; *come to an agreement* Mt 20: 2, 13. *Fit in with, match* Lk 5: 36.*

συμφώνησις, εως, ἡ *agreement* 2 Cor 6: 15.*

συμφωνία, ας, ἡ in Lk 15: 25 may be *music, orchestra*, or an *instrument*, perhaps the double flute.*

σύμφωνος, ον *agreeing* ἐκ συμφώνου *by agreement* 1 Cor 7: 5.*

συμψηφίζω *count up, compute* Ac 19: 19; pass. *be counted* 1: 26 v.l.*

σύμψυχος, ον *harmonious, united in spirit* Phil 2: 2.*

σύν prep. w. dat. *with* Mt 25: 27; 26: 35; Mk 2: 26; Lk 1: 56; Ac 5: 1, 26; Ro 6: 8; 1 Cor 15: 10; Phil 1: 23. Nearly equivalent to καί Lk 20: 1; Ac 3: 4; Phil 1: 1. *Beside(s), in addition to* Lk 24: 21.

σύναγω—1. *gather* (*in*), *gather up* Mt 13: 47; 25: 24, 26; Lk 3: 17; 15: 13; J 6: 12f; 15: 6.— 2. *bring* or *call together, gather* Mt 22: 10; 25: 32; Mk 2: 2; 7: 1; J 11: 47; 18: 2; Ac 13: 44; 14: 27; 1 Cor 5: 4.— 3. *invite* or *receive as a guest* Mt 25: 35, 38, 43.—4. *advance, move* Mt 20: 28 v.l.

συναγωγή, ῆς, ἡ—1. *place of assembly*—a. the Jewish *synagogue* Mt 4: 23; 10: 17; Mk 6: 2; Lk 6: 6; 21: 12; J 18: 20; Ac 17: 1, 10, 17; 22: 19.—b. a Christian *synagogue* can also be meant in Js 2: 2 (see 4 below).— 2. (*the congregation of a*) *synagogue* Ac 6: 9; 9: 2.—3. συναγωγὴ τοῦ Σατανᾶ *synagogue of Satan* Rv 2: 9; 3: 9.—4. *a meeting* of Jews for worship Ac 13: 43. The preferred interpretation for Js 2: 2 is that it refers to the *meeting* of a Christian congregation (see 1b above).

συναγωνίζομαι *help, assist* Ro 15: 30.*

συναθλέω *fight* or *contend beside* Phil 1: 27; 4: 3.*

συναθροίζω *gather, bring together* Lk 24: 33 v.l.; Ac 12: 12; 19: 25.*

συναίρω *settle* (*accounts*) Mt 18: 23f; 25: 19.*

συναιχμάλωτος, ου, ὁ *fellow-prisoner* Ro 16: 7; Col 4: 10; Phlm 23.*

συνακολουθέω *follow, accompany* w. dat. Mk 5: 37; 14: 51; Lk 23: 49; J 13: 36 v.l.*

συναλίζω in Ac 1: 4 this word is variously understood: συνᾰλίζω *eat* (*salt*) *with*; συνᾱλίζω *bring together*, pass. *come together*; as another spelling for συναυλίζω mid. *spend the night with, stay with*.*

συναλίσκομαι *be made captive together with* Ac 1: 4 v.l.*

συναλλάσσω *reconcile* Ac 7: 26.*

συναναβαίνω *come* or *go up with* Mk 15: 41; Ac 13: 31.*

συνανάκειμαι *recline at table with,* *eat with* Mt 14: 9; Mk 2: 15; Lk 14: 10, 15.

συναναμείγνυμι *mix up together,* pass. *mingle* or *associate with* 1 Cor 5: 9, 11; 2 Th 3: 14.*

συναναπαύομαι *rest* or *find rest with* Ro 15: 32.*

συναναστρέφομαι *associate, go about with* Ac 10: 41 v.l.*

συναντάω *meet* w. dat.; lit. Lk 9: 18 v.l., 37; 22: 10; Ac 10: 25; Hb 7: 1, 10. Fig. *happen* Ac 20: 22.*

συνάντησις, εως, ἡ *meeting* εἰς συνάντησίν τινι *to meet someone* Mt 8: 34 v.l.; J 12: 13 v.l.*

συναντιλαμβάνομαι *help, come to the aid of* w. dat. Lk 10: 40; Ro 8: 26.*

συναπάγω pass., fig. *be led* or *carried away* Gal 2: 13; 2 Pt 3: 17. τοῖς ταπεινοῖς συναπαγόμενοι Ro 12: 16 may mean *accommodate yourself to humble ways* or *associate with humble folk.*

συναπήχθην 1 aor. pass. ind. of συναπάγομαι.

συναποθνῄσκω *die with* Mk 14: 31; 2 Cor 7: 3; 2 Ti 2: 11.*

συναπόλλυμι *destroy with* mid. *perish with* Hb 11: 31.*

συναποστέλλω *send at the same time* 2 Cor 12: 18.*

συναρμολογέω *fit* or *join together* pass. Eph 2: 21; 4: 16.*

συναρπάζω *seize violently, drag away* Lk 8: 29; Ac 6: 12; 19: 29; 27: 15.*

συναυλίζομαι see συναλίζω.

συναυξάνω pass. *grow together, grow side by side* Mt 13: 30.*

συνβ- see συμβ-.

συνγ- see συγγ-.

σύνδεσμος, ου, ὁ *that which binds together*—1. *bond* that holds something together—**a.** lit., of sinews Col 2: 19.—**b.** fig. Eph 4: 3; Col 3: 14.—2. In Ac 8: 23 σύνδεσμος may mean *bond, fetter* or *bundle.*

συνδέω *bind* (*with*) or *imprison* (*with*) Hb 13: 3.*

συνδοξάζω pass. *be glorified with someone, share in someone's glory* Ro 8: 17.*

σύνδουλος, ου, ὁ *fellow-slave* lit. and fig. Mt 18: 28f, 31, 33; 24: 49; Col 1: 7; 4: 7; Rv 6: 11; 19: 10; 22: 9.*

συνδρομή, ῆς, ἡ *running together, forming* of a mob Ac 21: 30.*

συνέβη 2 aor. act. ind., 3 sing., of συμβαίνω.

συνεγείρω *cause someone to rise up with another* fig. Eph 2: 6; Col 2: 12; 3: 1.*

συνέδριον, ου, τό *the high council, the Sanhedrin,* the highest indigenous governing body in Judaea Mt 5: 22; Mk 14: 55; Lk 22: 66; J 11: 47; Ac 5: 21, 27, 34, 41; 23: 1, 6, 15, 20, 28. *Local council* Mt 10: 17; Mk 13: 9.

συνέδριος Ac 5: 35 v.l. is probably an error for σύνεδρος, ου, ὁ *member of a council.*

συνείδησις, εως, ἡ—1. *consciousness* 1 Cor 8: 7a v.l.; Hb 10: 2; 1 Pt 2: 19.—2. *moral consciousness, conscience, scruples* J 8: 9 v.l.; Ac 23: 1; 24: 16; Ro 2: 15; 9: 1; 13: 5; 1 Cor 8: 7b, 10, 12; 10: 25, 27–29; 2 Cor 1: 12; 4: 2; 5: 11; 1 Ti 1: 5, 19; 3: 9; 4: 2; 2 Ti 1: 3; Tit 1: 15; Hb 9: 9, 14; 10: 22; 13: 18; 1 Pt 3: 16, 21.*

συνεῖδον 2 aor. act. ind. of συνοράω.

συνειδυῖα, fem. perf. act. participle of σύνοιδα.

I. σύνειμι (from εἰμί) *be with* Lk 9: 18; Ac 22: 11.*

II. σύνειμι (from εἶμι) *come together* Lk 8: 4.*

συνείπετο imperf. mid. ind., 3 sing., of συνέπομαι.

συνεισέρχομαι *enter with, go in(to) with* J 6: 22; 18: 15.*

συνείχετο imperf. pass. ind., 3 sing., of συνέχω.

συνέκδημος, ου, ὁ *traveling companion* Ac 19: 29; 2 Cor 8: 19.*

συνεκέρασα 1 aor. act. ind. of συγκεράννυμι.

συνεκλεκτός, ή, όν *chosen together with* subst. *the one who is chosen* 1 Pt 5: 13.*

συνεκπορεύομαι *go out with* Ac 3: 11 v.l.*

συνελαύνω *drive, force, bring* Ac 7: 26 v.l.*

συνεπιμαρτυρέω *testify at the same time* Hb 2: 4.*

συνέπιον 2 aor. act. ind. of συμπίνω.

συνεπίσκοπος, ου, ὁ *fellow-bishop* Phil 1: 1 v.l.*

συνεπιτίθεμαι *join with others in an attack* Ac 24: 9.*

συνέπομαι *accompany* w. dat. Ac 20: 4.*

συνεργέω *work (together) with, cooperate (with), help* Mk 16: 20; 1 Cor 16: 16; 2 Cor 6: 1; Js 2: 22. τοῖς ἀγαπῶσιν τὸν θεὸν πάντα συνεργεῖ εἰς ἀγαθόν Ro 8: 28 means *everything helps* (or *works with* or *for*) *those who love God to obtain what is good*) unless ὁ θεός is read after συνεργεῖ, in which case the sense is *in everything God helps* (or *works for* or *with*) *those who love him to obtain what is good*.*

συνεργός, οῦ, ὁ *fellow-worker, helper* Ro 16: 3; 1 Cor 3: 9; 2 Cor 1: 24; Phil 2: 25; 1 Th 3: 2; Phlm 1, 24.

συνέρχομαι—1. *come together, assemble, gather* Mt 1: 18; Mk 3: 20; Lk 5: 15; Ac 1: 6; 16: 13; 22: 30; 1 Cor 11: 17f, 20; 14: 26. —2. *come, go* or *travel with* Lk 23: 55; J 11: 33; Ac 1: 21; 10: 23, 45; 21: 16; 25: 17.

συνεσθίω *eat with* Lk 15: 2; Ac 10: 41; 11: 3; 1 Cor 5: 11; Gal 2: 12.*

σύνεσις, εως, ἡ—1. *the faculty of comprehension, intelligence, shrewdness* Mk 12: 33; Lk 2: 47; 1 Cor 1: 19.—2. *insight, under-*

standing Eph 3: 4; Col 1: 9; 2: 2; 2 Ti 2: 7.*

συνεστώς perf. act. participle of συνίστημι.

συνετάφην 2 aor. pass. ind. of συνθάπτω.

συνετέθειντο pluperf. mid. ind., 3 pl., of συντίθημι.

συνετός, ή, όν *intelligent, wise, with good sense* Mt 11: 25; Lk 10: 21; Ac 13: 7; 1 Cor 1: 19.*

συνευδοκέω *agree with, approve of, consent to, be willing* Lk 11: 48; Ac 8: 1; 22: 20; Ro 1: 32; 1 Cor 7: 12f.*

συνευωχέομαι *feast together* 2 Pt 2: 13; Jd 12.*

συνέφαγον 2 aor. act. ind. of συνεσθίω.

συνεφίστημι *join in an attack* Ac 16: 22.*

συνεχύθη 1 aor. pass. ind., 3 sing., of συγχέω.

συνέχω—1. *close by holding, stop* Ac 7: 57.—2. *press hard, crowd* Lk 8: 45; 19: 43.—3. *hold in custody* Lk 22: 63.—4. pass. *be tormented by, suffer from* Mt 4: 24; Lk 4: 38; 8: 37; Ac 28: 8. *Be distressed, be hard pressed* Lk 12: 50; Phil 1: 23.—5. pass. *be occupied with, be absorbed in* Ac 18: 5.—6. For 2 Cor 5: 14 *urge on, impel* or *hold within bounds, control.* Cf. Ac 18: 5 v.l.*

συνζ- see συζ-.

συνήδομαι *(joyfully) agree with* Ro 7: 22.*

συνήθεια, ας, ἡ *custom, habit* J 18: 39; 1 Cor 11: 16; *being accustomed* 8: 7.*

συνῆκα 1 aor. act. ind. of συνίημι.

συνήλασα 1 aor. act. ind. of συνελαύνω.

συνηλικιώτης, ου, ὁ *a person of one's own age, a contemporary* Gal 1: 14.*

συνηρπάκει pluperf. act., 3 sing., of συναρπάζω.

συνθάπτω *bury with* Ro 6: 4; Col 2: 12.*

συνθλάω *crush (together), dash to pieces* Mt 21: 44; Lk 20: 18.*

συνθλίβω *press together, press upon* Mk 5: 24, 31.*

συνθρύπτω *break* fig. Ac 21: 13.*

συνίημι or συνίω *understand, comprehend, gain an insight into* Mt 13: 13–15, 51; 15: 10; 16: 12; Mk 4: 9; 6: 52; 8: 17, 21; Lk 2: 50; 18: 34; Ac 7: 25; Ro 3: 11; 2 Cor 10: 12; Eph 5: 17.

συνίστημι, συνιστάνω, συνιστάω —**I.** transitive, act. and pass.— **1.** *present, introduce, (re)commend* Ro 16: 1; 2 Cor 3: 1; 4: 2; 5: 12; 6: 4; 10: 12, 18; 12: 11.— **2.** *demonstrate, show, bring out* Ro 3: 5; 5: 8; 2 Cor 7: 11; Gal 2: 18.—**II.** intransitive, pres. mid. and perf. act.—**1.** *stand with* or *by* Lk 9: 32.—**2.** *continue, endure, exist, consist, be composed* Col 1: 17; 2 Pt 3: 5.*

συνίων pres. act. participle of συνίω (see συνίημι).

συνκ- see συγκ-.

συνλ- see συλλ-.

συνμ- see συμμ-.

συνοδεύω *travel with* Ac 9: 7.*

συνοδία, ας, ἡ *caravan, group of travelers* Lk 2: 44.*

σύνοιδα *share knowledge with, be implicated* Ac 5: 2. σύνοιδα ἐμαυτῷ *I know with myself, I am conscious* 1 Cor 4: 4.*

συνοικέω *live with* 1 Pt 3: 7.*

συνοικοδομέω *build together with* pass., fig. *be built up* Eph 2: 22.*

συνομιλέω *talk, converse with* Ac 10: 27. *Live with* 1 Pt 3: 7 v.l.*

συνομορέω *be next (door) to* Ac 18: 7.*

συνοράω *perceive, become aware of, realize* Ac 12: 12; 14: 6.*

συνορία, ας, ἡ *neighboring country* Mt 4: 24 v.l.*

συνοχή, ῆς, ἡ *distress. dismay, anguish* Lk 21: 25; 2 Cor 2: 4.*

συνπ- see συμπ-.

συνρ- see συρρ-.

συνσ- see συσσ-.

συνσπ- see συσπ-.

συνστ- see συστ-.

συνταράσσω *throw into confusion, disturb* Lk 9: 42 v.l.*

συντάσσω *order, direct, prescribe* Mt 21: 6; 26: 19; 27: 10.*

συνταφείς 2 aor. pass. participle of συνθάπτω.

συντέλεια, ας, ἡ *completion, close, end* Mt 13: 39f, 49; 24: 3; 28: 20; Hb 9: 26.*

συντελέω—**1.** *bring to an end, complete, finish, close* Mt 7: 28 v.l.; Lk 4: 13.—Of time *come to an end, be over* Lk 2: 21 v.l.; 4: 2; Ac 21: 27; perhaps Mk 13: 4 (see **2** below).—**2.** *carry out, fulfill, accomplish* Ro 9: 28; Hb 8: 8; perhaps Mk 13: 4 (see **1** above).—**3.** pass. *give out* J 2: 3 v.l.*

συντέμνω *cut short, shorten, limit* Ro 9: 28.*

συντεχνίτης, ου, ὁ *one who follows the same trade* Ac 19: 25 v.l.*

συντηρέω—**1.** *protect, defend* Mk 6: 20. Pass. *be saved, preserved* Mt 9: 17; Lk 5: 38 v.l.—**2.** *hold* or *treasure up (in one's memory)* Lk 2: 19.*

συντίθημι mid. *agree* Lk 22: 5; *decide* J 9: 22; Ac 23: 20. *Consent* Ac 24: 9 v.l.*

συντόμως adv. *briefly* Ac 24: 4; short ending of Mk.*

συντρέχω *run together* Mk 6: 33; Ac 3: 11. *Run with, go with* 1 Pt 4: 4.*

συντρίβω *break, shatter, crush*— **1.** lit. Mt 12: 20; Mk 5: 4; 14: 3; J 19: 36; Ro 16: 20; Rv 2: 27. *Bruise, wear out* Lk 9: 39.— **2.** fig. Lk 4: 18 v.l.*

σύντριμμα, ατος, τό *destruction, ruin* Ro 3: 16.*

σύντροφος, ου, ὁ *foster-brother, intimate friend* Ac 13: 1.*

συντυγχάνω *come together with, meet, join* Lk 8: 19; Ac 11: 26 v.l.*

Συντύχη–σφραγίζω 211

Συντύχη, ης, ἡ *Syntyche*, a Christian woman Phil 4: 2.*

συνυποκρίνομαι *join in playing the hypocrite* w. dat. Gal 2: 13.*

συνυπουργέω *join in helping* 2 Cor 1: 11.*

συνφ- see συμφ-.

συνχ- see συγχ-.

συνψ- see συμψ-.

συνωδίνω *suffer agony together* Ro 8: 22.*

συνωμοσία, ας, ἡ *conspiracy, plot* Ac 23: 13.*

Σύρα, ας, ἡ *the Syrian woman* Mk 7: 26 v.l.*

Συράκουσαι, ῶν, αἱ *Syracuse*, a city on the east coast of Sicily Ac 28: 12.*

Συρία, ας, ἡ *Syria* Mt 4: 24; Lk 2: 2; Ac 15: 23, 41; 18: 18; 20: 3; 21: 3; Gal 1: 21.*

Σύρος, ου, ὁ *the Syrian* Lk 4: 27.*

Συροφοινίκισσα, ης, ἡ *the Syrophoenician woman* Mk 7: 26.*

συρρήγνυμι *dash (together)* Lk 6: 49 v.l.*

Σύρτις, εως, ἡ *the Syrtis*, two shallow gulfs along the Libyan coast in North Africa Ac 27: 17.*

σύρω *drag (away)* J 21: 8; Ac 8: 3; 14: 19; 17: 6; *sweep away* Rv 12: 4.*

συσπαράσσω *pull about, convulse* Mk 9: 20; Lk 9: 42.*

σύσσημον, ου, τό *signal* Mk 14: 44.*

σύσσωμος, ον *belonging to the same body* Eph 3: 6.*

συστασιαστής, οῦ, ὁ *fellow-insurrectionist* Mk 15: 7 v.l.*

συστατικός, ή, όν *introducing, commendatory* συστατικὴ ἐπιστολή *a letter of recommendation* 2 Cor 3: 1.*

συσταυρόω *crucify (together)* with pass., lit. Mt 27: 44; Mk 15: 32; J 19: 32. Fig. Ro 6: 6; Gal 2: 19.*

συστέλλω—1. *draw together, limit, shorten* 1 Cor 7: 29.—2. The

meaning of σ. in Ac 5: 6, 10 v.l. is probably *cover up, wrap up*, but other possibilities are *snatch up* and *take away*.*

συστενάζω *lament* or *groan together (with)* Ro 8: 22.*

συστοιχέω *correspond* Gal 4: 25.*

συστρατιώτης, ου, ὁ *fellow-soldier* Phil 2: 25; Phlm 2.*

συστρέφω—1. *gather up, bring together* Ac 28: 3; 17: 5 v.l.— 2. *be gathered, gather, come together* Mt 17: 22; Ac 10: 41 v.l.; 11: 28 v.l.; 16: 39 v.l.*

συστροφή, ῆς, ἡ *disorderly* or *seditious gathering, commotion* Ac 19: 40. For 23: 12 *mob* or *plot* are possible.*

συσχηματίζω *form* or *mold after* pass. *be conformed to, be guided by* Ro 12: 2; 1 Pt 1: 14.*

Συχάρ, ἡ indecl. *Sychar*, a city in Samaria J 4: 5.*

Σύχεμ indecl. *Shechem*—1. fem., a city in Samaria Ac 7: 16.— 2. masc., son of Hamor Ac 7: 16 v.l.*

σφαγή, ῆς, ἡ *slaughter* Ac 8: 32; Ro 8: 36; Js 5: 5.*

σφάγιον, ου, τό *victim* to be sacrificed, *offering* Ac 7: 42.*

σφάζω *to slaughter* Rv 5: 6, 12; 13: 8. *Murder* 1 J 3: 12; Rv 5: 9; 6: 4, 9; 13: 3; 18: 24.*

σφάξω fut. of σφάζω.

σφάλλω pass. *slip, stumble, fall* Mt 15: 14 v.l.*

σφόδρα adv.*very (much), extremely, greatly* Mt 2: 10; 17: 6, 23; 19: 25; Mk 16: 4; Lk 18: 23; Ac 6: 7.

σφοδρῶς adv. *very much, violently* Ac 27: 18.*

σφραγίζω *(provide with a) seal*— 1. lit. Mt 27: 66; Rv 20: 3.— 2. fig.—a. *seal up* to keep something secret Rv 10: 4; 22: 10.— b. *mark (with a seal)* to identify Eph 1: 13; 4: 30; Rv 7: 3, 4f, 8. In J 6: 27; 2 Cor 1: 22 there is the added connotation 'endue

with power from heaven'.—
c. *attest, certify, acknowledge* J 3:
33.—**d.** σφραγισάμενος αὐτοῖς
τὸν καρπὸν τοῦτον Ro 15: 28
may be translated *when I have
placed the sum that was collected
safely (sealed) in their hands.**

σφραγίς, ῖδος, ἡ *seal, signet*—
1. lit.—**a.** *seal* Rv 5: 1f, 5, 9;
6: 1, 3, 5, 7, 9, 12; 8: 1.—**b.** *the
instrument with which one seals,
a signet* Rv 7: 2.—**c.** *the mark* or
impression of a seal 2 Ti 2: 19;
Rv 9: 4.—**2.** fig. *that which
confirms, attests* or *authenticates,
certification* Ro 4: 11; 1 Cor 9: 2.**

σφυδρόν, οῦ, τό *ankle* Ac 3: 7.**

σφυρίς, ῖδος, ἡ an alternate form
of σπυρίς.

σφυρόν, οῦ, τό *ankle* or *heel* Ac 3:
7 v.l.*

σχεδόν adv. *nearly, almost* Ac 13:
44; 19: 26; Hb 9: 22.**

σχῆμα, ατος, τό *form, outward
appearance* 1 Cor 7: 31; Phil 2: 7.**

σχίζω *split, tear, divide*—**1.** lit.
Mt 27: 51; Mk 1: 10; 15: 38;
Lk 5: 36; 23: 45; J 19: 24;
21: 11.—**2.** fig., pass. *become
divided* or *disunited* Ac 14: 4;
23: 7.**

σχίσμα, ατος, τό *split, division*—
1. lit. *tear* Mt 9: 16; Mk 2: 21.—
2. fig. *division, dissension, schism*
J 7: 43; 9: 16; 10: 19; 1 Cor 1:
10; 11: 18; 12: 25.**

σχοινίον, ου, τό *rope* or *cord* J 2:
15; Ac 27: 32.**

σχολάζω *have time* or *leisure*—
1. *devote oneself to, give one's
time to* 1 Cor 7: 5.—**2.** *be
unoccupied, stand empty* Mt 12:
44; Lk 11: 25 v.l.*

σχολή, ῆς, ἡ *school* Ac 19: 9.**

σχῶ 2 aor. subj. act. of ἔχω.

σῴζω *save, keep from harm,
preserve, rescue*—**1.** *preserve* or
rescue from natural dangers and
afflictions—**a.** from death Mt
14: 30; 27: 40, 42, 49; Mk 13:
20; Lk 6: 9; 9: 24; J 11: 12;

Ac 27: 20, 31.—**b.** *bring out
safely* J 12: 27; Hb 5: 7; Jd 5.—
c. *save* or *free from disease* or
from demonic possession Mt 9:
22; Mk 5: 23, 28, 34; 10: 52;
Lk 8: 48, 50; 17: 19; 18: 42;
Ac 4: 9; 14: 9; Js 5: 15.—**2.** *save*
or *preserve from eternal death,
from judgment, sin, bring salvation, bring to salvation*—**a.** act.
Mt 18: 11; Lk 7: 50; J 12: 47;
Ro 11: 14; 1 Cor 1: 21; 7: 16;
Tit 3: 5; Hb 7: 25; Js 4: 12;
5: 20; 1 Pt 3: 21.—**b.** pass. *be
saved, attain salvation* Mt 24:
13; Mk 10: 26; Lk 13: 23; 18:
26; J 3: 17; 5: 34; Ac 11: 14;
15: 1, 11; Ro 8: 24; 11: 26;
1 Cor 5: 5; Eph 2: 5, 8; 1 Ti 2: 4.
—**3.** Certain passages belong
under 1 and 2 at the same time
Mk 8: 35; Lk 9: 24; 9: 56 v.l.;
Ro 9: 27; 1 Cor 3: 15.

σῶμα, ατος, τό *body*—**1.** *body* of
man or animal—**a.** *dead body,
corpse* Mt 27: 52, 58f; Lk 17: 37;
J 19: 31, 38, 40; Ac 9: 40.—
b. *the living body* Mt 5: 29f; 6:
25; Mk 14: 22; Lk 11: 34; Ro 4:
19; 7: 24; 8: 10, 13; 12: 1; 1 Cor
5: 3; 6: 20; 11: 24, 27, 29; 15:
44; 2 Cor 5: 6, 8, 10; Gal 6: 17;
Col 2: 11; Hb 13: 3; Js 3: 3.—
2. pl. σώματα *slaves* Rv 18: 13.—
3. Paul speaks of various kinds
of bodies in 1 Cor 15: 35, 37f,
40.—**4.** the body as *the thing
itself, the reality* Col 2: 17.—
5. The church is pictured as a
body, or the *body of Christ* Ro 12:
5; 1 Cor 12: 13, 27; Eph 4: 4,
12, 16; Col 1: 18, 24.

σωματικός, ή, όν *bodily, corporeal*
Lk 3: 22; 1 Ti 4: 8.**

σωματικῶς adv. *bodily, corporeally*
Col 2: 9.**

Σώπατρος, ου, ὁ *Sopater,* a
Christian from Beroea Ac 20: 4.
See Σωσίπατρος.*

σωρεύω *heap* or *pile up* Ro 12: 20.
Pass. *be filled with* 2 Ti 3: 6.**

Σωσθένης, ους, ὁ Sosthenes—
1. leader of a synagogue in
Corinth Ac 18: 17.—2. a 'brother'
of Paul 1 Cor 1: 1. It is possible
that 1 and 2 are the same man.*
Σωσίπατρος, ου, ὁ Sosipater, a
friend of Paul Ro 16: 21. He
may be the same man as
Σώπατρος (Ac 20: 4).*
σωτήρ, ῆρος, ὁ Savior, Deliverer,
Preserver—1. of God Lk 1: 47;
1 Ti 1: 1; 2: 3; 4: 10; Tit 1: 3;
2: 10; 3: 4; Jd 25.—2. of Christ
Lk 2: 11; J 4: 42; Ac 5: 31;
13: 23; Eph 5: 23; Phil 3: 20;
2 Ti 1: 10; Tit 1: 4; 2: 13; 3: 6;
1 J 4: 14; 2 Pt 1: 1, 11; 2: 20;
3: 2, 18.*
σωτηρία, ας, ἡ salvation, deliverance, preservation—1. generally,
preservation, deliverance Lk 1:
71; Ac 7: 25; 27: 34; Hb 11: 7.
—2. salvation brought by Jesus
Christ as Savior Lk 1: 69, 77;
19: 9; short ending of Mk; J 4:
22; Ac 13: 26, 47; Ro 1: 16;
10: 1, 10; 2 Cor 1: 6; 6: 2; Eph
1: 13; Phil 1: 28; 2: 12; 1 Th 5:
8f; 2 Th 2: 13; 2 Ti 2: 10;

Hb 1: 14; 2: 3, 10; 9: 28; 1 Pt 1:
5, 9f; 2 Pt 3: 15; Jd 3; Rv 7: 10.
σωτήριος, ον saving, delivering,
bringing salvation Tit 2: 11.
Neut. as subst. τὸ σωτήριον
salvation Lk 2: 30; 3: 6; Ac 28:
28; Eph 6: 17.*
σωφρονέω—1. be of sound mind,
be in one's right mind Mk 5: 15;
Lk 8: 35; 2 Cor 5: 13.—2. be
reasonable, sensible, serious Ro
12: 3; Tit 2: 6; 1 Pt 4: 7.*
σωφρονίζω encourage, advise, urge
Tit 2: 4.*
σωφρονισμός, οῦ, ὁ moderation,
self-discipline, prudence 2 Ti
1: 7.*
σωφρόνως adv. soberly, moderately, showing self-control Tit 2:
12.*
σωφροσύνη, ης, ἡ—1. reasonable-
ness, mental soundness Ac 26:
25.—2. good judgment, self-control specifically decency, chastity
1 Ti 2: 9, 15.*
σώφρων, ον, gen. ονος prudent,
thoughtful, self-controlled 1 Ti 3:
2; Tit 1: 8; 2: 2. Chaste, modest
2: 5.*

T

ταβέρναι, ῶν, αἱ (Latin loanword:
tabernae) tavern, shop, store
τρεῖς ταβέρναι Three Taverns,
a place on the Appian Way, 33
Roman miles from Rome Ac 28:
15.*
Ταβιθά, ἡ indecl. Tabitha, a
Christian woman Ac 9: 36, 40.*
τάγμα, ατος, τό class, group 1 Cor
15: 23.*
τακήσομαι 2 fut. pass. ind. of
τήκω.
τακτός, ή, όν fixed, appointed
Ac 12: 21.*
ταλαιπωρέω lament, complain Js
4: 9.*

ταλαιπωρία, ας, ἡ distress, trouble,
misery Ro 3: 16; Js 5: 1.*
ταλαίπωρος, ον miserable, wretched
Ro 7: 24; Rv 3: 17.*
ταλαντιαῖος, α, ον weighing a talent
(about 58 to 80 lb.) Rv 16: 21.*
τάλαντον, ου, τό talent; first a
measure of weight (58 to 80 lb.),
then a monetary unit whose
value differed considerably in
various times and places; $1,000
is frequently given as an ap-
proximate figure for its value.
Mt 18: 24; 25: 15–28.*
ταλιθά (Aramaic) girl, little girl
Mk 5: 41.*

ταμεῖον, ου, τό—1. *storeroom* Lk 12: 24.—2. *innermost, hidden* or *secret room* Mt 6: 6; 24: 26; Lk 12: 3.*

ταμιεῖον, ου, τό *hidden, secret room* Mt 24: 26 v.l.*

τανῦν see νῦν.

τάξις, εως, ἡ—1. *fixed succession* or *order* Lk 1: 8.—2. *(good) order* 1 Cor 14: 40; Col 2: 5.— 3. *nature, quality* κατὰ τὴν τάξιν *according to the nature of* = *just like* Melchisedek Hb 5: 6, 10; 6: 20; 7: 11, 17, 21 v.l.*

ταπεινός, ή, όν *low* fig.—1. *of low position, poor, lowly, undistinguished* Lk 1: 52; Ro 12: 16; 2 Cor 7: 6; Js 1: 9.—2. *of emotional states, etc. subservient, abject* 2 Cor 10: 1. In a good sense *lowly, humble* Mt 11: 29. Subst. Js 4: 6; 1 Pt 5: 5.*

ταπεινοφροσύνη, ης, ἡ *humility, modesty* Ac 20: 19; Eph 4: 2; Phil 2: 3; Col 2: 18, 23; 3: 12; 1 Pt 5: 5.*

ταπεινόφρων, ον, gen. ονος *humble* 1 Pt 3: 8.*

ταπεινόω *lower, make low*—1. lit. *level* Lk 3: 5.—2. fig.—a. *humble, humiliate* Mt 23: 12; Lk 14: 11; 18: 14; 2 Cor 11: 7; 12: 21; Phil 2: 8.—b. *humble, make humble* in a good sense Mt 18: 4; Js 4: 10; 1 Pt 5: 6.—c. pass. *discipline oneself* Phil 4: 12.*

ταπείνωσις, εως, ἡ—1. *humiliation* Ac 8: 33; Js 1: 10.—2. *humility, humble station* Lk 1: 48; Phil 3: 21; Hb 11: 20 v.l.*

ταράσσω—1. lit. *stir up* J 5: 4 v.l., 7.—2. fig. *stir up, disturb, trouble, throw into confusion* Mt 2: 3; Mk 6: 50; Lk 24: 38; J 11: 33; 12: 27; 13: 21; 14: 1; Ac 15: 24; 17: 8; Gal 1: 7; 1 Pt 3: 14.

ταραχή, ῆς, ἡ *disturbance*—1. lit. *the stirring up* of the water J 5: 4 v.l.—2. fig. *disturbance, tumult, rebellion* Mk 13: 8 v.l.*

τάραχος, ου, ὁ *disturbance, com-* *motion* Ac 19: 23. *Mental agitation, consternation* 12: 18.*

Ταρσεύς, έως, ὁ *(a man) from Tarsus* Ac 9: 11; 21: 39.*

Ταρσός, οῦ, ἡ *Tarsus,* capital of Cilicia in southwest Asia Minor Ac 9: 30; 11: 25; 21: 39 v.l.; 22: 3.*

ταρταρόω *hold captive in Tartarus,* thought of as a place of divine punishment lower than Hades 2 Pt 2: 4.*

τάσσω—1. *place* or *station*— a. *appoint to* or *establish in an office* Ro 13: 1.—b. used with a preposition *put someone in charge of* Mt 8: 9 v.l.; Lk 7: 8. *Assign,* pass. *belong to* Ac 13: 48. *Devote* 1 Cor 16: 15.—2. *order, fix, determine, appoint*—a. act. and pass. Ac 15: 2; 18: 2 v.l.; 22: 10.—b. mid. = act. Mt 28: 16; Ac 28: 23.*

ταῦρος, ου, ὁ *bull, ox* Mt 22: 4; Ac 14: 13; Hb 9: 13; 10: 4.*

ταὐτά = τὰ αὐτά *the same things,* only as v.l. in Lk 6: 23, 26; 17: 30; 1 Th 2: 14.*

ταφή, ῆς, ἡ *burial-place* Mt 27: 7.*

τάφος, ου, ὁ *grave, tomb*—1. lit. Mt 23: 27, 29; 27: 61, 64, 66; 28: 1.—2. fig. Ro 3: 13.*

τάχα adv. *perhaps, possibly, probably* Ro 5: 7; Phlm 15.*

τάχειον a variant spelling for τάχιον (ταχέως 2).

ταχέως adv.—1. positive ταχέως *quickly, without delay, soon* Lk 14: 21; 16: 6; 1 Cor 4: 19; Phil 2: 19, 24. *Too quickly, too easily, hastily* Gal 1: 6; 2 Th 2: 2; 1 Ti 5: 22.—2. comparative τάχιον—a. *more quickly, faster* Hb 13: 19. With gen. of comparison J 20: 4.—b. without comparative meaning *quickly, soon, without delay* J 13: 27; 1 Ti 3: 14; Hb 13: 23.—3. superlative τάχιστα ὡς τάχιστα *as soon as possible* Ac 17: 15.

ταχινός, ή, όν *imminent, swift,* 2 Pt 1: 14; 2: 1.*

τάχιον, τάχιστα see ταχέως 2 and 3.

τάχος, ους, τό *speed, quickness, swiftness, haste* Lk 18: 8; Ac 12: 7; 25: 4; Rv 1: 1; 22: 6.

ταχύς, εῖα, ύ—**1.** adj. *quick, swift* Js 1: 19.—**2.** the neut. sing. ταχύ as adv. *quickly, without delay, soon* Mt 28: 7f; Mk 9: 39; Lk 15: 22; J 11: 29; Rv 2: 16; 22: 7, 12, 20.

τέ enclitic particle—**1.** used alone *and* J 4: 42; Ac 2: 37, 40; 4: 33; 6: 7, 12f; 10: 22; 23: 10; 1 Cor 4: 21; Hb 6: 4f; 12: 2.—**2.** τὲ—τέ, τὲ—καί *as—so, not only—but also* ἐάν τε γὰρ ζῶμεν ἐάν τε ἀποθνήσκωμεν *so, not only if we live, but also if we die* Ro 14: 8b. 'Ιουδαίοις τε καὶ Ἕλλησιν *not only to Jews but also to Greeks* 1 Cor 1: 24. Cf. Ac 2: 46; 17: 4; 26: 10, 16. τὲ καί *often means simply and* Lk 23: 12; J 2: 15; Ac 1: 1; 4: 27; 5: 24; 21: 30; Ro 1: 12; Hb 5: 1, 7; 10: 33; Js 3: 7.

τεθλιμμένος perf. pass. participle of θλίβω.

τεθνάναι, τέθνηκα perf. act. inf. and ind. of θνήσκω.

τεθραμμένος perf. pass. participle of τρέφω.

τεῖχος, ους, τό *wall, city wall* Ac 9: 25; 2 Cor 11: 33; Hb 11: 30; Rv 21: 12, 14f, 17–19.*

τεκεῖν 2 aor. act. inf. of τίκτω.

τεκμήριον, ου, τό *convincing proof* Ac 1: 3.*

τεκνίον, ου, τό *(little) child* fig. J 13: 33; Gal 4: 19 v.l.; 1 J 2: 1, 12, 28; 3: 7, 18; 4: 4; 5: 21.*

τεκνογονέω *bear* or *beget children* 1 Ti 5: 14.*

τεκνογονία, ας, ἡ *the bearing of children* 1 Ti 2: 15.*

τέκνον, ου, τό *child*—**1.** lit. Mt 7: 11; Mk 13: 12; Lk 1: 7; 15: 31; Ac 7: 5; 1 Cor 7: 14; 2 Cor 12: 14; Col 3: 20; Rv 12: 4f. More generally, *descendants, posterity* Mt 2: 18; 27: 25; Ac 2: 39; 13:

33; Ro 9: 8a.—**2.** fig. Mt 3: 9; 23: 37; Mk 2: 5; J 1: 12; Ro 8: 16f, 21; 9: 7; 1 Cor 4: 14, 17; Gal 4: 19, 25; Eph 5: 8; Phlm 10; Tit 1: 4; 1 J 3: 1f; 2 J 1.

τεκνοτροφέω *bring up children* 1 Ti 5: 10.*

τεκνόω *bear (a child)* Hb 11: 11 v.l.*

τέκτων, ονος, ὁ *carpenter, woodworker, builder* Mt 13: 55; Mk 6: 3.*

τέλειος, α, ον *having attained the end* or *purpose, complete, perfect* —**1.** of things Js 1: 4a, 17, 25; Hb 9: 11; 1 J 4: 18. τὸ τέλειον *what is perfect* Ro 12: 2; 1 Cor 13: 10.—**2.** of persons—**a.** *full-grown, mature, adult* adj. 1 Cor 14: 20; Eph 4: 13; subst. Hb 5: 14. For 1 Cor 2: 6 the sense may be *adult*, or it may belong under b below.—**b.** *the initiate* into mystic rites, perhaps 1 Cor 2: 6 (see **a.** above); probably Phil 3: 15; Col 1: 28.—**c.** *perfect, fully developed* in a moral sense Mt 5: 48a; 19: 21; Col 4: 12; Js 1: 4b; 3: 2.—**d.** of God as absolutely *perfect* Mt 5: 48b.*

τελειότης, ητος, ἡ *perfection, completeness* Col 3: 14; *maturity* Hb 6: 1.*

τελειόω—**1.** *complete, finish, accomplish, bring to its goal, perfect* J 4: 34; 5: 36; Ac 20: 24; Hb 2: 10; 5: 9; 7: 28.—*Make perfect* J 17: 23; Hb 9: 9; 10: 1; 11: 40; 12: 23; Js 2: 22; 1 J 2: 5; 4: 12, 17.—*Spend* Lk 2: 43. *Fulfill* J 19: 28.—Pass. *reach one's goal* Lk 13: 32.—**2.** *consecrate, initiate* Phil 3: 12; such passages as Hb 2: 10; 5: 9; 7: 28 may perhaps be classed here (see 1 above).

τελείως adv. *fully, perfectly, completely* 1 Pt 1: 13.*

τελείωσις, εως, ἡ *perfection* Hb 7: 11. *Fulfilment* Lk 1: 45.*

τελειωτής, οῦ, ὁ *perfecter* Hb 12: 2.*

τελεσφορέω *bear fruit to maturity* Lk 8: 14, 15 v.l.*

τελευτάω *die* Mt 2: 19; 22: 25; Mk 7: 10; Lk 7: 2; Ac 7: 15; Hb 11: 22.

τελευτή, ῆς, ἡ *end*, a euphemism for *death* Mt 2: 15.*

τελέω—**1.** *bring to an end, finish, complete* Mt 7: 28; 11: 1; 13: 53; Lk 2: 39; 2 Ti 4: 7; Rv 11: 7. *Come to an end* Rv 20: 3, 5, 7. *Find consummation* 2 Cor 12: 9. —**2.** *carry out, accomplish, keep* Lk 18: 31; Ac 13: 29; Ro 2: 27; Gal 5: 16; Js 2: 8.—**3.** *pay* Mt 17: 24; Ro 13: 6.

τέλος, ους, τό—**1.** *end*—**a.** in the sense *termination, cessation, conclusion* Mk 3: 26; 13: 7; Lk 1: 33; 22: 37; Ro 10: 4; Hb 7: 3; 1 Pt 4: 7; probably 1 Cor 10: 11 (see 3 below).—**b.** *end, goal, outcome* Mt 26: 58; Ro 6: 21f; 1 Ti 1: 5; Hb 6: 8; Js 5: 11; 1 Pt 1: 9.—**c.** adverbial expressions. τὸ τέλος as adverbial acc. 1 Cor 15: 24; 1 Pt 3: 8.—ἄχρι τέλους, ἕως τέλους *to the end, to the last* 1 Cor 1: 8; 2 Cor 1: 13; Hb 3: 6, 14; Rv 2: 26.—εἰς τέλος *in the end, finally* Lk 18: 5. *To the end* Mt 10: 22; Mk 13: 13. For 1 Th 2: 16 *forever* or *decisively, fully.* In J 13: 1 the meanings *to the end* and *to the uttermost* are combined.—**2.** *(indirect) tax, customs duties* Mt 17: 25; Ro 13: 7; perhaps 1 Cor 10: 11 (see 1a above).

τελωνεῖον a variant spelling for τελώνιον.

τελώνης, ου, ὁ *tax-collector, revenue officer* Mt 5: 46; 10: 3; 21: 31f; Mk 2: 15f; Lk 3: 12; 5: 27; 7: 29, 34; 18: 10f, 13.

τελώνιον, ου, τό *revenue* or *tax office* Mt 9: 9; Mk 2: 14; Lk 5: 27.*

τέξομαι fut. mid. ind. of τίκτω.

τέρας, ατος, τό *portent, omen, wonder* Mk 13: 22; J 4: 48; Ac 5: 12; 14: 3; Ro 15: 19; 2 Cor 12: 12.

Τέρτιος, ου, ὁ *Tertius*, a Christian, helper of Paul Ro 16: 22.*

Τέρτουλλος, ου, ὁ *Tertullus*, the Roman eparch under whom Onesimus was martyred Phlm subscr.*

Τέρτυλλος, ου, ὁ *Tertullus*, an attorney Ac 24: 1f.*

τεσσαράκοντα or τεσσεράκοντα indecl. *forty* Mt 4: 2; J 2: 20; Ac 1: 3; 23: 13, 21; Hb 3: 9; Rv 11: 2; 21: 17.

τεσσαρακονταετής, ές *forty years (old)* τ. χρόνος *a period of forty years* Ac 7: 23; 13: 18.*

τέσσαρες, neut. τέσσαρα, gen. τεσσάρων *four* Mt 24: 31; Mk 2: 3; Lk 2: 37; J 11: 17; Rv 4: 4.

τεσσαρεσκαιδέκατος, η, ον *fourteenth* Ac 27: 27, 33.*

τεσσερ- see τεσσαρ-.

τεταρταῖος, α, ον *happening on the fourth day* τεταρταῖός ἐστιν *he has been dead four days* J 11: 39.*

τέταρτος, η, ον *fourth* Mt 14: 25; Mk 6: 48; Ac 10: 30; Rv 4: 7. τὸ τέταρτον *the fourth part, quarter* 6: 8.

τετραα- see τετρα-.

τετράγωνος, ον *(four-)square* or *shaped like a cube* Rv 21: 16.*

τετράδιον, ου, τό *a squad of four soldiers* Ac 12: 4.*

τετρακισχίλιοι, αι, α *four thousand* Mt 15: 38; 16: 10; Mk 8: 9, 20; Ac 21: 38.*

τετρακόσιοι, αι, α *four hundred* Ac 5: 36; 7: 6; 13: 20; 21: 38 v.l.; Gal 3: 17.*

τετράμηνος, ον *lasting four months* of a period of time J 4: 35.*

τετραπλοῦς, ῆ, οῦν *four times (as much), fourfold* Lk 19: 8.*

τετράπους, ουν, gen. **ποδός** *four-footed*, subst. τὰ τετράποδα *four-footed animals, quadrupeds* Ac 10: 12; 11: 6; Ro 1: 23.*

τετραρχέω *be tetrarch* Lk 3: 1.*

τετράρχης, ου, ὁ *tetrarch*, title of a petty dependent prince, whose rank and authority were lower than those of a king Mt 14: 1; Lk 3: 19; 9: 7; Ac 13: 1.*

τέτυχε perf. act. ind., 3 sing., of τυγχάνω.

τεφρόω *cover with* or *reduce to ashes* 2 Pt 2: 6.*

τέχνη, ης, ἡ *skill, trade* Ac 17: 29; 18: 3; Rv 18: 22.*

τεχνίτης, ου, ὁ *craftsman, artisan, designer* Ac 19: 24, 25 v.l., 38; Hb 11: 10; Rv 18: 22.*

τήκομαι *melt, be melted, dissolve* 2 Pt 3: 12.*

τηλαυγῶς adv. (*very*) *plainly, clearly* Mk 8: 25.*

τηλικοῦτος, αύτη, οῦτο *so great, so large, so important* 2 Cor 1: 10; Hb 2: 3; Js 3: 4; Rv 16: 18.*

τηνικαῦτα adv. *at that time, then* Phlm subscr.*

τηρέω—1. *keep watch over, guard* Mt 27: 36, 54; 28: 4; Ac 12: 5; 24: 23.—2. *keep, hold, reserve, preserve* J 2: 10; 17: 11f, 15; Ac 25: 21; 1 Cor 7: 37; 1 Ti 6: 14; 2 Ti 4: 7; 1 Pt 1: 4; Jd 1, 13; Rv 3: 10; 16: 15.—3. *keep, observe, pay attention to* Mt 23: 3; 28: 20; Mk 7: 9; J 9: 16; 14: 15, 21; 1 J 3: 22, 24; Rv 3: 8, 10; 12: 17; 22: 7.

τήρησις, εως, ἡ—1. *custody, imprisonment* or *prison* Ac 4: 3; 5: 18.—2. *keeping, observance* 1 Cor 7: 19.*

Τιβεριάς, άδος, ἡ *Tiberias*, a city on the west shore of the Lake of Gennesaret; the lake is sometimes named after the city J 6: 1, 23; 21: 1.*

Τιβέριος, ου, ὁ *Tiberius*, Roman emperor 14–37 AD, Lk 3: 1.*

τίθημι and τιθέω—I. active and passive—1. *put, place, lay*—a. generally *lay* (*away*), *set up, put* (*away*) Mt 12: 18; 27: 60; Mk 16: 6; Lk 11: 33; 14: 29;

J 11: 34; Ac 3: 2; 13: 29; Ro 9: 33; 14: 13; 2 Cor 3: 13; 2 Pt 2: 6.—b. special expressions— τιθέναι τὰ γόνατα *bend the knee, kneel down* Mk 15: 19; Ac 7: 60; 21: 5.—*Place before someone, serve* J 2: 10.—*Put aside, store up, deposit* Lk 19: 21f; 1 Cor 16: 2.—*Take off, remove* J 13: 4. *Give* (*up*) 10: 11, 15, 17f; 1 J 3: 16.—θέτε ἐν ταῖς καρδίαις *make up* (*your*) *minds* Lk 21: 14. —*Present* Mk 4: 30.—2. *make* Lk 20: 43; Ac 13: 47; Ro 4: 17; 1 Ti 2: 7; Hb 1: 2. *Appoint* J 15: 16.—II. middle—1. *put, place, lay*—a. *arrange, fix, establish, set* Ac 1: 7; 1 Cor 12: 18; 2 Cor 5: 19. *Put* Ac 5: 18, 25.—b. ἔθεντο ἐν τῇ καρδίᾳ *they kept in mind* Lk 1: 66, but the same expression in the 2 sing. *contrive in your mind* Ac 5: 4. Similarly *resolve* 19: 21.—2. *make* Ac 20: 28; 1 Cor 12: 28. *Reach* Ac 27: 12. *Destine* or *appoint* 1 Th 5: 9; 1 Ti 1: 12.

τίκτω *bear, give birth* (*to*)—1. lit. Mt 1: 21, 23; Lk 2: 6f, 11; J 16: 21; Gal 4: 27; Rv 12: 2, 4f.— 2. symbolically *bring forth* Hb 6: 7; Js 1: 15.

τίλλω *pluck, pick* Mt 12: 1; Mk 2: 23; Lk 6: 1.*

Τιμαῖος, ου, ὁ *Timaeus* Mk 10: 46.*

τιμάω—1. *set a price on, estimate, value* mid. *for oneself* Mt 27: 9b. Pass. 27: 9a.—2. *honor, revere* Mt 15: 4, 8; Mk 7: 6; 10: 19; J 5: 23; Eph 6: 2; 1 Ti 5: 3; 1 Pt 2: 17. (*Show*) *honor* (*to*), *reward* J 12: 26.

τιμή, ῆς, ἡ—1. *price, value* Mt 27: 6, 9; Ac 5: 2f; 7: 16; 19: 19. τιμῆς *for a price* 1 Cor 6: 20; 7: 23.—2. *honor, reverence, respect* J 4: 44; Ac 28: 10; Ro 2: 7, 10; 12: 10; 13: 7; 1 Ti 6: 1; 2 Ti 2: 20f; 1 Pt 2: 7; 3: 7; Rv 4: 9; 5: 13; 21: 26. *Respectability* 1 Th 4: 4. *Place of honor, office*

Hb 5: 4. *Honorarium, compensa-*
tion may be the sense in 1 Ti 5:
17, though *honor* or *respect* are
also possible.—The expression
οὐκ ἐν τιμῇ τινι Col 2: 23 is
probably *they are of no value in.*

τίμιος, α, ον *valuable, precious,*
costly, of great worth or *value*
1 Cor 3: 12; Js 5: 7; 1 Pt 1: 19;
Rv 17: 4; 18: 12, 16. *Held in*
honor, respected Ac 5: 34; Hb 13:
4.

τιμιότης, ητος, ἡ *costliness, abund-*
ance of costly things Rv 18: 19.*

Τιμόθεος, ου, ὁ *Timothy*, a friend,
traveling companion and co-
worker of Paul. His career can
be outlined by reference to
these passages: Ac 16: 1; 17:
14f; 18: 5; 19: 22; 20: 4; Ro 16:
21; 1 Cor 4: 17; 2 Cor 1: 1;
Phil 1: 1; Col 1: 1; 1 Th 1: 1;
2 Th 1: 1; 1 Ti 1: 2; 2 Ti 1: 2;
Phlm 1; Hb 13: 23.

Τίμων, ωνος, ὁ *Timon* Ac 6: 5.*

τιμωρέω *punish* Ac 22: 5; 26:
11.*

τιμωρία, ας, ἡ *punishment* Hb 10:
29.*

τίνω *pay, undergo* 2 Th 1: 9.*

τίς, τί gen. **τίνος** (the acute accent
on this word never changes to a
grave) interrogative pron. *who?*
which (one)? what?—**1.** subst.—
a. τίς *who? which one?* Mt 3: 7;
22: 42; 26: 68; Mk 2: 7; 11: 28;
J 18: 4, 7; Ro 7: 24; 1 Cor 9:
7; Hb 1: 5; 3: 16–18.—*Who?* in
the sense *what sort of (a) person?*
Lk 5: 21a; J 1: 19; 21: 12; Ac 11:
17; Ro 14: 4.—*Who, what* as a
substitute for the relative pron.
Ac 13: 25 v.l.; perhaps Js 3: 13.
b. τί *what?* Mt 17: 25a; 21: 28,
40; Mk 10: 3, 17; Lk 10: 27;
J 18: 38; Ro 10: 8.—διὰ τί,
εἰς τί, πρὸς τί, χάριν τίνος all
mean *why?*—*What sort of (a)*
thing? Mk 1: 27; Col 1: 26;
Eph 1: 19; 3: 18.—*Which of*
two? Mt 9: 5; Mk 2: 9; Lk 5:

23; 1 Cor 4: 21; Phil 1: 22.—
Elliptical expressions J 1: 21;
11: 47; Ro 3: 3; 1 Cor 5: 12. On
τί ἐμοὶ καὶ σοί, see ἐγώ.—
What as a substitute for the
relative pron. Mk 14: 36; Lk 17:
8; Ac 13: 25; 1 Ti 1: 7.—
2. adj. *what?* Mt 5: 46; Lk 14:
31; J 2: 18; Ac 10: 29; 2 Cor 6:
14–16.—**3.** adv.—**a.** τί; *why?*
Mt 6: 28; 7: 3; Mk 4: 40; Lk 19:
33; J 18: 23; Ac 14: 15; 1 Cor
10: 30; 15: 29b, 30.—**b.** τί in an
exclamation *how!* Mt 7: 14 v.l.;
Lk 12: 49.

τὶς, τὶ, gen. **τινός** enclitic, indefinite pron. *Anyone, anything;*
someone, something; many a one
or *thing.*—**1.** subst.—**a.** τὶς,
τινές *someone, anyone, somebody*
Mt 12: 29, 47; Lk 7: 36; J 2: 25;
6: 46; Ac 5: 25; 2 Cor 11: 20.
Pl. *some* Lk 13: 1; Ac 15: 1;
1 Cor 6: 11; 2 Th 3: 11.—τὶς *a*
certain man, etc. Lk 9: 49; J 11:
1; Ac 18: 7; Ro 3: 8; 1 Cor 4:
18; 2 Cor 2: 5; 11: 21. *A person*
of importance Ac 5: 36.—**b.** τὶ,
τινά *something, anything* Mt 5:
23; Mk 13: 15; Lk 7: 40; J 13:
29; Ac 4: 32; Ro 15: 18; 1 Cor
10: 31. εἶναί τι *be* or *amount to*
something 1 Cor 3: 7; Gal 2: 6;
6: 3.—**2.** adj.—**a.** *some, any, a*
certain, often omitted in translation into English Mt 18: 12;
Lk 1: 5; 17: 12; 23: 26; Ac 3: 2;
8: 34; 10: 5f; Ro 9: 11; 1 Cor 1:
16; Hb 4: 7.—**b.** serving to
moderate or heighten ἀπαρχήν
τινα *a kind of first-fruits* Js 1:
18. δύο τινάς *perhaps two* Lk 7:
18. Cf. Hb 10: 27. βραχύ τι
(only) a little 2: 7, 9.—**c.** *some,*
considerable Ac 18: 23; Ro 1: 11,
13: 1 Cor 11: 18; 16: 7.—
d. τινές *several* Lk 8: 2; Ac 9:
19; 10: 48; 15: 2; 17: 5f.

Τίτιος, ου, ὁ *Titius* Ac 18: 7.*

τίτλος, ου, ὁ (Latin loanword:
titulus) *inscription, notice*, giving

the reason for condemnation J 19: 19f.*

Τίτος, ου, ὁ *Titus*—1. friend and helper of Paul 2 Cor 2: 13; 7: 6; 8: 6; 12: 18; Gal 2: 1, 3; 2 Ti 4: 10; Tit 1: 4.—2. surnamed Justus Ac 18: 7 v.l.

τοιγαροῦν inferential particle *for that very reason, then, therefore* 1 Th 4: 8; Hb 12: 1.*

τοίνυν inferential particle *hence, so, indeed* Lk 20: 25; 1 Cor 9: 26; Hb 13: 13; Js 2: 24 v.l.*

τοιόσδε, άδε, όνδε *such as this, of this kind* 2 Pt 1: 17.*

τοιοῦτος, αύτη, οὗτον and **οὗτο** *of such a kind, such (as this)* Mt 9: 8; Mk 6: 2; 9: 37; Ac 26: 29; 1 Cor 5: 1; 15: 48; 2 Cor 12: 3; Gal 6: 1; Eph 5: 27; Tit 3: 11; Phlm 9; Hb 7: 26; 11: 14; Js 4: 16.

τοῖχος, ου, ὁ *wall* Ac 23: 3.*

τόκος, ου, ὁ *interest* on money loaned Mt 25: 27; Lk 19: 23.*

τολμάω—1. followed by the inf.— **a.** *dare, have the courage, be brave enough* Mt 22: 46; Mk 12: 34; Lk 20: 40; J 21: 12; Ac 5: 13; 7: 32; Ro 5: 7; Phil 1: 14. —**b.** *bring oneself, presume* Ro 15: 18; 1 Cor 6: 1; 2 Cor 10: 12; Jd 9.—2. abs. *dare, be courageous* Mk 15: 43; 2 Cor 10: 2; 11: 21.*

τολμηροτέρως Ro 15: 15 and **τολμηρότερον** 15: 15 v.l. both mean *rather boldly.**

τολμητής, οῦ, ὁ *bold, audacious man* 2 Pt 2: 10.*

τομός, ή, όν *cutting, sharp* comparative **τομώτερος** *sharper* fig. Hb 4: 12.*

τόξον, ου, τό *the bow* as a weapon Rv 6: 2.*

τοπάζιον, ου, τό *topaz*, a bright yellow precious stone Rv 21: 20.*

τόπος, ου, ὁ *place, position, region* —1. lit. Mt 14: 35; 26: 52; Mk 1: 35; 15: 22; Lk 16: 28; J 5: 13; 11: 48; 20: 25; Ac 6: 13; 12: 17; 16: 3; 27: 2; 1 Cor 1: 2;

Rv 2: 5. *Room* Lk 2: 7; 14: 9, 22. Pl. *regions, districts* Mt 12: 43; Mk 13: 8; Ac 27: 2.—2. in special meanings—**a.** *place, passage* in a book Lk 4: 17.— **b.** *position, office* Ac 1: 25a.— **c.** *possibility, opportunity, chance* Ac 25: 16; Ro 12: 19; 15: 23; Eph 4: 27; Hb 12: 17.—**d.** ἐν τῷ τόπῳ οὗ ἐρρέθη αὐτοῖς *instead of their being told* Ro 9: 26.

τοσοῦτος, αύτη, οὗτον and **οὗτο** *so great, so large, so far, so much, so strong,* etc.—1. used with a noun Mt 8: 10; J 14: 9; Hb 12: 1; Rv 18: 7, 17. Pl. *so many* Mt 15: 33; Lk 15: 29; J 12: 37; 1 Cor 14: 10.—2. without a noun—**a.** pl. τοσοῦτοι *so many people* J 6: 9. Cf. Gal 3: 4.— **b.** sing. τοσούτου *for so much* Ac 5: 8. Correlative τοσούτῳ . . . ὅσῳ *(by)* so much (greater, more, etc.) . . . *than* or *as* Hb 1: 4; 10: 25. Cf. 7: 20–22.

τότε adv.—1. *then, at that time* Mt 2: 17; 13: 43; 27: 9, 16; 1 Cor 13: 12; 2 Cor 12: 10; Gal 4: 8, 29; 2 Pt 3: 6.—2. *then, thereupon, thereafter* Mt 2: 7; 4: 1; 12: 22; 13: 26; 21: 1; 26: 65; Mk 13: 14; Lk 24: 45; J 11: 6, 14; Ac 1: 12; 17: 14.

τοὐναντίον = τὸ ἐναντίον.

τοὔνομα = τὸ ὄνομα.

τουτέστιν = τοῦτό ἐστιν.

τράγος, ου, ὁ *he-goat* Hb 9: 12f, 19; 10: 4.*

τράπεζα, ης, ἡ *table*—1. lit. Mk 7: 28; Lk 22: 21, 30; 1 Cor 10: 21; Hb 9: 2. Specifically for money-changers Mt 21: 12; J 2: 15; *bank* Lk 19: 23.—2. fig. *a meal, food* Ac 6: 2; 16: 34.

τραπεζίτης, ου, ὁ *money-changer, banker* Mt 25: 27.*

τραῦμα, ατος, τό *a wound* Lk 10:34.*

τραυματίζω *to wound* Lk 20: 12; Ac 19: 16.*

τραχηλίζω pass. *be laid bare* Hb 4: 13.*

τράχηλος, ου, ὁ neck, throat Mt 18: 6; Mk 9: 42; Lk 15: 20; 17:2;Ac15:10;20:37;Ro16:4.*

τραχύς, εῖα, ύ rough, uneven Lk 3: 5; Ac 27: 29.*

Τραχωνῖτις, ιδος ἡ, ἡ Τραχωνῖτις χώρα the region of Trachonitis, a district south of Damascus Lk 3: 1.*

τρεῖς, τρία three Mt 12: 40; Lk 1: 56; J 2: 19; 1 Cor 13: 13; 1 J 5: 7.

Τρεῖς Ταβέρναι see ταβέρναι.

τρέμω be afraid, fear Mk 5: 33; Lk 8: 47; Ac 9: 6 v.l.; 2 Pt 2: 10.*

τρέφω—1. feed, nourish, support, provide with food Mt 6: 26; 25: 37; Lk 12: 24; 23: 29; Ac 12: 20; Js 5: 5; Rv 12: 6, 14.—2. rear, bring up, train, pass. grow up Lk 4: 16.*

τρέχω run—1. lit. Mt 27: 48; Mk 5: 6; Lk 15: 20; J 20: 2, 4; 1 Cor 9: 24a, b.—2. fig. strive to advance, make progress Ro 9: 16; 1 Cor 9: 24c, 26; Gal 2: 2; 5: 7; Phil 2: 16; Hb 12: 1. Spread rapidly 2 Th 3: 1.

τρῆμα, ατος, τό hole, eye of a needle Mt 19: 24; Lk 18: 25.*

τριάκοντα indecl. thirty Mt 13: 8; Mk 4: 8; Lk 3: 23.

τριακόσιοι, αι, α three hundred Mk 14: 5; J 12: 5.*

τρίβολος, ου, ὁ thistle Mt 7: 16; Hb 6: 8.*

τρίβος, ου, ἡ path Mt 3: 3; Mk 1: 3; Lk 3: 4.*

τριετία, ας, ἡ (a period of) three years Ac 20: 18 v.l., 31.*

τρίζω gnash, grind Mk 9: 18.*

τρίμηνος, ον of three months subst. τὸ τρίμηνον (a period of) three months Hb 11: 23.*

τρίς adv. three times Mt 26: 34, 75; Mk 14: 30, 72; Lk 22: 34, 61; J 13: 38; 2 Cor 11: 25; 12: 8. ἐπὶ τρίς three times or (yet) a third time Ac 10: 16; 11: 10.*

τρίστεγον, ου, τό the third story Ac 20: 9.*

τρισχίλιοι, αι, α three thousand Ac 2: 41.*

τρίτος, η, ον third—1. as adj. Mt 16: 21; 27: 64; Mk 12: 21; Lk 18: 33; Ac 27: 19; 2 Cor 12: 2; Rv 4: 7.—2. as a subst. τὸ τρίτον the third part, one-third Rv 8: 7–12; 9: 15, 18; 12: 4.— 3. adv. (τὸ) τρίτον for the third time Mk 14: 41; Lk 23: 22; J 21: 17; in the third place 1 Cor 12: 28. τρίτον τοῦτο this is the third time J 21: 14. ἐκ τρίτου for the third time Mt 26: 44.

τρίχες nom. pl. of θρίξ.

τρίχινος, η, ον made of hair Rv 6: 12.*

τρόμος, ου, ὁ trembling Mk 16: 8; 1 Cor 2: 3; 2 Cor 7: 15; Eph 6: 5; Phil 2: 12.*

τροπή, ῆς, ἡ turn(ing), variation, change τροπῆς ἀποσκίασμα Js 1: 17 may be shadow of variation or darkening, which has its basis in change.*

τρόπος, ου, ὁ—1. manner, way, kind Ac 15: 11; 27: 25; Ro 3: 2; Phil 1: 18; 2 Th 2: 3; 3: 16; Jd 7. ὃν τρόπον in the manner in which = (just) as Mt 23: 37; Lk 13: 34; Ac 1: 11; 7: 28; 2 Ti 3: 8.—2. way of life, conduct, character Hb 13: 5.*

τροποφορέω bear or put up with Ac 13: 18.*

τροφή, ῆς, ἡ nourishment, food—1. lit. Mt 3: 4; Lk 12: 23; J 4: 8; Ac 9:19;Js 2:15.—2.fig., of spiritual nourishment Hb 5: 12, 14.

Τρόφιμος, ου, ὁ Trophimus of Ephesus, a friend of Paul Ac 20: 4; 21: 29; 2 Ti 4: 20.*

τροφός, οῦ, ἡ nurse, possibly mother 1 Th 2: 7.*

τροφοφορέω care for (as a nurse) Ac 13: 18 v.l.*

τροχιά, ᾶς, ἡ wheel-track, course, way fig. Hb 12: 13.*

τροχός, οῦ, ὁ wheel Js 3: 6.*

τρύβλιον, ου, τό bowl, dish Mt 26: 23; Mk 14: 20.*

τρυγάω *pick* or *gather* (*grapes*) Lk 6: 44; Rv 14: 18; *gather the fruit of* 14: 19.*

τρυγών, όνος, ἡ *turtle-dove* Lk 2: 24.*

τρυμαλιά, ᾶς, ἡ *hole, eye* of a needle Mk 10: 25; Mt 19: 24 v.l.; Lk 18: 25 v.l.*

τρύπημα, ατος, τό *eye* of a needle Mt 19: 24 v.l.*

Τρύφαινα, ης, ἡ *Tryphaena*, a Christian woman Ro 16: 12.*

τρυφάω *lead a life of self-indulgence, revel, carouse* Js 5: 5.*

τρυφή, ῆς, ἡ *indulgence, revelling* 2 Pt 2: 13. *Luxury, splendor* Lk 7: 25.*

Τρυφῶσα, ης, ἡ *Tryphosa*, a Christian woman Ro 16: 12.*

Τρῳάς, άδος, ἡ *Troas*, a seaport city in the northwest corner of Asia Minor Ac 16: 8, 11; 20: 5f; 2 Cor 2: 12; 2 Ti 4: 13.*

Τρωγύλλιον, ου, τό *Trogyllium*, a town south of Ephesus Ac 20: 15 v.l.*

τρώγω *eat* Mt 24: 38; J 6: 54, 56–58; 13: 18.*

τυγχάνω—1. *meet, attain, gain, find, experience* Lk 20: 35; Ac 24: 2; 26: 22; 27: 3; 2 Ti 2: 10; Hb 8: 6; 11: 35.—2. intr. *happen, turn out*—a. *happen to be, find oneself* Lk 10: 30 v.l.—b. εἰ τύχοι *if it should turn out that way, perhaps, probably* 1 Cor 14: 10; 15: 37.—c. τυχόν (acc. absolute, aor. participle) *if it turns out that way, perhaps, if possible* 1 Cor 16: 6; Lk 20: 13 v.l.; Ac 12: 15 v.l.—d. οὐχ ὁ τυχών *not the common* or *ordinary* (*one*), i.e., *extraordinary* Ac 19: 11; 28: 2.*

τυμπανίζω *torment, torture* pass. Hb 11: 35.*

τυπικῶς adv. *typologically, as an example* or *warning* 1 Cor 10: 11.*

τύπος, ου, ὁ—1. *mark* J 20: 25a, b v.l.—2. *image, statue* Ac 7: 43. —3. *form, figure, pattern* Ro 6:

17; perhaps *content* Ac 23: 25. —4. (*arche*)*type, pattern, model* —a. technically Ac 7: 44; Hb 8: 5.—b. in the moral life *example, pattern* Phil 3: 17; 1 Th 1: 7; 2 Th 3: 9; 1 Ti 4: 12; Tit 2: 7; 1 Pt 5: 3.—5. the *types* given by God as an indication of the future Ro 5: 14; 1 Cor 10: 6, 11 v.l.*

τύπτω *strike, beat*—1. lit. Mt 24: 49; Mk 15: 19; Lk 6: 29; 18: 13; Ac 21: 32; 23: 2.—2. fig. Ac 23: 3a; 1 Cor 8: 12.

τύραννος, ου, ὁ *despotic ruler, tyrant* Ac 5: 39 v.l.

Τύραννος, ου, ὁ *Tyrannus*, an Ephesian Ac 19: 9.*

τυρβάζω mid. or pass. *trouble oneself, be troubled* Lk 10: 41 v.l.*

Τύριος, ου, ὁ *the Tyrian* Ac 12: 20, 22 v.l.*

Τύρος, ου, ἡ *Tyre*, an important seaport in Phoenicia Mt 11: 21f; 15: 21; Mk 7: 24, 31; Ac 21: 3, 7.

τυφλός, ή, όν *blind*, adj. and subst.—1. lit. Mt 20: 30; Mk 8: 22f; Lk 6: 39; J 9: 1, 18, 24; 10: 21.—2. fig. Mt 23: 16f, 19, 24, 26; J 9: 40f; Ro 2: 19; Rv 3: 17.

τυφλόω *to blind, deprive of sight* J 12: 40; 2 Cor 4: 4; 1 J 2: 11.*

τυφόομαι *be puffed up, conceited* 1 Ti 3: 6; 6: 4; 2 Ti 3: 4. But τ. in 1 Ti 6: 4 can also mean *be blinded, be foolish* or *stupid*.*

τύφω pass. *smoke, smolder, glimmer* Mt 12: 20.*

τυφωνικός, ή, όν *like a whirlwind* ἄνεμος τυφωνικός *a typhoon, hurricane* Ac 27: 14.*

τυχεῖν, τύχοι 2 aor. act. inf. and opt., 3 sing. of τυγχάνω.

Τυχικός, οῦ, ὁ *Tychicus*, a friend and companion of Paul Ac 20: 4; Eph 6: 21; Col 4: 7; 2 Ti 4: 12; Tit 3: 12; Eph subscr.; Col subscr.*

τυχόν 2 aor. act. participle, neut. acc. sing., of τυγχάνω.

Y

ὑακίνθινος, ίνη, ινον *hyacinth-colored*, i.e. dark blue (dark red?) Rv 9: 17.*

ὑάκινθος, ου, ὁ *the jacinth* or *hyacinth*, a precious stone, perhaps blue in color Rv 21: 20.*

ὑάλινος, η, ον *of glass, transparent as glass* Rv 4: 6; 15: 2.*

ὕαλος, ου, ἡ or ὁ *glass, crystal* Rv 21: 18, 21.*

ὑβρίζω *treat in an arrogant or spiteful manner, mistreat, scoff at, insult* Mt 22: 6; Lk 11: 45; 18: 32; Ac 14: 5; 1 Th 2: 2.*

ὕβρις, εως, ἡ—1. *shame, insult, mistreatment* 2 Cor 12: 10.—2. *disaster, damage* Ac 27: 10, 21.*

ὑβριστής, ου, ὁ *a violent, insolent man* Ro 1: 30; 1 Ti 1: 13.*

ὑγιαίνω *be in good health, be healthy or sound*—1. lit. Mt 8: 13 v.l.; Lk 5: 31; 7: 10; 15: 27; 3 J 2.—2. fig. *be sound or correct* 1 Ti 1: 10; 6: 3; 2 Ti 1: 13; 4: 3; Tit 1: 9, 13; 2: 1 f.*

ὑγιής, ές acc. ὑγιῆ *healthy, sound*—1. lit. Mt 12: 13; 15: 31; Mk 5: 34; J 5: 4, 6, 9, 11, 14f; 7: 23; Ac 4: 10.—2. fig. Tit 2: 8.

ὑγρός, ά, όν *moist, pliant, green* Lk 23: 31.*

ὑδρία, ας, ἡ *water jar* J 2: 6f; 4: 28.*

ὑδροποτέω *drink* (only) *water* 1 Ti 5: 23.*

ὑδρωπικός, ή, όν *suffering from dropsy* Lk 14: 2.*

ὕδωρ, ατος, τό *water*—1. lit. Mt 3: 11; Mk 9: 41; 14: 13; J 5: 3f, 7; Hb 10: 22; 2 Pt 3: 5; Rv 1: 15.—2. fig. J 4: 10f, 14; 7: 38; Rv 7: 17; 21: 6; 22: 1, 17.

ὑετός, ου, ὁ *rain* Ac 14: 17; 28: 2; Hb 6: 7; Js 5: 7 v.l., 18; Rv 11: 6.*

υἱοθεσία, ας, ἡ *adoption* (of children), only in a religious sense Ro 8: 15, 23; 9: 4; Gal 4: 5; Eph 1: 5.*

υἱός, οῦ, ὁ *son*—1. in the usual sense—a. lit. Mt 1: 21; Mk 6: 3; Lk 15: 11; Ac 13: 21; Gal 4: 30. *Offspring* Mt 21: 5.—b. more generally *descendant* Mt 1: 20; Ac 5: 21; 10: 36; 2 Cor 3: 7, 13; Hb 11: 22. Of one who is accepted or adopted as a son J 19: 26; Ac 7: 21.—c. fig.—α. of a pupil, follower, etc. Lk 11: 19; Hb 12: 5; 1 Pt 5: 13.—β. of the members of a large group Mk 3: 28; Ac 13: 26; Eph 3: 5.—γ. of those who are bound to a person by close ties Mt 5: 45; 23: 31; Ro 8: 14, 19; Gal 3: 7, 26; Hb 2: 10.—δ. υἱός with gen. of the thing, to denote one who shares in this thing Mt 8: 12; 9: 15; Mk 3: 17; Lk 16: 8; J 17: 12; Ac 4: 36; Eph 2: 2; 2 Th 2: 3.—2. in various combinations as a designation of the Messiah and a self-designation of Jesus—a. *Son* of David Mt 9: 27; 21: 9, 15; Mk 10: 47f; 12: 35, 37; Lk 18: 38f.—b. (*the*) *Son* of God Mt 2: 15; 3: 17; 27: 43, 54; 28: 19; Mk 3: 11; 9: 7; Lk 1: 35; 10: 22; J 1: 49; 3: 16–18, 35f; Ac 13: 33; Ro 1: 3, 4, 9; Hb 5: 5.—c. ὁ υἱὸς τοῦ ἀνθρώπου *the Son of Man, the Man*, always as a self-designation of Jesus Mt 8: 20; 9: 6; Mk 8: 31, 38; 14: 21; Lk 9: 22, 26, 44, 58; J 1: 51; 6: 27, 53, 62; Ac 7: 56; Rv 1: 13; 14: 14.

ὕλη, ης, ἡ *wood* Js 3: 5.*

ὑμεῖς nom. pl. of σύ.

Ὑμέναιος, ου, ὁ *Hymenaeus* 1 Ti 1: 20; 2 Ti 2: 17.*

ὑμέτερος, α, ον *your*—1. *belonging to or incumbent upon you* Lk 6: 20; J 7: 6; 8: 17; 15: 20; Ac 27:

34; 2 Cor 8: 8; Gal 6: 13; subst. Lk 16: 12 v.l.—**2.** for the objective gen. τῷ ὑμετέρῳ ἐλέει *by the mercy shown to you* Ro 11: 31. νὴ τὴν ὑμετέραν καύχησιν ἣν ἔχω *by the pride that I have in you* 1 Cor 15: 31. τὸ ὑ. ὑστέρημα *that which is lacking in you* 16: 17.*

ὑμνέω—**1.** trans. *sing the praise of* Ac 16: 25; Hb 2: 12.—**2.** intrans. *sing a hymn* Mt 26: 30; Mk 14: 26.*

ὕμνος, ου, ὁ *hymn* or *song* of *praise* Eph 5: 19; Col 3: 16.*

ὑπάγω—**1.** *go away* Mt 4: 10; Mk 5: 34; 8: 33; J 6: 67; 18: 8; Js 2: 16. *Go home* Mt 8: 13; 20: 14; Mk 10: 52.—**2.** *go* Mt 9: 6; 18: 15; 26: 18; Mk 1: 44; 14: 13; Lk 10: 3; J 7: 3; 9: 11; 21: 3; Rv 13: 10; 14: 4.— Especially of Christ's going to the Father J 7: 33; 8: 14; 14: 28; 16: 5a, 10, 17.

ὑπακοή, ῆς, ἡ *obedience* Ro 1: 5; 6: 16; 16: 19, 26; 2 Cor 10: 5f; Hb 5: 8; 1 Pt 1: 2, 22.

ὑπακούω *listen to*—**1.** *obey, follow, be subject to* w. dat. Mk 1: 27; 4: 41; Ro 10: 16; Eph 6: 1, 5; Phil 2: 12; 2 Th 3: 14; 1 Pt 3: 6.—**2.** *open* or *answer* (the door) Ac 12: 13.

ὕπανδρος, ον *under the power of a man* ἡ ὕπανδρος γυνή *the married woman* Ro 7: 2.*

ὑπαντάω (*come* or *go to*) *meet* w. dat. Mt 28: 9; Mk 5: 2; J 4: 51; 11: 20, 30.—*Oppose* Lk 14: 31.

ὑπάντησις, εως, ἡ *coming to meet* εἰς ὑπάντησιν *to meet* w. dat. or gen. Mt 8: 34; 25: 1; J 12: 13.*

ὕπαρξις, εως, ἡ *that which one has, property, possession* Ac 2: 45; Hb 10: 34.*

ὑπάρχω—**1.** (*really*) *exist, be present, be at one's disposal* Ac 3: 6; 4: 34; 19: 40; 28: 7, 18; 1 Cor 11: 18. τὰ ὑπάρχοντα *property, possessions* Mt 19: 21;

Lk 8: 3; 11: 21; 19: 8; 1 Cor 13: 3.—**2.** *to be,* as a substitute for εἶναι Lk 8: 41; 9: 48; 16: 14; Ac 7: 55; 21: 20; 22: 3; Ro 4: 19; 1 Cor 7: 26; Gal 1: 14; Phil 2: 6; Js 2: 15.

ὑπείκω *yield, give way, submit* Hb 13: 17.*

ὑπελείφθην 1 aor. pass. ind. of ὑπολείπω.

ὑπεναντίος, α, ον *opposed,* in Col 2: 14 *against.* οἱ ὑπεναντίοι *the adversaries* Hb 10: 27.*

ὑπενεγκεῖν 2 aor. act. inf. of ὑποφέρω.

ὑπέπλευσα 1 aor. act. ind. of ὑποπλέω.

ὑπέρ prep. w. gen. and acc.— **1.** w. gen.—**a.** *for, in behalf of, for the sake of* Mt 5: 44; Mk 9: 40; J 11: 50–52; Ac 21: 26; Ro 5: 6–8; 8: 31; 16: 4; Col 1: 7, 9; Phil 1: 7; Hb 2: 9.—**b.** w. gen. of the thing *in behalf of,* but variously translated: with ἁμαρτιῶν *in order to remove the sins* Gal 1: 4; Hb 7: 27; 10: 12; with ζωῆς *to bring life* J 6: 51; with δόξης *to reveal the glory* 11: 4; with ὀνόματος *to spread the name* Ro 1: 5.—**c.** *in place of, instead of, in the name of* Ro 9: 3; 2 Cor 5: 14f, 21; Phlm 13.— **d.** *because of, for the sake of, for* Ac 5: 41; 21: 13; Ro 15: 9; 2 Cor 12: 10; Eph 5: 20; Phil 1: 29.—**e.** *above and beyond* may be the meaning in Phil 2: 13; *in* is also possible.—**f.** *about, concerning* J 1: 30; Ro 9: 27; 2 Cor 1: 7f; 12: 5.—**2.** w. acc. *over and above, beyond, more than* 1 Cor 4: 6; 2 Cor 1: 8; Eph 1: 22; Phlm 16, 21. *Superior to* Mt 10: 24; Lk 6: 40; Phil 2: 9. *Than* 2 Cor 12: 13; Hb 4: 12. *More than* Mt 10: 37; Gal 1: 14.— **3.** ὑπέρ as adv. *even more* 2 Cor 11: 23.

ὑπεραίρομαι *rise up, exalt oneself, be elated* 2 Cor 12: 7; 2 Th 2: 4.*

ὑπέρακμος, ον *past one's prime, past the bloom of youth* if it refers to the woman; *with strong passions* if it refers to the man 1 Cor 7: 36.*

ὑπεράνω adv. *(high) above*, as improper prep. w. gen. Eph 1: 21; 4: 10; Hb 9: 5.*

ὑπεραυξάνω *grow wonderfully, increase abundantly* 2 Th 1: 3.*

ὑπερβαίνω *transgress, sin* 1 Th 4: 6.*

ὑπερβαλλόντως *surpassingly, to a much greater degree* 2 Cor 11: 23.*

ὑπερβάλλω *go beyond, surpass*; the participle ὑπερβάλλων, ουσα, ον *surpassing, extraordinary, outstanding* 2 Cor 3: 10; 9: 14; Eph 1: 19; 2: 7; 3: 19.*

ὑπερβολή, ῆς, ἡ *excess, extraordinary quality or character* 2 Cor 4: 7; 12: 7. καθ' ὑπερβολήν *to an extraordinary degree, beyond measure, utterly* Ro 7: 13; 2 Cor 1: 8; Gal 1: 13. καθ' ὑπ. ὁδόν *a far better way* 1 Cor 12: 31. καθ' ὑπ. εἰς ὑπ. *beyond all measure and proportion* 2 Cor 4: 17.*

ὑπερεγώ for ὑπὲρ ἐγώ 2 Cor 11: 23; see ὑπέρ 3.

ὑπερεῖδον 2 aor. act. ind. of ὑπεροράω.

ὑπερέκεινα adv. *beyond* w. gen. 2 Cor 10: 16.*

ὑπερεκπερισσοῦ adv. *quite beyond all measure, as earnestly as possible* 1 Th 3: 10; 5: 13 v.l. W. gen. *infinitely more than* Eph 3: 20.*

ὑπερεκπερισσῶς adv. *beyond all measure, most highly* 1 Th 5: 13; Mk 7: 37 v.l.*

ὑπερεκτείνω *stretch out beyond, overextend* 2 Cor 10: 14.*

ὑπερεκχύν(ν)ω *pour out over*, pass. *overflow* Lk 6: 38.*

ὑπερεντυγχάνω *plead, intercede* Ro 8: 26.*

ὑπερέχω—1. *have power over, be in authority (over), be highly placed* Ro 13: 1; 1 Pt 2: 13.—2. *be better than, surpass, excel* w. gen. Phil 2: 3; w. acc. 4: 7.—3. τὸ ὑπερέχον *the surpassing greatness* Phil 3: 8.*

ὑπερηφανία, ας, ἡ *arrogance, haughtiness, pride* Mk 7: 22.*

ὑπερήφανος, ον *arrogant, haughty, proud* Lk 1: 51; Ro 1: 30; 2 Ti 3: 2; Js 4: 6; 1 Pt 5: 5.*

ὑπερλίαν adv. *exceedingly, beyond measure* as adj. οἱ ὑπερλίαν ἀπόστολοι *the super-apostles* 2 Cor 11: 5; 12: 11.*

ὑπερνικάω *win a most glorious victory* Ro 8: 37.*

ὑπέρογκος, ον *of excessive size, haughty, bombastic* 2 Pt 2: 18; Jd 16.*

ὑπεροράω *overlook, disregard* Ac 17: 30.*

ὑπεροχή, ῆς, ἡ—1. *superiority* καθ' ὑπεροχήν *as a superior person* 1 Cor 2: 1.—2. *a position of authority* 1 Ti 2: 2.*

ὑπερπερισσεύω—1. intrans. *be present in (greater) abundance* Ro 5: 20.—2. trans. *cause to overflow* pass. *overflow* 2 Cor 7: 4.*

ὑπερπερισσῶς adv. *beyond all measure* Mk 7: 37.*

ὑπερπλεονάζω *be present in great abundance* 1 Ti 1: 14.*

ὑπερυψόω *raise to the loftiest height* Phil 2: 9.*

ὑπερφρονέω *think too highly of oneself, be haughty* Ro 12: 3.*

ὑπερῷον, ου, τό *upper story, room upstairs* Ac 1: 13; 9: 37, 39; 20: 8.*

ὑπετάγην 2 aor. pass. ind. of ὑποτάσσω.

ὑπέχω *undergo* Jd 7.*

ὑπήκοος, ον *obedient* Ac 7: 39; 2 Cor 2: 9; Phil 2: 8.*

ὑπήνεγκα aor. act. ind. of ὑποφέρω.

ὑπηρετέω *serve, render service, be helpful* w. dat. Ac 13: 36; 20: 34; 24: 23.*

ὑπηρέτης, ου, ὁ *servant, helper, assistant* Mt 5: 25; Mk 14: 54,

65; Lk 4: 20; J 7: 32, 45f; 18: 18, 36; Ac 13: 5; 26: 16; 1 Cor 4: 1.

ὕπνος, ου, ὁ sleep lit. Mt 1: 24; Lk 9: 32; J 11: 13; Ac 20: 9; fig. Ro 13: 11.*

ὑπό prep. w. gen. and acc.—**1**. w. gen. by, denoting the agent or cause Mt 1: 22; 8: 24; J 14: 21; Gal 1: 11; 1 Cor 10: 29; Rv 6: 13; at the hands of Mk 5: 26; 2 Cor 2: 6.—**2**. w. acc. under, below Mt 8: 8f; Ac 4: 12; Ro 6: 14f; 16: 20; 1 Cor 9: 20; 15: 25, 27; Col 1: 23; (below) at Js 2: 3; about Ac 5: 21.

ὑποβάλλω instigate (secretly), suborn Ac 6: 11.*

ὑπογραμμός, οῦ, ὁ model, example 1 Pt 2: 21.*

ὑπόδειγμα, ατος, τό—**1**. example, model, pattern J 13: 15; Hb 4: 11; Js 5: 10; 2 Pt 2: 6.—**2**. copy, imitation Hb 8: 5; 9: 23.*

ὑποδείκνυμι or **-ύω** show, prove, set forth Lk 6: 47; 12: 5; Ac 9: 16; 20: 35. Warn Mt 3: 7; Lk 3: 7.*

ὑποδέχομαι receive, welcome, entertain as a guest Lk 10: 38; 19: 6; Ac 17: 7; Js 2: 25.*

ὑποδέω mid. tie or bind beneath, put on (footwear) Mk 6: 9; Ac 12: 8; Eph 6: 15.*

ὑπόδημα, ατος, τό sandal, footwear Mt 10: 10; Mk 1: 7; Lk 15: 22; 22: 35; Ac 7: 33.

ὑπόδησαι 1 aor. mid. imperative of ὑποδέω.

ὑπόδικος, ον answerable, accountable Ro 3: 19.*

ὑποδραμών 2 aor. act. participle of ὑποτρέχω.

ὑποζύγιον, ου, τό donkey, ass Mt 21: 5; 2 Pt 2: 16.*

ὑποζώννυμι undergird, brace with cables around the hull Ac 27: 17.*

ὑποκάτω adv., as improper prep. w. gen. under, below, down at

Mt 22: 44; Mk 6: 11; J 1: 50; Rv 5: 3, 13.

ὑπόκειμαι be found, lit. 'lie below' Lk 6: 42 v.l.*

ὑποκρίνομαι pretend, make believe Lk 20: 20.*

ὑπόκρισις, εως, ἡ hypocrisy, pretense, outward show Mt 23: 28; Mk 12: 15; Lk 12: 1; Gal 2: 13; Js 5: 12 v.l.; 1 Ti 4: 2; 1 Pt 2: 1.*

ὑποκριτής, οῦ, ὁ hypocrite, pretender, dissembler, lit. 'player-actor' Mt 6: 2, 5, 16; 7: 5; 23: 13–15; Mk 7: 6; Lk 6: 42; 12: 56; 13: 15.

ὑπολαμβάνω—**1**. take up Ac 1: 9. —**2**. receive as a guest 3 J 8.— **3**. reply Lk 10: 30.—**4**. assume, think, believe Lk 7: 43; Ac 2: 15.*

ὑπολαμπάς, άδος, ἡ probably window Ac 20: 8 v.l.*

ὑπόλειμμα, ατος, τό remnant Ro 9: 27.*

ὑπολείπω leave remaining pass. be left (remaining) Ro 11: 3.*

ὑπολήνιον, ου, τό vat placed beneath a winepress Mk 12: 1.*

ὑπόλιμμα a different spelling for ὑπόλειμμα.

ὑπολιμπάνω leave (behind) 1 Pt 2: 21.*

ὑπομεμενηκώς perf. act. participle of ὑπομένω.

ὑπομένω remain, stay (behind) Lk 2: 43; Ac 17: 14.—Remain, stand one's ground, hold out, endure Mk 13: 13; Ro 12: 12; 1 Cor 13: 7; Hb 12: 2, 7; Js 5: 11; 1 Pt 2: 20.

ὑπομιμνήσκω—**1**. act. remind J 14: 26; Tit 3: 1; 2 Pt 1: 12; Jd 5. Call to mind, bring up 2 Ti 2: 14; 3 J 10.—**2**. pass. remember, think of w. gen. Lk 22: 61.*

ὑπόμνησις, εως, ἡ remembering ἐν ὑπ. by a reminder, i.e., as I remind you 2 Pt 1: 13; 3: 1. Remembrance ὑπόμνησιν λαμβάνειν receive a remembrance = remember 2 Ti 1: 5.*

ὑπομονή, ῆς, ἡ—1. *patience, endurance, fortitude, steadfastness, perseverance* Lk 21: 19; Ro 2: 7; 5: 3f; 8: 25; 2 Cor 12: 12; 2 Th 3: 5; Js 1: 3f; 5: 11; Rv 2: 2f; 13: 10.—2. (*patient*) *expectation* Rv 1: 9.

ὑπονοέω *suspect, suppose* Ac 13: 25; 25: 18; 27: 27.*

ὑπόνοια, ας, ἡ *suspicion, conjecture* 1 Ti 6: 4.*

ὑποπιάζω a variant spelling of ὑπωπιάζω.

ὑποπλέω *sail under the lee of* an island Ac 27: 4, 7.*

ὑποπνεύσας 1 aor. act. participle of ὑποπνέω.

ὑποπνέω *blow gently* Ac 27: 13.*

ὑποπόδιον, ου, τό *footstool* Lk 20: 43; Ac 2: 35; Hb 1: 13.

ὑπόστασις, εως, ἡ—1. *substantial nature, essence, actual being, reality* Hb 1: 3.—2. *confidence, conviction, assurance, steadfastness* 2 Cor 9: 4; 11: 17; Hb 3: 14; 11: 1.*

ὑποστέλλω—1. act. *draw back, withdraw* Gal 2: 12.—2. mid. *draw back in fear* Hb 10: 38. *Shrink from, avoid* Ac 20: 27. *Keep silent about* 20: 20.*

ὑποστολή, ῆς, ἡ *shrinking, timidity* Hb 10: 39.*

ὑποστρέφω *turn back, return* Lk 1: 56; 4: 14; Ac 8: 25, 28; 12: 25; Gal 1: 17; Hb 7: 1; *turn away* 2 Pt 2: 21.

ὑποστρωννύω *spread out underneath* Lk 19: 36.*

ὑποταγή, ῆς, ἡ *subjection, subordination, obedience, submission* 2 Cor 9: 13; Gal 2: 5; 1 Ti 2: 11; 3: 4.*

ὑποτάσσω *subject, subordinate*—1. act. 1 Cor 15: 27a, c, 28c; Eph 1: 22; Hb 2: 5, 8a.—2. pass. *become subject* Ro 8: 20a; 1 Cor 15: 27b, 28a; Hb 2: 8c. *Subject oneself, be subjected* or *subordinated, obey* Lk 2: 51;

10: 17, 20; 1 Cor 14: 34; 15: 28b; 16: 16.

ὑποτίθημι act. *lay down, risk* Ro 16: 4; mid. *suggest*, or *order*, or *teach* 1 Ti 4: 6.*

ὑποτρέχω *run* or *sail under the lee of* Ac 27: 16.*

ὑποτύπωσις, εως, ἡ *model, example, prototype* 1 Ti 1: 16; *standard* 2 Ti 1: 13.*

ὑποφέρω *bear* (*up under*), *submit to, endure* 1 Cor 10: 13; 2 Ti 3: 11; 1 Pt 2: 19.*

ὑποχωρέω *retreat, withdraw, retire* Lk 5: 16; 9: 10.*

ὑπωπιάζω *strike under the eye*—1. lit., in a weakened sense *annoy greatly, wear out* Lk 18: 5.—2. fig. *treat roughly, torment, maltreat* 1 Cor 9: 27.*

ὗς, ὑός, ἡ *the female of the swine, sow* 2 Pt 2: 22.*

ὑσσός, οῦ, ὁ *javelin* J 19: 29 v.l.*

ὕσσωπος, ου, ἡ and ὁ also ὕσσωπον, τό *the hyssop*, a small bush with highly aromatic leaves, used in purification J 19: 29; Hb 9: 19.*

ὑστερέω—1. act.—a. *come too late, miss, be excluded* Hb 4: 1; 12: 15.—b. *be in need of, lack* Lk 22: 35.—c. *be less than, be inferior to* w. gen. of comparison 2 Cor 11: 5; 12: 11. *Be inferior, lack* Mt 19: 20; 1 Cor 12: 24.—d. *fail, give out, lack* J 2: 3. ἕν σε ὑστερεῖ *you lack one thing* Mk 10: 21.—2. pass. *lack, be lacking, go without* Lk 15: 14; Ro 3: 23; 1 Cor 1: 7; 8: 8; 12: 24; 2 Cor 11: 9; Phil 4: 12; Hb 11: 37.*

ὑστέρημα, ατος, τό—1. *need, want, deficiency* Lk 21: 4; 2 Cor 8: 14; 9: 12; 11: 9; Col 1: 24. *Absence* 1 Cor 16: 17; Phil 2: 30.—2. *shortcoming* 1 Th 3: 10.*

ὑστέρησις, εως, ἡ *need, lack, poverty* Mk 12: 44; Phil 4: 11.*

ὕστερος, α, ον used as a comparative and superlative—1. as

adj., comp. *latter, second* Mt 21: 31. Superl. *last* 1 Ti 4: 1, though *later* is also possible.—**2.** neut. ὕστερον as adv., comp. *in the second place, later, then, thereafter* Mt 21: 30, 32; Mk 16: 14; J 13: 36; Hb 12: 11. Superl. *finally* Mt 21: 37; 26: 60; Lk 20: 32; *last* Mt 22: 27.

ὑφαίνω *weave* Lk 12: 27.*

ὑφαντός, ή, όν *woven* J 19: 23.*

ὑψηλός, ή, όν *high*—**1.** lit. Mt 4: 8; Rv 21: 10, 12; *uplifted* Ac 13: 17. Comparative ὑψηλότερος Hb 7: 26.—**2.** fig. *exalted, proud, haughty* Lk 16: 15; Ro 11: 20; 12: 16.

ὑψηλοφρονέω *be proud, haughty* 1 Ti 6: 17; Ro 11: 20 v.l.*

ὕψιστος, η, ον *highest, most exalted*—**1.** in a spatial sense Mt 21: 9; Mk 11: 10; Lk 2: 14; 19: 38.—**2.** *the Most High*, i.e. God Mk 5: 7; Lk 1: 32, 35, 76; 6: 35; 8: 28; Ac 7: 48; 16: 17; Hb 7: 1.*

ὕψος, ους, τό *height*—**1.** lit. Eph 3: 18; Rv 21: 16. *High place, heaven* Lk 1: 78; 24: 49; Eph 4: 8.—**2.** of rank *high position* Js 1: 9.*

ὑψόω *lift up, raise high*—**1.** lit. Lk 10: 15; J 3: 14; Ac 2: 33.— **2.** fig. *exalt* Mt 23: 12; Lk 1: 52; Ac 5: 31; 2 Cor 11: 7; Js 4: 10; *make great* Ac 13: 17.

ὕψωμα, ατος, τό *height, exaltation* Ro 8: 39. *That which rises up, pride* 2 Cor 10: 5.*

Φ

φαγεῖν, φάγομαι 2 aor. act. inf., fut. mid. ind. of ἐσθίω.

φάγος, ου, ὁ *glutton* Mt 11: 19; Lk 7: 34.*

φαιλόνης, ου, ὁ *cloak* 2 Ti 4: 13.*

φαίνω—**1.** act., intrans. *shine, give light, be bright* J 1: 5; 5: 35; 2 Pt 1: 19; Rv 1: 16; 8: 12; 18: 23; 21: 23.—**2.** φαίνομαι— **a.** *shine, flash* Mt 24: 27; Phil 2: 15.—**b.** *appear, be or become visible, be revealed* Mt 9: 33; 24: 30; Hb 11: 3; Js 4: 14; 1 Pt 4: 18.—**c.** *appear, make one's appearance, show oneself* Mt 1: 20; 6: 5, 16, 18; Mk 16: 9; Lk 9: 8.—**d.** *appear as something, appear to be something* Mt 23: 27f; Lk 24: 11; 2 Cor 13: 7. *Be recognized* Ro 7: 13.— **e.** *have the appearance, seem* Mk 14: 64.

Φάλεκ, ὁ indecl. *Peleg* Lk 3: 35.*

φανεῖται fut. mid. ind., 3 sing. of φαίνω.

φανερός, ά, όν—**1.** adj. *visible, clear, plainly to be seen, plain, known* Mt 12: 16; Mk 6: 14; Ac 4: 16; Ro 1: 19; 1 Cor 3: 13; Gal 5: 19; Phil 1: 13; 1 J 3: 10. —**2.** τὸ φανερόν subst. *public notice, the open* Mk 4: 22; Mt 6: 4 v.l., 6 v.l. ἐν τῷ φ. *outwardly* Ro 2: 28.

φανερόω *reveal, make known, show* Mk 4: 22; J 7: 4; 17: 6; 21: 14; Ro 1: 19; 3: 21; 2 Cor 2: 14; 5: 10f; Eph 5: 13f; 1 Ti 3: 16; Tit 1: 3; Hb 9: 8, 26; 1 J 1: 2; 2: 28.

φανερῶς adv. *openly, publicly* Mk 1: 45; J 7: 10; Ac 10: 3.*

φανέρωσις, εως, ἡ *disclosure, announcement* 1 Cor 12: 7; 2 Cor 4: 2.*

φανός, οῦ, ὁ *lantern* J 18: 3.*

Φανουήλ, ὁ indecl. *Phanuel* Lk 2: 36.*

φαντάζω *make visible*, pass. *become visible, appear* τὸ φανταζόμενον sight, spectacle Hb 12: 21.*

φαντασία, ας, ἡ pomp, pageantry Ac 25: 23.*

φάντασμα, ατος, τό apparition, ghost Mt 14: 26; Mk 6: 49; Lk 24: 37 v.l.*

φανῶ 2 aor. pass. of φαίνω.

φάραγξ, αγγος, ἡ ravine, valley Lk 3: 5.*

Φαραώ, ὁ indecl. Pharaoh, title of the Egyptian kings, then a proper name Ac 7: 10, 13, 21; Ro 9: 17; Hb 11: 24.*

Φαρές, ὁ indecl. Perez Mt 1: 3; Lk 3: 33.*

Φαρισαῖος, ου, ὁ Pharisee, lit. 'separatist,' member of a Jewish sect that interpreted the Torah with great strictness and urged Jews to keep it zealously Mt 3: 7; 5: 20; 9: 11, 34; 23: 26; Mk 2: 16; 3: 6; Lk 7: 36f, 39; Ac 23: 6–9; 26: 5; Phil 3: 5.

φαρμακεία, ας, ἡ sorcery, magic Gal 5: 20; Rv 9: 21; 18: 23.*

φαρμακεύς, έως, ὁ mixer of poisons, magician Rv 21: 8 v.l.*

φάρμακον, ου, τό magic potion, charm Rv 9: 21 v.l.*

φάρμακος, ου, ὁ magician Rv 21: 8; 22: 15.*

φάσις, εως, ἡ report, news Ac 21: 31.*

φάσκω say, assert, claim Ac 24: 9; 25: 19; Ro 1: 22; Rv 2: 2 v.l.*

φάτνη, ης, ἡ manger, stall Lk 2: 7, 12, 16; 13: 15.*

φαῦλος, η, ον worthless, bad, evil, base J 3: 20; 5: 29; Ro 9: 11; 2 Cor 5: 10; Tit 2: 8; Js 3: 16.*

φέγγος, ους, τό light, radiance Mt 24: 29; Mk 13: 24; Lk 11: 33.*

φείδομαι—1. spare w. gen. Ac 20: 29; Ro 8: 32; 11: 21; 1 Cor 7: 28; 2 Cor 1: 23; 13: 2; 2 Pt 2: 4f.—2. refrain from 2 Cor 12: 6.*

φειδομένως adv. sparingly 2 Cor 9: 6.*

φελόνης an alternative spelling for φαιλόνης.

φέρω—1. bear, carry—a. lit. and fig. Lk 23: 26; Hb 1: 3.—b. bear patiently, endure, put up with Ro 9: 22; Hb 12: 20; 13: 13.— c. bring with one, bring along Lk 24: 1; J 19: 39.—2. bear, produce Mt 7: 18; J 12: 24; 15: 2, 4f.—3. move out of position, drive lit. Ac 27: 15, 17; rush 2: 2. Fig. be moved 2 Pt 1: 21b; move on Hb 6: 1.—4. bring (on), produce—a. bring (to), fetch Mt 14: 11, 18; Mk 6: 27f; 11: 2, 7; J 4: 33; Ac 4: 34, 37; 14: 13; Rv 21: 24, 26.—b. bring, utter, make J 18: 29; 2 Pt 1: 17f; 2: 11; 2 J 10; be established Hb 9: 16. Reach out J 20: 27.— c. bring or lead Mk 1: 32; 7: 32; 15: 22; Lk 5: 18; J 21: 18; Ac 5: 16.—d. of a gate, lead somewhere Ac 12: 10.

φεύγω—1. lit. flee, seek safety in flight Mt 8: 33; Mk 14: 50; 16: 8; Lk 21: 21; J 10: 5, 12; Ac 27: 30; Js 4: 7; Rv 9: 6.— 2. escape Mt 23: 33; Lk 3: 7; Hb 11: 34; 12: 25 v.l.—3. flee from, avoid, shun 1 Cor 6: 18; 10: 14; 1 Ti 6: 11; 2 Ti 2: 22.— 4. vanish, disappear Rv 16: 20; 20: 11.

Φῆλιξ, ικος, ὁ Antonius Felix, a freedman prominent in the reign of the Emperor Claudius; he was procurator of Palestine about 52–60 AD. Ac 23: 24, 26; 24: 3, 22, 24f, 27; 25: 14.*

φήμη, ης, ἡ report, news Mt 9: 26; Lk 4: 14.*

φημί—1. say, affirm Mt 8: 8; 13: 29; Mk 9: 12; Lk 7: 44; J 9: 38; Ac 8: 36; 25: 5, 22; 1 Cor 6: 16; 2 Cor 10: 10; Hb 8: 5.—2. mean by one's statement Ro 3: 8; 1 Cor 7: 29; 10: 15, 19; 15: 50.

φημίζω spread (a report) by word of mouth Mt 28: 15 v.l.; Ac 13: 43 v.l.*

Φῆστος, ου, ὁ Porcius Festus, successor to Felix (see Φῆλιξ) as procurator of Palestine; the date of his death was probably in the early 60's. Ac 24: 27; 25: 1, 4, 9, 12–14, 22–24; 26: 24f, 32.*

φθάνω—1. come before, precede 1 Th 4: 15.—**2.** arrive, come Mt 12: 28; Lk 11: 20; Ro 9: 31; 2 Cor 10: 14; Phil 3: 16; 1 Th 2: 16.*

φθαρῇ 2 aor. pass. subj., 3 sing., of φθείρω.

φθαρήσομαι 2 fut. pass. ind. of φθείρω.

φθαρτός, ή, όν perishable 1 Cor 9: 25; 15: 53f; 1 Pt 1: 18, 23; mortal Ro 1: 23.*

φθέγγομαι speak, utter, proclaim Ac 4: 18; 2 Pt 2: 16, 18.*

φθείρω ruin, corrupt, spoil 1 Cor 3: 17a; 15: 33; 2 Cor 7: 2; Eph 4: 22; 2 Pt 2: 12; Jd 10; Rv 19: 2; pass. be led astray 2 Cor 11: 3.—Destroy 1 Cor 3: 17b.*

φθινοπωρινός, ή, όν belonging to late autumn Jd 12.*

φθόγγος, ου, ὁ sound, tone Ro 10: 18; 1 Cor 14: 7.*

φθονέω envy, be jealous of w. dat. Gal 5: 26; cf. Js 4: 2 v.l.*

φθόνος, ου, ὁ envy, jealousy Mt 27: 18; Ro 1: 29; Gal 5: 21; 1 Ti 6: 4; Tit 3: 3; Js 4: 5.

φθορά, ᾶς, ἡ ruin, destruction, dissolution, corruption Ro 8: 21; 1 Cor 15: 42, 50; Gal 6: 8; Col 2: 22; 2 Pt 2: 12; depravity 2 Pt 1: 4; 2: 19.*

φιάλη, ης, ἡ bowl Rv 5: 8; 16: 1–4, 8, 10, 12, 17.

φιλάγαθος, ον loving what is good Tit 1: 8.*

Φιλαδέλφεια, ας, ἡ Philadelphia a city in west central Asia Minor Rv 1: 11; 3: 7.*

φιλαδελφία, ας, ἡ brotherly love fig. Ro 12: 10; 1 Th 4: 9; Hb 13: 1; 1 Pt 1: 22; 2 Pt 1: 7.*

φιλάδελφος, ον loving one's brother 1 Pt 3: 8.*

φίλανδρος, ον loving her husband Tit 2: 4.* ⟍

φιλανθρωπία, ας, ἡ love for mankind, kindness Tit 3: 4; hospitality Ac 28: 2.*

φιλανθρώπως adv. benevolently, kindly Ac 27: 3.*

φιλαργυρία, ας, ἡ love of money, avarice 1 Ti 6: 10.*

φιλάργυρος, ον fond of money, avaricious Lk 16: 14; 2 Ti 3: 2.*

φίλαυτος, ον loving oneself, selfish 2 Ti 3: 2.*

φιλέω—1. love, have affection for, like Mt 6: 5; 10: 37; 23: 6; Lk 20: 46; J 5: 20; 11: 3, 36; 12: 25; 15: 19; 16: 27; 20: 2; 21: 15–17 (see ἀγαπάω 1); 1 Cor 16: 22; Tit 3: 15; Rv 3: 19; 22: 15.—**2.** kiss Mt 26: 48; Mk 14: 44; Lk 22: 47.*

φίλη, ης, ἡ see φίλος 2.

φιλήδονος, ον loving pleasure 2 Ti 3: 4.*

φίλημα, ατος, τό a kiss Lk 7: 45; 22: 48; Ro 16: 16; 1 Cor 16: 20; 2 Cor 13: 12; 1 Th 5: 26; 1 Pt 5: 14.*

Φιλήμων, ονος, ὁ Philemon, a Christian who probably lived at Colossae; owner of the slave Onesimus Phlm 1; subscr. and title.*

Φίλητος, ου, ὁ Philetus 2 Ti 2: 17.*

φιλία, ας, ἡ friendship, love Js 4: 4.*

Φιλιππήσιος, ου, ὁ the man from Philippi, the Philippian Phil 4: 15; title.*

Φίλιπποι, ων, οἱ Philippi, a city in Macedonia, location of the first Christian church founded in Europe Ac 16: 12; 20: 6; Phil 1: 1; 1 Th 2: 2; 1 and 2 Cor subscr.*

Φίλιππος, ου, ὁ Philip—**1.** son of Herod I; he was tetrarch of several districts northeast of Palestine; died 33/34 AD. Mt 16: 13; Mk 8: 27.—**2.** the first husband of Herodias Mt 14: 3; Mk 6: 17.—**3.** one of the twelve apostles Mt 10: 3; Mk 3: 18; Lk 6: 14; J 1: 43–46, 48; 6: 5, 7; 12: 21f; 14: 8f; Ac 1: 13.— 4. one of the seven 'deacons' in Jerusalem Ac 6: 5; 8: 5–13, 26–40; also an evangelist 21: 8f.

φιλόθεος, ον loving God 2 Ti 3: 4.*

Φιλόλογος, ου, ὁ Philologus Ro 16: 15.*

φιλον(ε)ικία, ας, ἡ dispute, strife Lk 22: 24.*

φιλόν(ε)ικος, ον quarrelsome, contentious 1 Cor 11: 16.*

φιλοξενία, ας, ἡ hospitality Ro 12: 13; Hb 13: 2.*

φιλόξενος, ον hospitable 1 Ti 3: 2; Tit 1: 8; 1 Pt 4: 9.*

φιλοπρωτεύω wish to be first, like to be leader 3 J 9.*

φίλος, η, ον—1. adj. kindly disposed, devoted Ac 19: 31.— 2. subst.—a. ὁ φίλος the friend Mt 11: 19; Lk 7: 6; 11: 6, 8; 16: 9; 21: 16; 23: 12; J 15: 13–15; Ac 10: 24; 27: 3; Js 2: 23; 4: 4; 3 J 15.—b. ἡ φίλη the (woman) friend Lk 15: 9.

φιλοσοφία, ας, ἡ philosophy Col 2: 8.*

φιλόσοφος, ου, ὁ philosopher Ac 17: 18.*

φιλόστοργος, ον loving dearly, devoted Ro 12: 10.*

φιλότεκνος, ον loving one's children Tit 2: 4.*

φιλοτιμέομαι have as one's ambition, consider it an honor, aspire Ro 15: 20; 2 Cor 5: 9; 1 Th 4: 11.*

φιλοφρόνως adv. in a friendly manner, hospitably Ac 28: 7.*

φιλόφρων, ον, gen. ονος well-disposed, friendly, kind 1 Pt 3: 8 v.l.*

φιμόω muzzle—1. lit. 1 Ti 5: 18; 1 Cor 9: 9 v.l.—2. fig. (put to) silence Mt 22: 34; 1 Pt 2: 15. Pass. be silenced, be silent Mt 22: 12; Mk 1: 25; 4: 39; Lk 4: 35.*

φιμώθητι 1 aor. pass. imperative of φιμόω.

φλαγελλόω = φραγελλόω Mk 15: 15 v.l.*

Φλέγων Phlegon Ro 16: 14.*

φλογίζω set on fire Js 3: 6.*

φλόξ, φλογός flame Lk 16: 24; 2 Th 1: 8; Rv 1: 14.

φλυαρέω talk nonsense about, bring unjustified charges against 3 J 10.*

φλύαρος, ον gossipy, foolish 1 Ti 5: 13.*

φοβερός, ά, όν fearful, terrible, frightful Hb 10: 27, 31; 12: 21.*

φοβέω only pass. **φοβέομαι**— 1. be afraid, aor. often become frightened—a. intrans. Mt 1: 20; 9: 8; 17: 6f; Mk 5: 36; 16: 8; Lk 2: 9f; 12: 4, 7; Ac 16: 38; 23: 10; Gal 4: 11.—b. trans. fear something or someone Mt 10: 26; Mk 6: 20; 11: 32; Lk 12: 5; 22: 2; J 9: 22; Ac 5: 26; Ro 13: 3; Gal 2: 12; Hb 11: 23, 27.—2. fear in the sense reverence, respect Lk 1: 50; 18: 2, 4; Ac 10: 2, 22, 35; 13: 16, 26; Col 3: 22; 1 Pt 2: 17; Rv 11: 18; 14: 7; 19: 5.

φόβητρον and **φόβηθρον, ου, τό** terrible sight or event, horror Lk 21: 11.*

φόβος, ου, ὁ—1. the causing of fear, that which arouses fear, a terror Ro 13: 3; 1 Pt 3: 14; perhaps 2 Cor 5: 11 (see below). —2. in a passive sense—a. fear, alarm, fright Mt 28: 4, 8; Lk 1: 12, 65; J 7: 13; Ac 5: 5, 11; 2 Cor 7: 5, 11, 15; 1 Ti 5: 20; Hb 2: 15; 1 Pt 1: 17.—Slavish fear Ro 8: 15; 1 J 4: 18.— b. reverence, respect Ac 9: 31; Ro 3: 18; 13: 7; 2 Cor 7: 1, perhaps 5: 11; Eph 5: 21; 6: 5; Phil 2: 12; 1 Pt 2: 18; 3: 2, 16.

Φοίβη, ης, ἡ Phoebe Ro 16: 1.*

Φοινίκη, ης, ἡ Phoenicia, the seacoast of central Syria; Tyre and Sidon were its most important cities. Ac 11: 19; 15: 3; 21: 2.*

Φοινίκισσα see Συροφοινίκισσα.

I. φοῖνιξ or **φοίνιξ, ικος, ὁ** *the palm-tree, the date-palm*—**1.** *the tree as such* J 12: 13.—**2.** *palm-branch, palm-leaf* Rv 7: 9.*

II. Φοῖνιξ, ικος, ὁ *Phoenix*, a *seaport city on the south coast of Crete* Ac 27: 12.*

φονεύς, έως, ὁ *murderer* Mt 22: 7; Ac 3: 14; 1 Pt 4: 15; Rv 22: 15.

φονεύω (*commit*) *murder, kill* Mt 5: 21; 19: 18; 23: 31, 35; Ro 13: 9; Js 4: 2; 5: 6.

φόνος, ου, ὁ *murder, killing* Mk 7: 21; 15: 7; Lk 23: 19; Ac 9: 1; Ro 1: 29.

φορέω *bear* (*regularly*), *wear*—**1.** lit. Mt 11: 8; J 19: 5; Ro 13: 4; Js 2: 3.—**2.** fig. 1 Cor 15: 49.*

φόρον, ου, τό see Ἀππίου φόρον.

φόρος, ου, ὁ *tribute, tax* Lk 20: 22; 23: 2; Ro 13: 6f.*

φορτίζω *load, burden,* with double acc. *cause someone to carry something* Lk 11: 46. Perf. pass. participle πεφορτισμένοι *those who are burdened* Mt 11: 28.*

φορτίον, ου, τό *burden, load*—**1.** lit. *cargo* Ac 27: 10.—**2.** fig. Mt 11: 30; 23: 4; Lk 11: 46; Gal 6: 5.*

φόρτος, ου, ὁ *cargo* Ac 27: 10 v.l.*

Φορτουνᾶτος, ου, ὁ (Latin name) *Fortunatus*, a Christian of Corinth 1 Cor 16: 15 v.l., 17; subscr.*

φραγέλλιον, ου, τό (Latin loanword: flagellum) *whip, lash* J 2: 15.*

φραγελλόω (Latin loanword: flagello) *flog, scourge* Mt 27: 26; Mk 15: 15.*

φραγῆ, φραγήσομαι 2 aor. pass. subj., 3 sing., and 2 fut. pass. ind. of φράσσω.

φραγμός, οῦ, ὁ *fence, wall, hedge*—**1.** lit. Mt 21: 33; Mk 12: 1; Lk 14: 23.—**2.** fig. *barrier* Eph 2: 14.*

φράζω *explain, interpret* Mt 13: 36 v.l.; 15: 15.*

φράσον 1 aor. act. imperative of φράζω.

φράσσω *shut, close, stop*—**1.** lit. Hb 11: 33.—**2.** fig. *silence* Ro 3: 19; 2 Cor 11: 10.*

φρέαρ, ατος, τό *a well* Lk 14: 5; J 4: 11f. *Pit, shaft* Rv 9: 1f.*

φρεναπατάω *deceive* Gal 6: 3.*

φρεναπάτης, ου, ὁ *deceiver, misleader* Tit 1: 10.*

φρήν, φρενός, ἡ pl. *thinking, understanding* 1 Cor 14: 20.*

φρίσσω *shudder* from fear Js 2: 19.*

φρονέω—**1.** *think, hold* or *form an opinion, judge* Ac 28: 22; Ro 11: 20; 12: 3a, 16a; 15: 5; 1 Cor 13: 11; 2 Cor 13: 11; Gal 5: 10; Phil 1: 7; 2: 2; 3: 15; 4: 2, 10.—**2.** *set one's mind on, be intent on* Mt 16: 23; Mk 8: 33; Ro 8: 5; 12: 3b, 16b; Phil 3: 19; Col 3: 2; *observe* Ro 14: 6.—**3.** *have thoughts* or *attitudes, be minded* or *disposed* Phil 2: 5.

φρόνημα, ατος, τό *aim, aspiration, striving* Ro 8: 6f, 27.*

φρόνησις, εως, ἡ—**1.** *way of thinking,* (*frame of*) *mind* Lk 1: 17.—**2.** *understanding, insight, intelligence* Eph 1: 8.*

φρόνιμος, ον *sensible, thoughtful, prudent, wise* Mt 7: 24; 10: 16; 24: 45; 25: 2, 4, 8f; Lk 12: 42; Ro 11: 25; 12: 16; 1 Cor 4: 10; 10: 15; 2 Cor 11: 19. Comp. φρονιμώτερος *shrewder* Lk 16: 8.*

φρονίμως adv. *wisely, shrewdly* Lk 16: 8.*

φροντίζω *be careful* or *concerned* Tit 3: 8.*

φρουρέω—**1.** *guard* 2 Cor 11: 32.—**2.** *hold in custody, confine* Gal 3: 23.—**3.** *guard, protect, keep* Phil 4: 7; 1 Pt 1: 5.*

φρυάσσω *be arrogant, haughty, insolent* Ac 4: 25.*

φρύγανον, ου, τό *thin, dry wood, brushwood* Ac 28: 3.*

Φρυγία, ας, ἡ *Phrygia,* a large

district in Central Asia Minor Ac
2: 10; 16: 6; 18: 23; 1 Ti subscr.*
φυγαδεύω—1. trans. *cause to
become a fugitive, banish from the
country* Ac 7: 29 v.l. (ms. E).—
2. intrans. *be a fugitive, live in
exile* Ac 7: 29 v.l. (ms. D).*
Φύγελος, or **Φύγελλος, ου, ὁ**
Phygelus 2 Ti 1: 15.*
φυγή, ῆς, ἡ *flight* Mt 24: 20;
Mk 13: 18 v.l.*
φυείς 2 aor. pass. participle of φύω.
φυλακή, ῆς, ἡ *a watch, guard—*
1. *guarding, watch* as an action
Lk 2: 8.—**2.** *guard, sentinel* as a
person Ac 12: 10.—**3.** *prison,* the
place of guarding Mt 5: 25;
25: 36, 39, 43f; Mk 6: 17; Lk 12:
58; 22: 33; J 3: 24; Ac 5: 19,
22; 12: 4, 6, 17; 22: 4; Hb 11:
36; 1 Pt 3: 19. *Haunt* Rv 18: 2.
—**4.** *a watch (of the night);* the
time between 6 p.m. and 6 a.m.
was divided into four *watches* of
three hours each Mt 14: 25;
24: 43; Mk 6: 48; Lk 12: 38 (the
watches are named in Mk 13:
35).
φυλακίζω *imprison* Ac 22: 19.*
φυλακτήριον, ου, τό *phylactery,*
a small box containing scripture
verses, bound on forehead and
arm by Jews during prayer (see
Deut 6: 8) Mt 23: 5.*
φύλαξ, ακος, ὁ *guard, sentinel*
Mt 27: 65 v.l.; Ac 5: 23; 12: 6,
19.*
φυλάσσω—1. act. *watch, guard,
defend—*a. φυλάσσειν φυλακάς
keep watch Lk 2: 8.—**b.** *guard*
someone to prevent him from
escaping Lk 8: 29; Ac 12: 4;
23: 35; 28: 16.—**c.** *guard,
protect, keep* Lk 11: 21; J 12:
25; Ac 22: 20; 2 Ti 1: 12, 14;
2 Pt 2: 5; Jd 24.—**d.** *keep,
observe, follow* a law, etc. Lk 18:
21; J 12: 47; Ac 7: 53; Ro 2: 26;
Gal 6: 13; 1 Ti 5: 21.—**2.** mid.
—**a.** *(be on one's) guard against,
look out for, avoid* Lk 12: 15;

Ac 21: 25; 2 Ti 4: 15; 2 Pt 3:
17.—**b.** *keep, observe, follow,* as
the act. in 1d above Mt 19:
20 v.l.; Mk 10: 20; Lk 18: 21 v.l.
φυλή, ῆς, ἡ—1. *tribe* Lk 2: 36;
22: 30; Phil 3: 5; Hb 7: 13f;
Js 1: 1; Rv 7: 4–8.—**2.** *nation,
people* Mt 24: 30; Rv 5: 9; 11: 9;
14: 6.
φύλλον, ου, τό *leaf* Mt 24: 32;
Mk 11: 13; Rv 22: 2.
φύραμα, ατος, τό *that which is
mixed* or *kneaded, (a lump* or
batch of) dough Ro 11: 16; 1 Cor
5: 6f; Gal 5: 9. *Lump* of clay
Ro 9: 21.*
φυσικός, ή, όν *belonging to nature
—1. natural, in accordance with
nature* Ro 1: 26f.—**2.** φυσικά
creatures of instinct 2 Pt 2: 12.*
φυσικῶς adv. *naturally, by instinct* Jd 10.*
φῡσιόω *blow up, puff up, inflate*
fig. 1 Cor 8: 1. Pass. *become
puffed up* or *conceited, put on airs*
1 Cor 4: 6, 18f; 5: 2; 13: 4;
Col 2: 18.*
φύσις, εως, ἡ *nature—1. natural
endowment* or *condition* Ro 2:
27; 11: 21, 24; Gal 2: 15; Eph 2:
3.—**2.** *natural characteristics* or
disposition Gal 4: 8; 2 Pt 1: 4;
perhaps Js 3: 7b (see 4 below).
—**3.** *nature* as *the regular natural
order* Ro 1: 26; 2: 14; 1 Cor 11:
14.—**4.** *(natural) being, creature,
species, kind* Js 3: 7a; probably
3: 7b (see 2 above).*
φυσίωσις, εως, ἡ *being puffed up,
pride, conceit* 2 Cor 12: 20.*
φυτεία, ας, ἡ *a plant* Mt 15: 13.*
φυτεύω *to plant* Mt 15: 13; Mk
12: 1; Lk 13: 6; 17: 6, 28; 1 Cor
3: 6–8; 9: 7.
φύω *grow (up), come up* Lk 8: 6,
8; Hb 12: 15.*
φωλεός, οῦ, ὁ *den, lair, hole* Mt 8:
20; Lk 9: 58.*
φωνέω—1. *produce a sound—*
a. *crow* Mt 26: 34, 74f; Mk 14:
30, 68 v.l., 72; Lk 22: 34, 60f;

J 13: 38; 18: 27.—**b.** *call* or *cry
out, speak loudly* Mk 1: 26;
Lk 8: 8, 54; 23: 46; Rv 14: 18.—
2. *call* someone—**a.** in the sense
address as J 13: 13.—**b.** *call to
oneself, summon* Mt 20: 32; Mk
9: 35; 10: 49; Lk 19: 15; J 1:
48; 2: 9; 9: 18, 24; 10: 3;
Ac 9: 41.—*Invite* Lk 14: 12.
φωνή, ῆς, ἡ—1. *sound, tone, noise*
Mt 2: 18; Lk 1: 44; J 3: 8; 1 Cor
14: 7f; Rv 4: 5; 6: 1; 8: 13b;
9: 9; 10: 7; 19: 6b.—**2.** *voice*—
a. generally Mt 27: 46, 50;
Lk 17: 13, 15; 19: 37; J 5:
25, 28; Ac 7: 57; 12: 14; Hb 3:
7, 15; Rv 5: 2. *Tone* Gal 4: 20.—
b. *call, cry, outcry, loud* or
solemn declaration Mk 15: 37;
Lk 23: 23; Ac 12: 22; 13: 27;
19: 34; 2 Pt 1: 17 f.—**c.** a *voice*
speaks from heaven Mt 3: 17;
Mk 1: 11; J 12: 28; Ac 7: 31;
22: 7, 9; Rv 14: 13: 19: 5.—
d. special cases: ἐπέστρεψα
βλέπειν τὴν φωνὴν ἥτις ἐλάλει
μετ᾽ ἐμοῦ *I turned around to see*
(to whom) *the voice that was
speaking to me* (belonged) Rv 1:
12. φωνὴ βοῶντος ἐν τῇ ἐρήμῳ
*hark! someone is calling in the
desert* Mt 3: 3; Mk 1: 3; Lk 3: 4.
John the Baptist applies these
words to himself *the voice of one
calling in the desert* J 1: 23.—
3. *language* 1 Cor 14: 10f; 2 Pt 2:
16.

φῶς, φωτός, τό *light*—**1.** lit.—
a. generally Mt 17: 2; Lk 8: 16;
J 11: 10; Ac 12: 7; 2 Cor 4: 6;
6: 14; Rv 18: 23.—**b.** that which
gives light, *light* (*-bearer*) Mt 6:
23; Lk 11: 35; J 11: 9; Ac 16:
29; Js 1: 17. *Fire* Mk 14: 54;
Lk 22: 56.—**2.** *light* as the ele-
ment and sphere of the Divine
J 1: 4, 7–9; 9: 5; 12: 35f, 46;
1 Ti 6: 16; 1 J 1: 5, 7b.—**3.** fig.
Mt 4: 16; 5: 14; Lk 16: 8; J 8:
12; Ac 13: 47; 26: 18; Ro 2: 19;
13: 12; Eph 5: 13; Col 1: 12;
1 J 2: 8–10.
φωστήρ, ῆρος, ὁ *star* Phil 2:
15. *Splendor, radiance* Rv 21:
11.*
φωσφόρος, ον *bearing* or *giving
light* subst. ὁ φ. *the morning star,*
Venus, fig. 2 Pt 1: 19.*
φωτεινός, ή, όν *shining, bright,
radiant* Mt 17: 5. *Full of light,
illuminated* 6: 22; Lk 11: 34,
36.*
φωτίζω—1. intrans. *shine* Rv 22:
5.—**2.** trans.—**a.** lit. *give light
to, light* (*up*), *illuminate* Lk 11:
36; Rv 18: 1; 21: 23; 22: 5 v.l.—
b. fig. *enlighten, shed light upon*
J 1: 9; Eph 1: 18; 3: 9 v.l.;
Hb 6: 4; 10: 32.—**c.** *bring to
light, reveal* 1 Cor 4: 5; Eph 3:
9: 2 Ti 1: 10.*
φωτισμός, οῦ, ὁ *illumination,
enlightenment, light* 2 Cor 4: 4;
bringing to light, revealing 4: 6.*

X

χαίρω—1. *rejoice, be glad* Mt 2:
10; 5: 12; Mk 14: 11; Lk 15: 32;
22: 5; J 3: 29; 16: 20, 22; Ac 5:
41; Ro 16: 19; 2 Cor 7: 9, 16;
Phil 1: 18; 3: 1; Col 1: 24.—
2. as a formula of greeting—
a. as a form of address χαῖρε,
χαίρετε *welcome, good day, hail*

(*to you*), *I am glad to see you*
Mt 26: 49; 27: 29; Mk 15: 18;
Lk 1: 28; J 19: 3; 2 J 10f; *good
morning* Mt 28: 9 and possibly
others.—**b.** elliptically at the
beginning of a letter χαίρειν
greetings Ac 15: 23; 23: 26;
Js 1: 1.

χάλαζα, ης, ἡ *hail* Rv 8: 7; 11: 19; 16: 21.*

χαλάω *let down* Mk 2: 4; Lk 5: 4f; Ac 9: 25; 27: 17, 30; 2 Cor 11: 33.*

Χαλδαῖος, ου, ὁ *Chaldaean*, an inhabitant of Chaldaea in Mesopotamia Ac 7: 4.*

χαλεπός, ή, όν *hard, difficult* 2 Ti 3: 1; *hard to deal with, violent, dangerous* Mt 8: 28.*

χαλιναγωγέω *guide with a bit and bridle* fig. *bridle, hold in check* Js 1: 26; 3: 2.*

χαλινός, οῦ, ὁ *bit, bridle* Js 3: 3; Rv 14: 20.*

χαλινόω *bridle, hold in check* Js 1: 26 v.l.*

χαλκεύς, έως, ὁ *coppersmith, blacksmith, metal worker* 2 Ti 4: 14.*

χαλκηδών, όνος, ὁ *chalcedony*, a precious stone, the exact nature of which is uncertain Rv 21: 19.*

χαλκίον, ου, τό (*copper*) *vessel, kettle* Mk 7: 4.*

χαλκολίβανον, ου, τό or χαλκολίβανος, ου, ὁ perhaps *gold ore, fine brass* or *bronze*; its exact nature is unknown Rv 1: 15; 2: 18.*

χαλκός, οῦ, ὁ *copper, brass, bronze*: the metal itself Rv 18: 12, or anything made of it: *a* (*brass*) *gong* 1 Cor 13: 1; *copper coin*, or simply *money* Mt 10: 9; Mk 6: 8; 12: 41.*

χαλκοῦς, ῆ, οῦν *made of copper, brass* or *bronze* Rv 9: 20.*

χαμαί adv. *to* or *on the ground* J 9: 6; 18: 6.*

Χανάαν, ἡ indecl. *Canaan*, the land west of the Jordan in the time of the patriarchs Ac 7: 11; 13: 19.*

Χαναναῖος, α, ον *Canaanite* (see the previous entry) Mt 15: 22.*

χαρά, ᾶς, ἡ *joy*—1. lit. Mt 28: 8; Lk 24: 41; J 16: 20–22; Ac 8: 8; Ro 14: 17; 2 Cor 7: 4; 8: 2; Gal 5: 22; Phil 1: 4, 25; Phlm 7; Hb 12: 11; Js 1: 2; 1 Pt 1: 8.

—2. fig.—a. *the person* or *thing that causes joy*, (*the object of*) *joy* Lk 2: 10; Phil 4: 1; 1 Th 2: 19f.—b. *a state of joyfulness* Mt 25: 21, 23; Hb 12: 2.

χάραγμα, ατος, τό—1. *a mark* or *stamp* Rv 13: 16f; 14: 9, 11; 15: 2 v.l.; 16: 2; 19: 20; 20: 4. —2. *a thing formed, an image* Ac 17: 29.*

χαρακτήρ, ῆρος, ὁ *reproduction,* (*exact*) *representation* Hb 1: 3.*

χάραξ, ακος, ὁ *palisade* Lk 19: 43.*

χαρῆναι, χαρήσομαι 2 aor. pass. inf., 2 fut. pass. ind. of χαίρω.

χαρίζομαι—1. *give* or *grant freely as a favor* Lk 7: 21; Ac 3: 14; 25: 11, 16; 27: 24; Ro 8: 32; 1 Cor 2: 12; Phil 1: 29; 2: 9; Phlm 22: perhaps Gal 3: 18 (see 3 below). *Dispense with, cancel* Lk 7: 42f.—2. *remit, forgive, pardon* 2 Cor 2: 7, 10; 12: 13; Eph 4: 32; Col 2: 13; 3: 13.— 3. *show oneself to be gracious* Gal 3: 18 (see 1 above).*

χάριν acc. of χάρις, used as a prep. w. gen., usually coming after the word it governs; *for the sake of, on behalf of, on account of*— 1. indicating the goal Gal 3: 19; 1 Ti 5: 14; Tit 1: 5, 11; Jd 16.— 2. indicating the reason χάριν τίνος *for what reason, why?* 1 J 3: 12. Cf. Lk 7: 47. Eph 3: 1, 14 may be classed under 1 or 2.*

χάρις, ιτος, ἡ—1. *graciousness, attractiveness* Lk 4: 22; Col 4: 6. —2. *favor, grace, gracious care* or *help, goodwill* Lk 1: 30; 2: 40, 52; Ac 2: 47; 7: 10; 14: 26; Ro 3: 24; 4: 4; 5: 20f; 11: 5f; Gal 1: 15; Eph 2: 5, 7f. *Credit* Lk 6: 32–34. *That which brings* (God's) *favor* 1 Pt 2: 19f.— (Divine) *grace* or *favor* in fixed formulas at the beginning and end of Christian letters, e.g. Ro 1: 7; 16: 20; 2 Cor 1: 2; 13: 13; 1 Th 1: 1; 5: 28; Hb 13:

25; 1 Pt 1: 2; Rv 1: 4.—**3.** *prac-tical application of goodwill, a (sign of) favor, gracious deed* or *gift, benefaction* J 1: 14, 16f; Ac 13: 43; 24: 27; 25: 3, 9; Ro 5: 2; 6: 14f; 1 Cor 16: 3; 2 Cor 1: 15; Eph 4: 29; Hb 10: 29; Js 4: 6; 1 Pt 5: 10.—**4.** of exceptional effects produced by divine grace Ro 1: 5; 12: 6; 1 Cor 15: 10 a, b; 2 Cor 8: 1; 9: 8, 14; 1 Pt 4: 10. Hardly to be differentiated from *power, knowledge, glory* Ac 6: 8; 1 Cor 15: 10c; 2 Cor 1: 12; 2 Pt 3: 18. —**5.** *thanks, gratitude* χάριν ἔχειν *be grateful* 1 Ti 1: 12; 2 Ti 1: 3; Hb 12: 28. In other expressions Ro 6: 17; 7: 25; 1 Cor 10: 30; 15: 57; 2 Cor 9: 15; Col 3: 16.

χάρισμα, ατος, τό *a gift (freely and graciously given), a favor bestowed*—**1.** generally Ro 1: 11; 5: 15f; 6: 23; 11: 29; 1 Cor 1: 7; 2 Cor 1: 11.—**2.** of special gifts bestowed on individual Christians 1 Cor 7: 7; 1 Ti 4: 14; 2 Ti 1: 6; 1 Pt 4: 10. Of *spiritual gifts* in a special sense Ro 12: 6; 1 Cor 12: 4, 9, 28, 30f.*

χαριτόω *bestow favor on, favor highly, bless* Eph 1: 6. κεχαρι-τωμένη *favored one* (in the sight of God) Lk 1: 28.*

Χαρράν, ἡ indecl. *Haran,* a place in Mesopotamia Ac 7: 2, 4.*

χάρτης, ου, ὁ *a sheet of paper,* i.e. *papyrus* 2 J 12.*

χάσμα, ατος, τό *chasm* Lk 16: 26.*

χεῖλος, ους, τό *lip*—**1.** pl. *the lips* Mt 15: 8; Mk 7: 6; Ro 3: 13; 1 Cor 14: 21; Hb 13: 15; 1 Pt 3: 10.—**2.** *shore* of the sea Hb 11: 12.*

χειμάζω *expose to bad weather, toss in a storm* Ac 27: 18.*

χείμαρρος, or **χειμάρρους, ου, ὁ** *winter torrent, ravine, wady* J 18: 1.*

χειμών, ῶνος, ὁ—**1.** *rainy and stormy weather* Mt 16: 3; Ac 27:

20.—**2.** *winter* Mt 24: 20; Mk 13: 18; J 10: 22; 2 Ti 4: 21.*

χείρ, χειρός, ἡ *hand*—**1.** lit. Mt 22: 13; Mk 3: 1; Lk 24: 39; J 20: 25; Ac 19: 26; 21: 11; 1 Cor 4: 12; Rv 9: 20; 20: 1. *Hand-writing* 1 Cor 16: 21; Gal 6: 11; Col 4: 18; 2 Th 3: 17; Phlm 19. Equivalent to *activity* Mk 6: 2; Ac 2: 23; 19: 11; Gal 3: 19. *Finger* Lk 15: 22. Perhaps *arm* Mt 4: 6; Lk 4: 11.—**2.** fig.— **a.** the *hand* of God, Christ, or an angel Lk 1: 66; J 3: 35; 10: 28f; 13: 3; Ac 7: 35, 50; 13: 11; Hb 1: 10; 10: 31.— **b.** *hostile power* Mt 17: 22; 26: 45; Lk 24: 7; J 10: 39; Ac 12: 11; 21: 11b; 2 Cor 11: 33.

χειραγωγέω *take* or *lead by the hand* Ac 9: 8; 22: 11.*

χειραγωγός, οῦ, ὁ *one who leads another by the hand, leader* Ac 13: 11.*

χειρόγραφον, ου, τό *certificate of indebtedness, bond* Col 2: 14.*

χειροποίητος, ον *made by human hands* Mk 14: 58; Ac 7: 48 v.l.; 17: 24; Eph 2: 11; Hb 9: 11, 24.*

χειροτονέω *choose* or *elect (by raising hands)* 2 Cor 8: 19. *Appoint, install* Ac 14: 23.*

χείρων, ον, gen. **ονος** comparative of κακός, *worse, more severe* Mt 27: 64; Mk 2: 21; 5: 26; Lk 11: 26; J 5: 14; 1 Ti 5: 8; 2 Ti 3: 13; Hb 10: 29.

Χερούβ, τό indecl., but pl. Χερου-βίν *cherub,* one of the two winged figures over the ark of the covenant Hb 9: 5.*

χήρα, ας, ἡ fem. of χῆρος = *bereft* (of one's spouse)—**1.** generally γυνὴ χήρα *a widow* Lk 4: 26. Subst. (ἡ)χήρα (*the*) *widow* Mk 12: 40, 42f; Lk 2: 37; 4: 25f; 20: 47; Ac 6: 1; 1 Cor 7: 8; 1 Ti 5: 3b, 4, 5, 11, 16; Js 1: 27.—**2.** of a special class in the Christian communities 1 Ti 5: 3, 9.

χθές adv., v.l. for ἐχθές *yesterday* in J 4: 52; Ac 7: 28; Hb 13: 8.*

χιζ' see χξζ'.

χιλίαρχος, ου, ὁ *military tribune,* commander of a cohort, about 600 men, roughly equivalent to major or colonel Mk 6: 21; J 18: 12; Ac 21: 31–33, 37; 23: 17–19; 25: 23; Rv 6: 15; 19: 18.

χιλιάς, άδος, ἡ (a group of) *a thousand* Lk 14: 31; Ac 4: 4; Rv 5: 11; 7: 4–8; 11: 13; 14: 1, 3.

χίλιοι, αι, α *a thousand* 2 Pt 3: 8; Rv 11: 3; 12: 6; 14: 20; the millennium 20: 2–7.*

Χίος, ου, ἡ *Chios* an island (with a city by the same name) off the west coast of Asia Minor Ac 20: 15.*

χιτών, ωνος, ὁ *tunic, shirt* a garment worn next to the skin, and by both sexes Mt 5: 40; 10: 10; Mk 6: 9; Lk 3: 11; 6: 29; 9: 3; J 19: 23; Ac 9: 39; Jd 23. Pl. *clothes* Mk 14: 63.*

χιών, όνος, ἡ *snow* Mt 28: 3; Mk 9: 3 v.l.; Rv 1: 14.*

χλαμύς, ύδος, ἡ *cloak,* used by travelers and soldiers Mt 27: 28, 31.*

χλευάζω *mock, sneer, scoff* Ac 2: 13 v.l.; 17: 32.*

χλιαρός, ά, όν *lukewarm* Rv 3: 16.*

Χλόη, ης, ἡ *Chloe* an otherwise unknown woman. οἱ Χλόης *Chloe's people* (slaves or freedmen) 1 Cor 1: 11.*

χλωρός, ά, όν—1. *yellowish green, (light) green* Mk 6: 39; Rv 8: 7; 9: 4.—2. *pale,* as of a person in sickness Rv 6: 8.*

χξζ' *six hundred sixty six* (χ' = 600, ξ' = 60, ζ' = 6). The v.l. χιζ' = 616. Rv 13: 18.*

χοϊκός, ή, όν *made of dust* or *earth, earthy* 1 Cor 15: 47–49.*

χοῖνιξ, ικος, ἡ *choenix,* a dry measure, almost = a quart Rv 6: 6.*

χοῖρος, ου, ὁ *pig, swine* Mt 7: 6; Mk 5: 11–13, 16; Lk 15: 15f.

χολάω *be angry* J 7: 23.*

χολή, ῆς, ἡ *gall, bile*—1. lit., of a bitter substance Mt 27: 34.— 2. fig. χολὴ πικρίας *bitter gall* Ac 8: 23.*

Χοραζίν, ἡ indecl. *Chorazin,* a place in Galilee Mt 11: 21; Lk 10: 13.*

χορηγέω *provide, supply* (*in abundance*) 2 Cor 9: 10; 1 Pt 4: 11.*

χορός, οῦ, ὁ (*choral*) *dance, dancing* Lk 15: 25.*

χορτάζω *feed, fill, satisfy*; pass. *eat one's fill, be satisfied* lit. Mt 14: 20; 15: 33; Mk 8: 4, 8; Lk 6: 21; J 6: 26; Phil 4: 12; Js 2: 16; Rv 19: 21. Fig. *be satisfied* Mt 5: 6.

χόρτασμα, ατος, τό *food* Ac 7: 11.*

χόρτος, ου, ὁ *grass* Mt 6: 30; 14: 19; Mk 6: 39; J 6: 10; Js 1: 10f; 1 Pt 1: 24; Rv 9: 4. *Blade, stalk* of grain Mk 4: 28. *Hay* 1 Cor 3: 12.

Χουζᾶς, ᾶ, ὁ *Chuza* Lk 8: 3.*

χοῦς, χοός, acc. χοῦν, ὁ *dust* Mk 6: 11; Rv 18: 19.*

χράομαι *use*—1. *make use of, employ*—a. w. dat. Ac 27: 17; 1 Cor 9: 12, 15; 1 Ti 5: 23; *make the most of, take advantage* (supply either τῇ δουλείᾳ or τῇ ἐλευθερίᾳ) 1 Cor 7: 21.— b. w. acc. 1 Cor 7: 31.—2. *act, proceed* 2 Cor 1: 17; 13: 10.— 3. w. dat. of the person and an adv. *treat a person in a certain way* Ac 27: 3.

χράω another form for κίχρημι.

χρεία, ας, ἡ—1. *need, necessity* Lk 10: 42; Hb 7: 11. χρείαν ἔχειν *have need* Mt 3: 14; 6: 8; Mk 11: 3; Lk 19: 31, 34; 1 Cor 12: 21, 24; Hb 5: 12; 10: 36.—2. *need, lack, want, difficulty* χρείαν ἔχειν *be in need, lack something* Mk 2: 25; Ac 2: 45; 4: 35; Eph 4: 28; Rv 3: 17.—In other expressions Ac 20: 34; Ro 12: 13; Phil 4: 16, 19.—3. *the thing that is necessary*

Eph 4: 29.—4. *office, duty, service* Ac 6: 3.

χρεοφειλέτης and χρεωφειλέτης, ου, ὁ *debtor* Lk 7: 41; 16: 5.*

χρή *it is necessary, it ought* Js 3: 10.*

χρήζω (*have*) *need* (*of*) Mt 6: 32; Lk 11: 8; Ro 16: 2; 2 Cor 3: 1.

χρῆμα, ατος, τό—1. pl. *property, wealth, means* Mk 10: 23, 24 v.l.; Lk 18: 24.—2. *money,* mostly pl. Ac 8: 18, 20; 24: 26; rarely sing. 4: 37.*

χρηματίζω—1. of God *impart a revelation* or *injunction* or *warning* Mt 2: 12, 22; Lk 2: 26 and 26 v.l.; Ac 10: 22; Hb 8: 5; 11: 7; 12: 25.—2. *bear a name, be called* or *named* Ac 11: 26; Ro 7: 3.*

χρηματισμός, οῦ, ὁ *a divine statement* or *answer* Ro 11: 4.*

χρῆσαι 1 aor. mid. imperative of χράομαι.

χρήσιμος, η, ον *useful, beneficial, advantageous* 2 Ti 2: 14; Mt 20: 28 v.l.*

χρῆσις, εως, ἡ *relations, function* Ro 1: 26f.*

χρῆσον 1 aor. act. imperative of κίχρημι.

χρηστεύομαι *be kind, loving, merciful* 1 Cor 13: 4.*

χρηστολογία, ας, ἡ *smooth, plausible speech* Ro 16: 18.*

χρηστός, ή, όν *useful, worthy, good*—1. adj.—a. of things *good, pleasant, easy* Lk 5: 39; Mt 11: 30; (*morally*) *good, reputable* 1 Cor 15: 33.—b. of persons *kind, loving, benevolent* Lk 6: 35; Eph 4: 32; 1 Pt 2: 3.—2. subst. τὸ χρηστόν *kindness* Ro 2: 4.*

χρηστότης, ητος, ἡ—1. *goodness, uprightness* ποιεῖν χρηστότητα *do what is right* Ro 3: 12.—2. *goodness, kindness, generosity* Ro 2: 4; 9: 23 v.l.; 11: 22; 2 Cor 6: 6; Gal 5: 22; Eph 2: 7; Col 3: 12; Tit 3: 4.*

χρῖσμα, ατος, τό *anointing* 1 J 2: 20, 27.*

Χριστιανός, οῦ, ὁ *the Christian* Ac 11: 26; 26: 28; 1 Pt 4: 16.*

Χριστός, οῦ, ὁ—1. as a title *the Anointed One, the Messiah, the Christ* Mt 2: 4; 16: 16; Mk 8: 29; Lk 2: 26; 4: 41; J 1: 41; 4: 25; Ac 3: 18; 5: 42; Rv 11: 15.—2. as a proper name *Christ* Mk 1: 1; 9: 41; Ac 24: 24; Ro 1: 4, 6, 8; Hb 3: 6; 1 Pt 1: 1–3.

χρίω *anoint* fig. Lk 4: 18; Ac 4: 27; 10: 38; 2 Cor 1: 21; Hb 1: 9.*

χρονίζω—1. *take time, linger, fail to come* (or *stay away*) *for a long time* Mt 24: 48; 25: 5; Hb 10: 37.—2. w. inf. following *delay, take a long time in doing something* Mt 24: 48 v.l.; Lk 12: 45. —3. *stay* (somewhere) *for a long time* Lk 1: 21.*

χρόνος, ου, ὁ *time* Mt 25: 19; Lk 8: 27; J 7: 33; Ac 1: 7; 14: 3, 28; 17: 30; Ro 16: 25; 1 Cor 16: 7; Gal 4: 4; Hb 5: 12; Rv 6: 11.— *Delay, respite* Rv 2: 21; 10: 6.

χρονοτριβέω *spend time, lose* or *waste time* Ac 20: 16.*

χρύσεος uncontracted form of χρυσοῦς.

χρυσίον, ου, τό *gold* 1 Cor 3: 12; Hb 9: 4; 1 Pt 1: 7; Rv 3: 18; 21: 18, 21.—*Gold ornaments, jewelry* 1 Ti 2: 9; 1 Pt 3: 3; Rv 17: 4; 18: 16.—*Coined gold* Ac 3: 6; 20: 33; 1 Pt 1: 18.*

χρυσοδακτύλιος, ον *with a gold ring* (or *rings*) *on one's finger*(*s*) Js 2: 2.*

χρυσόλιθος, ου, ὁ *chrysolite,* the yellow topaz Rv 21: 20.*

χρυσόπρασος, ου, ὁ *chrysoprase,* an apple-green quartz Rv 21:21.*

χρυσός, οῦ, ὁ *gold* Mt 2: 11; 10: 9; 23: 16f; Ac 17: 29; Rv 9: 7; 18: 12.

χρυσοῦς, ῆ, οῦν *golden, made of* or *adorned with gold* 2 Ti 2: 20; Hb 9: 4; Rv 1: 12f, 20; 9: 13, 20; 21: 15.

χρυσόω *gild, adorn with gold* Rv 17: 4; 18: 16.*

χρώς, χρωτός, ὁ *skin, surface of the body* Ac 19: 12.*

χωλός, ή, όν *lame, crippled* Mt 11: 5; 15: 30f; Mk 9: 45; Lk 14: 13, 21; J 5: 3; Ac 3: 2; 14: 8. τὸ χωλόν *the lame leg(s)* Hb 12: 13.

χώρα, ας, ἡ *country, land*—**1.** *district, region, place* Mt 8: 28; Mk 6: 55; Lk 15: 13–15; Ac 10: 39; 13: 49; 16: 6; 26: 20.— **2.** *the (open) country* in contrast to the city J 11: 55; Ac 8: 1.— **3.** *(dry) land* in contrast to the sea Ac 27: 27.—**4.** *field, cultivated land* pl. Lk 21: 21; J 4: 35; Js 5: 4. Sing. *land, farm* Lk 12: 16.—**5.** ἐν χώρᾳ καὶ σκιᾷ θανάτου *in the land of the shadow of death* Mt 4: 16.

Χωραζίν see Χοραζίν.

χωρέω *make room, give way*— **1.** *go, go out* or *away* lit. Mt 15: 17; 20: 28 v.l. Fig. *come* 2 Pt 3: 9.—**2.** *go forward, make progress* J 8: 37, though *find place* is also possible.—**3.** *have room for, hold, contain*—**a.** lit. J 2: 6; 21: 25. μηκέτι χωρεῖν *there was no longer any room* Mk 2: 2.— **b.** fig. χωρήσατε ἡμᾶς *make room for us* 2 Cor 7: 2.—*Grasp, understand, comprehend, accept* Mt 19: 11f.*

χωρίζω—**1.** act. *divide, separate* Mt 19: 6; Mk 10: 9; Ro 8: 35, 39.—**2.** pass. *separate (oneself), be separated* of divorce 1 Cor 7: 10f, 15.—*Be taken away, take one's departure, go away* Ac 1: 4; 18: 1f; Phlm 15.—In Hb 7: 26 κεχωρισμένος means not only that Christ is *separated* from sinful men, but that he is also *different* from them.*

χωρίον, ου, τό *place, piece of land, field* Mt 26: 36; Mk 14: 32; J 4: 5; Ac 1: 18f; 4: 34, 37 v.l.; 5: 3, 8; 28: 7.*

χωρίς adv.—**1.** used as an adv. *separately, apart, by itself* J 20: 7.—**2.** as an improper prep. w. gen. *without, apart from*—**a.** w. gen. of the person *apart from someone, far from someone, without someone* J 1: 3; 15: 5; Ro 10: 14; 1 Cor 4: 8; 11: 11; Eph 2: 12.—*Besides, in addition to* Mt 14: 21; 15: 38.—**b.** w. gen. of the thing *outside (of) something* 2 Cor 12: 3.—*Without, apart from* Mt 13: 34; Lk 6: 49; Ro 3: 28; 7: 8; Phil 2: 14; Phlm 14; Hb 4: 15; 9: 28; 10: 28; Js 2: 20.—*Besides, in addition to* 2 Cor 11: 28.

χωρισμός, οῦ, ὁ *division* Ac 4: 32 v.l.*

χῶρος, ου, ὁ *the northwest* Ac 27: 12.*

Ψ

ψάλλω *sing, sing praise* Ro 15: 9; 1 Cor 14: 15; Eph 5: 19; Js 5: 13.*

ψαλμός, οῦ, ὁ *song of praise, psalm* Lk 20: 42; 24: 44; Ac 1: 20; 13: 33; 1 Cor 14: 26; Eph 5: 19; Col 3: 16.*

ψευδάδελφος, ου, ὁ *false brother* 2 Cor 11: 26; Gal 2: 4.*

ψευδαπόστολος, ου, ὁ *false apostle* 2 Cor 11: 13.*

ψευδής, ές *false, lying* Ac 6: 13; Rv 2: 2. Subst. *the liar* 21: 8.*

ψευδοδιδάσκαλος, ου, ὁ *false teacher* 2 Pt 2: 1.*

ψευδολόγος, ον *speaking falsely, lying* subst. *liar* 1 Ti 4: 2.*

ψεύδομαι—**1.** *lie, tell a falsehood* Mt 5: 11; Ac 5: 4; 14: 19 v.l.; Ro 9: 1; 2 Cor 11: 31; Gal 1: 20;

Col 3: 9; 1 Ti 2: 7; Hb 6: 18; Js 3: 14; 1 J 1: 6; Rv 3: 9.— **2.** (try to) deceive by lying, tell lies to, impose upon Ac 5: 3.*

ψευδομαρτυρέω bear false witness, give false testimony Mt 19: 18; Mk 10: 19; 14: 56f; Lk 18: 20; Ro 13: 9 v.l.*

ψευδομαρτυρία, ας, ἡ false witness Mt 15: 19; 26: 59.*

ψευδόμαρτυς, υρος, ὁ one who gives false testimony, a false witness Mt 26: 60; 1 Cor 15: 15.*

ψευδοπροφήτης, ου, ὁ false prophet Mt 7: 15; Mk 13: 22; Ac 13: 6; 1 J 4: 1; Rv 16: 13.

ψεῦδος, ους, τό lie, falsehood, lying J 8: 44; Ro 1: 25; Eph 4: 25; 2 Th 2: 9, 11; 1 J 2: 21, 27; Rv 14: 5; 21: 27; 22: 15.*

ψευδόχριστος, ου, ὁ a false Christ or Messiah Mt 24: 24; Mk 13: 22.*

ψευδώνυμος, ον falsely called 1 Ti 6: 20.*

ψεῦσμα, ατος, τό lying, untruthfulness, undependability Ro 3: 7.*

ψεύστης, ου, ὁ liar J 8: 44, 55; Ro 3: 4; 1 Ti 1: 10; Tit 1: 9 v.l., 12; 1 J 1: 10; 2: 4, 22; 4: 20; 5: 10.*

ψηλαφάω feel (about for), touch, handle, grope after Lk 24: 39; Ac 17: 27; Hb 12: 18; 1 J 1: 1.*

ψηφίζω count (up), calculate Lk 14: 28; Rv 13: 18.*

ψῆφος, ου, ἡ pebble, vote Ac 26: 10; used as an amulet Rv 2: 17.*

ψιθυρισμός, οῦ, ὁ whispering, gossip, tale-bearing 2 Cor 12: 20.*

ψιθυριστής, οῦ, ὁ whisperer, tale-bearer Ro 1: 29.*

ψίξ, χός, ἡ bit, crumb Mt 15: 27 v.l.; Lk 16: 21 v.l.*

ψιχίον, ου, τό a very little bit, crumb Mt 15: 27; Mk 7: 28; Lk 16: 21 v.l.*

ψυγήσομαι 2 fut. pass. ind. of ψύχω.

ψυχή, ῆς, ἡ soul, life; it is often impossible to draw hard and fast lines between the meanings of this many-sided word.—**1.** lit. —**a.** of life in its physical aspects —**α.** (breath of) life, life-principle, soul Lk 12: 20; Ac 2: 27; 20: 10; Rv 6: 9; 8: 9; 20: 4.—**β.** earthly life itself Mt 2: 20; 20: 28; Mk 10: 45; Lk 12: 22f; J 10: 11, 15, 17; Ac 15: 26; 27: 10, 22; Phil 2: 30; 1 J 3: 16; Rv 12: 11.—**b.** the soul as seat and center of the inner life of man in its many and varied aspects, desires, feelings, emotions Mk 14: 34; Lk 1: 46; 12: 19; J 12: 27; 1 Th 2: 8; Hb 12: 3; Rv 18: 14; heart Eph 6: 6; Col 3: 23; mind Phil 1: 27.— **c.** the soul as seat and center of life that transcends the earthly Mt 10: 28, 39; 11: 29; 16: 26; Mk 8: 35–37; 2 Cor 12: 15; Hb 6: 19; Js 1: 21; 1 Pt 1: 9; 2: 11.—**d.** ψυχή sometimes expresses a reflexive relationship and may be translated self Mt 26: 38; Mk 10: 45; J 10: 24; 2 Cor 1: 23; Rv 18: 14.—**2.** by metonymy that which possesses life or a soul, creature, person Ac 2: 41, 43; 3: 23; 27: 37; Ro 2: 9; 1 Cor 15: 45; 1 Pt 3: 20; Rv 16: 3.

ψυχικός, ή, όν pertaining to life, in this case the life of the natural world rather than the supernatural.—**1.** adj. unspiritual 1 Cor 2: 14; Js 3: 15; physical 1 Cor 15: 44.—**2.** subst. τὸ ψυχικόν the physical 1 Cor 15: 46. ψυχικοί worldly men Jd 19.*

ψῦχος, ους, τό cold J 18: 18; Ac 28: 2; 2 Cor 11: 27.*

ψυχρός, ά, όν cold—**1.** lit. Mt 10: 42 v.l. τὸ ψυχρόν cold water

10: 42.—2. fig. *cool, cold* Rv 3: 15f.*

ψύχω pass. *grow cold, be extinguished* Mt 24: 12.*

ψωμίζω *feed* Ro 12: 20. In 1 Cor 13: 3 the meaning is either *dole out* or *fritter away.**

ψωμίον, ου, τό *(small) piece* or *bit of bread* J 13: 26f, 30.*

ψώχω *rub* Lk 6: 1.*

Ω

Ω, ὦ *omega*, last letter of the Greek alphabet Rv 1: 8, 11 v.l.; 21: 6; 22: 13.*

ὦ interjection *O!* Mt 15: 28; Mk 9: 19; Ac 1: 1; Ro 2: 1, 3; 11: 33.

'Ωβήδ v.l. for 'Ιωβήδ.

ὧδε adv.—1. *here* in the sense *to this place, hither* Mt 8: 29; 22: 12; Mk 11: 3; Lk 19: 27; J 6: 25; Rv 11: 12.—2. *here* in the sense *in this place* Mt 12: 6, 41f; Mk 14: 32; Lk 4: 23; 15: 17; Ac 9: 14; Col 4: 9; Hb 13: 14.— With the local meaning weakened *in this case, on this occasion, under these circumstances* 1 Cor 4: 2; Rv 13: 10, 18; 14: 12; 17: 9. ὧδε . . . ἐκεῖ *in one case . . . in the other* Hb 7: 8.

ᾠδή, ῆς, ἡ *song* Eph 5: 19; Col 3: 16; Rv 5: 9; 14: 3; 15: 3.*

ὠδίν, ῖνος, ἡ *birth-pain(s)*—1. lit. 1 Th 5: 3.—2. symbolically Mt 24: 8; Mk 13: 8; Ac 2: 24.*

ὠδίνω *suffer birth-pangs, bear amid throes* Gal 4: 19 (fig.), 27; Rv 12: 2.*

ὦμος, ου, ὁ *shoulder* Mt 23: 4; Lk 15: 5.*

ὠνέομαι *buy* Ac 7: 16.*

ᾠόν, οῦ, τό *egg* Lk 11: 12.*

ὥρα, ας, ἡ—1. *time of day, hour* Mt 14: 15; 24: 36, 50; Mk 6: 35; 11: 11; Lk 12: 39f, 46; Rv 3: 3.—2. *hour*—a. as a (short) space of time Mt 20: 12; 26: 40; Lk 22: 59; J 5: 35; 11: 9; Ac 5: 7; 2 Cor 7: 8; Gal 2: 5; Phlm 15; Rv 9: 15; 18: 10, 17, 19.— b. as a moment of time named from the hour that has just passed. The period of daylight was divided into twelve 'hours' (more than 60 minutes each in summer, less than 60 minutes in the winter); the 'first hour' was approximately six a.m., the second was seven, and so on. Mt 20: 5, 9; Mk 15: 25; Lk 23: 44; J 1: 39; 4: 6; Ac 3: 1; 10: 30; 22: 13; 23: 23; 1 Cor 4: 11.—3. *the time* of an occurrence Mt 8: 13; 18: 1; Mk 13: 11; Lk 1: 10; 10: 21; J 2: 4; 7: 30; 12: 23; 16: 21; 19: 27; Ac 16: 33; Rv 11: 13; 14: 7, 15.

ὡραῖος, α, ον *beautiful, fair, lovely* Mt 23: 27; Ac 3: 2, 10; Ro 10: 15.*

ὠρύομαι *roar* 1 Pt 5: 8.*

ὡς adv.—I. as a comparative particle *as, like* Mt 26: 39; 27: 65; Mk 10: 15; 1 Cor 3: 15; 7: 17; 13: 11; Eph 5: 28, 33; Col 3: 18; 1 Th 5: 2; Hb 11: 29. *How* Lk 24: 35; Ro 11: 2; 2 Cor 7: 15.—II. as a conjunction denoting comparison, *as* Mt 6: 10; 13: 43; 22: 30; Mk 4: 36; Lk 3: 23; 12: 27; 15: 19; J 7: 46; Ac 23: 11; 25: 10; 1 Pt 3: 6. ὡς θάλασσα *something like a sea* Rv 4: 6. ἤκουσα ὡς φωνήν *I heard what sounded like a shout* Rv 19: 1, 6. ἀρνίον ὡς ἐσφαγμένον *a lamb that appeared to have been slaughtered* 5: 6.—III. ὡς introduces the characteristic quality of a person, thing, action, etc., *as* Lk 16: 1; 23: 14; J 1: 14;

Ro 1: 21; 3: 7; 9: 32; 1 Cor 3: 10; 4: 7; Col 3: 23; 2 Th 2: 2.— *As one who, because* Ac 28: 19; 2 Pt 1: 3.—**IV.** Other uses of ὡς—**1.** as a temporal conjunction—**a.** *when, after* Lk 1: 23, 41, 44; J 2: 9; 4: 1; Ac 5: 24; 10: 7, 25.—**b.** *while, when, as long as* Lk 12: 58; 24: 32; J 12: 35f; 20: 11; Ac 1: 10; 8: 36; 21: 27.—*Since* Mk 9: 21. —**c.** ὡς ἄν *when, as soon as* Ro 15: 24; 1 Cor 11: 34; Phil 2: 23.—**2.** as a conj. denoting result *so that* Hb 3: 11; 4: 3.— **3.** as a particle denoting purpose *in order that* Ac 20: 24; Hb 7: 9. —**4.** *that,* after verbs of knowing, saying, etc. Lk 6: 4; 24: 6; Ac 10: 28; Ro 1: 9; Phil 1: 8; 1 Th 2: 11a.—**5.** with numerals *about, approximately, nearly* Mk 5: 13; Lk 1: 56; J 6: 10, 19; Ac 13: 18, 20; Rv 8: 1.— **6.** in exclamations *how!* Ro 10: 15; 11: 33.—**7.** with the superlative ὡς τάχιστα *as quickly as possible* Ac 17: 15.

ὡσάν *as if, as it were, so to speak* 2 Cor 10: 9.*

ὡσαννά indecl. *hosanna* (Heb. or Aram. 'help' or 'save, I pray') Mt 21: 9, 15; Mk 11: 9f; J 12: 13.*

ὡσαύτως adv. (*in*) *the same (way), similarly, likewise* Mt 20: 5; Mk 12: 21; Ro 8: 26; 1 Cor 11: 25; 1 Ti 2: 9; 3: 8, 11.

ὡσεί—**1.** particle denoting comparison *as, like, something like* Mt 3: 16; 9: 36; Mk 9: 26; Lk 22: 44; Ac 2: 3; 6: 15; Ro 6: 13.—**2.** with numbers and measures *about* Mt 14: 21;

Lk 3: 23; 9: 14; 23: 44; Ac 1: 15; 19: 7.

Ὡσηέ or Ὡσῆε, ὁ indecl. *Hosea;* metonymically of his book Ro 9: 25.*

ὡσί dat. pl. of οὖς.

ὥσπερ (*just*) *as* Mt 6: 2, 7; 18: 17; 24: 27, 37; J 5: 21, 26; Ac 2: 2; Ro 5: 19; 2 Cor 8: 7; Hb 9: 25; Js 2: 26.

ὡσπερεί *like, as though, as it were* 1 Cor 4: 13 v.l.; 15: 8.*

ὥστε—**1.** introducing independent clauses *for this reason, therefore, so* Mt 12: 12; Mk 2: 28; Ro 7: 4, 12; 1 Cor 3: 7; 5: 8; 15: 58; 2 Cor 5: 16f; Gal 3: 9, 24; Phil 2: 12; 1 Th 4: 18.—**2.** introducing dependent clauses— **a.** indicating the actual result *so that* Mt 8: 24; 27: 14; Mk 1: 45; 2: 12; J 3: 16; Ac 1: 19; 2 Cor 1: 8; Gal 2: 13.—**b.** indicating the intended result *for the purpose of, with a view to, in order that* Mt 10: 1; 27: 1; Lk 4: 29; 9: 52; 20: 20.

ὦτα nom. and acc. pl. of οὖς.

ὠτάριον, ου, τό *ear* Mk 14: 47; J 18: 10.*

ὠτίον, ου, τό *ear* Mt 26: 51; Mk 14: 47 v.l.; Lk 22: 51; J 18: 10 v.l., 26.*

ὠφέλεια, ας, ἡ *use, gain, advantage* Ro 3: 1; Jd 16.*

ὠφελέω *help, aid, benefit, be of use (to)* Mt 16: 26; Mk 7: 11; 8: 36; 1 Cor 13: 3; 14: 6; Gal 5: 2; Hb 4: 2. *Accomplish* Mt 27: 24; J 12: 19. *Be of value* J 6: 63; Ro 2: 25.

ὠφέλιμος, ον *useful, beneficial, advantageous* 1 Ti 4: 8; 2 Ti 3: 16; Tit 3: 8.*

ὤφθην 1 aor. pass. ind. of ὁράω.